PENGUIN BOOKS

London: City of Disappearances

'Of all cities, London most powerfully touches the imagination. It is the landscape for these stories because no other place has the same capacity for labyrinthine obliquity. It elicits wonder and horror in equal measure. In Blake's words, it has become "a human awful wonder of God"'
The Times

'Hugely enjoyable, hilarious, frightening, strikingly macabre, seductively amusing, brilliant, hair-raisingly evocative. Anyone who wants a vivid taste of the old, real London, in all its coarseness, darkness, sensuality and wonder, will delight in this book' *Daily Telegraph*

'Make Sinclair the modern city's most vital chronicler'
Evening Standard

'A deeply personal journey through the city's forgotten nooks, crannies and stories' *Metro*

'Some writers have become obsessed by an event – a crime, a disappearance, an accident – and are drawn back to its location again and again as if puzzling out the mystery of London itself' Peter Ackroyd, *The Times*

LONDON

CITY OF DISAPPEARANCES

EDITED BY

IAIN SINCLAIR

PENGUIN BOOKS

PENGUIN BOOKS

Published by the Penguin Group
Penguin Books Ltd, 80 Strand, London WC2R ORL, England
Penguin Group (USA) Inc., 375 Hudson Street, New York, New York 10014, USA
Penguin Group (Canada), 90 Eglinton Avenue East, Suite 700, Toronto, Ontario, Canada M4P 2Y3
(a division of Pearson Penguin Canada Inc.)
Penguin Ireland, 25 St Stephen's Green, Dublin 2, Ireland
(a division of Penguin Books Ltd)
Penguin Group (Australia), 250 Camberwell Road, Camberwell, Victoria 3124, Australia
(a division of Pearson Australia Group Pty Ltd)
Penguin Books India Pvt Ltd, 11 Community Centre, Panchsheel Park, New Delhi – 110 017, India
Penguin Group (NZ), 67 Apollo Drive, Rosedale, North Shore 0632, New Zealand
(a division of Pearson New Zealand Ltd)
Penguin Books (South Africa) (Pty) Ltd, 24 Sturdee Avenue, Rosebank, Johannesburg 2196, South Africa

Penguin Books Ltd, Registered Offices: 80 Strand, London WC2R ORL, England

www.penguin.com

First published by Hamish Hamilton 2006
Published in Penguin Books 2077
1

Editorial and selection copyright © Iain Sinclair, 2006
All rights reserved

The Acknowledgements on pp. 641–3 constitute an extension of this copyright page

The moral right of the editor has been asserted

Typeset by Rowland Phototypesetting Ltd, Bury St Edmunds, Suffolk
Printed in England by Clays Ltd, St Ives plc

A CIP catalogue record for this book is available from the British Library

ISBN 978–0–141–01948–2

www.greenpenguin.co.uk

Penguin Books is committed to a sustainable future
for our business, our readers and our planet.
The book in your hands is made from paper
certified by the Forest Stewardship Council.

Looking for someone is, as psychologists have observed, perceptually peculiar, in that the world is suddenly organized as a basis upon which the absence of what is sought is bodied forth in a ghostly manner. The familiar streets about my house, never fully to recover from the haunting, were filled with non-apparitions.

Iris Murdoch

You don't disappear, you reappear, dead.

Ed Dorn

CONTRIBUTORS

AnnBAERJ.G.BALLARDSteveBEARDKi
kiBENZONPaulBUCKVahniCAPILDEO
KeggieCAREWPeterCARPENTERBrian
CATLINGMarcVaulbertdeCHANTILLY
ThomasDeQUINCEYKathiDIAMANTDrif
fieldBillDRUMMONDGarethEVANSTib
orFISCHERAllenFISHERAnthonyFREW
INRanaldGRAHAMBillGRIFFITHSLee
HARWOODStewartHOMERichardHUMP
HREYSPatrickKEILLERMariusKOCIEJOW
SKIAndrewKÖTTINGTonyLAMBRIANOU
MalcolmLETTSRachelLICHTENSTEINAlex
isLYKIARDJonathanMEADESMichaelMO
ORCOCKAlanMOOREJeffNUTTALLNick
PAPADIMITRIOUChrisPETITTomRAWO
RTHDerekRAYMONDGeorgeW.M.REYN
OLDSNicholasROYLEAnthonyRUDOLFJa
mesSALLISSukhdevSANDHUJohnSEED
WillSELFAnnaSINCLAIRIainSINCLAIR
WilliamSINCLAIRStephenSMITHAvram
STENCLMartinSTONERuthVALENTIN
EAlanWALLClaireWALSHMarinaWARN
ERBenWATSONJohnWELCHCarolWIL
LIAMSSarahWISEPatrickWRIGHT

CONTENTS

PREFACE: SMOKE AND MIRRORS

She told us there was a disappearance every eleven seconds
and taped everything we said.

DON DELILLO

At first it was cats and dogs. Snapshots blown up and pinned to trees, municipal noticeboards: 'Bodger. I am a tanned male Staff with white chest and little black nose, much loved by my family and friends.' London is a kennel city populated by vanished animals, kidnapped domestic pets. Self-published, premature obituaries have been wrapped around surveillance poles, pasted to electrical junction boxes. Killer mutts killed in the course of duty: as if one dog had eaten another until there was only a single beast, the dog of dogs, left in town. Dog-shaped absences are felt as a warm wind playing around your ankles. Snatched pooches. Porn-star poodles. Privileged pussies converted into winter gloves or given over to laboratory technicians for evil experiments, scent extraction. Extraordinary rendition. Extinguished darlings can be cloned and replaced. They leave their traces everywhere. Under and around a bench, beside the Regent's Canal in Hackney, I notice a thick mat of grey fur; the site of an epic grooming session. Animals, heard at night, yelp in empty buildings. Tooth marks can be found in the branches of trees where pit bulls once hung, strengthening their jaws for combat: the obscene fruit of twilight.

Now the temperature has changed, pit bulls are forgotten. Their patrons, bereaved, have retreated deeper into Essex. Photographs of disappeared humans, victims of the latest outrage, multiply across plywood fences that protect the latest grand project. Life drains from the image like hope from a dying eye. Memory-prints of the lost are arranged, in the hope that such a ritual will restore the

I

missing person, the loved one: daughter, brother, husband, father. The disappeared of the First War were named and published on English memorials because they were not here; their bodies, what was left of them, could not be returned from the battlefield. In our present climate of shoulder-shrugging amnesia, we have memorials to memorials, information posters telling us where the original slab has been stored. Heritage replaces the memories which should be passed on, anecdotally, affectionately, from generation to generation, by word of mouth.

It is difficult to explain, this conceit: a 'city of disappearances'. J. G. Ballard thinks of the centre of London as a redundant mausoleum; he can't understand why anyone would concern themselves with its erasure. He has never set foot in Spitalfields or visited Wapping. Why should he? Better to promote an accident of civil engineering like the Westway, a fairground ramp enlivened by tired fictions. What disappears, driving west, is not the road but the landscape that surrounds it: overbuilt, undermanaged. The ramp is the skeleton of a theme-park dinosaur. A fairground ride closed by safety inspectors: too predictable, too boring. A concrete folly in a skateboard jungle of cranes and diggers. A government-sanctioned sprawl of retail colonialism dumped between slip roads. Better this fancy, Ballard suggests, three minutes skimming above the houses, Hilton hotels, railway lines and stadia, than whatever happens down below in the dirty human streets. Three minutes of nervous reverie before the weight of things, the impossibility of escape, strikes us dumb once more.

By soliciting contributions to an anthology of absence, I hoped that the city would begin to write itself (punningly, in both senses): a Canetti fabrication, a documentary chronicle with a multitude of anonymous authors. A revival of the 'Mass Observation' project, perhaps, without the greedy voyeurism of poverty snoops and Home Counties elitists infiltrating northern industrial towns. You have to belong to a place before you are qualified to speak. I am a tolerated provincial who has outstayed his welcome, the liberties of Hackney (where we are all passing through). *London: City of Disappearances* was a book I couldn't construct, except by proxy. I nudged potential contributors. I made suggestions: paintings that had been stolen or destroyed (like Graham Sutherland's Churchill portrait fed into the boiler), bombed libraries, persons who stepped out for a newspaper and never returned, dusty reputations, found objects for which, as yet, no satisfactory explanation has been forged. Poets – I have a weakness for poets' prose – responded warmly, they would start that very day: underground rivers, the Odeons of childhood, detective work on the careers of fellow poets of even more fabulous obscurity. The promised pieces never surfaced and I was not cruel enough to harry denizens of the netherworld. It was their decision, to hold back, to keep their discoveries from prying eyes. If they had succeeded in teasing out the history of some junkie angel, published in heaven, the integrity of the initial disappearance would be threatened. Better to leave well alone. One celebrated and prolific London author, pestered beyond endurance by my invitation to dredge, yet again, into the old memory sludge, replied by postcard: 'Alas, I have nothing.'

The poet Lee Harwood, from whom I bought paperbacks in his days in Charing Cross Road, at Better Books (or so I think I remember), cannot substantiate Paul Buck's claim to have worked in the same shop. 'I guess Paul must have been there when I was away somewhere.' He does however recall Buck's attempts to fascinate young women: 'I'm a sadist.' 'Ah, the murky past,' Harwood muses. While Buck, infiltrating the same city of shadows, believes that Harwood was out of circulation, in hospital. Harwood, challenged, pictures the scene: 'I was locked up in that hospital just east of Mile End tube. (The chief psychiatrist was an ex-concentration camp victim. He seemed to have learned a lot from his captors in the way he treated his patients! A Burroughs nightmare.) So the pieces of the puzzle *at times* fit together.'

More frequently, they do not: we revise, talk ourselves up, airbrush the shame. Tale-tellers, those with a gift for public relations and self-promotion, take over the production, fabricate a mythology and sell off the doctored footage. Alexis Lykiard's role in the celebrated 11 June

1966 poetry readings at the Albert Hall remains woefully under-described. Jeff Nuttall, an inspirational figure to his peers, never made it on to the stage. With John Latham (the intense, mad-eyed sculptor/philosopher), Nuttall had got himself up in an Aztec costume stitched together from books. They were going to fight a duel. Alex Trocchi, the master of ceremonies, forgot to signal their entrance. Latham, suffering from heat exhaustion, fainted in the wings. An attendant barred Nuttall's path. Later, in what must have been a very bad night for this functionary, he discovered the two artists soaping each other down in Sir Malcolm Sargent's private bathroom.

The book of disappearances assembled itself as a deflected autobiography, scripted by an automatic pen in an end-of-the-pier booth in an out-of-season resort. Friends and friends of friends sent me the missing chapters of a book I was incapable of writing. With a Charing Cross Road dealer, I visited Nuttall in Hebden Bridge, helping to clear his library (a not infrequent occurrence). He was on the move again, evacuating the trash of identity: magazines, lavishly inscribed (and stained) booklets from other poets, multiples of his own samizdat titles. Hebden Bridge, on the road between Halifax and Rochdale, was an outstation of the reforgotten, a penal colony of cancelled creatives, drift-culture marginals. The London poet and publisher Asa Benveniste, a significant figure at that golden moment in the 1960s when books from presses such as Trigram, Goliard and Fulcrum outperformed their mainstream rivals, opened the front room of his terraced house as a shop: personal holdings and the relics of his press were offered for sale. I would have to revise Ed Dorn's tag: you don't reappear, dead – you reappear in Hebden Bridge; rolling a thin cigarette, peddling your most precious possessions. And sporting a metaphorical beret.

When I listed some of Nuttall's books in a (long-vanished) magazine put out by an equally long-vanished book-runner, Driffield, I was contacted by a man who worked for a fast-food franchise in Gloucester Road. The burger joint was obviously a front for other, even speedier activities. This man, pock-marked, chivalrous, struck me as an exemplary customer. He crossed town to collect his purchases, paid cash on the nail (no haggling), brought cookies (he was known to my children as the 'Cookie Man') and champagne. What's more, he left the best of the books behind him, in my safe-keeping. I have them still, a complete run of Nuttall's *My Own Mag* (with all the Burroughs contributions). Then he vanished. Into South America, so he hinted. Once, after a number of years, he returned: more cookies, more champagne, a private viewing of his holdings. A handshake at the door and out into the night. Never heard from again. My wife thinks the Cookie Man might have perished in the newsreels of the Mexico City earthquake. I can't convince myself that he had any corporeal existence. The literate burger-slave bailed me out at a point when I was frantic to get a big book finished. And then, charity performed, he stepped from the frame: a shapeshifter with a carrier bag of goodies and a roll of crisp, high denomination banknotes.

For the bookish, London is a book. For criminals, a map of opportunities. For unpapered immigrants, it is a nest of skinned eyes; sanctioned gunmen ready to blow your head off as you run for a train. When the city of distorting mirrors revealed itself, through its districts and discriminations, I discovered more about London's past as a reworking of my own submerged history. Stephen Smith's investigation of Paul Raymond, skin impresario and property speculator, brought back one of my more unlikely occupations from years spent taking on anything and everything as a way of learning about the metropolis. I was a short-lived stagehand at Raymond's Revuebar. A mature student (lifelong) from the School of Art and Technical College, where I had been teaching in Walthamstow, got me in. I wanted to experience the difference between the public face of Soho entertainment and the back door (pit, sweatbox, slum). The glitz of front of house, where the businessmen and Japanese tourists eased their elbows and sharpened their gaze, was balanced by the narrow quarters allocated to the stage staff, the (un)dressing rooms of the gravy-coloured dancers. My fellow labourers, efficient, diminutive, muscular, were mostly Australians in green-striped T-shirts, puncturing cans and sitting around a small television set.

Smoke machines. Dry ice. Wet leather bikinis. Motorbikes on stands. The drench of steaming bodies and industrial perfume countered cigar fug, the testosterone soup of the unseen punters. We were the ashtray of the vanities. Pounding sound, cracking whips, coloured lights flashing on chrome: androids of the night. We darted forward, as the curtain closed, to pick up discarded wisps of costume that were like skin changes, surgical dressings improvised from unsuitable materials: vinyl, peeled dog, diamanté. We skidded on sweat pools.

Will Self's lively account of a street incident outside the pre-transported Charing Cross Hospital (where he was born in 1961) keyed up recollections of a different order. I accompanied my wife, eleven years after the yowling novelist's first appearance in the city, for the birth of our first child. We got a booking up West because the Natural Childbirth antenatal classes we attended were held there: yogic exercises that might have been developed by Mike Leigh, a dummy babe of sinister aspect and a comprehensive account of everything that could possibly go wrong. Instruments of delivery laid out for inspection. The classes were like a suburban wife-swapping club, licensed to go no further than inflicting Chinese burns on the smooth thighs of potential partners, to whom you had just been introduced. Raw biology, immortal longings and a mug of hot sweet tea: the English way.

The ambulance carrying us from Hackney – another discontinued courtesy – broke down, half a mile shy of its destination. We walked, with our bundle of nightwear (sponges to suck, soap, warm socks), down the middle of the street, into a building where assorted junkies and headbangers were lying on the floor, waiting for admittance. We stepped over them and on, eventually, to a room where we were left alone: to come to terms with this improbable but inevitable situation. What a privilege it was, being so close to the heart of things, watching the cockroaches crawl across damp plaster, with someone to call on if required; within the throb and pulse of the nocturnal city, the ghosts of empire. A daughter, disgruntled, red-faced, came into the world. I slid home, on private rails, finding London an altered landscape. I saw, that one time, more truly into the dream of things: Strand, Fleet Street, Smithfield, Bunhill Fields. A route that became a mantra for the years that would follow.

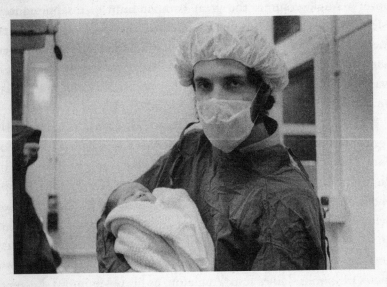

I'm haunted by the way more vivid memories overwrite my own. Ann Baer visiting the exiled German painter Ludwig Meidner in Golders Green: a young woman having her portrait painted as an act of patronage, in order to keep a difficult artist afloat in difficult times. Meidner's terrifying visions, made before the First War, demonstrated the tremble that lies beneath the confident fabric of long-established cities. Future detonations are experienced by neurotic seers before they actually happen: crumpled buildings, crushed humans, the sun like a melting eye. Meidner left Germany for London, with his wife, Else, also a painter. A fretful relationship. They held a joint exhibition, years later, which I saw, at the Ben Uri Gallery in St John's Wood. I copied a couple of lines from the catalogue into my notebook: 'Since their art did not make enough money for the Meidners to survive in London, they were dependent on assistance from well-wishers and charitable organizations. Else eventually accepted a position as a servant with an elderly woman in Sydenham.' That catalogue has now vanished. There must be a library somewhere – like the Gray's Inn Road cellar that Malcolm Letts describes – where all the missing books of London are assembled, three-deep on the shelf, welded together by subterranean ooze: a single volume, the great compendium of disappearances. Meidner caught that instant of fracture, the rip in the temporal membrane, before it was obvious to less agitated citizens. Trapped here, reputation occulted, he studied Blake and began to write. I was honoured to have his painting *Apokalyptische Landschaft* (1913) on the cover of the first edition of my novel *Downriver*.

The most deeply buried of all the mind-dramas reactivated by contributions to the anthology started with Chris Petit's account of Kim Philby's house in Crowborough. Philby was a professional of disappearance, presenting a false self, keeping his doctored script afloat on alcohol: living with the strangeness, in his circle, of not being a walking disaster, not coming visibly apart as the years rolled on; not having the underworld of predatory homosexuality, class on class, still proscribed, as a smokescreen. Petit uses that ghost, spook of spooks, James Jesus Angleton, as his posthumous dreamer: the world is a conspiracy of the ungodly. Life and career: a futile attempt to write himself out of the story. Angleton's visit to Philby's wife, Aileen, in Crowborough, the Strindbergian theatre of that two-hander, brought it back. A rented flat in Sandycove, alongside Joyce's tower, on the southern rim of Dublin Bay. Early 1960s. We didn't know what we'd walked into: all the loose ends of unresolved literary and cultural projects that needed somewhere quiet in which to atrophy or resurrect themselves. Xeroxes of late Modernism in a provincial backwater, still hag-ridden by the Church and the well-oiled machinery of political corruption. Casualties of the peace treading water, watching the horizon: runaways and failed suicides. You couldn't talk about disappearance in this context. We were off the map in a place that held resolutely to its fabricated past. A willed disappearance, a voluntary submersion, doesn't count. At the top of the house was a poet, escaped from South Africa, biding her time, plucking a guitar, waiting for the move to Hampstead. Beneath her, a nurse, battered mistress of a northern novelist whose books were being turned into films, plays. A convalescent putting her life back together, after experiencing the torrid integrity of this man's acted-out Lawrentian dynamic. She had the bruises, the limp, to prove it. And then, in the spacious ground-floor flat, the sprawled daughters of a shadowy American presence in Ireland (military, diplomatic, CIA). They were picking up the graces of an unde-manding education, inquisitive about alien lifestyles, innocently promiscuous.

Stepping away from material too eager to be transcribed, I came out of the garden gate and down to the rocks. A gaunt woman in Bermuda shorts, legs drawn up, was already sitting there; our neighbour. She nursed a permanent glass of something iced and clear, vodka. It was my first taste and I learned to appreciate that the spirit was better not taken by the tumbler if there was still business outstanding in what remained of the day. Even among the electively lost, this woman was the paradigm. Unlike the rest of them, people were actually looking for her; journalists, investigative teams, ghost-writers with mousetrap chequebooks. She hadn't dis-appeared, not this time, she was hiding: and therefore, more than ever, aware of herself, her difficulties, a life snatched away, without explanation, one January night in 1963. Here, in the next house, was Eleanor Philby, the third wife of the Third Man: dark glasses, headscarf for the street (she never went out). Beirut had just hap-pened, the headline disappearance. When there is a choice, for the woman left behind, London or Moscow, she makes an instant decision: Dublin. What Eleanor noticed about the men in the secret world was 'their watchfulness, but also a surprising tenderness'. 'You tend to compensate,' she wrote, in her account of her marriage, 'by the intensity of your sex-based relationships.'

The blinds were permanently down, the television was on. The vodka kept coming. They must have been doing an afternoon series of Preston Sturges movies; it was hard to tell, reception was hit and miss. Drift footage, mirthless high spirits on trains: *The Palm Beach*

Story. 'Films,' wrote W. G. Sebald (in 'Kafka Goes to the Movies'), 'far more than books, have a way of disappearing not just from the market but from the memory, never to be seen again.' I didn't watch a Preston Sturges film, from that time in Eleanor Philby's flat, until June 2005 – when I dug up a DVD of *Sullivan's Travels.* Our television seances were a ruse for holding a three-way conversation (the Third Man silent as a Buddha); the pearly-grey screen became a window into an American past about which I knew nothing. Glamorous figures exchanging quips. Hollywood plutocrats toying with Marxism, boasting about meeting Brecht and Greta Garbo at a dinner party in Salka Viertel's Santa Monica salon. Things Eleanor said, my film-buff remarks: they allowed us to avoid any form of direct interrogation. 'Communism, communism, this picture is the answer to communism.' 'With a little sex in it.' Veronica Lake, tactfully robed and framed, pregnant, was cast against the wishes of the studio bosses. There is a black cook and a big-time director, played by Joel McCrea, who decides to go hobo, on the road, *Grapes of Wrath* with following caravans and attendants. 'What do you know about garbage cans?' barks the money man. And when at last McCrea takes his place – chain gang, swamp convict – with the wretched of the earth, they are all redeemed by viewing some Disney slapstick. The American dream: the point at which savagery gives way to sentiment. The paradox of fang-rotting sugars and perfect white teeth.

Eleanor Philby, if she successfully erased her memories, clipped the labels from her clothes, stayed out there on the rocks, might have been a figure to set beside the 'Piano Man' of Sheppey. People cannot simply disappear, abdicate from the soap opera of the city; they must reappear: even the ones who have never been seen before. Like Kaspar Hauser, the changeling of Karlsruhe, or the peasant poet John Clare adrift in London, figures with no history continue to arrive out of some black hole: space-time anomalies. On a beach in the Thames Estuary, a man is discovered, in a wet evening suit with all identifying marks removed: one of the drowned, walking out of the river. His hair is erect, spiky; he hasn't shaved in a couple of days. White shirt, no tie. The look seems to be calculated, borrowed from David Lynch – but the expression contradicts any facile explanation. A second life for a person who has avoided the preliminaries.

Here, and more convincingly present than the magician David Blaine in his high glass coffin, is a being to trouble the imagination. Blaine's performance was mired in banality, he made himself a target; he was attached by an umbilical cord to City Hall and the media hose. A volunteer for the virtual pillory, the soft crucifixion of tabloid headlines, this self-hostaged American floated on the sweet stink of narcissism: underwritten by burger sweat and bad electricity. Too many safety lines, too many cables. It took the novelist Nicola Barker to redeem the project (before moving on, I'm sure, to the Piano Man).

The revenant's expression tells us nothing, a passenger from nowhere. He is lodged in the Medway Maritime Hospital at Gillingham, where he draws detailed impressions of a grand piano. Unhesitating marks on paper, found in later times, will be a passport to the City of Disappearances. There are so many achieved and aborted quests, our soundtrack is as busy as a screwball Preston Sturges comedy. But, as noise fades, we are left with a gazetteer of erasures, each disappearance represented by a random object or image: a cabinet of curiosities. The military hairbrush that once belonged to Franz Kafka (as recorded by Kathi Diamant). Paul Buck's photograph, pigeons in Trafalgar Square, from which his mother has been excluded. Kiki Benzon's Camden Lock shoes, the ones that can't be found a second time. Jeff Nuttall's daughter, in his story, running away to London: how was that episode resolved? Marius Kociejowski's discovery of a 'blank Gretna Green marriage certificate'. A fading VHS tape of a deleted Channel 4 documentary, *The Cardinal and the Corpse*, in which dead London writers like Derek Raymond and Alexander Baron (along with the Kray associate Tony Lambrianou) keep on talking, still at the pub table, trying to fix the topography of forgotten films.

I thought the book might, in the end, be defined by pieces

that didn't appear. Nicholas Royle's extended tale, a novella, was promised but it didn't arrive. As deadline followed deadline, I considered publishing his postcards, the teasing hints of what was to come: Picasso etchings, Soho drawings, a promotional card for *Baby Oil and Ice* (an account of 'striptease in East London'). And then, story delivered, Royle discovers, in a secondhand paperback of Kafka's *The Castle*, a folded, photocopied poem: 'The Disappearing City (Prague, 1938–London, 1988)' by Nicholas Drake.

'At dawn the storm troops execute the clocks.'

Another search is initiated. Everyone is keen to point out – as is the poet of 'The Disappearing City' – that he is not *that* Nick Drake, the suicided lyricist, the one whose sister played the woman in the first (television) version of J. G. Ballard's *Crash*. Another person entirely, stroke victim, so they say, prizewinner. (The poet, run to ground by Royle, denies it. The confusion here is with yet another Nick, the playwright Nick Darke.) Did Drake do a book on Yeats for Penguin (author's details not on file)? I met the original, the now celebrated singer/songwriter, my first time on radio, late 1960s, *The John Peel Show*. I had an 8 mm Bolex in my woolly shoulder-bag, I was keeping a film diary, but security wouldn't let me shoot while the show was on air. No images of Peel or Drake, just the empty studio, an associate playing the various parts, faking it: an unreliable memory. The show was taped – it might have some value now – but that tape is lost. Too much time has been wasted searching for it, for all the other photographs, poems, totems. Never go back. Emulate Basil Bunting and burn the letters before the pests get at them. Free up the researchers. At the finish, even the cabinet of curiosities will betray us; all we can ever know is the shape the missing object leaves in the dust – and the stories, the lies we assemble to disguise the pain of an absence we cannot define.

[I. S.]

WEST END FINAL

THE STALKING GHOST

In the late 1930s, as an ex-art student, I was often in the West End of London, a frequenter of galleries and exhibitions. I became aware of a man who attended the same events. From the first moment I noticed him, I felt that his face was familiar. He was a man of medium height, black haired, black eyed, with a look so ravaged by horror and grief that it was startling. He surely had been to hell and back. So regular were his appearances that I light-heartedly referred to him as my Ghost. I do not wish to imply that he was in any way pursuing me, nor I him; the encounters (barely that) were quite by chance, and not always in art exhibitions.

One evening, having a drink with friends at the Café Royal, I noticed him, melancholy, dark and tormented, at the next marble table. On another occasion, alone in the Lyons Teashop in Piccadilly, engrossed in what I was reading, I felt a slight chill. I looked up to discover my Ghost sitting at the pink glass table, directly in front of me.

Again, I was travelling with a friend to stay with her relatives in Coventry; a gloomy journey on a gloomy November evening. We took a corridor train with sliding doors that gave access to each carriage. As the train rattled through the Midlands, the door to our compartment was slid open; my Ghost stared in, shut the door immediately and disappeared.

War came. Lives were in upheaval. One evening, back in the Café Royal, I saw my Ghost, this time in uniform. Years passed, the war was over. I was walking down Shaftesbury Avenue with the friend who had shared my train journey. 'He looks familiar,' she said. A man in the crowd, in civilian clothes. 'It's my Ghost,' I replied, 'out of the army.'

No further sightings took place until 1952, at the private view of the Mexican Exhibition at the Tate Gallery. Passing from one room to another, I recognized my Ghost in dinner jacket and black tie.

He approached me, as if to shake my hand; realizing he did not know me, he dropped his hand and sidled off. 'Ah,' I thought, 'if he's been haunting me all these years, perhaps I've been haunting him.'

Next day, I spotted him coming out of the post office on the corner of Knightsbridge and Wilton Place. A few weeks later I saw him in Southampton Row. I was then working for the Ganymed Press, near Holborn, and thought that, sooner or later, as he seemed to be in the 'art world', my man would be sure to turn up. He did. One day, returning to the office after lunch, I was confronted by my Ghost sitting at the desk. My assistant was on the phone to my boss, who was upstairs. 'Mr Roberts,' she said, 'Mr Mervyn Peake is here to see you.'

[Ann Baer]

ANN OF OXFORD STREET

Being myself, at that time, of necessity a peripatetic, or a walker of the streets, I naturally fell in more frequently with those female peripatetics who are technically called street-walkers. Some of these women had occasionally taken my part against watchmen who wished to drive me off the steps of houses where I was sitting; others had protected me against more serious aggressions. But one amongst them – the one on whose account I have at all introduced this subject – yet no! let me not class thee, Oh noble-minded Ann —, with that other order of women; let me find, if it be possible, some gentler name to designate the condition of her to whose bounty and compassion – ministering to my necessities when all the world stood aloof from me – I owe it that I am at this time alive. For many weeks I had walked at nights, with this poor friendless girl up and down Oxford Street, or had rested with her on steps and under the shelter of porticos . . .

One night, when we were pacing slowly along Oxford Street, and after a day when I had felt unusually ill and faint, I requested her to turn off with me into Soho Square. Thither we went; and we sat down on the steps of a house, which to this hour I never pass without a pang of grief, and an inner act of homage to the spirit of that unhappy girl, in memory of the noble act which she there performed. Suddenly, as we sat, I grew much worse. I had been leaning my head against her bosom, and all at once I sank from her arms, and fell backwards on the steps. From the sensations I then had, I felt an inner conviction of the liveliest kind that, without some powerful and reviving stimulus, I should either have died on the spot, or should, at least, have sunk to a point of exhaustion from which all re-ascent, under my friendless circumstances, would soon have become hopeless. Then it was, at this crisis of my fate, that my poor orphan companion, who had herself met with little but injuries in this world, stretched out a saving hand to me. Uttering a cry of terror, but without a moment's delay, she ran off into Oxford Street, and, in less time than could be imagined, returned to me with a glass of port-wine and spices, that acted upon my empty stomach (which at that time would have rejected all solid food) with an instantaneous power of restoration . . .

Some feelings, though not deeper or more passionate, are more tender than others; and often when I walk, at this time, in Oxford Street by dreamy lamp-light, and hear those airs played on a common street-organ which years ago solaced me and my dear youthful companion, I shed tears, and muse with myself at the mysterious dispensation which so suddenly and so critically separated us for ever . . .

About fifteen shillings I had employed in re-establishing (though in a very humble way) my dress. Of the remainder, I gave one-quarter (something more than a guinea) to Ann, meaning, on my return, to have divided with her whatever might remain.

These arrangements made, soon after six o'clock, on a dark winter evening, I set off, accompanied by Ann, towards Piccadilly; for it was my intention to go down as far as the turn to Salt Hill and Slough on the Bath or Bristol mail. Our course lay through a part of the town which has now totally disappeared, so that I can no longer retrace its ancient boundaries – having been replaced by Regent Street and its adjacencies. *Swallow Street* is all that I remember of the names superseded by this large revolutionary usurpation. Having time enough before us, however, we bore away to the left, until we came into Golden Square. There, near the corner of Sherrard Street, we sat down, not wishing to part in the tumult and blaze of Piccadilly. I had told Ann of my plans some time before; and now I assured her again that she should share in my good fortune, if I met with any; and that I would never forsake her, as soon as I had power to protect her . . . I hoped to return in a week, at furthest, and I agreed with her that, on the fifth night from that, and every night afterwards, she would wait for me, at six o'clock, near the bottom of Great Titchfield Street; which had formerly been our customary haven of rendezvous, to prevent our missing each other in the great Mediterranean of Oxford Street. This, and other measures of precaution, I took; one, only, I forgot. She had either never told me, or (as a matter of no great interest) I had forgotten, her surname. It is a general practice, indeed, with girls of humble rank in her unhappy condition, not (as novel-reading women of higher pretensions) to style themselves *Miss Douglas*, *Miss Montague*, &c., but simply by their Christian names, *Mary*, *Jane*, Frances, &c. Her surname, as the surest means of tracing her, I ought now to have inquired; but the truth is, having no reason to think that our meeting again could, in consequence of a short interruption, be more difficult or uncertain than it had been for so many weeks, I scarcely for a moment adverted to it as necessary, or placed it amongst my memoranda against this parting interview; and, my final anxieties being spent in comforting her with hopes, and in pressing upon her the necessity of getting some medicine for a violent cough with which she was troubled, I wholly forgot this precaution until it was too late to recall her . . .

I quitted London in haste, and returned to the Priory; after some time I proceeded to Oxford; and it was not until many months had passed away that I had it in my power again to revisit the ground which had become so interesting to me, and to this day remains so, as the chief scene of my youthful sufferings.

Meantime, what had become of Ann? Where was she? Whither had she gone? According to our agreement, I sought her daily, and waited for her every night, so long as I staid in London, at the corner of Titchfield Street; and during the last days of my stay in London I put into activity every means of tracing her that my knowledge of London suggested, and the limited extent of my power made possible. The street where she had lodged I knew, but not the house; and I remembered, at last, some account which she had given of ill-treatment, from her landlord, which made it probable that she had quitted these lodgings before we parted. She had few acquaintances; most people, besides, thought that the earnestness of my inquiries arose from motives which moved their laughter or their slight regard; and others, thinking that I was in chase of a girl who had robbed me of some trifles, were naturally and excusably indisposed to give me any clue to her, if indeed they had any to give. Finally, as my despairing resource, on the day I left London I put into the hands of the only person who (I was sure) must know Ann by sight, from having been in company with us once or twice, an address to the Priory. All was in vain. To this hour I have never heard a syllable about her. This, amongst such troubles as most men meet with in this life, has been my heaviest affliction. If she lived, doubtless we must have been sometimes in search of each other, at the very same moment, through the mighty labyrinths of London; perhaps even within a few feet of each other – a barrier no wider, in a London street, often amounting in the end to a separation for eternity! During some years I hoped that she *did* live; and I suppose that, in the literal and unrhetorical use of the word *myriad*, I must, on my different visits to London, have looked into many myriads of female faces, in the hope of meeting Ann. I should know her again amongst a thousand, and if seen but for a moment. Handsome she was not; but she had a sweet expression of countenance, and a peculiarly graceful carriage of the head. I sought her, I have said, in hope. So it was for years; but now I should fear to see her; and her cough, which grieved me when I parted with her, is now my consolation. Now I wish to see her no longer, but think of her, more gladly, as one long since laid in the grave – in the grave, I would hope, of a Magdalen; taken away before injuries and cruelty had blotted out and transfigured her ingenuous nature, or the brutalities of ruffians had completed the ruin they had begun.

[Thomas De Quincey]

BRIDGE OF SIGHS: THE RAYMOND REVUEBAR

Paul Raymond shifted fractionally in the hot tub, and a droplet of perspiration fell from a ringlet. His signature bouffant had thinned a little at the crown, it was true, but it still flowed to his shoulders like al dente vermicelli. (What was it about purveyors of gentlemen's entertainment and their barnets? Stringfellow was the same.) 'More Krug, Steve?' offered Raymond, propping himself on an elbow and reaching for the sweating bucket.

I raised a wrinkled thumb. 'Be rude not to, Paul,' I said. Not for the first time, I reproached myself for misjudging my host. Like many others, I had been ready to believe the caricature of the publisher as a miserly misanthrope, passing his declining years by stroking gold bars in his lonely condo. Through the wreaths of my cigar smoke, I considered the still-vital octogenarian in front of me and wondered that anyone could doubt his credentials as a liberator of post-war London, who had brought a welcome dose of honesty to our confused and hypocritical attitudes to sex.

At that moment, the Japanese doors sighed ajar, and stepping towards us through the nimbus of moisture and tobacco came Lorelei and Roxanne, shrugging off their robes, and then Susie and Lucy, and Tammy and Sammy . . .

Dear reader, it wasn't like that. No, it wasn't that way at all. I'll admit that when I began to chronicle the disappearance of the

20

Raymond Revuebar, Britain's original strip joint, I half expected – do I mean hoped? – to wind up in a steamy spot alongside its founder. But in the event, the clinch I found myself in with Paul Raymond was a long way from the pleasures of the assisted Jacuzzi. On the contrary, I felt the hot breath of the powerful Raymond organization on the back of my neck. The business of the Revuebar was titillation, the tantalizing withholding of juicy material. In this respect, Raymond and his people had a holistic approach, as much a feature of the boardroom as of the dimly lit cockpit of the stage itself. A man by the name of Carl Snitcher, who is chief executive of Raymond's property empire, Soho Estates, has a practised way of saving your time and his when you inquire whether Mr Raymond might be willing to – 'No, he wouldn't,' says Mr Snitcher, before you've even finished asking if Raymond would speak to you in person. Despite this, I was soon standing in the lobby of a mansion block in Piccadilly that didn't look worth the money it must cost to live there: I knew that Raymond had a bachelor pad near the Ritz Hotel and by chance I had stumbled on the right place at the first time of asking. In the hallway, which had been camouflaged in a colour scheme of sub-fusc, I secured the displeasure of the door-men, and indeed others on the Raymond payroll, with a patently under-rehearsed story about 'an appointment'. Nonetheless, I found myself returning more than once to Arlington Street, SW1, blowing on my hands and stamping my feet and hoping for a glimpse of the man who had revolutionized London's nightlife, not to mention the opportunity to snatch a word, if you'll overlook the expression.

But all of this lay ahead of me when I set out to chart the decline of Raymond's fleshpot. It was due to be reincarnated as a gay bar. Out were going all the trappings and appurtenances of the old hetero mosh pit, one supposed: the hoppy kegs in the cellar; the desultory puck of air-freshener in the well of the urinals, the Velcro carpets. And in were coming toney, tongue-in-cheek fixtures and fittings, as demanded by a more sophisticated clientele. I wondered what all this reminded me of, and realized hotly that it was what you read about in every other phonebox in London. The Revuebar was pre-op.

From the south, the club was approached by way of Shaftesbury Avenue, which was effectively the grid reference of the magical destination 'London's West End'. Turning off this theatrical thoroughfare into Rupert Street, the visitor all at once beheld the scintillating signifier of the Revuebar itself: the name of the gaff, spelled out in neon. There was talk of preserving this throbbing masthead, but it was out of sight behind scaffolding in 2005 and Westminster Council said it had no knowledge that the sign would be listed. The northern means of access to Raymond's pleasuredome was from Berwick Street, a tributary of mighty Oxford Street. People from out of town were well advised not to go too far to the west along this strip before making a left, and in any case a change of direction was overdue by the time one reached Marks & Sparks, coincidentally the site of the pox doctor where Thomas De Quincey bought his first wrap of opium. Assuming that you were safely proceeding along Berwick Street, the sight of market barrows and the nosegay of fruit on the turn announced that the Revuebar was close at hand. Strictly speaking, it was not on Berwick Street itself but at 11–12 Walker's Court. The revamp of the venue saw not only its name removed but also proud armorials such as 'The Festival of Erotica' torn down. The onlooker found his eye drawn to a relic of an earlier life, a plaque for 'Maurice House'. It was little wonder that the old name had fallen into disuse: 'Maurice House, Walker's Court' had the ring of warden-controlled accommodation rather than an amphitheatre of unwithered flesh. The plaque had come to light on the club's one architectural conversation piece, the bridge over Walker's Court. The bridge is an enclosed walkway, suspended above a narrow strand of sex shops and Italian caffs, and as far as I can see it's the only reason for calling Walker's Court a court at all. It is a *low* bridge, so low that a man standing on the pavement beneath might almost brush the underside of it with his outstretched fingers. In any other setting, this squat rampart would be ugly, laughable: a dirty cladding of concrete which attempts to imitate stone without remotely coming close. The whole thing is too heavy for the supporting buildings to bear, aesthetically if not structurally.

With its leaded bay windows, it is a mockery of a romantic fantasy, Ivanhoe's penthouse. But by virtue of its very improbability, it casts a strange spell. A folly such as this might awaken in a man's breast a courtly daydream of a beautiful exotic dancer trapped in a tower, who offers to let down her hair extensions to any punter bold and trim enough to shin up them and claim her.

Despite Soho's renown or notoriety as London's red-light zone, history shows that it took a while to get the old girl in the mood. As late as Elizabethan times, Soho was nothing but water-meadow, and the story goes that it acquired its name only in the late seventeenth century, when the Duke of Monmouth, who had a place in the West End, uttered the rallying cry of 'So-hoe!' at the Battle of Sedgemoor. When Casanova himself had digs in Greek Street, the Soho we know today was still no more than a twinkle in his roving eye. In fact, it wasn't until the nineteenth century that the place got a reputation for carnal pursuits. Prostitutes working the Strand and Haymarket repaired to rookeries with their temporary patrons. These comings and goings were recorded by Robert Louis Stevenson in *The Strange Case of Dr Jekyll and Mr Hyde*. Not only a horror classic but also a prototype account of Soho low-life, the story notes that the typical thoroughfare boasted 'a gin palace, a low French eating house, a shop for the retail of penny numbers and twopenny salads, many ragged children huddled in the doorways, and women of many different nationalities passing out, keys in hand'. By the end of the First World War, Soho had determinedly made its bed, and has been lying in it ever since. Girls were to be found on the streets from the late afternoons, as shops and offices closed for the day. From midnight until cockcrow, a shift of heavily made-up older ladies patrolled Glasshouse Street, no more than a garter's throw from the Revuebar. As the novels of Graham Greene remind us, many of Soho's prostitutes between the wars were French or Belgian, known locally as Fifis. Gangsters set up stables of girls on Rupert Street and Brewer Street. Ed Glinert, a one-man gazetteer of London, says that coitus was frequently interruptus thanks to 'men with cameras bursting in and taking shots that could be used for blackmail'. By the 1950s, there were an estimated 5,000 working girls in Central London. A policeman walking up Shaftesbury Avenue one evening encountered 100 girls soliciting before he'd got as far as Cambridge Circus. These scandalizing antics were not to be endured. The forty-shilling fines handed down to prostitutes were having no effect, so these sanctions were reinforced by the big stick of imprisonment for third-time offenders. The result was that working girls were swept off the street overnight.

This was the hygienic, hosed-down scene that confronted the new owner of Maurice House, the thirty-three-year-old Paul Raymond. In the late 1950s Raymond was a former comb salesman and a failed mind-reader. But he had experienced a eureka moment on the variety circuit when he realized that he could persuade a couple of girls who were sharing the bill with him to take their tops off for an extra ten shillings each, an outlay which he more than recouped at the box office. Raymond was born Geoffrey Quinn in Liverpool in 1925: he shared his birthday with the noted authors J. G. Ballard and Tibor Fischer. Chalk it up to healthy adolescent curiosity, if you will, or to a precocious talent for his future line of work, but at fourteen Raymond was peeping through a keyhole as his aunt undressed. He was educated by the Jesuit brothers at St Francis Xavier's College in Liverpool, the alma mater of Gerard Manley Hopkins. 'If there's any spanking on the curriculum of Raymond's clubs and his magazines,' said the *Liverpool Post*, 'we know where he got the idea from.' Raymond left school at fifteen and went to work as an office boy with the Manchester ship canal before a brief spell down the mines (he lasted a week).

Wartime found him doing his best to avoid national service by force-feeding himself sandwiches of saccharin before his medical. A pal had told him that chain-eating sugar butties would fool the unsuspecting stethoscope into picking up signs of a heart condition. But Raymond was passed 'A1 fit' and joined the RAF as a bandsman. During his two years in uniform, he supplemented his forces pay by flogging grooming products as well as nylons and petrol coupons.

'I was a total spiv,' he has said of this period of his life. The demobilized Raymond made a living of sorts in show business, first playing the drums in a dance band and then setting up as a clairvoyant after buying the act from a clown on Clacton Pier. The fee of £25 included a book of secret codes, a crib of apparently workaday phrases with which the mystic's assistant could guide the great Raymond to his uncanny insights. Not that he went by that name on stage: if he and his then partner had been lucky enough to have their own dressing room, the name on the door would have been Mr and Mrs Tree (as in 'mystery'). Poor takings suggested that Raymond had no future in the mind-reading business. The masterstroke of putting topless women in front of a paying audience came to him not a moment too soon. In 1951, he went on the road with the Festival of Nudes, his own personal tribute to the rather better-known carnival which was then attempting to raise post-war spirits.

The Revuebar, which opened in 1958, was not the first London venue to feature nude shows. Around the corner at the Windmill, women had stood and shivered in the altogether for years: famously, the Lord Chamberlain had decreed that the models were not allowed to move. Raymond spotted a loophole in the ruling and registered his Revuebar as a club: the striptease had arrived. Raymond and his activities excited the loathing of papers such as the *Daily Mail* from the outset. In 1961, Raymond was fined £5,000 for keeping a disorderly house. The judge censured the 'filthy, disgusting and beastly' Revuebar. But the business was an unstoppable success: by 1965, its owner had made half a million pounds. Raymond grew rich on membership fees, as Soho's old faces duly noted. 'Made millions out of standing orders,' the underworld figure Billy Howard told his son as they stood in Walker's Court, admiring the photos of 'attractive showgirls, scantily clad in feathers and sequins'. 'To get in you have to be a member. Most of the customers have got a few bob, they're down here for conferences or meetings, they have a few drinks and end up here. Fill in the membership form with their bank details and every year it comes out. Most of them only ever go in the place once, but they just keep on paying.'

Carelessness, or embarrassment, kept the bankers' drafts rolling in. According to Michael Connor, who wrote a biography of Howard, *The Soho Don*, 'Bill obviously thought the way Paul Raymond had achieved this cash flow was a clever angle. The operation itself . . . was stylish. Not only were the sets a talking point, Mickey Spillane, the American thriller writer, had remarked that the Girl in the Golden Fish Tank was the sexiest girl he had ever seen.'

The terrible burden of conceiving and bringing to the stage Paul Raymond's increasingly spectacular productions was borne for half a lifetime by the Revuebar's former artistic director, Gerard Simi. 'I have lived with spangles, with glitter, but I am not duped. I see through it.' I found Simi taking some time off at his home in north-west London before committing himself to new projects. He was telling me about video directors with whom he'd recently had some dealings. 'They are so pretentious,' he went on. 'You meet them and they are all talking about "my work". Well, here is my work, thirty years of work.' Simi ran a hand over transparent wallets of photographic prints, a fraction of the 3,000 images he had saved from the Revuebar and which he hoped one day to bring to the public between the covers of a coffee-table book. One snap captured a pair of young women in minimalist sportswear apparently undergoing a searching workout. Simi was 'persevering' with a text to accompany his glossy souvenir. 'I write better English than I talk,' he said, the accent of his Corsican childhood unmodulated by long exposure to the stews of Soho. In the bearded middle-aged man it was possible to descry the young hoofer who had arrived penniless in London. 'I had a saucepan, to cook food in the hotel. I suppose it was illegal.' Simi has calculated that the curtain rose 22,000 times on his shows. 'More than *The Mousetrap*,' he said. In excess of two million people came to gawp at his productions. How many routines had he choreographed at the Revuebar? Pah, too many to count, perhaps 1,000. Raymond, the former vaudeville turn, had prided himself on being an impresario. As well as the Revuebar, he bought the Whitehall Theatre and transferred a successful farce called *Pyjama Tops* from the United States, throwing in added nudity. Its success led to a run of shows including *What, No Pyjamas?* and *Yes, We Have No Pyjamas*. Despite their emphasis on bare skin, the plays were judged to be oddly wholesome by the critics. Sex was on show but it was also sent up. Raymond's most ambitious production was the *Royalty Follies of 1974*, which cost £300,000 to put on, a princely sum thirty years ago. The climax saw a live dolphin removing a woman's bikini with its bottlenosed snout. Like Raymond's other blockbusters, the *Follies* was rolled out to what might be called the legitimate theatre, and the dolphin played for many nights at the Royalty on Kingsway, now the Peacock Theatre. The responsibilities of backstage staff included installing a tank for the mammal, and lowering semi-naked models through trapdoors in the proscenium arch, which had been purpose-built to allow airborne entrances: 'tart traps' as they were inevitably known. The official history of the Peacock claims that the dolphin failed to adapt to its new life in showbusiness. 'Sadly, the conditions proved far from congenial for poor Flipper, who passed into legend as the only ghost the theatre boasts: a spectral squeaking, not unlike a crying baby, to be heard desolately wailing in its now abandoned and rusted prison . . .'

Gerard Simi's role behind the scenes was recognized in 1997 when Raymond sold him the Revuebar. 'I made money out of it, £7 million a year,' Simi told me. Around us were some of the fruits of his labour. Tropical fish pouted like showgirls from behind their glass. Simi's living room was dominated by a huge television set. Behind its shutters, it was like a deserted chateau. The money had bought Simi time to develop his gifts as a portraitist. On an easel, a work in progress celebrated an unabashed gym-rat who was entwined in a sash or perhaps a bedsheet. Yes, the money had been good, but where had it gone? 'By the end of Saturday night, we had all this money,' said Simi. 'By Monday, most of it had disappeared, on this and that.'

By the time Raymond had unloaded the Revuebar, it was the centre of his empire in name only. He had enriched himself by diversifying into men's magazines. At the self-consciously classy end of his adult library – I'm thinking of titles such as *Mayfair* and *Men*

Only – editorial was shoehorned between the pin-ups, in an echo of Hugh Hefner's *Playboy*. Heartbreakingly, this convention is observed to the present day, as though the staff have a touching faith in the taste and breadth of interest of their readership, or simply cannot bring themselves to break it to the old boy about the unconscionable charcuterie that is the mainstay of rival publications.

Not even Raymond's portfolio of one-handed journals could compare with the property business that he was building. Ironically, his opportunity came after a crackdown on the proprietors of sex boutiques, the successors of Conrad's Adolf Verloc and his 'dim shop with its wares of disreputable rubbish' in the London of *The Secret Agent*. The purge drove many tenants out of Soho in the mid 1970s. In their wake, property prices fell, and Raymond followed along behind, buying up Soho by the street. By the time he was done, it was estimated that he owned between a third and a half of the area. In recent years, his assets have included the freehold to Ronnie Scott's, Sugar Reef and Soho House. Nor had he severed his ties with the Revuebar entirely, it turned out. In one of the last interviews he gave, he told the *Estates Gazette* in 1990 that he had made his initial venture into property as long ago as 1958, to prevent his club from falling into the hands of Soho villains. 'It was the time of Jack Spot, Billy Hill and other gangsters. The wrong type of people were beginning to encroach on me. The protection racket said I wouldn't last more than three weeks, so, to safeguard my interests, I bought the freehold.' Raymond said that it was the best deal he ever did. There was still one last little drink in it for him in 2004, when he put up Gerard Simi's rent from £150,000 a year to £275,000.

It would have been even more but Simi managed to talk Soho Estates down from their original figure. However, the landlord wanted the new rate backdated to cover the nine months it had taken to conclude negotiations. 'It was an astronomical sum,' Simi told the *Independent* at the time. 'But still I managed to find it. I was only two or three days late. But they sent the bailiffs round one night, saying, "We are coming to close your place." That was the thanks I got for keeping the Raymond Revuebar alive. I was very, very disappointed.'

Carl Snitcher pointed out that the rent rise at the Revuebar had been agreed, not imposed. 'So we agree it between us and then that's the rent, and so it does go up. But that's the real world. And then what do you say, as a landlord, in circumstances in which everyone has agreed a rent? That, for sentimental reasons, you won't enforce it?'

Simi didn't want to talk about it any more, he said, about how he came to sell up and the Revuebar finally closed its doors after nearly half a century. The far Finchley Road was a susurrus through his French windows. 'It's not about finding work. I could go and work in Austria *now*.' Simi snapped his fingers. But he mourned the sophistication that had been the hallmark of his shows, the choreography, the sparkle. 'There is no market for striptease today. The boys all used to come down to see us in Soho on a Saturday night but they don't come any more. They think it's all one big gay village now. Lap-dance bars have taken a lot of the business away, so have the sex shops. People go in there for a quickie, as I call it.'

Simi told me that he still spoke to his old boss on the phone. But later he admitted that it had been several years since they'd had a conversation. 'He lives very quietly, counting his money,' he said. 'You know the customers always used to ask me, "Show me the seat where Paul Raymond sits," but the truth is that we hardly ever saw him. He liked to give the impression that he loved the club, arriving in his Rolls Royce, but really all he was interested in was the bottom line.' Raymond became one of the richest men in the world, with a personal fortune estimated at £600 million in 2004. But his personal life was less enviable. His relationship with his two sons had been strained. A famous affair with the former porn star Fiona Richmond was a distant memory. 'She has a family now,' Simi said. Raymond's daughter, Debbie, who had seemed likely to inherit the empire, died of a drugs overdose in 1992, and the old man was seldom seen in public again after that. John Walsh of the *Independent*, covering the funeral of the writer Jeffrey Bernard at Kensal Green five years later, reported that Raymond had turned up to pay his respects to a fellow Soho legend. Walsh found him 'unrecognizable'. Carl Snitcher of Soho Estates wrote to the *Evening Standard* in January 2004 to correct a story that the paper had run about Raymond. 'Although he doesn't come into the office all that often, he is still the chairman of the company and is involved on a daily basis with matters pertaining to the business,' wrote Snitcher. 'To say that he "spends most days in his dressing gown, dyes his shoulder-length hair yellow and doesn't cut his fingernails" is untrue. Last week he attended his granddaughter's eighteenth birthday party in fine form. His fingernails were cut, he was not in a dressing gown and his hair was certainly not yellow.'

Raymond didn't lack for posh grub, living as he did between the Ritz and Le Caprice. He could take his constitutionals in Green Park. When I went into his apartment building and said, 'I'm here to see Paul Raymond,' one of the doormen dialled the penthouse. But it was no good. 'I'm afraid he's not in,' said the doorman, giving me a wary look. I thought of the long-running *Private Eye* cartoon strip which had celebrated Bernard and the Coach and Horses in Soho, with its invariable caption: 'Jeff been in?' I wrote to Paul Raymond care of his condo and I'm still waiting for a reply.

The day came when the Revuebar was reopening. It was a fully-fledged gay bar now: it was post-op. I hesitated to tell Gerard Simi that I had an invitation to the launch party but he said he wanted to hear all about it. He made me promise to ring him and tell him how it went.

As is often the way with these things, the grand opening of Too2Much became a last-minute rush. The boys and girls who had been taken on behind the bar and in the cloakrooms arrived on time, but their hot pants didn't turn up. I heard all this from a strapping cigarette girl called Joy, a nice lad in leopard skin and a stovepipe hat. The essential layout of the Revuebar, and many of its fixtures, had been retained. In the red plush of a wall, I made out what looked like a circular panel. Had it once held a lifebelt, for use in emergencies in the dolphin tank? I opened the panel to find a rack of fuseboxes. In the larger of the two bars, Gerard Simi's beloved proscenium arch had been preserved – would I really call him and tell him this, I wondered – but the curtain would not be rising that night. There would be no writhing floor show, no naked motorcycle display team. Instead, there was a metal pole on either side of the bar, as though what everyone was actually attending was the launch party of a fire station. Pole-dancing! The stainless shafts were as infra dig as a teasmade in the bedroom of a country house. In the small upstairs bar, beneath a mirrored ceiling, I selected a cocktail and a seat. Woody Allen's professed wish to be reincarnated as Warren Beatty's fingers came to mind: there must be men out there – sad men, if you like – who wouldn't mind coming back as the Naugahyde on the Revuebar's storied banquettes. The club was at the back of the mind of every fond survivor of the Swinging Sixties, and anyone else who toasts that era. Its bump 'n' grind revues, which anticipated 'live bed shows', were like a photographic negative of John and Yoko beneath a coverlet the colour of inno-cence. (The connection between Raymond and the Beatles was cemented in 1967, when scenes for *The Magical Mystery Tour* were filmed at the Revuebar.) In the States, home of *Playboy*, the girls had large hair and good teeth and all lived with Hef on a bunny ranch. In London, after air raids and rationing, our sexual proving ground could hardly fail to be less sunny, less redolent of vitamins in the milk, and so a different kind of menagerie had emerged. Pigeon-chested, gyrating in their 'birdcages', the girls of the Revuebar might have been strutting their stuff in a wheezy-making coop or loft. It was all of a piece, somehow, when a 1970s television series inspired by Raymond's Soho was called *Budgie*.

I might add that it took me a long time to make my way from the main bar to the smaller one. Between the one and the other, I pushed through a door and was transfixed to find myself floating above London in a glass gondola, just as high off the ground as a man's outstretched fingers could reach. From my aerial bathyscaphe, I looked down in wonder on the serried blazons of Soho. There was the sign for Slinkys – 'for the liberated and enslaved: corsets, rubber,

leather, lingerie, SM equipment . . .' – and over there, the fluorescent earnest for the Café Roma (the classic espresso bar was another
threatened tenant of the West End). I was on the bridge over
Walker's Court, now revealed as the bridge of sighs at the University
of Life. Not unlike Leonardo DiCaprio in *Titanic*, you might think,
I travelled on through the night in the prow of Paul Raymond's
abandoned flagship.

Each man kills the thing he loves, as a Soho low-life might tell
you in his cups. Then he would wake up and scrounge a cigarette
and remind you of the punchline, the unillusioned motto of red-
light districts the world over: what's love got to do with it?

[Stephen Smith]

HEART OF THE MATTER

Charing Cross Road, I must have walked up and down it two or
three thousand times. Perhaps ten thousand. Who knows? How to
calculate a figure with any form of accuracy when it traces back
forty years to my early teens? Can't I make a stab in the dark, like
Simenon when he purported to have had sex with 10,000 women
in his 'need to communicate'? A figure later reduced to around
1,200 by his second wife. Whatever the number, this dynamic road
plays a major part in my autobiography. It has been a spine to my
life, as it is to Central London. Or, alternatively, the aorta, the main
artery of the body. My life would have been very different if Charing
Cross Road hadn't been there to support and launch me.

As a young child my grandma used to take me to Trafalgar Square
to feed the pigeons, followed by tea in Lyons Corner House. The
photographs, reinforced by family stories, tell me that's what we
did. I have absolutely no memory of those events aside from the
images. Did we only go that far? What else did we do? Didn't we
set foot in the Charing Cross Road? I could ask my sister, she's a
wealth of information on childhood memories. But I won't. I don't
need to remember the forgotten.

To walk. Always that pleasure. Even now. Another street will just not do; if chosen, it's for the exotic nature of the detour, not to experience the pulse of my life. This street has become an addiction. I've needed it 'to communicate' with myself, to make me understand the complexities and confusions of my life, though I cannot say that I realized that point until I was around nineteen. I had chosen a college in Chelsea because of its image, a sense of 'bohemia' – the Chelsea Set, with their Chelsea boots, those Cuban-heeled wonders bought from Anello & Davide, the theatrical footwear shop that was once to be found in Charing Cross Road. I had also chosen Soho as another fixed point for its sense of risk and sexuality – enhanced by its Italian delicatessens (my mother came from south of Rome), though probably as a ruse to cover my sexual awakenings and leanings.

Great Newport Street came to my attention as a jazz home for Ken Colyer's Studio 51. Not that I favoured that form of New Orleans 'Trad Jazz' – but I was aware, each time I walked past, a few yards away in Charing Cross Road, that jazz was played there. I did get to visit it later when a friend of mine, the poet Pete Brown, formed a band, one of many, that included the then session musician Johnny McLaughlin.

Studio 51 was to catch my eye again when I came across Patrice Chaplin's book *Albany Park* (the area of Sidcup that borders on where I live). I discovered that she grew up a couple of streets from where I'm now sitting at my desk. Her story plots the course of an escape from the suburbs to the wider world, via early trips to London to visit Studio 51 and other nearby jazz haunts and all-night cafés around Soho. Later she was to venture to America, to the West Coast, and marry – into the famous film family whose surname she now bears.

More in keeping with my mood was Ronnie Scott's, at that time in a basement in Gerrard Street. I was too young to visit the club, and the knowledge that it was in Chinatown didn't help. Any image of Soho, no matter how sordid, I have always felt comfortable with, but all images of Chinatown spooked me in those days, and perhaps still do.

Charing Cross Road was where people in the music business could be seen, walking to Denmark Street or elsewhere. Heads turned when someone like Hendrix in his multicoloured clothes would pass. On one occasion, in June 1967 at the Saville Theatre, round the corner in Shaftesbury Avenue, Hendrix opened his set with the title number of *Sergeant Pepper*. The album had been released that week. The audience, which included the Beatles, were amazed. Perhaps Hendrix had heard it at UFO, the underground club where all the great musicians used to come, and where *Pepper* would have been played on the sound system between live sets. Not would have been, but *was*: I was there that Friday night. Like many major albums it was played straight through. Hendrix only needed to hear something once to absorb it for future use.

Earlier, when I was at college, I found myself attached to the street as another world of dreams opened. I had been approached by a woman who looked like Sophia Loren. She wanted me to model for her agency, the Marjorie Jones Agency, which had its office at the end of Charing Cross Road, along William IV Street. At college I had not been aware of many gay men, now I was faced by a room entirely occupied by gay male models. My preference was always female and I tended to park myself in their changing room. I started my part-time occupation at the same time as a woman who later came to fame on the silver screen: Charlotte Rampling.

In my short stay as a model I was offered free hairdressing, and used to go to one of the best, Robert James, who had a little salon upstairs in an alleyway opposite Studio 51. An alleyway that led to Chinatown. But having my hair cut too frequently left me feeling the draught. I wanted my hair back. From that day I've never stepped inside a hairdresser's shop, though for many years I saw photos of myself extracted from hairdressing magazines and stuck in their windows.

*

Shape for 1965—
Mod means modernity
and moderation

MOD BECOMES MODEL

by ROBERT JAMES

I soon determined that I would much prefer to work in a bookshop. As far as the Charing Cross Road was concerned that meant Better Books, which was more like an Arts Centre, given that there were benches for people to sit on and a coffee machine. My fellow workers were all poets: Bob Cobbing, Lee Harwood, Anthony Barnett, Paul Selby. Our visitors, visitors as much as customers, were poets, writers, artists, and all manner of famous faces. The shop was more than a shop. Downstairs, in a squalid and damp cellar, theatre events occurred. Or, more precisely, Jeff Nuttall's 'People Show' started its illustrious history. The 'People Show' was the most extreme form of fringe theatre, what many might term 'performance art'. I witnessed shows that were a total assault on the senses. I saw Laura Gilbert hanging upside down from a meat hook, suspended next to the whole side of a cow that had been strung up for a few days, left to fester and rot, perhaps even to achieve a maggoty state. 'A Nice

35

Quiet Night' was the title. Laura swung from the rafters, distraught, racked with tears, baited by Mark Long and John Darling – until a member of the audience tried to intercede and confront the pair, insisting they take her down. The terror was real, nothing to do with acting. Mark and John turned on this man, a well-known psychiatrist, and berated him. 'Who said this was acting?' In another show, 'Golden Slumbers', Laura walked around naked, except for black fishnet stockings and a rose taped high on her navel, besieging Syd Palmer, who lay in bed, playing with himself, while Mark and John stuck their heads through a backdrop and added comments. The words might have gone, but the visuals remain clear before my eyes, whether wide open, or tightly closed. Today Nuttall's presence is there for all to see, larger than life, acting in films like Peter Greenaway's *The Baby of Macon*.

For poetry readings, we drew curtains across the shelves to prevent excessive stealing. Stealing was rife from the professionals. No matter how hard we watched them during the day they always managed to secrete books under their coats, art books in particular, as they turned and made for the front door. We couldn't challenge them unless we had proof. Occasionally one of us would walk to the door if we suspected a professional at work and stand there, to let them know we were wise to their activity, the gauntlet thrown down for them to take the risk of being confronted. Checking the shelves after their departure, we could not believe a book could vanish despite close scrutiny. Poets were the most incompetent book thieves, or 'borrowers', as one told me some years later. We watched them clumsily sticking books away in a bag, or beneath their jackets. If only they had asked, they would have received a good deal. Many a poet or artist – David Medalla, for example – would spend the day seated on a bench, reading and making notes as if in a regular library, and then appear with a volume and ask if we had a less expensive, shop-soiled copy of the same. For some reason we used to find just such a copy on the floor, a footprint on it. Not worth its price, now. Sold. Or Heathcote Williams, who used to turn up a few minutes before closing, whisk around the shelves collecting a pile of books, place them high on the counter. Bob Cobbing would glance at the pile, then at his watch – fifteen minutes after closing time – and nominate a rough estimate. Heathcote would leave to devour another trove of earthly delights. Arts patronage at its best.

On Friday nights I worked at UFO, the club at the top of the street. We stayed open most of the night, pushing on until everyone was dead on their feet. I used to depart around five in the morning, observing the remains of the audience collapsed in corners, waiting until public transport started. For me it was a matter of walking down the road and, keys in hand, entering Better Books, to stretch out on a bench and snooze until the others arrived, just before ten-thirty.

Memories of the shop come and go. Customers like the actor James Coburn – who didn't believe we actually knew our stock: no need to check the shelves for *50 poems* by e. e. cummings. Jean-Paul Belmondo was wary that we recognized him at all. Burroughs announced himself with: 'I'm William Burroughs.' Francis Bacon, never prepared to look for anything, always asked us to search and fetch.

When our wing of the shop was closing down, the cream being folded back into the more traditional sections of the shop next door, I bought up or removed some of the remaining copies of magazines like *Kulchur*. I used a borrowed car, one Sunday, to take away a handful of boxes. I was instructed to do that, otherwise loads of rare items would just be junked. As I understood it, the owners were closing us down because we were losing money, or not making enough profit (their role as unwitting arts patrons was not appreciated). They justified their decision by stating that they disliked the prominence given to Burroughs and his *Naked Lunch*. Of course, once they had disposed of the thriving but nasty avant-garde aspect to their shop, they sold Burroughs's books like any other. Why turn away sales? The shop that remained under the illusion that it was Better Books never recovered, even though it limped on, in one form or another, for years. All the loyal customers transferred their allegiance to Indica, run by Barry Miles in Southampton Row. And later northwards to Compendium, in what was then a peripheral area called Camden Town.

I was fortunate to find a bookshop that gave me my first steps into the world I wanted to enter. One of those who led me deeper into this world was Colin Wilson. In my teens I had discovered his book *Adrift in Soho* in the local library. It was that title, with the salacious word 'Soho' and its implications and propositions, that made me pluck it from the shelf. Reading a copy I later acquired, I note that the pub opposite Better Books, Molly Moggs, on the corner of Old Compton Street, was one of the first places at which Wilson's hero stopped when he descended on the metropolis in the 1950s. 'The whole city,' he adds, 'was a part of the great unconscious conspiracy of matter to make you feel non-existent.' But Wilson had a presence in my life. The novel led me to *The Outsider* and the pursuit of various references (Sartre, Camus, Nietzsche); each leading to further paths, avenues, alleyways, fields, vistas. A personal labyrinth, a paradise to my imagination. Wilson's books had a considerable part to play in determining my direction in life.

Another bookshop, better known than anywhere I worked, was Foyles. The shop was famous for its accumulation of stock, no clearance sales, back stock lost among endless shelves; no stock-taking. You could find books, out of print for years, still at the original prices. Here was a dream outlet for small and independent publishers who could always send in a rep to top up the stock, deliver them in the afternoon with a bill to be paid a few days later. A system I knew very well when I worked for Fulcrum Press, publishers of David Jones, Basil Bunting, Robert Duncan, Ed Dorn, Allen Ginsberg, Gary Snyder, Lorine Niedecker, Tom Raworth, Lee Harwood, Tom Pickard and numerous other notable or reforgotten poets. Foyles solved many a cash-flow problem.

The name suggests antiquarian quaintness, dominated by its formidable lady owner. This might have been true, but with its chaotic organization, and perhaps because of its low-pay practices, members of staff had other ways to secure a more clandestine reputation. Stories abound of drunken lunch hours, after-hours sprees. In the early 1990s, when I was friendly with various staff members, I would drop in to hear about the sexual activities that occurred in darkened corners, in cupboards, under the stairs, in the toilets. On more than one occasion I walked smack into couples half perched on the edge of their pleasures. Sympathetic members of the higher echelon were adept at turning a blind eye, remarking that it was just young people having fun, no different from their own youth. Lines of cocaine along the counter probably didn't strike home.

Bookshops have risen and fallen over the years on Charing Cross Road. At different times I have frequented one more than another, but the road has always been a road I can't keep away from. Each bookshop, when I'm standing outside it, is like a bookcase. Each offers memories and obsessions. Reading a building is like casting one's eye over a bookcase, looking for something that is not to be found, an item on the top shelf, hidden on the cornice. On a window ledge. A word, a turn of phrase, that remains frustratingly out of reach.

Further down the road, a decade ago, I was gazing up at the façade of one particular building, checking to see if I had the right number, as I had to deliver a package to a friend of a friend, who would take it across to Germany. I recalled that I had visited that same block of apartments many years before, a block I must have passed time and again and entirely forgotten. Not that the young woman had slipped my mind, or the events of our relationship, often extremely humorous. I have never again seen such an enormous bed, one that unfurled from an equally enormous sofa. Unfortunately, it wasn't her own apartment, but one she was looking after for a few weeks while the wealthy owners were abroad.

The thought recurred when I read that T. S. Eliot used to have a flat there, or the use of one, as a secret retreat when he wanted to escape from his wife. I wonder whether his memories were as pleasant as mine.

Do I pursue the implications for a trip down a road in my memory? Or do I leave it to 'decay'? Decay is a major factor in the thinking and composition of Morton Feldman. 'Decay, departing landscape, this expresses where the sound exists in our hearing – leaving us rather than coming towards us.' Decay as an aspect of memory, as a key to forgetting, is my interest. Do we always wish

to have our memories refreshed? The nuisance of photographs is that they create revivals of our memories, not always just single notes, sometimes complex chord impositions, opening out vast arrays that we never really wanted to revisit. The photograph of my grandma in Trafalgar Square, of me with her in Trafalgar Square as a child, has always been an early remembrance. At that time family photographs were a rarity, we cling to those we have in our possession. There is a photograph of my mother in Trafalgar Square too, feeding the pigeons, taken at the same outing: my sister has it framed on display in her home. I try to reimpose that image in preference to the one of my grandma that has been lodged in my head for far too long – particularly since I discovered, after my mother's death, the abominable way that my grandma treated her. It started when she arrived in this country to join her husband. Her telegram was ignored and she was left stranded on the doorstep until my father returned from work. I cannot forgive my grandma, teetering on the edge of the abyss in my esteem, countless excuses offered to justify her persistently disagreeable behaviour. It seems so unfair that the reward for her approach to life should be longevity, and that she should not only see her husband into an early grave, but also outlive her son, my father.

Until recent times there was only a trace of cinema in Charing Cross Road, one of the sleazy outlets of the Jacey chain. I can barely remember occupying a seat, except to sit and watch Yoko Ono's *Bottoms* film, which had a short season, its billboard viewable from Better Books. I went to see if I could recognize the characteristics of my own posterior on the big screen, wobbling along, shot in the early hours, after a session at UFO. I was taken back to an impro- vised studio in a Mayfair flat. Today there are only the passing faces of those in the film trade, their editing rooms and offices in this area. Always intriguing to note how films can change the location when they adapt a novel. Watching *The Russia House*, in connection with some research on Lisbon, I noticed how panoramic shots across the Alfama offered a sunnier and more acceptable disposition than the more subdued but piquant setting of John le Carré's novel.

How to erase that image of my grandma, that image of me with my grandma, feeding pigeons in Trafalgar Square? I seek the photo. It isn't here; I must have already taken the decision, some years ago, to exclude it from my collection. Perhaps my sister has it? Don't inquire. I can't erase the photograph from my memory. I can't pretend it doesn't exist. Not writing about it doesn't cancel its existence. I should accept that life is not only the pleasant images. Each street has aspects that might be unsavoury or that might create unsavoury memories. That I wish to exclude my grandma from my memory, for all her nastiness, not only to myself, but also to the rest of my family, particularly my mother, has become paramount. It has crept up on me without warning. It fills my head like a bulging burden. And so, instead of writing about a street in upbeat terms, touching on happy memories, hopes and aspirations, I find a lingering aftertaste of my grandmother traced on the screen, the canvas, the page. Despite my efforts to grind her into the earth, I find her eidolon becoming dominant. It seems to be growing beneath my feet – as if a dehydrated image, having been watered, swelled up out of all proportion. I even discuss my grandma with my sister, as we drive to the supermarket on one of our regular shopping trips.

When I was a teenager I was taught a method of accomplishing feats of memory, recalling numbers, objects and names in order. I was called upon to treat it as a party piece. I think the book my father used was called *The Art of Memory*. No, it was more salacious, something like *How to Improve Your Memory*. A garish yellow cover. Not that I had a bad memory. In fact I think it's good, just unfortunate.

Perhaps what is really niggling away inside me is that particular photo of my grandma, not all photos of her. No others seem as offensive as this one. Why should this be? Because the set of two photos is taken from the same outing, only a few years after my mother had arrived from Italy. It is obviously taken by a street photographer. It looks very professional. Very glamorous. My mother is dressed up for a day out, as they did then, just after the war. My mother is feeding the pigeons in the same way as my grandma, except that my grandma has me with her. I have seen other photos taken through the years of my grandma, but in this one I am with her, not with my mother. She might have rejected my mother, but she had not rejected me. She was probably paying for the day out and she wanted me, alone, to be her possession in the photo. That is obviously what is upsetting. A rare 'proper' photo, as they say, rather than the usual informal family snaps. A posed image that would undoubtedly survive because it looked crisp and professional. I have to be fixed in a smile with my grandma. That's the point, the real issue I have to come to terms with.

My activities in the poetry world overlapped with performance art. Kathy Acker was another who traversed writing and art, a part and product of the New York scene. Her readings were performances and her writing techniques were as much inspired by the visual arts as by literature. Though we met in Amsterdam in the late 1970s, then in Paris, pursuing a correspondence before she moved to London, it was rare to see her around town. Our paths diverging rather than crossing. The last time we met was in the Charing Cross Road. We were both on the way to other appointments, but promised to make contact again, to have an extended conversation. It never happened, illness and death intervened. Kathy was a writer who painted with words. Beckett said it was the shape of the sentence that was more important than the meaning.

I remember the way I had to divorce myself from my family and start afresh. Perhaps it is the suburbs. Hanif Kureishi, who comes from the neighbouring town of Bromley, notes: 'Culture is rather sneered upon in the suburbs. You're considered to be getting above yourself or it's seen as pretentious or financially not viable.' Only when you have established yourself, not necessarily in the arts world, but within yourself, is it possible to live again in the suburbs – where you can work in peace, making sorties to the centre . . . to the Charing Cross Road.

My memory is untrustworthy. Studio 51 was not a haunt of Patrice Chaplin: as I appreciate when I browse her book again. Other clubs and coffee bars are noted, but not the one I felt sure was included. Does it matter? Other memories have surfaced and played a role in the walk along the road. The choice is to keep writing, to pursue what I've been trying to pursue – while I am walking on the edge, there is still that chance to find something more.

Maple syrup. Out of the blue I think: maple syrup. When we

went to Lyons Corner House it wasn't to have afternoon tea, or cakes or scones, but to have waffles with maple syrup, something I had never had anywhere else. That was our childhood treat. No wonder I've lost the taste for waffles over the years. I could have chosen other locations to explore, but each would have a different emphasis, each would have turned up different reminiscences, even if they would not have been at the heart of the matter like Charing Cross Road.

[Paul Buck]

'Heart of the Matter' by Paul Buck is extracted and adapted from a much longer essay on the Charing Cross Road entitled 'Street of Dreams' that was written for a French publisher, and still awaits publication.

BETTER BOOKS

It feels as though times of intense energy and experiment come in waves. And in between are periods of consolidation or just 'treading water' or even a strong conservative reaction reversing it all. This is how it seems in the Arts, at least, though maybe it's a continual process and that sense of waves is more to do with personal history than anything else.

But for me the mid 1960s were one of those wave crests. (Younger readers' eyes glaze over at this point.) And one of the main centres, catalysts, for all this energy in London was the bookshop at 94 Charing Cross Road started by Tony Godwin, who had also revolutionized the design of Penguin Books. It was called Better Books. It was two shops really. One had a more general stock and the other, in the basement, specialized in poetry, film, drama, but most of all books on what was new, whether it be John Cage or Timothy Leary. It was near unique as a shop where you could find those rare imports and 'little press' books and pamphlets and heaps of duplicated/ mimeographed magazines bursting their staples. It was a place of discoveries.

From about 1964 the shop, or the second shop, which was by then in a separate premises just around the corner in New Compton Street, was managed by a series of people who were involved in far more than just the book trade. The list includes the poet and publisher Bill Butler, editor and writer Barry Miles, concrete poet, sound poet, publisher and instigator Bob Cobbing – and, briefly, myself. It was a fluid organization. For some periods I worked as bookshop assistant, others as a packer, and even as a manager. Between times I'd wander off for stays in the US or Greece, and then come back to a Better Books job. Among other workers at the shop I remember the writers Anthony Barnett and Paul Selby and the poet and artist's model David Kozubei.

What made Better Books so very special for me? It was a whole series of events held there that opened my and many other minds to all sorts of new possibilities, new worlds. It was Gustav Metzger putting small mechanical sculptures in the window that over the days were to destroy themselves and did. It was columns, totem poles, of burned books created by John Latham. It was the London Film Makers' Co-op putting on a showing of Kenneth Anger's films, including *Scorpio Rising*. It was Andy Warhol and Gerard Malanga showing some of their films. It was poetry readings by the 'New American Poets' such as Kenneth Rexroth, Allen Ginsberg, Gregory Corso, Lawrence Ferlinghetti, Jerome Rothenberg – as well as British poets like Bob Cobbing with performances of his sound poems, or the Austrian sound poet Ernst Jandl.

It was Jeff Nuttall taking over the basement and creating an installation, a miniature world that you entered by pushing your way through a tunnel set with phone directories. After that was a narrow passage lined, either side, floor to ceiling, with TV sets. Walls of blurred sound and distorted images. Then a seemingly peaceful grotto with a fountain, fake flowers and grass, and a dish with a piece of rotting meat. You eventually got out by crawling along a narrow pipe and sliding down into a round nest filled with chicken feathers. All the senses had been assaulted during your journey. (On the opening night the art critics didn't appreciate ending up covered in feathers, nor did they appreciate an over-enthusiastic Nuttall associate pouring paint on them through cracks in the floor above.)

The shop, because of these events and because of the range of books and magazines it held, became a magnet for anyone interested in new writing, new ideas, new directions. This in turn made it an important meeting place for the like-minded and not so like-minded – along with the usual sprinkling of nutters. It would be a centre not only for people in London but also for those outside, who,

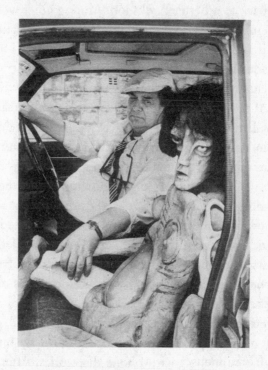

when visiting, would usually call by to inspect the latest publications. Jim Burns would even come down on a Saturday all the way from Preston just to check out what had come in.

The shop itself finally closed in the early 1970s after going through a series of owners, including the publisher John Calder. The times changed and there was now a different atmosphere from the heady free-ranging 1960s with its welcome foolishness, its optimism and its experiments, good and bad. In a way it had lit a fuse for much that would appear in future years.

There's no moral to this story. A fire flared up. It came, it went, and the people involved – those who survived in one piece – followed their own paths, overlapping at times, at others solitary. A shared, often distorted, often blind memory, but a memory that had an edge.

[Lee Harwood]

THE SINGING TED

Tom Raworth could be said to be the first English poet to deliberately assault the structure of language and come up with something quite new; the first considerable English poet whose professionalism refused the defining standards of established disciplines and attached itself to the high position of attacking the profession itself. English genius has been driven to absurdity by madness and perversity. English genius has never been urbanely at home with absurdity, with the unreasonable, with the unsystematic, with the illegal. Raworth spent a good deal of energy making sure that important American work was smuggled into the land. He published it in his magazine *Outburst* at a time when such writing was unavailable elsewhere, when the academic world was almost perfectly sealed. He was in fact first known as an editor and typographer; no one knew he was a poet in 1960. When his poetry did emerge in the late 1960s he could be seen to be facing towards Paris rather than New York. Consequently his closest influence is Gertrude Stein.

Like Stein, the area between the lines is a no man's land. Unlike Stein, whose lines are mono- or biolithic, the interaction of images within the line (or stanza) is rich and ultimately romantic. The multilevel interplay of images has a long-standing tradition in Rimbaud, Lautréamont, the Surrealists, Arp, Schwitters. But all these previous image-spinners were hysterics, grotesques. There is no menace in Raworth's imagery. There is no Freudian symbolism. There is no alarm. All Raworth's images have a seductive pull on the senses. They colour the inward retina, they tickle the palate, they wake half-forgotten sounds in the ear. Thus they have the lucidity of small jewels and the whole poem, built on its intervals of disconnection, is most delicately decorated, the fine handiwork of a master criminal, a consummate piece of cool.

The kind of cool that is Raworth's particular vehicle is not American, is not so physical, is not so swinging or black. It is the cool which is the articulation of pride and arrogance that the young of the English working class formulated for themselves in the 1950s. It is the cool of the drape suit and the blue suede shoes. Tom Raworth was, and remains as far as attitude goes, a Ted.

The current image of Teds, now that the teenage culture has spread into a far greater diversity, is one of antediluvian crudity. They are regarded, if anything, as synonymous with rockers. In the 1950s the reverse was the fact. Rockers were practically dressed, for the open air, for dirty bikes and transport cafés. They were scruffy, nomadic and loud. Teddy boys had cultivated an elaborate etiquette, an incredible pitch of vanity. They were foppish.

Raworth's home and his family are in turmoil. Wife and kids are shrieking everywhere. There is no money and there is no food. Tom stands before the mirror. Without any effeminacy he is quietly seeing to the hang of his tie, combing his hair, his moustache. It isn't that he's going anywhere or that anyone is coming to see him. It isn't that he's unaware of the turmoil around and the issues indicated. He is just putting first things first, seeing to his own image with a certain calm authority.

This urbanity is founded on the clear ground afforded by an icily preserved toughness, even a cruelty. The voice always even, in anger, in love, the same balanced note. A little throaty, as though cigarette smoke had but hours ago dried tears. The statements short and summary, near-whispered out of a scarred mouth . . .

*

'The first job we did together was an Estate Agents. A friend had
an aunt working there, and she told him a house had been bought
for cash one Saturday afternoon and they hadn't had time to bank
the money. We met at the dance hall with a vague idea of establishing some sort of alibi. At eight-thirty we left, stole a van from
the car park (the only motor with the keys left in it) and drove
there. The office was on the main road and the lights were on all
night. Parked the van in a side street and went down the road at
the back. A narrow lane along the back of the building. We counted
off the windows. Pitch black. Don went over the wall first while
Joe and I crouched behind it. Silence. Ten minutes passed and Joe
got nervous. Let's go he said. Don't be a cunt I told him, what
about Don? Leave him he said. I shoved him. Do what? What if he
had some sort of accident in there? You want us to just piss off and
leave him? Get over there and see what's happening. He went over
the wall. I waited. Five minutes. Then a crash of breaking glass. I
started to walk away, but no one came, nothing moved. So I went
back and climbed over. Reached the back of the office, avoided
pieces of broken glass on the ground and climbed in. Don and Joe
were in the back room looking at the safe. What happened? I asked
Don. I got here, he said, I take out the pane all carefully, I lay it
down, then what does this four-eyed git do but come tramping
along like a fucking elephant and walks straight over it. Joe blinked.
Prick I said to him. He blinked again. And look at this fucking
thing Don went on, pointing at the safe. It was immense. Until
that moment I'd not really thought about it. Had imagined it as
something about the size of a biscuit tin that we could cart out to
the van and crack later. But it looked larger than a fridge. One
keyhole and a handle. Well we're not going to open that Don said,
unless we shove this cunt's thin head in the crack and use him as a
fucking lever. He nodded at Joe, who was trying to lift an enormous
adding machine from one of the desks. We can get a fiver for this
he said. Don pushed him. You tiny-minded bastard that's just about
your mark. You think I want to risk two years for a fucking glorified
abacus? Joe stared at him. You think you're really hard he said, if

49

I had my shooter here you wouldn't be so bleedin flash. Piss off I told him, I bet you stand in front of the mirror every night waving it about and thinking you're Dillinger. Oh you two piss me off he said, always bleedin nagging. Then I lost my temper. Stamped on his foot, and as he bent, kneed him in the mouth. Two of his teeth came out and my leg began to bleed. Fuckin HELL Don said, where the fuck do you think you are? We'll have the law round before we've even nicked a pencil. OK I said. And helped Joe up. You SHIT he kept saying, what you do THAT for? Don was moving around the room: it must have been the manager's office. We can take these . . . he pointed to two small typewriters. And that cigarette box, that lighter. Have a look through the desk . . . I did. There were a couple of paper knives, stapler, some odds and ends. You want to try that? I asked, pointing at the safe. I did he said, it's locked well enough. We couldn't open it. Even from the back? He shook his head. Maybe if we had the tools and more time. But not after all that row. Better take what we can and go. Look for your teeth I said to Joe. If the law find them they'll use them as evidence. If they can bear to touch them said Don. We left and drove back. Dumped Joe near the dance hall. Arranged to meet him in the morning to sell the stuff to a dealer in Woolwich. What shall we do now? Don asked. I don't feel much like going home. Nor me. Let's have a motor somewhere. We can put this back in the morning.'

Essex University. Summer arts festival. Groups, poets, dancers. Over the golden lea somebody is roasting an ox in the afternoon heat. They are not roasting it very well. The outdoor auditorium, with grass steps and concrete steps, carries overtones of Roman ruins and Nuremberg mistakes. The university pop group amiably does its crust. I am MC. Tom, Val and friends sit among the sparse audience and turn on. Later there is beer and more beer. All the people I meet are on the verge of dislocation. I am. My thirteen-year-old daughter has disappeared, run away to London. Having completed my MC job I have half an urge to take a swift train to London and search for her up and down the bowels of night-town. But the relief of getting off the concrete stage lets in the anxiety. The anxiety mixes with that of others and lets in the alcohol. The bar is a row of social knots and in each of these social knots people are laughing and drinking back sudden lets of tears. Tom, the practised stoic, is even jaunty among this. So that when finally I don't catch the train to London, and my remorse accentuates my complete hopelessness about my daughter, when finally I'm carried from the bar weeping like a lost toddler, it's Tom who carries me. 'Cheer up, Jeff,' he says, with that even, throaty voice. 'Two best writers in the land, you and me. All is not lost.' Like much of what Tom says, the remark reaches a point subtly beyond irony, as though the joke were not so much the exaggerated claim as the ludicrous truth of it.

He put me to bed in a lecturer's luxurious office-study. Mysteriously I awoke in a cottage. All the birds in the world were singing out over the fields of cabbage. The world was alight.

It's difficult for me to imagine Tom Raworth without thinking of light. Some people are most readily imagined in beds, or pulpits, or motor cars. Tom is most readily seen in environments of light. Somehow the sparseness of his movements and the dry unsparing way he selects his remarks, his bold version of himself, emergent out of shyness – 'Manchester's a long black wall. I drove along it once. That was Manchester, somebody said' – accentuates the liquidity of a place, and the liquidity of a place is sheer light.

The nerve of Tom, like any nerve, is quickened by pain. 'Come in,' says Val at the door, with a black eye. 'I want you to bloody well see this.' She takes me in and shows me Tom. Tom's face is purple today. The eyes are terrible, the whites all red. There is a density to the flesh of his temples as though the veins beneath had congealed. The tiny fronds of his unaccounted scars stand white and delicate. 'Hi Jeff,' says Tom, his voice like a machine's. 'And shall we all drink tea?' I ask.

The room where they lived then was big and sparse. Tom kept the Methedrine in neat glass jars. It was before drugs were fashionable or even commonplace. Tom was cheerful with drugs, confident always, accepting none of the hysteria stemming from the laws about drugs, accepting none of the hysteria stemming from the law about anything. Methedrine, thought now to be the most dangerous of the narcotics, contrives just that sense of warm flight and total licence that lets a writer replace his craft with his invention.

There were new books all the time at Tom's. The kids kept coming in and Val would scream them back out again so that she and Tom could carry on their marriage like a couple of knife fighters.

Between bouts Tom paced the room. He sat on the couch in perfect profile, even his repose was poised. He stood before the mirror and pulled no face, just stood looking. He played a lot of Tamla Motown records. He moved ever so slightly to the rhythm. He made collections of postcards and souvenirs. He arranged his books as he arranged his face, impeccably. Much of the time he was impervious to interruptions of his thinking and his looking. The rest of the time he could be murderous. He would never answer the door. He would sometimes not see people. He could coolly abuse a friendship in a way that somehow made a friend doubly loyal. There was a man called Mike who was unlimitedly tolerant.

'Seen this?' asks Tom.

'Oh don't get out that fuckin book,' shrills Val. 'It's horrible, horrible.'

Tom shows me a book of photographs of war wounds, lips ripped off the gum, eyeballs lidless, skinned bone.

'Interestin,' says Tom.

At that time I thought Tom had done the A6 murder. The first time I met Tom was at a party where the murder widow was present. There she was, sitting beside me on the divan, and there was Tom, cool, dry-talking, with an impressive and almost imperceptible scar, curiously bloodless among the winey flushes. 'Are you terribly unhappy with your husband?' I asked sourly. 'I think so,' she said, 'when you consider that he was murdered.' The revelation and my own absurdity in the situation was like something written by Tom. I couldn't get it out of my head that this was an ironic situation

Tom had contrived, to meet me, anonymous in the presence of his victim's widow. Tom introduced me to Genet's novels.

Tom Raworth produced *Outburst* and made poetry available to Englishmen. With Barry Hall he set up Goliard Press. Edward Lucie-Smith wanted to strike an agreement with Goliard Press to print books edited by him and financed by the German scrap dealer George Rapp. Rapp went around to the press and was talking about putting money into it. Barry and Tom were printing, and Rapp was trying to find out some sort of basis for agreement. But all his chat had at the back of it the idea of editorial control. Finally he said something like 'I don't understand you. What do you think the best arrangement would be?' And Tom said, 'Just give us the money and fuck off.' That was the end of that.

Later, when Goliard merged with Jonathan Cape, Tom hauled himself off to Essex. No efficient criminal can sign treaties with the legislators. No lone dog comes to the hearth. The possibilities are terrifying.

[Jeff Nuttall]

A SERIAL BIOGRAPHY

They were taking up the paving stones along the street. The skin is so thin; the earth and trees so powerful. With one heave the houses could all come down. So easy to wear a groove in the brain; the same relays click each time. For six weeks now there's been a poster on the wall near my home. In large black letters it says SUMMER ENTERTAINMENTS IN PARKS, and each time I read it as SUMMER ENTERTAINMENTS IN PARIS. Same thing with Shopfitters which I always read as Shoplifters. When I sense I'm going to bump into someone on the pavement the only solution is to look away and keep walking in a straight line. Once the eyes hold, all those dance steps and the final collision is inevitable.

*

August 1966. Staring with my eyes out of focus (in this dark do I focus on anything?) through the train window. Raindrops trickling down look like floating puffballs. As we pick up speed their tracks swing towards the horizontal. Each back garden has thrown out a brick wall towards the train and captured a tree. Dark embankments, the earth dark. Looking back as the track curves, a narrow bridge vanishes into the foliage on either side, slightly out of true. Entering the tunnel. A grease smear on the window. My reflection blurred.

The way it *could* have gone, thinking like that. But no way left for the audience. What I want is a kaleidoscope, not a telescope. Now, their tracks merging with the gloom, the drops move across the glass like ball-bearings over black oil. Not right for this time.

What I must do. Is. Investigate the shape of a life. Somehow reach the solid body. Like the machine they use at Locks for fitting bowler hats. A nest of movable rods that finally reproduces the true shape of a head. Every bump. To push them all in until I reach something solid. Round and round, like peeling an onion. Like this . . . like that . . . I hate those phrases. The first try can't be true. Each time plane down another area. As time runs out I need a record. Truth and the ear. The vanity itself part of the fact. The struggle to get the thing, and not the many neat and true-looking other terminations. This is the body of what went on when we met, underneath the words. The real feelings, seasons, weather. The other noises that were more important to me as we talked. To leave myself open, with trust. I shake your hand. And again it is impossible. I know even now there are things I will leave out; things I will distort. But that is also the truth. If the skeleton is false in parts I can't remove or replace them now. Sunlight on the road as she met me that morning. Sometimes she couldn't remember. There was a card from Ron she said. Oh yes she said, he said Frank O'Hara died two days ago.

At least I was never arrested for anything *good*. That month I had to stop myself because I was convinced Americans were incapable of love, listening to them talking to their wives, the same words we use, I couldn't believe it. Because they've never been bombed. That was after I found out Pearl Harbor was on Hawaii, not the mainland, and all the time I'd been giving them credit for that at least. Losing cohesion, my arms and legs slightly out of time. I went to the library and took out books I already had at home.

There was this man, she said, and, you know, his left eye was somehow turned, all you could see was the red. And at school, when somebody wouldn't share something, cakes, sweets, we'd say think of Freddy Lane's watery eye when you're eating that.

There were peacocks in Danson Park at the beginning of the war, in an enclosure next to the Olde Englishe Rose Garden. The trams went down to Woolwich, a jumble of tracks at the terminus in the square. Picking my way across them coming home. When they remade the road, after the trolleybuses started, we used the tarry wood blocks on the fire that winter. Spitting stones across the room as they burned.

Jimmy I met in the West End. He'd been drifting around there for years. Had got a job in a shop selling pornographic books, films and photographs. He was only the front man; the job lasted until the shop was raided. The average time between raids was four months, but a friend of his had lasted seven. Of course the shop never closed; just changed name and manager. He said it was interesting for the first couple of days. Odd people coming in, and looking through the stock himself. But after that it was a drag, sitting there six days a week. But the money was good. £5 a day cash, no tax, no insurance stamp, no deductions. So he was making £30 a week clear. The day he was arrested he would get £50 and the £5 daily would continue until his trial. The owners of course paid all costs, fines and so on. If he was sent to jail, £5 a day would be paid into an account for him while he was inside. And there was a bonus system. £20 extra a week if the shop's takings exceeded £100 a day . . . and he got that bonus every week he was there. I'll tell you something he said to me. I'll tell you what the best-selling photograph is this week. It's a bird dressed in a frogman's suit, all you can see is her eyes, and she's tied to this kitchen chair with a piece of rope. All the old boys are going nutty over it. Can't understand it. I mean what can they get out of that?

[Tom Raworth]

DEREK RAYMOND REMEMBERS ROBIN COOK, HIS EARLIER SELF
The Carpenters Arms, Cheshire Street, 1992

I got off a boat called the *Gloucester City*, which was carrying grain, pig-iron and a 1934 Rolls Royce. It docked at Avonmouth. I was completely broke. Mrs Cook the First had taken literally everything I had. So I got on the train, arrived in Paddington and I'd got two shillings, max. I went round to the French – 'cos I thought to myself at least I can afford one of Gaston's halfs of bitter because they were only one-and-a-penny in those days. I ordered at the bar. Everybody said: 'Well, haven't seen you for a minute or two. Thought you were dead.' It was as if I'd never been away.

I was drinking at the bar when a young fellow, who'd been at Eton with me by the way, came up and said, 'Well, how's it going, Morrie?' And I said, 'A bit unsteady, actually.' He said, 'Would you like a job?' So I said, 'You bet!' I thought, I don't care what it is, this can't go on. I'd got ninepence. He said, 'Right, finish that off. Have a glass of champagne. Just got time for a bottle.' I said, 'Good.'

He said, 'Right – taxi.' And we were speeding off. We'd picked up some other people – who I found out were my future fellow directors. I said, 'I wonder if anybody, since we're in this together, could lend me a fiver?' Which was quite a lot of money in those days. 'A fiver?' Alan Peel reached his hand into his pocket, pulled out a roll of notes, about £300, and said, 'Have that.' He said,

'There's plenty more where that came from.' And by five o'clock that evening I was managing director of five property companies. I signed all the share certificates, all the transfers, all the company documents. The lot.

The retiring chairman, who was a poor old MP, can't remember his name, said: 'Gentlemen, are you trying to commit financial suicide?' And I said, 'My dear fellow, you've just committed it.' We were in business.

And what an extraordinary business it was. I was leading a totally different life. At twenty-seven you don't mind at all. I was associating with people I didn't know existed, except by reading about them in the newspapers. I'd always wanted to write, though I'd never been successful at it. I thought, 'I'm living a novel a day here.'

When we were doing banking, which was my thing, people would come round and say, 'We shall be needing £15,000 in cash by midday.' I had to go to the bank – you needed nerves of steel – and say, 'Well, Mr Smith, I think we should probably be moving this from No. 1 account into No. 3.' 'Oh, that's quite all right, Mr Cook.' What we were doing in the property business, we had five sites. We owned the sites. We were making 'starts' on houses and then selling them. Actually they were only about two bricks high, but, according to the company prospectuses, they were all ready to walk in, everything except the latchkey. We were taking deposits on continuing building work. The work, once we took over, quickly ground to a halt. No builders were actually contracted. We were basically working for someone called Charles Da Silva, brilliant conman. I saw him fifteen days before he died and we went back over all that. He said, 'You know, my dear fellow, what fun that was.' Black as your hat, Charles. Oxford. His uncle was High Commissioner of Ceylon. What a lovely man! Terrific! A remarkable person. He was always known as the Colonel. I used to watch him in action. My heart used to bleed for the punter, because I could see it twelve foot high on the wall. I couldn't understand why the punter didn't see it. It was like a rabbit mesmerized by a snake. But what the Colonel couldn't do, he couldn't gamble. I mean he was racing all the time. Used to live in front of the television, for the racing, and he never got it right. Never had less than £5,000 on a horse. Never. 'What's running at Worcester Park at half past three? Right, I think we'll have Hind Legs.' I'd say, 'Charles, I'm no great racing expert . . . you can't possibly win.' 'I've got a very hot tip.' That's why Charles needed me to go banking the whole time.

In my quest for information, I found myself doing the most remarkable things. As a result of which I invariably ended up skint. I had a taste for very expensive girlfriends. I did actually find myself, 1965, with a girlfriend on my hands who was costing me more and more. I ran into Bobby Katz and he said, 'Why don't you have a go at selling books? Porn.' I said, 'Terrific.'

We were in the French – where else? All my operations started there. Headquarters. So he said, 'Come up and get started in St Anne's Court,' which is where it was all happening in those days. The very first day I was working a man dashed in with blood all over him and a gun in his hand. Luckily he ran out again. You got some peculiar people. So much so that at one point we had a notice up behind the counter saying THE FOLLOWING MPS WILL NOT BE SERVED. Two Conservative, two Labour. Like a football match, two all! We had magistrates among our regulars, the most amazing people. MPs used to come in and say it was for a parliamentary inquiry. Bobby said, 'They're trying to get something for nothing. Bloody MPs, who needs them? Wankers. They won't be served.' Every time we took £100 in the shop, bottle of champagne. Pop. Terrific!

The harmless stuff was all out the front and then the heavy punishment, bondage and the movies were in the back. It was what they call 'visual and explicit'. I did suggest to Bobby that it might be interesting to have something a bit more upmarket. 'Upmarket?' he said. 'Look, this place has to run to so much profit per square centimetre. I know what the punters want. They're queueing up.' I could see his point. I miss Bobby. I was very fond of Bobby. There are stories I can't tell in public. They still make me split my sides. I can't really tell them. A pity.

CHARING CROSS HOSPITAL

It matters where you are born. Not just the country or the city, the burg or the hamlet – but the precise location, its height above terra firma, its positioning in the welter of the world; for this is the still point at the exact centre of the ever-expanding shock wave of your life.

For years it mattered to me that I had been born in the Charing Cross Hospital. Not, you understand, Ralph Tubbs's air terminal for the pathologically grounded on the Fulham Palace Road, but the old Charing Cross Hospital, slap-bang in the middle of London. Here, I fondly felt, I was ushered/expelled into life but paces from the Strand, the high-tension cable which connects the financial and regal powers of the land. Here, I considered, I was within dandling distance of the eight fake statues of Queen Eleanor that mark the spot where – Dr Johnson averred – 'The full tide of human existence is to be met.' Here, I was convinced, on a clear day of profound stillness, Bow Bells might be heard, their brassy clanging hammering me into the shape of a Cockney.

It pleased me to believe that Benjamin Golding's hospital, founded in 1818 in Suffolk Street, and transliterated a few years later to 28 Villiers Street, was my fount. I liked even more the vile Terry Farrell development the Thatcher era shat down atop Charing Cross Station, and which I felt certain obscured my very origins with its lumps of concrete, curvilinear steel and smoked glass. Liked it, not least because I ascended the windy decks while it was under construction, in my then capacity as a lowly corporate puffer, and looked out on the bend of Thames, pewter under a leaden winter sky.

How wrong I was – about everything. It wasn't until I set out to discover precisely where I was born that I found out the painful truth: far from old Charing Cross Hospital being razed, it has instead been transmogrified . . . into a police station. I was propelled into the world two hundred yards north of where I had thought –

and so the wonky trajectory of my life was amply explained. I identified the building from a photograph in the Museum of London archive. It occupies the triangle formed by Agar Street, William IV Street and Chandos Place, and is now separated from the hubbub of the Strand by a scarified, paved area. Designed by Decimus Burton, the foundation stone of the new old Charing Cross Hospital was laid in 1831. Decimus Burton, purveyor of sculpted blocks of hard cream to the Regency and then the Victorians. Decimus Burton, whose fantasies on the neoclassical stud Regent's Park and line the margins of Hyde Park. Decimus Burton – the Terry Farrell of his day.

I suppose there is a niceness to this disappearance: pioneering healthcare replaced by paranoid law enforcement; blind birth giving way to the blinkered investigation of death. There's a niceness also about the way that the new Charing Cross Hospital compromises the debatable land of Fulham and Hammersmith, dragging the centre of town out there, only for it to be Dead on Arrival. The new Charing Cross Hospital is a very nice hospital, it has hundreds of beds, it treats all comers. It has a pioneering transgender clinic – but no facilities for examining its own metamorphosis.

I went to see the old hospital – and, cycling along Exeter Street, was honked loudly from behind, then shouldered into the kerb by a monstrous American SUV. 'What the fuck d'you think you're doing?' I bawled at the driver, and he, not understanding that this was a rhetorical question, halted with a squeal, got out, came over to where I was struggling to dismount, said, 'Who d'jew fink I am, some fucking punk?' Then hit me in the face. Salt blood and toothy fragments filled my mouth. A stagehand from the theatre on the left was shouting – a mobile phoner outside the restaurant on the right was shouting as well. The anti-sophist was already back in his shooting brake and squealing around the corner. I had received a natal blow and was breathing heavily. I stood in the ever-expanding shock wave of my own life, and – since the stagehand had got the licence number – I called the police. After all, it's not often you get the opportunity to summon help from your birthplace.

A day later I went to speak to the detective constable in charge of the case. She wanted to get photographs of my extremely minor injuries and flesh out my statement. Being in the lobby of the police station felt like a homecoming. I could imagine my father, that quint-essential interwar man, striding up and down the stage-shaped space, under the smoked-glass sconces, while waiting for news of my arrival. Behind the duty desk there was a board full of missing-persons notices and appeals for assistance in murder inquiries: Camilla Gordon last seen alive leaving the Blue Bunny. DO YOU RECOGNIZE THIS MAN? (Yes, of course I do, he looks exactly like a forensic pathologist's reconstruction of a decomposed murder victim – I'd recognize him anywhere.) But there was no flyer reading: Charing Cross Hospital, last seen leaving Charing Cross in a westerly direc-tion. In the corner a revolving strip of pinprick red lights made the slogan: IF YOU HAVE BEEN THE VICTIM OF A THEFT WHERE FORCE HAS BEEN USED TO STEAL YOUR PROPERTY PLEASE INFORM THE STATION OFFICER YOU HAVE PRIORITY OVER OTHER CALLERS.

The detective constable I'd come to see pitched up and ushered me in. I followed her down a distempered corridor, coated with a carpet so flat and dun that it looked spread rather than lain. Doors opened off to the right, affording glimpses of offices full of obsolete computer equipment and paunchy administrators. Water-cooler tanks, blue, ribbed, plastic, lay on the floor like the discarded shells of a liquid bombardment. To the left there were windows, in their metal frames I saw the metallic mangle of police vehicles jumbled up in the triangular yard. We went upstairs.

In a tiny cubicle of a room as featureless as a desert, we were joined by the snapper. She wore a brown woolly and brown corduroy trousers; was she, I wondered, deliberately camouflaged? She encour-aged me to roll back my lip and show my chipped tooth. The flashbulb exploded. Into the charged atmosphere, I made the light-hearted remark 'I was born here, y'know.' The snapper, the DC – they took it well. 'There's been a lot of smoking done in this room,' the cop said, and I wondered: 'Before or since?'

I wasn't sorry to leave the nick – I never am. When I was born, in 1961, I had a congenital inguinal hernia. My mother wasn't able to feed me – they had to put me on a drip. I lay for six weeks – or so she assured me – in 'a little cage', until I was old enough for them to operate. As I strode along the Strand I wondered what had happened to the little cage; had it, like the hospital, transmogrified? Or was it perhaps still here, being used by the Met to contain tiny offenders?

[Will Self]

THE GAZETTEER OF DISAPPEARANCES & DELETIONS

CHARING CROSS CATHEDRAL, SW1

In the 1970s, a London Buses ticket inspector based at Charing Cross fascinated tourists with tales of how the (nineteenth-century) Eleanor Cross on the station fore-court was the spire of a great cathedral that had sunk into the marshy land close to the river.

[Sarah Wise]

THE STUCCO COLUMNS OF COUTTS & CO., WC2

The pillars of the Nash-designed bank headquarters, at 440 Strand, disappeared in 1973 during refurbishment. Charles Dickens used to lounge against them, as a hungry factory boy on his lunch break, in 1824. They were resur-rected by architect Frederick Gibberd in his gardens at Harlow, where, now draped in ivy, they doze their days away.

[Sarah Wise]

SWALLOW STREET, W1

Swallowed up by the creation of Regent Street in 1821: 250 homes and 700 shops lost, thousands displaced. The ghost of Swallow Street runs along the centre of Regent Street. Regent Street divorced Mayfair from Soho once and for all. The minimal number of eastern entrances into Soho was a design ploy to keep the London mob away from Nash's glorious shopping street.

[Sarah Wise]

THE FISHWIVES OF TOTTENHAM COURT ROAD, WI

In 1841, journalist Charles Knight wrote of them: 'In Tottenham Court Road, which still retains the character of a market, they stand in long rows as the evening draws in, with paper lanthorns stuck in their baskets on dark nights, and there they vociferate as in the old times . . . "Mackerel alive!" "New Wall Fleet oysters!"'

[Sarah Wise]

NIGHTMORE STREET, WCI

Maisie Bishop's Tic-Toc Club was in the basement of No. 21. Members included Dylan Thomas, Francis Bacon, Patrick Hamilton, Julian Maclaren-Ross, Henry Williamson and other literary luminaries of the 1940s and 1950s. The Colvin brothers (Jimmy and 'Wicksy') based their radio play *Nightmare Street* on the murder of Nigel Fox-Patterson, advertising manager of the *News Chronicle*. Fox-Patterson's body was found hanging from the area railings on 13 October 1946. At first thought to be suicide, it soon became clear that this death was the result of foul play. Johnny Nicholson, bookmaker cousin to the notorious Walworth Nicholsons, was arrested when it was discovered that the deceased owed him a substantial sum of money. Gordon Amis, cousin of the more eminent Kingsley, was also detained and later released. After months of evidence gathering, there was no prosecution.

Nightmare Street remains a popular play on the repertory circuit, featuring, as it does, characters clearly based on contemporary originals. The BBC recorded a television version as a real-time experiment which was said to have influenced Hitchcock and inspired his film of Patrick Hamilton's *Rope*. See also: Dan Farson's *Hanging on Their Words* (1962) and J. Michael Harrison's *What Maisie Didn't Know* (1966).

[Michael Moorcock]

GOLDEN PLACE, WC2

Best known for the 'Warrens' on its north side, Golden Place was notorious as a thieves' sanctuary, being technically Portuguese soil. A charter had been granted by Charles I to the Contessa d'Ecreta, an adventuress associated with *L'École des Fleures*, a secret society pursuing alchemical experiment and the search for the Emerald Stone – itself said to be a form taken by the Holy Grail (otherwise documented as the 'Roone Staffe'). Originally the haunt of quacks and 'hereticks', Golden Place degenerated into a haven for criminals. It was returned to England by the Portuguese government in 1934. The Warrens endured as a slum of evil reputation while various government agencies debated jurisdiction and responsibility. Much of the area was flattened by German incendiary bombs in 1941. The offices of the Inland Security Services (IS4) now occupy the site.

[Michael Moorcock]

THE VENUE UNDERGROUND, LITTLE MONMOUTH
STREET, WC1

Originally (1954) opened as the Jazz Cellar. In the early 1960s it changed its name to the Cellar and later to the

Basement. It was where the Beatles first performed in London, but was better known for its association with the Rolling Stones and the Who. The Deep Fix were resident there until 1977, when the Venue decided to feature nothing but punk bands such as the Adverts, Siouxsie and the Banshees and Needle. It is now chiefly associated with rap and hip-hop.

[Michael Moorcock]

THE REGENT STREET COLONNADE, SW1

The destruction is complete. One of the most striking features of modern London has been cut off its face, and a great public injury committed, to gratify a score of persons who fancy they will be individually benefited by the removal of the colonnade. Now that the mischief is done, some of our contemporaries are raising their voices against it. The *Daily News* says, 'The poor Quadrant! Has no one a kind word to say for it before it goes? Shall we part from it without a friendly word – a sad, or at least a respectful, farewell? There are many among us old enough to remember what the space now covered by the Quadrant was before the Prince Regent and the Prince of Architects invaded it. The narrow streets, the wretched hovels, the dens of infamy (we may almost say) that stood upon its site – who did not rejoice in their destruction? There sprang up in that place the finest street in Europe, and the largest colonnade. A diversity of opinion may exist as to the merits of the work in detail, but there can be none as to its effects as a whole. The Quadrant has been one of the features of London – not a foreigner but asked for it; not a print shop abroad but would display in its window an engraving of it, good, bad or indifferent. One of our national characteristics is to affect a depreciation of things in which we really feel a pride. On the whole, however, the feeling of Londoners has been by no means generally unfavourable to the Quadrant.'[1]

[Sarah Wise]

SCHMIDTS, WI

And then there was Schmidts on Charlotte Street, staffed entirely by lawyers from Vienna, who assured you that an empty room was full, advised against the duck as 'terrible', and then sat down to update you on the friend you'd brought in once, almost ten years ago, and who dropped in last summer on his way to Nigeria.

[Ruth Valentine]

THE RING

Ann Baer gave me my first job, at the Ganymed Press. I was nineteen. I was a pretty terrible employee, for all kinds of reasons; not least that my husband, after his release from prison, used to hang around outside, threatening to make trouble. The Ganymed Gallery was next to the *New Statesman* building and shared a common hallway. Every few months an elderly man would enter the gallery through our front door and then pass on, through a side door, into the *Statesman* office. He always carried a shabby shopping bag and his tie was held together with a ring. We were told never to speak to him or give any acknowledgement of his presence. He was to be treated like a familiar ghost. He came through the Ganymed entrance to avoid speaking to anyone at the *Statesman* front desk. He was Leonard Woolf. The ring had belonged to Virginia.

[Claire Walsh]

BIBLIOMANIA

THE TESTAMENT OF CHARLOTTE B.

I

*England is the paradise of women, the hell of horses and
the purgatory of servants.*

ENGLISH PROVERB

'There is no such thing as chance,' Schiller writes, 'and what seems
to us merest accident springs from the deepest source of destiny.' A
woman salvaged from another time, and the story she relates – one
of rape, dark intrigue and abduction – may seem a touch familiar,
it may even produce a doubtful smile, but as much as can be proved
happens to be true. I do not think I exaggerate when I say that what
follows had a decisive influence on my thinking with regard to how,
on occasion and *for a while only*, we enter curious intersections of
time and space. I am not given to spiritualism or parapsychology
and, indeed, at the sound of those words will run a mile, but I do
think there is in this universe of ours something more powerful
than chance. There is even, I suspect, an area where poet and
physicist think and act as one. After all, what is the making of a
fine simile but a brief habitation of some kind of interstice? I am
reluctant, though, to allow my thoughts on the matter to congeal
into theory, preferring, as Keats does, 'to move between uncer-
tainties'.

Should one, in what purports to be the investigation of a historical
document, resort, as I'm about to do, to the personal pronoun? I
offer my defence without being asked to: the issues raised by certain
events of a couple of hundred years ago are resolved in the present
and in the present only and, necessarily, *through me*. A haunting is
what they comprise and, as in all ghost stories, a ghost is not a ghost
until it has a living audience. Also, there needs to be an outcome, a
place where all the loose strands are neatly tied together and these,

for better or worse, required my presence. Should events have proved otherwise, had these papers fallen into hands other than mine, what follows would have been the analysis of a social document, another sheaf for the departments of eighteenth-century studies. I would suggest that circumstance has turned them into something else. On the other hand, I do not wish to mystify, stump or bamboozle because to do so would be to drain a good story of a potency that is found only in the real. I'm not out to produce atmospheres.

I used to work for the antiquarian bookseller Bertram Rota, a distinguished London firm that had its origins in the person of Bertram Dobell; he it was who established the authorship of a manuscript that came into his possession. It was the work of the Elizabethan poet and mystic Thomas Traherne. I will make no such claims for the manuscript that came into my hands but it was through my happy association with this firm that I was more modestly rewarded. The history of the book trade is one of remarkable discoveries. A bookseller is not quite as surprised as he ought to be by the way objects move through time and space. Perhaps it is because he is, by virtue of what he does, the net lowered into the water, the bigger the fishes he catches the better, the more profitable. On 13 May 1988, during preparations for a change of premises, my colleague Peter T. Scott called me over to look at some papers that had just been exhumed from a cupboard where they had been lying for some fifteen years. Should they be kept or jettisoned? Actually, like any experienced bookseller, he had caught from the papers before him a whiff of importance. These were originally in the stock of another bookseller, 'Dusty' Miller, and when he retired the firm I worked for acquired them. This happened when I was still living in Canada with no thoughts either of staying there or of moving to England. It was only by chance or, rather, over a bottle of wine, perhaps two bottles, that some years later I came to work for this most English of companies. I had been there almost a decade when the present discovery was made. I relate all this as a demonstration of unlikelihood. The papers that are about to concern us had been lying under my nose during all that time.

They included:

1) Several military commissions, signed by George III, in the name of Captain John Hitchcock.
2) An account of expenses, totalling £53.15.1, incurred by Hitchcock's funeral in 1823.
3) A blank Gretna Green marriage licence.
4) A letter, dated 26 February 1821, written by 'Charlotte B.', and accompanying this, in the same hand, a manuscript of several folded leaves, which had once been sewn together to make a booklet of twenty-eight pages.
5) Another letter, which, judging from the contents and style, probably dates from the turn of the nineteenth century and is from a man, possibly a notary (his surname is illegible, but he shall be remembered by his first and middle names, Edward Tyrell), to a Reverend J. B. Watkins of St James's Rectory, Dover; the letter, of which only the second page survives, describes the above items.

Subtract items 1, 2 and 3 and begin with No. 5. Edward Tyrell makes mention of 'a curious feminine manuscript', which he might have read through were it not, he claims, that his eyes gave out by the end of the second page. He feels assured enough in his doubts, however, to state that what he is now sending Reverend Watkins is 'an imitation of the stories which eighteenth-century novelists used to incorporate in their stories, e.g., the *Memoirs of an Unfortunate Lady*'. It was to this feminine manuscript that my attentions were directed. It was, incidentally, only inches away from the open mouth of a refuse sack into which was flung anything of unimportance.

The covering letter, headed 'Private', begins:

'I fear, my dear General, your first impression on opening this packet will be that I am making you an extraordinary present & that I am taking a liberty with you which an acquaintance so long suspended does not authorize. To this I have nothing to plead but the gratification I *myself* feel, & though I am aware this could be no plea to your reason or your justice, I think it will be one to your friendship & kindness: for you have told me you still take an interest in my happiness & I am no longer of an age to be the object of *professions* – I *must* believe you – I should not, however, have chosen this time to offer you the resemblance of a form once dear to you, but for the very precarious state of my health & the desponding notions I entertain of the future. Since I last wrote I have rapidly declined, I took cold after bathing (which it seems neither habit nor precaution will enable one to do in this climate with impunity) & my Cough is daily becoming worse – I have not passed a Spring in England since 1814 & both the opinion of my Physicians & my own feeling make me look forward with considerable dread [. . .] God knows then how this may end – the Doctors say my lungs are as yet untouched, but that they are in so very delicate a state as to give grounds from apprehending the result of the next three months if I am exposed to the usual vicissitudes of an English climate [. . .] I will not say that the original romance of my nature might not have some share in this strange constancy – to love without *hope* – an *object*, a Being who was become almost an imaginary one to me – one of whom I could hear only through the voice of fame; to cherish a secret passion for a man whose character & profession were well calculated to associate enthusiasm with mystery – was not only a very seducing state of mind to a girl of my disposition – but it was the most fortunate turn I could have taken – yes, my dear General, I owe to this affection that the most dangerous years of my life were protected from Vice & that I have through so many difficulties & disadvantages raised myself to a situation in society which if not splendid is honorable – & that with a very moderate fortune I enjoy more consideration than many who are great & affluent. My fear, my hopes, my wishes have followed you through a long & glorious career & there was a something of exaltation in this interest which would of itself have preserved me from debasement.'

The style is pleasing enough, the sincerity of feeling unassailable, but it was not until my perusal of the following passage that something like a shudder moved through me.

'I should vainly attempt to describe the anxiety I suffered during the Mahratta War of 1803. I never could read a dispatch from India without trembling – never could I venture to read one in the presence of any third person – I believe I may reckon amongst my happiest moments that in which I once saw your name to a short report (I think of killed & wounded but I forget from whence) for it assured me of your safety – nor did I suffer less during the Wars of the Mysore. [. . .] – During the greater part of the years 1814–15 I was in Holland – Germany – Italy – Switzerland – God knows where & did not hear of your Campaign, nor its results till the Spring of 1816 [. . .] The Hero of Nepaul little imagined that his early friend was on the 15th of May 1816 giving a Ball in celebration of the anniversary of his treaty after the reduction of Malown, to some of the prettiest women in Paris – But forgive me – I have wandered half over your Peninsula in recalling the tender & Constant concern I have ever felt for your safety & your fame.'

It was as if the post had arrived over a century and a half late. I knew immediately from the historical details and dates, all of which were precise, *exactly* to whom she was writing. There is a single detail later in her manuscript, where proof would be absolute, where she had scratched through the recipient's name, which when held up to the light is clearly visible. The 'Being' she idolized was my great-great-grandfather on my mother's side, Sir David Ochterlony. Some months earlier, I had stood beside Ochterlony's crumbling mausoleum in the haunting European cemetery at Meerut, north of Delhi, and for the past year or so I had been gathering materials on his life.

Ochterlony is one of the most fascinating historical figures to have never had a biography fully devoted to him. Although I had accumulated notes on his military career, and in particular his victory over the Gurkhas, the man himself remains one of those enigmatic figures of whom history leaves little more than a silhouette.

I possess a painting of him in full military dress, probably painted at around the time Charlotte writes her letter. There is nothing much revealed in the face, a certain vulnerability perhaps beneath the stiffness of the pose, something a bit glazed across the eyes, but this could be a fanciful reading. In truth, it is probably little more than a likeness. There is a copy of the painting, which I saw exhibited not so long ago at the National Army Museum. The note beneath it stated the subject never married. I protested. I was not listened to. Accompanying my painting are portraits of two young women, presumably his daughters. The written labels on the back of them describe them as having been born the Princesses Gorgii of Greece, a country that did not exist at the time. The Greek served to disguise the presence of Indian blood, which, ironically, is easily enough discernible in the paintings themselves. A military gentleman, now deceased, who began to write a biography of Ochterlony, showed little interest in the information I had to offer him, which related to his subject's domestic affairs. I feel sure it is an area of the life he was not prepared to countenance. When I first broached the subject with my great-aunt, in whose possession the paintings then were, informing her we had an Indian ancestor she expressed her delight at the idea, adding, 'I wouldn't want to be of mixed blood, though.' 'Aunt Helen,' I said, 'you *are*.' 'Oh,' she replied, bringing the conversation to a close. I had released all thirteen elephants from the family closet. Although the temptation, if one is a male, is to mentally project oneself into the harem it ought to be remembered that in the real world of eighteenth-century India husbands were expected to take responsibility for their wives.

When Charlotte writes her letter to Ochterlony in 1821, and believes herself to be dying, he, nearing the end of his life, is already a sad figure, prone to terrible depressions. There are accounts of him quitting the dinner table in tears. The simple fact is that British rule in India had cast him to the side. Already he had begun to unhinge, both physically and mentally, and in the following year he suffered a major collapse. Also, he was crippled with severe gout. Ochterlony was in fact only sixty-six years old and had been in India for forty-six years. A year later he was dead. It is melancholy to observe in what contrasting lights Charlotte imagines him.

I began to read through the pages of the manuscript to see what I could glean of Ochterlony's life, and as my disappointment rose what emerged in the absence of any news of him was a narrative of considerable power. It was now Charlotte who claimed me, and I wondered at these two lives that were linked together as though by means of a most delicate clasp. The 'Unfortunate Lady' is, judging from internal evidence, approximately sixty years old at the time of writing. She believes she is dying, probably from consumption, and is now writing to the first love of her life, a boy she knew when she was barely sixteen and whom she has not seen since. The letter is studiously composed, whereas, as we shall see, the accompanying manuscript shows signs of having been hastily put together, as though the writing of it were a battle against the writer's reluctance to do so. What the manuscript loses in the epistolary grace of the former it gains in directness, almost modern in tone, which gives her story its particular emotional drive. Although Charlotte may not, as she claims, have conquered vanity (she loves dropping names – Lord Harris, the Duke of Wellington, Mr Pitt, 'this vixen of a Queen [Caroline]', etc., etc. –), she is, as she approaches death, free of the strictures polite society places upon her. She is remarkably frank. She has improved her station in life, through a good marriage we may suppose, but it is to where innocence took a tumble, the years from 1779 to 1784, that she now returns. She wishes to make her case clear. The audience she chooses is both near and far enough to make this possible, and the audience also happens to be famous. What we have here is not simply the case of a female suppliant seeking a hero, for although she may be in awe of him, in this remembrance of someone she once knew having risen to fame there is a vindication of her own worth. We know more than she does, however. She is spared the knowledge that she is writing to a broken man.

The rest of the covering letter is written in some confusion and the tone becomes a touch shrill at times: 'Good God, what you must think of me, to believe that I who could so young & inexperienced resist the object of my first my fondest affections, & when I was eighteen months older, with my understanding more cultivated & a perfect notion of the consequences, voluntarily throw myself into the arms of a Libertine half mad & half fool – & who has been my ridicule and aversion.' She refers a couple of times to a 'Mr H—', but whether he is the above-mentioned Libertine is not immediately clear. The main thrust of her concluding remarks concerns her virtue.

'I doubtless have had many [faults] of both omission & Commission, yet it is most true – that no woman ever had more strictly the virtue of the sex than myself. I thank God that I am naturally cold – my passions have been all in my heart – an ardent love of literature – constant occupation – early disappointment – early calamity – have tended to give me a sort of disgust – to the relations of love (as it is called) & Gallantry which I have seen possess in the world [. . .] You will see, my dear General, that I have through my life held in great dread the violent passions of men [. . .] & such has been the impression made on me by such scenes that I never heard a profession of love however respectful & decent without shuddering & repugnance.'

I took the manuscript home and began making a typed transcript straight from the page, and it was in the slow fashion, word by word, that an incredible adventure took shape.

2

'It was about eighteen months after your departure,' Charlotte writes, 'that I concluded if you had been disposed to write I might expect to hear from you.' Ochterlony sailed out of Portsmouth Harbour on the *Lord North* on 15 July 1777. This much I had learned from my earlier researches. This is the date upon which we may construct a chronology of all that happens to Charlotte. She assumes, correctly, that the average run to India and back was eighteen months and that the *Morning Post* to which she later refers would publish details of ships' arrivals and departures. She was not to know, in this month of January 1779, that the *Lord North* had sailed on to China and that it would be some weeks yet before news of its return to England. Charlotte describes how she applies for help from a Mrs Green, the wife of a small timber merchant. We know she lives south of the Thames because she speaks of their crossing the river to go to No. 5 New Palace Yard where, Mrs Green told her, she would find a file of *Morning Posts*. A boy meets them at the door and Mrs Green explains to him that the man at whose house they are is a family friend and that their purpose is to see the *Morning Posts* that are kept upstairs in the drawing room. She then leaves Charlotte to go through the papers, saying she has to go to Bridge Street to do some errands.

'I had not the slightest suspicion. Lights & Coffee were brought by the Boy & the Coffee being already poured out I took some – almost immediately after I accidentally opened a Book (for at that time I was ignorant of all the etiquettes which forbid looking at Books) & to my great terror I saw Mr H—'s name – Still I did not suppose I was in his House (for I knew he lived in Parliament Street) yet I was alarmed & began to examine the room – on the chimney piece was a trinket which I had refused the day before – I no longer doubted where I was – my Head began to be heavy, & bewildered & terrified I flew to the door with the intention of getting away – at this instant this wretched man entered – I screamed dreadfully & I know not how it happened but in a violent effort to reach the door I struck my head: in an instant I was deluged with blood from my nose & the blow & the Laudanum together deprived me of my senses – oh General – what monstrous passions must a man feel who could abuse such a situation – I never think of this without an indescribable sensation of disgust & horror.'

Within the space of a few lines Charlotte describes not only her rape, by the aforementioned Mr H—, but also her accidental opening of a book. I do not wish to muffle the terrible blow she receives but the aside is a fascinating one. The reading of novels, and especially 'fancy works', as Charlotte calls them elsewhere, was not recommended for women. Steele notes, 'insensibly they lead the Heart to Love. Let them therefore [. . .] be avoided with Care; for there are elegant Writers enough on Moral and Divine subjects.'

The *Spectator* warned women against reading novels, which along with chocolates, and especially in the month of May, were believed to inflame the blood.

'It was many hours before I became sensible of the outrage I had suffered – on first coming to myself – I was strongly convulsed – my Head was swollen – my white dress covered with blood & torn to pieces – my ankle sprained, one of my arms bruised – it is impossible to imagine a more pitiable object – my mind was a chaos of misery & I was in extreme bodily pain – I recollected too the alarm of my poor Mother – I was distracted by every sort of anguish – but I was helpless – I could not even turn on the soffa where I was placed – I sank again into a state of torpor & was put to Bed by a woman who I found afterwards had been in no way accessory to my sufferings – I saw no one else & Mr H— did not venture to approach me – but he began to be terrified at the state I was in – yet did not dare to call in medical aid.'

She describes in some detail how over the next few days she sinks in and out of consciousness and is then removed, by carriage, to another place where she is tended to by medical people. She recovers just enough for her to be able to decide she will inform the physician of her plight but no sooner is she ready to do so than he is mysteriously discharged.

'While I was planning some means of escape Mr H— came. It was a dreadful scene – he deplored his violence – offered every sort of reparation – acted one moment like a Madman the next like a person really penitent – he had brought a small Bible with him & Pistols – protesting if I would not take an oath to conceal what had passed that he would shoot himself – this I refused – but said if I should have some Books & work I would remain & consider of it. The Books & needles & threads were brought me & after cutting out capital letters to compose Mr Beaufoy's address I sewed them on a blank leaf – together with my own name – & a sentence descriptive of my situation cut from the Prayer book which I had desired to have. This paper I found means to give to the Apothecary who I learned after was a Mr Saunders of St James's Street – he had probably remarked something extraordinary & readily went to Mr Beaufoy – proper authority was immediately obtained – & Mr B—'s carriage & Housekeeper was sent to take me away – for the people of the house made no resistance.'

What follows is a lengthy description, fascinating to any student of legal history, of the charges that are brought against Mr H— and how the prospect of seeing him hanged, together with the humiliation she would feel in becoming an object of public scrutiny, results in the charge being changed from a criminal to a civil one. Mr H— is made to give his word of honour that he'd never attempt to see Charlotte again and now follows a 'peaceful' interlude during which time her mother dies. Charlotte is provided with a servant and she resumes her studies. What happens some months later is enough to make the sceptical reader scratch his head a little.

'One Evening about ten o'clock just as I was preparing to go up stairs – the servant made a pretext of some Household want for the morning to go out & returning hastily she said there was a great fire up the street which she believed was at Mary Belson's the woman who had nursed me & of whom I was very fond – instinctively almost I put on my cloak & ran out with the maid – there was in fact the light of a fire but at a great distance – but she drew me to the water side saying it was quite *visible* from thence – in an instant I was muffled in a Boat cloak – put under a tilt & rowed off into the Thames – the whole was so rapid – so sudden – that I am not sure I even screamed & I had Westminster Bridge before I could disengage my Head & mouth – so as to beg the men to put me on shore – they were very brutal fellows & only muttered something about "Women running away from their Husbands" – the only person in the Boat besides the rowers I could discern was a Mulatto who kept telling me I should not be hurt. I was excessively terrified, for my idea was that they were going to drown or to murder me in some way – it was in vain I cried & entreated – there were no Boats about at that Hour & when at last I was landed in a lone place I expected no other than that the Mulatto was going to assassinate me – so that when I was hurried into a carriage it was rather a relief to me otherwise. A few minutes brought me to the back entrance of a large Mansion situated in the midst of pleasure grounds – I saw no inhabitants but a grey-headed man & his wife who took me up stairs in a state of passive terror – for I was really as much astonished as frightened – I had made an attempt to call for assistance in coming from the water side but if you recollect the *locale* – you will know it must have been useless [. . .] A paper was put in my hand which I saw was Mr H—'s writing, conjuring me to tranquillize myself for the night & protesting I should meet with no molestation – I found there was no remedy & hoping to get away in the morning & my cloaths being very wet & draggled by my struggling in landing I consented to go to Bed & have them dried. The room was covered with a sort of fresco paper representing the ruins of Ancient Rome & after fastening the Doors carefully I lay down, & worn out & harassed I sank into an uneasy slumber – but I had scarcely forgotten myself when I was awoke by the opening of a Door at the Head of the Bed – it formed the representation of an Archway in the Campo Vac[c]ino & unless closely inspected was not visible – so that it had escaped my search – you will imagine – what it would be so painful for me to trace. Suffice it to say that towards morning in some effort to escape I was thrown from the Bed on the corner of a chair & one of my ribs broken – I fainted from suffering & was for three months attended by a surgeon, a Mr Churchill (the brother of the poet), in a nervous fever.'

Although I believed what Charlotte wrote – in the way one senses a story too outlandish to be true must be true – the many questions raised here demanded answers. I would accept nothing I believed. It was fortunate that Charlotte provides so many clues, for there is barely a page of her manuscript on which she does not mention a name or a place. These I realized would need to be verified. A hundred facts do not constitute a true story, however, and truth may be composed of many smaller fictions. It would be the rare author who did not, to some extent, re-invent his own life; verity becomes version, yet in Charlotte's account there is remarkably little speculation. The events she describes are dramatic enough to survive her own interpretation of them. Charlotte is at the mercy of 'a Libertine half mad & half fool' whom she refers to throughout as 'Mr H—'. What she gives us with much 'Œconomy' of language is a character so exquisitely demonic as to make us wonder whether she did not invent him. Fortunately, she provides the two addresses where he lived – 5 New Palace Yard, Westminster, and Peterborough House near Parsons Green, which was then outside London. She mentions in passing that this last, her 'magnificent Prison', was once 'the haunt of Pope & all the Wits of that day'. Whatever truth her story contained depended largely on my being able to identify the inhabitants of these two houses. The local history library in Fulham was the obvious place to go.

I asked the librarian in Fulham about Peterborough House. She looked through her records and found a small file. I asked her where the house was, for I was determined I should visit the place, but she informed me it had been demolished. She pulled out some descriptions of the place, first John Bowack's in his topographical guide *The Antiquities of Middlesex* (1705), which describes Peterborough House thus: 'This seat is a very large, square, regular pile of brick, and has a gallery all round it upon the roof. 'Twas built by a branch of the honourable family of the Monmouths and came to the present Earl in right of his mother, the Lady Elizabeth Carey, Viscountess De Aviland. It has abundance of extraordinary good rooms with fine paintings, etc., but is mostly remarkable for its spacious gardens, there being above twenty acres of ground enclos'd: the contrivance of the grounds is fine, tho' their beauty is in great measure decay'd. And the large cypress shades, and pleasant Wilderness, with fountains, statues, etc., have been very entertaining.'

A watercolour of the house, done in 1794, which the librarian showed me, suggests that the house had not changed much since Charlotte's time. The walls were sparkling white and the roof a handsome blue. It was there that Charles Mordant, Earl of Peterborough, lived until his death in 1735 and, yes, entertained most of the literati and wits of the time, including Addison, Swift, Pope, Locke and Bolingbroke. Swift makes reference in several of his letters to the hospitality he received there and even wrote a poem beginning,

> Mordanto fills the trump of fame,
> The Christian world his deeds proclaim,
> And prints are crowded with his name.

In 1727 Voltaire spent three weeks there, and, to make matters curiouser, it was only a short distance from the villa where Samuel Richardson lived from 1758 until his death in 1761. The depiction of oppressed heroines was, of course, Richardson's forte. I asked the librarian who lived in the house.

'Why, the Earl of Peterborough, of course.'

The 4th Earl, also named Charles, lived at Peterborough House until his death in 1779. It seemed just then that Charlotte's story was about to collapse.

'No, wait a minute,' the librarian said, pulling out some further bits of paper, which included an advertisement for the house, now owned by Robiniana, Countess Dowager of Peterborough, to be sold by private contract by Messrs Robson & Harris of Lincoln's Inn.

A FREEHOLD CAPITAL MANSION HOUSE

with the spacious and convenient outhouses, offices, stabling for 12 horses, dairy, dog kennel, very extensive pleasure grounds tastefully laid out, and large kitchen-garden, well cropped and planted with the choicest fruits, hot-houses, green-house, ice-house, and fruit-house, with exceeding rich meadow lands, close adjoining; the whole containing above 40 acres.

'Yes,' the librarian continued, 'it says here that Peterborough House was sold in April 1782, to Richard Heaviside, a timber merchant. He lived there until 1795 and he sold the house, in 1797, to a John Meyrick, who demolished it and replaced it with a second Peterborough House.'

Heaviside, *Heaviside*.

The name was almost too good to be true, the very stuff of Restoration comedy. 'H' for *Heaviside*. I must allow for coincidence, I reasoned, and besides, the dates, according to my first calculations, fell a little late. I had reckoned the year of Charlotte's first misadventure to be 1780 and her second one a year or so later. My next step was to check the Fulham rate books, and there, in the column for 27 July 1781, Heaviside makes his first appearance. So he had been living there, possibly as a lessee, prior to the sale. According to the rates he paid, £17.16.6 (a figure exceeding even that exacted from the bishop), he must have been one of the wealthiest men in the borough. The rate book for the previous year indicates 'empty of occupier', so Heaviside could have moved in at any point after July 1780. It should be noted, too, that the names of ratepayers were entered in the books well in advance of monies being collected. I now had a Mr H— in the right place at the right time; all I had to do now was check the New Palace Yard address. The Guildhall Library holds old business directories. A 1782 edition lists Richard Heaviside, timber merchant, New Palace Yard, Westminster. Also, during these researches, I identified many of the people she mentions in her narrative, Mrs Green who led her to New Palace Yard, for example. The *London Business Directory* for 1778 lists Thomas Green, timber merchant, of Cuper's Bridge, Lambeth, which would have been very close to where Charlotte lived. Mark Beaufoy, a Quaker from Bristol, was a vinegar merchant in Cuper's Garden. He began his career by distilling hard liquor but was so appalled by Hogarth's depictions of Gin Lane that he turned to the making of 'mimicked wines' and vinegar. The poet Charles Churchill gave his younger brother, John, financial assistance to train as a surgeon. These are just some of the names that I was able to identify over the following months.

I had identified Mr H— more easily than Charlotte may have wished anyone to. Perhaps justice has been done. Does she spill more clues than she means to, or is she mischievously spreading them? I suspect that she is, despite the years closing over her and despite her obvious intelligence, uncommonly naive. It is this very combination of strength and vulnerability that makes her so attractive a figure. There is no secret that so breaks as the one most tightly reined in, but we must remember she is writing not for literary detectives but privately for a man she once and perhaps *still* loves. She struggles with the problem of what not to include in her narrative – that which most pains her, that which the world should not accidentally see and that which would mean little to someone as far removed as Ochterlony is. The joke on her is that she unstitches her own secrets while making them.

So where did we leave Charlotte?

'Surely General, sorrow does not kill or I must have sunk under these accumulated afflictions – I can hardly imagine a more desolate, a more forlorn creature than I felt myself at this time – I no longer complained – I no longer wept – my heart was half broken – the elasticity of my mind destroyed – & helpless & despairing I submitted to whatever was deemed necessary for my preservation. Mr H—'s mother was extremely kind to me, Mr Churchill really acted like a father, he brought his daughters to see me, & so interested one of the most respectable families in the Vicinage for me [. . .] all this while the evil genius of my life behaved very decently – never attempting to see me alone, & I lingered on in this strange situation till I was confined. On my recovery my position was changed & I now had a new embarrassment – I knew not where to go or what to do – I confess to you, though it is contrary to all experience, all one has read or heard of, that this offspring of fraud & violence did not inspire me with the maternal tenderness of which I *have* an idea – it was associated with degradation & misery & what I felt for it was rather pity than fondness & I deemed it a moral duty to preserve it if I could (for it was a female) from being as wretched as myself. I did not nurse it – & it was only brought to the House occasionally – I had bribed the woman who nursed me to send letters to my father & Mr B— but I could receive no answers for I found after, that the woman had betrayed me. Not knowing this I concluded I was given up – and at last I made a species of arrangement with

Mr H— by which he agreed never to intrude on me, or to bring me any visitors – I had a wing of the House to myself – sombre groves & bright Parterres – music – Books – whatever I desired [. . .] I was become wild, savage as it were, & could not often be induced to receive anyone.'

Clearly, she was living in a strange situation. With time, however, Heaviside returns to his old tricks.

'I was at times also subject to frantic intrusions from Mr H—. He was leading a very dissipated life – he endeavoured I believe to forget me & the atrocity of his conduct together, but it is certain he entertained a passion for me little short of insanity & which probably my coldness & aversion tended to encrease. He was once dangerously ill & made a Will by which he bequeathed me the whole of his property but nothing could conquer the dislike, the horror (I may say) with which I beheld him.'

What are we to make of Heaviside? What is his problem? A man so absolute in what he does is not without interest, possibly charm. This is not to excuse him, his crimes are heinous, but the risks he takes to secure Charlotte are so immense that in the end even her father is silenced. Heaviside must be judged in his time, and although the noose might have spared Charlotte much sorrow there is little doubting his ardour. He lies, he cheats, he breaks bones, but otherwise he is prepared to give Charlotte what he thinks she desires, even the education she so highly values. Dissipated he may have been, but Heaviside manages to keep the books balanced. He was an immensely successful merchant, and as such was part of a social phenomenon then taking place. The merchants quickly rose to power, social barriers were broken, and upstart traders moved into grand houses. Heaviside, about whom I learned little, was born in 1754 in Bishopsgate. His father was a saddler of some repute. The son moved into timber. And into politics too. In the 1780 General Election he ran in two constituencies and lost in both. At some point he was made Justice of the Peace, a position that had more to do with local prestige than actual justice. In 1800, he married Elizabeth Ann Proctor. A son was baptized in 1804. Richard Heaviside died in 1815.

He was, in terms of the social framework we have put him into, typical of the age. Whatever else he was, Charlotte has made him flesh and blood.

Now comes a critical turning point in her life.

'In this way I went on for more than two years till the Child died & I had no longer any reason for remaining [. . .] I then began to affect a desire to see plays & operas & to have valuable trinkets to appear at them – I pretended fancies for things which I had never worn or wished to wear, until in the course of a few months I procured enough for my purpose. Being now so far supplied as not to have the appearance of wanting to beg or borrow I related the whole of my story (which they had never heard from me) to Mr & Mrs S— & entreated their assistance in finding me some cheap place where the produce of my trinkets would support me for a year or a year & a half till the first search & the first rage of Mr H— should be over & I could claim the annuity. They entered into my project with the most benevolent Zeal & one of their friends a woman of fashion who was then on a tour of pleasure found & took for me a small cottage in Glamorganshire between Neath & Swansey & for which Mrs S— insisted on paying the first year in advance.'

She makes her escape and then begins a blissful interlude. I was to have one rather less so. I had already made considerable advances in my research, even though it had been barely two weeks since the discovery was made, but there were gaps in the typescript I prepared, certain words, which, no matter how hard I teased them, resisted decipherment. Whose property, I wanted to know, should have sunk in the Bay of Bengal? Which Roman Campo was depicted on the fresco of a certain bedroom? Who was the Frenchman the guillotine took away from Charlotte? Whose house was supposedly in flames? I passed the manuscript to my colleague John Byrne, who is an expert in autograph materials and whose eye is much sharper than mine. Meanwhile, I had written to the three Heavisides in the London telephone directory, asking them if they could supply me with any biographical information on this figure who might have been an ancestor of theirs. Surely, I reasoned, Heaviside was not a common name. I may have gone too far, but my fascination was such that I was now willing to go trampling through the private gardens of complete strangers. Only one Heaviside answered: 'Thank you for your letter. I am seventy-one years old, born Londoner. My father was originally born in Durham City. His father was in a wealthy iron business in Darlington. He, like the prodigal son, left home & came to London about 1900. He married an actress. They had a son. She died, then he married my mother. Yours faithfully ———.'

Monday morning I was back at work and found myself wading through the silences of my colleagues. There was something they were not telling me. A few minutes later, John Byrne walked in and all was made clear. There were cuts and bruises all over his face. The previous Thursday evening he had been brutally set upon in Pimlico Road and left bleeding in the middle of the street, and he had taken from him the black leather bag containing the original of Charlotte's manuscript. This was, in terms of what matters to me, a loss beyond loss. It seemed a mocking irony that from the violence of one century Charlotte should have disappeared violently into this. My wife drove around Pimlico in a futile attempt to find a discarded black leather bag. She even peered into the courtyard of one of the nearby housing estates. I sank into a kind of despondency and that week I dreamed about the manuscript, it must have been several times, and in those dreams I saw only the written pages, nothing surrounding them. I struggled with a memory of the shaped peculiarities of Charlotte's hand, and one night a *P* turned into a *V* and the word Vaccino came into focus. The next morning I consulted a plan of Ancient Rome, something I should have done in the first place, and there it was, the Campo Vaccino through the frescoed representation of which Heaviside made his dramatic entrance. Still, despite various other small mysteries I solved that week, there was the underlying knowledge that gone for ever was the proof that such a manuscript had existed in the first place.

I had resigned myself to the loss of Charlotte, and I had even persuaded myself that recent events were merely a continuation of the same evil that had befallen her. The mind constructs its own mysteries, it does so for the sake of coherence sometimes, and in a curious way I found myself not wishing to find the manuscript. I was to feel the same way when later I fretted over who Charlotte might have been. Would I be puncturing the mystery? I think in both instances I was proved wrong, for no sooner is one mystery solved than another is made. The detective story with all its loose ends so neatly tucked in is for sophisticated simpletons. The truth is always odder.

Charlotte, now aged twenty, describes a period of peace.

'I lived in a sort of enchantment & there was nothing great or glorious which my fancy did not ascribe to you – & this is so true that your image is even now as much connected with the Bay of Briton Ferry as with the scenes in which I really saw you – in which I first loved you. It was here too my habits of order – of arrangement – & study were formed such as they still continue – my homely breakfast of herb tea – or milk and bread – was always decorated by mountain flowers – & the repast which I called dinner & which was seldom anything more than Potatoes – an Egg or Oysters – was served with all the ceremony of a dinner *en règle*. I dressed regularly with as much neatness as though I were to be seen – rose as early as though I had a thousand occupations & bathed in all weathers twice a week – in this inoffensive way I lived above a year – the poor people were much attached to me for though I had nothing to give I worked for them & when they were ill often cured them by simple remedies – I met with no sort of evil or embarrassment, the natural energy of my mind kept me from ennui & I had a good collection of books – Johnson's Poets – Hume – Gibbon, Robertson & many of our best authors both in History & ethics. But alas a Cloud was fast approaching which must soon change this serene sky to gloom.'

Charlotte is down to her last ten pounds; her father and Mr Beaufoy, both perhaps under the influence of Heaviside, no longer support her; she speaks not a word of Welsh and although she could teach she cannot bear the idea of being 'surrounded by *dirty* children'. She returns to Peterborough House where she is placed under the protection of Heaviside's mother, who stipulates that her son remain in Kent. Arrangements are made for her to go abroad to a convent. Soon enough, however, her oppressor returns.

'Moreover the ungovernable passions of Mr H— rendered the House often a scene of nightly disorder – for in these frenzies he would break open the doors – get in at the windows & commit all sorts of outrages – so that I was often obliged to make one of the maids sleep in my room.'

At last, and I will spare the reader the complexities relating to her obtaining an annuity, she makes her escape. 'Thus, my dear General, I have brought you through the most melancholy part of my History . . . my residence in the Convent – my Marriage – & all the subsequent events you may (if I live) learn by degrees –.' The ending is not wholly satisfactory, all sorts of roots are left dangling in the air, but then this was not meant to be literature.

A week after the loss of the manuscript John Byrne received a phone call at work. It was Westminster police station. A policeman discovered a black leather bag in an open space in the middle of a housing estate just down the road from where the mugging took place. It was the very place where my wife had a brief look. It had been lying there for several days in the rain and not a single person was curious enough to investigate. I heard John Byrne ask after the contents of the bag. The bag itself was in a sorry state and all the papers inside had been either torn to pieces or else seriously damaged by water. Well, *almost* all of them. Charlotte's manuscript, which had been tucked in between a copy of *The Times*, because it was written in iron-based ink on handmade paper, was barely affected.

Quality is a passport to permanence.

3

The search to discover Charlotte's identity was not an easy one. At one point I had her eloping to Gretna Green with the notorious 7th Earl of Barrymore (a worthy successor to Heaviside). I never did get to the bottom of that blank Gretna Green marriage licence. I contacted the Bristol Record Office to find out who lived at 7 Pritchard Street and was informed that it was a Mrs Rachel Biggs. This, I assumed, must be the relative Charlotte mentions in her narrative. At least I had a B—, though. 'B' for *Biggs*. A friend of mine, Wendy Saloman, confounded matters somewhat by turning up a Will in the name of Rachel *Charlotte* Williams Biggs. The path from one Charlotte to another is too labyrinthine to retrace, especially in an age abounding with Charlottes, and, quite frankly, I could not have strayed further in my researches.

A couple of months later, I checked the British Library Manuscript index under 'Biggs' and found an entry for some letters from a Mrs R. C. Biggs to William Windham (1750–1810), who was a leading statesman and secretary at war under Pitt. When the letters arrived at my desk I saw immediately they were in Charlotte's hand. So the Rachel Biggs at Pritchard Street *was* the right one. I suspect that after Charlotte made her final escape from Heaviside she reverted to her original first name as a kind of subterfuge. She may have been the Charlotte Williams, daughter of John and Mary, who was baptized at St Sepulchre, Holborn, on 10 December 1761. There were Williamses everywhere, and nothing regarding them is absolutely certain, but a John Williams paid rates in Lambeth and a Mary died there in 1780.

Much mystery still surrounds Charlotte. Only once, in her correspondence with Windham, does she mention a husband: 'Mr Biggs has been lingering above eighteen months & is now in so deplorable a state that my only hope of his surviving the Winter is taking him to a milder climate [. . .] There was a time when Peace with the French Emperor would not have been remembered in my orisons, but I confess I am little of a Heroine & think more of my Husband than my Country.' The correspondence with Windham stops there, with this one and only mention of the husband who for now must remain a shadowy figure. Six years later, on 15 May 1816, presumably widowed, she is in Paris throwing a ball in honour of Ochterlony. What was she doing there so soon in the wake of Waterloo? Was she one of the fashionable ladies who followed the war almost to the brink of battle? In 1821 she is in Pritchard Street, Bristol, and the only other record I have found is that she died in a Versailles lodging house on 24 February 1827.

Not too long after he had been constrained to resign his high political office and was then planning a return to England, Ochterlony died in Meerut on 15 July 1825. One account has him turning against the wall, muttering, 'I have been betrayed.' Richard Heaviside died in 1815. A couple of years after the discovery of Charlotte's manuscript, while wandering through Bath Abbey, I noticed a tablet on the wall dedicated to the memory of Richard Heaviside.

HUJUS COLUMNAE SEPULTUS EFT
AD PEDEM, RICARDUS HEAVISIDE
ARMIGER. IN AGRO DUNELM NATUS,
QUI BATHONIAE OBIIT I2MO
APRILLIS. A.S. MDCCCXAMUM
AGENS LXII R.I.P.

Bristol, Bath. Mr H— had remained geographically close.

[Marius Kociejowski]

GRUB STREET

Milton Street, located midway between the Barbican and Liverpool Street Station, is a curious place these days. Not somewhere anyone would head for unless there was necessary work to be done there, or necessary money to be had. It appears to have almost no identity at all. There is one large building with tinted glass, kept in good repair, which has various signs relating to possibilities of access, but none whatsoever indicating what the building is for or what the people in it might do. The premises might represent one of those sphinxes of modern finance, both expressionless and inscrutable. The people inside would probably be devoting themselves to taking large amounts of money and, by alchemical means, turning it into even larger amounts of money. On the other hand, it has been rumoured that it might be one of our larger utilities, keeping its head down in a dangerous world. Whatever they do in there, they've decided to keep quiet about it.

Not so the eponymous Mr Milton, who was no relation at all to the poet of *Paradise Lost*, though the latter did in fact spend some time in this street in the early 1660s. This other Milton, unlike the owners of the tinted-glass sphinx, wanted his identity to be known, and so he bestowed his name upon the place so that posterity should remember: this was the man who abolished Grub Street when he took over the lease and renamed it in 1830. He evidently thought nobody would mind much, though if the original street were still in place it would surely have been heritaged into a theme site by now: the half-timbered, garreted homes of eighteenth-century scribblers and pamphleteers. There might even be character-assassination kits for the schoolchildren, each of them togged out in miniature periwigs, being given exercises such as: 'Write the nastiest attack you can think of upon the deputy prime minister, paying particular attention to any unpleasant personal or bodily characteristics you might have noticed.' This was the sort of brief that was all too common down the street during its heyday. The writers who made it their domicile were often the literary equivalent of the lumpen proletariat. They were verminous, both in body and soul.

What remains of Milton Street these days is only a sad little rump of what was once a considerable thoroughfare stretching from Fore Street to Chiswell Street. Samuel Johnson was characteristically terse and magisterial in his *Dictionary*: 'Grub Street: Originally the name of a street near Moor-fields in London, much inhabited by writers of small histories, dictionaries, and temporary poems.' G. A. Coole's *Walks through London* is almost elegiac. The place, he says, 'so long proverbial as being the residence of sorry authors, being spared by the great fire, still preserves several specimens of the old gloomy and uncomfortable mode of building. From this street has proceeded an infinity of wit and humour: perhaps authors were poorer in former days than at present, and therefore chose this cheap part of the town for their residence. Here, before the discovery of printing, lived many of those ingenious persons who wrote the small histories then in use; also, the A, B, C, or Abecies, with aves, creeds, graces, &c. When the art of printing multiplied black-letter copies *ad infinitum*, and stationers – whose name is derived from their being stationed at the corners of streets, particularly about Smithfield, Grey Friars wall, Paul's cloister, Barbican, and other places – became booksellers, and chose for their residence Little Britain and Aldersgate-street; authors chose Grub-street for their station, from its vicinity to the different presses and publishers.' This makes the whole thing sound positively homely, in a downtrodden but literate sort of way, a poor man's Yaddo two centuries back. The Augustan satirists took a rather different line.

The members of the Scriblerus Club, particularly Pope, Swift, John Arbuthnot and John Gay, delighted in the besmirched topography of London, though their imaginative delight was entangled in a permanent waltz with their moral disapproval. Their writing grew out of those streets, and the streets were famously crooked and rancid, like so many of the figures inhabiting them. Had Christopher Wren been permitted his classical re-gridding of London after the Great Fire, it is interesting to speculate as to how different this satire would have needed to be. The unplanned, awry, unpredictable lawlessness of London's streets itself became emblematic of the shambles of human chaos and desire that was domiciled there. Neoclassical the Scriblerites' precepts might have been, but their imaginations feasted upon a mighty Gothic bustle, and their loves and hates were continually channelled by an obsession with naming, both personal and topographic. In Pope's case the ceaseless catalogues and litanies of names seem at times to amount to something not far off a nominal psychosis.

London for these writers was a series of mnemonics, and the mere mention of a tavern, a street, even a particular house, conjured up a mode of life, a set of associations, even a raft of political affiliations. They could pretty well smell the names and taste the air of every rendezvous. So what did Grub Street mean? It carried a more complex significance than we are likely to assign to it today. Hired pens; words bought up by the quire; pamphlets commissioned for purposes of malice and turned out without much in the way of diligent research or caveat by those whose animus was therefore vicarious. The paid scribblers of the day, less salubrious and less well shod than Wapping's present crowd, though whether ultimately any less scrupulous is open to question. The street has become associated for ever with the word 'hack'. Yet 'hack' here has an intriguing genealogy. Deriving as it does from a hackney horse, as in hackney carriage, and therefore something put out to hire, the term is used throughout the eighteenth century to mean a sorry creature, raddled and worn-out, a jade. In the pages of the *Spectator* the word meant the driver of a carriage, a usage that emigrated to America. By a characteristic transfer this shifts over to the literary realm and by 1774 we have Goldsmith writing: 'Here lies poor Ned Purdon . . . who long was a bookseller's hack.' The first instance recorded in the *OED* of a usage in terms of writing rather than merely selling books is in 1798: 'The paper to which he was a hack.' And the first explicit reference connecting hack (in its abbreviated form) with Grub Street comes from Macaulay in 1831: 'The last survivor of the genuine race of Grub Street hacks.' Grub Street housed them; it certainly didn't invent them, even though the narrator of Swift's *Tale of a Tub* is called the Hack. Johnson's *Dictionary* doesn't refer to writing at all under his entry for Hack; it is merely a matter of putting oneself out for hire. But the next meaning of the word listed, and one that was current at the time, is prostitute, for the hack sold his brain and his lexicon in exactly the same way that a drab sold her body.

So the inhabitants of Grub Street were thought of as writers only in the technical sense of earning a living, and a meagre and precarious one, by pumping out words to be printed. Hence Grose in 1795: 'A Grub-street writer means a hackney author, who manufactures books for the booksellers.' So they were not 'writers' in the sense that Alexander Pope or Jonathan Swift were. There is a curious relationship between money and writing here. One could get money from writing, but one shouldn't merely *write for money*. Pope financed his little Palladian villa down near the Thames at Twickenham, grotto and all, from the proceeds of his version of the *Iliad*, which should surely make the present age think twice before patronizing that one. A lot of money was made out of the huge success of *Gulliver's Travels*. And yet neither Pope nor Swift was 'writing for money'. The motley crew who were hacking it and roistering down in Grub Street were seen to be the hired hands of the ephemeral literature of the day, simultaneously employable and disposable. Their names were writ on water, and filthy enough water it was, given the ad hoc sewerage system operative in London at the time. Things have already changed, the great Augustan pillars are already starting to fall, when Samuel Johnson shakes his mighty head and exclaims that no man but a blockhead ever wrote *except* for money.

The lapse of the Licensing Act in 1695 effectively ended censorship. From now on newspapers and magazines started to hit the streets and coffee houses, and pamphlets began to appear with great frequency too, vicious and biased as they all too often were, and were intended to be – but someone had to write them. Many of those who did the writing lived in and around Grub Street. The periodicals thrived upon the generation of opinion. It was for this that they were simultaneously praised and reviled. The production of opinion on a manufacturing if not precisely an industrial scale began in the early eighteenth century. Milton's sense of the meaning of the word less than a century before is worth noting. In *Areopagitica* he writes: 'Opinion in good men is but knowledge in the making.' In other words it is the scaffolding, the provisional structure, for sure knowledge. That's in good men. The implication seems to be clear, that in less good men, or straightforwardly bad ones, it is that which substitutes for real knowledge. This latter sense starts to grow vehement a little later. Thus Sir William Temple five years before the Licensing Act fell into desuetude: 'Nothing is so easily cheated, nor so commonly mistaken, as vulgar Opinion.' Or as Dean Swift, Temple's one-time secretary, put it a little later still: 'The Bulk of Mankind is as well qualified for *flying* as *thinking*.' The very name of the *Spectator* was meant to convey a certain stepping back from such a sea of opinion, from the tumultuous sway of temporary beliefs which governed the minds of those unanchored in tradition and learning. It's the *Spectator*, after all, not the *Listener*, ocular, then, not aural; there was an attempted lofty separation from the noisy tumult. Addison and Steele's prose seeks to be fastidious, scrupulous, choosy: this is, as it were, an anti-journalistic journalism. Steele even wrote an essay in the *Tatler* in 1710 on the dangers of reading newspapers: 'What I am now warning the People of is, That the News-Papers of this Island are as pernicious to weak Heads in *England* as ever Books of Chivalry to *Spain*; and therefore I shall do all that in me lies, with the utmost Care and Vigilance imaginable, to prevent these growing Evils.' But the mores of Grub Street pointed mostly in the other direction. The scandalous polemics were often lethal, and often very funny, but 'fastidious' is not a word that would spontaneously rise to the lips to describe them. Most of them have disappeared for ever, but then the word 'journalism' as applied to periodical literature means something for the day, borrowed originally from the French word *jour*, just as the word 'ephemeral' also comes from the Greek word for day. *Ephemera* are insects that live only for twenty-four hours. And the use of the word *journal* to signify a daily newspaper appears for the first time in English in Pope's *Dunciad*, a poem greatly devoted to the ephemeral and insect-like creatures swarming around Grub Street. Its grubs, perhaps, the infestation of larvae feeding upon that feculent climate of opinion. (In fact the word 'grub' might originate from a refuse ditch, known as a 'grub' or 'grube', which ran alongside it, though it has also been argued that the street once belonged to a man named Grubbe.)

An eighth of the population of England and Wales lived in London at the time. The topography might have been limited in reach, but it certainly wasn't in content. And it was, for many of these satirists, an infernal one. Grub Street was within easy walking distance of both Newgate and Bedlam. The damned and the insane were always to hand. It could in any case be hard to tell the difference sometimes. In Hogarth's sequence *The Rake's Progress* it is financial ruin that leads to the mental variety. First you lose your money, then your wits. The whores and lawyers of London are only too happy to lift one thing or the other out of your trousers for you. And the essence of London for these writers was the City, even though Pope, for one, hardly ever went near it. Anti-Catholic legislation helped keep him rusticated down in Twickenham. Much that is eminent in the City now was novel then. The Bank of England, for example, the Old Lady of Threadneedle Street, was a very young lady indeed at that time, having only been brought into the world in 1694. Since her founding was based upon the concept of a national debt against which the government could raise financial resources 'upon a Fund of Perpetual Interest', there were many who looked upon this newfangled way of paying for the state's ventures as not far off a national larceny. The rage of Ezra Pound against such a monetary system in the twentieth century was matched by the rage of many an Augustan in the eighteenth.

The dissonance that generates much of the literature is the jostling of one category and class of person and property against another; educated against uneducated; good writer against bad; money against poverty. As Yeats put it in another context: 'Great hatred; little room.' This is that combination of physical proximity and social distance which Ian Watt speaks of in *The Rise of the Novel*. For the truth is that Cripplegate was a sordid place, filled with pestilence and disease. Counterfeiters, whores and thieves thronged its streets and back alleys. The sense of sewerage, actual and metaphorical, is never far away in the satirists' writings. Jeremy Taylor as early as 1630 associated the locale with disease: 'The Quintescence of Grubstreet, well distild through Cripplegate in a contagious Map.' The estate agents hadn't gone to work as yet.

This sense of a pestilence affecting both body and intellect, with Newgate and Bedlam only minutes away, is crucial in Pope. Here he is at the beginning of his Epistle to his fellow Scriblerian John Arbuthnot:

> Shut, shut the door, good John! fatigu'd I said,
> Tye up the knocker, say I'm sick, I'm dead.
> The Dog-star rages! Nay 'tis past a doubt,
> All Bedlam, or Parnassus, is let out:
> Fire in each eye, and papers in each hand,
> They rave, recite, and madden round the land.

But the real gazetteer of the persons and locality of Grub Street and environs is the *Dunciad*. As already noted, Grub Street was very conveniently situated for Bedlam, and Bedlam was a place of public spectacle. Johnson thought it a useful experience to go and study the chained and bawling inmates, as useful as studying, for example, a public execution. And there was a particular animus to Pope's onslaught, since Grub Street was, among other things, a place of conventicles, and so by definition of dissent. But then if pressed Pope would have had to admit that as a Roman Catholic he saw the whole of the established Church in England as a vast conventicle. But the real animus came from the literary not the religious angle. And Pope's own justified belief in the excellence and scruple of his writing set its face absolutely against a slackness of linguistic practice he came to believe was enshrined in Grub Street and everything associated with it. To the vast monumental witlessness, the cocksure prattle, the self-important vaunting of his day, he gave the name of Dulness.

It is impossible to overestimate the amount of personal animus here. If there were ever to be a posthumous election to the role of president of Nietzsche's republic of resentment, Pope would surely be among the front-runners. The first hero of the *Dunciad* was Lewis Theobald, whose criticisms of Pope's edition of Shakespeare in 1726 were both severe and, as it happens, almost entirely accurate: Pope had been cavalier in his role as editor. So this fellow's 'dulness' was largely his pedantry, and as we know pedantry is someone else's precision, usually when directed at oneself. For the ultimate version of the poem Theobald had to make way for Colley Cibber. Cibber had attacked Pope's dramatic practice and infuriated him in the process. The attacks on both these writers were seriously unfair, libellous, scabrous and unrelenting, and yet somehow the poem rises above its undoubtedly frequent meanness of spirit to achieve something glorious and lasting: a demolition of the tawdry machinery of letters as it functioned in Pope's time, and found its parodic Parnassus in Grub Street. The Empire of Emptiness and Dulness is a marvellous creation, and still rings a great many contemporary bells. 'Dulness' does not at all mean a lack of intelligence. On the contrary, there is often (as Wittgenstein was fond of remarking about Cambridge) enough intelligence to feed the pigs. It is not the basic mental machinery that is at fault, but the object or objects to which it is put. For example:

> Keen, hollow winds howl thro' the bleak recess,
> Emblem of Music caus'd by Emptiness.

There's no shortage of that these days either, where all the lights are flashing and there's nobody home. It's probably grown louder in the intervening years.

These lines from one of the earlier versions of the poem convey the complexity of what is being attacked:

> Hence hymning Tyburn's elegiac lay,
> Hence the soft sing-song on Cecilia's day,
> Sepulcral lyes our holy walls to grace,
> And New-year Odes, and all the Grubstreet race.

From the sacred music to the 'soft sing-song', for we must at all costs keep those feet a-tapping with good cheer. Presumably there was a version of Andy Williams and *Sing Something Simple* in Pope's day too, even if there were no public broadcasters pumping out reality TV, quiz games and endless programmes about house make-overs. The vast machinery of a culture based upon the immediate assuaging of desire rather than the clarification, or even the exten-sion, of cultural need – this is Pope's target here. And in that sense, Grub Street might have gone, but the real object of the attack undoubtedly remains. The target is also 'scribbling', which means the production of words for print, words which have no other purpose than to preclude the possibility of an intermittent silence in which thought might occur. The Twickenham edition of Pope's poem has this touching note: 'For there cannot be a plainer indi-cation of madness than in men's persisting to starve themselves and offend the public by scribbling . . . when they might have benefitted themselves and others in profitable and honest employments.' Mmm. An interesting evening might be passed speculating as to which scribblers might gain entry into Pope's empire today.

The combination of clamorous mouthings and infernal din brings the *Dunciad* to a climax in Book Four. It is simultaneously a noise of self-acclamation and abasement before the gods and goddesses of this world, of whom Pope was not unduly fond. The noise coincides with the extinction of intellectual light:

> Lo! Thy dread Empire, CHAOS! is restor'd;
> Light dies before thy uncreating word:
> Thy hand, great Anarch! lets the curtain fall;
> And Universal Darkness buries All.

So was Pope calling for the destruction of Grub Street? If so his wish was granted topographically, but not spiritually, and certainly not in the sense of burying the Scribblers once and for all. They have simply multiplied and found new addresses. Where once their pens scratched, now their keyboards tap. Where once their candles waxed and waned, now their screens shine an unearthly blue light into the open-plan office and the Barbican apartment. Some of the prattle, including much of the Higher Prattle, is better paid than it used to be. So maybe there is a sort of progress after all.

The term could later be claimed as, in a sense, an emblem of one's hard work and lack of reward as a writer, as, with much anguish, in Gissing. Or here in Emerson: 'At present I am perfectly Grubstreet, but then I have the pleasure of earning every penny I spend.' There was even for a while a noun of membership, 'Grub-streetian', and an even grander adjective of ascription: 'Grubstreet-onian'. And yet, to return to the beginning, there is an oddity we didn't remark upon. It is in the nature of Johnson's famous entry.

Johnson's *Dictionary* was first published in two volumes in 1755, a little over ten years after the complete *Dunciad* in 1743. And the entry, as already noted, begins: 'Grub Street: Originally the name of a street near Moor-fields . . .' Originally. But Grub Street wasn't to be renamed Milton Street for another three quarters of a century. Why the elegiac tone? Because Grub Street had already become mythic. The grass had grown, not around the topography, but around the metaphor. To be in *Grub Street* was not necessarily to be in Grub Street, Cripplegate. It had become a spiritual distemper and a condition of life. Hegel famously said that the owl of wisdom flies at twilight. Perhaps the legend becomes most legendary at the very moment when its physical reality is about to vanish. A legend, in the nature of the word, is something to be read.

We have had a similar phenomenon in the last few decades. It was once called Fleet Street. In a sense, like Grub Street, it still *is* called Fleet Street, even though the presses are no longer there. *Private Eye* runs a column called 'Street of Shame'. It's hard to imagine them renaming it 'Wharf of Shame'. And yet the constel-lation that was Fleet Street has also gone for ever, and it is hard to see how it could ever return. Hard to see how Wapping can restore such a unique combination of talent, wit, repartee, institutional cor-ruption and degenerative nocturnal behaviour, ready for immediate transcription into club-land anecdote and raucous memoir. Now the cars take you back and forth from home to office, office to home. You can listen to the news; talk into your mobile if you've hit the big time and the chauffeur's driving. Stare out of the window at the postmodern blocks whose skins of reflective material might give you back a brief image of yourself inside your motor, only for an instant though, before the lights change colour and you accelerate away again. Leaving the topography behind you.

[Alan Wall]

VANISHING HERO,
VANISHED PLACE

We think we are living in the world, when in fact we are being positioned in perspective . . . The hero, the ruler, the superstar, the millionaire, the expert . . . how often have they sold out all they held most dear?

RAUL VANEIGEM: *The Revolution of Everyday Life*

In Woburn Walk, Bloomsbury, where Yeats once resided long ago, can be found the excellent Aquarium Gallery. A small but significant exhibition, entitled 'Pax Britannica: A Hellish Peace', was shown there, featuring work from 'distinguished artists who do not believe in war as a means towards peace, who deplore organized aggression and the killing of innocent civilians and soldiers'. Among those included were Richard Hamilton, Ralph Steadman, Gerald Scarfe, Sir Anthony Caro, Steve Bell, Billy Childish and Martin Rowson. On the evening of 31 March 2004 over a dozen poets read in protest against the American and British 'coalition' involved in the invasion of Iraq.

Reading with other literary friends, colleagues and acquaintances, on what turned out to be an extraordinary night, I was glad to re-encounter some writers I liked but hadn't seen for years, notably Adrian Mitchell and Ruth Fainlight. Conspicuous by his absence, however, was the latter's husband, Alan Sillitoe. This was scarcely a surprise in the light of what Sillitoe had recently written about the so-called 'war' against Iraq, but it did give me both reason for wonder and cause for regret.

I recalled the only time I'd actually met Sillitoe. This was back in the late 1970s at the Arvon Foundation's Yorkshire centre, Lumb Bank, where I was tutoring a writing course. The Sillitoes and their young son, David, appeared one day accompanied by Ted Hughes, whose family house the centre had previously been. A brief but convivial enough occasion, or so I remembered it. As a writer in my thirties, engaged by then on his own seventh or eighth novel, I was naturally interested to meet the internationally celebrated author of *Saturday Night and Sunday Morning* and *The Loneliness of the Long-Distance Runner*.

Those days, I was more naive than I am now, but I still thought I knew better than to identify authors with their fictional protagonists or projections. Not that I necessarily expected to be introduced to some dour, pugnacious hulk from the Midlands. Nor had I really imagined he'd be any kind of angry misfit – brash brawler or working-class hero. I'd not have been disconcerted, though, to meet somebody cast more in the mould of characters incarnated by Tom Courtenay or Albert Finney – the combative Brit stars of films based on Sillitoe's influential books.

Sillitoe himself, however, seemed no rebel, appearing shy, pallid and frail. Thin mousy hair was slicked across his scalp. Slight of build, he was suited, quite surprisingly, in a three-piece outfit complete with waistcoat; across the waistcoat pockets, very visible, hung a fob-watch and chain. For an autodidact who had left school at fifteen, this might have been regarded as mere affectation: or had he playfully reinvented a personality? When it was a question of drawing down a sash-window, some awkward wrestling ensued. He seemed hardly able to perform this simple act. I also noted a pair of round gold-rimmed spectacles, more mannered than cool. Sillitoe struck me as reserved and somewhat precious, a little short on humour.

Not given to hero-worship, I tend to be sceptical rather than readily impressed. It's true we had nothing much in common, apart from the English language. I was a foreigner, a perpetual outsider, classless exile from an utterly different country and culture. But Sillitoe's breakthrough early writing had struck home. Anger at injustice, principled and dogged endurance, resistance to exploitation or the bullying tactics of corrupt Authority – all these I could recognize. Alas, fame, money and the years intervene, and most of us sell out somewhere along the line. Individuals setting out as working-class heroes, writing and raging with wit and power, ending up as self-indulgent, drunken old codgers! I don't suggest that the undignified ageing process – the near-deathly hankering for honours, wealth, comfort, popularity and the like – has yet caught up with Sillitoe, though my initial misgivings resurfaced after reading his comments in *Authors Take Sides on Iraq and the Gulf War* (Cecil Woolf, 2004).

Flashback to 1937. Nancy Cunard edited and published her questionnaire, much imitated, inviting nearly 150 authors to comment and take sides on the Spanish Civil War. Only five supported Franco; two of whom (had I been alive then) I'd probably still have read but no longer respected. Both, predictably, were elitist reactionaries; both must sincerely have believed in the quasi-mystical Rightness (no pun intended) of their cause. Yet Arthur Machen and Evelyn Waugh defended an irrational illegal crusade: by their armchair assent to fascism, these untypical British representatives of *la trahison des clercs* let their readers know they stood for removing democracy and installing dictatorship.

By 2004, Bush and Blair, another pair of far less intellectual yet quite fervent believers (both in God and themselves), can scarcely make shift to defend their own irrational and illegal crusade. Having pre-emptively removed one ugly dictatorship, they plan to replace it, at countless human cost, with another. Who truly credits the botched British and American arguments, the crude, noxious lies? Who falls for this rotten arm- and word-twisting, the hate-filled propaganda pumped out daily with the pilfered oil?

These rhetorical questions bring me back to the reading in Woburn Walk, and to Cecil Woolf's questionnaire. For I was distressed by the comments of one writer who, among only two or three others, has wholeheartedly supported the illegitimate, pre-emptive attack on Iraq. Alan Sillitoe stoutly declares himself 'in favour of the war in Iraq'. Seven bad enough words (and note the last four, themselves making up a phoney definition of the conflict), but Sillitoe concludes: 'One can only congratulate the United States forces, and the soldiers of Great Britain. And, as for settling things in the Middle East, if this won't help the process nothing will. Israel and the West must stick together.'

Leading up to those appallingly blinkered statements, Sillitoe has the gall to quote Milton. He enlists the great radical out of context and into his own dubious cause. Cavalierly annexing a well-known chorus from the elegiac epic *Samson Agonistes* – quite as if it's a separate piece, standing on its own – Sillitoe next informs us, mistakenly and clearly deliberately, that this is 'a poem . . . called "The End of Violent Men"'.

It seems to me that Sillitoe wilfully misses the vital point here. Surely Samson himself, the great rebel vilified and confined like Vanunu in vindictive and dreadful isolation, is far from cowardly: humiliated, yet defiant in his blind desperation, Samson may be reckoned the original suicide bomber. How ironic that the arche-typal hero-as-victim, the bold fighter for freedom, viewed by the blind and disappointed Milton as the instrument of divine justice, should be an Israeli(te)! Ironic too that Sillitoe signally fails to distinguish between oppressor and oppressed: if he thinks Sharon's Israel, financially and militarily supported by the US and UK, is the underdog of the Middle East, I doubt we inhabit the same planet.

Writers must speak out and not sell out, since free speech matters more than 'free' enterprise, and if you compromise with the truth, you end up compromised yourself. Emily Dickinson believed 'Truth is so rare, it's delightful to tell it,' but published almost nothing in her lifetime. Our own so-called free press would have appalled and repelled her. Best keep your heads down and keep silent, or give the public what it's supposed to want. Upwardly mobile they may be, the working-class heroes of the twenty-first century, but they can't all have vanished.

Nothing is in vain. Heroes vanish as they must, but they're never forgotten. Even this late in the day there are 'flowers for the rebels who failed'. If there seems nothing much left to cheer about, it's always worth continuing the struggle, continuing at least to raise a fist and shout. Where, though, is the new young breed of revolutionary with the fighting spirit and the fire? Declare yourselves without delay, poets and radicals! Be ready to write your hearts out and bring some hope to this confused, war-ravaged world of inevitable entropy, futile greed, needless hate and careless love.

[Alexis Lykiard, May Day 2004]

THE LIFE OF IT

It is such a thing of hints and echoes. One lunchtime four or five years ago in Walthamstow, East London, where I was teaching, I had gone into a secondhand bookshop. It had some pretensions – 'modern first editions' wrapped in cellophane – and I got into conversation with an old man who was selling off some books. He started talking about Soho, in the old days. He used to drink there and he knew them all. He reeled off a list of names, Soho Bohemia. The next time I was there, I bought Nina Hammett's memoirs, *Is She a Lady?*, and I found he had made a bookplate, scratchily drawn and duplicated. Talking to this elderly cockney before he went back to his council flat on the outer fringes of London, I felt, even at this distance from the centre and some fifty years later, how Soho exerts a ghostly pull.

Upstairs in the public library in Hendon. It's 1959. I am seventeen years old and wondering where have all these paintings come from? Abstracts. It's as if they've flown in through the windows and alighted here on the walls in this North London suburb. I wander around, bemused. There are some pamphlets, and one of them I still

106

have. It's a local poetry workshop, the early days of Bob Cobbing's Writers' Forum. More than forty years later, I get it out again. Looking back it's as if I were peering in at something as I read those poems – a suburban literary group in the 1950s, these moments of private intensity, sadness and frustration mostly, being briefly shared and exposed.

1967. I have a tiny bedsitter in a house in Islington and am working on part-time contracts in various FE colleges. The other residents of the Islington house include two writers or would-be writers. They are both Canadian. Jim wants to be a novelist. He is in his thirties and lives upstairs. Charles Hatcher, in his early fifties and lodged in the basement flat, is a poet. Jim had thrown up a steady job in insurance, on an impulse as he would have us believe, and taken off for Paris. This would have been at the end of the 1950s but so far as Jim was concerned it was still the Paris of Hemingway and Scott Fitzgerald. The other, older man was already installed in Paris when Jim got there, staying, as they used to, in a cheap hotel. There was an expatriate literary scene and Charles could publish his Poundian poems in *Merlin* and *Botteghe Oscure*. He spent time in Tangier, on the edge of the Burroughs and Trocchi circle. Now he drifts between Paris and London, his movements dictated in part by financial considerations – his principal source of income appeared to be bits and pieces of freelance journalism for UK-based publications, mainly scientific fillers composed for partwork encyclopaedias, a genre that he once summed up in an often used phrase, 'The human brain is about the size of a grapefruit.' For Charles, as for Jim, the mythic pull was Paris, and I still have the copies of *Shakespeare and Son* by Sylvia Beach, and *The Passionate Years* by Caresse Crosby, books that embody the pre-war myth of literary Paris and which Charles had apparently failed to return to London libraries and had subsequently passed on to me in part-exchange for one of the small loans he requested from time to time. I read the Sylvia Beach only the other day, and I can sense the attraction. James Joyce's publisher, she knew absolutely everyone, and there they all are swimming into and out of her shop in a perpetual golden afternoon; and the illustrations – cobbled streets and traditional shopfronts on the left bank, faded signs and deeply etched shadows in the black-and-white photographs – exhale a powerful sense of nostalgia for a vanished period.

Charles never spoke of Canada save vituperatively and he never once mentioned his family. I don't know quite what it was he was getting away from. Talking to him I got glimpses of that expatriate literary life, and from time to time I would look in the folder at his carefully typed poems. I feel sure he never offered unsolicited work anywhere, and his only two publications, apart from his appearances in *Merlin* and one or two other magazines in Paris, were two pamphlets he brought out himself. One was written in French and was about a computer, and the other was called *How to Kill Poets*. He showed me how to do it, getting the poems typeset – there was a thing called the IBM composer, a glorified electric typewriter that re-created, more or less, the effect of traditional print. You paid someone to type them, then took the setting home and pasted it up, sticking the bits down with cow-gum and drawing pale blue guidelines, which wouldn't show up when they photographed it to make a plate. Then you took it to be printed, and you brought the sheets home and, to save money, collated them yourself. Charles had rigged up a home-made long-arm stapler to bind his pamphlet. Carefully I copied him at every step, borrowed his stapler and produced a pamphlet of my own – and this, I now see, was the genesis of the poetry press I was to set up ten years later and which I have been running sporadically ever since.

Meanwhile Jim tapped away upstairs. He had completed his novel while living in Paris and was trying to get it published, and now he was putting together a series of television scripts, and getting nowhere – I don't think he ever published anything at all. Two men marooned on the outermost margins of a dreadfully potent myth, the 'literary life'; and how it does lie in wait for you . . .

Still 1967. 'Over to You' at Writers' Workshop, upstairs in a pub in Covent Garden, and a shaggy-haired individual comes out and reads a long poem, 'A Young Girl's Arse is a Type of Eternity'. It is set in New York – he has just come back from there – and uses a long, swinging line to hymn the praises of his girlfriend's anatomy. I recognize him as the man I had met several years before at Jimmy's, a cheap Cypriot restaurant in Soho, which amazingly still seems to be there. That must have been in 1961. I was nineteen and, following a breakdown, was a patient in a mental hospital in Surrey. I came home every weekend and I had been taken to Jimmy's by my friend Simon, who was at Chelsea Art School. I can recall every detail of what was a perfectly ordinary evening, but for me was a glimpse, a sense, of some new possibility, something beyond the strange, shut-in life I had been living. There was a girl who claimed to be the latest girlfriend of a famous poet. There was a medical student drowning his sorrows – he was about to be thrown out of medical school. And there was this friend of Simon, Donald Gardner, a poet just back from Italy where he had, in theory, been doing research after taking an English degree at Oxford.

So I go up to Don after the reading and I introduce myself and mention Simon, and Don says why don't we go over to the Arts Lab in Drury Lane and eat in the restaurant there? We have our meal and then, looking down from a balcony, we see below us John Lennon in a white suit being shown round. He's capering about in front of some pictures with a little group of people round him. Don has just come back from New York, bringing the message with him – because it always comes from somewhere else. He is the repository of this truth and is bringing it to us. There is a group he's starting at the Arts Lab, called Guerrilla Poets, and every week we'll meet and read our work to one another, and we'll read out on the street as well.

Don was an incarnation of the 1960s, approaching it with a revivalist fervour. And I became a sort of follower. Every Wednesday I would turn up and we would sit upstairs in a circle and each person would read one poem. There was generally no discussion of the poems – we were simply witnessing for the faith. It was a very odd group. There was an elderly man who came all the way from

Brighton, moving uncertainly into the cannabis-scented haze of the Lab, seemingly oblivious to most of what was going on around him. There was a middle-aged woman who wrote poems in impeccably rhyming quatrains and who had been published in *Country Life* and who, it became clear, was schizophrenic. There were occasional street readings as well – but I wriggled out of those. Julian Beck's 'Living Theatre' was the next thing. It blew Don's mind and he had to be the English Living Theatre. From time to time I had news of them. They would sit down in the road and all start to howl. The word was no longer enough.

1969. In Lyons, teaching and still in the word-state, sitting up late at night with this writing-self. The writing speaks from an inner remoteness, my self speaking to myself as if from an enormous distance: word-silence, a lake of language. From that year I remember a sense of plenitude edged with regret. There is the sensuous amplitude of France but at the same time something about this expatriate life that did not work. I knew it would not do. There is a sadness about it, embodied in some of those who had stayed on. Like them I could all too easily just drift.

I came back from France after a year, and once more was living in London, continuing to exist in that odd state where words could make me happy. 'Arranging the nouns of furniture in a sunny room . . .' I wrote in one of my poems. The bedsitter life – as if you've escaped from the scene of the crime, a carefully orchestrated flight. It is as if I went around in this small cloud of words. I generated words everywhere I went, writing them down at odd moments, on buses, in the street. It was a question of clearing a space to be in, to achieve a moment of pure autonomy. Aged ten or eleven, reading Buchan in the dormitory in my Sussex prep school, I remember in particular *Prester John*, the mythical 'secret' king of Ethiopia. I was a 'John', so was this my fantasy? Had I been chosen, 'crowned', in secret? Because where I actually was, it was all too often nowhere, and I carried that sense of nowhere around with me like a perverse form of sustenance. In imagination you had to be somewhere else. Not wanting to be where you are is the beginning of all this business.

Back in London after my year in France. It's the middle of the afternoon and I've just come out of the Underground at Oxford Circus. The class I'm teaching – French for 'bilingual secretaries' – is in Riding House Street, off Regent Street, and here's Don, standing in the doorway of a shop and wearing a long robe – a North African djellaba – and when he sees me he starts intoning my name: 'John Welch, John Welch.' It's like a priestly incantation – I believe his father, like mine, was a clergyman – and it echoes down Oxford Street. I pause, baffled. There's something mocking about this display. I am the lost sheep – well, I did always duck out of the street readings. A woman who works in the shop is standing just behind him and laughing. I can't think of anything to say, so I turn away and, with this derisive salutation still sounding behind me, hurry up Regent Street to my class.

There was one final meeting, an odd, shadowy encounter. It was the early 1980s, just after we'd moved into our house in East London. I ran into him in the street one autumn evening just as it was getting dark. There was a girl with him, his daughter I believe, a gawky figure in her early teens, and I was touched by the way she looked up at him, her look of loving admiration. Now he makes me think of Arnold's 'The Scholar Gipsy' – well, Don had been at Oxford, and I have always found it a particularly haunting poem. He was living in Holland now, he said. It was better there. I didn't invite him back. Maybe I felt my big newly acquired house wouldn't be approved of, and that mocking greeting from six or seven years back was still sounding in my ears.

What became of them all I can't imagine. Is Charles forever haunting the edge of things? I have recently come across two fleeting references to him, one in Jeff Nuttall's *Bomb Culture* and one in a biography of Samuel Beckett, where he is referred to, in passing, as a member of the expatriate scene. The last time I saw him was in Paris, around

1972. Things seemed bad. He was in a dreadful little room, the phone had been cut off and he had no money. Maybe there are people who simply wish to disappear.

And what of earnest, uncomplaining Jim, who eventually took to making jewellery and selling it on the pavement – even here he was a bit late in the day, the hippy moment was passing. There they were, these shadowy figures who had been my introduction to something – but, paradoxically, something that they themselves were excluded from. There is this being, a spectator, on the outside looking in and wondering what the rules are. This 'outsiderishness' is transmuted into literary ambition, the notion that there is a magical world which you gain entry to by virtue of your work and where as a consequence you are 'recognized'; you are seen. Hence the 'literary life' with its interminable fantasies of inclusion and exclusion.

[John Welch]

DRIFFIELD: MISSING PRESUMED MISSING

Our mutual friend: the man in the middle. There was a photograph I liked to look at, from time to time, three bookdealers in a parking lot outside the City Airport in Silvertown. Playing their part: black coat (me), beret (Martin Stone) and kilt (Driffield). But we weren't dealers any more, we'd gone public. The photograph had been reproduced in a newspaper before it vanished. Martin took time out, the cure, and came back to the trade, in another country. I exploited fading memories, polished the myths, a writer of fiction. Driff experimented with a new career: disappearance.

Without him, the chemistry didn't work. Stone floated, Driff sank. They said, the men on the telephone, that he was dead; drowned, suffocated, stopped heart. I wasn't convinced. That would be too easy. He'd climb out of the river one day, covered in mud, white mouth still moving, tongue too fat for his head. Dry spittle at the corners of the snarl, breath of life. Our mutual friend, the revenant. He'd been there for centuries, in the city markets, the charity pits, plotting some means of escaping the wheel of fate. Thinking up a fresh identity.

The calls came at irregular intervals in the years after his vanishing act, but they weren't from *him*. Driff groupies. Tired journalists trawling through the back files, suffering late-afternoon spasms of nostalgia. The 'Drif bin in?' moments in the life of a man who never touched a drop and who avoided, wherever possible, pubs, bars, dives, dens: the noise, the conversation. The smell. He was fastidious after his fashion.

'A Surrey asylum, for definite. Lobotomy. Brain like boiled lettuce.' Said an old boy who claimed to have almost met Driff once, getting thrown out of a shop. Plenty of choice, asylums in Surrey. Where to start? Too obvious, I thought. He'd emerged from a funny farm in the first place, why go back? Unless it was to avoid prison. Plea of mitigation. Time out for a few years. Special diet on religious grounds. Access to a decent library. He'd miss the bicycle, one of his minor Wellsian enthusiasms, but otherwise the regime would suit him. Professionals paid to listen. Too easy, too communal. Driff was a solitary with a taste for the society of children and older women, imagined innocence alternating with feisty experience (disposable income, property).

Dead was favourite. Topped himself, as promised. Death or America. *That couldn't be right.* They wouldn't let him in. But still the phone fetishists relayed messages, as if I'd asked them for information. As if I were actually looking for the man. Gone is gone. And stays gone – until there is a major shift in the microclimate of the city: portents appear, scribblings on walls, faces in smoky mirrors, someone familiar in the background of a newsclip. Driffield was the Bin Laden of the book trade: a self-publicist sought by people who didn't want to find him, not really. Much better all round if he stays in his cave, his safe house, incubating mischief, symbolizing absence. A discredited era staked by this vampire's spike. Making the world more interesting for the rest of us. Driff's invisibility generated funds, books of disappearance. New maps were drawn up on the principle of X-does-not-mark-the-spot.

It would have to be close to the river, the dealer's return. Giant poster outside Tate Modern, that was my first hallucination, featuring his glowering face: beetle-browed and up for it. Pachydermic hide impervious to insult. Lemon-sucker's mouth: a suicide rictus undone by gravity. Deep groove between the eyes. An alien who has known better times: Max Beckmann. Painter, cabbalist. Driff's doppelgänger, Beckmann saw life as a triptych: one panel for public viewing, two held back for the initiated. The darkness, the symbols, the savage rituals. Lead books and wax fruit filled with blood. On the inside of a greasy trilby, held in murderer's hands, Beckmann has inscribed the most secret word: LONDON.

Searching the Beckmann poster for clues to the whereabouts of the missing bookdealer, I tried to find that badger's streak of white, the scar gifted by a workman on a building site (who showed his appreciation of a clumsy witticism by hitting young Driffield with a wheelbarrow). Not there, not him. Beckmann is a crude approximation, an avatar dying in New York while my colleague, our disappeared night-visitor, was still a child. Driffield behaved like the *subject* of a painting, not a painter; no subtle and strategic observation of things, performance.

Beckmann's right hand, angled to the hip, is sausage-thick and delicately camp. Fist clenched: to stop him punching your lights out. Only the cigarette is wrong, dead wrong, smoking was never one of Driffield's vices. No character was less interested in admission to the culture club, the academy. When Driff squeezed himself into black tie he looked like a Shoreditch bouncer, aggravated by the necessity of keeping his back to the action. The naked women snaking around silver poles. His problems began with Bloomsbury book fairs, the locked cabinets of antiquarian dealers. From most of which he had been barred under six or seven aliases. They would hear him coming from the next aisle and hide their wares under a blanket.

The public Driffield (Liberian registered) was a vegetarian autodidact. A serial vanisher. Think: Abel Magwitch. Back from the colonies, blistered, between penal stretches. Cash-rich from undisclosed sources and overdressed for it. Pockets padded with wads of temporary gelt. Back from the river, back from the dead. A flasher: one fifty-pound note wrapped around a Swiss roll of fives. Driffield talked about close encounters with the police, mistaken accusations of murder, expulsion from America. His yarns amused the Kray gofer and memory man, Tony Lambrianou, when they sat together, old lags, competitive narcissists, in a Cambridge Heath Road barber shop. (Lambrianou, exiled from his native Hackney, died across the river: an afterlife of attending gangland funerals and mournful television confessionals. Getting the suit out of hock, practising the Look in an empty mirror.)

'You must have done something to be thrown out of a country,' said Lambrianou, with a twitch of envy. 'You don't get thrown out of a country for nothing.'

Driff preened. The vocal register was pure Kenneth Williams (Williams ventriloquizing Ross Kemp). 'I'd like to go round the world collecting documents saying: "You've been asked to leave the country." I'm the nuclear cargo nobody wants.'

Certainly his wardrobe had that sheen: irradiated silk, fissile mohair. He spent hours every morning deliberating between racks of matching socks, shirts, pocket handkerchiefs that would put Lord Bragg on his mettle. The Imelda Marcos gear absorbed all the space, in numerous fly-by-night accommodations, left over from the books (unshelved, floor to ceiling, awaiting incineration). When he was no longer able to squeeze into the room, his libricide's coffin, Driff moved on: Richmond, Southall, Acton, Notting Hill Gate, Belsize Park, Hackney. It was his stated ambition to circumnavigate London, a wall of books, a paper-trail M25. (He didn't drive, because you couldn't read while you travelled. And you required a verifiable Christian name and an address for the licence.)

The famous Driffield costumes: they looked like a dare. Like a coarse-grained Aryan parody of a Jewish comedian. A *Punch* cartoon from the bad old days. A punchline with no preliminary justification. Checks so loud the tailor offered complimentary earplugs. Thick yellow ties with horses' heads: Max Miller. Anaemic cableknit sweaters with salmon-pink plus fours. A migraine-inducing sense of colour, accidentally Fauve: deep-blue shirt (white collar slashed like Thatcherite wide boy), tie haemorrhage. Fedoras, cloth caps, Homburgs. Gangster coats from the 1950s – *Night and the City* – draped around coal-heaver shoulders. Carnation erupting like a challenge. 'You looking at me?' (If not, why not?) A *Carry On* bookie with literary ambitions. A discounted villain trolling for a ghost-writer, someone to listen to the fiction of his life. Driffield, hitting town, the dawn run through the street markets – Camden Passage, Cheshire Street, Portobello, Camden Lock – was as much a performance artist as Oscar Wilde. Dyslexic wardrobe. Everything authentic but misplaced. And it didn't fit, not quite. Disparate elements had spent too much time accommodating other men's bodies, the deceased and the Oxfam generous. In full sail, Driffield was sartorial Esperanto. A display case of revamped pictorial dust-wrappers: Sapper, Sax Rohmer, P. G. Wodehouse, Tom Wolfe.

Golfers who didn't golf and white-suit dandies who never took a holiday. He had an outfit for every occasion and no reason to utilize them. Driffield didn't do occasional. He was always *on*, in transit, mid-monologue. The over-considered clothes didn't complement the shaven head. A mad butler who had butchered the upstairs folk, then raided their dressing room: hunting pink, riding boots, blazer and boater. Nobody in England owned more club ties for clubs to which he did not belong.

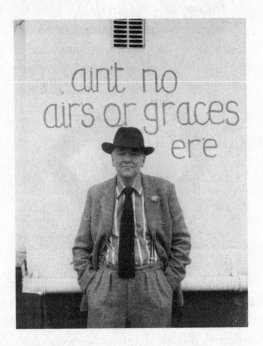

'I'm a yuppie,' Driff boasted. 'There's no limit to the upwardness with which I'd like to be mobile.'

You'll notice that I'm talking about him in the past tense. As if he were dead. That was always his intention, his boast: to finish it on 9/9/99. He sold tickets to a public suicide, his final act of theatre. There were plenty of takers, hoping for the best: revenge, debts settled, quality stock hooked from the smouldering ashes. Driff would be self-immolated on that mound of unsold books, blaming the punters who wouldn't pay his inventive prices. By the date of the bonfire, he would be the only book scout left in England who didn't use a computer. (The day I get my first email from Driffield will be the day I know there is life after death.)

Histories of suicide, papers on suttee, he collected them (as a rehearsal). Coffin catalogues, mourning outfits, funeral customs: big-time (big-money) necrophilia. Driff had a thing about Indian 'ladies'. He collected those too: first the sepia albums of earnest ethnographers and then the young women themselves. Hence the Southall connection.

He registered (glowing references from totally fictitious account-ants) with a Southall marriage bureau. And began to visit households where bank-books were audited, contracts signed in blood, before the first chaperoned date could be arranged. He had the clothes, the readies, the relish for spicy vegetarian feasting. The young ladies, he said, were charmed by his high-caste manners: box at Covent Garden, floral tribute and long cab ride home.

Southall was where the first contracts were taken out on his life. The threat was serious enough to excuse Driff's migration to 'darkest Dalston'. Slighted bookdealers, low-lifers on stalls or dozing in provincial shops, couldn't afford professionals of violence. And, in any case, the posh ones were amused by his presumption. He was a character to be invited to dinner on a slack weekend. A bit of rough with a nice line in sawn-off aphorisms, knee-capping puns. The ruder the better. Tough-minded old ladies, who dealt in serial killers and Ripper relics, doted on Driff: the authentic reek of Newgate and Tyburn.

I met the man for the first time in the book-jungle subterranea of the 1970s (unpensioned hippies, premature punks) and very soon found myself taken on as one of his chauffeurs. He needed dozens, wearing us out with merciless days on the road, Penzance to Glasgow. His foibles included patronage of the cheapest B&Bs, no food during the hours of daylight, gallons of black coffee – and hefty vegetarian dinners, with consequent flatulence, only when there were no shops left. No private dealers to be coaxed from their beds. He didn't sleep but lay awake all night, muttering, lights on (suicide watch); radio tuned, full volume, to the World Service.

Blinking, first hint of the rosy fingers of dawn, at a dirty window, I would be just in time to catch him marching off down some endless country road, in quest of newsprint: all the broadsheets, plus trade papers and local rags. Skimmed and abandoned by seven o'clock. His map-reading technique was Situationist, street plan of Paris imposed on the canals of Venice. Crude memories of Petersfield (Hants) rigorously applied to Peterborough (Hunts). Most towns have stations. One river is very much like another. A tree is a book waiting to happen.

Beneath the bluster, the sit-down/stride-along monologues, was an austere moralist, a roundhead. Driff recognized no ethical dilemma in scamming bookshops any way he could, while, at the same time, denouncing dealers who committed such cardinal sins as closing for lunch, offering weak coffee, expecting you to pay a market price for the plunder you carried away. 'Bookdealing,' he announced, 'is a form of big-game hunting.'

He went everywhere, searching for books on golf, embroidery, trade catalogues, skin-diving, forgotten novels by John Lodwick (all novels by John Lodwick). He was highly visible (when he crossed the border, still wearing his kilt, they stoned him in the street). Some dealers welcomed his witchfinder-general visitations, others trembled. Several took their annual holidays when he was rumoured to be in the neighbourhood. The brave went to law. Without much joy: Driff employed a titled brief with terrifying notepaper (one of his subverted toffs, a title and a pukka address).

In this skinhead peripatetic you have something the English choose to celebrate: a rogue (with a heart of brass), a turn (funny clothes, loud voice). But stare into those eyes: a little too real for television. Mania too convincing. They couldn't package him, hyperventilating, lens-licking like David Dickinson, the Lovejoy character on *Bargain Hunt* – although Driff had the taste for pin-stripe suits that looked as if they were designed by the Highways Agency.

If he had a home, I was never invited to inspect it. He visited you, that was the contract. He spoke in capital letters with audible exclamation marks. He loved wordplay, dipped into *Finnegans Wake* when he'd finished the day's newspapers. He discovered the secret of perpetual motion: greasy spoon for post-market coffee, curry house late at night and a man to service the bike. His addiction started with Saturday-morning jumble sales in church halls, ex-changing insults with anoraks and outpatients, fist fights with old ladies; then the trawl of charity shops, outer suburbs and south coast. Books, condition and edition unimportant, to feed the furnace of his promiscuous curiosity.

Driffield became the first cyclist to successfully ram-raid an Oxfam. When he travelled outside London, if he had exhausted his current roster of chauffeurs, he took trains. He was the only human to understand the system. Like Count Dracula, he hoarded outdated guidebooks, timetables. Much of his life was spent arguing discounts and special-offer tickets with railway inspectors on a branch line in Lancashire (heading off, yet again, to the wool shop in Morecambe that kept books in the back room). A 'Driff special' was a courtesy title conferred on anywhere off the map that looked like landfill, stayed open all hours and charged prices that kept the proprietors a centimetre above the starvation line.

During our long drives, eyelids propped with toothpicks, I listened to the often contradictory snippets of a back story, a fabulously unreliable CV. He might, once, have had a father – a naval officer? He lived for a time, as a child, in Malta. He definitely had a mother and a sister, south of the river. They sometimes agreed to store his books in garages or spare rooms. He'd been expelled from a dozen schools. He liked taking the children of friends on lavish expeditions: theatres, days in the country, helicopter rides. He worked for the post office and made a rapid, strategic exit to the United States. From which he was expelled. There were anarchist connections in the 1960s. With a couple of other freaks he operated a free bookshop in Notting Hill: total failure. Nobody could be persuaded, even then, to take stock away. If it was free, it was worthless.

Then there was that name: Driffield. Something found on a Yorkshire or Gloucestershire road sign (meaning 'manured field'). Or in a charity-shop novel, *Cakes and Ale* by Somerset Maugham. He had a cameo, so he told me, in Richard Neville's *Playpower* – under an earlier flag of convenience. The man was Shakespearean in the way he treated his signature: Driffield, Dr Field, Dryfeld. This was before he had his e. e. cummings period and went lower case. Ducking under the perimeter fence of the culture, he decided on 'drif field'. Lower case like an ibis hotel or a Chelsea crimper. His book, when he produced it, was estuary-casual in its use of grammar, spelling, apostrophes.

In 1984 Driffield published a guide to: *All the Secondhand & Antiquarian Bookshops in Britain*. It was pocket-sized, surreal in arrangement, barely indexed (random geography, opening hours, phone numbers). Swiftian in savagery, composed in hieroglyphics, unreadable (literally), the little blue book was an immediate success. (Driff outperformed Mao.) Vapours in the provinces. Writs. Physical threats. Cash (in advance) from optimistic subscribers. Now he had to carry a large pair of scissors in his luggage, to deal with the mound of newsprint. The broadsheets: *he was in all of them*.

At £4.50 the book was a steal. Whacked-out journalists (serial sentimentalists) loved it, they loved Driff. He was ruder than they were and didn't have problems with copy-editors. Or mortgages. Tax returns. Wine merchants. Coke dealers. Ex-wives. Current children. He was immediately elected to the pantheon of English eccentrics: the monocle-sporting, arm-waving explainers who hide behind bow ties and amusing hats. Driff got his radio spots, fawning profiles by Lynn Barber, Francis Wheen and Richard Boston. He appeared on television, alongside the customized, multicolour bicycle. He was outrageous on demand. And he wasn't fussed about a fee. He would have paid to appear on screens he viewed only while queueing for a Chinese takeaway. The little blue book shifted more than 25,000 units.

Now Driff was a victim of his own success. He had to travel the country (plus Ireland): every shop, every cellar with a shelf or two of books. The shorthand got shorter, the tone more abusive. Aberystwyth: 'Judging by body temp, shop seems to have expired in 1930.' Hay-on-Wye: 'I could smell a bargain, the pity was I had a cold that day.' Birmingham: 'Owner has been unwell recently with bad back (possibly caused by turning on the customers once too often).'

Mainstream publishers, recognizing a rare gift for clocking up column inches, came sniffing. But Driff had already found a way to dispose of the loot brought in by the success of the guidebook. He launched a magazine: *driffs: The Antiquarian and Second Hand Fortnightly*. It ran for twenty-two issues and closed with an extract from my first novel, *White Chappell, Scarlet Tracings* – in which a pale Driffield Xerox was a major character.

Fiction was the flaw that undid him. Driff sold his guide to a proper publisher, pocketed the cheque and vanished. Delivering nothing. Rogue contracts, in those days, could be written off as entertainment expenses. Commissioning editors also. 'This magazine is now owned by a Workers' Collective,' he announced. 'Mr driffield and his debts have departed. All inquiries for Mr Driffield should be addressed to La Paz, Bolivia.'

Aka: Hackney.

The original disappearance was a stunt. Driff could be found, as ever, checking in with his dealer of choice, the person presently known as John Adrian (decamped to Spain), in Cecil Court, or at 'Any Amount of Books' in Charing Cross Road: canvas plumber's bag stashed behind counter, while he prodded incoming stock, cashed cheques, played chess – or made an unsecured loan from the till.

The final issue of the magazine carried a boxed ad.

> SEEKS NEW CAREER AS A WORK OF FICTION.
>
> I will be a character in your novel, essay or poem.
> All parts accepted.
> MY MOTTO: If I can't make it in real life I'm
> determined to make it as a work of fiction.
>
> APPLY DRIFFIELD BROADMOOR.

Driff talked a lot about asylums. He'd once been handed over to child psychiatrists; beyond that, who can say? He knew the geography of the criminal wards. He had friends – lifers, psychos, killers – that he visited on a regular basis. He could describe the security precautions at Grendon Underwood, the 'liquid cosh' regime. He was intimate with Rule 43. And had the kind of pulsing temples, eel-fat veins, you caught yourself scanning for scorch marks. Prisons, madhouses: he collected them. Anything by Tony Parker.

The upswing of mania. Then the downside: black dog (collects Robert Burton, *The Anatomy of Melancholy*). Room painted in black gloss, oilcloth blinds. There were long periods when he vanished from view. Driff, in short sharp hits, was a stimulating and intriguing companion: misinformation on everything. An encyclopaedia of prejudices. Tics, twitches. Gimmicks.

But there was a streak of fierce libertarian humanity that would surface in the most unlikely locations. Inflicting himself, after hours, on a desperate, cold-turkey dealer in Stamford (Lincs), a man sweating for a fix, he invaded the private house. Thin kids shunted from sight. More books, more haggling: Driff got his way. Then, as we drove out of town, he insisted on making a detour to the appropriate offices to leave a letter accusing the wretched dealer of child abuse, misuse, neglect. The kids in pyjamas, the wife, wanting, quite reasonably, to be shot of the pests in the living room. Anonymous (capitalized) denunciation delivered, we were back on the road. Phone calls to be made, pockets heavy with dirty coins.

We exploit the world in our special ways. I took this episode and ran it, with fictional trimmings, as the opening of my first novel. I was reacting to Driff's invitation: 'Make me fabulous.' He was a character looking for text. He had to confirm his continued existence by seeing his name in print, on a daily basis. Better to be slandered than ignored.

By the 1991 edition of the guide, he had taken to using a false author photo: portrait of a doom-embossed Raymond Carver. The sleeve notes read: 'he struggled against alcoholism. His death "faked" in 1988 upon discovering he was the twin of driffield with whom he has a new incarnation as chauffeur.'

Here, at one stroke, were two of Driff's prime obsessions: the theatre of suicide ('see what you've made me do') and the conceit of employing writers as chauffeurs – so that they can transcribe, Boswell-style, his dazzling monologues. He would pass, directly, into that other dimension, fiction. And become what he had always been, an entirely mythical creature.

When he flew off his bike, unsubtle pothole, close to Arthur Machen's bachelor set, and landed on his head, they took him into hospital. 'No real damage,' said the quack, 'the road's fine, hairline crack. But you'll have to give up the booze. How many bottles a day are you on?' The teetotal skinhead, it seems, had a liver like slate. He made Derek Raymond look like a milksop.

Shortly after this, the blackouts began. Sometimes on trains, sometimes on the street. And once, puffing hard, up on the pedals, on a roundabout outside Taunton. Driff's consciousness was spotted with darkness. He did look like Carver now, life-shocked, electively posthumous. He looked like everyone. You could tag him (like De Quincey's 'Walking Stewart') seven times in any London expedition. He was justifiably proud of his Hyde-like exterior, but what did it signify? A reformed boozer, junkie, child molester? His friends were loyal. There was no halfway house: baseball bat under the counter or lifelong adoration (whatever the provocation).

I still got the calls, but they no longer came from railway stations, Carlisle, Crewe, ferries to the Orkneys; he lived, ate, slept, in his office. Creditors combed the streets with copies of Carver paperbacks, staring at silvertop skinheads. He no longer dropped in, late at night, at my home in Hackney, fishing treasures from his bag, gulping a pint of ink-black coffee – and pedalling away up Queensbridge Road in a straw boater. It took me a while to work out that he had a bolthole in the neighbourhood.

Driffield rented a flat from friends – and then, as part of a Channel 4 documentary, he let in a film crew. His secret life was exposed: the racks of clothes, the walls of unshelved books, the desk, the phone. Bills mounted. Driff's method of book-searching was simple: keep ringing – America, Australia, Japan – until the title is located. From his window he could see the minatory hulk of the German Hospital, where Joseph Conrad was brought, after his Congo ordeal, to recuperate: mentally, physically. Beside his bed Conrad kept the diaries that seeded *Heart of Darkness*.

Think of the vanished Driff as Kurtz. The Brando version. Heavier, half-naked, sweating in the dark. Reading by candlelight as his demons gather around him. Ambulances, squad cars. Beams from surveillance helicopters. Some splinter of Polish iron infiltrated his soul. He talked of Lodz. And decided to write a novel. He sent me a typescript.

This blatant autobiography was a way of dealing with the painful and complicated situation in which he now found himself. Driff's novel was a kind of tabloid *Lolita*: plus demented humour, relentless windbagging. A drama of secret passion that lurches towards the climax of a restaurant dinner with the loved-one's parents – when, at last, the truth comes out. A counter-current is provided by a sequence of verbatim letters, the author's apologia. Which an editor would probably insist on cutting down or reshaping. But, given Driff's high profile, his attraction for blue-chip journos, there was no reason why the book couldn't be in the shops by Christmas.

The typescript went to my agent. A contract was being discussed with J. K. Rowling's publishers when the call came from a kiosk in the thick of the traffic. Driffield was withdrawing the novel. He wanted to extend the letters. The story of forbidden romance and star-crossed lovers was returned. It vanished, along with the author. Who left behind him rumours of a flight into Poland. I didn't believe a word of it. Not with those bookshops, the ex-Polish dealers I'd met in London. One of whom had landed a pretty decent blow on Driff's nose in a market misunderstanding. Or threatened to do it. Nobody could remember.

The Southall families were still after him. As was his former Hackney landlord. And a posse of Old Bill. Creditors were closing in. Journalists wanted the story of his vanishing act. Publishers were still waiting for the revised guidebook. Accountants. Lawyers. Folk who had laid out serious cash for undelivered collectables. After the usual three months, lying low, Driffield would surface. Not this time. Three years passed, five. Not a whisper.

Agents reported a thinner, long-haired, vagrant Driffield, alien as Howard Hughes, combing the remnants of the Cheshire Street Market. A frozen stare of non-recognition as he brushed past them. An urban ghost. Next time he would be ruddy-cheeked, silent, toothless. Most recognized the bicycle, not the man.

After a few years, hammering away at various books, I experienced moments of regret for the wandering life, the dawn markets, and I thought about Driffield. The other great runner of the period, Martin Stone, was back from the dead, or at least from Paris. Honoured, re-toothed, respected: the subject of a private-press hagiography put out by a Californian millionaire and the dedicatee of a popular memoir by John Baxter. The sharper Martin's luminous outline became, the blacker the hole left by Driffield.

Spending time on the south coast, I made inquiries in surviving bookpits. A confederacy of the spurned. Decent characters support-ing an unsupportable lifestyle. 'Not been seen,' they said. Clive Linklater, the man from St Leonards, author of a lively booktrade paperback (they're all writers now, they have the time), promised to put the word out. He wasn't hopeful.

Then, when I'd given up all hope of making contact, a message on my answer machine. A dealer in modern first editions, based in West London, had heard about my quest. He might have something to tell me. I rang back, left word. He was away, holiday, book fair, on the prowl.

After another series of answer-phone pleasantries, I got him. He'd seen Driffield. He thought it was him, he was almost sure of it. In Ealing. A one-way street with two charity shops. A bit older, a bit thinner: there was no mistaking that red sweater, hunched shoulders, the weight of skull. Frown of adamantine concentration.

'Did you speak to him?'

Intake of breath.

'Well, you know. The rumours . . .'

The dealer, driving away, passed Driffield on his bike. Bulging panniers. Everything as it ever was. So the man *is* out there in London, muttering, rehearsing his memoirs as he pedals. Working on another novel? Plotting a more auspicious date for his suicide?

He'll be filleting all the broadsheets, the Sunday supplements, I know that. Combing the shelves of charity shops for a cheap read, arguing with the custodians of tat. He might notice this small tribute. Then the phone will ring again, a gruff voice correcting my manifold errors. 'This is quite disgraceful. I demand full damages and a printed retraction. That sweater wasn't red, it was *rufous*.'

[I. S.]

THE DEALER MARTIN STONE
INTERVIEWED
Passing through the City Airport,
Silvertown, 1992

Once I was very enthused by that life. It was something that replaced a life of rock and roll and a going from town to town. Instead I hunted books. It was, in the beginning, more thrilling – and also one felt more noble because you were not increasing yourself, you were finding other people and making a bit of a living on the side. It was exciting. It was archaeology. You were discovering a forgotten, perhaps neglected, past. Bringing minor writers into the light. Essentially, of course, one would love to find a D. H. Lawrence manuscript, but in Stafford that was not available. So you bought something lesser, as is thought. And then made a sale by explaining what it was in some half-arsed way. And it worked and you could do it again the next day – something which no longer happened for me in music.

Now that world has passed. It's a question of people knowing more about things. Everything has been discovered – or at least priced. The greater world is not interested in you and what you have discovered. It's yesterday's thing.

Dealers change, they turn into something else. Driffield puts on a kilt but he isn't a Scotsman. He vanishes. I might move to Paris, try to be a Frenchman or a French bookseller – which is vastly different from being an English bookseller; it's more civilized but less exciting. It's more cut and dried. You can't be a scavenger any more. There's a little man in the village who knows the book is worth £4.75, so I don't want to go to his village any more.

A pity. A pity. But perhaps we've already discovered everything. A quick visit to the Bath Book Fair seems to confirm this. I'm not sure, I think not. I'm sure there are minor things out there, waiting for us.

A small world. It meant nothing. A world that has now been brought into the bigger system of things. It's a business and I'm not a very good businessman. I'm sorry. But I'm sure there is something that would set my heart afire once more. I don't doubt it. The good thing about being a bookseller is you can carry on. You can be an old bookseller. You can't be in many professions and be ninety years old. A ninety-year-old bookseller is revered. A ninety-year-old rock-and-roll musician is laughed at. A ninety-year-old banker is inept. Bookselling is a good job for an old man.

THE GAZETTEER OF DISAPPEARANCES & DELETIONS

THE ARTHUR SIMPSON LIBRARY, N4

First you are a man, a woman. Then you are a member of the public but, through certain acts, you might become more so, more public, might be busy in the world and so become more seen, more thought of as being known. Either way, you die. But, having been seen by more than just the family and the mirror, there is a strong chance you could continue. The place previously occupied by your body needs to be inhabited but, given that the cycle of things relies on a migration between forms, it makes sense that you too shift. You might become a hospital, a school, a park; you might find yourself a Barratt Close in Chingford, a no-through road in a no-through dormitory. Or, luck on your side, you might become a library.

Arthur Simpson became a library because he was one already, in spirit and enterprise. There's a photograph, buttoned work coat and tie of course, a neat sweep of hair, a little like Tim Roth or Gary Oldman if they'd been pre-war, with a glint in the eye to camera and plans in mind that could not be held purely by the day job, worker and union organizer in the Woolwich Arsenal (it made sense, he'd survived 1914–18, guess that might break you, turn you or make you value the public realm and the means by which it had been, then, preserved).

And his schemes are hinted at, perhaps, in the hand on his photographed hip, in the gaze. He seems sensitive beyond his classification. He was brooding, it turns out. On books, stacks of them, shelves and shelves. First step, become a councillor, Lower Holloway, then get on the Committee; Libraries and Museums, Islington in the 1950s, chairman in four years. Now get to work. Commission branch outposts across the borough's poorest quarters, add children's spaces, reading gardens. Committees mean commitment. He'd inscribed the libraries on his heart, as they said at the time.

It's the old, true vision, too much vision for council suits today. Libraries bring worlds in, books open the estates, offer an axle to the community to engine itself forward; they're safe havens, they resist capital, they are liberal spaces, democratic. Simpson got it, made it here and here and there. Set a final one in motion, for Tollington, the deprivation zone. Then retired, 1959, then died as if he had retired to die, as if the books had been his blood (they had).

So he became his books, in 1960 born again on Hanley Road, a model undertaking, a blessing in brick and ink. They planted rose trees at his birth, put the building up for an award. There was a sense of worth. And so he lived forty-four more years, deepening the neighbourhood, gifting its people a shelter and a path. Until a council (Liberal Democrats but neither in this case) went high-street chrome and glass with a showcase thinkstore flagship that meant the Tollington operation was dead. Cash-flow erasures, excuses around access, better, shinier, more CDs . . . all the usual, but this time round no

Simpson at the helm, no lover of the literature, the word, but Kempton (James), who thought the library budget could be better spent on a one-off backhander to the people, a Waterstone's voucher for everyone right now! (Think election promises of standpipes to some shanty in the sticks outside of Cairo.)

The campaign of defence was model too, it kept the same high bar as that which it sought to save. And who they got onside; Hornby, Lessing, Morpurgo, Rayner. Petitions and protest. An angry love that still could not halt the tearing down of ideas, of education, of part of what it means to be civilized, humane, a society even. They shoot horses, don't they? But they execute many futures when they empty the barrels on a library.

Sure, this is a small, short story in the city's schema, a corner conversation with the past and what it means in this so present tense. The city ebbs and flows and much is lost and gained. But Arthur Simpson's second death should be remembered; he did not need to pass once more, he could be with us still, the roses of his books blossoming again and again among the young, green minds.

[Gareth Evans]

THE WHITECROSS STREET TEMPLE OF REASON

One of many Radical London debating societies and reading clubs set up in the wake of the French Revolution. The Temple of Reason was one of the largest, and was created in 1796 within the premises of Nichol's sale room, near the Barbican; it had a large collection of Non-conformist, Radical literature. Its members – artisans, working men and middle-class intellectuals – furnished the library at their own expense.

[Sarah Wise]

THE FRENCH BOOKSHOP, CHARING CROSS ROAD, WC1

Founded by Pierre Quirole in 1905, this small but well-stocked shop became, during the Second World War, the meeting place of various exiled French citizens, chiefly writers and journalists, including Georges Bataille, Jean-Luc Fromental, Louis Murail, Boris Vian – and, briefly, Françoise Stein. From this address was published the weekly journal *Refusé*. After the liberation the shop continued to flourish, thanks to the interest of English readers in certain aspects of continental writing. The business was taken over by Colletts and absorbed into their main shop in 1967, by which time few readers could be found for untranslated literature. Quirole himself had returned to France in 1925 and later emigrated to the US, where he was to die in the Chicago bombing, while observing a meeting of the German–American Bund (9 September 1933).

[Michael Moorcock]

THE WEATHER IN THE STREETS

The woman who looked like my wife walked past the shop again. She stopped at the window. I was sure it was her, then sure it was not when she looked up and saw me watching. If she was surprised to see me she gave no sign. She went on looking in the window, then came in. The bell rang as she closed the door. I nodded, she said nothing: two strangers, a brief acknowledgement.

She wandered around, went down to the basement. I watched her on the monitor. On the black-and-white screen she looked more like her old self. She bought a first edition of *The Weather in the Streets*. I wrapped it carefully. Again I couldn't be certain. She was thinner. I looked her in the eye as I handed over the book. She held my gaze, hers betraying no sign of recognition. Perhaps she was ashamed to find me reduced to working in a bookshop. My sitting, her standing, the exchange of money: I couldn't think of a question that didn't sound ridiculous. I wondered if she had set out to ignore me, to humiliate me. Her unspoken message was: whether I was your wife or not, I'm a stranger now.

[Chris Petit]

THE CELLAR IN GRAY'S INN ROAD, WCI

But his chief hobby was to collect books, a weakness of which he was most heartily ashamed . . . There are stories of Uncle Charles as a young man slinking upstairs with armfuls of books, which he hid under the bed. They were still there when he died, hundreds of them. In fact the bed actually rested on books. The walls of his room were covered with them. The rest were stored in an enormous damp and dingy cellar beneath some shops in Gray's Inn Road, and tended by a bricklayer of grubby appearance and uncertain habits. It was the bricklayer's business to spend his evenings opening the various packages which had been thrown down the stairs by delivery boys during the day, and to arrange them on the shelves, and as Uncle Charles appeared to be the mainstay and support of most of the secondhand booksellers in London, the bricklayer could not keep pace with the deliveries, and the accumulation of unopened packets was at times enormous. It was very rarely that anyone else was allowed to enter that cellar. I do not think the owner spent much time there. If a particular book was asked for he promised readily to get it, but more often than not it was never found. The odd thing is that I rarely saw Uncle Charles with a book in his hand, except in the evenings, when he went to sleep and let the book fall into the fireplace. I used to think that perhaps he read in bed, but his room, as I was to learn later, was a wretched attic with a pent roof rising abruptly above his pillow, so that he cannot have sat up in bed or even, except with great difficulty, have read lying down. But in spite of all this he must have been at heart a genuine book lover, and in his early days he read widely and well, for he had more than a passing acquaintance with English literature. Probably he commenced, as most ordinary book collectors do, with the honest intention of reading everything he bought, but, in his case, the difficulty of storage, the dread of being found out, and the craze for accumulation combined to overwhelm him, and the flood just swept him away. I should like to be able to record that Uncle Charles worshipped his books, cataloguing and arranging them with love and affection until even the dust on them was precious in his eyes, but I am driven to the conviction that he was ashamed of them. He was certainly ashamed of that cellar . . .

It was now my lot to go through the cellar and clear out the bedroom. To a book lover the experience was both horrifying and exciting. The conditions under which the books were housed were appalling. The cellar was damp and very cold. There was a small gas stove and no light except for a couple of gas burners, a small table and one chair. Every inch of the walls was covered with shelving, on which the books were arranged two and sometimes three deep, according to some obscure method known only to the worthy bricklayer. Books were piled high on the floor and stowed away in the most inaccessible corners. The cellar had two of the essentials of a good library and two only – books and quiet. I laboured there on Saturday afternoons for a whole winter, dusting, polishing, listing, sorting, removing some of the more precious books and burning other items. As for peace, I might have been buried in a tomb instead of working just below a busy London street. So profound was the quiet that a brother who helped me out on a few afternoons (quoting, I think from *The Anatomy of Melancholy*) claimed to have heard a bookworm calling to its mate. I have never seen so many books in my life . . . The books, oddly enough, had suffered on the whole little internal damage, although the bindings were faded. The bricklayer may have been an indifferent librarian, but he packed books as he laid bricks. It only needed cement to make them into a solid block. No damp could penetrate such a mass. Over everything was a thick coating of dust which formed, I suppose, a kind of natural protection.

[Malcolm Letts]

SECRET HISTORIES

THE STILETTO OF FICTION;
OR, THE CHINAMAN

No flights were called. Everywhere snowed up. Departures turned into a campsite, bad weather all over, a lot of it in his head, whole memory terrains cut off by the adverse conditions. What came to him was unbidden, cranked-out stuff over which he had no control: the flickers of a dying man, except he was dead already and awaiting departure.

What he had not appreciated was death's variable offensive in life: how close it had been to attacking: *it could have happened any time, not necessarily when it did.* From his own life he could see road accidents missed by seconds, imminent river drowning from slipping while wading, at least two KGB plots that could have gone either way, and so on and so on, including nights when he could have died simply from his body packing up with the alcohol ingested, and, damn it, even now he missed cigarettes.

What to say of the gaunt young James Jesus Angleton, counter-espionage master in the making, and of his arrival in Rome in 1943 as head of American counter-intelligence at the age of twenty-seven? Alone at night in the office, thin and sleepless chain-smoker, the Ivy League aesthete read modern poetry on the job and projected a Romantic angst, convinced he was dying Keats's death from consumption.

A wartime photograph shows him in London, outside the South Kensington Hotel, thin and anxious, the loner already used to keeping his distance. We see something of the man's vanity. Photographs of his early mentor and Nemesis, the traitor Kim Philby, show a less specific sense of dress. London schooled Angleton in the art of deceptive appearance, taking things seriously while appearing not to, learning what was worth taking seriously. Angleton was keen to understand the nuances of such a highly coded society. It wasn't cleverness the British taught but advanced deviousness. Espionage as the art of the lie: where the trick was not to make the lie a thing in itself but a shadow of the truth, so the telling was not an isolated fabrication but a comfortable variation of the truth. Truth was not an absolute but a commodity.

Angleton would state that William Empson's *Seven Types of Ambiguity* was a sufficient preparation and introduction for a career in counter-espionage.

During his London wartime training at Ryder Street (known fondly as the school for spies) he was assessed by familiar names: Kim Philby, Malcolm Muggeridge and Graham Greene.

The Yankee Angleton was schooled in British irony, thanks to his time at a British boarding establishment (Malvern College), and knew it was a protection of personal space as much as a literary conceit.

Greene's verdict on Americans: insufficient geography.

In the Red Lion off Jermyn Street, Philby told Angleton that Greene had once suggested a roving brothel as an intelligence front in Sierra Leone.

Greene looked modest and said the proposal had been turned down. Greene's new idea was to use an ex-pornographer named Scattolini with Vatican connections.

'What a cherry that would be,' Greene said. 'Vatican security is as tight as the Virgin's crack.'

He knew of an operation run in Lisbon by an agent code-named Garbo who with the help of a good map, a Blue Guide and a couple of standard military reference books had fooled the Germans into believing his detailed reports on Britain's defences were the work of a national spy network.

'Made the whole thing up from thousands of miles away and, bugger me, the Germans bought it hook, line and sinker.'

Angleton had lost count of how much they had drunk; God alone knew how many pints of watery English ale and at least five Scotches.

Philby asked if Angleton knew what a Chinaman was.

'A left-handed googly.'

Greene looked irritated. 'I thought Yanks weren't supposed to know about cricket.'

Philby said, 'All right, Mr Know-it-all. What's a googly?'

Angleton told them it was an off-break delivery, disguised by sleight of hand to resemble a leg-break action, deceiving the batsman into thinking the ball would break the opposite way from the one it would really turn.

Philby said, 'You offer the other fellow three googlies. He gets one chance to read it, one to play it and the third you give him the real leg-break, which he misreads and doesn't know where he is, if you get my drift.'

The stiletto of fiction was what Angleton learned to insert into any operation, by way of information and disinformation. The lie must embrace the truth. 'Wild lies, gentlemen, are of no use to us,' he would say. 'Rectal thermometers would not be able to detect the heat being given off by a well-placed lie.'

A solitary light in the window of an otherwise dark street in Rome, 1944: Lieutenant Angleton's office, two-thirty in the morning. He was familiar with Fitzgerald's *Sleeping and Waking* and Hemingway's *Now I Lay Me*, referred to by Fitzgerald in *The Crack-Up*: 'In the real dark night of the soul it is always three o'clock in the morning, day after day.'

He kept files on everyone, including himself.

Nocturnal Angleton greeted the dawn with a mixture of relief and dread: the exhaustion of another day. Dawn over Rome rooftops never failed to remind him of Murnau's *Nosferatu*.

In 1956 Angleton was in London. He had heard stories about Philby: that he had been more or less down and out, drinking harder and hanging on. He had applied for jobs and been turned down. His wife, Aileen, had been abandoned in Sussex while Philby stayed in

London, either alone or with a woman, and scrounged a living at the lowest end of Fleet Street while Aileen underwent a series of breakdowns.

Several times over the years when passing through London Angleton had found his finger poised to dial Philby and each time he had gently replaced the receiver.

By the summer of 1956 the situation had changed. Philby had been offered a proper job as a correspondent with the *Observer* newspaper and was shortly to go abroad. Angleton presumed this signalled his return from the cold and re-employment by the secret service. He let his finger complete the dialling, nervous about what to say.

He had only the Sussex number. It was a Saturday. Philby would be at home because it was the children's school holidays. The phone rang a long time and Angleton was about to hang up when it was picked up rather than answered because he was greeted by silence. He thought he must have woken Philby from a drunken stupor. He could hear breathing. Angleton repeated his name several times and asked if that was Adrian. Formally, and formerly, he had called Philby Adrian not Kim.

'I was hoping to meet up again, come down and see you all.' He struggled on, wondering if Philby was punishing him by refusing to talk.

Aileen eventually spoke, sounding dismal. Angleton wasn't sure if she even remembered who he was. She told him her husband would be there the next day but seemed unable to extend any invitation. Out of morbid curiosity, and cursing himself as he said it, Angleton invited himself to lunch, which he immediately regretted, knowing he would spend the time between dreading the encounter. He had been reading Jean Rhys, copies of whose books he had found secondhand in Charing Cross Road for a shilling, in the cheap boxes out in the street, and he had been reluctantly captivated by her gloom and depression, and he couldn't help wondering if his telephone call had fallen under her spell. Rhys was obscure, a lost writer, whom Angleton remembered from before the war. She was a dipso and neurotic and a lover once of Ford Madox Ford; but she wrote like an angel and didn't deserve to be forgotten. Philby had better be there, he thought.

He changed his mind several times but took an old train that rattled its way through dreary suburbs, stopping at every station. There was a heatwave. On one platform he saw a man wearing a knotted handkerchief on his head. When the weather was too hot for the old city, London was like burned toast. Brightness made its buildings appear naked and ugly. He could see into the backs of terraced houses and their gardens, some fanatically neat. People were indoors and a torpor hung everywhere.

He carried on with Jean Rhys. What he read struck him as intensely un-English because so unironic. She seemed particularly in tune with emotional short-changing, and, by extension, the humiliation and excitement of masochism. There was nothing conventionally realistic about her except her ennui. Her startling, surreal juxtapositions reminded him sometimes of Buñuel: collisions of dreams, weather, ghostly eroticism and bourgeois reality, represented by the financial transaction and the cold geometry of British architecture. As the train drew into his station at Crowborough he read: 'One day the fierce wolf that walks by my side will spring on you and rip your abominable guts out. One day. One day.'

The taxi, an ordinary saloon with a sign on its roof, lacked the loud, knocking diesel engine of London cabs, the driver a young man with a DA haircut. Previously, in a moment of mild hilarity, Angleton had been forced to explain to Allen Dulles that DA in England didn't stand for District Attorney but duck's ass, or arse in the case of his driver. Angleton was so nervous he could see the tremor in his hand as he lit his cigarette. It had been over five years.

The house was at the end of a lane that looked like it would usually be muddy, and was surrounded by rhododendrons grown out of control. It was a large Edwardian affair, not pretty, gloomy even in bright weather. Angleton sweated uncomfortably into his suit. The gravel drive, also neglected, was rubbed bare in parts and full of weeds. The tiny stones crunched under his soles. He worried he had given the taxi driver too large a tip.

He endured a long wait before anyone answered. The electric bell didn't work so he used the knocker, in the end rapping loud enough to wake the dead.

At last Aileen opened the door and recoiled as though she were expecting Angleton to attack her.

He had bought flowers from a stall outside the station in London. They had wilted in the heat and from the state of Aileen he could see there was no point in presenting them.

'Are you all right?' It was a stupid question. She was dressed, but barely, wearing only a heavy winter skirt and a blouse with the buttons done up wrong, no shoes or stockings, and her hair was wild and sticking out. She wore no make-up and looked miserably thin. One hand was grubbily bandaged.

'It's Jim Angleton,' he said. He could have been Father Christmas for all she knew. 'We spoke yesterday. I've come to see Kim.'

Lunch was out of the question; that was obvious. And so, he feared, was Philby. Aileen was alone. Philby, it turned out, had taken all the children off on an outing. Angleton couldn't decide whether Aileen had failed to pass on his message or if Philby was snubbing him.

He suggested a cup of tea, which he offered to make. She reluctantly stepped back. As he crossed the threshold Angleton had the feeling of stepping into a tomb. The hall was dark and cheerless, the decorations institutional, the carpets thin. They went into a large kitchen at the back of the house, which overlooked a huge, wild and neglected garden, hemmed in by oppressive cypress trees. In the middle of a lawn a tent had been pitched.

Aileen stood with her arms folded, staring at a square of sunlight on quarry tiles. They drank their tea black. The only milk had long turned rancid.

'Whose is the tent?' he asked in a desperate attempt to strike up conversation. Aileen always had been difficult and Angleton suspected she disapproved of him because he belonged to her husband's drinking chums and, as such, was an excuse for him not to come home.

The tent belonged to her husband, she said. She called Philby her husband, not by his name. Angleton was slow to grasp that Philby slept in the tent and not in the house when he was staying.

She was quite mad, Angleton decided. He laboured to establish the facts of her life, which were hard to extract apart from Aileen bitterly hating where she was. Her mother had bought the place, trying to help, but Aileen was cut off and alone when the children were away at school, and the neighbours, most of them retired civil servants from India, were unfriendly or depressed to be home.

Aileen used the word 'depressed' and Angleton feared she had no idea what a state she was in. She was a woman of forty-five, no more, who looked like she had accelerated ahead a couple of decades. She was already living out the old age Angleton dreaded was waiting, alone in surroundings that manifested her madness.

He wanted to leave but fell captive to Aileen's dangerous eyes and her damaged, animal smell. He feared her frustration and sexuality and experienced the unwelcome temptation of a Burgess-style bacchanalia following his response to her pass. Whatever impulses were usually hidden in decorum and ritual seemed close enough to scratch.

Angleton counted the cigarettes he had left while Aileen fretted about money and how it slipped through her fingers. The school fees and her housekeeping kept disappearing, she had no idea where until she decided Philby was stealing it to support his fancy woman in London.

It was theft, Aileen said, because most of the money came not from him but her mother. Her mother had a private detective on Philby's tail to see how much he was spending on this other woman. Christ! thought Angleton. It sounded like a terrible and twisted version of *The End of the Affair*. What a desperate situation, with Aileen and her mother paying someone to spy on Philby! The irony wasn't lost on Aileen, who said it was about time her husband received a dose of his own medicine.

They drank and Aileen asked, 'Do you find me attractive?'
Angleton lied and talked about his family.

Aileen said, 'I don't care if I drink myself to death, I really don't.'

She sounded almost happy about it and for a while talked lucidly about her isolation, which had increased since crashing her car through a shop window in Crowborough. The abscess on her thumb meant she could no longer drive, which had been greeted with some relief in town. Angleton recalled Aileen in the early days of Washington and her brittle vivacity, always on the border of being neurotic but attractive, and her friendly bickering with Philby as he cooked supper for the children and they drank their gin. He had envied their casual domesticity.

She told Angleton how Philby had always made out she couldn't cope and now he was telling everyone she was mad.

'He wants to destroy me because I know the truth,' she said. 'That's why he has abandoned me. Because I know.'

Angleton the fox sniffed the scent. A deep animal impulse made him want to put Aileen out of her misery to spare her from further shame and demoralization. She was a burden and a victim and he understood why Philby found it impossible to be around her. He had destroyed her for everyone else. Logic demanded that he, Angleton, should extract her confession and leave after killing her.

The homicidal moment passed as had the earlier one of lust. Both left him shaken. He wasn't used to being exposed to his darkest innermost feelings. He took stock and told himself to be careful or at the very least he would find himself arrested for being drunk and disorderly.

He corralled his feelings knowing they had nothing really to do with Aileen. They were about him finally confronting his old friend's treachery, the man on whom in so many respects he had modelled himself, which raised the question what unexamined treacheries might lurk in his own heart. If Philby was susceptible who wasn't?

Aileen gabbled on, slopping drink into their glasses; she was not a careful drunk. Gin would be licked off the table before the end of the day. Her husband was a bad man, she said, and a bad father. At first Angleton thought Aileen's accusations would be restricted to Philby bagging the best room in the house for his study and his squeamishness when having to dress the children's cuts. Philby had her seeing a psychiatrist, she said in a matter-of-fact tone: one of his Russian agents.

'There,' she said, 'I've said it.'

Angleton looked at her, in the oasis of post-confessional calm.

'Everyone was so in thrall to Kim they never saw the obvious. Kim lies. He lies all the time. He lies about his women. He lied about Burgess. Don't you see? It's because he lies he had to be a spy, and turning traitor was another excuse to lie. My husband is a born liar.'

She gave a sharp bark of laughter as though she had delivered the punchline to a long and painful joke.

'Can't any of you men see that?' she accused Angleton. 'Do you lie to your wife?'

'My wife is not someone you lie to.'

Aileen stared at him with barely repressed fury. He waited for her invective but what came out was very different from what he was expecting.

'I couldn't bear the children to go to Russia!'

Angleton thought she was hiccuping but she was crying, inasmuch as someone so desiccated could produce tears. He took her hand and said, 'Tell me.'

She had sent a telegram to the Foreign Office telling them her husband was the Third Man, she said. It was all-out war between them now and she wished he had never told her.

'Told you?'

Aileen looked at him levelly, not drunk for the moment. 'Yes. He told me everything and now he thinks he has been weak and has to destroy me.'

It had made all the difference, for a while. Philby was desperate and had nowhere to turn, least of all to her, having ruined her life as much as his. They were both at the end of their tethers and one night he had got drunk and instead of keeping the stopper in, as he always did, he came out with the simple announcement that it was all true.

'As soon as he had said it I could see he regretted it. He put on a brave face and we pretended everything was better for being clearer, but Kim has forgotten how to trust. He said what he'd told me wasn't true. He said he had been having a nervous breakdown. Then, seeing what he had done, he turned against me once and for all.'

Aileen descended into incoherence as the afternoon wore on. She was so far gone Philby would have no trouble persuading everyone that her accusations were the ravings of a lunatic, yet Angleton was in no doubt. In Philby's betrayal and abandonment of Aileen he saw the larger truth. He thought Aileen in her derangement knew what he suspected: that Philby had confessed to her secure in the knowledge he could destroy her afterwards.

It was the start of his slow vendetta against Philby. He had him watched by Miles Copeland in Beirut, waiting for the right moment. Whether Philby picked up his scent Angleton never knew, but he defected only days before Angleton meant to close the trap. He had reckoned on conducting Philby's debriefing in person.

Aileen showed no signs of waking. Angleton called a taxi and spent the time waiting in Philby's room at the top of the house. Aileen was right. It was the only pleasant spot, a high window with views of the forest. In the garden, Angleton could make out the lines of an abandoned tennis court among the grass, like archaeological markings from another civilization. There was a stand-up Victorian desk and Kim's books, looking well read as always. He noticed an identical copy of *Good Morning, Midnight*, surprised less by the coincidence than its being there at all. Kim had always confessed to never reading fiction. There was plenty to choose from on the shelves. Oh well, thought Angleton, another lie, one of those simple lies that kept one's hand in. He doubted Aileen would tell Philby about his visit (or even remember it) and, if she did, whether Philby would make contact. After their drunken three-day bender in Rome all those years ago he remembered them deciding if they weren't friends they would have to be enemies. So be it.

He continued with Rhys on the train to London, relieved after Aileen to get back to fiction.

Long after came the insight he lacked. He had often been struck by the fact of his reading Rhys that day yet had made no direct connection to the similarity between her world and Aileen's. Had he read *The Wide Sargasso Sea*, published in 1966 as her fortunes revived, he would have better appreciated Aileen as one of Rhys's haunted figures, and as such unreasoning, and seen how he was part of that world of dubious masculine patronage which he congratulated Rhys for writing about so well.

That night at his hotel he slept early from exhaustion and had a vivid dream of Philby at his most persuasive and charming, but with another dimension. Philby was transparent. Angleton could see right through him. He woke sweating and lay awake a long time thinking he had betrayed Aileen, not only by sneaking away like a thief. The day's events lingered with a strange clarity and hardly a day after passed without him thinking of her. She was gone little more than a year later, worn away.

Lying there, smoking in the dark, cleansed of any illusion and feeling the first not unpleasant stirrings of a cold anger of vindictiveness, Angleton finally read Philby's ploy, understood for the first time what he referred to afterwards as Philby's Washington feint. Philby knew the Americans were spy hunting and another investigation was underway for British moles, not least because Angleton had told him, indiscreetly, over lunch. Fearing exposure, or perhaps as a defensive reflex action, Philby had deliberately let Burgess loose on him, knowing Angleton was secretly jealous because Burgess represented fun, which he, Angleton, most certainly didn't. Burgess was uncensored, Angleton the censor, offering dull companionship, erudition, good shop and table talk but never the smut and the giggles, boisterous scrapes and breathlessness. Distracted by the appalling Guy, Angleton had overlooked the evidence mounting against Philby, allowing himself instead to be blinded by his dislike of Burgess, refusing to see Philby in the equation of treachery.

In terms of Philby's previous parlance, Burgess was the Chinaman. Philby had played Burgess as his Chinaman and Angleton had never read it.

[Chris Petit]

THE GLC ABOLISHED

Time to wake up again. The usual bears at the window. Could the daylight too be growing?

> A solemn morning.
> The monster goats
> stir, in the out-fields.

> And in the day again
> Past the window, warm, and in
> the light plant-down shifts and stirs.

I am thinking of small things as I take breakfast, like any other day. Suddenly to stop. As tho I had forgotten why I should be uneasy. Or what sorts of foolery are afoot, with the smell of discord.

> On the hills
> the wolves and foxes lie down and discuss
> what more the government can possibly do for them

It is as tho something is taken away from you, and the thief returns to punish you for carelessly losing it. What can you say? Yet there is something more than just grotesque about this day; it is self-defeating:

> The mouth of the dragon
> twists
> to bite its own tail.

For today, the government will make a city disappear. No more London, not even a shire to take its place! I open the windows of my friends' flat to watch the transformation, uncertain what is happening.

> Exhilarating?
> over the plants,
> the mountain range.
>
> In the width of windows
> viewing the warm brick
> the sides of the mountains.
>
> There the houses
> are folded and waved
> in a complex of mountains.
>
> The wall that is faces of houses
> is plain and square: such brick
> in new mountain-building.
>
> Curves keystoned,
> brick arches in roman threes
> like mountains, ancient, again.
>
> present as a curtain wall
> that are cliffs
> and ridges
>
> And at night
> the lights are here then there
> in the caves of the face.

[Bill Griffiths]

THE GAZETTEER OF DISAPPEARANCES & DELETIONS

HOLYWELL MOUNT

Upon the site of the women-only Augustinian priory of St John the Baptist (built in the 1130s, close to a spring; dissolved in the 1540s), Parliamentarians constructed, in 1642, an earthwork from which to defend London against Royalist troops entering the capital from the east. The Mount was just west of where Curtain Road crosses Great Eastern Street. Another version of the Mount's origins has it that during the 1665 plague the driver of a cartload of corpses accidentally overturned his vehicle, and no one was willing to handle and dispose of the bodies. The pile remained, was soon scattered over with earth on which weeds began to grow; before long, the people of Shoreditch were using it as a general refuse dump. The Mount was levelled in 1787 and became a private burial ground, until being cleared for housing and manufactories.

[Sarah Wise]

RESURRECTION MEN

A specialist trade, now defunct. Until the 1780s, London anatomists and their students, for the most part, dug their own dissecting material from the grave. But as the medical profession's desire to be viewed as respectable gentlemen grew, so body-snatching became increasingly outsourced to Resurrectionists, or Resurrection Men – commonly regarded as low-life by the surgeons they supplied, and pariahs by the working men and women they lived among. The 'Guildhalls' of the Resurrection Men were such disappeared pubs as the Fortune of War, in Giltspur Street, opposite St Bartholomew's Hospital (destroyed by redevelopment, 1910); the Bricklayers Arms, where New Kent Road became Old Kent Road (Bricklayers' Roundabout is near the spot); and the Rockingham Arms off Newington Causeway (long gone). 1832 saw the beginning of the end of the profession, with the passing of the Anatomy Act, which made available to surgeons the bodies of those who died in the workhouse (or other public institutions) unclaimed by relatives or friends.

[Sarah Wise]

THE PORCHESTER TOWER, WESTBOURNE GROVE, W11

This Gothic folly was built in 1820 by Sir Hector Reed, who owned large tracts of land on both sides of the West Bourne River. The tower's most famous resident was Paul Black, known as the 'London Spymaster'. Operating from an antique shop in Kensington Old Church Street, Black ran a complex intelligence operation for his Soviet paymasters, but was also a double agent working for MI6. He sold limited editions of Ezra Pound to James Jesus Angleton and Victorian detective fiction and pornography to Graham Greene. An affable man of ambiguous sexuality, Black was implicated in the IRA bombing of the Kensington Café in 1971. The restaurant, he later revealed, was never the intended target. A runner, dealing in fantastically inventive and obscene drawings of 1940s film divas, had left his shop with the wrong parcel. Black wrote his memoirs in 1982 and returned to Kiev in 1996, where he still runs a successful business, trading in icons. His house, in some disrepair, was given to the National Trust shortly before he left England for the last time.

Fully restored, the Tower is once more in private ownership, rented by the Trust to Prince Omar bin Faud.

[Michael Moorcock]

THE ZODIAC HOUSE, ORMINGTON PLACE, SWI

Residence of the variety, stage and cabaret performer
known as 'Monsieur' (sometimes 'Count') Zodiac. This
illusionist and conjuror was an albino, unusual among
human beings for his crimson eyes and his bone-white
hair. He was said to be an Austro-Hungarian aristocrat
who lost his estates after the First World War; or perhaps
a Serb whose lands were divided in the formation of
Yugoslavia. Another rumour associated him with 'Crimson Eyes' (the 'Mirenburg Ripper'). Known for his
elegance and courtesy, Zodiac was fictionalized by
Anthony Skene as 'Monsieur Zenith', an opponent of his
'metatemporal detective', Sir Seaton Begg. He is thought
to have died in a direct hit during a London air raid in
September 1941, at the Kennington Empire, while performing his famous Bronze Basilisk illusion. The police
became suspicious and searched the house in Ormington
Place, near Victoria Station, finding a considerable quan-
tity of opium and arresting Zodiac's Japanese manservant,
who was subsequently interned on the Isle of Man.

The house is now a museum of things occult, magical
and illusory. It can be visited in the summer months
between 11 a.m. and 5 p.m. and during the winter months
between 10.30 a.m. and 4 p.m. The museum displays
some of Zodiac's illusions, as well as a full set of his
evening clothes.

[Michael Moorcock]

DERRY & TOMS ROOF GARDEN, W8

This elaborate roof garden was created in 1938 when the department store was first opened. Consisting of an aviary and themed gardens – such as the Tudor garden, the Spanish garden, the Old English garden and the Japanese garden – it also featured a large tearoom, on whose terrace customers frequently arranged to meet. Lady Shapiro was said to have favoured the roof garden for her assignations with Sir Frank Cornelius, the post-war property developer. A liaison which was brought to light in the 1950 divorce case with its lurid testimonies from valets and maidservants, its torn photographs of headless men in hotel rooms. The episode marked the beginning, some media scholars assert, of tabloid journalism and the cult of celebrity exposure.

Mary Quant and Sir Richard Branson are among the better-known custodians of the garden in recent times. Now the property of a private club, the roof gardens are occasionally opened to the public. Times and details of visits are announced on the relevant website.

[Michael Moorcock]

OLD LONDON

A BOX OF LITES: A CASE OF FOGS

For Our London Fathers.

The carpenter's sleeping hand did not fumble, floating over his frail dreaming wife, without disturbance, to smother the almost waking clock: with the certainty of an auctioneer. Four-thirty in the morning. Nothing yet moves in the street outside. It is past death's last visit and before the shudder of birds. He gains balance and slides out from his side of the bed. Reinforced by a board beneath it, intended to straighten his back, the bed is as hard and as stiff as his liver. In advance of a broken hip and in retrospect of a fractured heart.

So this is how the day begins. Quietly moving in the bedroom and kitchen. Carrying his shoes to the street door, steadying the tilt of furled sleep with a tot of rum, before leaving. The weight of the drink's thick darkness inverting the hourglass of this new day.

The house is set in a long road of homes, each one alike, each painted to be different. It is north of the centre, so he follows gravity, down, to his work. But that is hours away; first he must establish his territory and his communion, turning the mechanisms of unseeing into his favour. He must begin the outward process of being seen by choice, seen by his workmates and overseers, even when he is not there. He must be unseen by ghosts. The inward chemical part is the exchange of blood for alcohol. This frost-covered morning was not the beginning of something, but just a moment in the continuous cycle, in which he kept absence in balance by dissolving identity.

London is a city that sleeps too much. This is the mould of its quality. A magnetic contract: to reinvent itself on the other side of dream, each day. And such dreams, smouldering against the tidal spine of the river, telling and retelling the tales that must be told to manifest a city's bones. Whispering the night architecture back into stone. Millions agree to follow the sun's pendulum, until their unconsciousness coalesces to a pure pulse that shadows the Thames. On a clear cold empty time like this you can hear them all sleeping. The cold has drawn a membrane and a cone to collect their occulted labours, focused to a splinter of ice that inscribes submerged voices on hissing tracks, invisible but firmly held to certain known places, especially bridges.

There is no fake continuity here, no driven constant enforced by an over-stoked engine; nothing runs on fear-shifts terrified of pause. It is structured by memories and the little fluids that trickle between them. There is none of that adolescent pretence of younger cities; those that 'never sleep'. Trying to convince the night that it is transparent to human desire, undreaming, matter of fact and ultimately tired. A braggart of awareness speckled with the lint of its cot. The blunt will of continuance believing it is cheating night, avoiding its depths and charging the city with power – when, in fact, the opposite is true. Drained and singing loudly to deafen out the faint but perpetual scratching at its virgin seams. The night workers in this city stay concealed. Hidden in locked buildings or toiling underground. Separate beings made more invisible when they leave their hidden labours.

The carpenter moves quickly for one so unfocused. The surrounding streets are no more than cardboard; disinterested sets painted in uniform colours. He never looks into the identities of the passing places, he never sees their unchanging – but feels it with an unspoken agreement of veracities. His crossings are no more than the elaborate fake journeys of his best-remembered childhood. Where, at Christmas, on a long-awaited visit to Santa Claus in one of the city's vast department stores, he was bought a ticket to a dream voyage. He would sit with six or seven other children in a wooden box, while a painted landscape on a canvas roll was wound past the windows and the box gentle-rattled in a pretence of motion. Something of the wonder of these shabby exciting illusions stayed with him. Something of their obvious artificiality was convincing and drove a wedge between himself and the agreed painted roll of reality, for ever. So that now, in the bleakest of streets, the act of movement was liberating and modestly audacious. He enjoyed his grim ritual, which would soon be rewarded by the warm sweet doze of oblivion. All drunks understand the righteousness of compensation, and the satisfaction of its achievement.

It was only the few doubtful others he met on his way that jilted his momentum; only the ones that met the gaze he was not giving. Those we would become, trying to cup the moisture of recognition from his passing eyes.

His relationship with ghosts paralleled his attitude to work; the balance of labour and freedom, individual choice and purchased employment, their time and his. The ancient craft of skiving. Of being there when you are not, or being elsewhere all of the time. Clocking into a system that was so common that it was not there at all. The art of detachment, liberty taken in small, irregular gasps. Powered by cunning and agreement. Tiny wilful fractures in the daily chain of earning.

The carpenter worked in the Law Courts. A village system of jurisprudence at the heart of the city. A microcosm hungrily copied throughout the world: antique, venerable, formal, layered and conservative. An intricate hierarchy structured on class and attainment, position and power – with the dignity, pomp and fairness of the armed forces, Oxbridge colleges and other efficient and unquestioning treadmills.

The courts were divided into various houses, halls and chambers. In them, the higher echelons of law workers performed their daily tasks, breeding and dividing conflict with razor-sharp pens. A regiment of administrators controlled the buildings, the flow of paper and other eddies of communication. Making sure that daily trivia did not impinge on the sacred motors. Below them were the craftsmen, messengers, butlers, maids, kitchen staff, cleaners and other general foragers and carriers and sweepers that kept everything turning and stable. They lived in the arteries that duplicated the corridors and halls. A lymphatic shadow system that scurried unseen and close to the blood. Many of the workshops and storerooms were underground or hidden in tightly folded courtyards; appendices that most never found or knew to exist.

The whole edifice was riddled with ghosts. So much friction of emotion braced into control and rubbed hard on the membrane of corporality. To which is added the concentration of meaning: for many of these termite workers, the Inns were their only life. A trusted existence safe from the outside world. Which always proved to be unstable, female and slippery. The constant solidity of the Inns gave a firm ground and a clear horizon. Uncluttered by the uninitiated flapping of families and other random systems. The binding principle was the regular and unspoken flow of alcohol. It drained, fountained and circulated through the entire village, from the Lords to the Boot Boys, giving a common wavering anatomy to all of them. Omnipotence that lifted and divided time. Brightening the middle and the end of each day – and, for some, the beginnings too.

The carpenter drank to suppress ghosts, to blind them from his day and the concealed part of his thoughts, which most assumed he never had. Sensibilities that over the years had become inconvenient or a source of argument. He was now without sexual drive, ambition or what is usually described as 'imagination'. These things had wilted, their pains and innocence soothed closed by the distant saintly smirk of drink, comforting and reducing the nagging sugars of humanity. This was part of the price of his conversion to transparency. The complex hungers of rich emotions sit heavily in the whilsting frame, that part of us that walks between flesh and spirit. That part of him that allowed the sanctum of hollowness.

Care must be taken where proximity grows. And yet he chose to wend his difficult path, leaving and returning through some of the most infested parts of the city. The old tenting grounds where markets grew before homes and businesses. He mapped his stagger between their haunted industry of passing, their saturated history of exchange. Markets that trade before first light, running meat, fruit, fish, flowers and grain to the core, while the rest of the city sleeps. Each market has its own pub or inn, bolted down to a different time, cutting no slack for this moment. Forever enacting the past in the future with little consideration for the present. Under the muscle of need, licensing laws and drinking times are barged aside, reverting to earlier frames, holding the ghosts that curl and bristle among the fog silhouettes of blur-men carrying grain, potatoes and oxen, or seriously drinking themselves towards midday.

St Bartholomew's is his first call. The market pub is swollen full of men, the temperature steams out against the cold breath of morning. A red boot bar where coffee and rum lace the tobacco smoke and the newly mowed smell of open carcasses. Although the conversation is loud and active, some drinkers just stare into the surface of their shimmering beer. All are regulars, all are known and some are not alive. Occasionally there are eddies of smaller tighter men, finishing shifts from the hospital across the square. Smithfield Market and St Bartholomew's Hospital have shared this tilted field for hundreds of years. The conjoined sewers beneath them are congealed with the blood of men and beasts. This swollen acre was once a festive home for execution, music, butchery, medical vision and debauchery; the wild joy of each element humped together, formally, in the ancient ruse of a three-day fair. The echoes of which can still be heard in voiceless shivers.

There is never conversation among the professional drinkers. Nods and minor gestures waft at shaggy recognition. By some reflex twitch of nerve, a drink is ferried from one drinker to another, by a barman who is more absent than any of them; it will be returned later on another calling. Other markets are shuffled into the carpenter's circuits. Leadenhall, Spitalfields, Covent Garden, Billingsgate sometimes distort his daily track. Today it is the Garden; the wet sun is lamely sucking at the colours of the bundled flowers and the earth smell of vegetables. Stems and leaves are slippery underfoot and he tiptoes carefully into the public bar, its heavy doors loud and levering against the day.

He is beginning to find equilibrium as he walks on, into the fiercely treed enclosure of Lincoln's Inn Fields. Smoke is rising from the burning cardboard homes. A daily ritual, the homeless destroying their previous night's shelter. Some of these constructions are elaborate, ingeniously crafted against the wind and frost. A collection of insulations and buffers: Adam's House in Paradise.

He walks through the empty bandstand, its positive structure giving sound to his presence. He does this every day – and, at the same point in the circular stage, a memory uncoils and flickers in the enclosed darkness of his skull: like a whisper of a spring set in a quivering pulse; a tiny wire maquette of a galaxy stretching one of its spiral arms. The memory is of the ocean, swollen, vast and disconnected. Something like water and wood fusing in a death or a blessing.

In one of his lunchtime sessions, in his usual corner of a pub in Chancery Lane (long since gone, having, over centuries, transformed from coffee house to pub, and now back into coffee house again), he overhears a conversation about cork. The pithy cuttings that seal valuable fluids. He recognized the speaker, having once or twice attempted communication with him, as a regular who was always talking. A person normally to be avoided or seen through. But now, for no reason at all, he was becoming hooked and entangled with the words. The talker was conjuring the impossible in a thick Polish accent. He speaks of the object: a model of a tomb crafted in cork, weighing nothing, its maker unknown.

The carpenter follows the talker across the square to the Soane Museum. It is one of three secret spaces that hide in the lofty houses that fringe the park. He knew of the Hunterian Museum of the Royal College of Surgeons. He sometimes drank with one of the porters. He had seen its delicacies of pathology, its twisted stumps of folk, its malign cradles of glass and alcohol. He had seen the book bound in human skin and the Sicilian dwarf scurrying under the shadow of the Irish giant. But mostly he has seen the Evelyn tables. Four vertical slabs of wood saturated in a dark treacle of varnish, encrusting the root like tracery that is forever glued to its surface. Remains of men. Nerve trees and arterial ladders pinned down for inspection, the rest of the carcass cut away, its density of purpose disposed. These whittled human drawings chilled and excited him in a way that he could never explain. When once being questioned, after staying with them too long, he gave the easy answer: 'I am a carpenter.'

And now, in balance, another wooden artefact had stolen his attention.

The cork models sit in the sunken darkness of the museum's subconscious, near an over-tanked sarcophagus, at the far end of the underground room. They are scaled constructions of Punic burial chambers. Boxed worlds. Bone dry and unreasonably tight. The carpenter's last rind of imagination was used up by these things. Conjuring the sea, the shipwreck and the raft he would have lashed together from the Evelyn tables, to save himself and the cork tombs. This is the memory that floods to him, every morning under the smoke-filled trees.

The empty bandstand, just before work, will be forgotten in seconds.

The daily round of work and hiding has begun with the first ritual of clocking in, punching time holes out of his named label. He knew where the uncomfortable places were. Most of the broken furniture came from there. His repairs kept him locked in association with a catalogue of invisible incidents. Sometimes, while concentrating on a splintered chair or a cracked window, he would realize he was no longer alone. He was sharing the room with a displacement that wrote its contours of nothing in human form.

> Yesterday upon the stair, I saw a man who wasn't there.
> He wasn't there again today. I wish that he would go away.

Sometimes they crept through the carefully layered protective skins of drink. Insinuating themselves against his whilsting frame, as if invited, as if kindred, as if warming their distance on his translucence. Everything in the rooms and corridors was complacent and eloquently engaged in the act of being still. Not breathing in this vulgar time. One of the rituals was rewarded by a tiny yearly stipend. The daily winding of an ancient clock, nested on a high dark shelf, and accessible only by a perilous ladder. This was to be his undoing. The mournful walnut-and-brass cluck counted the moments away, reeling the accident in: face to face. But for now he is safe and the day gently spills towards evening. A couple of drinks to rectify freedom and prepare for the journey back. Which will remain unbroken until the Oakdale. This is a bad time between drinks and sanctum, the way home is not level. The ragged shadows are hungry and struggling against weak gravity.

Returning is a different matter, its form distorted by a saline of time. It is not the reverse or opposite of setting out, but an entirely other ritual. The carpenter's way back to his wife and numbered house was drenched in mishap. The balance of humours slewed, swilling him into bait. Even worse, his crooked path was trespassed by an unkindness of sleep. A purple-black undercurrent that is beyond conscious control and knows its place of attack with uncompromising bilious guile. For this solitary man, it was lived underground: waiting in the shuddering echo of the Piccadilly Line. It should have been the sleep of fatigue that, in its innocent stage, offers the collapsing of time as a gift, letting the homecomer doze away the lagging boredom, scooping a chunk of dismal event out of its trapped sequence. But this was an angry and vindictive other, gnawing with contempt for any citizen who had spilled or wasted its benediction. A worse cruelty was the absence of dreams. So he rattles in a little smudged light of the worming train, speeding under the vast city. There is no rest. His gummy doze is full of chiselling joints, shudders that pretend to be falls, slips from the edge of sentience. The other passengers don't notice his eyes holding on to consciousness, between heavy-lidded blackouts.

He leaves the train at Manor House, one of the deepest stations in London, and walks the final yards, past his front door, looking down, towards the next street and the Oakdale Arms. It is eight-thirty in the evening and he will drink here for another hour.

166

Rotating his mood into a woollen jubilance, blotting out the day, the journey and tomorrow; but worst, the embarrassment of having to spend a short blurry time with his wife. His dinner has been in the oven warming since seven o'clock. The time at which he should have arrived home. By ten the food will be soldered to the plate, desert hot. This tragic sadness occurs every day and is the only act of exchange between man and wife. It is another clocking in, a silent treaty of failure. The ultimate emotional manifestation of invisibility.

The morning and the alarm clock wait. The other clock at the Inns of Court will watch for three more years, before he falls. When he is taken to hospital, his routine is snapped. The staff are on strike and he is becoming delirious as the pain and the DTs chew into him. He becomes simultaneously transparent and solid. The carefully preserved balance wheeling into overspill. The ghosts find him. His family stare through an absence. He is caged in a cribbed bed, high sides restrain him. The dropped food and broken plates are swept under his bed. Domestic and nursing staff are protesting in the streets.

He gibbers, rages and swoons. The cot is shaking apart, while his family, catatonically locked in obligation, are sitting close by, unable to see the man in the creature that dissolves before them. The vigil lasted a week, until he was no longer there and the room was filled with a smouldering gas of shadows.

Many of the places, acts and histories have gone since his time. Some have changed beyond recognition. But the layers that describe and bind us are still permeable. Those that are here have a duty to those that are almost here, and those that have been, and especially to those in between. The carpenter can finally be found, downing the invisible, gradually sobering towards yesterday, in and between: the Blue Anchor, the Seven Stars, the George IV, the Ship, the Fox & Anchor, the Wicked Wolf, the Bishop's Finger, the Sutton Arms and the Oakdale and all those others that pretend to be gone.

[Brian Catling]

THE DISAPPEARED PHARMACIST

How unmeaning a sound was opium at that time! what solemn chords does it now strike upon my heart! what heartquaking vibrations of sad and happy remembrances! Reverting for a moment to these, I feel a mystic importance attached to the minutest circumstances connected with the place, and the time, and the man (if man he was), that first laid open to me the paradise of Opium Eaters. It was a Sunday afternoon, wet and cheerless; and a duller spectacle this earth of ours has not to show than a rainy Sunday in London. My road homewards lay through Oxford Street; and near 'the *stately* Pantheon' (as Mr Wordsworth has obligingly called it) I saw a druggist's shop. The druggist (unconscious minister of celestial pleasures!), as if in sympathy with the rainy Sunday, looked dull and stupid, just as any mortal druggist might be expected to look on a rainy London Sunday; and, when I asked for the tincture of opium, he gave it to me as any other man might do; and, furthermore, out of my shilling returned to me what seemed to be a real copper halfpence, taken out of a real wooden drawer. Nevertheless, and notwithstanding all such indications of humanity, he has ever since figured in my mind as a beatific vision of an immortal druggist, sent down to earth on a special mission to myself. And it confirms me in this way of considering him that, when I next came up to London, I sought him near the stately Pantheon, and found him not; and thus to me, who knew not his name (if, indeed, he had one), he seemed rather to have vanished from Oxford Street than to have flitted into any other locality, or (which some abominable man suggested) to have absconded from the rent. The reader may choose to think of him as, possibly, no more than a sublunary druggist; it may be so, but my faith is better. I believe him to have evanesced. So unwillingly would I connect any mortal remembrances with that hour, and place, and creature that first brought me acquainted with the celestial drug.

[Thomas De Quincey]

NOVA SCOTIA GARDENS

*In 1831, the obscure region of Bethnal Green known as Nova Scotia
Gardens had notoriety thrust upon it, when body-snatchers John Bishop,
thirty-three, and Thomas Williams, twenty-six, moved in; alas, they
did not restrict themselves to snatching corpses from graves, having
found an ingenious way of ensuring that the human flesh they delivered
to London's surgeons was as fresh as it could possibly be.*

Nova Scotia Gardens has never appeared on any map. It never will.
No one has used the name since the late 1850s. While it lived, the
acreage it occupied was marked on maps as 'Garden Grounds' or
'The Gardens', if it was named at all; often, it is shown as empty
space, dotted with a few cartographic icons of trees and a scattering
of dwelling houses.

It lay not far to the north of St Leonard's Church in Shoreditch
High Street, and was bordered to the west and north by the curve
of Hackney Road and to the south by Crabtree Row (today's
Columbia Road). It was overlooked by the Birdcage pub, which is
still to be found at the spot where Columbia Road makes a sudden
jerk to the left.

The level of the Gardens' ground was slightly below that of the
surrounding streets, and so some locals also referred to the place as
the Hackney Road Hollow. Another early name for the territory
was Milkhouse Bridge – probably/possibly in connection with a
farmhouse constructed on the spot during the Restoration period.
At the start of the eighteenth century, the Gardens were 'Goodwell
Garden'; by 1746 – the year of the publication of John Rocque's
famous map of London – they appear to be largely unbuilt-upon
fields, on the fringes of the Huguenot settlement of Spitalfields, to
the south. It is unlikely, but not impossible, that the punctilious
Rocque would have failed to indicate that housing occupied the
site; but Stow's *Survey of London* (1603) refers to some houses

recently built just to the north of St Leonard's Church upon 'the common soil – for it was a leystall' (dunghill), and if this is a reference to the Gardens, it would indicate that the development was Jacobean in origin.

By the early 1800s the older horticultural and food-related names of the surrounding lanes and roads (Crabtree Row, Birdcage Walk, Orange Street, Cock Lane, Bacon Street, Sweet Apple Court) were being joined by the martial, naval and colonial references of the brick-built terraces springing up in the vicinity. The Gardens had become Nova Scotia Gardens, and near by was Virginia Row, Nelson Street, Gibraltar Walk and Wellington Street.

The Gardens comprised a number of cottages which by 1831 were noticeably quaint; they were interconnected by narrow, zigzagging pathways. In July 1830, John Bishop, a prolific body-snatcher, or Resurrection Man [see 'Resurrection Men', p. 152], had rented No. 3 Nova Scotia Gardens from its owner, Sarah Trueby, living there with his wife and three small children; one year later, Trueby rented No. 2 to a young man just out of Millbank Penitentiary – Thomas Williams had served four years of a seven-year sentence for stealing a copper pot.

Nos. 2 and 3 formed a semi-detached unit and were not in among the labyrinth of Nova Scotia Gardens, but close by Crabtree Row and near to the main entrance into the Gardens. John Bishop's house, No. 3, had a side gate, opening on to a path known locally as The Private Way, and the house was entered by a back door, close to a coal-hole. No. 2 opened directly on to the largest path, connecting the Gardens to Crabtree Row. A four-inch brick wall separated the dwellings.

Each cottage consisted of two upstairs rooms, a downstairs parlour, eight foot by seven, a smaller room from which the staircase rose, and a small wash-house extension. The downstairs window overlooked the back garden. The roof of Nos. 2 and 3 sloped sharply down from the front of the building to the back, and this may indicate that the cottages were built – like so much housing in Bethnal Green, Shoreditch and Spitalfields – as homes for weavers:

the lack of an overhanging front gable would allow light to pour into the upper rooms, which may once have contained hand-looms.

Each cottage had a thirty-foot-long, ten-foot-wide garden, divided from its neighbour by three-foot-high wooden palings, in which was a small gate. At the end of each garden was a privy. In the garden of No. 3 was a well to be shared by Nos. 1, 2 and 3, though in fact the residents of many of the cottages could have reached it easily; it was halfway down the garden and comprised a wooden barrel, one and a half foot in diameter, sunk into the soil. The generous size of these back gardens, together with the fact that mulberry trees appear to have been growing there, may reflect an earlier use as tenter grounds, to stretch and dry silk; silkworms lived on mulberry leaves [see 'Silkworms', p. 274].

The ground on which the cottages perched was described by one 1831 commentator as 'former waste – slag and rubbish', and it is possible the cottages had been built on the site of a brickfield, of which there had been a great many in Bethnal Green in the eighteenth century, supplying the fabric of the ever-expanding capital city. The earth would be torn up and baked into bricks in kilns built on site. Another theory is that the Gardens had once been allotments, and that the cottages had developed from a colony of gardeners' huts or summer-houses.

The Gardens and their surrounds had, during the 1664/5 plague visitation, seen some of the highest mortality figures in the capital. In 1831, its old reputation for poverty and despair was returning. Letters from Londoners concerned about conditions in this part of the East End – unpaved, undrained, unlit – were starting to appear in the newspapers. The *Morning Advertiser* printed a complaint about the filth outside the violin-string workshop in Princes Street, just south of Nova Scotia Gardens – a mess (mainly comprising offal) that was five foot wide and one foot deep; while 'An Observer' wrote to the same paper to report the level of filth in nearby Castle Street.

But the most calamitous era for Nova Scotia Gardens was still to come. When John Bishop and Thomas Williams were arrested, on

7 November 1831, after delivering a suspiciously fresh corpse to King's College Anatomy School in the Strand, Police Superintendent Joseph Sadler Thomas searched Nos. 2 and 3 for evidence that would back his hypothesis that Bishop and Williams had advanced from grave-robbery to 'Burking' (after Edinburgh's infamous murderers-for-dissection Burke & Hare), in their bid to supply the surgeons. Superintendent Thomas would later say that he had found Nova Scotia Gardens 'remarkable'; that there was not a street lamp within a quarter of a mile of the place; and that he considered No. 3 itself to be 'in a ruinous condition'.

The examining magistrate asked Superintendent Thomas whether it was true, as he had heard, that Bishop's house lay 'in a very lonely situation', the sort of place where evil deeds could be committed unseen. Thomas had had to reply that in fact the Gardens was 'a colony of cottages', and that one had only to step over the small palings in order to have access to at least thirty other dwellings.

In Bishop's cottage, Thomas had come across two chisel-like iron implements, each with one end bent into a hook; a bradawl with dried blood on it; a thick metal file; and a rope tied into a noose. They looked incriminating, but the police officer knew that they were simply the paraphernalia required by a Resurrection Man. He knew that a court would recognize them as such, too.

No. 3 had contained surprisingly little else: a rickety old cupboard, the marital bed, a large pile of dirty clothes in one corner of the parlour, a child-sized chair, a few household bits and bobs.

Thomas decided to search the well in Bishop's garden; it was covered over by planks of wood, on to which someone had scattered a pile of grass cuttings. From the bottom of the well he fished out an object that proved to be a shawl wrapped around a large stone.

Thomas had found nothing of note in Williams's cottage, No. 2, but from the bottom of its privy in the garden he retrieved a bundle: unwrapped, it comprised a woman's black cloak which fastened to one side with black ribbon, a plaid dress that had been patched in places with printed cotton, a chemise, an old, ragged flannel petticoat, a pair of stays that had been patched with striped 'jean' (a heavy, twilled cotton) and a pair of black worsted stockings, all of which appeared to have been violently torn or cut from their wearer. There was also a muslin handkerchief, a red pin-cushion, a blue 'pocket' (a poor woman's equivalent of a purse, or small, everyday bag) and a pair of women's black, high-heeled, twilled-silk shoes. The dress and chemise had been ripped up the front, as had the petticoat, which also had two large patches of blood on it. The stays had been cut off in a zigzag manner.

On Thursday 24 November, nearly three weeks after the arrests, two admission booths were set up outside Bishop's House of Murder, as No. 3 Nova Scotia Gardens was now known. The police had asked Sarah Trueby, owner of Nos. 1, 2 and 3, if some arrangement could be made whereby visitors could enter the House of Murder, five or six at a time, paying a minimum entrance fee of five shillings – a move officers hoped would prevent the house being rushed by the hundreds who were thronging the narrow pathways of the Gardens and straining to get as close to the seat of the horror as possible. Sarah Trueby's grown-up son told the police that he was concerned about his family's property sustaining damage and asked the officers if they could weed out the rougher element in the crowd. Somehow, some kind of pretence of decorum was achieved, and it was reported that 'only the genteel were admitted to the tour'. Nevertheless, the two small trees that stood in the Bishops' garden were reduced to stumps as sightseers made off with bark and branches as mementoes – ditto the gooseberry bushes, the palings, the few items of worn-out furniture found in the upstairs rooms, while the floorboards were hacked about for souvenir splinters. An elegantly dressed woman was seen to stoop down and scoop up water from the well in which the macabre find had been made, in order to taste it. Local lads were reported to have already stolen many of the Bishops' household items, and around Hackney Road and Crabtree Row a shilling could buy the scrubbing brush or bottle of blacking or coffee pot from the House of Murder.

*

Bishop and Williams died for their crimes, and their bodies then suffered the fate of executed murderers: they were anatomized by London's surgeons. The 'Case of the London Burkers', as it became known, brought Nova Scotia Gardens another, unflattering, name: for the remainder of its life it would be known as Burkers' Hole, and a myth arose that the cottages communicated with each other via a warren of cellars and subterranean passages – a vivid image of how London's criminal fraternity were felt to be able to move around unseen along secret pathways of their own making.

In the late 1830s and 1840s Nova Scotia Gardens was one of the slums traversed by such sanitary reformers as George Godwin (founding editor of the *Builder* magazine); Dr Southwood Smith (who took the Earl of Shaftesbury to see how the cottages regularly flooded because they were so low-lying); Henry Austin (Charles Dickens's brother-in-law); and Dr Hector Gavin (author of the compendium of East End fever haunts *Sanitary Ramblings*, 1848). By the late 1840s a refuse collector was using Nova Scotia Gardens as his official tip, accumulating a vast mound of waste – all manner of metropolitan rubbish, including human and animal dung – from which the still destitute residents of that part of Bethnal Green came to salvage some sort of living. Godwin decided that 'an artistic traveller, looking at the huge mountain of refuse which had been collected, might have fancied that Arthur's Seat at Edinburgh, or some other monster picturesque crag, had suddenly come into view, and the dense smell which hung over the "gardens" would have aided in bringing "auld reekie" strongly to the memory. At the time of our visit, the summit of the mount was thronged with various figures, which were seen in strong relief against the sky; and boys and girls were amusing themselves by running down and toiling up the least precipitous side of it. Near the base, a number of women were arranged in a row, sifting and sorting the various materials placed before them. [See 'Fairies', p. 178.] The tenements were in a miserable condition. Typhus fever, we learned from a medical officer, was a frequent visitor all round the spot.'

'Refuse' was Godwin's euphemism for human faeces; Dr Hector Gavin described the same scene as 'a table mountain of manure' and 'excrementitious matter', which towered over 'a lake of more liquid dung'. Gavin complained that the Gardens had become 'a resort for all the reprobate characters in the vicinity on Sundays, who there gamble, fight, and indulge in all kinds of indecencies and immoralities. The passersby on Sundays are always sure to be subjected to outrage in their feelings, and often in their persons.'

Half a century later a nostalgia column, 'Chapters of Old Shoreditch', in the local newspaper, the *Hackney Express & Shoreditch Observer*, featured an aged local resident's eyewitness memory of 'the fearful hovels . . . once so famous in the days of Burking – a row of dilapidated old houses standing back from the line of frontage and in a hollow, with a strip of waste land in front, on which was laid out for sale flowers, greengrocery and old rubbish of all kinds'.

Royalty came to gawp at the natives too, and discovered that nature always finds a way: Princess Mary Adelaide, Duchess of Teck – granddaughter of George III and mother-in-law to the future George V – recalled of the Gardens: 'There was a large piece of waste ground covered in places with foul, slimy-looking pools, amid which crowds of half-naked, barefooted, ragged children chased one another. From the centre arose a great black mound . . . the stench continually issuing from the enormous mass of decaying matter was unendurable.'

But the most important visitor to these foetid regions was Angela Burdett-Coutts (1814–1906), millionairess, philanthropist, baroness (from 1871) and, for two decades, close friend of Charles Dickens. Together, the baroness and the novelist would take long night-walks to some of the 'vilest dens of London' during the 1840s and 1850s; and from time to time the 'Ruins' (yet another local name for Nova Scotia Gardens) featured on their East End itinerary; to Burdett-Coutts it was 'the resort of murderers, thieves, the disreputable and abandoned'. In 1852, she bought Nova Scotia Gardens for £8,700. She intended to raze the cottages and in their place build salubrious homes that would lead to the moral, spiritual and physical improvement of the dwellers of Burkers' Hole. But she had not been informed that the refuse collector was legally entitled to stay on the land – no matter who owned it – and to use it as he saw fit until 1859. It was only in that year that she was able to set about her grand project. She employed architect Henry Darbishire to create Columbia Square, a magnificent five-storey block of one-, two- and three-room apartments, housing 180 families who paid between 2s 6d and 5s a week in rent; there were shared washing facilities and WCs on each floor, and a library, club room and play areas. Every summer, Burdett-Coutts chartered two steam trains to take the entire estate to a garden party at her Highgate villa, Holly Lodge. A waiting list of families keen to move into the flats quickly grew.

Columbia Square was an odd amalgam of industrial-dwellings-style tenements on to which were grafted the pinnacles and pointed arches of Gothic; plain yellow stock bricks were dressed with Portland stone and terracotta mouldings. What followed next was even more exotic: Columbia Market, built just to the west of the Square between 1863 and 1869, was a Castle Perilous extravaganza that included 36 shops and 400 market stalls for local traders and costermongers. The costermongers were specifically catered for in Columbia Market; where previous philanthropic housing ventures had created no room or facilities for the costers' donkeys, Burdett-Coutts built stables for the animals, and sheds for the barrows they pulled. She helped to found a sort of union, the Costermonger Club, which presented her with a small silver donkey in thanks; this would remain one of her most treasured possessions.

Columbia Market looked like a miniaturized cathedral and came complete with pieties painted on the walls, such as 'Speak everyman truth unto his neighbour', and orders forbidding swearing, drunkenness and Sunday trading. It went bust within six months.

The baroness's housing, however, continued to be popular for nearly 100 years, but Columbia Square was finally condemned as unfit for human habitation in the 1950s; the Market died alongside it (Britain's heritage bodies having not yet realized their lobbying skills), and Henry Darbishire's masterpieces fell to the demolition ball in 1960.

Today, the Dorset Estate (named after the Tolpuddle Martyrs) is Nova Scotia Gardens' latest incarnation, though, like all the others, it's not a name that's likely to stick. Its architect, Berthold Lubetkin, is probably most famous in this, his adopted nation (he fled the Soviet Union, arriving in Britain in 1931), for the Penguin House at London Zoo. On the site of Bishop and Williams's depredations, the staircase that soars through the nineteen floors of Sivill House (completed in 1966) has distinct echoes of the penguins' Modernist home.

There are sadder, nastier echoes: in 2002/3 four people were murdered at Sivill House within a nine-month span. Psychogeography? I think not. Isolated tragedies, with poverty playing at the very least a walk-on part.

Time has written some very odd features on to the face of the Gardens: the zigzags of the colony of tiny, quaint cottages; the mid nineteenth-century hillock of shit; the philanthropic towers of Angela Burdett-Coutts; and, now, the stark geometry of post-war high-density housing and Lubetkin's monoliths.

[Sarah Wise]

THE GAZETTEER OF DISAPPEARANCES & DELETIONS

IN THE DAYS OF HOGARTH; OR, THE MYSTERIES OF LONDON

In those times, nearly every shop, warehouse or commercial establishment was marked by its particular sign. In many instances, these signs were emblematical representations of the trades carried on in the houses ... But there were also many cases in which the signs were not symbolical of special trades, and were merely used as distinctive characteristics of various commercial establishments. Thus representations of bears, lions, dogs, crowns, bee-hives, wheat-sheaves, &c, were hung up as signs; and the progress of luxury introduced a refinement even into this department – so that the streets of London at the period of which we are writing were filled with green dragons, golden elephants, blue bears, red lions, yellow dolphins, and such like incongruous inventions.

[George W. M. Reynolds, 1849]

FAIRIES

A disappeared trade: a London-wide community of women who made a living sifting the city's rubbish dumps, given the Cockney ironic name of 'Fairies'. Described by a London City Mission welfare worker in 1905 as 'strong, coarse women . . . knee-deep in dust. That which passes through the sieve goes to help make bricks, while that which remains in the sieve goes to burn the bricks. The pots, pans, kettles and dead animals are picked out and placed on one side.' The Fairies worked alongside 'Bobblers' – men who shovelled the rubbish into their sieves. If she rose to the top of the profession, a Fairy was said to have become a 'Queen'; the job often passed from mother to daughter.

[Sarah Wise]

HOCKLEY IN THE HOLE, ECI

A district removed during the 'Clerkenwell Improvements' of the mid 1850s. The Hole (at the lowest part of today's Ray Street) was a tiny valley into which the nearby Fleet regularly flooded; 'hock' meant miry. From the seventeenth century Hockley was famous for its bear gardens and small amphitheatre, in which cock- and dog-fighting spectacles took place, and bears, bulls and don-keys would be baited and tormented – sometimes by having fireworks tied to them.

[Sarah Wise]

LINCOLN'S INN FIELDS SHANTY TOWN, WC2

In 1988, as rough-sleeping in the UK increased dramati-cally, hundreds of homeless people put up their tents and cardboard-box 'bashes' in the gardens of Lincoln's Inn Fields. This metropolitan shanty town was forcibly cleared and its inhabitants dispersed in March 1993.

[Sarah Wise]

GRESHAM CLUB, E4

The Gresham was a gentleman's luncheon club, estab-lished in the nineteenth century, and functioning in 1969 in much the same way as a hundred years before. Meg and I, dedicated Marxists, reluctantly abandoned our miniskirts for waitresses' black and white, and set about trying to undermine the false consciousness of the perma-nent staff, to little effect. The gentlemen, city types and assorted worthies, undoubtedly shaping the fate of smaller nations, sat in their dull dark suits at refectory tables. 'Miss,' one would cry, 'my napkin ring is missing.' And we sifted through the engraved silver christening rings and tortoiseshell and probably whalebone and meteorite, because gentlemen could not be expected to eat without their own napkin ring before them. The food was predict-able, public-school dinners: veal, ham-and-egg pie, steak-and-kidney pudding, spotted dick. I stopped by a balding man with glasses, my order-pad at the ready. 'My usual.' He went on with his conversation. 'It's my first day;

perhaps you could tell me what your usual is?' 'I am Lord Carrington,' he said. 'Find out.'

[Ruth Valentine]

LIVESY WALK, BROOKGATE, EC1

Running between Leather Lane and Brookgate Market, Livesy Walk is best known for its eighteenth-century inn, the Three Jolly Dragoons – where, legend has it, Dick Turpin and Tom King held court during the Golden Age of the Tobeymen (mounted highway-robbers whose exploits were finally brought to an end by the introduction of the electric tram). A few tobeymen continued to waylay trams run by the London Universal Transport Co., though the famous cry of 'Throw down your lever' was a myth propagated in such boys' papers as *Thrilling Tramway Yarns* and *The Dick Turpin Library*. Livesy Walk was later the residence of Edward Holmes, Desmond Reid and a number of authors, all of whom worked for the Amalgamated Press, which was situated near by. Between 1910 and 1914, the Walk was the fictitious address of the 'office boy's Sherlock Holmes', Sexton Blake. Arnold Bennett lived here for a short time, after his return from France in 1912.

[Michael Moorcock]

COVENEY'S YARD, EC3

Although the Elizabethan courtyard has now disappeared, the name is still attached to the Brookgate flats (built in 1990). Until the early years of the twentieth century the Yard was best known for Coveney & Child's Medical Supply Stores – the chief importers of opium and morphine, suppliers to London society (including many theatrical celebrities). George Grossmith refers to 'Coveney

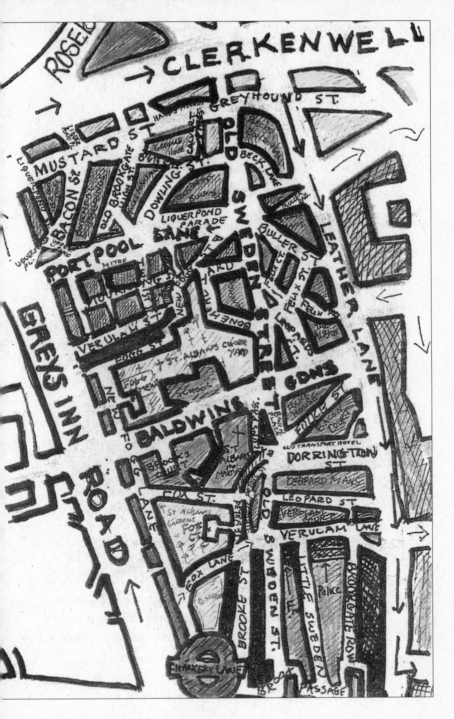

TALES of the TRAMWAYS

A Monthly Magazine of Adventure, Mystery and Education
featuring the famous
'Knight of the Line' -- DICK TURPIN

JULY 1976   PRICE ONE SHILLING   Vol. VIX No. 3

DICK TURPIN SOLVES THE MYSTERY OF THE

MURDER on the ORPINGTON EXPRESS!!
By Agatha Coltrin

70

A Tale of the Romney Marsh lines

The final issue of *Tales of the Tramways*. 'A kind of popular
fiction unique to London' – Cyril Connelly. Hugely popular
in the 1920s and 1930s, *Tales* had by 1970 become primarily a
comic book.

the Younger, the Happiness Monger' in one of his comic songs. De Quincey mentions 'Coveney's Comfort' in a footnote to his second revision of *Confessions of an English Opium Eater*. For a short time, in the 1870s, Coveney & Child enjoyed the prestige of a royal warrant.

[Michael Moorcock]

THE OLD MOON & STARS, FOXES ROW, E3

Named for Sir John Moustiere, the first Huguenot judge in London, the Old Moon & Stars was originally a coffee shop. It is mentioned by Goldsmith in an essay published in the *Monthly Review* (1758). (The New Moon & Stars is located in Dykes Street, Smithfield, and is notable for its 'blood worms' – the black sausages that are still sold, on request, in the teeth of Euro regulations.)

The Old Moon & Stars became a public house during the middle part of the nineteenth century and was noticed by Dickens in several articles for *Once a Week*. The association with *Master Humphrey's Clock* is recalled in dubious memorabilia. A framed document claims that in the first draft of the tale Dickens portrays Adjutant Slate holding court in the pub.

The house sustained some damage during the Blitz but was restored in 1965. The proprietor, Tommy Mendes, had a reputation in the East End as a bare-knuckle boxer. He can still be brought downstairs to talk to customers who are making a disturbance. In recent years, thanks to a relaxation in the licensing laws, fifty kinds of absinthe have been made available – including the famous 'Red and Yellow' (95 p.c. proof).

[Michael Moorcock]

THE LAST SEWER

1

The last sewer I was working at
was the sewer at Blackfriars-bridge that
played the deuce with me that did

we pulled up an old sewer had
been down upwards of 100 years &
under this a burying-ground we dug
up I should think one day about
seven skulls & as to leg-bones
oh a tremendous lot of leg-bones
to be sure I don't think men
has got such leg-bones now the
stench was dreadful we knocked off day-
work & was put on to night-
work to hide it after that bout
I was ill at home for a week

2

we nails our lanterns up
to the crown of the
sewer when the slide is
lifted up the rush is
very great & takes all
before it roars away like
a wild beast we're obligated
to put our heads fast
up against the crown &
bear on our shovels so
not to be carried away
& taken bang into the

Thames there's nothing for us
to lay hold on if
taken off our legs there's
a heavy fall about three
feet just before you comes
to the mouth if we
was to get there the
water is so rapid nothing
could save us

3

Great black
rats as
would frighten
a lady into
asterisks to
see
of a sudden

[John Seed/Henry Mayhew]

'A DESERT IN THE HEART OF LONDON'

The extensive and complicated network of lanes, courts
and alleys covering the area bounded east and west by
Bell Yard and Clement's Inn, north by Carey Street, and
south by the Strand and Fleet Street, lately containing a
population more numerous than that of many Parliamentary boroughs, is being fast deserted. A few of the winding
thoroughfares are not yet disturbed, but several of old
and worse than equivocal notoriety – and in which, a few
weeks ago, passage was rendered somewhat difficult by
the human swarms whose modes of existence are among
the unsolved social mysteries – are now almost uninhabi-
ted, only a house or two remaining, in exceptional cases,

where a brief extension of term has been granted. Massive padlocks guard every door. The glass on the first and second floors has been smashed in by unforbidden missiles discharged as parting salutes by the more juvenile emigrants, and the grimy, stooping, unwholesome buildings wear an aspect of weird gloom, contrasting strangely with their recent animation, when every doorway and window arrested passing attention with grotesque and sordid samples of human nature. The ground taken by the authorities intrusted with the arrangements for the new 'Palace of Justice', or, in plain English, the new law courts and offices, includes nearly thirty lanes and passages, the names of some of which will be familiar to all who have made acquaintance with the topography of London. Among them is Clement's Lane, the south part of which, nearly up to King's College Hospital, comes down. Here still stand some old houses, the very peculiar, perhaps unique, character of whose construction is worthy of a visit. One of them is remarkable as the scene of one of those Royal intrigues and misdeeds which figure in the *Mémoires pour Servir* of Charles II and his Court. Then there is Bell Yard, the seat of newsvendors, law booksellers and printers ... Next come Middle and Upper Serles Place, with Lower Serles Place, formerly Shire Lane; Ship Yard, mentioned more than once in the chronicles of seventeenth-century roysterings; Crown Court, a dilapidated passage ... with its noisy and dangerous neighbour, Newcastle Court.

The main frontages to come down are, northwardly, nearly the whole of the south side of Carey Street, and, southwardly, the eastern and western extremities respectively, the north side of the Strand and Fleet Street, crossing Temple Bar. The pulling down of the south frontage will probably be deferred until some way has been made in the removal of the passages to the rear. By the displacement of so many hundreds of poor families, the unhealthy courts about Drury Lane, Bedfordbury, the Seven Dials and other localities, already reeking and noisome with excess of numbers, have become more overcrowded than ever. The rents of the most miserable rooms have materially risen, and another entanglement is added to the difficult problem, 'How and where are the poor to find suitable dwellings?'

[*The Times*, 12 November 1866]

'LOST GRAVE OF WILLIAM BLAKE FOUND IN LONDON'

The keeper, the Irishman, was unusual. He was there when you needed him, but otherwise invisible. When Bunhill Fields was the subject, this man was always mentioned by initiates. Some said he was an artist, a painter. They didn't know his name, had never set eyes on his work. There was a distance, certainly, between the person who stood, so obligingly, before you, and whoever came, by accident or whim, to the old Nonconformist burial ground on the edge of the City. The unlucky Cromwells, he had those on tap. He would unlock a low gate and lead you to the relevant memorial, the chipped or erased tomb. He had the stories, without the compulsion to inflict them on you. And he did his job, quietly and efficiently: the gardening, sweeping, toilet cleaning. The brewing of regular mugs of tea.

A slight figure in baseball cap and overalls, you may have noticed him ghosting through television films, local-interest documentaries. The man solved one of the mysteries of the place. Who, I wanted to know, left flowers on the grave of William and Catherine Blake? There was no such tribute for Daniel Defoe or John Bunyan. Pass through as early as you like, they were there, in a jam jar; fresh, modest. A splash of colour against the grey. 'That's me,' he confessed. But I think the coins which have recently made an appearance are *not* him. Brown. Leaving a stain when they are lifted – so that new tributes can be placed, next morning, in exactly the same position. Three groups of coins on the rim of the thick slab: five at each end and seven on the highest part, the curve. I'd have made something of that once.

The keeper rubbed his nose with a knuckle and confirmed what I'd read in *The Times* (16 April 2005), Blake wasn't here. The much-loved memorial was just that, a prompt marking nothing, marking absence. Two 'amateur sleuths' – Carol Garrido, a landscape gardener, and her husband, Luis, a law graduate – had 'used records from *Bunhill Fields Burying Ground Order Book* to find the grave's coordinates'.

The present memorial had been set up in 1960, an episode of civil pride, to smooth over minor bomb damage, after the Blitz. Fading newspaper photographs of moustache-and-black-hat dignitaries, taped to the window of the keeper's hut, made it absolutely clear: the dedication ceremony happened elsewhere.

We looked at mute grass and away to the west, beyond the line of trees, to the obelisk of St Luke's, Old Street. Not a trace. Not one degree of the original heat. A communal grave: even in death, a shared tenement for the Lambeth poet. I read out the list of names, co-tenants of this Clerkenwell pit: Margaret Jones (37), Rees Thomas (53), Edward Sherwood (53), William Blake (69), Mary Hilton (62), James Greenfield (38), Magdalen Collin (81) of Bethnal Green Road, Rose Davis (58).

The Necropolis Company took a million-pound contract to clear the slumbering dead, in strong green bags, from beneath St Luke's. Winter rains turned earth to muddy soup. Kosovans were employed – willing, active workers – to feel, blind, for bones, scraps of cloth, coffin wood. And then the logged remains, details entered in an antique ledger, were taken out to the suburbs and bull-dozed into a mass grave. Which was soon returfed and rolled.

'They're everywhere,' said the man who made the film. 'London is a great mound of bones. We are walking on the faces of the dead.' Before Brookwood, the funeral trains out of Waterloo, and the suburbanization of death, our immediate forefathers were much closer to the sur-face. Hands reached out of the ground, literally: Hoxton urchins were challenged for wearing small fists of signet rings. Respectable matrons, walking nervously through churchyards, skidded on human skin, mortality's leather.

Blake was put to earth with a charabanc of East Enders, recent immigrants from the Celtic fringe. No alcove in St Paul's, no effigy in winding sheet. No heritage plate (like a royal-blue satellite dish), not then. And better so. Beyond the reach of vulgar curiosity. A stone postcard in the shade of a fig tree. And the company of other distinguished absentees. All under the patronage, the casual and affectionate custodianship, of this Irishman, my guide. His daily jam jar of garage flowers.

[I. S.]

THE VEGETATIVE BUNYAN

After completing our three-and-a-half-day hike, Epping Forest to Glinton, in pursuit of the 'peasant poet' John Clare, I returned to London and Bunhill Fields. My companion, Renchi Bicknell, had broken away from a solitary expedition he was undertaking, as a way of restor-ing his sense of place, after a period spent in India: he was walking, in a kind of disembodied reverie, from Boston (on the Wash) to Abbotsbury in Dorset. A raw-food diet left him floating several inches above the ancient flags. To keep himself grounded, he looked for difficulty and filled his pockets with the relevant stones.

That triangulation, Blake-Defoe-Bunyan, covers it. Everything in old London, in England, moves out from here. A shaded enclosure, a green passageway: beyond the City walls the melancholy susurration of the non-conforming dead.

The relief panel on Bunyan's generous monument is what we are both after, what we have been doing all these years: the Pilgrim, his back horseshoed by a grotesque burden, leans on a staff. It's what Jeff Kwinter, the rag-trade magus, said to me, years ago: 'You're always schlepping something across town. That's your karma.' Books, cameras, unwieldy kit. Blake's version of the Pilgrim, stooping under a maggoty chrysalis rucksack, reading as he walks, was the frontispiece of my first London book, *Lud Heat*.

The sleeping figure of Bunyan, face to the rising sun, has been groomed. He is no longer the vegetative god, the albino sacrifice: lichen for nose hair, black fur to emphasize the cheekbones. White plaster crumbles as the traveller, the tinker, breaks out of his mummy case. The cracked skull leaks light. It dissipates, quietly, noticed only by the scholarly Irish custodian, keeper of the stones. It drains across the darkening burial ground; over lesser Cromwells and other forgotten exiles; over Milton's death chamber, the small markets and lost theatres of metatemporal London.

Bunyan is the emblem of transformation. Another floater: kept in place by the anvil-weight of his sepulchre. His eyes are pads of emerald moss. Wavelets of chalk hair flow back into the empty tank. Accidents of dust and corruption sculpt a white mask, a flash into negative. Anorak groups are brought here to witness a continuing absence. They confirm it with cameras.

Gerda Norvig, in an account of Blake's illustrations to *The Pilgrim's Progress*, sees this image of Christian with his burden as a form of entrapment: the man peering short-sightedly at the book is *himself captured* within the pages of another book, at which we, tentative readers, also peer. This gaze is not easily broken. Bunyan's carapace disintegrates, a memento to the passage of time – but the panel with the Pilgrim is fresh and bright. The author's death dream realized: framed.

'A storm is brewing,' Norvig tells us. 'The man is bent double with wakeful pain and anguish, he wears ragged trousers and a torn shirt, and his limbs show extreme muscular exertion as if he were straining upwards against the equal and opposite downward force of his burden.' No escape. We have come to a place that describes, flawlessly, the place to which we have come. So: disappear into the image, the stone mirror. Or stand here for ever, confirmed in your ignorance.

[I. S.]

EASTENDING

LOU ESTERMAN
Wednesday 2 March 2005

It's a dark cold late afternoon. It's sleeting, at times snowing. My breath's white as I stand outside 226–228 Mile End Road, across the road from Stepney Green tube station. Forty-four years ago there was a monumental masons here or about here.

226 is now '2 Tasty Halal Meals' and 228 is the 'Golden Dragon – Chinese Food to Take Away'. Was it 228? Or 226? They both seem newer buildings even though in yellow brick and local style.

As I write this in a notebook the sleet makes the ink dissolve and run down the page. I take refuge in a telephone box to finish writing.

I've forgotten the name of the masons so need to check this up. I walk through the sleet and rain west along the Mile End Road to the Whitechapel Library by Aldgate East tube. It's closed.

Friday 18 March 2005

A hot sunny spring day. I go to the Whitechapel reference library to check the *Kelly's Directory* for 1961 but am referred to the local-history library in Bancroft Road. So I walk this time east along the Mile End Road to the fine but now very neglected library. (The place where, in my late teens, I discovered American literature. William Carlos Williams, John Dos Passos, William Faulkner, and so many more. That was from 1958 onwards.)

The library has a 1962 *Kelly's Directory* and there I find – '216–218 Harris & Son Monumental Masons, E1'. I was looking at the wrong building. The memory was wrong. The monumental masons' showroom and yard was four doors west of where I'd thought.

I walk back and find it's 'Lucky Groceries Ltd – Rahim Bros'. A two-floor building painted white – now a greying off-white – with a big and spacious Bangladeshi grocery on the ground floor. I can see out the back a large loading yard where the stone yard used to be. Another Jewish monumental mason has disappeared, leaving only A. Elfes Ltd at 17 Osborne Street at the bottom of Brick Lane. (They specialized in polished black granite, beside the usual and cheaper white marble. If I remember right.)

Satisfied with my searches I walk back west along the Mile End Road and stop for a beer at the Blind Beggar opposite London Hospital. Sat there I suddenly realize this was the pub where Jack the Hat was murdered. Or was he? The next day, phoning Robert Sheppard, I find Jack the Hat was killed by Reggie Kray in Stoke Newington. It was George Cornell who was shot in the Blind Beggar – by Ronnie Kray for calling him 'a fat poof'. The bullet was still lodged in the jukebox until recently, or so the legend goes. One more mangled memory.

This is a memory of a memory of a memory. Box in a box. Picture within a picture. Borges and the Camp Coffee bottle.

Summer to Winter 1961

Needing work I saw a handwritten notice LABOURER WANTED in the window of Harris & Son, a monumental masons opposite Stepney Green tube. I went in and got the job. Starting as a labourer, polishing large slabs of marble, I soon moved up to be a monumental mason's mate. There were four masons and six or seven labourers. We made elaborate marble and granite gravestones – half the inscription would be in Hebrew, the other half in English. Blacklead lettering on the white marble and blacklead or gilded lettering on the red granite headstones. My own work was to prepare and sandblast the simpler decorations for the cheaper headstones, paint temporary grave markers on white marble tablets with the names and dates of the deceased, and to do the lead lettering. (Soot was used to cover small imperfections in the lettering when the rabbi was due to inspect the stones.)

One of the masons, Lou Esterman, to this day remains an ideal for me. A neat-built man about five foot nine and in his early forties, I'd guess. He was a superb stonemason. He faultlessly cut the long inscriptions. He would carve wreaths of flowers and flowing decorations on a slab of marble, after making the briefest of pencil sketches on the stone. And yet, with all this natural skill and flair, he was never smug or opinionated. He always seemed open and looking. He always had a generous spirit. He had that beautiful gift of, for want of a less clumsy phrase, intellectual humility. This, I realized, was what one should hope for more than anything else, what an education should teach more than anything else.

If in a lunch break I should be sitting in the stone yard looking at a book of Picasso's paintings, there would be none of the usual mockery then current, the jokes about how a monkey could paint better, and so on. Lou would want to discuss why Picasso had made a painting the way he did. He'd want to work it out. I've found the same willingness and freshness since then, and nearly always among craftsmen like the bookbinders when I worked in a library. I found it too when I finally met Tristan Tzara. Tzara epitomized the questing spirit, never taking anything for granted but always searching and pushing the boundaries further. But Lou was really the first to directly show me this. I love and dearly respect such clear modesty. We never met again after my time in the yard, but the seed had been sown. That memory I get right and will continue to do so.

[Lee Harwood]

AVRAM NACHUM STENCL

This essay is dedicated to the memory of Majer Bogdanski, who died on 4 September 2005.

In 1965, East London historian Bill Fishman called this extraordinary man 'the last of the dreamers of the ghetto'. Eighteen years later Avram Stencl was found on the streets of Whitechapel, where he had collapsed. He was dressed like a beggar, penniless, practically unknown. He died shortly afterwards. Bill said Kaddish at the funeral. He still cannot talk about Stencl without tears in his eyes: 'That he should end his days like this is such a tragedy. We have forgotten London's foremost Yiddish poet.'

I first heard Stencl's name in my grandparents' house in Westcliff-on-Sea (or Whitechapel-on-Sea, as many called it). My grandfather had been a great friend. They were *Landsleit* who met in White-chapel and shared a mutual passion for the Yiddish language. After the war, like many others, my grandfather moved the family from the bombed-out streets of East London. Their new home in Essex became a refuge and a meeting place for the artists, poets and radicals of the Jewish East End.

Stencl regularly visited my grandparents' seaside home. My father remembers seeing him sitting in the front room, arguing passion-ately with my grandfather, laughing, playing cards, talking of art, politics and friends. 'He was like a warm and affectionate uncle. Stencl would pinch my cheeks, vigorously, and speak at great speed in Yiddish. I only ever understood half of what he told me. He always brought flowers for my mother, who adored him. As soon as he arrived, she'd put a plate piled high with steaming hot *hamisha* food in front of him, whilst lamenting the holes in his jumper and his fingerless gloves. To her it was a *mitzvah* to feed him, an honour to have such a great man in her house.' As far as my grandfather was concerned, Stencl was a genius. 'Poetry was the most important thing in his life.'

This was the most romantic statement I had ever heard. Half-remembered details of Stencl fuelled my teenage fantasies of the Jewish East End. Determined to discover this landscape for myself, I moved there after finishing a Fine Art degree at Sheffield Univer-sity. Then, during many years tracing the remnants of Jewish Whitechapel, my fascination with Stencl grew. It seemed impossible to talk about the vanished East End without hearing about him. Elderly people spoke of him with the greatest affection. 'He was a great poet.' 'A real gentleman.' 'A righteous person who never walked past a beggar without giving him something.' 'A legend.'

For a decade I filled box files with newspaper articles, recorded interviews, images and stories about his life. I began to construct a brief biography. Avraham Nachum Stencl was born in 1897, in Czeladz, a small mining town in southern Poland. Descended from a long line of Hassidic ultra-orthodox rabbis, he attended Yeshiva and grew up in an atmosphere steeped in Jewish learning. From a very early age he knew that he wanted to be a poet.

In 1917, when he received his military call-up papers, he left home with his father's blessing. He moved to Holland and joined a Zionist community – with the intention of emigrating to Palestine as a pioneer. Personality clashes influenced his decision to leave the community. He began travelling in Germany, living and working with peasants, writing poetry about people and landscape. He moved to Berlin in 1921, just when Franz Kafka and his lover, Dora Diamant, were settling in the city. Stencl was in love with Dora – according to her biographer Kathi Diamant. They shared a common background, coming from ultra-orthodox Hassidic communities in the same area of Poland. In Berlin they met at the Romanische Café. Stencl said: 'For those fleeing from the pogroms in the Jewish Ukrainian *shtetls*, from the famine in Russian cities, and from the revolution, a kind of Jewish colony formed itself in the west of Berlin and the Romanische Café was its parliament. It was buzzing with famous Jewish intellectuals and activists, well-known Jewish lawyers from Moscow and Petersburg, Yiddish writers from Odessa and Kiev, with party-leaders from the extreme left to the extreme right wing – it buzzed as in a beehive.'[1]

Stencl stayed in Berlin for fifteen years, writing poetry. He published many books in the 1920s and 1930s. His achievement was acknowledged by the literary establishment. Thomas Mann was one of his greatest admirers. He lived a bohemian, café life, while enjoying an intense relationship with expressionist poet Else Lakser-Shuler (who was twenty-eight years older than him). He slept rough on park benches and on friends' floors. He wrote constantly and took occasional jobs – as a farmhand or in a cemetery.

In 1936, accused of being a communist, he was arrested and tortured by the Gestapo. On his release, he escaped to England. It is rumoured that he was smuggled out in a coffin, by an athlete returning from the Berlin Olympics. Or perhaps with the aid of a former lover, the German schoolteacher Elisabeth Woeheler, who learned Yiddish and translated much of his poetry. Woeheler died in 1974 and left Stencl all her money.

Talking about Germany, Stencl said: 'I loved the country, I walked and talked with philosophers and poets of all faiths. Then Hitler came with his storm and hatred. That is all I want to remember now.'[2]

Stencl's first English home was in Hampstead, where he may have attempted to meet up with his old friend Dora Diamant. He said: 'I don't like the attitude of the Jews there. We were hearing about the pogroms in Poland and the troubles and they carried on laughing, going about their business. So I took a taxi and said take me to Whitechapel. The driver was Jewish and we conversed in Yiddish. When I saw Whitechapel, the streets, the people, I felt like I was coming home. The driver helped me find a room and I've lived here ever since.'

Stencl arrived in Whitechapel just before the war. Coming from the rich culture of Berlin, this part of London could have been a disappointment. But Stencl loved it dearly. The vibrant Jewish street life – markets, cafés, Yiddish theatres – became the inspiration for much of his poetry. He called Whitechapel his 'holy acres', his 'shtetl', his 'Jerusalem in Britain'. He began to publish *Loshn un Lebn* (*Language & Life*), a monthly journal of Yiddish writing. He not only worked as editor, he also provided many of the contributions. Israel Narodcizcky, who ran a commercial press on the Mile End Road, printed the journal without charge. During the war, when the bombing affected the production of other papers, most Yiddish writers in England published in *Loshn un Lebn*.

Stencl survived on money made from selling the magazine outside meeting places, cafés and lecture halls. He cried: 'Koyfts a heft!' (Buy a pamphlet!) His constant presence at Jewish events made him a familiar face. He stood, in all weathers, making his pitch – even approaching people who worked in the markets. He has been described as a beggar. Emanuel Litvinoff said that 'his work became humiliating as the community that supported him died away'.

Stencl is frequently recalled, at his usual table in a Lyons tea shop, scribbling in a notebook. Or walking the streets of White-chapel, tipping his hat to everyone he met. He achieved a mythical status. His voice reminded people of the world they had left behind. His dedication to the preservation of Yiddish made him a legend.

In 1936, with the help of Dora Diamant, Stencl established the *literarische shabbes nokhmitogs*: regular Saturday meetings now called the 'Friends of Yiddish'. Communists, anarchists, Bundists, Zion-ists, the orthodox and the secular, famous writers and factory workers, all attended these gatherings. Stencl managed to keep this wild mix of Yiddish speakers unified. 'He began the meetings with a loud bang of his fist on the table, promptly at three, and then a short speech often based on current affairs or something from the Talmud or Kabbalah.'[3] Guest writers came from abroad, others performed the Yiddish classics. They sang or discussed politics. Meetings were noisy, demonstrative. No subject was taboo, so long as it was discussed in Yiddish.

My grandfather met Stencl at one of these affairs. The only recorded evidence I have of their friendship is a few minutes of video from a documentary, shot in the late 1970s.[4] It shows Stencl, my grandfather (Gedaliah Lichtenstein) and Majer Bogdanski sing-ing at a Friends of Yiddish meeting at Toynbee Hall. This is indeed the only film I own of my grandfather. Overwhelmed to discover such rare footage, I take stills of the three men. I am amazed to see how much alike they appear.

I know my grandfather travelled to the East End every Saturday to attend the Friends of Yiddish meetings. He continued this practice

Avram Nachum Stencl

Gedaliah Lichtenstein

Majer Bogdanski

until Stencl's death in 1983 – by which time, he also suffered from ill health. He died three years later. Stencl's only surviving relative, his great-niece, Miriam, donated his writings and personal effects to SOAS (the School of Oriental and African Studies). After a lengthy correspondence with the curator, and the production of letters of reference from the British Library, I received permission to inspect the Stencl archives.

Last summer I examined the contents of more than eighteen boxes marked: 'A/521728: A. N. Stencl – Poet of Whitechapel'. Most were filled with papers, printed and handwritten in Yiddish. Not being able to unlock the language, I concentrated on two boxes of ephemera: photographs, passports, newspaper articles, letters in English and other languages.

At the top of the first box was a fat brown envelope containing personal documents. A tea-stained 'final demand' gas bill covered with handwritten script. A receipt for a donation, made by Stencl, to Great Garden Street Synagogue. Evidence of payments for lost library books. A street map of Berlin. Invitations to literary events connected with the Yiddish language. Membership cards for the Beaumont Day Centre Luncheon Club. Personal letters in Yiddish from Paris, Jerusalem, Poland, New York, Amsterdam. Receipts from Jerusalem hotels.

Apart from the domestic bills, most of the papers seemed to relate to some form of Jewish life. There were notes from the Burial Society of the United Synagogue: 'a guidance of persons visiting graves'. A pictorial calendar of Israel (dated 1973). A 1951 catalogue from a Jewish art festival. Flyers for Yiddish concerts and plays that he attended. I found a special grant awarded to Stencl, by the United Synagogues, to obtain kosher foods for Passover in 1970. And there were letters of thanks from numerous Jewish charities for donations.

In the second box were letters – dated 1951 – from a woman called Julie, all in English. In one letter she writes: 'You are very wicked, but you are also a dear. I forgive you some of your many sins because you send me chocolate and because you make me laugh.' Julie could not read or speak Yiddish and seemed to have little appreciation of Stencl's poetry. The letters quash the myth that Stencl could not speak or understand English. He must have communicated successfully with this woman, but the relationship was obviously troubled and fizzled out after a few months. Stencl remained a bachelor till his death.

Another dusty pale blue envelope contained letters in Yiddish, yellowing pages, faded ink, from his father (I presume in Czestochowa) to a Berlin address. Later I found a telegram from Czestochowa, dated 1920. 'Heint fater gestorben = kadsz.' Which Bill Fishman translated for me: 'Father died today = Kaddish.' A stern reminder to Stencl from his family: to fulfil his religious duties by saying a prayer of mourning.

Preserved inside a pink envelope were several birthday cards and New Year cards from 'Your niece Miriam and family'.

Tucked between newspapers was a red leather British passport (1970). A small black-and-white photograph of the now familiar poet and a description of the man. Name: STENCEL – Abram Nachum. Born: Czeladz, Poland. 9.1.1897. Occupation: Poet/ Writer. Height: 5'8". Eyes normal, nose long, complexion fresh. Address: 7 Greatorex House, London E1.' The stamps inside reveal the only evidence of trips abroad, visits to Israel.

From newspaper articles mentioning Stencl, I scribbled down fragments, as I tried to build a portrait of the man. 'His presence is convincing; of medium height in his shabby brown suit he has the stooping shoulders of the Talmudic scholar. His features vitalize the frame. Intense blue eyes under once-fair greying hair; a small hawk nose brooding over full lips in a square jaw; the traditional gesticulation for emphasis and a quick change of expression from an almost beatific smile to mild anger provoked by any sign of flattery' (Bill Fishman, *Elam*, 1965). 'His work breathed the spirit of the great rabbis; it was saturated with Hebrew knowledge and wisdom' (Mr Goldsmith, *Jewish Chronicle*, 31 March 1967). 'He went on writing poetry, sometimes in despair but with a steady and sustained flicker of hope that one day his legacy would be found valuable. Not to go on, to remain inactive while facing the threatened disappearance of yet another Yiddish-speaking community, would be to allow Hitler yet another posthumous triumph' ('A. N. Stencl – Poet of White-chapel' by S. S. Prawer, *TLS*, 3 May 1985). 'The occasion was the 25th anniversary celebration of *Loshn un Lebn*, London's only exist-ing Yiddish periodical, but it was really a testimonial to the last angry Yiddisher, Stencl' (*Jewish Chronicle*, 27 March 1964).

The most revealing article was one that described a room Stencl once rented. It reads like a mirror image of the abandoned room of the orthodox scholar David Rodinsky. 'On the mantelpiece of a shabby little room in Philpot Street, in the heart of Whitechapel, is a reproduction of Rembrandt's *Self-Portrait* taken from an illustrated London magazine, a newspaper cutting showing a photograph of two old Jews with long white beards who surrendered in the old city of Jerusalem in the recent fighting, and a postcard-size repro-duction of Chagall's painting of *Jerusalem*. Stacked on the floor in a corner are old issues of a Yiddish magazine called *Loshn un Lebn*. Other Yiddish magazines and books fill a shelf in another corner. A small table by one window in the room is completely cluttered with Yiddish newspapers. There is in addition, one chair, a narrow bed and a small chest of drawers. Nothing else' (*Jewish Chronicle*, 23 January 1949. Unnamed special correspondent).

One of the boxes was filled with correspondence, in English, about the Friends of Yiddish meetings. Many of the letters mentioned a man named Majer Bogdanski – who would be singing at the event. I had heard of Majer before and knew that he had set a number of Stencl's poems to music.

In September 2000, thanks to an invite from my friend Bill Fishman, I met Majer at the annual dinner held at King's College, Oxford, to celebrate the end of the Yiddish summer school. The first time I saw Majer he was sitting on a bench in the walled garden of the college, wearing a tired jacket, trousers slightly too short and a flat cap. His eyes were closed and he rocked back and forth as if in prayer, while singing a haunting Yiddish melody.

During the meal in the banqueting hall, a number of academics got up to speak. Unaware that he may have been causing offence, Majer continued to sing in Yiddish at the top of his voice, banging the table vigorously with his fists.

Bill Fishman told me that Majer had taken over as the chairman of the Friends of Yiddish after Stencl died. 'He's the real thing,' said Bill, 'truly one of the last of the Mohicans, a dying breed, you should speak with him.'

I talked with Majer for most of the evening and asked if he wanted a lift back to Whitechapel in my car. He was eighty-eight years old and more than capable of travelling by train, but he graciously accepted my offer. I discovered that Majer was from the same area of Poland as my grandfather. He was a fascinating person with a story that includes a stint in the gulags after being captured by the Russians while fighting in the Polish army. 'We were the first to have been there and survived,' he told me. After many personal tragedies, including the loss of his wife and child, Majer made his way to Whitechapel. He worked as a tailor and took evening classes in music. He is now considered to be one of London's greatest Yiddish singers and songwriters. Like Stencl and my grandfather, Majer represents so much of what was great and good about the Jewish East End.

We became friends and met on many occasions. So I became concerned when letters I sent were unanswered and his phone line appeared to be dead. I was relieved to find out, through another member of the Friends of Yiddish, that Majer had moved, by his own choice, into a Jewish old people's home, near Gants Hill in Essex.

I visited him at the first opportunity. I found the home, a vast uninspiring brick building, incongruously tucked between a row of suburban 1930s semis, in a side street near the Gants Hill round-about. The fortress-like exterior reminded me of synagogues I had seen in Eastern Europe. Security was tight. After rigorous questioning by a stern-looking nurse, I was led through carpeted corridors smelling of disinfectant to Majer's room.

As soon as I reached the third floor, I heard his voice, still powerful after several heart attacks and a recent operation to have a pacemaker fitted. I stood for a few moments outside his door, listening until he reached the end of his song. I knocked. Majer was sitting in a large electric-blue wing-back chair. In his hand was a notebook with his latest composition, a Polish poem set to music. As he got up to greet me, I was shocked to see him almost doubled over. He had been so fit and upright. He kissed me passionately on both cheeks and led me towards the only other chair in the room.

'Well, what do you think?' he said.

'It's OK,' I replied. 'More manageable for you. But where are the books?'

'All gone. I donated them to the Spiro Institute.'

His sparsely furnished flat near Tower Bridge had been filled with books.

'They were in the bedroom, the cupboards, everywhere,' he said. 'Every surface was covered. I'm pleased they are somewhere safe, not in the dust-heap.'

Majer had moved, reluctantly, into the home, when he realized he could no longer cope alone.

'I'm ninety-two years old now. I have great trouble with the heart. My confidence has gone. I no longer go out without an escort. The greatest part of the day I spend sleeping. The only place I go is the Friends of Yiddish meetings – with Haim Neslen, who has taken over as chairman. He takes me there and back.'

We began to talk of happier times and the first Friends of Yiddish gathering Majer had attended.

'It was in 1947, the year I came to London, in the basement at Henriques Street, the Baron Beaumont Settlement. There was barely room to stand at the back. Stencl led the meeting and I talked with him afterwards. He told me he put out 250 chairs and still people had to stand. Back then he was quite a superstar. Many came to hear him read his poetry. He was a prolific writer, one of our best. The first time we met, he invited me to sing. I've been singing at these Saturday meetings ever since. I knew an awful lot of *steibel ligun*, songs sung in small synagogues in the back rooms of houses. The Hassidim passed these songs from mouth to mouth but never wrote them down. So I wrote down fifty-four from memory and I began to sing them at the Saturday afternoon meetings. Then I began to compose new songs. I have composed hundreds of songs, all in Yiddish, and published four books.

'In the old days, when the meetings were full to capacity, we went en masse, at about five o'clock when the meeting ended, to one of ten places, and chewed over the whole thing, really heated discussions for many hours. We took the programme to pieces, more tea, then another two hours arguing. There were plenty of these tea places, particularly on the Commercial Road, but most often we went to Lyons, a huge place near Aldgate station. It was where Stencl wrote his poetry. You have to think hard when you read those poems. He writes about many things, an awful lot about love – and when he writes about love, it's with real passion. I have composed music to a number of his poems. He lived for his literary works.

'In the years I knew Stencl his appearance didn't change too much. He wasn't too nicely dressed but he didn't want it. He nearly always wore a shabby old suit, tie and trilby hat and the pockets of his jacket bulged with poems and papers. He was quite handsome, ruggedly so, with piercing blue eyes. He was charismatic. He attracted people to him. He had a temper and would curse vehemently in Yiddish if someone wronged him, but he didn't hold a grudge against anyone. We came from the same part of Poland, but from entirely different backgrounds. His family were learned Talmudists, mine were working people. I came from a long line of cabinetmakers, he came from a long line of rabbis. So we had completely different upbringings, although we both came from orthodox households. Stencl studied for a much longer time with his father. He was a very learned man, a great Talmudist, no rabbi could catch him out. He was not exactly a religious man, he didn't observe all the 613 commandments, but he was definitely at home in the synagogue. Wherever there was a Jewish gathering, even if they didn't speak a word of Yiddish, he was there. He was among the

Zionist gatherings, he for a time sympathized with the communists, although he wasn't a communist. He was at home with the Bundists. He edited *Loshn un Lebn* and he himself had to sell it. This is partly why he was there at the door of every Jewish gathering. People just bought it, they couldn't say no to him, he was so lovely. It cost only a few pence and many couldn't read it even, but they bought it because of the charming way he approached people.

'He lived a modest life in various cheap rented rooms around Whitechapel and was bombed out a number of times. He finally got a council flat in Greatorex Street, which was very near to my workshop in Wilkes Street and he'd often drop by for kibbutzing, just chatting – but the Saturday afternoon meetings were always our main point of contact. Slowly the meetings got smaller as people began to leave Whitechapel. A few would still make the effort and come from further away – but as the audience died off, the hall became too big. Halls got smaller and smaller until we ended up in the Toynbee Hall, which must have been the tenth venue. We still meet there every Saturday at three o'clock. The principle of the meetings is the same: everything must be conducted in Yiddish. We read and discuss Yiddish prose, poetry, essays, as well as singing songs. Until the 1950s, even in the 1960s, there were plenty of performers. Nowadays we have very few, and those that do come learned their Yiddish at university, they didn't grow up speaking it. I try to encourage everyone to participate by asking them to read or say something. There is no restriction on what we discuss or perform, as long as it is in Yiddish. Yiddish songs of all types, Yiddish literature, even articles in newspapers. This Saturday there were only ten, which is now considered to be a good audience. A few weeks ago there were eighteen. There has only been one time since Friends of Yiddish began that we didn't have an audience. It was a cold winter Saturday in the early 1970s and only Stencl and myself showed up. I asked him, "Well, is this it?" And he answered, "While I live, never!" And it's never happened since.

'The meetings are still run in the same way they were in the 1940s, apart from one new addition. After Stencl's death, I took over as chairman and I followed the exact same pattern he had – except he used to inaugurate meetings by talking about current affairs. I established the custom of reading something by Stencl, a poem, an essay. We like to keep his memory alive and this is the way we do it.'

As we talked Majer kept checking his watch, it was nearly time for his evening meal. We walked downstairs together and parted outside the canteen. I asked him if he had held any concerts at the home. 'Because of the pacemaker I can no longer play the violin,' he told me, 'and that I regret very much.' With a wide sweep of his hand around the beige-coloured, empty dining hall, he said, 'This is it for me now. I shall be here until I die.' I watched his tiny hunched figure shuffle painfully over towards an awaiting dinner lady. I left the building with a new determination to start Yiddish lessons at the soonest possible date.

[Rachel Lichtenstein]

WHERE 'WHITECHAPEL' STOOD

The ruin where the church once stood
Lit strangely by the electric lamp,
Tucked under bushes in a dark corner
Head on fist, sleeps the tramp.

Tired from roaming about all day
He lies in the middle of his journey,
The moon hangs in his ragged face
A lamp torn down from its post.

I fear that like the neglected tramp
I too will yet lie somewhere here
And with him wander sad away
Before the day dawns grey

[Avram Stencl]

DORA'S STORY: LOST AND FOUND

On one spring day in 1940, hundreds of women and children disappeared from the streets of London. Early in the morning of 27 May, as the world's eyes focused on the evacuation of Allied forces from the beaches at Dunkirk, police, accompanied by members of the Women's Voluntary Services, knocked on doors throughout Great Britain. Thousands of women between the ages of sixteen and sixty were informed that they could pack a suitcase, one per adult, before they were arrested and imprisoned. Days later, thousands of them were shipped out of the country.

With the outbreak of war, the British Home Office had ordered all alien residents with German and Austrian passports to appear before police tribunals, where they were placed into one of three categories: A, B or C. Class A enemy aliens were considered dangerous and immediately arrested. Those classified as B were considered of questionable loyalty and kept under supervision. They were allowed to remain free, but were subject to certain restrictions: they were not to go beyond a five-mile radius of their homes without police permission and had to surrender any potential espionage items such as cameras, maps and binoculars. Class C aliens were classified as refugees from Nazi oppression and went completely free.

Churchill's attitude towards the refugees hardened as reports of German fifth-column infiltration poured across the North Sea. Public opinion turned against the 70,000 German and Austrian refugees in Great Britain as newspaper headlines fuelled a rampant anti-refugee paranoia. Even Oxford University got in on the act, issuing an official statement that 'all aliens are a potential menace and should be interned'. It was true that some real Nazi sympathizers were among those arrested and interned, but the vast majority of Britain's 'enemy aliens' were Jews and other refugees fleeing Hitler.

One day before the Dutch resistance collapsed, Churchill called for the round-up of enemy aliens. 'It would be much better that all these persons should be put behind barbed wire,' he said. On 15 May 1940, all male Class B aliens between the ages of sixteen and sixty were arrested. When the Home Office Secretary announced the arrests in the House of Commons, many felt he had not gone far enough. As one MP asked: 'Is the female of any species not generally more dangerous than the male?' Members of the House of Lords concurred that 'women spies are much more dangerous than men'. And so, on 24 May, a secret memorandum went out from the Home Office to all chief constables in Britain, ordering the internment of all B women to begin the following Monday at seven in the morning.

Dora Diamant (Dymant-Lask) was one of them. She and her six-year-old daughter, Marianne Lask, were arrested in their Islington flat on Carysfort Road and taken to the grim gates of Holloway Prison. They were locked in a cell block with hundreds of other German-speaking women, who, in at least one respect, were just like her: Jewish refugees with German or Austrian passports who had been classified as B enemy aliens. In her battered suitcase Dora carried some warm clothes, medicines for Marianne and her only treasure, a holy relic in the form of a man's military-style hairbrush, the only possession she had been able to keep of her love affair with Franz Kafka.

Dora had come to England only the year before, after crossing from the Hook of Holland eight or nine times before she was finally admitted. Fleeing Berlin in 1936 for what she still believed to be the workers' paradise, she had arrived in Moscow at the height of Stalin's purges. Following a miraculous escape from the Soviet Union and a harrowing journey through Nazi-occupied Europe that had lasted months, Dora reached safety in England, with her desperately ill daughter, in 1939, exactly one week before Germany invaded Poland. Her imagined safe haven had turned into a trap. Not once, as an active Jewish communist in Nazi Germany or as the outspoken wife of a imprisoned German Trotskyite saboteur in the Soviet Union, had Dora been arrested or incarcerated. She had escaped Hitler and Stalin, only to wind up a prisoner in England.

Two days after their arrest, Dora and Marianne were among the more than 3,200 women and children shipped off to hastily set up detention camps on the Isle of Man, where they spent the next year at the Women's Internment Camp at Port Erin. Because she was 'Kafka's Dora', Dora was rescued from the Isle of Man by Professor Dorothy Emmet, a philosopher at the University of Manchester, in the late summer of 1941.

When Dora returned to London, what she found in the bombed streets of the once vibrant Jewish East End was a new purpose: the preservation of the Yiddish language. She joined forces with the poet A. N. Stencl in the co-founding of the Friends of Yiddish. 'Immediately after her arrival she associated herself with our work,' Stencl wrote in a tribute to Dora in his Yiddish journal, *Loshn un Lebn*. 'She held lectures at the Shabbat afternoons, read from Yiddish literature, especially the classics. Dora's readings of portions of Yiddish stories, for instance the poem "Monish", were always a *Yontif*, a holy day, at the Yiddish literary Sabbath afternoons.'

When he came to England as a young refugee from Poland, Majer Bogdanski met Dora when he participated in Friends of Yiddish meetings as an audience member. Fifty years later, Bogdanski still recalled magical Saturday afternoon meetings after the war, when 'each meeting was an event'. He would press himself against the wall at the back of the crowded room, to see Dora at the front of the hall, as he said, 'the star of the show'. After Stencl's death, Bogdanski took over the leadership of the group, which has survived to the twenty-first century. Frail in his mid nineties, he regularly attended and performed poetry and prose readings at the meetings of Friends of Yiddish, which are still held every Saturday afternoon at three o'clock at Toynbee Hall in Whitechapel.

Throughout the 1940s, Dora wrote reviews and articles for *Loshn un Lebn* on the 'impoverished' Jewish theatre of London, which she saw as another aspect of the Holocaust. With the murder of one third of the Yiddish-speaking population, Dora did what she could to keep the promise and future of the language alive. Turning her focus to the younger actors, whom she saw slipping away, lured to more professional and lucrative opportunities on other stages, Dora wrote: 'A strange and very disturbing phenomenon has shown itself for some time: A kind of extinction – heaven help us – of young talents. As soon as a young acting talent is discovered – and one barely has a chance to taste it – and already we've lost the child. Be very careful, London Jewish Theatre directors,' Dora warned, 'that a ship – not with sour milk, but actually with cream – will sail away from you. Pinje Goldstein, our most talented, original comedic character actor, may go to America. This has happened with the very gifted Tamara Solomov, now with the Habima in Palestine. So it has been with Fela Feld – and what about our Shiomoh Kohen? How many Shiomoh Kohens does the Jewish stage have?'

Despite her best efforts, the Yiddish world of 'Jewish art' was vanishing before her eyes, unable to survive the postmodern world, born in the apocalyptic end to the war. A discontinuity brought about by the cataclysmic events of 1945 had changed the very composition of the universe. With the birth of the atomic age, the old world of Yiddish had dimmed and was dying. Dora saw herself as 'engaged in a bitter struggle to preserve that bit of honesty and purity that we possess'. A cherished dream had come true with the birth of a Jewish nation, but it had not helped the Yiddishists' cause. Israelis spoke Hebrew, the revived and updated ancient language of the chosen people, as the language of the future. Yiddish was scorned by the Israeli literati, shunned as the old-fashioned jargon of a victimized people.

In the dark performance halls of Whitechapel, Dora continued to wage her battle 'against forgetting'. She urged the Jewish community on to greater creativity and artistic expression, producing and directing conferences, meetings, readings and shows in which she acted several parts, as one observer wrote, 'deploying in front of a public to whom ancient, almost forgotten emotions had to be recalled'. It was dispiriting and disheartening to see the audiences grow older and dwindle as no new artists appeared. But, as Dora reflected, 'What can you do? Out of great need and misery you take what is given – and you shrug your shoulders. One must, after all, keep the soul alive. So you give in. However, this "giving in" is the saddest part of our hopes and struggles.'

When she learned she was dying, Dora began to write her memories of Franz Kafka. She realized she must do what she could to clear up the distortions and misunderstandings surrounding him and his literary intent. Her journals are a testament to her undying love for the man, not the writer, who by then had risen to world fame. After Dora's death in August 1952, her eighteen-year-old daughter typed up the two journals and gave the originals to Marthe Robert, Kafka's French translator. It wasn't until 2000 that Dora's journals were discovered, first the original in Paris, and then in 2002 the typed copy turned up in Berlin. The original of the second journal, written in the darkest moments of Dora's life, is still missing.

Dora died on 15 August 1952, and was buried in a vast treeless cemetery on the eastern outskirts of London. Her funeral was described by Marthe Robert in the Paris journal *Evidences*: 'No writers or journalists attended her funeral. The news had not reached them; only those with whom Dora had worked, played and sung were now crying openly under the rain in the big East End Jewish cemetery. All those who knew her were aware of the importance of her presence, not only because of the great writer whose life she shared – for one brief year, or, if one wishes, for almost thirty years. The figure of Dora does not come under literary history, not even for those who saw in her a reflection of Kafka's light. She spread her own light . . . she was still spreading it in the Jewish milieu of Whitechapel.'

Dora's grave remained unmarked, without a tombstone, until 1999. It was not only a matter of not having the money. According to Kafka's niece, the late Marianne Steiner, who was at Dora's bedside when she died, Marianne (Dora's daughter) didn't want a headstone. 'Mother isn't there,' she said. According to Dora's friends, neither they nor Marianne ever returned to the cemetery again. For almost five decades, the location of Dora's grave, a solitary rectangle of bare rocky earth between tall granite tombs and white marble slabs, was forgotten.

Zvi Diamant, Dora's only living nephew, had no idea that 'Kafka's last love' was his aunt until 1996. Born in 1947 in the release camp at Dachau to Dora's older brother, David, Zvi moved to Israel when he was two years old. David died in 1960, before Zvi's thirteenth birthday. Zvi first became intrigued with Dora when he received a yellowed newspaper article, with 'this beautiful love story of Franz Kafka and Dora Diamant'.

Because of the coincidence of their shared last name, Zvi began to research. He soon discovered that they were indeed related and began to wonder: What happened to Dora after Kafka died? Did she survive the Holocaust? Did she marry? Did she have children? Are they still alive? Determined to find answers, he turned to the internet. There he learned that Dora had married 'a certain Lask' some time 'between 1926 and 1936' and had given birth to a daughter, Marianne. He also learned that Dora had died in 1952 and was buried in London, but he could find no information on his cousin Marianne.

Zvi wanted to find Dora's grave in London, but was told that many Kafka scholars had looked for it but no one had found it. The next year, in late September 1998, Zvi contacted me on Yom Kippur Eve, in answer to a letter that I had written to him, telling him about the results of my more than a dozen years of in-depth research into Dora's life. When Zvi learned the sad news of Marianne's death in 1982 and the location of Dora's unmarked grave, which I'd found in 1990, he felt he must do something. Believing himself to be the only living relative of Dora, he decided that he must 'repair this wrong' and provide them both with a tombstone. A date was set for the stone setting: 15 August 1999.

Three months later, on the forty-seventh anniversary of Dora's death, a memorial-stone setting was held at Dora's unmarked grave at the United Synagogue Cemetery on Marlow Road in East Ham. From Berlin came members of the Lask family, Dora's *mispoche* from Israel included Zvi, his wife, Shoshi, and their four children, a cousin and her family, and Dora's half-sister, Sara Baumer, with her daughter, Tova Permutter. In all, more than seventy-five people from the UK, Germany, Israel, Holland and the United States came to honour Dora's memory. The reception afterwards offered a moving testament to the power of the Yiddish language, with a performance of a story by Dora's favourite author, I. L. Peretz, given by ninety-four-year-old Majer Bogdanski. Few in the audience knew Yiddish, yet everyone understood, as Kafka said, instinctively, the depth of the emotion.

Dora's daughter was not forgotten. Although her ashes are interred at Hoop Lane in Golders Green, Marianne's name was included on Dora's white marble tombstone. The large stone is engraved with both their names, along with a quotation from one of Kafka's closest friends: 'Who knows Dora, knows what love means.'

[Kathi Diamant]

JOSEF RUDOLF, MY ZEIDA
(Dealer in Secondhand Clothes and Army Surplus)

The present texts are based on the transcriptions of tape recordings I made in 1975, when Josef was at least ninety-two years old. My role model as a poet is Charles Reznikoff, who deployed a maximally or perhaps minimally free verse when transcribing documentary texts in two astonishing books: *Holocaust* (taken from the Nuremberg Trials Records) and *Testimony* (taken from American law-court records). Also, I acknowledge the way Claude Lanzmann laid out the original French transcript of his film masterpiece, *Shoah*. My own words – titles, comments, notes, questions – are in italics. Eventually the sequence (with full notes) will be integrated into a book about my grandfather.

Long ago I corresponded with Charles Reznikoff, the exact contemporary of the lost grandfather of Anglo-Jewish poets, Isaac Rosenberg, except that Reznikoff lived on till 1974. I told the American poet about my grandfather and that I intended writing about Josef one day. Reznikoff was encouraging, and for sure intuited that I saw him as a poetic grandfather. To this day, this great and self-effacing poet does not appear in any mainstream anthologies. My own Menard Press published Milton Hindus's book on him, and also one of his poems as a Jewish New Year card, which sold out quickly, partly because the Reznikoff family and in-laws bought so many copies.

Josef Rudolf was born not later than 1883 and perhaps as early as 1880 in Kalusz, a *shtetl* near Stanislawow, a small town in the easternmost province of the Austro-Hungarian Empire, East Galicia, now West Ukraine. The family moved to a village called Dolpatow, where his father kept an inn, and then to Stanislawow itself, his mother's town.

East Galicia became Poland in the wake of the First World War. It was occupied by the Nazis in 1939, then by the Soviet Union in 1941. After the war, it became part of the Ukrainian republic within the Soviet federation. Ukraine is now independent. Josef arrived at Hamburg Docks in 1903 or 1904 or 1905 (more research needed), en route for London. The journey from his home region involved changing trains at Oswiecim, Auschwitz (see also section 26 below).

When his mother, Rosa Vogel Rudolf, arrived here for his wedding to Fanny Flashtig in 1912, her boat was moored offshore at London Docks. He couldn't wait to see her, so he rented a rowing boat and rowed or was rowed over for a reunion. His way of speaking English was typical of his generation of Jewish immigrants, although his sexual frankness was surely rare.

Zeida is the Yiddish word for grandfather and is derived from *dyadya*, the Russian word for uncle, and is etymologically related to *dedushka*, grandfather. Grandmother in Yiddish is *bubba* or *bobba*, with its obvious etymology. Fanny Flashtig was known by us as 'Bobba Dolf'.

A chance reference to immigration officers in an email from a friend today reminded me of my grandfather's naturalization in 1924. The bobby walked the short distance from the police station in Leman Street to 52 Little Alie Street, where the family lived upstairs. Presumably he had an appointment. 'Say after me, Mr Rudolf, "How now brown cow."' Zeida replied: 'How now brown cow,' doubtless in his best English, which was probably not as good as the heavily accented Polish Jewish Yiddish English he spoke to me fifty years later. 'Very good, Mr Rudolf. I shall recommend to the Home Secretary that you should receive your papers.' Bureaucracy only kicked in when it was discovered that his nationality, Austrian, no longer existed, at least not for him, since his home town was now in independent Poland. But there was a solution: he must become a Pole – for three weeks – before he could become English.

I

Apropos an old photograph in a book I showed him of pre-war Polish Jews:

A good thing no Jews live in Vietnam.
There are in Hong Kong.
My mother's half-sister,
Yenta Vogel, married Captain Adolf Spatz,
and went to Hong Kong.

Why did he photograph these poor Jews?
They all look like monkeys.
I didn't see one good-looking person in this book.

Photo of a shul (synagogue):

AR: *It's very old.*

Everything is old. It's only a picture.

2

Apropos a mention of Moses:

Moses was a nice-looking man.
If they will put a picture of him in a *shul,*
people might think he's a God, like Jesus.

3

It happened in a family related to us:
one man married a woman and the brother fucked her.

AR: *Is it allowed?*

If you're doing something wrong, you're not worried if it's allowed
    or not.
She liked it better with the younger brother, that's all.

AR: *And the older one didn't know?*

No, but the family knew about it.
It happens everywhere.
It happens all the time.
(*sotto voce*)
It happened once
in an old story:
someone didn't know he was fucking his mother.

4

I was on the board of management of Hambros Synagogue
(*in Commercial Road*)
for twenty-five years.
There was a man on the board called Hart
who didn't like one called Fox,
and said to him:
You are fox in the name, and fox in the game.

5

When you say your name is Rudolf (*Mayerling*),
the world thinks Prince Rudolf.
He would have been king but they killed him.
Her father found him in the bedroom with her and killed him
    with a bottle.
The king (*Franz-Josef*) had many women, but he wasn't a bad man.
He was religious and he believed the Jews killed Jesus.
Jesus was a communist, and he preached against the religion,
    you understand.
Yehuda (*Judas*) was a bastard, Yehuda was a blackguard,
he came running from the scaffold where they hung Jesus,
crying *mazal tov*, they've hanged him.

6

A Jew in them years, you could kill him like a cat.

A Jew in them years, they killed them all out.

A book tells people
to take a couple of Jews and kill them like rats.

Prejudice against the Jews is all over the world.
I didn't look for problems.
Look, one Jew another Jew doesn't like, so why should a *Yok*
    like a *Yid*?
(*offensive terms for non-Jew and Jew*)
The Jews too are bastards. They kill one another.

7

You shouldn't talk about a father to his son.
You shouldn't talk about a son to his father.
To keep the peace, forget about the trouble.

8

Zeida did his military service in the Austro-Hungarian cavalry:

I dreamed I was in the army on my horse,
in a charge.
Suddenly two more riders
entered the dream
and pulled my horse to one side
while the others charged on
to be destroyed.
I woke up.

9

In my *shul*
one *Shabbes*
(*Ashkenazi Hebrew pronunciation of the word for Sabbath*)
there was a wise old man.
He put his finger in his mouth.
What are you doing? I asked.
I'm fooling my arse.
I smoke tobacco
against constipation.

AR: *What was his name?*

Zeida cackled.
You *potz.*
(*Yiddish word for prick, literally and metaphorically, as in English*)

Yankel Kakka, that was his name.
Yankel Kakka.
(*Jack Crapp, the name of a Gloucestershire cricketer when I was a child, is an accurate and perfect translation*)

10

Life gets in the way.

AR: *Gets in the way?*

Yourself. Life gets in the way of yourself.

11

Old man Klinghoffer was a *groisse potz,*
bought a thousand pounds worth
of blue silk at ten shillings a yard.
Had to sell at half a crown.
I showed him the ropes.
He became paralysed
and could do nothing.
He died soon after.
His wife was a *yachne* (*gossip*) but she was more clever.

12

I met a Jew from Mesopotamia.
He liked a pretty girl in my workshop, Lucas Street,
in the first Great War.
(*East End street rebuilt after being bombed in the Second World War*)

Her father [was] dead, she asked me
should she marry him?
I had to make sure
he was a Jew:
he said the Kaddish for her father,
so he was.
Why not? I said.
But she decided not to.
He became engaged to a plain girl
and fucked her mother.
(*presumably knowingly*)

13

In the old days, when you died, they broke a plate and buried it with you. You wanted the world, and all you took away was a broken plate. It's supposed to be at twelve o'clock in the night, dead souls come together and *daven* (*pray*).

A man passes by the *shul* at midnight. He hears or maybe thinks he hears the souls calling him over to the *Torah* (*metonym for the Holy Ark*). He goes to the rabbi. In them days, the rabbi always lived near the *shul* or over the *beis hamidrash* (*small prayer-house*).

'What shall I do?' he asks the rabbi. The rabbi says: 'You can go in, they will give you an honour, you can take an *aliyah* ('*ascent' to assist in the Reading of the Law, an honour*), but make sure you go in backwards.'

14

Zygfryd (*his nephew Zygfryd Rudolf, later of Los Angeles*) is a bastard. When he came to England, he didn't show respect to the family. I can quarrel with you today, but if I got respect for you I won't lose my temper with you in front of your family.

My brother, Zygfryd's father, Shmuel, was in Carlsbad for a holiday. I visited their house in Stanislawow when I was on leave from the army. I found Zygfryd fucking the servant. When he finished, I told him, do whatever you want to do, go to the fields, but don't do nothing wrong in your own house.

She was good-looking. Oh, she was good-looking. I said to her that when his parents come home I won't tell nobody, but you ought to be ashamed. And I asked her: he persuaded you or he didn't persuade you? He did persuade her. That's all right then, I said.

When I was a sergeant in the cavalry, I went to a brothel in Przemsyl near the Russian line, to round up the men after a day's leave. 'Soldiers out.' I noticed a pair of army boots under a bed, and summoned the man: your name, soldier? Isaac Rudolf. He was a distant relative, but not under my command, so he could stay. There were a million soldiers in Przemsyl.

15

I remember a soldier who had syphilis.
Pieces were falling off of it.
They kept him for experiments, how long he can live.
They fed him on water rolls, no fats in them.
They kept him alive till the whole dirty blood went.
Then they start feeding him with good things,
to make the body go back good, you understand.
Take an apple, inside is a worm.
You open it, you take out the worm, to preserve the apple.

16

If she's not clean and you've got some matter there on top of the skin of your *shmekel* (*willy, affectionate, unlike potz*), you should wash it off with your piss. Your piss only works on your own blood. It's so strong it eats up the dirt. You got to do it straightaway.

The doctor advised soldiers
that when you go to a whore and it comes up
he shall wash in the piss,
the piss is so strong.
My piss wouldn't be good for you,
your piss wouldn't be good for me.

17

Why couldn't you be a doctor, you *potz*? You work in the house all
day. If I would be a young man I would rather do anything than
what you do, working at home translating. That's what I think.

18

Am I born from a stone? [*or*: If I am born from a stone]
I never had a mummy.
Why did my mother left me,
Left me alone
And I aint got where to go.
The best would be
You shall take me there.
I mustn't do that no more.

19

I can't sleep.
If I'm laying in bed
thinking too much
I suffer insomnia.
The doctor told me I mustn't do that no more.
So I'm trying to forget about it.
(*This describes what happened when he wrote his only poem* [*section 18
above*]. *Sure enough, he stopped writing poems*)

20

The pike is a clever fish,
the king of the fish.
He lives off little fish.
Other fish lives on worms.
He tastes good.
He's an expensive fish.
But the head is no good.
They don't throw the head away, they boil it.

We had no sea. We had big rivers.
For gefilte fish, you can fill any fish.
Take for instance an English fish, a bream.
I would say it comes from the carp family.
It's a fat fish.

We dined at each other's houses in turn,
two brothers, two sisters. (*he and his London siblings*)
I bought fish, carp,
from Tom's in the Lane. (*Petticoat Lane*)
Live fish. At the end of the week
live fish
thrown back into their
(*word missing; unclear on tape*)

When we were boys
we used to go to the water.
The fish, they don't swim about;
at the edges
during some grass you put your hand in
and you'll find a fish. That's where they sleep.
If you went in the water
and looked for a fish
sometimes there was a snake there.

You put your hand in
and you can feel if it is a fish, a frog or a snake.
The snake didn't bit you in the water.
I used to catch fish like that.

21

At one point I put myself down, describing myself as a shmok:

Why do you say that? You're a clever boy and you make
    yourself small.
You're not enough proud of yourself. You're a learned man.
You've got everything what God gives, and you don't appreciate.
If you call yourself *shmok* people will hear and call you *shmok*.
You are higher than somebody else because you are
    an educated man.
A person ought to call himself more than he is.
It's a fools' world. If you're too good they shit on you.
Keep yourself higher than others, not exactly without manners,
You've got to have manners as well.
Think yourself a *mensch*.
If you're not a rich man, you'll be a rich man.
Your father says a clever word:
if a person understands his position
the battle is half won.
You understand your position, you know how to act.

22

The gypsies didn't come from Egypt.
They came from somewhere.
The government didn't allow gypsies to the army.
They got no rights.
The gypsies weren't whores, they were thieves.

The government didn't give them civil rights, and they didn't try
   to get rights.
They go every time to another place.
Garlic is good for you, protects you against gypsies and diphtheria.

23

AR: *Were your friends in London all Galicianers?*

A nice man was by me a friend, I didn't care from where he came.

AR: *What do you consider yourself, an Austro-Hungarian, an English-*
   man or a Jew?

I consider myself nothing.
I says a person is nothing.
I was an Austrian patriot when I was young.
I thought I was *Moishe Groiss* (*Big Moses, a big shot*) but I wasn't.
A job you couldn't get there.
They took one out of a thousand
for a civil service job.

24

Hershel Ostropoler was a clever bugger.
(*He was court jester to an eighteenth-century Hassidic rabbi who was*
a rich depressive)

25

Renee has tomatoes the whole length of her garden.
(*His daughter, in whose Hendon house he lived for many years as a*
widower)

26

Auschwitz is a junction.
All the trains from the whole of Europe
go to Auschwitz.
From every part of the world
you've got to change at Auschwitz.
That's why those bastards
made a concentration camp there.
I've been through Auschwitz many times.
You can't go to my home
unless you pass through Auschwitz,
except if you go to Vienna.
But that way it costs longer.
The straight cut is through Auschwitz.

27

My father worked in agriculture.
He had horses.
He had a mill.
Made beer from hops. Young trees.
They aint got no coalmen there. You cut your own wood.

My father had a licensed inn.
Sold brandy.
You pay over your nose.
Tobacco belonged to the government.
They gave you 5 per cent.

My father had a head for business.
He rented property for seven years from a lord.
They were very rich there,
Potockis and Rozvadovskys,
some of them had twenty villages.

My father had shop licences to rent,
he passed them to old soldiers.
They had to be at least half a mile apart, to make a living.
Here you can have one shop next to the other
because it's in private hands.

My father had five sons.
If all of them had been in the army,
he could claim a pension.
My father had small businesses.
He had a head for business.

28

In Austria, it wasn't good prospects for young people. A Jew wants
more than food, a Jew wants prospects. You can't have prospects in
a country what is too poor for prospects. They can't have fifty
Yiddisher clerks taking twenty jobs. If I would be an official, and I
got the chance of taking clerks, I might take a *Yid*, give him a
chance. Between a good *Yok* and a bad *Yid* I choose the *Yok*,
between a good *Yid* and a good *Yok* I choose the Jew. It's not right,
but I would take him. Why should I give a Jew a job if two *Yoks*
are waiting? Here in London once was a job: a sailor, a soldier and
a Yiddisher handyman, they want to be a postman. The post wants
one postman, and three men wanted the job. Why should they give
it to the Jew? The sailor was on the sea and the soldier was in the
army. You got to consider things. That's the way to do it.

29

In London, I been in the Jewish shelter in Mansell Street till one
o'clock at night. My brother Jonas run about till he found me sitting
outside the shelter. I was sick of sleeping on the floor. I was two
weeks on the floor sleeping in Hamburg, and on the ship third class
was no joke. Jonas brought me from the shelter to his lodgings. He

took all my clothes and threw them in the dustbin because he was afraid I was not clean from the boat. He gave me a shirt, and he told his wife, Bertha, and she gave me three shirts and three vests and three pants.

I had lodgings in Lucas Street. In Jubilee Street. In East Mount Street, back of the London Hospital. In Jewish families. I'm orthodox. A brother-in-law and sister came to London to take me to America. I said I won't go. I can exist in London as well. I had got to know my future wife. My mother visited twice, for my wedding and my brother's wedding, but my father wouldn't come because it wasn't *froom* enough here. She came for two weeks. I kept her for four weeks. She was anxious to go back and look after the younger children. My father had thirteen children to keep, five from the first wife, eight from my mother. She went home out of pity for him, *rachmonos*: he was twenty years older. She was going to come again, but war broked out and nobody came no more from there. My parents died in their own beds, before Hitler came.

I had no trade. I met a man. For five pounds he said he would teach me to be a cutter and designer. Who will keep me for a month, I said? For that five pounds I could be in America not here. Still, I learned how to operate a trousers machine. I was paid in secondhand clothes what I could sell. I sent home money to my parents. In them years you could start a big business with fifty pounds. As a machiner I earned three or four pounds a week.

I was learning to be a machiner in my brother's workshop in Lucas Street. I started with ten shillings to pay my lodgings. Then I went out to work, in all sorts of places, and earned a pound, two pounds. Uncle Jonas paid my lodgings. Afterwards I paid him back. My brother-in-law Uncle Abba was my partner for thirty-three years in Lucas Street, and I lived in 16 Sutton Street.

I went past there once when I was working in your Uncle Leon's printing shop in Sun Street, three or four years ago. I was with Leon's driver Alan and I smoked a cigarette and thinking what happened in them days. Before we was married, Grandmother lived in 67 Chambers Street and Prescott Street. In the old days we went everywhere by bus. London Hospital to Marble Arch cost fourpence. Cheaper than the Underground. When I was working by Leon, and we would need to go to the City, I used to say to Alan go through Chambers Street. He says to me something happened here that you won't tell me. I said my girl lived here and I got married from this place.

[Anthony Rudolf]

THE QUAYSIDES OF BRICK LANE: WALKING WITH EMANUEL LITVINOFF

Time was, when the ships used to dock by Tower Bridge, and the immigrants into England could disappear without further ado among the streets and courts of the East End, there to begin life afresh. But all that had changed. Now, a permit was required from the Home Office . . .

ROLAND CAMBERTON, *Rain on the Pavements*

We were standing just a few hundred yards east of Brick Lane, in London's East End, and the narrow road stretched out between two rubble-strewn voids. The council had provided a new sign to confirm that this was indeed Fuller Street, but there was nothing left to see.

Not so, however, for the figure who gazed up from the pavement, his hands slicing the air as he hammered a world back into the emptied scene. He put a terrace of two-storied houses along both sides of the bulldozed street, and squeezed whole families into cellars beneath the road. Up at the far end he sketched in a taller tenement, named it Fuller Street Buildings, and then stared at it until it was fairly 'boiling' with humanity. Children started yelling, sewing machines rattled, and there was a constant chatter of Yiddish. Exasperated neighbours took to banging on thin walls and ceilings with broomsticks, and the air was thick, even in the cold damp of winter, with the interfused smell of drains, sour pickles, garlic and overflowing dustbins in the back yard.

Who was this man – spry but of considerable age – who walked through a temporarily slumped corporation's building site, repossessing it as a village that was, in his own words, 'remote in spirit from the adjacent cosmopolitanism of the great city of London', and altogether more like the small Jewish towns that were once 'scattered across the lands of Eastern Europe', each one fatally 'hemmed in by ancient curses'?[1] And why – now just as then – do we know so little about him?

As a child Emanuel Litvinoff lived in Fuller Street Buildings, but nowadays he perches a few miles to the west, in the sunken grandeur of Bloomsbury's easternmost bastion, Mecklenburgh Square, where he leases a small flat in a building used to house overseas students and their dependants. When I visited him towards the end of 1992, Litvinoff lived in an obscurity that owed little to geography or the length of the corridor leading to his door. To reach him, it was necessary to skirt the jostling vanity fair that is literary life in England, sidestepping the prize-giving ceremonies, the celebrity tennis matches (Barnes was still playing Amis in those distant days) and the chatter about Philip Larkin's dismal social attitudes, then being adroitly publicized by his literary executors. Eventually, I pushed a numbered bell and the man who had once written a Thames Television play named *The World in a Room* peered out and said, with a guarded smile, 'Come in.'

Litvinoff's books may have fallen out of print in the 1980s but some of them drew exuberant praise before that, and a few have even sold rather well. In the late 1960s and early 1970s, he was one of Britain's leading television dramatists: an accomplished exponent of the single-studio play, a now all but extinct genre which Litvinoff used to dramatize social prejudice. But television is, in his own regretful description, 'so much steam on glass', and no one should be expected to remember any of that. Yet Litvinoff has also been a contrary figure: insisting on asking awkward questions and never signing up for the compliances of the successful literary career. He was even a misfit stylistically, addressing fundamentally modern themes, but declaring that he did so as a storyteller ('you can't just jettison tradition or discount the problem of communication') and dismissing most avant-garde experimentation as the fashionable trickery with which self-indulgent writers attempt to make up for their lack of social imagination. Litvinoff was born in London in 1915, but he has never regarded himself as an English writer.

'There has always been a parochialism about English writing,' he remarks, explaining that the Whitechapel in which he grew up demanded a broader outlook. His celebrated autobiographical account of his childhood in the Jewish East End, *Journey through a Small Planet* (1972), was shortly to be republished.[2] Warning that little trace now remained of the community he had known, except for a few 'occasional relics, such as you'd find after a volcanic eruption or an earthquake', he was prepared to take me round nonetheless; and to follow the thread of his life through streets that, if they survived at all, now belonged in more recent immigrant worlds.

In the Tube going east under the City of London, Litvinoff talked of his parents, who had journeyed to London from Odessa in 1913. Like many of the Jewish immigrants who came up the Thames travelling 'steerage' in what might as well have been cattle boats, they had hoped to reach America, but ended up being dumped in a Whitechapel ghetto that was already densely populated by Jews who had fled persecution in the Russian Empire – an emigration that had become a terrified mass exodus in the early 1880s, thanks to the brutalities licensed by Tsar Alexander III and his notoriously anti-Semitic minister of the interior, Count Nicholas Ignatieff.

Emanuel remembers his father only as a tinted photograph on a vanished wall in Fuller Street Buildings. He was apparently a low-grade sweatshop worker who nevertheless thought of himself as an intellectual. Politically, he was an anarchist, who had probably been involved in student activity in Odessa. He went back to Russia during the First World War. Obliged, like other male 'aliens' in Whitechapel, to choose between serving in the Tsar's army in the East or with the British on the Western Front, he got caught up in the Russian Revolution and never returned: 'The things we know about him are extraordinarily romantic. He seems to have organized a band of freebooters, which minted money, and stole horses.' The group eventually made their way to Archangel and arranged passage on a boat leaving for London early one morning. Litvinoff's father arrived too late and was last seen on the shore: a receding figure waving frantically from the quayside. Obliged to fend for herself and her four sons alone, Emanuel's mother took to her sewing machine and worked as a home dressmaker. She haunts Litvinoff's pages as the 'resident ghost' of his childhood. Exhausted by endless drudgery and the five additional children that followed remarriage, she speaks out from a succession of grim flats (after Fuller Street, the family lived in Hackney's Mare Street and Sandringham Road in Dalston), issuing the despairing admonitions so vividly captured by the son she only saw going off the rails.

Emerging from Bethnal Green Underground station, Litvinoff took his bearings from a terrace named Paradise Row and then launched off down Bethnal Green Road. He remembered how as a child he used to run up and down this mean street to Bethnal Green Library, fetching the books that, as an untutored but 'omnivorous' reader, he would choose by title alone.

After pausing to tug a weirdly shaped shop back into its pre-war incarnation as Smart's picture palace, where he saw the first talkies, Litvinoff turned to seek out the brick Victorian heights of the institution he knew as Wood Close School. The Jewish parents of that time stressed the importance of having 'a good trade in your hands', but the intelligent kids only had to look at their own parents to realize that this meant being condemned to a life of 'humiliating drudgery'. The only escape lay in the local grammar school: it was 'through scholarship that you escaped the dread fate of the factory and sweatshop'. Litvinoff was on course for this elevation: indeed,

as he walked around the school, glancing at Bangladeshi children
in their bright red uniforms, he remembered winning the Bethnal
Green essay competition on the theme of 'What I did on my
holidays'. His tactic, as he explained, was 'to play on the sympathy
of the judges at the beginning' by making it quite clear that his
family had been in no position to offer him any holiday at all. But
though he was at the top of the class, and generally something of a
star pupil, he was defeated by the exam. Children were really 'fighting for their lives', and Litvinoff was ambushed by nerves – to such
an extent that he couldn't even hold the pen. He failed repeatedly,
and the future disappeared.

By the time we walked past the Carpenters Arms, still seedily
associated with the Kray twins, young Emanuel was sliding steadily
into dereliction. He had renounced his passion for reading, finding
nothing in books but a painful reminder of lost opportunities.
A trade scholarship checked his descent for a while, but, in what
he would later describe as 'my first serious experience of anti-
Semitism',[3] he was refused admittance to the school of lithography
he hoped to attend ('The one question I did not apparently answer
to the interviewer's satisfaction was that relating to my religion'). So
he ended up learning shoemaking as the only Jewish student at Cordwainers' Technical College near Smithfield: a place that is known
to readers of *Journey through a Small Planet* for the abiding stench
of the offal yard next door, and for the headmaster who spent
morning assemblies twisting mocking variations out of Litvinoff's
alien name: Litintoot, Litmuspaperoff, Lavatoryoffsky . . . Litvinoff
left as soon as he was legally able and was soon sleeping rough, or
in doss-houses. As he recalls, 'if you were down and out in the
1930s, nothing existed for you. You could die on the pavements.'

It was in this condition that Litvinoff drifted westwards towards
Soho. Having slept in the 'beggars crypt' of St Martin-in-the-Fields,
he would make his way over to the Café Royal in Regent Street,
where he stole past the commissionaires for a free wash in the
gentleman's cloakroom, winning a smile on the way through from
a knickerbockered George Bernard Shaw. He remembered catching

an apprehensive glance from Wyndham Lewis, striding along Piccadilly in black cloak and wide-brimmed hat; and visiting a basement café named the 'Dive' in Frith Street to scrounge a fourpenny plate of minestrone off Aleister Crowley, who sat there in tweeds, playing chess and looking altogether more like an English country gentleman than the notorious occultist, pervert and diabolical 'Great Beast' of widespread reputation.

Jewish Whitechapel was a hard place, and ardent in its pursuit of redemption. Standing outside the chained and deserted building that once served as the Working Man's Synagogue in Cheshire Street, Litvinoff observed that, while he had not been held by the rabbi with his Talmud and Hebrew lessons, he had certainly dallied with both Zionism and also 'the red day of reckoning' promised by the ghetto's apocalyptic brand of communism. It was from a left-wing vantage point that he saw the black-shirted Oswald Mosley working the East End in 1936 – a 'toff' aping Mussolini and using 'a prissy upper-class English voice'[4] to rally his hate-filled fascist followers from his stronghold in Bethnal Green's Roman Road. But he wasn't among the Whitechapel Jews who went off to fight the fascists in the Spanish Civil War. Indeed, he remembers laughing at the idea that this untrained and malnourished band of volunteers would be an asset for the International Brigade.

His next messianic affiliation began when he was befriended in a Soho café by a woman, recently deceased, whose name he was still reluctant to divulge. Though only a little older than Litvinoff, maybe twenty-one or so, she seemed to live in a different age. She dressed in old-fashioned clothes, and was, as he recognized only with hindsight, an uncompromising Jewish chauvinist. A skilled astrologer, she drew her acolyte into a world of esoteric divination reached through the exotically mixed media of Kabbalah, psychometry, automatic writing, meditation, and seance-like attempts to re-enter past lives. It was, Litvinoff remembered, all a bit too much: 'I used to get the feeling that I could enter into madness. If you're an untrained young mind, struggling with the complexities of the Kabbalah, and if your sexual initiation is all mixed up with this . . .'

So there he was, trudging through the 1930s, undernourished, often without food for days, and 'hallucinating' or having 'some kind of nervous breakdown' as he went: 'I would be standing in front of a shop window, and suddenly it would feel dark. People would look spectral, and the world was spectral.' He remembers 'out-of-the-body experiences', when a moment of time would suddenly seem 'stretched out to infinity', and other fugue-like occasions when he suddenly slipped through the historical fix of the city, 'stumbling into a little pocket of time'. He might be walking down the street, or perhaps approaching the Jewish soup kitchen off Bishopsgate, when suddenly he would look up and find the cars gone, and horse-drawn traffic in their place. In this condition, he saw Jewish immigrants arriving from Russia, and tenements melting away mysteriously, to be replaced by older cottages with little gardens. He remembers asking a man the date and, on being told it was 1890, going into a haberdashery shop and looking at children's exercise books for verification. Litvinoff's first poem was among the ghostly manifestations of that time. It appeared quite unexpectedly, when he was working in a furniture factory in Wembley. Perhaps it was down to the glue-pot, with its 'rather extraordinary, intellectually aphrodisiac' fumes, but the romantic words suddenly appeared, as if from nowhere: 'Farewell O Queen of the Night/ Dark Mistress of my Cosmic Dreams.' Litvinoff laughed at the memory of these overripe lines, remarking that, while he had long wanted to be a writer, he had never been interested in poetry, only knowing the stuff he had learned by rote at elementary school: '"The boy stood on the burning deck," that kind of thing.'

By the mid 1930s he had a room over the Finchley Road and a piece-work job as a fur-nailer, which enabled him to put in four or five hours a day, and devote the rest of his time to pursuing his renewed literary ambitions. He completed a long novel about the East End, written in 'a kind of fever' when he was just over twenty, and named *Of Time Wearied* after Thomas Wolfe's epic *Of Time and the River*. In one of many unpublished manuscripts, Litvinoff has described how Elias Canetti visited him in the darkened room where he would be sitting at his long-carriaged Remington, 'typing out the interminable novel I was convinced was a work of genius that would win for me instant fame. Trance-like, I spoke of the need to shape one's life into an instrument through which the voice of God would utter, a trumpet of prophecy, of my dream that an angel stood at my shoulder while I wrote the story of my generation on to the page in illuminated letters like the Book of Kells.' Canetti listened and then declared the young author 'a schizophrenic artist', leaving him to hunt through dictionaries to find out just what this meant. Litvinoff burned that ambitious novel in a characteristic fit of embarrassment shortly after the war.

As we wandered through the crowded street market of Petticoat Lane, Litvinoff pointed to the Jewish physiognomy of some stall-holders, and then proposed that one of the most insidious effects of racism is to make victims see themselves through their persecutors' eyes. It may not really show in *Journey through a Small Planet*, but Litvinoff left Whitechapel on a wave of revulsion that he described, most memorably, in the 1960s: 'Every time a woman with a foreign accent made a scene on a bus, or two men argued loudly in Yiddish over a business deal, or a music-hall comedian got a few laughs by jamming a bowler-hat over his ears and retracting his neck into his shoulders, I was miserably ashamed.' He found the Jewish names on shopfronts 'grotesque and provocative: the Kosher signs and Yiddish lettering were embarrassing advertisements of alienation; there was too much huckstering in street markets; the flies crawling over exposed meat and groceries were proof of ingrained backward-ness and squalor. I was equally affronted by the sight of a Hassid walking through the street in outlandish garb, impervious to the effect of his own strangeness, and of the herring-women down the Lane, plunging their chapped and swollen fingers into the open barrels of pickled fish.'[5]

The Second World War changed everything. To begin with, Litvinoff registered as a conscientious objector, but he changed his mind as soon as Hitler's purpose became clear to him and urged the War Office to hasten him into active service. The authorities had different ideas, parking Litvinoff alongside other mistrusted 'aliens' in the Pioneer Corps, first in Ulster and later as an officer in West Africa and Egypt. Barred from directly fighting the fascists, Litvinoff went to work on the poetic front. 'Conscripts; a Symphonic Declaration', published in 1941, retains some of the apocalyptic character of his early 'schizophrenic' period: the young khaki poet imagines the young rising up into 'the great open spaces of unthought where newness is', challenging 'the champions of unchange' and insisting on a 'prayer of human suffering' that rings out above 'the loud dogmatism of revolution/ And of hucksters selling patriotism to the mob.' In 'Re-Dedication' he declaims, 'We saw truth shining through the shabby compromise/ and closed our eyes.'

A few pieces printed in the anthology *Poems from the Forces* brought a letter from Herbert Read, who then published Litvinoff's slim volume *The Untried Soldier* in the Routledge New Poets series. Some of his poems were broadcast by the BBC and there was further interest from John Lehmann, publisher and homosexual patron of young literary strivers from the East End. Litvinoff went to meet him at his residence in Park Lane, and was embarrassed to find himself being offered sherry and cigarettes by 'a blond Nordic giant with exquisite manners' in a silk dressing gown ('I didn't know where to put my hobnailed boots and soon departed'). He also heard from Dr Alex Comfort, at that time a young anarchist poet and novelist, with whom Litvinoff was soon on good terms.

Yet Litvinoff's budding reputation as a neo-romantic poet did little to alleviate the difficulties of the late 1940s. He had married during the war, and had no idea that his wife would soon step out on to the catwalk as Cherry Marshall, a leading fashion model who eventually went off into a life of her own. The couple lived with their young children in a damp basement flat and Emanuel eked out a living by reviewing for the *Guardian*, the *Tribune*, the *Spectator* and other papers. He tried radio too, proposing a series of short programmes inspired by a café philosopher named Schulberg, a 'Yiddish Socrates' known for his aphorisms ('If God made you a

Jew you don't need a hobby'; 'Every fool is convinced he is going to give birth to a genius,' etc.), who worked as a dues collector for the Jewish Burial Society and frequented Goides, a Whitechapel café patronized by East End Jewish intellectuals. Litvinoff's plans for a longer series named *Harry's Delicatessen* were scrapped after July 1947, when a 'near pogrom mood' developed after British authorities in Palestine hanged three Jewish terrorists for an attack on Acre Prison, and two British sergeants were captured and hanged in retaliation. Litvinoff was quickly reduced to ghost-writing – first the memoirs of an eminent surgeon, who recommended that his scribe should adopt a properly English name if he wanted to get on; and then more literary works for Louis Golding, the best-selling Anglo-Jewish novelist for whom Litvinoff wrote three books, including *To the Quayside* (1954), a novel in which he took Golding's Mancunian cast of characters but used them to dramatize his own concern for the European Jews who, having survived Hitler, had faced new barriers as they tried to reach Palestine. Litvinoff would also try a comic novel ('everyone was writing one in those days'). Entitled *The Swello Girl*, this never-published satire was inspired by the ubiquity of tits and bums in advertising: it featured a buxom television presenter who became an instant celebrity after accidentally falling out of a low-cut dress.

Meanwhile, the once-denied memory of Whitechapel kept reaching forward from the back of Litvinoff's mind. Reanimated by the fact of Nazi mass murder, it would pass stern judgements on his literary endeavours. As he once wrote, 'I had climbed out of that ghetto on a ladder of books, inadequately self-taught, only to settle into the myopic confines of a Hampstead rented room scribbling bad poems.'

As his post-war writing developed, Litvinoff would range far and wide across Europe, yet every road seems to lead him back to the rejected square mile of the Jewish East End. In his novel of post-war Berlin, *The Lost Europeans* (1960), we wander through the communist Eastern sector of Berlin (a city that Litvinoff had visited in 1955 and 1957), only to arrive at another 'claustrophobic tenement' which evokes the 'vulgarity, the noise and overspilling vitality' of slum life in Whitechapel, even though its poverty has a contrasting and far more pitiful 'picked-to-the-bone' quality.[6] In *To the Quayside*, Louis Golding's character Elsie Silver walks up the rue d'Hauteville in Paris and is suddenly surrounded by 'the smell of warm boiled brisket of beef, and chopped fried fish, and yellow cucumbers in great glass jars, and cheese-cake, and red horseradish ... It was home sweet home again'.[7] We turn to the first page of *The Bare Knuckle Breed*, a book of historical boxing stories that the straitened Litvinoff ghosted for Louis Golding, and find ourselves in the squalor of Whitechapel's Horse Shoe Alley, falling through successive time warps until the smell of fields and hedges is in the air and Bethnal is 'still somewhat Green'.[8]

As we walked down Brick Lane, scouring the Bangladeshi detail for the odd remaining Jewish residue, I asked Litvinoff how he answered the charge of nostalgia. As a writer who came to identify so deeply with the lost world of Jewish Whitechapel, how did he avoid becoming a million times more parochial than the English tradition from which he had felt so dislocated? Litvinoff conceded that you do indeed have to be very careful about the 'sentimentality' of a Jewish memory that lingers over bagels and herrings from the barrel, while choosing to forget that the East End was in many ways a 'frustrating and verminous' place, which people wanted nothing more than to leave. Yet he also insisted on a 'real grief at the passing of the ghetto'. 'You've lost a world,' he explains: 'a living, vital, throbbing community, with enormous dignity, neighbourliness, fellowship and integrity.' Its demise, moreover, was like the 'death of a living creature': although it had the economic and institutional basis to have survived much longer, the Jewish East End was effectively killed off by the wartime bombing.

Litvinoff has never thought of himself as 'an East End writer' – resisting a category embraced by some of the left-wing Jewish novelists who wrote about Whitechapel in the 1930s and 1940s. He stands back from Willy Goldman, author of *East End My Cradle* (1940) and *The Light in the Dust* (1944); and he shudders as he remembers the representation of Jewish Whitechapel offered in Simon Blumenfeld's *Jew Boy* (1935), screeching 'Twenty to Eight' in horrified mockery of the bawling mother who wakes the work-shy hero in the opening paragraph of that crudely realist novel. As the title of his own memoir suggests, Litvinoff recalls Jewish Whitechapel as 'a small planet' – a place which was at once miniature and epic in scale: a square mile into which a vast twentieth-century world had been squeezed, and where 'people spoke of Warsaw, Kishinev, Kiev, Kharkov, Odessa as if they were neighbouring suburbs'. As he says of growing up in that two-roomed flat in Fuller Street Buildings: 'You were sitting in the kitchen or on your mother's knee, and what were they talking about?' He counts off a few possibilities: the failings of Russia's pre-Bolshevik Kerensky government; the sayings of a much-loved rabbi in the Ukraine; the vividly remembered brutalities of a pogrom somewhere on the Black Sea; or the relative merits of Lenin and Trotsky, both of whom were said to be good for the Jews. 'You really imbibed with your mother's milk a sense of the wider world out there – a world that was still reaching in to touch you.'[9]

Litvinoff has an eye for the glowing Whitechapel fragment that lights up a wider world. In *Faces of Terror*, a much-praised trilogy of novels about the Russian Revolution and its consequences (initially commissioned by Thames Television as plays, which were never made), he started with the 1911 Siege of Sidney Street, in which the British authorities shot it out with Latvian communists who were hoping to finance their revolutionary activities with the 'redistributed' wealth of British capitalists. The first book in the sequence, *A Death out of Season* (1973), takes the siege and the violently miscarried robbery that precipitated it, and enhances the story with the help of old East End speculation – factually incorrect, but true in an imaginative sense – which turned the fugitives into anarchists and linked their activity to an abortive Tsarist plot to assassinate the British monarch, thereby closing the country to the exiled revolutionaries who gathered there. In the next two books, *Blood on the Snow* (1975) and *The Face of Terror* (1978), Litvinoff projected his company of locally gathered characters through the Russian Revolution and the Stalinist Terror. A small, if much fabled, Whitechapel experience is used to trigger a narrative that travels through the defining events of the early twentieth century.

If Whitechapel gave Litvinoff a day-to-day awareness of distant historical convulsions, it also bequeathed him abiding themes that would outlive the ghetto in which they were found: his sympathy for victims of all kinds, and his concern with 'not politics per se, but a kind of morality that is often expressed in politics ... You couldn't grow up in the Jewish East End without having also lived inside the necessity of that morality.' Unlike many more conventional figures of English fiction, Litvinoff's characters are displaced and often unable to integrate lives that have been broken and scattered by the continental shifts of twentieth-century history. Some have nothing left but hatred and bitterness: Litvinoff designates them 'the thin sour fruit of the ghetto'.[10] Others are threadbare idealists, overtaken and defeated by history's corruption of their cause. They crackle with the 'neurotic tension' of those who feel alien wherever they are. Litvinoff's Europe is seen from the quayside and prison cell: it has more frontiers than reassuring landscapes, and its cities are known less by their stately monuments than by tenement blocks and the shabby cafés in which 'all the world's foreigners' gather.

Halfway up Princelet Street, where, in 1992, one house was still a battered Bengali leather factory while the next glowed as an architectural icon restored and re-Englished by New Georgian conservationists, we stepped through double doors into another pocket of forgotten time: a Huguenot weaver's house that had been converted into the tiny synagogue of a since dispersed East European *chevra*. Litvinoff, who had not been here before, peered around in an amazed shock of recognition. Searching through the names painted on the balcony for families he might have known, he mutters that this dark place is indeed 'full of ghosts'. We climbed upstairs to visit the garret that was once home to David Rodinsky, an eccentric and, by posthumous reputation, somewhat prophetic figure who stayed on as caretaker after the closure of the synagogue. A student of remote and archaic languages who used to wander the streets pressing coins into the hands of the poor, Rodinsky was rumoured to have walked out one day and vanished, leaving behind the jumbled and evocatively time-warped room that had recently been cleared out in the interests of architectural restoration.

This gentrifying myth of the dematerializing immigrant is of little interest to Litvinoff, who understands Jewish disappearance in the incomparably greater terms demanded by the Holocaust. Such is the brute historical fact that really distinguishes Litvinoff's post-war rendering of Whitechapel, giving his response to the death of the ghetto a character quite distinct from merely sentimental nostalgia or the frisson sought out by 'ripperologists' and Ackroydian 'psycho-geographers' in more recent years. As Litvinoff explained at a writers' symposium in Israel in the 1960s, the Holocaust had the effect of 'generalizing' his memories of Whitechapel, turning them into recollections of an extinguished 'tribal community'.

If the war reformed Litvinoff's memories of Whitechapel, remembered now as part of the murdered Yiddish culture of Eastern Europe, it also reinforced his distance from the British mainstream. In explanation, he refers back to events that took place at a distant quayside during the Second World War. Litvinoff was stationed with the Pioneer Corps in Ulster when he heard about the *Struma*, an old cargo boat that had left Romania in December 1941, packed with nearly 800 Jewish men, women and children who had made their way to the Dalmatian coast in desperate flight from the Nazis.

Having broken down at sea, this overloaded vessel was eventually towed into Istanbul harbour, where its passengers hoped to disembark so that they could travel overland to Palestine, but the Turkish authorities wouldn't let them off the boat unless the British agreed to admit them to Palestine. Cabled in London, the British Colonial Office would have none of it, declaring the fugitives to be 'illegal immigrants' who 'exceeded the quota'. There were to be no concessions even for the children. After weeks of hellish wrangling, a Turkish warship towed the *Struma* out of Istanbul harbour and abandoned it in the Black Sea, where in February 1942 it exploded and sank with only a single survivor. It would emerge, many years later, that the *Struma* had been torpedoed by a Soviet submarine acting on Stalin's orders. For Litvinoff, this shameful episode had the shocking effect of 'blurring the frontiers of evil'. The merciless officials in London had become 'Hitler's accomplices', and there was only one conclusion to be drawn: 'Never again would I be able to think of myself as an Englishman, or face uncertainty about my identity.'

So Whitechapel lived on in Litvinoff's mind: not just an evocative lost world but an abrasive insistence on inconvenient truths and awkward questions. His most notorious clash with the English mainstream occurred in January 1951, when Sir Herbert Read invited him to read at an inaugural poetry reading for the Institute of Contemporary Arts. A long-standing and even devout admirer of T. S. Eliot (he would later claim to have 'needed Eliot as a man needs food'[11]), he had been horrified when, in 1950 or so, he bought a copy of Eliot's recently published *Selected Poems* and opened it to find that it included a number of anti-Semitic verses written before the war. In the 1920s and 1930s, Litvinoff remarked, anti-Semitism was more or less endemic, but he was appalled, only a few years after the Holocaust, to find Eliot republishing his lines about 'money in furs' and the 'protozoic slime' of Bleistein's 'lustreless, protrusive eye'. After reading the book on the Tube, Litvinoff had gone home and written a poem entitled 'To T. S. Eliot' – indeed, he remembered how it seemed to write itself in less than an hour. When he got up to announce the poem at the ICA reading, he was mortified to hear Read say, 'Oh good, Tom's just come in.' He nearly faltered when he looked up in time to catch Eliot's welcoming smile, but decided that 'the poem had a right to exist', and read it to the packed but silent room:

So shall I say it is not eminence that chills
but the snigger from behind the covers of history,
the sly words and the cold heart
And footprints made with blood upon a continent.[12]

'All hell broke out' as soon as Litvinoff had finished. Sir Herbert Read, whom Litvinoff describes, with a sharp East End eye for compromise, as 'the anarchist knight', remarked that, had he known in advance, he would never have allowed the poem to be read: 'I have known Tom Eliot as a friend for many years and there is nothing at all to justify this crude and unprovoked attack.' Litvinoff's unpublished account of this event tells how Stephen Spender stepped in to say that 'As a poet as Jewish as Litvinoff, I deeply resent this slander.' David Gascoyne also rose to 'express dismay and amazement at the obscenity that had just been committed'. Shouted down as he tried to explain himself, Litvinoff decided that he couldn't just slink away, so he went and sat next to his wife as the storm raged. He admits to feeling 'a kind of regret about it . . . about the circumstances'. He also remembers Eliot getting up to leave, and one member of his adoring, dumbstruck entourage glancing at Litvinoff on the way out and spluttering in helpless outrage: 'Good God! He's with a beautiful girl!'

Litvinoff went home shaken. And that night his telephone kept ringing. Reuters had put the story on the wire, and papers all over the world wanted to know more. Dannie Abse, who was at the reading, heard T. S. Eliot mutter, 'It's a good poem, it's a very good poem,'[13] but that judgement was not widely shared at the time. Indeed, Litvinoff found himself 'stigmatized as a talentless younger poet trying to achieve notoriety by attacking an eminent poet'.

His criticism of T. S. Eliot was sharply condemned on the letters page of the *Jewish Chronicle*, and there were further objections in 1959/60 when he published *The Lost Europeans*. The first to appear under his own name, this novel was concerned with Jews going back into post-war Berlin. People objected to its portrayal of Jewish hate, its supposedly tactless revival of animosities that were best let lie, and its use of homosexuality to suggest the artificiality of relationships in that guilty but already forgetful and divided city. Asked about these condemnations, Litvinoff told a joke. Two Jews are lined up in front of a firing squad, and one of them starts protesting about his rights. He demands a last cigarette, and the blindfold to which he is also entitled. But his companion takes him by the sleeve and begs him, in a pacifying tone, not to make trouble. Perhaps that was always how established Anglo-Jewry's advice sounded to the rude and noisy East European newcomers of the Whitechapel ghetto.

Yet, for a while, Litvinoff prospered. The film rights to *The Lost Europeans* were sold, even though the film, which was to have starred Dirk Bogarde, never got made. There was a time when home was a six-bedroom house in Abbots Langley, Hertfordshire, with a Swiss maid, and a Ford convertible in the drive. In the late 1960s, Litvinoff told the Zionists at a symposium in Tel Aviv that he was content to live among generally 'mild, tolerant English people' in 'an urbanized English village' where he was 'not conscious of segregation from my neighbours'. But while his second novel, *The Man Next Door* (1968), was all about English country life, it was an anti-idyllic affair hardly calculated to flatter those neighbours. It concerns a Jewish family who, having made good in the Whitechapel lingerie trade ('Alluriste Ltd'), move into Maidenford, a village that would have been quite charming were it not for the vast sausage factory that, in a reprise of the stinking offal heap next to the Cordwainers' Technical College, fills the air with the heavily symbolic stench of pork production.

The arriving newcomers are studied by their neighbour, a middle-aged and all but redundant vaccum-cleaner salesman named Harold Bollam. Like Litvinoff, Bollam has spent time in West Africa and he comes equipped with the degenerate attitudes Litvinoff had found among some of his fellow officers during the war: men who humped their way through hot and sodden nights on long-suffering black girls, and then woke up to enact a grotesque parody of colonial domination on the other unfortunate natives they were saving from barbarism. Bollam is a pastoralist of the racist variety, for whom the sight of 'pure countryside' communicates 'a deeply religious feeling as if you'd been cleansed through and through', and he greets his infuriatingly successful new neighbours with an escalating campaign of rape, arson and murder.

Human vanity being what it is, there are writers who seem to choose their themes for strategic reasons – skipping from one massive historical event to another in order to demonstrate their command of a world that is never larger than their ability to endow it with new significance. A year or so before our walk through Whitechapel, Martin Amis had chosen to revisit the Holocaust and, in *Time's Arrow* (1991), to throw time into reverse so that the gas ovens in Nazi concentration camps actually gave life to their murdered 'victims'.

Litvinoff, who lacks such literary facility, declared himself horri-fied by the thought of this conceit. His themes have the heavy and perhaps old-fashioned quality of obsessions, curses, responsibilities that he is sometimes unable to shoulder. Sitting in the Market Café on Fournier Street, he recalled the unfinished work, the destroyed and discontinued manuscripts, the hundred ways he had found of cutting himself down from behind. Then he shrugged and recalled Orwell's observation that every life feels like a failure when seen from inside: 'I didn't have the ambition and drive you need if you want to be a noted author . . .'

Yet it was not entirely his fault that his experience could not easily be tailored into a steadily advancing literary career. As he once explained, the 'proletarian' life of Jewish Whitechapel had scarcely prepared him to get on even with the more 'deracinated' and flexible European Jews who later turned up in London as refugees from Hitler – stylish, urbane and often strikingly 'erudite' newcomers who 'swam in the mainstream of European culture',[14] and needed only a period of acclimatization to adjust themselves. Certainly, this kind of 'failure' has been the lot of more than one writer from the interwar Jewish East End. I mentioned Roland Camberton, whom

Litvinoff thought he had probably last seen wearing a smart suit and disappearing, perhaps with some relief, into a job in the Reader's Digest organization. Camberton's novel *Rain on the Pavements* (published by John Lehmann in 1951) features a character named 'Uncle Jake'. Known as the 'bad lad' of the family, he had resisted both work and marriage, and spent his time talking socialism and anarchy, using his 'mortgaged bicycle' to pedal back and forth between the public library and innumerable meetings of left-wing political parties. Irreligious, unhoused and a 'perpetual student', Uncle Jake ends up as an education officer in the RAF: married with two children, living on the base and keeping his distance from London and the disavowed projects of his youth, including the single novel he had managed to get written and published ('a heartbreaking business undertaken in hopelessly unfavourable conditions') before giving up. Entitled *Failure*, this 'thin, ill-printed, yellow-wrapped volume' had proved entirely true to its name. It had sold only 300 copies, one of which could still be found at the British Library, providing unread testimony to the lost world of pre-war Jewish Hackney: 'the labour exchanges, the public libraries, the parks, the bed-sitting rooms, rain on the pavements, fog over the railway yards, and Uncle Jake in an old mackintosh cycling immortally, eternally, towards dreams more real than the reality in which they had been forgotten'.

Litvinoff shrugged again, saying that one of the reasons he had devoted so much energy to the campaign for Soviet Jewry, in which he played a leading role after his visit to Moscow in 1955, was because he didn't feel that his literary writing was an adequate justification for his existence. 'I suppose I've never stopped failing the scholarship,' he said, remembering those distant years, just up the road, at Wood Close School.

We walked on past the gaunt bulk of Hawksmoor's Christ Church, too late to investigate the old gentleman's lavatory in front of the church steps: an underground amenity, which had been bought as a potential wine bar by an Asian entrepreneur at the end of the 1980s and was then in sporadic service as an experimental art space run under the name of 'Strike'. Down near the bottom of

Brick Lane, we turned east into Old Montague Street. This, as Litvinoff remarked, had once been the very heart of Jewish White-chapel, and its vivid life has been transferred into his novels, where children still throw balls at old tin cans, bald mongrels wander about, and the 'melancholy strain of evening prayers drifts across from the synagogue'. In the *Faces of Terror* trilogy, a down-at-heel anarchist bookseller called Hoffman has his shop here, selling revolu-tionary literature to a shabby clientele that includes Special Branch detectives trying to pass as working-class intellectuals, and Russian Embassy officials who come to keep an eye on the émigrés who are considered to be 'the most dangerous agitators in Europe'. Hoffman's shop is the site of heated argument between the anarchist tradition that was once so strong in the Jewish East End, and the Bolshevik Terror that would soon enough stamp it into the ground.

The redolent names of Green Dragon Yard and Black Lion Yard were preserved on brand-new street signs, but nothing else was left. 'There's no point going any further,' said Litvinoff, as the past evaporated in front of him. Yet we persisted, heading in the direction of one remaining place where Hoffman's struggle continues. We passed Whitechapel Library, where Litvinoff had unveiled the blue plaque to the poet Isaac Rosenberg, and turned into Angel Alley – an infamous slum in Victorian times, but now only squeezed by the expanding Whitechapel Art Gallery. At the end of this narrow way, we stepped through a cave-like entrance into a building that resounded with the sound of thrashing printing machines. The walls of the tightly curved staircase were covered with posters advertising diverse liberationist causes, and above that we stepped into the Freedom Bookshop – another tight little room, where the spirit of Kropotkin lives on.

Litvinoff had demonstrated that it is possible to straddle different eras and continents as you walk down a city street. But he now assumed the surprised look of a man who has suddenly been kid-napped by his own imagination. The books and pamphlets were piled high all around him. They expounded the anarchist theory of organization, and traced the beleaguered practice of mutual aid through the Spanish Civil War and then on into such unlikely refuges as allotments, holiday camps and alternative business networks. One offered a critique of the green theory of deep ecology, recommending that the plane trees of London – those purely decorative 'symbols of moral superiority' that Litvinoff sees outside his own window in Mecklenburgh Square – should be uprooted and replaced by apple trees, which, in Henry Thoreau's phrase, are surely 'the most civilized of all trees'.

After pondering this unexpected place, Litvinoff approached the man behind the desk, and asked for news of his old friend Alex Comfort, known here for what he was before 1972, when he turned his anarchism into a best-selling primer, *The Joy of Sex*. Seeing a stack of imported books by the late George Woodcock, then still thriving as the grand old man of Canadian Literature, he remembered another quayside proposition: when Woodcock was leaving for Canada, he had invited Litvinoff and his wife to join him on the anarchist literary commune he hoped to establish there.

After glancing at his watch and announcing that he had to meet his young son from school, Litvinoff remarked that he felt as if he had been in 'an extraordinarily intense dream. You could get home and find that the place you had just been had never existed.' He then vanished into the Underground at Aldgate East.

[Patrick Wright]

'EVERY DAY ABOVE GROUND IS A GOOD DAY'
Carpenters Arms, Cheshire Street, 1992

TONY LAMBRIANOU (*an East End face*): You remember the King's Road? What was it? Nothing. Now it's famous – for what? For the people who made it.

ROBIN COOK (*aka Derek Raymond*): That's right. You've got to go back thirty years.

TL: It's funny to hear you talking about that, Robin. It's the culture. It'll never ever come back. That's the tragedy of today. We're never going to get it back as it was.

RC: It was a brilliant sort of thing. Like a meteor. Phew!

TL: It went.

RC: It burned out, didn't it? Went pop like a light bulb.

TL: That is the tragedy of it today, looking back. I mean, you represent Chelsea to me. The way you're dressed. You understand that life.

RC: We saw it from the underside of things.

TL: You've had a good life. You've had an interesting life.

RC: Oh certainly.

TL: The first time I saw you, I thought: 'Here's a man who's been both sides of the fence.'

RC: Ah yes. A pub I used to drink in a lot, the Star. Belgravia. Remember that? Paddy Kennedy's place. You've got Charlie Mitchell, all that mob. Billy Hill.

TL: You remember them times do you?

RC: Yes, I used to drink there. First floor. Ground floor was only for the punters. First floor for the real mob and the law. Cos you've got the law one end of the bar and the rest of us at the other end. You've got Kennedy in-between. He was the guvnor.

TL: The villains at that time were more or less exactly what the papers wanted them to be. I've always said that. We had this war going on with Jack Spot and Billy Hill in the West End. Do you remember all that?

RC: Very much so.

TL: In all the papers. What was going to happen next?

RC: I'm sixty or so. I can go well back to the 1950s.

TL: These were *people*. I mean they came from the Italian part. You can see the way they used to dress even today. I watched. Every Friday night on BBC2 they're doing the Cagney film and the Bogart film. You see the way they dress, the sharpness of it stands out. I watched one last week. What was his name?

RC: George Raft, remember him?

TL: He came down with us. He came over to meet the Twins, didn't he? Met him at the Colony Club. He was one of the smartest men. One thing, going back to Billy Hill, they were all immaculately dressed people. Never anything out of place. You prided yourself on that. That was what it was all about. And there's still, luckily, a few of us around who dress to that style today. I don't think that'll ever die out. Never. Never in a million years. It's marvellous, to me.

I always remember a film that made a big impression in my life. *Angels with Dirty Faces*. Don't know if you've ever seen that? It was about the Dead End Kids. Remember them? They took Cagney to the chair because he wouldn't grass. And all the kids sitting there watching it. Do you remember that classic film? You've got James Cagney like he controlled all the rackets in America. He came from what's called the 'wrong side' of New York. Brooklyn? The Bronx? It was the Bronx. And you had all these kids and when he came out of prison they glamorized him and he winds up murdering some-body. I think it was a copper. He was in it, O'Brien. What was his name, the actor? Tom O'Brien, I think it was. Pat. You had Pat

O'Brien, he played the part of the priest who pleads with him to say, 'Look, I don't want to die. I don't want to die.' He wanted Cagney to say 'I don't want to die. Please don't do it to me.' He disappointed all the kids. That's how the film ended and you see Pat O'Brien smiling, like he done it for him. He knew the truth. The film was made in 1933. If you ever get a chance to see it, it's absolutely blinding.

RC: Remember the original *Scarface?* 1932 that was.

TL: Who played the original? They've had Al Pacino in it since then.

RC: Ah, that's the remake.

TL: To me, the original was the best.

RC: I liked the Al Pacino one. Have you seen it?

TL: No, I ain't. I like the original.

RC: Go and see it. Go and see it. You won't regret that. I've seen it thirteen times on video.

TL: Another film that's dear to me was *A Kid for Two Farthings.* Do you remember that?

RC: 'Montana, I believe you speak from the heart. Every day above ground is a good day.' Oh it's terrific. You ought to see it. You've got me going now.

TL: *A Kid for Two Farthings.* Do you remember that? Done in Brick Lane. Diana Dors. Can you remember that?

RC: What was it called?

TL: *A Kid for Two Farthings*. She was in it, Diana Dors. In the 1950s. Done in Brick Lane. It winds up, the little girl dying at the end of it. I've never seen the film on television or nothing, but it always stood out in my mind. About Brick Lane. It was done mostly round here. The stallholders and that. Incredible, incredible.

RC: Did you see the Bentley/Craig film the other day?

TL: Do you know what? That left a big impression on me as a kid. You know something? I remember that very well, the Bentley and Craig case.

RC: So do I. Same sort of age.

TL: From that day onwards, I remember that case. How old was I? 1950?

RC: When were you born?

TL: 1942.

RC: 1942? Oh well, I was thirty-one.

TL: I was about ten when that came on and nobody ever thought he would hang, Derek Bentley. Do you remember that? That case, it always stood out in my mind as a youngster. Nobody could believe what was happening, the hanging was out. Do you remember that? Hangings was the thing, Pentonville, Wandsworth. I remember Ruth Ellis, the scenes outside the prisons. It was news, headlines. Them things certainly stood out in my mind, especially the Bentley/Craig case.

RC: That stuck in my mind.

TL: The Ruth Ellis case.

RC: It was the week I was called up, the trial. Just gone into the army. I remember that vividly, 1949.

TL: Talking about the army, I know a lot of men I was behind in prison who done the army.

RC: No choice, National Service.

TL: They had, some of them, never committed acts of violence in their life. I know some from the Korean War onwards. And when they released them from the army they turned out to be bank robbers. Some committed murder because they'd trained them how to use violence. They knew how to do it. I know a man today who stands in prison. I won't name him, he was in the Korean War, and to my mind he's done twenty-five years. A man who never did nothing wrong. I won't name him because he's still away. He went out and committed murder. Before he went in the army he would never have dreamed of committing acts of violence. I sat there in Durham Prison with this bloke, he was telling me about it and it was unbelievable. Until he went in the army, he was a straight, mild man and from that minute onwards he started to murder. Incredible.

It's like what's happening now with America. They bring them back from the wars, I bet a lot of them turn out to be going to crime because they've been trained how to kill, to be cunning.

You still buying them French cigarettes? Are they French, them ones?

RC: Yeah. Do you want one?

TL: I was in Paris the Christmas before. Spent New Year there.

RC: I won't say I know Paris as well as London, but very nearly.

TL: It has a magic about it. I'd always wanted to go. Must go back, have a look around, because the history, it's out of this world.

RC: Mind you, the bars aren't worth a London pub. Tell you that for nothing.

Enter Driffield (a bookdealer, employing RC as driver)

D: Young Robin, out.

TL: Robin, see you again.

RC: I'll be back, Tony.

THE LOCKED CASE

An extraordinary moment. Even though I'd planned it with some care. The man in the big cap coming straight towards me, hurrying, the approach to Fenchurch Street Station, out of an old fiction and into a new: Gerry Goldstein. With Pat of course, his wife. A few steps behind. A little warm, well wrapped – coat, scarf, woolly jersey, prepared on this mild day for savage weather, prepared to leave London. Sort of. To entrain for the Estuary, Tilbury Town. The opening of my novel, all those years ago, in the nightmare of Thatcher. Gerry as primary witness, participant and telephone connection: the shift from bookdealing to factoring memory into a publishable form. At every event, every notorious gathering, Gerry was in the next room, on the stairs, at the kitchen table. A nice boy, they said. The Peakes, Donald Cammell, Malcolm McLaren, Sid Vicious, Michael Moorcock, Mick Jagger, Marianne Faithfull. Looped anecdotes on tap. 'Remember?'

We did our walks, once every seven years, through the City, Ludgate Hill, Smithfield; hospital, church, café, always that, tea and cigarettes, a late breakfast eaten fast, condensation on greasy windows. Gerry had a particular way of smoking, two fingers in a stubby V, cigarette up close to the bitten nails. Head down. Eyes staring off into the middle distance. He knows he's being photographed. But the look of the man, dark hat, small scar on left cheek, overcoat, has a residual sadness. Here and gone. John Bunyan's sculpted feet sticking out from a hospital blanket of snow as Gerry strikes a pose in Bunhill Fields.

Sometimes we tried Les the Junkman on Roman Road, if we could catch him open: dead shoes, scratched records, horizontally stacked books keeping the walls up. W. G. Sebald in his essay 'Moments musicaux' speaks of 'searching through a box full of old photographs in a junk shop near Bethnal Green underground station'. Photographs that might provoke memory, challenge a meandering narrative; evidence gathered before the crime has been committed. Recklessly, we give our trust to images. And treat stories as stories. All books in the end become fiction. I have every sympathy for Sebald's impulse, to collaborate with London, its murkier districts, by finding postcards or handwritten scraps that might, eventually, be teased into a meditation, a lecture. Cards from a shoebox in Cheshire Street suggested the form and numerology of my novel *Downriver*: twelve tales of imploded colonialism, exotic imports, unappeased crimes, political mendacity.

Gerry, always a character in search of a scribe, and Sebald, a fastidious ghost, coincide in the junk shop of the tall, moustached, preoccupied Les. Les is more custodian than vendor, collector rather than distributor of artefacts. His first instinct is to snatch back a potential purchase: 'Piss off.' Sebald has the confidence and the skill to shape a doctored autobiography, recalling what he needs to recall, making flux definitive in leisurely fatalistic prose. And then taking the blush off the thing, even this modest form of confession, by having his words translated. Gerry doesn't enjoy such luxury: he's on the move, the phone, talking talking talking. And reading too. In the crack of the day, hungrily seeking out pointers, clues, names.

Cabbalistic signatures: Canetti, Kersh, Emanuel Litvinoff. The Litvinoff trilogy was a particular favourite, rings of ghetto history diminishing into Europe's forests, cities, settlements. Into Russia. I have a photograph of Gerry and Pat getting Litvinoff, on a return visit to the haunts of childhood, to sign copies of the first editions of those books. Litvinoff is wearing just the kind of baggy Soviet cap Gerry favours as he hustles towards Fenchurch Street. The veteran author is bright-eyed, birdlike, sharp to the edge of sarcasm, hurt perhaps by the world's persistent refusal to grant his work a proper evaluation. He's sallow, tanned by electric light. You wouldn't believe that he went out much. The streets surprise him. A production assistant, annotating this material for a television documentary, describes him as: 'Asian man on railway bridge.'

One person from the past Emanuel won't talk about is his half-brother, David. Gerry mentions the funeral. It was the last time he saw Emanuel. But Emanuel has nothing to say about the incident. Gerry was a good friend of David Litvinoff, a person whose name turns up in the memoirs (gangland and showbiz), gambling, yakking, scamming: a conduit, a prankster with his phone wired to a reel-to-reel tape-recorder. Gerry owned several hours of Litvinoff tapes. He remembered what he wanted to remember. It shifted, the story, with the years, the audience. David vanishing, coming back with wads of unexplained cash. Runs at the country. Trips abroad. The Welsh tramp on whom Harold Pinter based his caretaker, Davies. Litvinoff and *Performance*. Litvinoff and the Krays. Litvinoff's suicide. The myth was treated by Jonathan Meades, by Colin MacCabe. Spun, trawled, analysed. Stories about stories: a man, his head shaved, hung from a window. A cheesewire grin. Gerry, rightly, felt a sense of ownership. The man, living or dead, was a friend. Gerry sat in a Cheshire Street pub, the Carpenters Arms, with the former Robin Cook. The Chelsea novelist took himself to France, worked in a vineyard and came back as Derek Raymond. Cook, moments earlier, was saying to an interviewer, sorry, he knew the name but had never run across this Litvinoff. Now he responds to Gerry's question. Telling him what he wants to hear.

'Where did you know David from then?'

'Oh well that was through Kim, gambling parties. Very much so. With the Krays in Esmeralda's Barn.'

'I remember that,' Gerry replies, 'in Knightsbridge, Walton Place. Yeah, I went there. I remember going there when I was about seventeen. Upstairs.'

Gerry, late in the day, told me where David Litvinoff was buried, out in Rainham, a long walk from the station. My visit became part of a book, as it was always going to, as Gerry knew and understood:

resented. No copyright on future memory. Snatches of dialogue, already written, are overheard on station platforms. Photographs are taken before the events they depict have been properly staged. Legendary characters pull away from the diminishing gravity of the books in which they are trapped. The only London constant is the weather, its shifts, the theatre of the clouds. The only way to free up a story is to start walking. To take a train somewhere you have never been and to recognize it, immediately, as the missing paragraph of a novel that should never be written.

The faraway looks of Gerry and Pat in their snatched portraits, black-and-white photographs, place them outside this mundane

circuit. They enact what I can only hint at. By the lives they led, the people they met, the endless rehearsals and repetitions of storytelling, they avoid the fix of time. They float. Two voices. Two versions of a shared past. This astonishing, long-lived and nurtured relationship: witnesses to a particular history. To London.

I had written, in part as a tribute to Gerry's dad, Pip, an even more animated fabulist, this train ride into the Estuary. Which is why, when Gerry rang, after months of sickness, heart, abdominal pains, asking about a walk, I suggested Fenchurch Street. An early start, in Gerry's terms, mid-morning. I had the sequence from my published novel, Pip Goldstein's arrival at the station, in place of his son, the journey to Rainham, stones on David Litvinoff's grave. And now as I set it up, I wanted to justify my theft by seeing Gerry come towards me, taking the place of his father, who had moved away from Whitechapel. Moved away from the ghetto. His telling of it: Jack Spot, Mosley's blackshirts, street markets, women, card games, clothes. 'You remember, Gerry, when we went to see David in hospital?'

Before Gerry and Pat appeared, as I stood at the entrance to the station, another person, a young neat contained man, approached, introduced himself. He was, by profession, an actor: one of the juvenile leads in an upcoming *Bleak House*. Now he has a role in the day's story. I won't gloss over his appearance, which was not part of my original template, the material I had already edited and needed only to live through and photograph. This man, like Gerry – a kind of tribute – wore a long scarf and a cap. (As did Pat, goose-white to Gerry's Donegal tweed.) The project, for the actor, was an uncommissioned work-in-progress, a documentary film on the life and legend of David Litvinoff. Gerry had been telling tales.

Things were shaping up nicely, a repeat journey in the direction of Rainham, Gerry and Pat playing themselves – and the actor, by his voluntary attendance, playing Litvinoff. To describe something, he would appreciate, is to become it. And so they approached, the Goldsteins, talking, gesticulating, greeting us with embraces. Introductions were made, after we had been through those moves.

Gerry explained the proposed outing, which had long ago been published, but which was not quite redundant.

Gerry has a camera, digital. Pat has a camera. The actor has a camera. The train *is* a camera, sweeping us away from cloying traces of brick and sentiment into Docklands, ice caves of political hyperbole and wastes that will become the latest nowhere, mustard-brick estates between pylons and landfill. The Goldsteins, jump-cutting, stereophonically, competitively, see little of this. They don't know where they are and have nothing to go on. They came to the Rainham funeral by car. 'What are those things?' Pat asks, confronted by a squadron of gas holders.

Old fictions, lost fictions. Revised fictions. Call them up as proof that we still remember, Joseph Conrad at Stanford-le-Hope. His displaced craft waiting on the tide, off Gravesend. The three caps, Pat and Gerry and the actor/documentarist, face the camera, under iron struts, a pattern of light and shadow, on the bridge that leads away from the dock at Tilbury Riverside. They look, very much, like dissidents coming out of East Berlin. Would you trust them, approve citizenship? The past is a burden revealed through stance and wearily complaisant half-smiles: Pat's bag, Gerry's shoulder pouch. Their papers, proof of identity. Before we walk out along the river path to East Tilbury, past the sign (white graffiti on concrete wall), beside which I photograph them – THICK AS THIEVES/ US, WE'D STICK TOGETHER/ FOR ALL TIME, AND/ MEAN IT – we stop for a drink, not wanting to exhaust the convalescent Gerry so early in the day. The World's End. A squat public house in the shadow of the fort and the power station.

This survival, which I associate with Magwitch's attempted escape in *Great Expectations*, his second flight, has now revised itself, self-consciously, as a prime example of London heritage. Memorabilia with no memory: Pepys murals, a limp view from Defoe's factory. Flags, swords, battle honours. We drink under a glass case in which is exhibited a battered quarto volume: SAMUEL PEPYS/ CHRONICAL OF/ THE GREAT FIRE OF LONDON/ 1666.

I want to examine this book; it belongs in the library of disappearances. Here is a version of Pepys that I've never come across. This is not the account in the *Diaries*. 'Some of our maids sitting up late last night to get things ready against our feast to-day, Jane called us up about three in the morning, to tell us of a great fire they saw in the City.' The diary entries are succinct, they cover eleven pages in my edition. The Tilbury trophy is something unknown and unrecorded – a late forgery or an illustrated private edition? But worth testing, sniffing over. An entry for the *Gazetteer of East London*. 'Chronical': is that a genuine archaism?

Gerry is game; the sun climbs, he flags. We take the train home from East Tilbury, leaving the mystery of the Pepys ledger to be resolved on another day.

In high summer, persuaded by a Dutch writer and his friend, an artist, a recorder of security personnel, I'm back at Fenchurch Street. This time we'll start at East Tilbury, the Bata factory, the church, the Coalhouse Fort and walk back, west, to Grays, Thurrock, Purfleet – stopping, if we time it right, at the World's End.

The mood is very different. The woman, spirited, present in a way that Pat and Gerry never could be, is alert to atmosphere. She is searching, openly, for material to exploit. She wants pieces of the world that conform to her way of seeing it. And, such is the intensity of her focus, these pieces duly appear. Our empty reverse-commute train, for example, is loud with ghosts. She mentions the fact, without emphasis. She understands what she's getting into. Without having read it, or having any requirement to read it, she's become that figure in a story of mine, 'Grays'. A woman who sets out with a copy of a book on *Conrad's Polish Background*. A vampire tale. This woman, dressed in black, ready to walk, performs the role – making us invisible, unnecessary. I stare out of the train window at a pale-wood fence, Rainham's Great Wall of China: it stretches for mile after mile. It's new and really rather . . . Dutch. Planks bright as Ikea floor tiles. The purpose of this new landscape feature is obvious: it masks blight. Smouldering landfill, discontinued industry, carcinogenic paddocks are hidden from the eyes of the Olympic commissioners. That's why the c-2-c train is so smart, roomy, air-conditioned and unreal. It's part of the pitch, the ruinously expensive and doomed 2012 bid. Doomed to be successful, condemning us to years of puff and spin as we creep towards the Great Project. Bleak times for those who are cheerfully off-message.

So we come back, through the Czech village of East Tilbury (next stop, Stanford-le-Hope), through the handpainted placards: SAY NO 2 THAMESGATE SCUM, THAMES GATE GET STUFFED. Through a Dutch landscape of poplars and ponds. To the river.

They are professional walkers, this couple: water bottles, sun cream, changes of shirt, cameras. The artist has been here before, obviously, the Bata factory is open to conceptualists. It's a compulsory visit: pre-development cash forced into the hands of those who are prepared to set-dress the latest piracy. Art first, shit later. Then art again: unfunded, disregarded. If they let you do it, get out – fast. You've been had. You're in the brochure.

The beach, below the Coalhouse Fort, is one of the best, half a mile of prime detritus, scoured and arranged by the tide. On a sort of altar, constructed from driftwood, somebody has laid out an exhibition of medicine bottles, reminiscent of Mark Dion's installation at the Tate (materials found on the foreshore). Chunks of coal are turning to tar in the day's sulphurous heat. The river is so low it belongs in a Ballardian fantasy, a post-apocalyptic London: war architecture, lookout towers with broken steps, lizards on hot stones. I explain to the artist that I'm looking for pieces of tile that have words, or bits of words, on them: I'm looking for a story, a sentence. Some way out of a narrative cul-de-sac. I find a shard of stained porcelain, the rim of a plate or dish, on which I discover an obelisk, perhaps a version of Nelson's column, with the word MORLEY'S. Interesting but no use. The only plunder worth carrying away relates to the Dutch artist, not to me. Two naked cherubs, twins, mounted on a white horse (legless). The rocker on which the horse once stood – it would have disqualified this object as kitsch – has gone, leaving just enough of the original to suggest a kind of celestial skateboard.

Twins, couples, duplicates, are the woman's subject. Later in the day, at the Port of Tilbury, we will be pulled up by a police car for the crime of photographing two women in lime-green tops, carrying green plastic bags, hair dyed red, passing two men, security personnel, walking in the opposite direction (yellow-green slipover jackets and yellow hardhats). 'Don't you know there's a war on?' the cop said, as he stepped from the car. 'This is a very sensitive place.' The artist refused to show any form of identity. She kept her faked card with the real photograph for Berlin, her next destination. I fobbed him off, as usual, with tales of the river and the production of a document proclaiming my membership of the Welsh Academy (Literature), Yr Academi Cymreig. It was that or the Video Box membership from Hastings. The mobile policeman confessed to living on Canvey Island. We parted on the best of terms.

The barmaid at the World's End, splendidly sullen, refused to pull a pint before the stroke of eleven. Much to the bemusement of another Dutch couple, tourists who had come ashore from a cruise liner, anchored at Tilbury and shortly to set sail for Spitzbergen. In the stern, nearly naked figures lounged on deckchairs, watching the oily river, the mirage of the deserted riverside parade. Container ships hugged the deep channel. Lorries filled the space alongside the B149 tea stall. Trucks rolled over the QEII Bridge. All of them Dutch, all of them operated by Geest. Which means, so I am told, ghost. Spirit.

The nice thing about my fellow walkers is that they take nothing for granted. 'The Romans crossed the river here,' I said (on the authority of a forgotten local historian). 'Are you sure?' said the man. 'There's a double moat around Tilbury Fort,' I offered. 'The best example of seventeenth-century military engineering in England.' (I quoted the postcard.) 'Probably Dutch,' I added. 'Now I believe you,' said the woman, when she saw with her own eyes the broad strip of water, the World's End on the far side.

The other thing about this couple was that despite the unforgiving heat, the roads I marched them down, the police interventions, miles of concrete wall along the riverbank, Barratt Estates, tower blocks of Grays, oil refineries, overgrown paths, thorns, broken glass, foodless pubs, grudging service: they never complained. They kept going to the finish, trailing a little by the end, it's true; but if I told them we were pushing on into the night, to reach Beckton Alp and the Northern Sewage Outfall, they would suck another water bottle, slap on the star cream, change a T-shirt and continue. 'Are you sure?'

The Dutch writer is not prepared to nurse his pint, his conceded peanuts and crisp powder, he demands the guvnor. The man responsible for the Pepys book in the sealed glass box. The woman has looked very closely at this thing: 'It's printed upside down.'

I take a tour of all the random mementoes that spell out: bogus history. A Pepys quote, in fake seventeenth-century script, is blocked by a notice: NO CHILDREN BEYOND THIS POINT PLEASE. A few sentences about a Pepys visit to 'Barkeing Church' dress the snug. You eat, if you get lucky, in an alcove of restored militaria. There is much talk of the Dutch Wars, raids on the Thames, the breaking of chains. But the clincher is the memory album. The curator of this riverside museum (in a genuine, low-ceilinged, black-beamed drinking den) has contrived a Joseph Cornell artwork from borrowed photographs, messages on postcards, snapshots found in car-boot sales. The downriver publican is an amateur Sebald documenting a fiction of war and loss and family: the karma of human melancholy and its impossible resolution. A young woman writes home from a teachers' training college in Swansea. A soldier has himself photographed before he returns to the trenches. An elderly man in regalia, perhaps Masonic, poses in a suburban garden: with the fatal confidence that undid Oscar Wilde when he chose to reveal himself in a velvet suit that made public the degree of his occult initiation. The compulsion, with these disparate elements, is to construct a narrative. And to relate that narrative to place. To authenticate lives that have no obvious connection with an undistinguished public house.

The publican appears and, without pressure, confesses: the Pepys book is a total fraud. He invented the title and had it blocked out on a ledger from a Tilbury junk shop. The book I wanted to investigate wasn't a book, it was a prompt card: CHRONICAL OF THE GREAT FIRE OF LONDON. (That 'al' ending must be a local variant, Francophobe. A car offered for sale, in East Tilbury, had DIESAL £495 painted on the window.) And, since the Pepys text had never been written, London fire was not yet brought to ground. It was still ahead of us, the disaster. The scorched air and blackened skin. Something was printed on those upside-down pages, some composition that must remain a private matter. The case was nailed and varnished. It would not be opened until the pub changed hands or was re-themed. This manifestation was another, very public, disappearance. A cheap trick. An attempt to make me describe an object that doesn't belong in the story. A plea to which, quite obviously, I will turn a deaf ear. Write nothing, say nothing. Tear up the photographs.

[I. S.]

THE GAZETTEER OF DISAPPEARANCES & DELETIONS

THE WAILING WALL OF STOKE NEWINGTON, N6

On General Election morning I'm wandering around Halkevi, a Kurdish and Turkish Community Centre that can be found along a busy street full of budget super-markets, spartan cafés, nail-design stores and boarded-up Edwardian chemists in Stoke Newington. It's an imposing building, an old Jewish garment factory whose industrial grandeur hasn't been entirely smothered by the tarpaulin and scaffolding that covers much of it as it undergoes renovation. By the late 1970s the ground floor was being used as a wedding venue by Turkish Cypriots, many of whom still recall the tunes and colour supplied by bands such as the Butterflies and the Cyprus Quartet whose musicians were local tailors and carpenters.

In those days it was a place of joy. That changed in 1986 when it became a hub for tens of thousands of Kurdish men and women escaping torture and government clampdowns back in Turkey. It was a home for those without a home, for those who dreamed of a homeland. A community of sorts was forged here, but one that was as much coercive as voluntary: centre officials would strong-arm locals into paying weekly levies. It became a PKK stronghold, a training camp for radical activists and future guerrillas who were taught to question their family loyalties and to regard them as less important than nation-building. Women in the area were so anxious that in desperation they tried to hide their sons from the Centre's panoptic eye.

In the mid 1990s Special Branch took to raiding the Centre. Today there are no security guards or amateur militia manning the front door, though a huddle of middle-aged men sipping tea around a table gaze at outsiders with not so much suspicion as surprise: this is a self-regulating environment, one whose dimly lit hall recreates the atmosphere of a provincial museum, where everyone knows each other. The snooker table, a near ubiquitous feature in Turkish and Kurdish social spaces, is deserted. On a pinboard are fastened notices offering cheap leases for kebab stores in Hull.

The sense of hushed desertion doesn't feel in any way intimidating; rather, it sets the stage for the contemplation of a striking section of the wall on the right-hand side of the hall. Here, protected by cheap plastic, are photographs of around fifty Kurdish men and women who have been fighting against the Turkish state. Young, moustachioed men in camouflage squatting on the ground; a carefully composed portrait of a slim-hipped young woman standing in an orchard; a group of soldiers hiding in a bunker; an enlarged photocopy of a broadsheet picture of a fighter with the newsprint on its reverse still visible. Some of them look barely out of their teens, while one resembles a septuagenarian philosopher-poet. Some look defiant, others smile or raise V-signs. Most carry rifles.

What they all have in common is that they are dead. And that they are all related to families who live in this area of London. Above the photos is a sign, in Kurdish: WE WILL NOT FORGET THEM. This is a martyr's memorial. A wailing wall that creates a foundation narrative for what it means to be Kurdish: the importance and the inevitability of death. The dead are not departed, it insists; they are among us, watching over and for us. The wall, seen along with the other photos of the jailed guerrilla leader Ocalan that hang throughout the hall, establishes the dominant mood of grief and collective struggle that underwrites this Community Centre.

The Kurds who attend this Centre are Muslims, but religion plays little part in their lives unless they're travelling abroad, in which case they use faith as a luck charm and drop in to the prayer room at Heathrow. The Centre's events coordinator is Yaşar İsmailoğlu, a Turkish Cypriot ex-soldier and former classmate of Ocalan who came to London during the power shortages of 1972. A poet who has published several volumes, he also set up the longest-surviving Turkish newspaper in the area, as well as a local football team. Activism is his life – and did for his adopted daughter whose photograph is included on the wall.

He is endlessly busy, full of good cheer, known to everyone in the neighbourhood. He finds it impossible to walk more than a couple of yards without bumping into a friend, colleague or co-conspirator. Yet talk to him for more than a few minutes, and a great melancholy enters the conversation: he dreams, he says, of mountains and of freedom. Here, in England, 'What we have lost is our enjoyment of living. It is exactly like a robot here. We come to work, then go home.'

We go to one of the many Turkish and Kurdish cafés that are found in the area. A clump of old and silent men cradle their coffees. 'In the social clubs here, it's just playing cards,' says Yaşar. 'They don't even talk. They're just killing time. There is no fun.' These places; many of them private and many acknowledged locally as drug dens, are far from the classic caffs that get celebrated by the aesthetic moribundists of the capital's psychogeographic fraternity. They're refuges from women, mosques for the faithless, retirement homes for the old and fatalistic.

There are few visible traces of the past as we wander around Stoke Newington, but Yaşar's memories function as a kind of architecture. As he recalls the protests he led, or huge marches that Halkevi orchestrated, the streets become momentarily filled up and populated by ghost communities. We observe pro-Ocalan, anti-imperialism graffiti and reflect on how these hasty, nocturnal scrawls represent an archive, never collected and often flypostered over, of local resistance. 'They are words,' Yaşar hazards, 'paragraphs – in the book of the Turkish Left.'

The siege mentality that enabled, however patchily or involuntarily, a sense of Kurdish community is on the wane. London-born teenagers, no longer animated by the dream of returning East, struggle with the law and with their parents. Halkevi, once a self-designated 'engine for a Kurdish new republic' and, according to Yaşar, local people's 'eyes, tongue and brains', has moved towards becoming a welfare organization that deals with spousal abuse, mental health, drug addiction and all the other ailments common among poor migrant populations.

Young Kurds embrace the amnesia of British pop

culture, its repudiation of anything as worthy or old-fashioned as politics. Unlike their elders, they're not assailed at night by dreams of beatings, electric shocks, prison-cell torture. Yaşar, who knows that a community is nothing without shared memories, is currently involved in an oral history project that involves the recording of first-generation settlers. The first batch of tapes arrived the day we met, but they proved to be faulty: the lighting was poor, the voices inaudible.

[Sukhdev Sandhu]

DR BARNARDO'S BOYS' HOME, STEPNEY CAUSEWAY, E1

Opened in 1870, demolished in 1970. From 1872 it featured a large sign, NO DESTITUTE CHILD EVER REFUSED ADMISSION – all because of 'Carrots'. John Somers (aka Carrots) was eleven when he knocked on the door of the Home one night in 1871. The refuge was full and he was turned away. Carrots had been on the streets since he was seven years old; whenever he earned money (by selling newspapers and cigarettes, or blacking shoes) his mother would find and rob him. Barnardo promised Carrots that he could have the first bed to become vacant, but a few days later a market porter found the boy's body in a sugar barrel in a passage leading to the river at London Bridge; the coroner found that he had died of exhaustion, exposure and lack of nourishment.

[Sarah Wise]

SILKWORMS

At its peak in the early 1820s, 20,000 home looms for silk-weaving provided a living for 50,000 Londoners. Silkworms can survive for sixty days on the leaves of the mulberry tree (at a push, they'll eat lettuce), and imported mulberries were often to be found in the back yards and gardens of Spitalfields and Whitechapel. (A beautiful, gnarled mulberry, some 300 to 400 years old, can be seen in the garden of the Hogarth House Museum in Chiswick, still flowering and fruiting.) Mr Antony Tagliabue was a prolific supplier of the worm larvae, from his premises at 31 Brook Street, Holborn.

[Sarah Wise]

BISHOPSGATE ARCHES, EC2

Despite being called 'a masterpiece of Victorian engineering', and being lauded by English Heritage, the Bishopsgate Goods Yard and its magnificent viaduct was bulldozed in 2004 for the East London Line extension – even though civil-engineering experts deemed the structure strong enough to take twenty-first-century rail traffic. In the 1890s the arches, at Wheeler Street and Brick Lane, became a temporary home to families who were unable to afford their rent or who were flitting between cheap lodgings in Bethnal Green and Shoreditch. They slept on the west side, while the police patrolled the eastern pavement, ignoring them. From five o'clock in the morning dockers and porters began to pass, and were known to throw down coins and even to offer their lunches to the neediest-looking children.

[Sarah Wise]

CALLAHAN'S, WHITECHAPEL HIGH STREET, E1

In 1909 Prince Kropotkin travelled to London to give a series of lectures on 'The Tyranny of Government'. He was refused admission into Britain until some Fabians, including Hubert Black, Edith Nesbit and James 'Big Jim' Callahan, interceded on his behalf, offering personal sureties for his good conduct, and the use of Callahan's Meeting Rooms, previously known for their association with Keir Hardie's Independent Labour Party.

Callahan became increasingly involved in questions of Irish Home Rule, returning to Dublin in 1914. He died, largely forgotten, in a botched robbery (or guerrilla attack) on Amiens Street Station, in 1921.

The Meeting Rooms, flourishing under their original name, continued to welcome anarchists (some of whom were to die in Spain). By the 1940s, Callahan's lost its political aspect and became a dance hall. When it was demolished in 1968, it was best known as a venue for 'Old Time' dancing and bingo. It enjoyed one final episode of public controversy when Frank Cornelius, standing as a Liberal candidate in the 1959 election, attacked the long-serving local member, Ian Rinkoff, for ballot-rigging, involvement with dubious property deals (under the guise of slum clearance), and part-ownership of a Maltese-run café/brothel in Cable Street. The café features in Alexander Baron's novel *The Lowlife*.

[Michael Moorcock]

MARRIAGES WHARF, E6

Marriages Wharf lay across the river from Marriage's Old Wharf at Gallions Reach. The old wharf was destroyed in the Arsenal fire of 1843 and William Marriage, grandson of the company's founder, rebuilt the wharf and warehouse so that it would be more convenient for the Custom House on the other side of the Woolwich Basin. Marriage was the chief importer and exporter of opium and the rarer spices. He financed a fleet of his own 'Poppy Clippers' and founded a hospice for destitute Chinese women in Albert Road. In the mid twentieth century Marriage's eccentric mansion, attached to the old warehouse, was still standing – but, by 1970, it had been demolished to make way for the GLC's Gallions Street development.

[Michael Moorcock]

MARRIAGE'S WHARF, E6   About 1930

JACK WILLIAMS

I

I picked up with a man
Jack Williams had no legs he
was an old sailor got frost
bitten in the Arctic regions I
used to lead him all about
Ratcliffe Highway & sometimes up as
far as Notting Hill with a
big painted board afore him a
picture of the place where he
was froze in I was with
him for fifteen months till one
night I said something when he
was a-bed didn't please him

277

he got his knife out &
stabbed my leg in two places

here are the marks

2

I can only see hisself sir
He's sure to give me any
coppers he has
in his coat-pocket
& that's a very great thing
to a poor man like me

3

It's no use
such as us
calling at fine houses
to know if they've
any old keys to
sell no we
trades with the poor

4

O yes I'll buy bones
if I have any ha'pence
rather than go without but
I pick them up
or have them
given to me
mostly

[John Seed/Henry Mayhew]

RATCLIFFE HIGHWAY MURDERS: THE FRENCH KNIFE

A most important discovery has been made within these two days which removes every shadow of doubt respecting the guilt of the late suicide Williams. It was proved before the magistrates of Shadwell Office that, three weeks before the murder of Mr Williamson and his family, Williams had been seen to have a long French knife with an ivory handle. That knife could never be found in Williams's trunk or among any of the clothes he left behind him at the Pear Tree public house. The subsequent search to find it has been unsuccessful. On Tuesday Harrison, one of the lodgers at the Pear Tree, in searching among some old clothes, found a blue jacket which he immediately recognized as part of Williams's apparel. He proceeded to examine it closely, and upon looking at the inside pocket he found it quite stiff with coagulated blood, as if a blood-stained hand had been thrust into it. He brought it down to Mrs Vermilloe, who instantly sent for Holbrook and another Shadwell officer to make further search of the house. Every apartment then underwent the most rigid examination for almost an hour and a half, when the officers came at last to a small closet where there was a heap of dirty stockings and other clothes, which being removed, they observed a bit of wood protruding from a mouse-hole in the wall, which they immediately drew out, and at the same instant they discovered the handle of a clasp knife, apparently dyed with blood; which upon being brought forth, proved to be the identical French knife seen in Williams's possession before the murders; the handle and blade of which were smeared all over with blood.

[*The Times*, 16 January 1811]

AT THE CROSS-ROADS: CABLE STREET AND CANNON STREET ROAD, E1

The mass hostility towards the corpse of John Williams, the supposed Ratcliffe Highway murderer, was of a bestial ferocity. The entire population of the district, as it appeared, rose with the aim of destroying him, dismembering his body and working every savagery upon the cold flesh. But the violence was formalized, a ritual was invented. A solemn procession moved out from St George's-in-the-East, where the suicided man had been kept overnight; a loop was made through the district, so that all eyes might witness the cart, its titled board and shameful cargo. With attendant horsemen and a straggle of pedestrians, the death-cart acknowledged the Marrs' Ratcliffe Highway shop, the scene of the crime, and then turned, along the western entrance to Hawksmoor's church, towards the chosen place of burial.

The board on which the body was arranged had been dressed with the murder weapons, the maul and the chisel – as well as the stake that would be driven through the dead man's heart. Thomas De Quincey, in his essay 'On Murder Considered as One of the Fine Arts', does not dwell on such details. Williams, he reports, 'was buried in the centre of a quadrivium, or conflux of four roads (in this case four streets) . . . And over him drives for ever the uproar of unresting London.'

[I. S.]

OBJECTS OF
OBSCURE DESIRE

THE MEIDNER PORTRAIT

Before the 1939–45 war I knew Michael Croft, later a figure in the London art world, Trustee of the Tate Gallery and owner of a collection of twentieth-century paintings. He was the son of Sir Henry Paige Croft, a Blimpish caricature, who made himself notorious in 1940 by advocating arming the Home Guard with pikes. Michael, in natural rebellion against his parental background, befriended and financially supported a number of refugee artists from Germany, many of whom were introduced to him by his sister Diana (who married Fred Uhlmann). As our mutual friend Charles Rycroft said, 'Michael is a refugee from his parents.'

I suppose the most famous artist he helped was Oskar Kokoschka, whom he commissioned to paint portraits of himself and his sister Posy. One of the other persons of interest was Ludwig Meidner, then quite elderly; a man with a great reputation as a 1914–18 war artist. There is a painting of trench warfare by Meidner in the Leicester Art Gallery, horribly realistic. What is amazing is that it is dated 1912. Meidner's work was truly prophetic.

Michael Croft asked me if I would sit for the exiled painter. I consented. At that time Meidner was living, with his wife Else and young son, in an attic room in Golders Green. I went there two or three times in the winter of 1939, one of the coldest I've known. It was freezing and I kept on my new, red, winter coat. Meidner proceeded to draw me. Else, his much younger wife, looked in. They had loud rows in German. She threw an orange enamel teapot at him, but missed. To me she appeared quite simply mad.

He spoke German and peculiar French. She spoke German and peculiar English. I spoke English and probably peculiar French. Meidner, as he drew, talked to me, in a sort of French, about the poems of Ossian (a mythical Celtic poet foisted on a gullible public, nearly 200 years ago, by Macpherson). The situation was absurd, surreal. Meidner revered phoney Scotch verse, which he had perhaps

283

read in a German translation. He punctuated rhapsodies on Ossian with personal comments on my face. 'Le front est monumental, mais la bouche est infantile.'

One such sitting, on a Saturday afternoon, was stopped rather abruptly. Meidner put on a tiny skullcap and took me down to a room where several elderly Germans were already seated at a table spread with strange cakes, some of which had cream cheese in the most unlikely places. Else was there as hostess, and also their son, whose bar mitzvah it was. I was the only non-Jew, the only non-German speaker. Socially, I was quite out of my depth.

The drawing Meidner produced was life-size, mostly in brown chalk, with bits of red chalk on the face and collar and bits of blue-grey for eyes and shadows. It was duly handed over to Michael Croft, who, I presume, paid Meidner. It was then expensively framed by another refugee, I think Polish, and presented to me. I never liked it. I was about twenty-five at the time and not ill-looking. The portrait made me look sixty, a person who had tried and failed to find consolation for a wretched life in oceans of alcohol. I accepted the unwelcome gift and put it away in a cupboard.

In 1940 there was a round-up of all German refugees in England. They were arrested and taken to camps on the Isle of Man; some of them as 'Friendly Aliens', some as 'Enemy Aliens'. All quite arbitrary. When Meidner was interned, there was a public outcry, questions in Parliament, and Kenneth Clark (Director of the National Gallery) pulled strings to get this innocent old man, this famous artist, released. (I thought at the time he was probably only too glad to be parted from his mad wife. He wouldn't have to worry where his next meal was coming from, fourteen herrings a week.) Meidner wrote to Michael Croft from the camp: 'This is an ideal community. Please send another sketch book.'

After the war, an old friend of mine, an artist herself, asked me what happened to that awful drawing. I took it from the cupboard (I had used the lovely frame for something more agreeable) and we both examined it. She asked if she might tear it up. I agreed, and she did so at once, saying, 'We should have done this long ago.'

Much later, my husband, Bernhard, another Jewish refugee, told me more of Meidner's reputation in Germany in the 1930s and how he had drawn a portrait of a female cousin, which Bernhard considered very good, very powerful. He felt that Meidner could not cope so well with my less emphatic Anglo-Saxon features. I am sure the trauma of being a refugee, the icy cold, the presence of his mad wife, must also have made drawing me very difficult.

Else Meidner was an artist too, of considerable reputation. I think they separated after the war and she went back to Germany. So did he, eventually. I never saw them again.

[Ann Baer]

THE STICKY PAD

A large green nylon zip-up bag preceded the rat-catcher as he stepped across our threshold at nine o'clock on Tuesday morning – prompt as a debt collector. The thin streak of mouth did not bend in greeting.

'What poison are you using?' he asked as he strode across the room, already it seems in pursuit of his prey.

'Sorex,' said I, 'but they're not eating it.'

'Grains like seeds?'

I showed him the packet: 'Controls all types of mouse, including warfarin resistant super mice'. The word 'warfarin' intrigued me. These mice were smart. They could gnaw a whole chunk of choc-olate off a loaded trap without tripping it. Same with cheese. I told the rat-catcher this but he showed little surprise or interest.

'You set the trap fine?' he asked. I assured him it couldn't have been finer.

'Mice are monsters,' he said.

'Sorry?' I said nonchalantly, wanting him to say it again.

'Rats eat anything. You never know with mice. They get so smart they don't even run along the floor. They scamper along the top of the skirting board. Sometimes they like to feed in a dark

private place. Sometimes they don't. Each mouse is different, see.'
The rat-catcher paused, sensing his audience. 'Calciferol and Difenacoum,' he liked the sound of them, 'if the Calciferol don't get
'em, the Difenacoum will. Hardens their kidneys.' His torch
flashed down backs of cupboards. 'You've got a lot of holes in your
floor.'

I remembered, when I was a child, nursing a sick mouse in a
matchbox with the lid half closed. I tucked it up with sheets made
of tissue and a pillow of cotton wool. When the mouse died the
matchbox made an equally good coffin. A lollypop stick made a
good headstone. I told all this to the rat-catcher.

'We'll try a multi-take poison first,' he said.

As the rat-catcher unzipped his green bag the noxious scent of
chemistry escaped.

'I can smell the poison,' I said. He looked at me quizzically.

'If this don't work . . .' he paused, 'we've other alternatives . . .'

'Which are?' I asked, knowing I had to.

'There's the sticky pad . . .'

'The sticky pad?'

'Not many people like using the sticky pad,' he said.

'What is it?' I asked, noting a millimetre curl raise the corner of
his mouth.

'It's a very sticky pad,' he grinned, plunging his hand back into
the green bag. He pulled out an off-white card with a sticky-back
lining and began to peel slowly.

'They get stuck on it, you see. But it don't kill 'em. You gotta
do that yourself. With a screwdriver or something. Bash 'em with
it. They could be wriggling and writhing around. They could get
caught on their back. Or just one leg could get stuck and they could
be scrabbling around and around. They could be squeaking . . .
squeak, squeak.' He squeaked through his nose. 'They could be
stuck by just their head and all their little legs could be going trying

to escape. You'd hear it squeaking under the fridge. Then you'd have to kill them yourself. A screwdriver's good.'

I tell you no word of a lie, this is what the rat-catcher said.

[Keggie Carew]

A CERTAIN PAIR OF SHOES: OR, THE UNIVERSE

but they were here, like only six months ago   they were here   they were here   you had them: here   displayed on this-here shelf   I remember because   yeah, I bought them   yes OK, consumed them, if you prefer, something like six months ago   why don't we just say gobbled   but I don't, no, expect your stock to be   but this time: black   I have a friend, see   see, look at this ready dosh, see   yeah I have this friend who when she saw mine she almost died so I said look next time I'm in London, which is now because I live here now see, so I say next time I'll march straight up to Camden Town and get another pair for you, for her like   yeah, this friend of mine except in black   New York   except she wants, yes, black   and plus plus but OK   platform, yes, but not exceedingly chunky heel   not, though, exceedingly   uh-huh: exceedingly   vinyl, masquerading as wood   obscene   real   convincing   Ye Olde Curiosity Shoppe kind of thing   a little man in a smoking jacket   maybe Raskolnikov if he'd've kept the loot   syntho-marble effect might go with a monocle and yeah, clip-clopping, seriously harkening back   you'd see them and hear like maybe the Goldberg Variations but performed by Kraftwerk   OK, nostalgic but not all annoyingly   you catch my drift   not like en route to the rave or anything   right   none of that crap, not referential but suggestive   not symbolic but allegorical, these, this pair   you know this pair?   'my kingdom for a'   and now you're telling me   you're saying   yup   yes, six months, I walked all along the canal, chips sopping   (rain and vinegar) harkening back and   black but   she's kind of an ex-goth, habits habits die hard you know and   but so now that's a vacant shelf you're showing me   OK yeah I see the fuchsia sequined sling-backs chord boots for the toeless eggshell soles, there   stressed polyamide clogs with nappa leather tassels   electronic legwarmers, OK (exceedingly)   fortune-telling loafers, velour and Plexiglas™   so then right these strap way up to   OK, the crotch and street-pumps that self-destruct musical laces (what, the theme from *Heartbeat*) stilettoidal sweat socks, Spurs, Gunners, OK   I'm, but see, a hockey gal   no: Escher invented stilts?   free matching red goggles   uh-huh that then is the cloven-foot look *Tatler* keeps on about   but sir mate Klaus   nice to meet you, Klaus   Klaus, yes, they're fabulous but what about   what about yeah   that pair, right   my pair   six months   only   black, but   not in stock   not in, like, stock   not now?   Klaus: ever?   but never?

[Kiki Benzon]

A SPARE PAIR OF BLACK OXFORDS

After he had gone I searched the flat for clues. Needles. Pills. Nothing would have surprised me, not that I really expected to discover anything beyond the absence of any serious trace of him that I did find. There were just a few ordered possessions: a row of books, all paperback, forgettable thrillers apart from a copy of De Quincey's *Confessions of an English Opium Eater*, and, in a wardrobe, a spare pair of black Oxfords . . . I thought of those shiny black shoes, the moon face and the secrets he carried. Though he had not been gone long, I could not picture him clearly.

[Chris Petit]

KNIFE/WAND

> I was playing with Macedonio's pocketknife, opening and closing it.
>
> J. L. Borges

When I was a child I jammed a knife into the safety valve of a pressure cooker. It wouldn't budge. But I refused to give way. I tried again, without success: the valve didn't yield. I dream of this. In the dream I get burned. I force down the valve. Wet heat leaves me with a stripe of scar across my forehead and down my cheek.

I woke from the dream to find that the markings had become fact. I had dreamed them into being. As I pressed the knife against the valve I punctured a membrane separating 'could have' from 'was'. This is how it must be. A scar of the past dreamed into reality. I walked. In the dream, connections occurred: no linking passages, only places. Names. A series of arrivals. Without staying or leaving, I advanced. Firsthand hindsight. The point of departure, lesson learned, but never the journey.

I aborted the urge to run. I knew, without thought, it was the wrong thing to do. I stopped: through fear, then persistence. If stuff was not going to behave then neither was I. Sitting here, I would perform magic. Time travel. Super-stasis. Drive a stake through my feet, scar the planet as it ground forward beneath me. At first: nothing. And then, as my shoes wore thin and blisters formed, pus streaked across time. I was going to see it all. Live retrospect.

Without a proper relish for the romance of enlightenment, I arrived at the answer: disappearance. My existence required the destruction of experience. As if experience confirmed existence. Without it I had nothing. People brought me television. Papers. Letters. People grew bored. They left. Knowledge was my enemy. I stayed on. Scratching at repetition, memory over muscle. Stinging my eyes, distorting vision: the seen became sore. My vital ember was lost in the frequency of its retelling. Disappearance was the scar forced upon me. A disfigured and immovable memory of a child with a knife, drawn by the sound of steam escaping from a pressure cooker. The map of a journey he resolves never to take.

[William Sinclair]

NINE ELMS COLD STORE

Although longer than it was broad or high, and from Vauxhall Bridge resembling a great sarcophagus, or the sole remaining buttress of a mighty defensive earthwork, the impression this disappearance leaves in my psyche is resolutely cubic. The Cold Store – a beehive of concrete beams; Venetian – blind-slatted; seeping. In certain lights the horizontal stria seemed to have a pattern of impressions, the bas-relief of some ancient Mesopotamian culture where frozen produce was needed for the afterlife. From the west, approaching along Nine Elms Lane, the Cold Store bore down on the puny drivers, dominating the Effra Road site, which until the erection of the foul St George Wharf was a rutted wilderness of coach and lorry park.

The Cold Store, over-toppling this mammon-forsaken stretch of South London littoral, so large that the one remaining building with a human scale in the vicinity – the tattered Victorian Conservative Club – was etched against it, as if its concrete hide were the grey-beige sky. Built in 1955, the Cold Store owed its Brutalist aspiration to the same jolt of post-war confidence which brought such triumphs as the still extant Stockwell Bus Garage. At its peak the Store held anything up to 16,000 tons of chilled meat, together with – as one of its admirers hymns it – 'some butter and cheese'. Ooh, I love that 'some butter and cheese': the churned-up products of the massacred beasts lying alongside them in freezing chancels and icy transepts.

However, by the 1980s, the Store was disused and until its demolition in 1998–9 it remained dormant, suffering only the periodic arousal of random acts of artistic aspiration. I have discovered evidence that an avant-garde album, *The Cold Store Tapes*, was recorded there in 1990; a sonic experiment in which guerrilla percussionists beat the rubble to produce echoic effects in the empty soundbox. There was also a 'pigment project' in the 1990s – I visualize splashes of Tyrian purple and cobalt blue across the pulverized canvas of the roof.

Vauxhall owes no one any favours. The Vauxhall Tavern, an upended oil drum of a gin palace, still belts out techno and high energy into the dark night of sodium flare and lead fume. Outside it, on the pavement, shaven-headed clones, naked to the waist, butt and paw at each other like mime-rutting bullocks, while the steel curtain of traffic endlessly unfurls beside them. A frenzied echo of the Pleasure Gardens which spread from here towards Lambeth Palace, and which lasted for two full centuries, the oiled, tarmac turd of Vauxhall Cross remains a zone of abandon. Clubs stud the railway arches – Crash, Flame, the Hoist – and on workaday mornings their denizens totter out into the commuter traffic, raccoon-eyed, clutching plastic water bottles.

1645. Nine eponymous elms along the turnpike, breweries, potteries and limekilns stain the riverine mud. To the south the magical district of North Lambeth, redoubt of Tradescant and Elias Ashmole. No blitz or innovation could leaven the heavy bread of this quartier, only now, with heavy pinion of the Cold Store removed, have bourgeois aspirations begun to soar. A preposterous giant tuning fork has been erected by the Council in lieu of a bus stop, the gull wings of St George Wharf above, hard evidence of mass faith in ever-rising property prices. December 2004. I stroll through the brushed-steel atria and columnar courtyards of the new development. In through a quarter acre of plate glass, an African security guard dozing behind his plinth. A vast plasma screen dominates the lobby, on it Sky News conducts an interview with the latest hack to have banged the former Home Secretary's former mistress. Where have they gone, those 16,000 tons of meat, some butter and cheese?

[Will Self]

COAL HOPPER, NINE ELMS LANE, 1979

In 1977 I started making a 'collection' of found architecture, mostly in London, which was the beginning of a line of inquiry that led me eventually to making films. The conceptual transformation involved in 'finding' a found object is fairly familiar but architecture, not being portable, is more difficult to appropriate in this way. Travelling around London (I was living in NW3, working in SW9, teaching part-time in E17 and visiting sites all over South London) I had encountered a number of buildings which I felt were attractive as structures with striking architectural qualities that were either not the result of conventional architectural activity, or, if they were, had perhaps not been seen by their designers in the way that I saw them. None were for sale, but even if any had been, acquisition seemed at first neither appropriate nor practical, so the collection consisted of 35mm colour slides.

The most familiar of these buildings was one that I knew as the Nine Elms Coal Hopper. This was the last surviving structure of

the Nine Elms Gas Works in Nine Elms Lane, between Vauxhall Bridge and Battersea Power Station. It was made of reinforced concrete, painted pink apart from the roof, which was light green, as if to suggest that it was copper (which it wasn't). It stood between the road and the river, as the coal had arrived by boat. In the late 1960s, Nine Elms Lane was a location of interest to a certain kind of architectural tourist (like Silvertown or Beckton, but easier to get to), so it was not a new discovery, but had perhaps become more visible. I had been redirected to it by a friend who commuted from Hackney (just a couple of streets from Iain, as it happens) to the architects' office of the Department of the Environment in Croydon. He had seen it from the train. I expect that it was admired by many people, but have not yet met anyone else who shared our enthusiasm.

It was demolished during the winter of 1979–80, by which time the site had been squatted by a car breaker, who was sufficiently intrigued by my interest in the building (and my interest in preserving it, which might have extended his occupation of the site) to permit access for the purpose of photography. I sent photographs to several people who I thought might support an effort to acquire the building and convert it to some cultural or hedonistic use, and received several replies, including one from Ove Arup,[1] who wrote: 'It is quite likely that there is a good case for the preservation of the Coal Hopper, but I could not express an opinion without going into much more detail and I am afraid that I really do not have the time to spare at present, but I wish you every success in your venture,' which I thought very kind in the circumstances. It was much too late to prevent demolition, as planning permission had by then just been granted to redevelop the site as an estate of light-industrial units. When the car breaker had been evicted, demolition began. It was difficult and very slow, as the building was too near the river for explosives and had to be knocked down with a ball and chain. This was the subject of the first film I ever exhibited, a short loop improvised for a party which turned out to be (for a different reason) a decisive personal moment. It was projected on an unplastered white-painted brick wall, so that it looked as if the film was knocking the wall down.

Gas-works architecture of this kind[2] now survives in London only as the ruins at Beckton, where the hoppers were transformed to represent Saigon for Stanley Kubrick. If I remember correctly, similar structures can be seen, undisguised, in *Facts and Fancies*, a promotional film produced for the Gas Council in 1951 by the great Richard Massingham. I recently deduced with the aid of an 1894 Ordnance Survey map that the 1897 Lumière films *Bateau à vapeur sur la Tamise* and *Départ d'un bateau sur la Tamise* were almost certainly photographed from Pimlico Pier, looking towards the Nine Elms Gas Works. One of the gasometers is visible, as is an earlier coal hopper, a tall structure on the waterfront distinguished by a series of curved roofs, probably corrugated iron.

The conversion of industrial structures to cultural and other uses is now a familiar feature of urban development. Tate Modern, as a converted power station (in which are examples of Bernd and Hilla Becher's photographs of industrial structures, including a series of coal hoppers), arguably owes its position opposite St Paul's, if not its existence, to the gas works which was established on the site by 1815, the predecessor of the first power station. Several gas works were built on or near the sites of London pleasure gardens, most of which were on or near the river.[3] The works at Bankside was built on a site which in the sixteenth century had been that of the Paris Garden, so that Tate Modern, as a place of resort, represents a return to something not so unlike this earlier use. Sometimes the connection is more direct. One of the assets of Vauxhall Gardens when it finally closed in 1859 was a gas works. Pleasure gardens were by then lit by enormous numbers of gas lights, and coal gas[4] was used to inflate balloons for the ascents that were a famous attraction at Vauxhall. Nobody seems to know the location of the Vauxhall Gardens gas works, but the Phoenix Gas Company later operated one immediately west of Vauxhall Bridge, which was perhaps that previously owned by the pleasure gardens.

[Patrick Keiller]

STONE COLLAR IN MORTLAKE

Friday, 23 May 1997: Alan Moore, still wearing 'something of the night' about his person, arrived early. He had decided to bivouac in a convenient hotel, so that he would be fresh for our walk, Hackney to Mortlake, in the morning. I realized, as soon as I saw him standing in the doorway with his bulging bag, that this time, without question, Alan *was* the story. (I'd done the walk several times before and worried at the locale: the meaning of that freestanding arch in St Mary's churchyard, the short stroll to Sir Richard Burton's stone tent. Nobody could tell me exactly where to find the bones of John Dee. Dr Dee was a subject I continued to approach but never managed to write about.) Now the tracings of our hike across London, tattooed on the skin of the Northampton visionary, would prove the day's narrative.

We had talked about Dee, Ashmole, seances, demonic possession, real frauds and true magic, for years; on the telephone, in letters, and on the infrequent occasions when our paths crossed at readings or performances (we were both dug deep into our own territories and emerged reluctantly – like snails with cities on our shoulders). I had imagined that Alan would be content to let me visit the churchyard on his behalf. Or that he'd cab upstream, one free-floating afternoon, with a mate and a camera. Not so. I suggested meeting him somewhere along the route, Putney or a riverside pub. But Alan wanted to do the whole thing. He stepped into the narrow house, equipped with a scrying mirror and a conjuror's kit of angelic tablets, books of the law, cabbalistic treatises. The full Harry Price awayday kit. Personal lightning attractors with which to claim safe passage through the Vessels of Wrath.

It was curious how this walk, a shotgun marriage between chiropody and alchemy, seemed to flow from obsessions that Alan and I, separately, exploited: Whitechapel conspiracies, surveillance in the City, the paranoid poetic of 'secret state' Lambeth and Vauxhall. Bad magic and worse feet, that's what London was about. The excuse for a range of greasy-spoon breakfasts, never better or worse, slowdeath in a lick of blood sausage, a mopped yolk. Newspaper headlines on white boards were instructions from alien intelligences: ARTIST GUILTY OF BODY-SNATCHING.

We were a thrift-shop Dee and Kelley, cupping our ears for whispers in the stone, knuckles of fossil code. I photographed convex mirrors outside generic burger joints and CCTV boxes on tall poles. Every step unpicked a previous fiction. Alan drudged, heroically, down the long detour that pretended to be a river path: cold stores and prisons for lost dogs.

As the sun dropped like the closing eye of a felled ox, Alan recovered. Evening light threaded the leaves, gilding the staggering magus's Dürer hair into a burning aureole. The world of appearances faltered and failed. I anticipated the lavender drench of Mortlake.

(Churchyard lavender, mashed hops from the brewery.) Walking was swimming. Target achieved, Alan fumbled with the scrying mirror: an oval of sky, church tower, self-portrait as one of the disappeared. You stick to the curved glass, you exit the river path. They find you, face down in the mud, pockets filled with stones.

This is a light that can neither be photographed nor described. Come so far and London loses its gravitational pull, the drag of dirty words and mean deeds. Between Mortlake and Richmond, reversing the ride Queen Elizabeth took when she wished to consult Dee, the Imperial geographer, is a green path. Leading you on, to follies and fountains, knot gardens and obelisks under flight paths. There is a post at Teddington that marks the limits of the tidal Thames. Or the point at which the story dies and exhausted writers, like horses, are changed, stabled, left behind.

[I. S.]

THORN IN THEIR SIDE: BRIAN HAW AND THE COMING OF THE DISAPPEARED

How does a man, this man, join the disappeared? He starts by arriving. With a sleeping bag, and a stick of painted signs, the word on cardboard, damp. Parliament Square, 2 June 2001. Blair again then, just days later, and all the four more years. It's too familiar now, too close to a kind of franchise of despair, but even then, in that now 'golden age' summer before everything changed, Brian Haw, Redditch father of seven, carpenter, merchant seaman, believer, could see the way it was all going, knew that extraordinary measures were required.

If you find yourself homeless, you find shelter – something dere-lict, somewhere so the sky is not your sheet, even just a doorway – you search for some place clear of thoroughfares, where sleep might breed less threat. But Mr Haw was not for this removal. He had not given up his life to go off-road. 'Peace on Earth, Goodwill to All', 'Stop Killing Kids', 'Let Iraq Infants Live'. If you break your being into pieces for justice and against the sinful sanctions on Iraq, against the cluster bombs that do anything but gather together, against the terrible unpicking of countries entire, then you accept the road is maybe a life long. You sleep under rain and ice and snow. Under blows from Marines, under the sometimes very heavy hand of the Met., 24/7, for four years. And counting. But more than sleep, you make the disgust visible. In placards, pictures, information, more. And soon they follow; uncounted articles, Sundays' photo shoots, Mexican radio, documentaries from Iran to CNN. With thousands from the planet-wide and folk from London town adding to the weave of pictures, poems, rage. You live on nothing except the goodwill of others, notes thrown down from passing cars. You win all the cases brought against you, in the High Court and the other halls of justice.

In short, you do not let the bastards get you down. You are an orator of anger and straight sense, but more than that, you simply are. Your secret is: that you refuse to leave. You stand against the war on terror, and first it stops with you. You will not be the terrorized. And slowly, you accumulate your own environmental time. Build it and they will come . . . You run the Square's length with a wall of words, the people's Commons, DU babies screaming you to speak. And now, at point of writing, you have so disturbed the 'peace' of Parliament that swathes of them, livid for you and your longest protest in this island's life, have gone all out to stitch up laws to oust you and those around who claim such rights to speak and act across the city's power-broking centre. You find yourself the likely first felon on the receiving end of the Serious Organized Crime and Police Act, with clauses scripted just for you. In this way, you link our power players straight to Pinochet and all the squalid rest who lift a person from their life and never set them down again, in grave or cell or any system filed. They want you absent, distant, gone, they want you disappeared.

But you will never leave because they want you to. And if they do erase you, others will arise, like stand-ins, Spartacus: I am Brian Haw, they'll say and they will be correct. For you have given protest your own body, face and sticking name. Marches come and marches go, but Haw, thorn, you remain. (www.parliament-square.org.uk)

[Gareth Evans]

TWENTY-FIVE MEMORY JARS

Objects left from a party.
An orchid and a postage stamp.
Billiard chalks dissolving.
A root and a china pig.
Pencil sharpener inside a model duck
    with a coil of wool, discarded from knitting.
Magnetic tape in a loop.
Chrysanthemum in formaldehyde solution.
Feathers and springs.
Pieces of iron found in the henhouse.
Salt container decomposing in saline.
Contents of an ashtray at the Royal Court Theatre;
    including bottle of gin, quarter-smoked cigarette,
crushed golden packet of filter cigarettes.
Fragments of a china flying duck and a saucer.
An aloe plant and tube of aloe ointment.
Bar magnets with container of chemicals including
    zinc and copper.
A water strainer with many coins.
Broken pieces of hallucinogenic mushroom.
Various pieces of metal.
A few bells.
A piece of chocolate with a compass.
Badges, medals.
Snuff.

A mole carcass and a jewelled fox's foot.
A flying-bomb battery, toy ambulance, toy car, plastic
    chain, a monster figure.
Piece of basalt and a game of competitive chance.
Lead glass balls and ballotini beads in water.

[Allen Fisher]

SOUTH OF THE RIVER

JUSTGONE

All cities are geological; you cannot take three steps without encountering ghosts bearing all the prestige of their legends. We move within a *closed* landscape whose landmarks constantly draw us towards the past.

GILLES IVAIN (pen name of Ivan Chtcheglov).

There I am talking to a book.
Head like a radio phone-in.
Holy God and for the love of Jesus.
Comes an invitation to participate.

He's en route from Warrior Square to back there, where, the remembering has been taking place.
Investigate.
Collaborate with the things he finds – cipher to the titillators that agitate his befuddled mind.
There, there, never mind.
'*He had to start all over again, he had to go back and start all over again, here he goes, here he goes, it takes you right back to when things are a lot clearer now.*'
Four score and four.
More: he wasn't, he was, he wasn't.
There.
Hym.
Nowgone, lookedfor and notfound.

Lost: one deadad's son.
Lumpen.
If anyone knows of his whereabouts or any other deadads' sons for that matter please contact someone that might know something that might lead to his being: kotting@deadad.abelgratis.co.uk. Gone.

Doggy carriage carrying.
Landscapes blurring.
Headspace whirring.
So, now to the lookback.
Where to put him?
Up there on the wallscrawl, next to Sammie Lee?
Author of herself and her:

```
hallo peoples my name is Sammie Lee I am 15 years of
age I come from New Cross No-one can fuck wid me
cause I'm a bad gal ya unnerstan skeen my tag name is
cutie and I am a skettel boom a shiner but only shine
for there bus fare (peoples dogs free),
```

Probably not,
or
Over there;   inside the phone box.
Slightly pre-bling.
The germ of blingbling and ting?
A sign plonkedinplace, reading:

```
If you want to bang me up I go to Blackheath
Bluecoats School if you want sex, shines or sex phone
me on 0181 694 **** we can have it anyway – Swimming
Baths  Bushes  Flats/Stairs  and  definitely  Buses
especially 53 Trains oh yea I forgot my vagina smells
like egg and I've got hairs on my breasts but I'll
wash just for you. And I only kiss girls/nothing else.
```

Don't talk to *her* she's rude. The unselfconscious innit wherewithal.
That might have been him? No, not at all. Never.
Yesteryears and a meandering inscape, outscape, upstairs, downstairs
and in that lady's chamber.
Moist,
d
e
e
p,

cocooning and clammy. Made him dizzy and then the offspring.
Her, the Garden *of*, our garden.
'*He* did it,' she once said, 'I was asleep, I wasn't looking where I was going.'
What to do? What a todo but that's jumping the gun.
Back to before-that.
To the he-wants-to-be-a-bloke.
Then.
Sporty and porting the early stages of a manhood.
Days spent in a transit van: scrap metal on Mondays, the Tiger's Head on Tuesdays, practise on Wednesdays and the markets of a weekend. (Thursday was his night off, indoors, perhaps Top of the Pops, a pickled egg, Beckett before bed.)
Ever the bloke rarely a mince.

Here he goes, here he goes, he'd just launch himself off –
A South London, paradise.
Head fairly full-to-overflowing with the cacophony.
From the Café Gallery to Downtown, from Deptford Beach to the Lion Roars to **Case** to `George Davies is innocent`, from Jim and Bob and John Irvine to Cash and Fred and Dorian Crook. D&C Metals and Salter's Paper to the Dog and Bell and selling wicker furniture with Jack Sharp in Deptford Market. From Amersham Road and **Being Karnal**, from Greenland Dock to Surrey Docks and the Seaman's Church, the Prince of Orange to the Mayflower, from the Rogue's Kitchen to the Old Den, from the Blue to `Spend-a-lot` (hairdressers). From Dilston Grove to Heilco van der Ploeug and Penfold's. He was well and truly there, see.

So to some scenes from the hasbeen life.
(Occasional apparatus a 35mm *Lomo* camera, comes instructing to take *Lomographs* instead of photographs; what a laugh.)

Lomograph as Post mortal snapshot.
Jaunt.
Billy Old steers his 'Hollywood' pleasure boat and Malcolm Hardy
speeding all wibbly wobbly on his 'Wibbly Wobbly'.
Pilot and drinker.
Pilot and drunk.

*'We toward London in our boat and thus I by foot to Greenwich and
in our way observing and discoursing upon the things of the Pepys
Estate.'*

Lomograph as Post studium snapshot.
The Thomas-à-Becket
Jack Sharp (now dead), sparring with Alan Minter,
father Terry beaming on,
me, all a fiddle as the Super 8's gone wrong.

Then g   aps in the memory. King Kurt and Julian Edward
Frances, Test Department and the Band of Holy Joy. Butch Minds
the Baby. Gordon House.
Love.
Head furniture and clutterup.
(Is this his *something intended*?)
City as cacophony and don't-give-up-on-me.
Cup of tea, a bun, thinly sliced ox tongue and Molin's cigarette
factory.
Tarradiddles and *'there was a dead body found in the Thames'* riddles:
Yonder comes the devil with his pitchfork and shovel he was digging
up potatoes in the turnpike road, riddles.

Another cavalcade of rethink springs up like the London Docklands
Development.
Corporation.
'All change.'

Cement the Land; mine is a place of faded grey mine is a place to pass away. Cement the land (**Being Karnal, 1982**).

Across the road you go. Evelyn Street in the rush hour. The city of lookback, the city of lookout! Speed humps and bollards. Let me go down there. I follow him and his 'oggle. He turns into Plough Way and he gets twelve-year-old girls dribbling their eversotough little boyfriends' seed, going: 'Like, knowhat I mean' and 'butters' and 'hench' then 'tonk' and whatever it was that Keisha was saying. 'She woulda went skeet and fickle *him* large,' so as an aside and because of the eyes, I like go: 'Yo! chattleup the tonks.' So they say: 'Comere'nsaythat.' Such fulsome banter.
So I'm thinking: Manthereafoolklutt.

But now to home. The flat. Red brick, yellow insides. An entrance to the rear. Puddled with piss in summertime and blocked with adolescent bliss in wintertime. The lift gleams with spittle the corridors with polish. Up to the sixth floor, the corridor, second on the left and in. Home, their home. Good-to-be-home, home. Bence House, Pepys Estate, home.

Lomographic triptych as witness to home, *there* home.
Sunrise to sunset
And a partial viewing of a specifically tuned consciousness.

We're inside: knick-knack bric-à-brac give the man a phone, hugger mugger with the memorabilia of their lives, lived together, home. And then the child. Sick-in-the-head, dribbling-rocking, life-will-never-be-the-same-again child. Forever at home child?

She can't walk and she can't talk and she drags us down with her to a world of loopy repetition: *Papa, Papa, Papa . . . It doesn't hurt, it doesn't hurt, it doesn't hurt.*
Despair.
But we're not there to hide.

We imbibe the paraphernalia that is vertical living. Thousands of us, shuffling and kerfuffling about our busy ness. The smell of the place, the heat and pace of the place. Spicy West African voices, warming, booming and then echoing:

Rejoice! Rejoice!! Rejoice!!! Isn't it a thing of joy to have known and seen the sacro-sanctity of the word of god?

(For further information phone 0171 or was it 0181?)

Outside, underneath the footbridge that connects us with Deptford Park, umbilical cord to the world of misdemeanour and misbehaviour and the Den, an old sheet flapping in the drizzle, it reads:

Marina your son wants to see you please mummy come home only 4 love.

The football-supporter wants his wife,
The football-supporter wants his wife,
A news flash from yours truly.
The wife doesn't want him or the child.

Look at me, look at me with my I'm-from-Deptford attitude. Blimey. People drift and they leave their marks – traces of their history – dog's droppings on the soul of the shoe. He's left a few in his time. What's that he's saying to himself? He's sat there watching. The inscape is gorgeous. Now all lit up and still no Gherkin. A reflection, half-truth and confabulation, a miracle of recollection. Him, the heavy-set shirehorse, meanderings then rememberings. Gripped by the possibilities of everything.

And I remember, I remember, I don't remember much at all, in fact I'm one of these people that remembers very little and he'd get to his feet and he'd go: 'Klipperty klopp, Klipperty klopp, Klipperty klopp, out with your cock, Klipperty klopp.' Docklands

Lomograph as still-life snapshot.
Jarman's Garden.
(Not Dungeness.)
The one from the *Last of England.*
We're crossing the river to get to the other side, don't ask me why,
the river's not wide but we're crossing to get to the other side.
The river's bend where little America looms you up opposite.
You'd think they'd keep canaries but they don't, they keep small
gorillas.

His psyche and its geography:
It takes me right back to when things are a lot clearer now.
Foggy wasn't the word for it, it was well muggy, exceedingly unpleasant.
See I remember he said;
He said, this my son is a sun, a prehistoric sun, and this my son is a
sign and it was round here, round here, that it all began.
All round here.
It takes me right back.
Something better come of this.
Something better come of this.

Lomograph as the comedy of spectacular reality.
The Redriff Community.
Gone.
No more the bingo. No more the weight watchers. No more the
gym. No more the bar. No more the trophies. No more the *social*
club.
(No more the Simon Hughes – our president and optimist.)

He looks to himself, hisself and that queer old bonce.
Come prick him you 'punctum'.
Memory leap out at him.
What was it like? How goes the foreshore?
Entice him with your sticky embrace, mudlarking him.
Sweet, sweet, river Thames.

Today the rapture offsets the jitters.
Hindsight as a heavyweight.
Perhaps he never would have left. His future is now in waves.
The memories his barnacles.

When it was very hard it was very hard. When it was soft it was
very soft. It was spilled all the time when it was spilled all the time.
Spillage. Here a bit there a bit everywhere a little bit. He mustn't lose
his head. He's been witness to his past and it's his heArt that quickens
when he walks on to the stage at the Lee Centre, Lee, the Tunnel
Club or the Fridge, Brixton; there he is again up at Cecil Sharp
House. Befuddled and ready to perform the thing that is his regurge.
His existence assimilation, his work the collation and this, his
performance, a bricolagic exaggeration.

Then there was Rotherhithe Baths.
Go to work on a swim.
Him, justgone.
A ride through the park, down the one-way streets to an egg,
on toast, mushrooms and a cup of tea.
Now seems wayback in a city full of ps's.

PS: To whom it may concern my daughter Harriet would
like to chance her scooter for something else. She
has already changed her scooter for another because
the wheel had fallen off. What's more this scooter
has broken. I am sorry I cannot be with my daughter
but I am unwell.

Moved.
Moved to.
Moved from.
Moved away.
All moves him.
What's more it's a reassure, a moving thought to think, that there

he is, his mind's eye, alone in the corridor that leads to the front door, writing a reminisce.

PPS: The clear sighted person who understands himself, explains himself, justifies himself, and dominates his actions will never make a memorable gesture. (**E. M. Cioran** – *A Short History of Decay*)

Once resolved, we are rewarded for our endeavours with the feeling of pleasure.
His heart was in Deptford and now it's near Bumptious Mansions, Warrior Square, up a side alley with othersuch there.
Justgone and hasbeen.
Disappeared.

Imagined Lomograph as a new Series.
He sees lots of fish swimming in the water.
And that little cod fish had a hole in the middle,
Tommy Doddler,
Tommy Doddler.

Look here comes Mr Stoppit.

[Andrew Kötting]

CRUSHED MEXICAN SPIDERS

Ahead of her, struggling up the stairs strugglingly was a mother and pushchair, laden with bags and a screaming kid. Homebound workers salmoned past without offering a hand, blinkered by visions of supper or respite.

The comatose staff of London Underground didn't think of helping the mother. She wouldn't be helping either. Ten years ago, when she had moved to London, she would have. Imperceptibly but perceptibly the city toxified you. Parking across strangers' driveways, not saying thank you when a door was held open for you, murder. Somehow it got you.

London informed you that you got nothing for a lifetime of decency; not a free glass of water. Not that behaving badly necessarily got you anywhere, but it was generally easier and more fun; and finally any career criminal from Albania or genocidist from Rwanda passing through London got the same medical treatment as you and better housing rights.

You didn't want to become the sort of person who didn't help an entoiled mother, but you became one. No one had helped her when she had needed it. And now her help muscles had withered away. Single mothers were especially annoying because of their dishonesty. Very few of them could hack it. They either leeched off friends and family, sucking in services and cash, or they botched it up, while maintaining how coping they were.

Outside, on the pavement, a Portuguese junkie was kneeling, while a buxom exorcist wielding a bible intoned with two back-up entreaters and sprinkled him with holy water.

Sidestepping the adjuration she threaded her way through the clumps of beggars, drug dealers, thugs and seething commuters that made up Brixton. She ran walking. To get home was all she wanted. The strength of the desire was almost alarming.

She had thought about getting out. She had been thinking about little else. And she hadn't just thought about it. Job applications. She was convinced she had sent more job applications than any other human being. They had failed. She had written more. They had failed.

Then, while she would have been happy leaving London, her boyfriend couldn't. Harun worked as a junior information officer at the Turkish Embassy, and just as he was coming to the end of his tour of duty, after three years, when she had been counting on escape, teaching English and getting a tan and a family, they had split up. She knew you couldn't have everything. Harun farted a lot and always had to be infallible on international affairs, but had a sense of humour and was punctual. Now she was again at the mercy of London's nightlife.

What was a night-out in London? Pleading your way into a club, past an earpiece which had grown a moron. Once inside you had to fight to get served, and then your money went as if you were surrendering it to bandits. She had only managed to get the deposit on her flat because of her inheritance from her grandmother. Her grandmother hadn't been well-off, but she hadn't been one for drinking, smoking, eating much, buying much, going to the cinema or indeed anywhere. She played bridge with old friends and was of a generation that worked or starved.

Everywhere she went, on holiday or on business, was better. Dublin, Copenhagen, Istanbul, St Ives, St Petersburg, Palermo. You name it, it was an improvement. You'd walk into a shop and the proprietor would say hello instead of assessing how much you would be attempting to steal. Everyone she knew talked of leaving London. Somewhere calmer. Somewhere greener. Somewhere sunnier. Somewhere else.

As she approached her house, she could see the lights on in the ground-floor flat that belonged to Gloria. Gloria, who was an interior designer, but who didn't seem to do any interior designing, not even in her flat. Her parents paid the bills, and Gloria had sex, noisily, with embarrassed men who were never seen more than twice.

In the basement flat were the Cooks. An elderly couple who had been living there for forty years; they effortlessly annihilated all the myths about the nobility of the white working class. They were sullen, smelly, fans of any manifestation of ugliness. Living in shit was evidently no problem for them, since they did nothing about the rubbish amassed, shin-high, in front of their door. For the first year she had greeted them, and been ignored. Twice, clandestinely, disgusted by the filth, she had gathered up the debris around their door. But then she gave up. Londoned.

The first floor was Rolf. An old, failed actor who lived on his own, he never had friends dropping by, because he was a bedridden inconsiderate miserabilist; a bedridden inconsiderate miserabilist, however, who had been an inconsiderate miserabilist long before he was bedridden. Yet he would never be one of those pensioners discovered long after the arrival of decomposition, because he was too unpleasant. A file of social workers shambled up to his flat, grimacing but reliable.

When she had moved in she had listened politely to Rolf's stories of being stranded in Ethiopia, playing third lackey in a film that had run out of finance, and explaining why he had to keep a pool table in the hallway, a full-sized one that made it difficult for the other residents to get past.

In his favour Rolf was at least under her flat. His bathroom regularly flooded Gloria's flat, but he wouldn't do anything effective about it. It was fascinating how you could not care at all about others and still be cared for. One summer when she had worked at a giant campsite in Normandy she had noticed how the decent customers got the nightmarish reps and how the decent reps got the nightmarish customers. Invariably the nightmarish reps never got the nightmarish customers any more than the decent reps got the decent customers.

Then, up on the second floor, she saw traces of light in her flat. Even though she assumed she must have left a light on in the morning when she left, she couldn't suppress a creep of anxiety. This was a city where everything was done to guarantee the liberty of burglars.

Although no one was watching her, or would be able to make her out in the dark, she felt ridiculous as she fumbled with the key in the top lock. The lock had never given her grief before, but no matter how many times she slipped the key in, it refused to turn. After several minutes of failure, it occurred to her that the locks must have been changed, so persistent was the lack of turning. Had there been a burglary during the day? If the locks had been changed why wasn't there a note? She chose to ring Gloria's bell to see what was going on.

Over the intercom, a male voice answered.

'Good evening,' she asked. 'Is Gloria there, please?'

'No Gloria here.'

Had Gloria moved out? Gloria had been in the house when she moved in, but they had never got on. She had first met Gloria fifteen minutes after she had magazined one unbelievably large hairy spider and given another unbelievably large hairy spider a taste of the nine hundred and sixty-six pages of the telephone directory. She had been agitated, because they were too big to be London spiders.

'I'm Gloria. You haven't seen two largish spiders have you?' Gloria, it transpired, bred spiders. She had always thought it was blank males who collected exotic or venomous creatures to make themselves more interesting or to feel powerful because they had one of the only five Armoured Mist frogs in the world stashed under their bed, as one suitor in a pub had recounted to her.

She had directed Gloria to the spider paste. 'Kelvin. Melvin,' Gloria had obituarized. 'I let them out for exercise,' she explained when asked how they had escaped. The hatred that Gloria had launched had been quite unjustified and unbalanced and relations hadn't much improved.

'Have the locks been changed?' she asked. 'I'm in the second-floor flat and I can't get in.'

'No one's changed the locks,' the male voice insisted.

'Could you let me in please?'

'I don't know who you are.' There was a receiver-replacing con-versation-terminating clack on the intercom. She pressed the other buttons, but no one responded. In the darkness she could just perceive that the names by the buzzers on the intercom looked different, but she couldn't make out the letters. She wondered what to do. Wait for someone to go in or come out? Call for a locksmith? It was cold.

As she wandered out into the driveway, she looked back up at her flat and she saw a woman at the window looking down at her. Shocked, she didn't quite know how to react. The interloper was a woman at the wrong end of middle age, unlikely to be a burglar, but very possibly mentally ill. The interloper was unfazed, observing her for a few moments before slowly retreating to the inner reaches of the flat.

She hit her own buzzer: 'Who are you?'

'Sorry?'

'What are you doing in my flat?'

'I don't know who you're looking for, but this is the second-floor flat.'

'I know. I've lived in it for seven years.'

'No. I've lived here for seven years.'

'If you don't let me in, I'll call the police.'

'If you don't go away, I'll call the police.'

'This has gone far enough.'

'This has gone far enough. If it's your flat why is it that I'm in here and you're out there?' Another conversation-terminating clack.

Was this some elaborate practical joke? Television chicanery? She looked around for concealed chucklers. If it was a joke, she would exact terrible revenge. She retrieved her phone from her bag, but, to top it all, it wouldn't work. Gagging with rage she strode over to the nearest payphone and called the police. After hanging on for several minutes, she explained that someone was in her flat. She then paced up and down in the driveway for twenty minutes, past the orange bathtub that had been there for months, and which, certainly, would be there for months to come. Eventually the police shot past with the sirens going. A few minutes later, they drove back and stopped in her driveway.

Two police officers emerged from the car with that caution police officers exhibit in case someone starts shooting at them. One was a policewoman who must have been the result of some equal-opportunity mania, almost a dwarf, tubby and with a look that said she couldn't believe she had been accepted for the job. The other was a towering, wall-wide veteran to whom she re-explained her predicament.

The police drew down the woman in her flat. Her name was Mrs Gardiner. Her name was inscribed by the bell. Mrs Gardiner swiftly produced correspondence from utility companies that enthroned her as the rightful occupant. The mystery man from the ground-floor flat maintained Mrs Gardiner had been living there for years.

They went upstairs to the flat – Rolf's pool table vanished – where her claim that the curtains in the back bedroom were red was proved wrong. All her belongings were gone. The flat had been totally redecorated, refurnished.

She was asked to provide any evidence that she lived there. She could have sworn she had a letter from her bank in her bag, but it was gone. Mrs Gardiner now studied her with the compassion reserved for the mentally ill who have just done something awful to themselves. The policeman couldn't have been more sympathetic as tears bunched in her eyes.

'I'd like to help,' said the policeman. 'But you see how it looks. This lady has proof of residence. You don't. Your keys don't fit any of the locks. The neighbours say they've never seen you before. Are you on some medication?'

Mrs Gardiner commented, 'She needs help.'

The rage and the weariness made her leave. She couldn't bear to see how they looked at her. She didn't know what to do. She walked over to the nearby newsagent run by a barely counter-high Asian woman who greeted her.

'You know me, don't you?'

'Of course,' the newsagent replied, but as soon as she replied she realized that she would have said the same thing to a complete stranger.

'Do you know what's going on over the road?'

'What's going on over the road? Something's always going on over there.'

Mechanically she started walking towards the Underground. She'd deal with this tomorrow. Stay with someone tonight and get on the case tomorrow, but none of her friends lived in the area. She tried her phone again: still not working. Stopping at the only working payphone, she tried her friends. The first attempts produced no reply. Then when she phoned Don, who was almost the last person on whose sofa she'd consider sleeping, a non-Don voice answered.

'Could I speak to Don?'

'You've got a wrong number.'

*

She punched the number again, extremely slowly to make sure she got it right, but only got the non-Don voice.

She took the Tube back into Victoria and went into the first OK-looking cheap hotel. All she wanted to do was curl up. The receptionist ran her credit card and then announced it was no good. With only a few pounds in cash, she went out to the cashpoint on the corner, and after she had tapped in her number three times, the machine ate her card.

It was now gone eleven and she took stock of how badly she stank. She made another round of phone calls. The numbers were unavailable, no one was there or an unfriendly voice would deny the person she was looking for. Finally, she returned to her office hoping to spend the night there, but when her key froze in the lock of the front door she wasn't surprised.

There was one last call to make, the one she dreaded most of all. When a strange voice answered her parents' number, she knew they were gone as well.

She caught the last train back to Brixton, and in the passageway between the two platforms, she sank down and gave way to tears.

[Tibor Fischer]

THE ABBEY

Did I?
or . . .
It *must* have been Doug.

Doug that dreamed the abbey.

An abbey of humps, just mounds
nothing you see
fields of fire-spawn, 'lion-seed, morning-stuff (tragocanth)
like so much
land forget

sun-planned derelict

I never

yes you did

you

it was obvious

like you could recover
submerged words

I said:
it was obvious
regular
symmetrical

we pretended them to be dragons' heads
or boxes with horses

something a buried castle

we play
we provide

you could balance and run

it wasn't just mud or tip-line
it was wall in it
solid, I could see it

we could all see it

nothing

until the men turned up, theodolytes, with yellow helmets, men
then

I told them.

*

To the escalator (on one side)
CRESS GARDENS . . . EARLY GRAPES . . . SUN
   PARADE OF HENRY VIII,
all that
and
TREATY OF . . . CHARTER . . . ABBEY
up the escalator.
also

we need celery, and delicatessen cheese choice
and pear pagodas,
beetroots in bottles only
for seasonal aisles
(take the past to pieces)

*

There was the good news.
There would be an abbey *and* a shopping centre.

Like having twins.

Like two-for-the-price-of-one.

Like:

Oh.

(That is good news)

*

For we deal with a living landscape.

Not just sweet sensuous hills, dips,
active hard-hat rivers
lilac-sided hymn survival
figures turning into
                      places pausing at
                              myths

Not imbued
    immanence
    measure
    motive
    or maybe even
    malice

the uselessly instructive baubles of a constitution

with its non-magnetic veins and sleeping/waking shifts
orifices, exits, that attribute and so on.

No way.

(Me, too, called out Shim.
I found a sword in the river.
It was Anglo-Saxon.
At least.
Or)

Better said,
somewhere we did not evolve,
a landscape we lived in,
conveyed life,
made to share our living
and every day

stones to jump

trawl rivers
knock the seeds out wide
at his gate

the playground
fittingly   churchground

merry-go-round

a Living Room

(sez Ulli)

thinking of all the past Living Rooms

it'll be different this time.

*

Of course, we always knew there was an abbey there, said
     officialdom.
The river site.
The proximity of the watermill.
Likely to be a traditional nexus of friendly (wallpaper) industry.
And again the river.
Some documents, but we lost them.
We didn't expect to actually be able . . .

*

The Sultan summoned his viziers.
'I want a map, a chart, a record of my kingdom.'
They began with lines.
Soon they had to add symbols.
For accuracy, the scale got more intense . . .
And after a heated meeting they agreed . . .
It could only be 1:1.

In some respects the result was cumbersome.

They unrolled a bit of it before the Sultan's throne.
He was delighted.
'Unroll it all!'

By comparison,
what is underneath
may now seem perfectly dull.

'Underneath – they said – there will be a series of stone foundations,
walls, that sort of thing.
Or there will be, when we finish.'

We respect our tangible monuments.
Maybe only outlines.
Bone-views.
But it has to be in stone.

There were diggers and barrows,
lots of trowels freshening up,
bits of string (big square, little square)
and more informed speculation than a betting shop
at the eve a great fight
which is relatively simple compared.
To?
crockery and earthed iron.
obols of baked tile, stains of réfuse,
anomalies of rubber . . .

Hang on – said the People of the Supermarket –
Can we move the whole thing six foot north?

*

It is easy to get lost.
To wander from one land to another in meander

The skill is

bike balance
girl friending

Till you grow
Alexander to the end.
The big trees in their heavy voices warn him
No you will never . . .
You cannot expect . . .
(Tell me, sez Alexander, what)
How you will never reach home . . .

                        *

Doug in the newspapers.
Probably not.

Went to look.
But not much to see.

Something of an outline?
Fat, wide edges, and
– not square –
a rounded termination
and then ditches and boxes.

The round eastern end is called APSIDAL.
This was the Abbey Chapterhouse.
                        *

Well,
the ghosts gone
that held the crossing to the eastern choir
are slowed
left no secure keepers.
The altar was long ago borrowed n garden ornament
dock & syrupy golden rod are rooted for where were stone claws
a house of squatters, snails.

                        *

Imagine a meeting
History and Carpark would be voiced, vying
With ideas of Everyman and influential was Multistore.
My Lady Wandle was
bubbling with anxiety, pie'd forecast, decks and
rolls, presentations, some matching figures, projections,
    basically
As to the past, dig up, gone, went, start now, economically.
Rumours. Druids. The round bit. I like that.
Zod this. Here store. Here carpark. Here muddy hole. In
    middle. Mad.

Everyman knew what Douglas wanted.
We want a moat.
We want a store, with lots of elephants and toys to ride on, for
    kids.
With carpark. That's the middle bit.
On the way out – you can see it – a basement scape. OK,
    under the service road. The ground-plan, the foundations,
    like in a cellar, we can view via window-holes, that will do
    fine.
The main road can come and embank right over the top, see . . .

Enough is enough.
The monks sleep in a spare petrol reservoir, right now,
The cemetery sheers from the escalator.
In a pile.
It has all worked out.

Reconciled

Like
the
little ring of tithes and vellum at the check-out . . .

[Bill Griffiths]

PLACE I

walked the entire straight road in sunlight
from the Elephant temple to the common at Clapham
 the road still flowed on out of town
  further than Wimbledon

Kennington palace scattered in a hundred directions
across market gardens and rockeries
a thousand distressed Protestant artisans

last decade's poets
 in the throats of our new Archbishops
 who too will fall suddenly when standing up to drink

Now it is Hog's Tide the great high Wednesday
 when the slaughter of our ancestors
is remembered in the jissom of our sons

 to the earth with tremendous struggles
 we too hug the gutter spin
 grabbing the drain rats from our throats

all day the new sirens sound
and the drink-flow and the
 babble is watered into drivel
 and the fact alone of our celebrating
  is not enough for these jerks

         [Allen Fisher]

PLACE IV

after the Sluice walked upstream
   along a connecting stream to Neckringer
(the course between Bermondsey Abbey & Thames)
parts of the flow are artificial
   to make matters worse
    Kent says the stream near the Elephant temple
   to be the Tygris
and this too partly artificial

took the bus south
I couldn't get to the matter of this
if our streams are becoming artificial
   our old sources will dry
and the trees we have planted to sup them
   will wither with them
nervously striking out for more nourishment
   to fill a poison flow
that they are no longer strong enough to filter

so that the many channels become alike
   and indistinguishable
and our course is one of habit
   disregarding any process we may need

                         [Allen Fisher]

UNEARTHING

Disappearing. Disconnecting all the visual cues that advertise the presence of a mind, a self that's here somewhere, already hidden. One way this may be accomplished, a technique he's previously playground bully-tested, is by standing still, ideally in some liminal location, in some threshold area, sheltering wall that edged the school-yard, cavern, hilltop, city limit, spaces between world and under-world, skyline and sky, streetlights and wilderness. Don't move. For almost sixty years don't move. Stand still and turn to urban furniture, to your own monument, to landscape. Bypass all the cultural motion sensors, become sub- or supra-liminal, white noise on the surveillance footage. In the country of the blind the one-eyed man is king, and, better yet, invisible.

Steve Moore, sat in the armchair opposite his bed with ballpoint pen and notepad, spiral bound, neat sloping capitals, each line a blue queue leaning forward, barely masking their impatience, as the book-crammed room around him pales unnoticed into dusk there on the top of Shooters Hill. Man with a foolish grin, perfectly still, as failing light adjusts to match his ash-slide hair, to match the wet-slate gleam his skin has, the South London moontan. Slowly, the defining edge is lost in grey on grey, a photo undeveloping. The textures vanish in obliterating gloss, details excuse themselves. Fine wrinkles spreading from the corners of his eyes, curved up around the brow, curved down around the cheekbones, face like a magnetic field. All this erased and then the body outline fades, the slight frame that conspires with posture to seem even slighter, basically an Adam's apple and its support system, melted, gone into the darkening of the cosy room, the manhutch with its pagan icon huddle. Finally the only light is this of the metropolis, the great black garden of a million flowers on fire spread supine and magnificent below his rear, north-facing bedroom window. This and moonlight.

Black on silver-dusted black the hill pokes up its positive yang terminal into the night's electrolyte, plated across the centuries with urban dream in a metallic rind. Seabed before the ice age, residues of fossil night-sweat crown the tumulus, a cradle-cap of gravel sheltering the clay and chalk beneath while all around wore down to lowland, marine aeons half-remembered still in seaside decors that incongruously dot the closes and steep lanes. Its sickle-shaped mass crystal-shot with *Selenites Rhomboidalis*, Shooters Hill is dreaming

London, dreaming London up: low on its northern slope a chalk fault that collapsed creating the Thames valley, gouging out a life-sump for the Neolithic swill to fill, the pallid Morlock scrum, chalk-mining chavs blowing their barter on bone bling in settlements at Plumstead, Woolwich, barnacled below the sleeping hill's north flank. Part of a queasy hypnagogic swirl erupting from its moonstone synapses the Stone Age shacks and faces flow like liquid, an accelerated morph seen from its geological perspective, turning into Bronze Age fishing villages and Trinovante squints. Riff-raff gets buried under middling heaps at Blackheath, kings and chieftains in great mounds up on the hilltop, sacred bulges on the hunched horizon. Five of these were flattened when they built the Lang Estate in the late 1930s but still one remains, a railed-off and grassed-over hump there at the junction of Plum Lane and Brinklow Crescent, sole surviving god of Shooters Hill and also dreaming, underneath the yellow weeds. Down on the far side is the boundary where the dream ends. Kent begins, and London disappears.

Back in the bedroom of the house where he's lived all his life, Steve Moore lies facing shelves of I Ching reference volumes, fast asleep on his right side so as to soothe that faltering gurgle in the ventricles, not half a dozen paces from the spot where he was born. Close to his face, upon a book-bare ledge, stands framed the gem-like miniature he painted during April 1989, a portrait of Selene, Greek moon goddess, moon herself, naked and white, the sable-stippled cunt, the eyes and lips that seem to move beneath the glass fogged by a silver aerosol, his every night-breath. There beside the picture rests the notepad and the ballpoint pen. Waking to dark or dawn's stone-blue he'll scrawl his dreams down, key words, phrases, image-prompts for later when they'll be typed up in full and added to the ring-bound stack, the log of an alternate life meticulously kept for more than thirty years with earlier entries dating from his childhood, messages from otherworldly scientists with winsome daughters on the planet Uniceptor IV. Faint tremors in balloon-thin eyelid skin betray the alien jostle taking place below, the nightlife. Skimming frictionless, his shoe-soles half an inch above the paving slabs, he slips through lamp-lit streets, disturbing analogues of those he grew among, walks to this day. To lift the plain black cover of a dream-file is to fretfully peel back a rectangle of tarmac from the skin of the locale, exposing a new stratum, laying bare a shadow neighbourhood beneath and making audible the creepy chat of shadow neighbours, ghost-train gossip, twilight ideologies.

He dreams the hill with different weather and new cellars. Giant roses hanging in the night sky over Plumstead or pellucid covered markets under Blackheath. The unnerving day-deserted cul-de-sacs and the 8,000-year-old woodlands just across the humming road become the sets of strange pre-title sequences for lost *Avengers* episodes. Diana Rigg, dead relatives and Hong Kong action movie stars move purposeful and sinister through semi-detached situations under lead skies. Elevator doors shrug shut before the lift slides sideways through unfathomable offices. Loveable horrors squirming in the garden pond. He takes a shit on the top deck of a 486 bus labouring towards the crest, sees roadside excavations of unearthly marble, massive buried architectures in a style he knows from somewhere, Greek or Babylonian Art Nouveau. He dreams a goatman, small and black, lounging insouciantly atop the back path's midnight hedge. He dreams his room, he dreams the three-by-five-inch portrait of the goddess within misting distance of his slumbering lips. He dreams the hill. The hill dreams London.

Arced across its crown is Watling Street, is Shooters Hill Road, the old Dover Road, along which channel the transforming energies leak in, foam downhill to engulf the capital. Julius Caesar's brief exploratory sortie during 55 BC had its first sight of the new principality from here, as did Agricola's more serious invasion force that followed later by almost a century. The same hushed apprehensions of a vast and brilliant counterpane below, untidily tucked under at the far horizion, messy and unmade, the river's copper ribbon spooled across it, crumpling towards the east and settlements like biscuit crumbs. The three great woods, Jack, Castle, Oxleas, rolling up the hill in black iron wave-fronts, smashing in a pale green spray across the peak and into Kent. Briefly, amid its breathless fluid tumble of alarming images, the hill hallucinates a filigree of Roman ideology, a loosely outlined golden threadwork stitched half-heartedly into the landscape's quilt, immediately unpicked, un-ravelled in a pungent woolly tangle of new Saxon place names, Eltham, Charlton, Plumstead, Woolwich, Welling. Sheters Hill? The road becomes a drovers' track, an overloaded artery to pump the meat and money up, the massive herds a grubby, lousy scarf wound out along its length. The gas-fat crowbait fallen into wayside ditches blurs to grease and blowflies, melts into the rockdream's rush and flicker, the frenetic lantern-show erupting in chalk scribbles, boiling clay, out of a subterrene unconscious, flash-frames in the blacked-out skull theatre of a buried Bronze Age god.

Jet coral, London is accumulated, squirms and grows in the detached gaze of the vantage. Royal successions in a strobe of ermine. On the cow track swarming spectres crackle into being and as soon are vanished, blazing specks and filaments scratched white upon the film's emulsion. Out a-Maying with one of his Catherines, Henry VIII attends a Robin Hood Fair, Shooters hill as medieval theme park, and meets players dressed as Robin, Friar Tuck, Will Scarlet, Bashful, Goofy. Soon thereafter Anne of Cleves crosses the hill and is immediately sent packing back the same way, failing to live up to the Hans Holbein PR package that preceded her. Archery ranges smeared across the lower slopes towards the east provide the shooters who will either give the hill its name or else will lend that name a spurious justification, and the sixteenth century whistles by, a rattling sideways rain of arrows.

At the ragged edges of Elizabethan London's proto-psychedelic swoon, murderers blossom on the steep road's wooded margins, springing up around the base of the armada beacon raised in 1588, cutpurses ripening to cut-throats, claret splashed across the turnpike and, inevitably, a new nickname: Hill of Blood, a missing psycho-tronic flick from Herschel Gordon Lewis, William Castle. Agent Orange options are employed to thin the bandit cover. Come the 1600s and the shearing of the hill commences, north side gradually reduced to Roundhead stubble. Come the eighteenth century and building starts, the place's fever-visions crystallized to lines and corners, brick growths thrusting through the shaven scalp, the coronet materializing one point at a time. First inns arrive, providing watering holes for drovers, boltholes for the highwaymen, and holes in general. Fanny on the Hill, the Catherine Wheel, Sun in the Sands, and then in 1749 the crowning glory of the Bull, palatial edifice erected on the summit with its glittering pleasure gardens, with its wells and fields and stables, its star chef and its extensive cellars.

Sumptuous hostelries and god-like view now make the dreaming hill itself a focal point for human aspirations, human dreams, as inns are followed by the follies, haunts and halls of hubris-sozzled toffs groping towards Olympus. Princess Charlotte dwells at Shrewsbury House, face underlit a ghostly scarab green by bubbling glass retorts, a first stab at extracting gas from coal. A little further down the hillside to the east, in the still-wooded reaches south of Watling Street, the widow of Sir William James raises a single-turret castle, Severndroog, in 1784, commemorating her late husband's naval victory over the pirate chieftain Conagee Angria at his Malabar coast sea-fort thirty years before. The tower looms up to peer between the treetops at the city spread below, brass sight-lines set into its wooden crow's-nest rail aligned with distant London monuments, with neighbouring counties, watching for the brigand hordes that may one day seethe from the backed-up drain of the metropolis, engulf the hill in rum, bum, concertina, cheap accessories. Just up the road, the Lidgbird family are owners of the land on which the Bull is standing, with their stately pile Broom Hall next door and on the right, while at the hill's foot by the gallows and the gibbet-fields are former Neolithic camps accumulating mass and muscle, the Royal Arsenal and Royal Artillery in Woolwich from the kick-off of the eighteenth century. Burned-powder notes perfume the nagging westerly, spark flintlock images of plunder, war and revolution in the free-associating stone subconscious, in its perilous, delirious mix.

Always a touchstone of imaginings and point of moonrise for

the ancient settlements, their dead kings hulking from its turf, the heap attracts new fictions now. Already a collage of other men's exploits and novelists' inventions, the Dick Turpin story is attached to Shooters Hill, the Essex Boy misplaced in a confusion over rumoured hiding places deep in nearby woods. Then, at the century's end during the 1790s, Sydney Carton's Dover-bound coach founders in the mudslide up towards the brink, its passengers dismounting terrified on the notorious bloodhill, made hysterically blind to the glaring façade of the Bull Inn, there at the peak for more than forty years by then. The fictions come, and next the fiction-mongers. During 1800, Wordsworth, barely thirty, has his cottage overlooking Woolwich Common underneath the hill, and as the villas of the middle classes start to fill the spaces between hilltop mansions in the early nineteenth century, Algernon Blackwood's future family home and birthplace buds among them. The new residents are prisoners in fairyland, commuters waiting for a train of neon rollergirls to carry them Starlight Express into eternity. They line up at the mounting block, stood knee-deep in a fertile scurf of faltered social visions, different fictions, no less wistful. Shooters Hill as healing spa or even enclave hilltop town, as site of a colossal pyramid, titanic mausoleum for the nation's Titan dead. The slowly spreading actual homes and streets, unwittingly, invariably, sink foundations deep into a pre-existent dreamcrust.

Steve Moore sleeps on wrinkled bedsheets made of a sand beneath Silurian seas. He sleeps, a dim encysted mass within the glacier ice, or cradled in the highest boughs of prehistoric forest. Mumbling, he rolls over into servant quarters in Broom Hall's east wing before the walls dissolve, are realigned into those of the quiet semi he shares with his elder brother, with his goddess, with his books, his work. The closed eyes, wearing an absence of spectacles, a hand pressed bloodless, tingling, between his knees and worlds away the woman-next-door's hall clock chimes another quarter-hour with brisk and brass enthusiasm inappropriate to the drowsing moment. Ageing-paper perfumes stew and simmer at the threshold of awareness, and the soft trough between lower lip and front teeth silts with curds of mango pulps, its citrus flinch smoothed into a thick equatorial honey, sweet and rounded as a Gauguin buttock. Everything he is, his biologic destiny, his father's stroke approaching that eighth hole, blood histories, his code embroidered on the pillow's edge in spittle threads.

Back in the 1880s his paternal great-grandfather is in Dublin putting down the Fenians, his granddad born there in the barracks to a mortal term obscure and brief, ended in 1919 with his eldest son, eleven-year-old Arthur James, becoming breadwinner. He never takes to 'Arthur', more a cleared throat than a name, preferring Jim. Hurries to work through Charlton's winter streets, head down, ears aching with the chill and mesmerized by his own schoolboy shoes, their rhythm on the pavement with its suede of frost, unable to believe this is his life, Frederick Boehm's, the company producing paper-size in Belvedere there on the river, just past Plumstead, just past Welling. Panting with the pace he leaves his breath behind him, frozen dragon embryos suspended in the dark and biting air.

More than a decade later, Jim's still with the same firm when their fit new secretary starts, Winifred Mary Deeks, nine years his junior, a tidy little bit of posh from the sedate, disputed borderlands where New Cross bleeds to Lewisham. She can't stand 'Winifred', all wisps and webs and spiders in the wedding cake, sticking with Mary. Delicate and lovely, paper in her blood with printers somewhere in the background stir and older brother, Francis, in Naval Intelligence while younger sibling, Donald, works his way up through the ranks at Foyles, ends up as a distributor of academic publications specializing in the Orient. They're stepping out together before long and Jim with his own family tree all guncotton and powder-burns hardly believes his luck. They wed in 1937 and start looking for a place to live, somewhere that's safe and self-contained above the grime and hustle and their eyes drift upwards inexorably towards the hilltop, where the sky fast-forwards into black and the full moon launches itself in ambush from behind the summit, flies up at the throat of night.

They find their des res in a muted cul-de-sac just opposite the melancholic front of the Memorial Hospital, erected circa 1920 on the side of the old Admiralty Telegraph where windmill vanes once clacked their urgent semaphore. New house, one of those knocked up in the 1930s where Broom Hall had stood, a previous owner bolted after eighteen months, no reason given. Jim and Mary take up occupation here in 1938, a perfect fit with the *Mrs Dale's Diary* ambience. Peace and quiet, a cousin on the Moore side of the family moved in next door and forest just across the Dover Road, itself barely a murmur. Future stretched secure before them and both of an age where all of this could still turn out to be a song, a Ronald Colman film, a musical, Darby and Joan who once were Jack and Jill. The hopes and dreams come with the elevation, then, within a year, so does the Luftwaffe.

The Roman observation point is now the highest land between Berlin and London. Jim, his father's barrack-room nativity just one twist further down the helical ancestral staircase, mans the rocket battery that's stationed on the golf course, uphill from the former gibbet-fields. Phosphorus tracers hyphenating giant blackness, boom and siren, recoil shuddering the green and distant firebursts pluming from the cower of the city. Their sole kill disputed, shared with other guns, the battery claims to have brought down only half a bomber: one-winged like a sycamore pod, just commencing its erratic spiralling descent on London when the rockets hit, the pilot's startled profile clearly visible in the exposed cross-section cockpit, open to an iron wind. Battle of Britain over with, the couple feel they can relax, allow themselves a modest and celebratory drink of future. First son, Christopher, arrives in 1943, spit of his dad, then 1944 and V-bombs, many of which fail to clear the hill. British Intelligence is leaking fake reports to Germany of rockets overshooting London, hoping that they'll underestimate instead and hammer Kent rather than W1. Back on Shot-Over Hill there's charred gaps, sudden spaces in the uniformly 1930s rows where architectural incongruities will one day rise from scorched earth. Shooters Hill becomes a surprise pot of bricks and offal at the far end of gravity's rainbow. Two doors down gets taken out while Jim is bathing. Bathroom ceiling comes down all in one piece, trapping him there in the tub but sparing him the rain of roof and chimney that immediately follows. That could have so easily been that, Mary a single parent, Chris an only child, and all the wave of possibility to come collapsed there into suds and rubble on the sopping lino.

Even with the war's end, understandably, the pair decide to wait and see if there are any more surprises . . . Nazi flying saucers piloted by Hitler's brain, or Fourth Reich mole-machines erupting through the pavement from the hollow earth beneath . . . before they risk another child. Stephen James Moore is born to a full moon on June 11th 1949, a crescent mark staining his forearm, there upon the crescent hill. Gemini, like his brother. Fire of air, the tarot Knight of Swords, the intellectual faculty in its most pristine and idealized aspect, almost mint condition on account of having been so seldom taken from its box and played with in the human mud. The corresponding tarot trump is number six, the Lovers, the alchemic principle of *Solvé*, or analysis. Of separation. Name the baby Stephen, with the name deriving from 'stephane', a type of crown usually favoured by Greek goddesses, most notably their lunar deity. His earliest memory is of September 20th the next year, 1950, fifteen months old, held up by his mother to look at a bright blue moon, this famous rarity occasioned by vast tracts of forest then ablaze in Canada. He will remember this for years, but as a dream, like floating slowly down the stairs into the hallway's umber, or the skeletal, androgynous old woman, lower face concealed by a bandanna, who unpeels into malign existence from the wardrobe door, abducts his hapless toys.

Time is discrete from space until the eyelids close. He's snoring in the fourth dimension as a gorgeous fractal millipede, his limbs a frilly Muybridge ruff, asleep on Duchamp's staircase. He's a Julia Set, an emerald gorgon fern unwinding from the luminous coelenterate complexity that is his mother, drifting there beside him in a grand fluid continuum, the albumen contained by spacetime's egg. Jewel-coral, with his tail in the zygotic damp, his head cremated dust scattered across the Brinklow Crescent burial mound, he's a subsidiary offshoot coiling from the parent form, evolving its own crenellated intricacies but forever tied to the maternal Mandelbrot. Moored fast. Back in the captured heat of his terrestrial bed one leg kicks out, dog-basket reflex, and along the overbody's snaking flank its insectile chaotic trim of arms and legs is rippled by a Tiller Girl convulsion. In suspension, monstrous in a lotus web above eternity, amid the gem anemones he dreams his life.

The awkward childhood, raised in low cloud up on the sequestered peak and cringing at the stark immensities about him. The most lightless, smog-bound days were called 'black puddings'. Is that dream or memory, that detail? Bawling from day one at nursery, singled out as best friend and primary prey by the four-year-old sexual sadist who, as luck would have it, lives two doors away; is inescapable. With each attempt to integrate himself into the baffling social jigsaw he discovers that his ears and mouth have fists in. Suffers military hazing rituals, punishment beatings, the full Deep Cut treatment, from the Cubs. With nowhere left to go unless he wants a kicking from the Brownies, he removes to the interior, the private bone-walled Wendy House, the great indoors of books and small ventriloquistic wars to annex mantelpiece or carpet, solitary games. Excursions with his mother through the gleaming neon afterdark, a thrilling adult land of purposeful, inscrutable activity adorned by burning smears of traffic light and Leslie Hore-Belisha's beacons, down to the Granada Cinema in Welling, 1958, nine years old, he wants to melt into the foyer's gold-and-crimson glow, into a lobby-card dimension of hand-tinted slave girls, burnished gongs, oiled musclemen. *Helen of Troy* commences his obsession with Greek myth, the *Iliad* read by the age of ten and then the hungry grey sponge in his head moves on from gods and legends to soak up the planets and the constellations named for them. Science, history, astronomy and classical mythology. In his retreat from fresh air and its various antagonisms, inadvertently he has become class swot, become more eminently punchable, practically begging for it. Oi, you. Yes, you. Giglamps.

Then escape, respite. He breezes his eleven-plus exams and lands himself at Roan School, traditional boys' grammar founded in Elizabethan times near Greenwich Park, a boffin undergrowth to throw off predators, to mask the tell-tale brainiac spoor and lose himself within. Lunchtimes alone in the Observatory, the Maritime Museum. Once discovered, fantasy is cultivated as a secret vice, a paediatric opium. Steve Reeves, *Goliath and the Vampires* after a preceding nudie featurette, that worn-out picture house in Lewisham, flypaper-coloured light, the kippered matron haunting the front booth. Retrieve the ticket from between her yellowed fingers without contact, mentally reciting a backdated birth-year just in case, then downhill following a weak-tea spill of torchlight into rustling black. Science fiction, too, attracts him with its lurid, buzzing pylon. *Man Against the Stars*, a Margulies anthology of yarns reprinted from *Astounding*, only two and sixpence, picked up like food poisoning while on a holiday to Guernsey. He divides himself between the academic analyst and pulp delinquent, a deliberate schism he will never see the need to mend.

Failing to realize that his interest in the scientific has collapsed to a vestigial cover story for his fascination with the fictional, he's carried through his schooldays caught in the remorseless current of the science stream, passing six 'O' levels a year early and then sluiced into a lab job, quality control at Rank Hovis McDougall, white-faced to find that at sixteen he's a flour-grader. This last year, since 1964, he's been attending meetings of the wilfully progressive London SF Group at someone's first-floor flat in Kilburn. Moorcock is around, there's talk of making an experimental sci-fi movie from Charles Platt and Langdon Jones and every week he rides the night-train home with John Carnell, then editing *New Worlds* and nurturing its fledgling new wave, living just downhill in Plumstead. How has he descended from those crackling, inspiring heights to this, a mere laboratory hunchback, hair a dusty preview of its later self, pay-packet burning fewer holes into his pockets than the everyday slop of sulphuric acid? He regrets his choice of occupation in a week, stays there for eighteen months, his jeans eventually reduced to smoking lace. Even his first taste of a girlfriend, their eyes meeting over the retorts through a corrosive steam, is not enough to hold his interest. 'Barbara or Louise' falls by the wayside, is supplanted by a new and more enduring passion, a new signal beamed from Uniceptor IV.

Early in 1965 he's turned out his first fanzine, *Vega*, printed and distributed by the BSFA, a British amateur science-fiction publishing association, thrown himself headlong into the bitchy, blotchy, endlessly enthusiastic circle-jerk of small-press magazines, as yet still unaware how closely he is following the fatal H. P. Lovecraft template. In the Charles Platt edited *Beyond* he first reads of the new Yank comic books, Stan Lee's crowd-pleasing formula of omnipotent losers. Yeah, you may be Nordic God of Thunder, but you've got a gammy leg. You'd trade your spider-sense and ability to run up walls for just ten minutes' tops and fingers. Mythic beings wearing science-fiction pants against a mournful and distressed Jack Kirby bowery, paranoid Steve Ditko skyline. How can he resist? Immersing himself in the garish newsprint flood that crosses the Atlantic by erratic spurts, as ballast, he drinks in the warm new smell of raw America. Swiftly acquiring a discerning eye he gravitates towards the somehow more distinguished product issuing out from the stable of Stan Lee's main rival, former Lovecraft literary agent Julius Schwarz. The science fiction here is old school, classical, romantic, perfect men and women on a field of stars, described with clean lines, Carmine Infantino's Cadillac-smooth sweep or Gil Kane's Michelangelo anatomies, weightless in sculpted plastic space. He's hooked, and, meeting amiable Brummie proto-comicfan Phil Clarke at 1965's London-based World S. F. Convention, he decides to put together the UK's first comics fanzine, *Ka-Pow #1*, dot-screened Adam West onomatopoeia, Ronco spirit-duplicated, purple carbon process, ghostly violet pages with a methylated bombsite tang. In 1967, fired by new resolve, he says goodbye to Rank Hovis McDougall, goodbye to Louise-or-Barbara, and seeks employment in the Funhouse.

Seventeen, and hanging up his flour-grader's hat to work as office boy for Odhams Press. Everyone tells him it's a bad idea. He starts there on May 1ˢᵗ to find HQ closed for the public holiday when he calls to collect his documents. Free games for May. A jumpy hippy kid, his chestnut hair cautiously inching past his collar, wallflower in the Perfumed Garden, within three months he's the junior sub-editor of *POW!*, Odhams's endearingly club-footed stab at duplicating Stan Lee's meteoric rise on this side of the pond. Here he hooks up with the evolving backbone of a future British comic scene, Steve Parkhouse and Mike Higgs, Kevin O'Neill, a pre-Pre-Raphaelite Barry Windsor Smith, and has to suffer an alliterative nickname in the slavishly reprised 'Smilin' Stan' style of Marvel Comics in the US: Sunny Steve Moore, with the planetary attribution so exactly wrong.

Co-organizer of the first comics convention in this country he is founder to an institution he will one day shun in horror, but back then it still seems such a good idea. He's hanging out at Britain's first comics and science-fiction bookshop, *Dark They Were and Golden Eyed*, a shimmering joss-stick-scented fug in Bedfordbury, then in Berwick Street, the offices of *International Times* next door, with Charles Shaar Murray or Mick Farren dropping in to pick up that month's *Silver Surfer* or swap counter-culture quips across the counter with 'Bram' Stokes, the archetypal bead-strung freak proprietor. By 1968 he's corresponding with Bob Rickard who within five years will launch the falling-fishes-and-spontaneous-combustion journal *Fortean Times*, he's glorying in the fizz of new ideas, new music, men upon the moon. In 1969 I met him for the first time, marvelling at his lunar lack of mental gravity, the slow and lazy arc of his creative leaps, the silver dust-plumes boiling up around his shoes, one small step for a man.

By now the exponential creep of his collection, comic books, paperbacks, pulps, fan publishing detritus, has necessitated a forced seizure of the big back bedroom from his elder brother, Chris, who's banished to the boxroom, a comfort-fit coffin just across the tiny landing. Chris is twenty-six by now, offsetting the swung-cat-free claustrophobia of his sleeping quarters with employment in the real world downhill, in his father's footsteps, with a job at the Hercules

Powder Company that Frederick Boehm's has by that time become. He'll stay there for another thirteen years then move to bar work for a while before he finds his true vocation as groundskeeper at the Golf Club, tidying the greens where his dad's rocket-battery was once positioned, crouched absorbed over this work beneath that merciless expanse of sky, pushing his chipped nails down into black soil, into the root-gauze, grounding himself, earthing, while way back in 1969, back home in Chris's former room, his younger sibling makes a fair fist at accomplishing the opposite.

An ivy carpeting of bookshelves has already claimed two walls for A. E. Van Vogt, Bradbury, Charles Harness, E. C. Tubb, Abe Merritt, the unusual suspects, covers mad with pink sand-cities and princesses, vacuum cleavage, chrome-dipped interplanetary cock, forever Saturn. Under the already sagging single bed his funnybooks are stacked, the lyric ray-gun romance *Adam Strange*, the E. C. science fantasies, Wally Wood's polythene-wrapped spacegirls with trans-solar darkness pooling under their amazing racks, Al Williamson's bright hypodermic cities soaring out of duotone-fogged fungus-jungle to impale the nebulae. Insidious four-colour radiation seeps up through the mattress from the piling pages, incubating benign crystal wireless tumours in the dozing brain, and through the fast glass of his new room's wide rear window London crawls like animator's putty, the British Telecom Tower, Canary Wharf, the Dome, the Wheel, the Gherkin, blossoming and melting in the Dan Dare spacesport seethe of the horizon. He begins to see the city from the opera-box perspective of a Chinese print, starts looking down upon it all.

In 2005 his closed lids dart and flicker, shifty REM, the thin skin blinds drawn hurriedly upon a Jungian suburban orgy going on below. Restless, he lifts from the untroubled, blissful deep-sleep sine-wave dip of the late 1960s into the uncertain toss and turn to come. In early 1969 Odhams is folded into Fleetway Publishing, IPC Magazines being the resultant amalgam, and he's one of the few staffers to survive the move. A close call, and an impetus towards diversifying, adding new strings to a bow he hopes to change by stealth into a harp. Commences writing scripts for comic weeklies, bonsai screenplays. *Wonder Car*, with art supplied by boyhood god Ron Turner, chief delineator of mid-1950s cosmic cop Rick Random, prescient name marking the future as a threshold of complexity. The 1970s are waxing and in his spare time he's working on superior fan publication *Orpheus* with Barry Smith, Steve Parkhouse, Ian Gibson, an experimental flux of words and images, attempts to wring some kind of a poetic from decaying orbits, damaged drives. 1972, in January, on a rare frost-bitten visit to Bob Rickard's place in Birmingham, he hits upon the winning mix of cannabis and late-night Hong Kong action flicks during a showing of *The Sword*, directed by and starring the adaptable Wang Yu. Between mandarin talons yellow magic grips his heart and he goes overboard, goes oriental mental and subscribes to *China Reconstructs*, pesters Uncle Don the book importer for impressive hardback tomes on Chinese history to crowd out the Ace Doubles, launches into a lifelong affair with the I Ching, eventual fellowship of the Royal Asiatic Society. Everything changes at the midnight matinée, at the box office with its moving lines. Fate hits the freeze-frame and the coins hang in the winter air.

He wants to make the jump from editorial offices and prospects that he fears may be unsound on to the listing death-trap scaffolding of a freelance existence. Editor of the impeccably hip fanzines *Stardock* and *Gothique* (back-cover collage portrait of Frank Zappa made from cops and corner stores and motorcades; an article on the right-wing agenda of the superman entitled *Popaganda; or, Why the Blue Beetle Voted for George Wallace*; Ramsey Campbell's penetrating piece on the grotesque in music, Saint-Saëns to the Velvet Underground), Stan Nicholls has established his Notting Hill Buddha frame at Bookends, a science fiction/comic/head shop out at Chepstow Place. He's offering a partnership, the opportunity to type up comic scripts during slack periods down in the bookstore's basement, too good to pass up, and those freelance assignments keep on coming, bolstering his false sense of security. *Curse of the Faceless Man*, text stories, jungle fables for the Swedish market, Tarzan of

Ikea, twenty episodes of sword-and-sorcery romp *Orek the Out-lander*. Things look every bit as bright for him as they had for his parents at their new house on the hill in 1948, but this time it's not doodlebugs or German bombers. It's the Met, the Obscene Publications Squad. No warning sirens and no backyard shelter for the R. Crumb cum-shots or the S. Clay Wilson severed pirate-dicks to huddle in until everything's over. There's no ack-ack shooting back: during all this his father dies, a golf-course stroke, just short of turning sixty-five. The pulmonary guns fire everything they've got into a popping strobe-lit heaven, emptying the chambers.

Busted, Bookends is shut down, 1973. He's writing comics to pay off five grand in business debts, but it's a largely loveless chore these days, the glitter long since rubbed from all the stern-eyed starmen, alter-ego icons for more optimistic times. Horror and weirdness, that's his tipple now. Bob Rickard's launched *Fortean Times*, a small-print black-and-white blast of excluded news, damned data and Hunt Emerson cartoons from the polymath clutter of his Birmingham bedroom, its shoebox morgue files full of thunder-stones and Owlmen, Morgawr, simulacra, Indrid Cold. Our man elects to pitch in with a study of the mystery beasts at large on Shooters Hill, black panthers, black dogs, Black Shuck, sighted mostly in proximity to the location's many water features, streams and mineral springs and the forgotten Ket or Quaggy rivers. He's attempting to relate all this to Taoist principles, the dark and watery Yin, the broken line, while almost unintentionally he begins to map the hill's imaginary contours and astral topographies for the first time, as if he's only just this moment realized where he is.

Meanwhile the days grind forward measured in worn-out type-writer ribbons. In 1974 he lands a gig at Thorpe & Porter's *House of Hammer*, scripts *The Legend of the Seven Golden Vampires*, captions oozing his still-burgeoning obsession with Cathay. 1975, he's writing endless children's annuals, documenting the Sex Secrets of Bangkok for a soft-core relaunch of *Tit Bits*, ducking furtively behind the mystifying pseudonym of Pedro Henry. When the work is thin, down to the Croxley onion-skin, he'll work a day or two for Bram

Stokes at the relocated *Dark They Were and Golden Eyed* along the faintly miserable defile of St Anne's Court. Conveniently, this is where the Charlie Fort crowd get together once a week to sort their clippings out by category, BVM or SHC or MIB. He has his hand read by a friend of Ion Will, the hero in Ken Campbell's *Fortean Caper*, and is told that when he's twenty-seven he will meet the woman he is meant for. Mantically misled, on reaching the appointed age in June 1976 he misidentifies a wan-but-personable co-worker at the shop as his intended but she's not, she's not. She's got a boyfriend, got a monkey, and the railtrack creases in his palm were wrong, led only to this disused branch line, this neglected siding.

In October, quietly, imperceptibly, the filmy and prismatic bubble of his life explodes, burst by a fingertip, from the outside.

He's bought an exorcism-sword on the first day of the new month, 108 Chinese coins, *cash* coins, the perfect geomantic number, square holes at their centres, bound together by red thread into the flat shape of a ritual blade, for banishing. A King of Swords, the Hebrew letter that's attributed to his tarot trump being Zain, a sword, his passion for sinology awakened by Wang Yu's *The Sword*, and now this. Clearly asking for it, he decides to use his new toy in a first-time improvised attempt at magic, winging it, asking for guidance and, if it's not too much trouble, a confirming dream. At four o'clock next morning he wakes up to darkness and a male voice whispering a single word into his ear.

'Endymion.'

At first it's gibberish, another false start like all that matchmaking palmistry, then he remembers where he's come across the word before, a book he'd not especially enjoyed, *Erotic World of Faerie*. It's a poem by John Keats based on a Greek myth, its last fifty lines written at Boxhill, one of the heights visible from Shooters Hill towards the south. It seems Endymion's a shepherd boy who falls in love with the divine Selene, goddess of the moon and Moon itself. Reciprocating his affections, she explains that since she is the queen of night and dreams, there are no means by which he might be with her always other than the death-in-life of an eternal sleep, an offer that he gratefully accepts, and that's it, more or less. Lucian has Endymion on the moon in his *True History*, as pirated by Karl Friedrich Hieronymous, Baron Von Munchausen, which leads to Robin Williams mugging his way through the role in Terry Gilliam's film adaptation. Frankly, none of this seems very promising.

Then the coincidences start, the library angels hurling some required book from the shelves down to the tiled floor at his feet. His life, his human narrative, begins to trespass on the draughty borderlines of the Fantastic as defined by Tzvetan Todorov, a literature of hesitation that refuses to decide between a rational or supernatural resolution. Henry James's *Turn of the Screw*: are spectral entities at work here or has the protagonist gone bonkers? Dreams and signs provoke him to investigate the source material, the unembellished myth, and he accumulates a massive library of classics that will match the still-expanding I Ching and science-fantasy collections, will necessitate surrendering another bedroom wall to academic kudzu. He tracks down the legend's pedigree to Mount Latmos in Turkey, the discovery of caves believed to be the hermit shelters of dream-oracles, *Luftmensch*, their lives spent in the presence of their lunar goddess, on the nod, perhaps dosed up on extracts of her sacred, visionary flower. Was this Endymion, his origin, or maybe an Endymion cult? Shooters Hill, Boxhill, Latmos, something about hills here, hills and caves. There at his research in his anchorite retreat upon the summit he constructs another joint and he considers, gradually identifies, as out beyond his window the decade winds down towards its discontented winter, its plutonium blond denouement. This is how it is at the approach of the uncanny, each progression in our comprehension of the concept like a footfall treading softly closer. This is how we act, no awe, no terror, just bland reassurance in our default certainty that this can't possibly be happening.

Meanwhile, back on earth, his native planet, things are going well. Regular work for 2000AD or Marvel Comics' UK satellite, Selene and a smattering of Olympeans cavorting with Tom Baker in the slick Dave Gibbons-crafted pages that he scripts for Marvel's *Dr Who*. Entire Selenic empires of argent imperatrices fall into decline in the back-story of *Laser Eraser*, penned for stylish independent *Warrior* in 1981. At this last publication's New Cross comic shop-cum-offices in 1982 he's ruinously smitten once again, picks up another damp and sputtering torch, another big-eyed china doll behind the counter of a mylar-lined emporium. While she's on holiday that summer he completes a first draft of the book-length piece of I Ching scholarship he's working on, *Trigrams of Han*, a drastic reinterpretation of the oracle which overturns, authoritatively, long decades of accreted dogma on the subject and proposes a more complex and sophisticated model, a mnemonic mapping of the ancient Chinese worldview in its convolute entirety, imagining that this is how one goes about impressing pretty girls. In 1984 with the demise of *Warrior* he moves with her to a shared house in Westcliff, Essex, the sole change of address he will make during his lifetime. Sticks it for three painful months and then comes home to the familiar bed, familiar view, familiar chair. His mother hasn't touched a thing. In 1985 he and his brother find one day they cannot wake her and the morning that she didn't make, its pencil-crayon light diffused on the unmoving eiderdown, death like her life demure, transacted without inconveniencing anyone. Mary, whom he took after. Every other night she still calls from the kitchen in his dreams.

The 1980s burn down, guttering, with so much gone and melted. Westcliff woman married with a kid, they still think of each other as good friends but, well, you know. His mum's gone too, these stabilizing female gravities, these planets breaking from his system, spinning off into the stars. The only woman who retains her influence upon him lives in Downing Street, is running down herself with super-villain tic in one eye, one hand now a pincer, will be gone within a year. The spring gusts on the hill's brow have a sense of resolution, a brave melancholia, an urge to something as yet without form. For reasons that he only poorly understands he has the sudden yen to dust off undeveloped drawing skills left on a high shelf since those early fanzine days, just for the exercise. Best start with something small. Small and erotic, to ensure that the enthusiasm needed to complete the project is maintained, Bog-Venus logic. Knows himself too well.

He starts to paint the body of the goddess, of the female that he first encountered in 1976, the foretold age of twenty-seven, couchant on a ground of turquoise night, naked except for her stephane, her crown, the spill of auburn splashing down upon her breasts, her shoulders. She sits unselfconsciously, her legs apart, *Déjeuner sur l'herbe*. He tries to make her face that of his recently lost love but here the licked-sharp brush refuses, cleaving to its own agendas. Diamond highlights animate the eyes, the gaze engaged, amused and up for trouble. For a while her smile eludes him, long nights' precious labour on her lips, the dawning knowledge that this graven image, this commandment-breaker, is the seal of an insoluble commitment. After something like a week she's finished, the addictive toil curtailed, contained within the narrow wooden limits of a prop-up frame to set beside the armchair he makes notes in, on the desk he types at, by his bed. *You saw me standing alone, without a dream in my heart, without a love of my own.* The shape made by her limp white limbs becomes a tender rune, an ampersand belonging to an alphabet of greater passion, stronger meaning, drinking in the energy of his attention, of his writing, of his work, his sex, his sleep, until the framed glass hums with it, lenses the trapped vibrations back into the room's air-pocket ambience, a high-pitched alpha drone on its periphery. Emotionally compressed, the bubble habitat heats up, exhibits sonoluminescence, starts to shine.

Over the next few years the sense of contact ebbs and flows, never recedes entirely while he's busy with the US colour version of *Laser Eraser*, earning, yearning, finishing *Trigrams of Han* and finding it a publisher on money that his mum has left, or grafting as a contract writer/editor for the going concern that *Fortean Times* increasingly has started to become. *Viz* magnate John Brown is the magazine's new publisher, its circulation rising as its genuinely interesting hardcore content dips, its articles on lexical linkages or its psychometric scrying of American arcana shunted out in favour of *X-Files*-related cover features, rubber Roswell autopsies. A bigfoot stumble, coughing in the dust of a bandwagon as it rumbles off to disappear for ever into Area 51. Meanwhile the postcard-sized framed portrait has become the portal where he stands and stares, replacing the grand panorama of the outer world beyond his bedroom window with its moonless view. She's there behind the glass, a different universe just millimetres from his fingertips, with everything she represents. Divine light. The romance of sorcery.

Aleister Crowley calls it a disease of language. Spot it from a mile off, the enflamed vocabulary, the light-headed syntax. Luckily, most of the population have been immunized by C. S. Lewis, Tolkien, J. K. Rowling, Buffy, by exposure to the virus in the form of a dead culture, something that will force no-nonsense antibodies to kick in without the danger of full-blown enchantment. Texts that act as disinfectant, language pasteurized for ordinary consumption, all the ontological blue mould scraped off, the strange loops of self-reference, the pathogens, words so far past their best-before date that they're crawling, they're alive. Virulent rhetoric is thus pro-scribed, no dirty intercourse allowed except for those professions where hot contact cannot be avoided, so effectively magic becomes less a disease of language, more an occupational complaint of writers. Stirring cloudy coffee at the tearooms tucked away in Castle Woods where Golden Dawn old boy Algernon Blackwood's family home once stood, he knows it's already too late for him, already in his bloodstream. He's high risk, susceptible, OTO positive, the I Ching work and covert goddess-worship markers of occult predisposition. Warily investigating, he affiliates himself in 1992 to a magical order, the Illuminates of Thanateros; their temple a New Cross recording studio. Chaos magic, though the name seems harsh. Bit of a mess at worst, more teen goth's bedroom than inchoate pre-creational abyss. He chants along with all the others for a while, recalls his lip-synched prayers at school assembly, then has the temerity to inquire of an order head if there's a reason why the ceremonial robes have to be black, is told in lieu of answer that it shows colossal ignorance to even ask. God, what if everybody questioned the most basic principles of ritual like that? It'd be chaos.

Clearly not for him, warmed over Austin Osman Spare without requirement to tread too close to the edge of the apocalyptic Brixton artist/shaman's risky line. He holds out for a month or two then jacks it in, though not without a certain fidgety dissatisfaction, an impatience with the numinous. You get all dressed up and she doesn't show. You turn up at the juju showroom to take magic for a test drive and can't get it off the lot, while all the senior salesmen stand around and suck their teeth. Maybe it hasn't got an engine, maybe that whole internal combustion thing was only crazy talk, and yet the promise in her eyes, behind the glass, beside the bed. There must be more to wizardry than this, this Gandalf-with-his-knob-pierced stuff. Where's the romantic rush, the Blake ache? Where's the Art?

At this point the narrator, up to now concealed behind the safety curtain, trying to keep out of it, must advertise his presence with a cough without allowing this to turn to a John Silence story, to a yarn where the intrepid house-on-haunted-hill investigator is reluctantly, predictably drawn in and made a witness to the awful outcome, to the vanishing, the giant hand from beyond. I've been along with him for most of the above, entranced and fascinated, following his lead, convinced that the smart money was on this unlikely scarecrow. *All about Eve*, him as Bette Davis. Follow him into the drug-fug of the 1960s underground and through the *Fortean* ruminations of the 1970s; into the comic-writing thing, his red corrections vivid and instructive lacerations on those first trial scripts, twenty-five years back. In the early 1990s with a three-lane pile-up of a marriage still receding in the rear-view mirror, following him into magic seems a good idea, a way to steer the vehicle of writing off the speedway of career into fluorescent wasteland. His forays in organized contemporary magical society, all his New Cross necromantic nights, are watched with interest. Let's see if this sends him mad or kills him before making any personal investment. Sharing his frustration and his disappointment when it fizzles out without result, late-night conversations as to what a genuinely modern magic worldview might entail, more literary and progressive, texts to represent the body of the god that may in some way then be treated or manipulated, Set/Osiris, Burroughs/Gysin, two cut-up techniques somehow reduced to one, the psilocybin dialogues blithely wandering through riff, hypothesis and rant towards a hidden precipice.

Visiting him. January 7th 1994, the cab ride up from Lewisham through Blackheath with its ghosts. The Bronze Age rabble who weren't on the list when they were handing out the hilltop burial mounds. Montague Druitt, cricketer and fit-up Ripper suspect with his astral doppelgänger David Lindsay, author of *A Voyage to Arcturus*, translucent fantasy that opens at a London seance then progresses into fiery allegorical terrain that characters must sprout new sensory organs even to perceive. The taxi shifts down, struggling up the hill towards its brink, and there is the familiar illusion that this raised, uncomfortably close horizon may have only sheer drop on the other side. Set down beside the road with rubies shoaling in the rush-hour dark, across from the Memorial Hospital, then those few paces down an almost hidden footpath and into the sheltering close, its paper-lantern light warm through the ring of pulled-to teatime curtains.

Welcomed in, cursory head-poke round the door into the soccer-highlight grumble of the living room to say hello to Chris, past fifty now and looking forward to early retirement from groundskeeping thanks to a pool-syndicate win some years earlier, a notable example of the elder sibling's striking-if-ambiguous relationship with probability and football, since he'll later lose one eye to flesh-eating infection in a minor wound sustained during his Sunday-morning kick-about. A game of two halves, clearly. After packing in the job he'll fill his time, he'll fill his half-share of the house with cacti, succulents, that most extraterrestrial of plants, speaking of an emotional reserve, survival in a hostile, dry environment, the water and the sweetness held inside. He and his brother with their amiably parallel existences will see the hilltop house become a border skirmish-zone, part of some age-old territorial war between the science-fiction paperbacks and the asclepiads. Exchanging genuine pleasantries with Chris, the next stop is his brother's room, the humming gem-field of its northern vista and signature two-note tinkle from the old and delicate tin wind chimes just inside the door.

Assume the customary position, semi-comfortable, slumped on the creaking bed while he sits beaming like an idiot or sensei in his armchair opposite. The conversation purrs to life from a cold start, part sputtered through a mouthful of the funny fungi, mildewed spider-roe, routine and purely recreational, a semi-regular and casual feature of the previous fifteen years. The talk drifts easily to magic in the slow three-quarter-hour approach to lift-off, something complicated, foggy, about gods as texts, linguistic entities, so if you intercut two texts together, say a god and goddess, then what kind of fusion might result, but wait a minute, wait a minute, that's not what he's saying, pay attention, it's this other stuff with one text seen as corpus of the goddess and the other one a purely purposive and causal piece of writing, a request, a spell, then cut them up and intersperse them so that god and goddess fuse together as hermaphrodite, as alloy, tempered gold and silver, chemic wedding, this is crucial, this is so important although actually that isn't quite what he's attempting to convey, we're at cross-purposes, it's more the notion of a statement of intent, a page of writing, then you take another page, an invocation to the god or goddess and you cut them up and shuffle them together so that purpose and divinity are one, so, let's see, that would mean that in the union of two passages composed to represent the male and female deities there would be a new sexual alchemy, is that right, and the struggle to express this, this is all so difficult and Jesus, man, we've just, we've just been through this, through this exact, this exact same conversation three three three times three times three times in a row.

The ceiling's gone, the room now opening upon a space above that isn't night, and something stoops, leans in from outside, gathering identity with its approach. It pushes its unfathomable face down into our aquarium, displacing world, spilling reality on heaven's front-room floor. We're flopping breathless on the holy carpeting.

This isn't meant to happen. We aren't doing anything, we're only talking and we stumble on an idea that turns out to be connected to another, then another, and the discourse makes its labouring progress upward from one concept to the next, completely unaware of climbing something's tail until it flicks, an active spirochete attending this disease of language. Dream-spine, knobbly with conceptual vertebrae but smooth as viscous liquid in its movement, living chain of muscular and dangerous notion, looping and recursive thought-meat winding, coiling back and forth upon itself, a current dragging helpless consciousness along its length in rippling peristalsis. Churning in this burning gold confusion, the awareness of having been swallowed by a snake of some kind is belated, useless, and we're riding the King's Highway, slamming primary-colour neon bumpers in the sephirothic pinball, shrieking like a roller coaster in the ricochet from zone to zone. Zone where both parties realize things could happen here, things that could shatter friendship irretrievably, and dare not speak the thought out loud. Zone where both parties realize simultaneously that they have been alone in this hallucination, none of this has really happened, that they have gone mad and all this time their colleague has been minding them, distressed, concerned, may have already called the ambulance, look, look at all that worry in his eyes. Zone like a room of dazzling white full of dead magi muttering outside of time and taller figures at the back, much taller, with the heads of animals.

The bookshelves there behind him are a hexagram with six unbroken lines, Ch'ien, the Creative, are a doorway where the brilliance bleeds through from a next room that's not there, a warren of such rooms stretching away above, below, on every side, a Hyper-London, an eternal fourfold town of lights. This is it, this is real, this lamp-glow that's inside the world like torchlight through a choirboy's cheeks, the mystical experience as Gilbert Chesterton's absurd good news, and it goes on for hours, goes on for ever. Later, as if there could be a later, separate strivings after sleep in a still-sizzling aftermath, each with identical eidetic imagery cascading, something between cooling printed circuitry and hieroglyphic stelae scrolling down behind the eyelids. And then in the morning you get up, you get on with your life, but it's a different one, at least at first, and all its streets are made a grey and glassy tracing-paper overlay, muting the colours of the rich design obscured beneath. Here sanity is on thin ice, here you could stick your foot right through the diagram. The safety buffer that's afforded by conjecture has evaporated. Sexing seraphs, noticing for the first time their startled, disapproving frowns at finding you with one hand up their frocks when you thought you were groping for a metaphor. Now everything is wonderful and hazardous, and nothing's hypothetical.

Increasingly, this includes his relationship with the tarot-scale image of the goddess resting on the shelf beside his bed. Where previously the conceit of a fond, romantic folly has provided insulation from the stark insanity of what he's been half entertaining, now the gloves are off. The poetry has jumped the fence and threatens rampage in his proudly maintained china shop of rationality. Todorov's definition of Fantastic literature as hesitation, as deferment of one's choice between a psychological or an unearthly explanation, has become his tightrope, and successful subsequent experiments with sorcery don't make things any better. She gets more real every night, is in his dreams, will sometimes break beyond the confines of the sexualized imaginary friend, of her allotted moon-nymph role, and show another face. He dreams he's in his room, almost aware that he is dreaming, almost lucid, kneeling by his bed to fumble underneath it for some misplaced *Planet Stories* pulp, and suddenly she's standing there behind him and he doesn't dare look round. Her voice, from over his left shoulder as he kneels, is not that of the young girl in his painting. This is someone older talking, someone graver with a ring of sad authority. 'There are bad times ahead, and yet because you love me, so shall I protect you. When you die, you will become a lily.'

He looks rough on visits to Northampton during 1995, passes out once or twice in public, and the magical experiments are steadily accumulating their own spooky aura. Lose each other for a moment in the busy main street's weekend shove, look round to find the other party gone, both struck by the same thought, what if we never saw the other man again? Magic is all about expanding the parameters of what is possible, and thin air suddenly seems like a possibility. That year he starts as editor of erudite and handsome *Fortean Studies*, a new journal launched by *Fortean Times* to make a home for all the fascinating academic stuff displaced by glowering spreads of Gillian Anderson, David Duchovny. Gleefully, he puts together dense anthologies of mysteries and marvels, wonders crowded to the margins by an influx of grey aliens and anal probes. The phantom Russian troops, 'snow on their boots', reported marching from the north of England during the Second World War to make a sneak attack on Germany. A self-penned contribution on the possible historic authenticity or otherwise of strange Chinese automata, the wooden oxen said to have been engineered by Chinese Merlin-figure Chuko Liang in AD 230 or thereabouts. Another piece of his on enigmatic and reputedly lunar secretions, some form of celestial cuckoo-spit known to antiquity as 'moon-foam'. This is much more like it. This is something he can get his teeth into, research and facts and dates and accurate investigation, publishing perfectionism. This is heavy, a huge intellectual anchor to prevent him drifting upwards, off into the mist, into the moonlight. Just in case, he adds some extra ballast: an exhaustive indexing by topic of *Fortean Times* for 1993 which will eventually lead to indexing the entire quarter-century of the magazine's duration, then *The Oracle*, a scholarly small-press journal of I Ching studies that he edits, then a massive bibliography of I Ching reference, from Crowley to John Cage, which he embarks on in collaboration, something for those idle moments.

Worried by his spazz-attacks and blackouts he checks with a doctor and in 1996 is told he has high blood pressure, though not that he's a high-risk cardiac catastrophe waiting to happen, which presumably they figure wouldn't help. He cuts down on the smoking and goes for a recommended walk each day around the hilltop, lanes and avenues he's not set foot in since his childhood. It's a revelation, the variety of architectural styles, the sudden incongruities in rows otherwise uniform that mark a buzz-bomb hit. Magnificently monstrous water tower, a red-brick fortress hulking there just past the Bull, and blue cut-paper torrents of hydrangea overflowing the low garden walls to spill into the streets. The postbox with a primitive horned stick-man sprayed in black upon its violent red. He taps into his family history, the blood-roots sunk into the blood-hill, reconnects with his environment and becomes reacquainted with its quanta, with its charge and spin, its strangeness and its charm.

Partway through 1998, while he's engaged, contentedly, in juggling his various and complex intellectual responsibilities, *The Oracle*, *Fortean Studies*, I Ching bibliography and the by now deranging *Fortean Times* index, his neglected love life coughs once, sits up naked on the slab and says 'Where am I?' just when everyone has given up on it. An e-affair, a dotcom romcom, a subscriber to *The Oracle* that he's been corresponding with who's fallen for him, wants to meet him. For God's sake, he's nearly fifty and he really doesn't need this; needs this desperately. She's an I Ching diviner teaching Taoist meditation and the yogic discipline Qi Gong. She lives in South America and if he'd care to he can pop out for a visit, stay there at her dad's coffee plantation for a while, her place in Rio or the beach house in Bahia. He's convinced that he's been given pages from somebody else's script, casting-department oversight, but still decides to play along, see how far he can get with normal human life before the error comes to light, before being unmasked as an impostor.

Late that summer he flies out to Rio and it's like a dream. She's beautiful, intelligent, and Qi Gong turns out to include a form of tantric sexual yoga in its repertoire, real tantra as opposed to Western magic's current usage of that term as esoteric code for 'had a wank' in case mum finds the Book of Shadows. While he's out there he smokes weed, plays poker, cultivates a taste for Scotch, unleashes an entire new personality, does everything but buy a derringer to hide, spring-loaded, up his sleeve. Sprawling beneath the stars on the plantation he discovers that the moon looks different from the Southern hemisphere, the crescent resting on its back, horns raised to gore the dark. He comes home with a proper haircut and a roguish glint, enjoys it all so much that he goes out again in 1999, invites her over for her first away match in 2000. England, understandably, is something of a shock to the Brazilian system. Life's a beach and then you hit South London, where the heatwaves bring her out in goosebumps. Meets and likes his one-eyed brother, Chris, whom thanks to errors in translation she'd assumed to be an evil Cyclops keeping Steve a prisoner in his lonely garret room, forced to hang underneath the belly of a ram if he should want to nip out to the shops, but even her relief does not endear the landscape to her. The astounding northern prospect of the city from his bedroom window is just city, lacking coast or mountains can't be called a view. The overcast skies, sunsets on a black-and-white TV when she's been used to colour. When she goes back home they part as lovers but at Heathrow there's a shift in indoor light, perhaps a misfire in the kiss, a premonition. Her black hair and coffee skin are melted, stirred into the milky pallor swirling there in the departure lounge.

Returning to his work he feels a certain apprehension in the air, a V-bomb hush that makes him restless, reckless. All this editorial responsibility will drive him bugfuck if he doesn't make a break, and so he quits *Fortean Studies* after Issue 6, concludes the indexing and bibliography, then extricates himself with honour from commitments to his *Oracle* subscribers and throws in the towel. He's got a couple of new projects on the go that will drain off the excess energy, a thorough excavation of the mythological Selene that might rescue the original text-body of the goddess from beneath a palimpsest of resprays, Robert Graves and Women's Mysteries, restore her to her former glory. This is something that's been brewing since 1976 but now he's getting down to business, loosely mapping out the necessary chapters, and then there's this other thing, this idea out of nowhere, for a novel. Something based upon the elements that have defined his life thus far, the hilltop solitude, the moon, the quarter-century back-catalogue of dreams.

He tinkers with the notion in the evenings, wants to craft an unadulterated night-work. Now that he's not smoking any more he finds he likes a glass of Scotch or three to help his mind uncoil into the still-coagulating narrative. Currently having something of a crush on the Elizabethans he's not listening to anything except gavottes, pavanes, speed garage harpsichord extravaganzas that put him in mind of his most cherished 1960s vinyl, Hendrix or the Yardbirds, a Jeff Beck deluge of notes. The sixteenth-century aural filigree infects his prose, informs his thinking with a tendency to the elaborate, an urge to decorate. By day he's come full circle, writing comic scripts for the increasingly nostalgic-sounding *2000AD*, the weekly publication traipsing nervously into its namesake year, the single dazed survivor of a home-grown comics industry that's suffered an extinction event, a migration of the native talent to America after the British comics boom exemplified by *Warrior*. The thriving field he'd given up flour-grading for all of those years ago is nearly dead, almost entirely vanished, the attendant fanzine scene turned into purple dust, all blown away, and somehow, when you think about it, this is probably his fault. In normal working hours he writes the space-Yakuza yarn *Red Fang* and the dark Ashton Smith-like *Tales of Telguth* as atonement, but when darkness falls he pours himself a shot, cranks up *Now That's What I Call Harpsichords* full volume and applies himself to his new secret labour, the new edifice he's building out of dark and drink and dreams, out of Elizabethan reggae and the hilltop's gutter-dust. He's even found a word, a name that's rattling around inside his head, a working title: 'Somnium'. Perhaps a city, lost. Perhaps an element not yet unearthed, not yet discovered.

Late 2000, early 2001, he gets the email from Brazil that he's been half expecting, breaking off the romance. They're in different hemispheres, they're under different moons. They need less space. He's upset, but the cracked chime in the gut is somehow muffled, or at least held in abeyance. What it is, he's picking up a lot of interference on the Venus waveband, garbled bursts of an emotive Morse he can't unscramble. Intermittently across the years he's been in casual, amiable contact with the yummy mummy that his botched

Westcliff elopement has become, is matey with her husband and her son, visits her maybe once a year, all that old heartache done with and behind him, pretty much. But now, with perfect or perfectly dreadful timing, her married life detonates and she's pinned underneath the rubble of divorce, no feelings in her numb extremities, calling out weakly, asking if there's anybody there. She badly needs some reassurance, as you do, to feel desirable, attractive and, OK, so if one night she hits the wine too hard and sends out some ambiguous signals then that's understandable. That's understandable to anyone who's been there, anyone but him. He gets the diagnosis wrong, completes the crossword clue that's in her late-night phone calls far too hastily, though he has no more than the first two letters, guesses 'loving' when in fact the answer's 'lonely'.

He's disoriented, lost, and all this sentimental sediment is filtered through the whisky into *Somnium*, the plot of which has by now crystallized into a mirror, is about a lovelorn writer who appears to be losing his mind on top of Shooters Hill. 'Appears to be,' so you can see that he's still clinging on to Tzvetan Todorov's Fantastic get-out clause, dangling from one end of the lifeline that was formerly his tightrope. This could yet resolve itself into a supernatural narrative rather than one of psychological collapse. *Turn of the Screw.* There's still that hesitation to hang on to, although frankly the sheer misery distilled into the prose makes it progressively more slippery, harder for anybody to maintain that vital grip, especially him. His main protagonist's a nineteenth-century author who's retreated from a doomed infatuation to seclusion in his rooms at the Bull Inn there on the hilltop. As a solace, a distraction from self-pity, he starts work upon a novel that's entitled *Somnium*, a wild romantic fantasy that's set on Shooters Hill during Elizabethan times. Already in this outline, in this book-within-a-book, the surface eddies that could deepen to a whirlpool are apparent but he presses on regardless. An Elizabethan knight, the hero of this second *Somnium*, rides to the hill upon a moonlit night and finds a hinge between two worlds, a different hilltop with a luminous marmoreal palace, giant architecture a stylistic hybrid between Mucha and Vitruvius, where dwells the incarnated lunar goddess Diana Regina. The affair develops as a convex version of Beardsley's erotic fantasy *Under the Hill*, and meanwhile in his room at the Bull Inn the bereft nineteenth-century author of all this is having dreams, with statuary and pillars from his novel found in cellars underneath the hostelry, and begins to lose sight of a line between his writing and reality.

Despite the dry-ice gothic cold front gathering around his life and fiction, it becomes quite clear that, speaking psychologically, the real twenty-first-century author of *Somnium* is setting up a flawless piece of slapstick for himself, becoming Michael Crawford at some gruesome halfway point between Frank Spencer and the Phantom of the Opera. He's got the roller skates, the plank, the tub of paste, the shopping cart. He's got the steep hill. All he needs is one good circumstantial shove, something the audience could see coming from a mile away, and a hilarious mix-up will most certainly ensue with him careening off into the laugh-track.

It's around this point that he receives a message from his Westcliff wisp of smoke, never exactly an old flame, inviting him as a much-valued chum to share her happiness at finding a new boyfriend, and it all comes down on him at once. The loss of his Brazilian woman, a deferred ache, and now this, the long shot everything was riding on, gone down at the first fence. He's drinking, riding on the redeye, and in *Somnium* his anguished nineteenth-century narrator's drinking too. He wants to die. He's dreaming blocks of excavated architecture from his novel just like his increasingly deranged protagonist, exquisite marble shards of an Elizabethan buried moon-town poking up from cellar floors, out of the hilltop dirt. His brother, Chris, is by now chairman of a local cactus-fanciers cabal, is seed-bank secretary to the International Asclepiad Society, is editor and publisher of the society's gazette, the same Gemini energy and King of Swords perfectionism as his younger sibling. Chris announces that he's travelling to South Africa during September, an asclepiad convention, perfect opportunity to find exotic specimens, weird flowers that stink like dogshit to attract the pollinating blowflies of a country without butterflies or bees. Chris plans to be away for a whole month, the first time his kid brother will have been alone there in the house that long, and right when ideologically he's at his most precarious extreme, could maybe use someone around the house to talk to who's not in his manuscript, not in his head. He goes the whole hog, plans to use the enforced solitude as background for a magical retreat, a scaled-down Abramelin ritual, withdrawal from the world into a strange hermetic space that in all likelihood turns out to be an observation ward.

His journal for September is a soberly recounted twilight travelogue, a disaffected radio-telescope view of our planet from some distant satellite. He rigorously records his nightly dreams and daily disciplines, the periods of meditation and the visualization exercises, yogic practices he learned in South America but has since customized to suit Selene-worship. Where he'd once sat with a human partner straddling his lap, their breathing circling the energy up through his chakras, down through hers, he tries the same thing now while he imagines his moon-deity astride him and it feels the same, the same sense of a shared force circulating, and he knows it's mad, he knows it's tragic, this imaginary love, this compensatory delusion, but he feels her gathering substance, feels her striving to break through. He's reading Alexandra David-Neel, the writings on Tibet, paying particular attention to her plainly told firsthand account of manufacturing a tulpa, a projected-thought form pictured with such vivid and sustained ferocity that other people can perceive it too. Can touch it. If he ventures out to buy provisions she accompanies him, her imagined form becoming gradually more stable, still there if he looks away and back again, the naked lunar goddess on his arm between the parked cars and the privet hedge, Delvaux by daylight. It's a famous Abramelin side effect, like Crowley up at Boleskine with spirits thronging on the terraces. They chat while strolling, trade the trivia of the crossroads and he hears her voice, her childish wonderment at the municipal and the mundane before they head back for their Qi Gong practice in the empty old house. Home alone?

Beyond his sphere of rapidly solidifying moonlight everyday life still goes on, but there's been a perspective switch. His moon-wife steadily gains actuality, but where's that coming from if it's not being siphoned somehow from reality itself? It seems that as his dream world has become more real, the real world has become a dream. There is an urgent phone call from the hilltop cactus club asking when Chris is coming home as it appears the treasurer has murdered his own mother and then tried to kill himself, Agatha Christie fiction, spatter on antimacassar and the spiny desert flora potted on a windowsill, green-grey, so difficult to dust. On the eleventh of the month he scrupulously makes his journal entry for that evening, noting length of time that meditations were sustained throughout the day with details of results, remarking casually in passing that apparently some hijacked planes have been flown into buildings in New York. His only comment is the observation that even apparently rock-solid mass consensual reality can flip into a new, unprecedented state as easily as can the shifting flow of situations in a dream or nightmare, just like that. He finishes the entry, stands and crosses to the window, blinking at the urban nebula suspended floating on the dark outside as he removes his spectacles and cleans them, wipes away the city that's reflected in each lens. Replacing them, he stands and listens to the silent bedroom for a moment, then he nods and chuckles in reply. Downstairs the woman-next-door's hall clock sounds the quarter hour.

September ends, and with it the retreat. His brother returns with a suitcase full of rare African monsters and becomes the cactus club's new treasurer, takes over from the previous incumbent, now incarcerated. Life at Jim and Mary's 1930s dream home soon gets back to normal, but with a Greek goddess lodging there in the back bedroom. He cuts down the drinking drastically and keeps up the Selenic ritual practices in one form or another, even now his hermitry is ended. His relationship with her becomes domestic, comfortable, as his relationship with his imagination similarly sees improvements, unsurprisingly when that's the faculty in him she represents. He's cut back on the madrigals and the Elizabethan authors to immerse himself within an absinthe-haze of decadents. Théophile

Gautier and Ernest Dowson and Richard Le Gallienne with that inspiring bifurcated afro 'do. He's crafting some of his best work, revising *Somnium* to weed out any self-indulgent soppiness and meanwhile making a return to US comic books with *Jonni Future*, elegantly purging all the too rich scientific romance and delicious *Planet Stories* cheesecake from his system in an unselfconscious paean to imaginative fantasy. He feels the goddess with him, he believes in her, of course he does, but he trained as a chemist. He's a Gemini, the *Lovers*, solvé or analysis, and he can't let himself off of the rationalist hook that easily. A King of Swords, he knows about the cutting edge of the discriminating intellect, knows about Occam and his razor. The most simple explanation for what's happening to him is obviously madness, the hypothesis requiring least elaborate unlikelihood or extra mathematical dimensions: he's a lonely old man on a hilltop who has lost his love, his bearings and his mind. A psychological denouement, no more sheltering in Todorov's convenient semantic stutter. No more hesitation.

Only one way he can play it now and that's Tibet rules. Only one way he can tell if she's a supernatural manifestation or the symptom of some brain disease, a tulpa or a tumour, and that's if somebody else can see her too. He takes the sullen, bad-complexioned Silverlink train up from Euston to Northampton, hails a cab from Castle Station and this whole account swerves unavoidably towards its Blackwood ending, stands revealed as a John Silence story all along, as *Secret Worship*, *Ancient Sorceries*, but in a different idiom, a different century. The coy narrator makes another entrance, pads his part, prepares to wrap things up with a traditional voice-over finish. 'When the hackney-carriage brought a much-loved colleague of almost four decades to my doorstep on that evening, I could not anticipate the philosophical experiment in which I should be forced to act my part, nor yet the terrible and marvellous event to which I should be made a witness.'

So he's sitting upright on my sofa, leaned against its back, his arms hung limp down by his sides, and he asks if I'm ready to begin and like a twat I say yes, and he shuts his eyes.

O chaire Selene. O chaire Selene. O chaire Selene. Oh no. Oh yes. Oh fuck she's blue, electric ultra-violet blue on her illuminated contours, see-through in the shadows like a special-effects hologram. She's riding him, she's straddling his lap, her narrow back is turned towards me and she's nothing like her picture, nothing like the way he sees her and describes her. Skinny as a rake she looks about fifteen, looks Turkish, naked, not even a moon-crown, a stephane, there's just a narrow band around her forehead, holding back her long hair that's blue-black, not auburn, and there at the front a solitary peacock feather sticking up but curling to a crescent at its tip. O chaire Selene. O chaire Selene. O chaire Selene. There's a confusion where their arms are. He's got four, the two still limp there at his sides and the translucent pair raised up and circling her waist, ghostly ring-heavy fingers resting at the small of her thin back. Her arms are likewise wrapped around him, tucked beneath his raised-up phantom limbs and passing through his real ones. Her head rests on his right breast, cranes round to look back over her left shoulder at me sitting here and gaping and her eyes, her eyes, her eyes are the one thing I recognize from the framed image that he keeps beside his bed, takes with him if he's visiting.

The gaze so full of sex and invitation and vitality that it's like stepping on a third rail, clenching both hands on a cattle fence, you can't let go, you can't let go. These are the violet eyes of beautiful Bohemia, this is the radiant face of Jazz herself and her perfume is Gaudi, is Magritte, is Baudelaire and Satie. Newgate's burning in the corners of her smile and we've all had her. There's no man or woman that I know who hasn't spent an hour, a night between her thighs lapping the moonfoam, drowning in her, worshipping, but not like him, not like this. She's theology in flames, her perfect archetypal arse a noon-blue apple shifting restless in his lap as she attempts to twist her torso round, fluorescence pooling in its hollows, tries to look at me across her shoulder, O chaire Selene, O chaire Selene, O chaire Selene and then he moves, he sits up on the sofa opening his eyes and she's dispersed, the signal breaks up in a luminous mauve talcum and we lose her . . .

'This is no good. She keeps telling me she wants to change position.'

'I could see her. She was straddling your lap and you'd got four arms, one pair up around her back and circling her waist. She'd got her head on your right shoulder. She was trying to turn it round and look back over her left shoulder at me. That was fucking unbelievable, man. Fucking awesome.'

'Yeah, that's just how we were sitting, but she wouldn't keep still, she was twisting round and looking at you. She says that she wants to get down off my lap so that she can sit facing you. Let me just put my glasses back on and get sorted.'

The remainder of the evening passes in convivial, illuminating dialogue or sometimes trialogue, with funny and disarmingly frank interjections that he relays from the empty space beside him at one end of the settee. Come one o'clock and they make their apologies, go off to bed while I sit up and have another joint before retiring, give the singing violet fire a chance to drain out from my nerve ends. In the morning they go back to London, slyly travelling on a single ticket, and I've missed my opportunity for a dramatic Blackwood-Machen-Lovecraft-Hodgson ending to the piece. 'Reader, I shot him.' No such luck. He's back on Shooters Hill completing his Selene study with a slew of comic projects looming up on the horizon, working his way through a fourth and maybe final draft of *Somnium*. Huge milky fragments of the buried hilltop citadel continue to be dug out in his dreams, hauled up from trenches by departed uncles, faecal muck wiped from the cryptic, perfect bas-reliefs. He'll soon have enough pieces to completely reconstruct the lunar palace, to impose it with his will upon the summit, a magnesium ribbon whiteness flaring over Eltham, lighting up the Progress Estate that the Lawrence killers came from in all likelihood, where once were housed canaries, female World War II munitions workers down from Woolwich Arsenal who'd been turned a brilliant yellow by the chemicals they handled. The eternal halls of Diana Regina reinstated thus, he'll walk beneath a grand triumphal archway where the relocated Bull now stands into a shining cloister, lose himself for ever in the whispering ballrooms, in the library of imaginary books, and that's the last that anyone

LONDON: CITY OF DISAPPEARANCES

shall see of him. Thin air's a possibility. His brother, Chris, will end up being fingered for his disappearance, what with all the homicidal cactus club connections and the sinister glass eye, an open-and-shut case.

He's happy. Yes, he's living in a dream but that's the deal, those are the rules, the only way that he can be with her. Rereading Keats's original *Endymion* he notices the poet's curious additions to the myth, a woman that the virginal Endymion has an affair with who is somehow necessary to prepare him for his union with the goddess, this brief love-interest referred to only as 'the Indian'. He thinks of his Brazilian beauty at her Qi Gong study centre and he wonders what to make of everything. There never was a shepherd called Endymion, no dream oracle in bygone Caria known by that name. These things, they only happen once, once in a blue moon. Latmos was a metaphor to represent the traffic-flume of Shooters Hill, its oracle caves rough-draft premonitions of his bedroom with its double-glazed mouth looking out across the ancient, sparkling city. He's Endymion. That's what the 4 a.m. voice meant, October 2nd 1976. It wasn't giving him a hint, it was identifying him. Keats's work was prophecy, a future legend channelled down the sightline linking Shooters Hill with Boxhill to the south. He's woken up to moonlight while the rest of us are still asleep, still tangled moaning in the clammy sheets of history and with vain phantoms keeping our unprofitable strife.

It's Friday, January 7th 2005, and in the bedroom's neutral smudge Steve Moore turns on his back and coughs, opens his eyes, kisses the portrait miniature good morning with the night-steeped glass like cracked ice to his lips. He checks his I Ching horoscope, the daily hexagram, this morning's being Kuan, or 'Contemplation', with its fifth line governing the week ahead. The text attached to this is 'Contemplation of my life. The superior man is without blame.' His breakfast is a muesli of heart pills in half a pint of decaf, health food, over which he mumbles a few words to Chris about arrangements for the shopping or the evening meal. The morning paper when it finally arrives is still awash with details of the Indonesian earthquake, surf's up, uh-huh, uh-huh, and so he goes upstairs to check his emails, to crack open the white Post Pak envelope containing his crisp printout copy of this manuscript. He lies back on the bed to read it with some eagerness and trepidation, it's about him after all, and mostly he enjoys it, likes the writing even though it's libellous, especially the physical descriptions when he'd previously believed himself to be a lithe Adonis in his early thirties. Some bits make him laugh, the passages concerning Westcliff and the failed Latin-American relationship elicit a faint wince, and some bits weird him out, especially this paragraph. Belatedly he realizes that it's the eleventh anniversary of that strange night back in the early 1990s when the roof came off, hair of the snake that bit him. He reads on, and reckons that the next bit's taking liberties, it's cheeky and manipulative and what's worse it's cheating.

He skims through these final pages, on to the conclusion, noting with increasing irritation and amusement that the narrative recounts how he concludes his reading, then goes out to take his morning constitutional along a route described precisely in the text that will deliver him to some lame and postmodern trompe-l'œil excuse for an ending, by the Brinklow Crescent burial mound. The thing is, even though he feels compelled to validate this true-up-until-now tale for the sake of friendship and his eye for a neat magical or literary conceit, he had been planning to go down the hill to the car-boot sale, see his personal Pirate of the Caribbean about hooky Hong Kong action DVDs, perhaps get better copies of some Shang-kwan Ling-feng movies he already has, but reading it spelled out in black and white like this he feels ashamed, deep in his wretched soul, that he should even think of abdicating his responsibility to furnish an important work with its appointed ending, just to further his embarrassing addiction to some Taiwanese bird-on-a-wire.

Grudgingly he thuds downstairs and gets his jacket, calls from the back door to Chris down in the greenhouse, explains with some difficulty the complex and metaphysical necessity for his excursion, only halfway through remembering that this was mentioned in the story, in the manuscript. He stands on the rear doorstep and looks down the hillside garden's terraced slope towards the wire-wool-coloured cumulus approaching over London from the north, deciding that he'd better take along his rolled umbrella, then recalls that this was mentioned too. He trudges back through kitchen, living room and hallway to step out into the sweet, familiar cul-de-sac. Insistently, the narrative demands that he walk up the footpath on to Shooters Hill Road. As he does so, on his right he passes near the bottleneck by which the close opens to Donaldson Road, just downhill, and thinks about the day last year when he'd glanced down towards the corner that he's crossing now from the front office window, Chris's coffin-room before their mum died and he moved into the big front bedroom. On the corner a blonde woman from some doors away that he knows well enough to say hello to was caught in a screaming fist-fight, possibly about a parking space or something, with a black girl from just down the street, before a neighbour came outside to intervene. The incident disturbed him, a behavioural lapse that the encircling houses hadn't seen before, not in his memory. Maybe with the working class dismantled or demoted to an underclass the hill's inhabitants dimly become aware they're on the bottom rung now, start reacting to the pressure from above just as their social predecessors did before them. He can feel a scummy tide-line creeping up the hillside as he walks along the short, dark corridor of trees that leads to Watling Street. How much of this tranquillity could wash away soon, could be gone?

Stepping out on to Shooters Hill Road opposite the grimy gate-posts of the old Memorial Hospital he pauses and considers a rebellion, thinks of turning downhill to his right rather than up towards his left, in flat defiance of the bullying manuscript's instructions, although actually it's pretty miserable down there. The day-care faculty for psychiatric outpatients at the old cottage hospital that's halfway down is boarded up, and at the bottom of the hill where the old gallows used to be the police station has been recently put up for sale. This is the spot Pepys mentioned back in 1661: 'I rode under a man that hangs at Shooters Hill, and a filthy sight it was to see how is the flesh shrunk from his bones.' The Hanged Man symbolizes a protracted and uncomfortable initiation, Odin dangling on the tree nine nights, the lunar number, to acquire the runic wisdom of the Norns. Thinking about it, he decides to turn left after all and stroll towards the Bull, up Shooters, Shooter's, Sheters, Shiters, Shuters or Shotover Hill, or Shoter's Held, or Shouters Helle, this last bringing to mind his neighbours and their noisy corner punch-up. Down in Woolwich, down in Plumstead, these days there are Gangsta turf wars, drive-bys, shooters gradually reclaiming the high ground named after them. He feels a slow, insidious encroachment in the air, suppresses a faint shiver. Then again, it's January.

Crossing Shrewsbury Lane where it joins the main road he walks on past the repositioned pub with Cretan crescent bull-horns raised up from its terracotta and a mounting block from the inn's old location further up the road cemented into place there by the kerb but wrong way up, set on its side with risers horizontal and treads vertical. It looks as if it's there for Escher's men or rolled-up centipedes to climb before they cross a pavement threshold and continue down among the water sources and sub-strata, down into the earth. A foot of topsoil, then a yard of dark brown clay, two feet of blue clay, thirteen feet of peat, river drift gravel eighteen feet, two feet of hard blue clay, soft yellow clay and sand in layers, one foot, and then forty feet down there's three yards that's 'hard grey sand with layers of tenacious clay of various hues, and shells', and under that there's dark green sand, round pebbles, Thanet sand and flint and chalk and intricately carved chunks of alabaster, the remains or germinating seeds of *Somnium*. Yesod, the lunar dream realm of the kabbalists, the Hebrew word that means foundation and suggests a different, buried moon. He sighs and carries on past the attractive late-Victorian semi with the patterned, decorative brickwork, standing where the Bull originally stood, continues on by the amazing and apparently Carpathian water tower towards the Eaglesfield Road turning, just ahead and on his left.

There on the corner, shabby and dilapidated, stands a handsome pre-war Modernist/Art Deco house. 'Four Winds', white-walled, flat-roofed, planning permission to demolish it and put up an apartment block long since applied for, probably not there much longer. Maybe this could be the house that Paul Buck's uncle lived in sixty years back. That was at this end of Eaglesfield Road, with a rumoured tunnel running from the air-raid shelter in his garden, underneath the road and into Castle Woods, another half-conjectural subsurface space. Earth movers, possibly, will find it while demolishing 'Four Winds' but myth requires a fragile quantum state, breaks down into river-drift gravel if observed, so either way it's finished, unappealingly resolved, and so on. A kind of socio-historic wind erosion, wearing all the elevation's visions, hopes and mysteries to grit then flinging them away, that's what it is. Resigned, he heads down Eaglesfield Road with the golf course where his father died and brother worked across the road upon his right, and Eaglesfield itself rising there on his left, the open parkland where sometimes he will escort the goddess so that she can see the squirrels, the surprising childlike streak in her that takes some getting used to. Eighteen months ago or more she startled him by asking for a teddy bear, a tiny one in scale with her small portrait, made him visit Hamley's to acquire a costly Hermann number suiting her specifics. Figured this for a sure sign of his decline into dementia, then found out about the handmaidens of Artemis, the bearskin costumes that they used to wear, so maybe after all there's meaning, even in this second-childhood stuff, maybe there's signal in the noise.

He passes on from Eaglesfield Road into Kinlet Road, then takes a left down Bushmoor Crescent past the current Shrewsbury House, re-sited from its previous location as the birthplace of piped coal gas and the home of Princess Charlotte, moved to this spot and once, years back, the location of the local library. He came here as a kid to plough through E. C. Eliot's *Kemlo* series of juvenile space adventures with their wacky jacket copy. 'What's the mystery of the Martian Ghost Run? "Bah! There *is* no mystery. It's just a boy's imagination!" laugh the chiefs of Space Satellite K, orbiting round the earth.' The subdued aisles were full of stars and rockets.

At the crescent's end he turns left into Mereworth Drive, its impressively diverse variety of shrubs and hedges planted in neat border strips between the pavement and the road, a quaintness he associates with crumpets and the 1950s, fireside rugs and cumbersome spread copies of the *Eagle*. A uniquely English dreamtime that is now almost extinct, the great diverse proliferation of imaginative periodicals gone with Dan Dare and Kemlo to oblivion. Bah! There *is* no mystery. It's just a boy's imagination. From the drive he turns left into Plum Lane and there straight across the road is Brinklow Crescent and the grassy railed enclosure of the Bronze Age chieftain's burial mound, the skullfaced, lugworm-bearded god of Shooters Hill, the promised end of his perambulation, of the story.

Why, he wonders, with the many resonant spots on the hilltop that there are to choose from, does his character-arc finish its parabola and dive into the dirt right here? Then he remembers the instructions in the will he had drawn up, his ashes to be strewn across the mound, a final fusion with the landscape he emerged from, one more angstrom added to the hill's height, some 411 feet, 8 inches, 85 points; 5 feet 1 inch higher than the gold cross of St Paul's Cathedral. When the smut and soot of him is rained into the foot of topsoil, with a bit of luck he'll filter down through the biodegraded remnants of the furze that great Linnaeus fell upon his knees and worshipped in, 'wrapped in a golden fleece of blossoms', down through all the brown and blue and yellow layers, through the solid and unrealized blueprint bore of 1810's projected tunnel under Shooters Hill to Blackheath, deep among the relic cupolas and shattered eggshell moon-domes of his downside palace, of his Nonsuch.

He stands motionless upon the corner of Plum Lane and Mereworth Drive, gazing at the hillock dead across the road uneasily and wishing he were done with this, squints homewards up Plum Lane to where it joins with Shrewsbury Lane, will take him back up to the Bull, the celebrated traveller's rest of eighteenth-century verse. 'At Zhooter's Hill we made a halt, for Polly's saddle was in vault; And Joe was dry, and so was I, but George was wondrous testy. Zo we went. Cherry, merry, into Kent, into Kent, Winking, blinking, down we went.' An unexpected shudder ripples through him to his tingling soles and runs to ground, a horror that is startlingly physical. He wants to go home, winking, blinking, but the manuscript contains a final pointless action that is in all probability included for no other reason than to make him look and feel ridiculous. He hesitates. Resentfully he follows his concluding orders and rotates in a half-circle with his back now turned towards the sulking lump. He's looking at an unremarkable semi-detached home very like his own, with on the left a massive oak tree that has overgrown the pavement, monstrous knuckled roots sunk in the tarmac put down to replace the slabs already ruptured and upturned. He wonders what to say if anyone emerges from the house and asks him why he's standing staring at it, please don't let it be some scared old woman who mistakes him for the still-at-large South London rapist, wonders how long he's expected to remain here. Feeling on his forehead the first splash of wet he creases it into a frown.

OK, let's freeze the picture there. Let's formalize it as a frame description. Final panel: he stands facing us, a head-and-shoulders frontal close-up in the centre foreground, light precipitation forming on his spectacles, a look of mild annoyance in his eyes. In the mid-ground that's just behind him Plum Lane is a dark stripe of macadam running left to right across the picture roughly level with his shoulders, with above that a thin, pallid band of path before the railings and the dead grass of the barrow. In the upper background are first trees and then the roofs and chimneys of the houses slightly further down the slope, with overall the great reach of the brimming granite sky, its vapour masses heading south across the city and towards us.

Pay attention to his spectacles, refracted light turning the puzzled eyes beyond the lenses into abstract clots of pearl and white. Just change the point of view a little, move an inch or so to one side or the other and the optical illusion fails. He comes to bits. You realize that the glasses are in fact a pair of dormer windows set into a housetop downhill, visible through parted trees that form the edges of his face, a patch of negative space strung across the gap between them. A wood pigeon swoops down through the area that formerly appeared to be his nose, his cheek, into the dappled sideburn shadows, and his swathe of silver hair is only raincloud mustering above the shiny tiles that were his brow. The corrugating wrinkles there beside his lips, the thin moustache and sparse goatee are random stains and shadows in the grave-mound's withered over-growth, vertical railings where there seemed to be lapels, his jacket melted into Plum Lane's damping tarmac and the whole Mae West room of his countenance disintegrates. No matter how much shifting back and forth you do, there on that dreadful corner just across the street from Brinklow Crescent, you won't find the magic spot again, won't bring him back in focus. There's nobody there, was never anybody there except a fluctuation in the visual purple, a perceptual misunderstanding, trick of moonlight.

Presently the view of London is erased by weather. Rain comes clattering down in bright tin sheets onto the empty street.

[Alan Moore]

THE GAZETTEER OF DISAPPEARANCES & DELETIONS

BERMONDSEY ISLAND

'A large swamp, with houses built upon piles,' according to the Earl of Shaftesbury, after his 1884 visit to the riverside part of Southwark, just east of today's Dockhead. 'The Venice of drains,' said the *Morning Chronicle*, in reference to its high mortality figures, caused by infectious disease. Dickens had created a furore in 1837 when he took Bermondsey Island as his inspiration for Jacob's Island in *Oliver Twist*: critics claimed nowhere was as bad as that. They were wrong. Once called Cupid's Gardens, the Island's wooden galleried buildings were Tudor, built on piles upon a creek that sometimes ran as red as blood (because of the leatherworks near by).

[Sarah Wise]

TRIPCOCK FLATS, SE28

Probably the best-known 'mud-larking' territory, once the domain of boys and girls who, until the 1900s, made a living digging in the oily mud along the Thames. Tripcock Flats was also notorious as a burial ground for murdered sailors who had the misfortune to drink at the Lady Margaret public house in Goldfinch Lane. The publican, James Sale, and his wife, Hannah, were thought to have killed more than forty 'homeward bounders'. The ghosts of the sailors are said to dance a hornpipe on the flats every summer solstice, to celebrate the hanging of the Sales at Southwark on 21 June 1824; an event witnessed and recorded by the poet John Clare on his third and final visit to London.

[Michael Moorcock]

THE TERMINAL CAFÉ, BRIXTON, SW18

Designed and fitted by Mendelsohn and Chermayeff (Modernist architects of Bexhill-on-Sea's De La Warr Pavilion), the Terminal Café was originally established for the exclusive use of tram-workers. It was attached to the celebrated Brixton terminus. Now rebranded, it is the flagship restaurant of former screen star Una Persson, and remains a favoured late-night dining experience with customers of the Roxy and other local venues.

[Michael Moorcock]

CAMBERWELL COLISEUM, HIGH STREET, SE12

One of the largest of the South London music halls, the Coliseum was built in 1890, became a cinema and bingo hall in 1970, and was demolished to make way for Enron's London headquarters in 1995. In its heyday the Coliseum featured Marie Lloyd, Gus Elen, Little Tich, Dan Leno, Una Persson, Gloria Cornish, Albert Chevalier, J. K. Elliot, Sonny Hale, Max Peters, Harry Lauder, Max Miller, Tommy Cornelius, Max Wall and Arthur Askey. It served as the setting for the BBC's *Stars of the Past* show, which ran from 1962 to 1969. Following the collapse of Enron, an attempt was made by the Society for the Preservation of Historical Comedy to acquire the building as a museum. The Coliseum proved to be an unsuccessful finalist in the television programme that decided, by popular vote, which British folly should be restored and retained.

[Michael Moorcock]

TURNER'S COTTAGES, STREATHAM, SW16

On the south side of Streatham Green, set back from London Road, this row of cottages (along with St Stephen's Church) is all that remains of the original village street – which, in 1924, was razed to make way for the new road to Tooting Bec (and the Cricketers at Mitcham). Protected by a preservation order since 1974, thanks to the efforts of Helena Mitford-Begg, long-time resident of Step Cottage (No. 7), the row has recently come under threat from an attempt to obtain planning permission for a canalside office/residential development. The canal, long buried, is being excavated and dressed as a sculpture park: the 'Genevieve Way'. Classic cars will be positioned as art objects along the old road from London to Brighton.

A plaque in honour of Henry Cornelius, director of the 1953 film *Genevieve*, will be unveiled by his nephew Sir Frank Cornelius (a major investor in the development).

[Michael Moorcock]

THE NOAH'S ARK, LONDON ROAD, NORBURY, SW16

Torn down to make way for office development, this pub was popular with between-wars 'race gangs', especially the Nicholsons (Joe and Jim). By the mid 1950s it was a Teddy Boy hangout and the scene of a bloody affray among members of the Brixton Chain Gang (whose weapon of choice, after the open razor, was a bicycle chain). Two were left for dead, twenty others required hospital treatment. Derek Bentley, Chris and Neville Craig were regular under-age drinkers.

But the most famous Noah's Ark 'face' is alive and well. He runs a restaurant in Portals Nous (Majorca) under his real name of Moses Collier. In the 1940s he was better known as 'Two Gun' Collier. He was an associate of the Notting Dale Cornell family and a rumoured enforcer for the Nicholsons. His restaurant is called the Gunslinger Saloon and serves Tex-Mex cuisine. His collection of Walther PPK .38 automatics is on display in the foyer.

In its final days, in the mid 1960s, the Ark hosted poetry and jazz evenings and was a haunt of counter-cultural dope dealers. The Carshalton poet (and parks' gardener) Chris Torrance launched his mimeographed collection *Diary of an Assassin* in a reading there with Lee Harwood and Zen monk Bill Wyatt.

[Michael Moorcock]

SIDCUP

In the 1950s and 1960s there was a small aviary in Sidcup Place. Cocky the cockatoo was its celebrity. I passed him every day en route to school on the western side of the park. On the northern side was the Sidcup Art School. Its students, in the late 1950s, included Keith Richards, Dick Taylor and other 'pretty things'. Barbara Charone notes in an early biography of Keef that he fed Cocky period pills or the odd benzedrine pill to make him more lively.

Commander Kenneth Drury, Head of New Scotland Yard's Flying Squad, was the highest-serving officer to be jailed for corruption. Fleet Street swamped our road, in the 1970s, to record this event. The first house in the road to afford an extension shows its age when set against today's much slicker conversions.

Pinter's 'Caretaker', the malodorous Davies, might have kept his papers in Sidcup, at the army offices in Halfway Street, but a new staging of the play would struggle to locate them. The barracks themselves have been erased, after being taken over by the Post Office in 1969.

Lord Waring's mansion in Footscray Meadows, burned and razed in October 1949, is a memory that exists not in photos but my head. I watched from the bathroom window as flames lit up the evening sky.

Coca-Cola tried to immortalize Sidcup with a sophisticated process of bottling tap water: marketed as Dasani Pure Water. More interesting was the botched break-in at the depot by some of the Stephen Lawrence suspects.

They tried to cart off 'empties', which their solicitor later advised them to describe as 'abandoned'.

All those shops, and details of places that slowly die with people and their memories, have been resurrected in a little volume. Written by Norman Hill, as an Easy English aid for French students, it is called: *Life in an English Suburb*. Hill chose Sidcup because he lived there. Sketches and interviews are recorded as 'a brief collection of impressions'. How many copies survive? Mine was found among bric-a-brac in a shop in Liège, Belgium.

A charity shop where one unearths books bearing library stamps, or non-returned school textbooks, turns up the copy of Breton's *Nadja* that I remember lending to someone who subsequently vanished. What are the chances of my inscribed copy surfacing in Sidcup in 2003, when I loaned it out in Maidstone twenty years ago?

[Paul Buck]

SHOOTERS HILL, SE18

When I was young, up to the age of nine or so, we used to visit our uncle on Shooters Hill. In the front garden there was a sort of air-raid shelter, a damp and dirty underground space, where Uncle kept three rifles and a couple of pistols, mementoes from the war. It was no more than five or six feet wide, ten feet long. A glorified tunnel. It had obviously been longer at one time, but had been roughly blocked at the far end with wood. We were told that it went beneath the road and emerged in the trees on the far side. Uncle explained that many animals had lived in and messed the tunnel, that no one used it any more. We couldn't explore. Today, almost fifty years later, I still mean to make a detour and walk the hill to discover that house anew. None of us remembers the number. I know it is near the top of the hill, because we were told that Dick Turpin and other highwaymen would have worked close by, stopping the coaches when the tired horses rested there.

[Paul Buck]

BAD NOISE

GARY HOLTON

Gary Holton died in his thirty-third year in the early hours of Saturday 25 October 1985. At an all-time low, he went drinking with a couple of old friends in the Warrington Hotel in Maida Vale. He died in a flat on the Chalk Hill Estate in Wembley.

He was an addict, a legendary drinker, had a problem with heroin. The *Sun* and other rags chronicled details of his sex life. He died in debt. As Lemmy the Motorhead axe-man put it: 'The bastard owed me a fiver when he died.'

He idolized Lenny Bruce. He was bad. He was the brother you never had. He was Pinter's Lenny: forever 'taking the piss'. Touring exploits with his band the Heavy Metal Kids read like banned out-takes from *Spinal Tap* or *Withnail & I*. The broken leg after falling off stage as support for Alice Cooper. Sacked as support for Kiss after laughing hysterically as Gene Simmons's hair caught fire. The last gig at the Speakeasy: Gary in white cowboy boots, pink poser pouch, Smith & Wesson bullet belts; Johnny Rotten in the front row chanting 'boring, boring'. The disastrous stand-in as lead singer for the Damned: no words known to any song apart from 'neat'.

Gary Holton has, for the following twenty years or so after his death, continued his work as shade. In the mid 1990s I flick on Radio 1: an interview with his widow is followed by his cover of 'Ruby (Don't Take Your Love to Town)'. The BBC ignore my subsequent persistent telephone inquiries. In Berwick Street vinyl outlets hitherto unknown bootlegs come my way ('HMK Live and Loud' and 'Sing It to Me'). Driving through Hackney past the then unrestored Empire I see HEAVY METAL KIDS LIVE chalked on a board outside a pub before the turn up into Dalston. The band (same name, RIP Gary, minus Gary) subsequently re-form. They have their own website. Gary's followers have assembled spooky 'voice collections' from *Auf Wiedersehen, Pet* and 'live' performance material from the Germany tour in 1976. It's all out there in a virtual world.

He's just a footnote in other stories. The glossy chroniclers of punk have hipper footage, other names. They all went down the Music Machine to hear him (TV Smith, Rat Scabies and the rest) before going off to form their own little gangs to play speeded-up R&B. A lost leader. Of punk or glam/pub/yob rock, take your choice. Only ever cited in homage to others. A mention in Mark Putterford's biography of Phil Lynott (for his involvement in the wonderful Christmas exploitation band the Greedy Bastards).

Otherwise, he's off the map. Take *Quadrophenia*, for example, the movie that announces the 1980s as it cynically recycles youth culture to make it marketable and safe. Sting and Phil Daniels are going one way and Gary the other: Holton is not even credited at the end and is replaced by a look-alike before the Brighton ruck. A ghost cameo as the 'aggressive rocker'. Sting moves smoothly on to soft-rock respectability with a hint of 'rough' and Phil Daniels takes on the mantle of Holton sound-alike for Brit Pop's nadir, Blur's *Parklife*. Mods and Rockers. Substitute for another guy . . .

The cover of his band's last album, *Kitsch* (one of those Hypnosis ones), has on the front a Holton look-alike (dusk, deserted country road) opening door of sports car (registration HMK3) and fluttered newspaper headline: POP STAR DIES IN CAR CRASH. On the back: identikit image, car registration HMK4 and newspaper title STRANGE TWIST OF FATE. Absolute kitsch, innit.

I'll help you out. Gary's best-known alter ego was Wayne Winston Norris. The Cockney carpenter in *Auf Wiedersehen, Pet*. The cheeky chappie with the shades and the dyed hair. As Holton described him: 'a wide boy, everybody's mate', with 'a set of values, just the wrong set'.

Holton died just after returning from Marbella during the filming of the second series. He was kept alive for the rest of it by a canny mix of long shots, look-alikes and voice-dubbing. Wayne reportedly dies of a rare heart condition. A 'son', Wyman, steps in to fill the gap. Sequels. We want more. Whatever happened to the likely lads, we don't want them back: crinkly, balding, turning fifty. A thousand thousand slimy things live on.

When he was in his pomp, as lead singer of the Heavy Metal Kids, there were replica Holtons at the gigs (stovepipe hat, 'Kid' coat, braces, fox stole, Wellington boots, etc.; touring Europe the band were tracked night after night by a Holton look-alike). There was a droog element to some of this.

After his death, I adopted 'Wayne Holton' as one of many liberating heteronyms for fanzine articles. W. H. was a lad insane, a rioter. I enjoyed his company.

Much was made of Holton's London street cred during his career. He was not a mockney. He was 'born and bred' in the East End: his father, Ernie, was an ex-boxer and owner of public houses. This helped him along. The luvvie knowingness of masks and personae as well as the much-valued diamond-geezer authenticity. He could move from Eddie Hairstyle in *The Knowledge* to Tennants Pilsner adverts: *Are you pulling my Pilsner?* His childhood progress explains a lot: posh school (Westminster), Sadlers Wells Opera Company, the Old Vic Company and the RSC at Stratford. The boy done good. On the stage from the age of eleven. He liked taking his clothes off (the lead in *Hair*) as well as dressing up. Good preparation for later 'hellraising'. One of the many roles became part of the interior furniture: the Dodger, Dickens's prototype 'loveable rogue'. Bless.

One of the many appeals of the Dodger persona is there in Dickens's original as well as the Bart 'free adaptation'. Adult and child are fused: the Dodger is man/boy, a song of experience/ innocence: 'as dirty a juvenile as one would wish to see, but he had about him all the airs and manners of a man ... he wore a man's coat'. He is a confusion of product and original. Much more fun than the cipher of innocence abroad, Oliver, and the sanitized middle-class world of the Brownlows. Appealing: the brother you never had.

The character is a bizarre take on Dickens's own father, John: the shield of other names (Mr Dawkins ... Jack Dawkins ... the

Artful . . .) slips at three points in the novel to 'John Dawkins', including the fateful delivery of Oliver to Fagin. Give the vowels a tweak and you have 'John Dickens', the father who betrayed young Charles to the blacking factory at Hungerford Stairs. The good bloke who was also a debtor, the big kid ('How long he is growing up to be a man'). The clubbable blagger desperate to be well liked.

The Dodger is one to be emulated, followed. Fagin advises Oliver, 'He'll be a great man himself; and will make you one too, if you take pattern by him.' Legions of future sentimentalized 'loveable rogues' in London culture have tucked in. From the cherubic grin of Dennis Wise, key member of Wimbledon's 'crazy gang' ('He could start a fight in an empty house': Sir Alex Ferguson), to the Krays, or other would-be goodfellas, who still 'look out for their own'.

Dickens (see his Preface of 1841) was anxious not to be seen to be condoning or glamorizing a world of crime (the public appetite already apparent in the lives of felons collected in the *Newgate Calendar*). So the Dodger is punished, but kept alive. Be honest, most of you had an image of him as the rozzas break down the door in the Lean version as they come a-looking for crazy Bill, or reprising on 'Consider Yourself' with the rest of the company. Instead the antecedent of 'lad culture' becomes a 'lifer', transported to Australia.

So, there in spirit as Ant and Dec welcome another C-list loser on to *I'm A Celebrity, Get Me Out of Here*. Johnny Rotten swearing? Shock horror.

The Dodger's first resurrection is Magwitch in *Great Expectations*, ready to turn Pip's world-views upside down.

Then on via David Lean, Carol Reed and Lionel Bart and any am-dram director near you to bless and curse generations of late twentieth-century players: Anthony Newley, Jack Wild, Davy Jones, Ben Elton, and . . . Gary Holton.

Holton's takes on the Dodger figure were various and often unsubtle. And the literary knowingness starts even before this. The Heavy Metal Kids was adopted as a name for the band upon the suggestion of 'manager' Ricki Farr (son of boxer, Tommy, who fought Joe Louis in his day). It is an in-joke that backfires, lifted from the works of William S. Burroughs. (We are in the era of Steely Dan, after all.)

The name is a curse: the band are not 'heavy metal'. The appellation is tightened to the Kids for the second album (knowing again: its title is 'Anvil Chorus').

The cover of the first 1974 album reveals Holton as Dodger with gang, blocking access to the *Oliver!* out-take cobbled alleyway. They are doing their best to look loveable and well 'ard. The poster insert shows Holton with empty bottle, trademark Dodger hat and coat, standing next to a dustbin, screwing out the camera. Only the clay pipes are missing. Cut their hair, get Bernie Rhodes in to consult on latest punk accessories, voilà: the Clash!

The pose of violence was taken seriously enough for there to have been a *Panorama* special (title: 'The New Criminals') with man-child Holton putting himself forward as a 'spokesman for a generation' of junior car thieves. In it the band play 'The Cops are Coming', a classic anglicized take on glam-gothic about a mock deadly encounter between a biker and the police that ends with a chain fight and the gleeful punch celebrating decapitation. How was anyone ever taken in? The kid was only kidding. The cult of the Dodger is remembered lyrically in a catchy little number 'Jackie the Lad' (Jack Dawkins, geddit). A tale of petty criminality and moral ambivalence, it was one of Holton's favourites on the live circuit.

The problem was that our cheeky chappie was going to meet another gang, led by Big Mal McClaren and fronted by another more ruthless frontman (an eluder, a cheat, an avoider, a surreptitious follower). Stand-up banter, funny outfits and songs (about nose-picking, the classic 'Bogey Woogie'; vomiting after excess drinking, the quietly restrained 'Spew Up'; and masturbation, 'Crisis') were no match for a knowing spike into abstract nouns like 'anarchy' and 'anger'.

Ronnie Thomas, the bassist for the Kids, relates the meeting in the Roebuck pub in the King's Road. Rotten, accompanied by two minders, 'undid this huge gold safety pin and put it on Gary's lapel. He then patted his cheek and said, "You've been ripped off, Holton . . . how does it feel?"'

Charley Bates sums it up. When the Artful is taken down and made a 'lifer' for a 'twopenny-halfpenny sneeze box' he is appalled at the likely injustice to the great one's reputation: 'nobody will know half of what he was. How will he stand in the *Newgate Calendar*? P'raps not be there at all.' And devotees of websites are out there to convince us that the dead man was greater than . . . Alex Harvey, Jimmy Pursey, Ian Dury, Jimmy Nail . . . you name it . . .

Twenty years on. Perhaps best not be there hereafter. He had his moment. His band's one real hit, 'She's No Angel', will never appear on *TOTP*2. We are instead destined to hear Robbie Williams, stand-in scally from Stoke, performing 'Angel' with nationwide club-land backing until the crack of doom.

[Peter Carpenter]

VANISHING ANGELS

'Where's Sally gone?'

He swivelled round, trying to scan the crowd. Some of them were sitting, some standing.

'Damn!'

'She'll be back.'

'She's got my colours.'

'Should be easy to pick her out.'

'Come on, Benny, she could be anywhere.'

'Benny! . . . Benny? . . . Bunny!' called a passing youth-citizen, a can of lager in his mitt, stars orbiting his head.

Benny took the can off him in a friendly sort of way and emptied the contents over his head.

'We cannot just scatter. Gorra maintain our presence.'

'Sure. She'll be OK.'

The Festival was a big chance to show solidarity, make a public mark, mend the image, build bridges.

*

'Danny, gerrus a coke, pal.'

'Me too.' Flicking a coin.

'And don't get lost.'

They were sat on a bank. Just high enough to make it look as though they were supervising something. Easy really, as the crowd was perfectly capable of looking after itself. Benny stretched back, aware the whole set-up was one of his better ideas.

An hour passed.

'Looks like we've lost Danny.'

They decided to retrace his movements. The catering was one crowd over and a bit of a hedge away.

'Time to eat,' Benny explained, in case it seemed he was anxious.

At the stall:

'Free,' he said.

'Nope,' said the caterer.

'Yes we are.'

He ducked a bit of hot fat aimed his way. Gave the van a little rock to test it. The server gave him a venomous stare.

'All of us.'

The chip hacker looked round for something heavier than a chip scoop, but all he found was a dog howling. Close too.

He slung the side door of the van open, took a look – 'That your dog?'

'He's hungry too.'

'Gerrim off the garbage. I've got chips.'

'He likes meat.'

A big bag of chips was shovelled up and passed over, a few stale burgers on top.

'Just get him out of it.'

'Sure.'

Danny's dog proved hard to shift. They had to improvise a lead out of a belt.

'Danny should look after him better.'

'You see my girl? Blonde, colours over her shoulder?'
The caterer just curled his lip.

They moved away to eat.
'Maybe someone's after us.'
Jed looked worried about Sally.
'Missing persons?'
'They're the ones trying to lose us.'
It seemed better to have a look round themselves. A patrol, Benny called it. In case the missing friends were sitting it out somewhere, or found new pals.

The music didn't make it easy to communicate, but they kept together somehow. Except the dog.

In the end, Benny placed them all together on the edge of the stage. 'That way they'll see us easily and know where to come to.'

It gave a smart sort of impression that somehow they were controlling the music, or at least filtering it. No one interfered.

For an hour or more. And then it was the dog broke the peace. He came bounding on to the stage shaking and banging a boot, mangled but recognizably –
'Eff!'
'D'you think . . . ?'
The air seemed to turn serious around them in the sound.
Jed dashed off to check.
The others pulled the dog and its relic off stage and, like a little army of improvised warriors, got hold of some space batons and tools – plenty about backstage.
They moved out of the public eye.

Jed made it back OK, one arm of his denim on fire, and some bulging bruises around his face.
'Danny – Sally – back of the hedge – foot off.'
They ran then, a band of comets through a scene now lit by generators and chasing floodlights.

There were six catering staff.

But all they'd say was:

'D'you think we'd eat that muck we make for you?'

[Bill Griffiths]

BATTLE OF MUDCHUTE

Real Audio stream

'There we were setting up the world's first truly multicultural rock'n' rave society, when the City of London moneymen did a deal with the Muslim monotheists and stabbed us in the back. Now look what's happened to all our ancient liberties! No more Glastonbury Festival, no more Wicker Man, no more Beaufort Hunt! I was born in this country and I don't even recognize it any more.'

Dr Double Oh No, Crown secret agent, occult cryptographer and head of Ukanian Stay-Behind rearguard cellnet.

Narrative voiceover

Previously, in *Rave Nation*, loads previously, it was 3000–2000 BCE in North West Europe. That's right. Before the Normans, before the Saxons, before the Romans – before even the Britons and the Celts – were the Afro-Atlanteans. Now these groovy little fuckers were the original technopagan vagabonds shipped into the Mediterranean trade network from Babylon via the Old Kingdom of Egypt. They were following their oracles towards the setting sun, in search of the precious incense ambergris which was reckoned an immortality drug. So they're passing through Cornwall, Ireland and the west coasts of Wales and Scotland on their way to Lapland and they get busy throwing down all their sacred tech – their trackways, earthworks, stone circles and long barrows.

Their shot-caller is a big fat bastard called Gogmagog. He is initiated into the mysteries of Isis and can get an indirect line that puts him through to Osiris, Lord of the Dead, and his crazy brother, Set. All the Old Egyptian deities move in the orbit of the Dog Star and are the zodiac avatars used by the Sirian breed of space aliens to communicate with their designated handlers on earth. All of this makes Gogmagog a real dab hand with proprietary Anubis interface code. The guy is a regular fucking demigod.

Anyway, years pass and all these Christian mainframes get dumped on the sacred sites of the Afro-Atlanteans by a bunch of monotheistic barbarians dressed in white sheets. The Crown/City duopoly gets going on the Thames. But old gods die hard and in 1582 true hacker and bisexual occultist Eddie Boy Krishna turns up on Dr Double Oh No's doorstep in Mortlake with a test tube of ambergris and an Anubis manual he says he found in the ruins of Glastonbury. Soon the two of them are trip partners grooving with the dead as they set up the Afro-Atlantean zombie circuits of the Old Ukanian Combine. Eddie worms his way into the Old Egyptian extranet while the Doctor starts running the Sirians without paying them like they were his pet monsters or something.

So, things are building to a climax. It's 1988 – the beginning of events covered in *Rave Nation* – and Eddie is chilling in the monotheistic state of Goa, recovering from some really bad experiences in the 1960s. He's got his bare feet up on the beach at Vagator catching some of the new electronic vibes when word reaches him that his old partner in crime is back in operation . . .

Full Motion Video
Drug lord flying in from his offshore island haven with coked-out wannabe supermodel in tow. He leans out from beneath the whirling blades: Hey, Eddie Boy, aincha heard? The Ibiza sound is the next big thing. Check out Clink Street.

Narrative voiceover
So Eddie catches the next plane to Heathrow and barrels through the jet lag to end up necking Substance E with a bunch of London wide boys suddenly eager to get oral on his bits. Damn! Where the fuck did this new drug come from? This is better than mandrake root. He has never partied so hard.

What do you know? Eddie grabs some Adidas shell-toes and starts running with the Inter City Firm, snipping locks on empty warehouses in the East End and putting down the competition with machete attacks and Stanley blade rushes. It's real small-time stuff but it gives him back his edge. Pretty soon he's got the local constabulary in on his scams and he's the lord promoter of every dodgy rave between Plaistow, Stratford and Poplar. He's keyed himself into the local extranet and pulled down the Karma Twins to put the frighteners on the indigenes. Everything is pretty fucking sweet.

Inevitably, Eddie gets bored. He hears the Doctor is hanging at the Dungeons on the Lea Bridge Road and one night they meet at Mudchute Common opposite City of London outpost east Canary Wharf. Designated venue the Crossroads of Anubis deep now underground.

Full Motion Video
Two sad old English blokes sniffing ambergris and smoking dried leaves in a crib done up like one of the back rooms at the Globe Theatre. It is earthy and damp.

EDDIE: How's tricks, matey? You don't look so good.

DOCTOR: I assure you the news of my demise was most et cetera. As a matter of fact . . . I'm back.

EDDIE: I dunno, man. You should lay off that kiddie porn.

DOCTOR: Very funny. Listen, Eddie, don't you realize what we're sitting on here?

EDDIE: Please don't say a gold mine. That whole El Dorado thing really freaked me out.

DOCTOR: *Edward!* Look, my Crown rating is still good. With

my intelligence contacts and your funny-money connections, we can put together the act again.

EDDIE: You want me back in the City of London?

DOCTOR: Not exactly. Have you seen the way the natives gobble down this Substance E?

EDDIE: You want me to set up the bathtub lab again?

DOCTOR: Bigger than that, Eddie. I'm thinking the old Raleigh network. Czech drug factories, MI6 spook runs, Caribbean money washes. The works.

EDDIE: Off-shore accountability. It figures.

DOCTOR: Plus, I'm thinking pharmaceutically indentured sex labour. The groundlings are already hooked. All we have to do is manufacture a scarcity and line up a new supply.

EDDIE: Brand name?

DOCTOR: Substance F.

EDDIE: Ooh, Doctor. What a comeback!

DOCTOR: We'll do a test run. If it works, then we'll get the old devil in on the act.

EDDIE: Gizza kiss, ya auld cunt.

Narrative voiceover
So that's how the Second English Revolution kicked off. Eddie gets his chemical kitchens up and running with raw materials squeezed out of Latvia and finished product cooked up in phoney biomedical

research labs in the Czech Republic. He's following the Benetton model with batch production runs and just-in-time delivery systems. The MI6 boys have their work cut out shipping the stuff into the country under the disapproving noses of Customs & Excise. Imports get so high it's embarrassing and the spooks have to keep cutting loose more and more bodies to keep their HM colleagues in the loop. Luckily, they've got the ICF and their newly loved-up ex-rival stadium gangs – the Bushwhackers in South London, fragments of the Highbury and White Hart Lane firms up North, the Headhunters out West – patched in on the ground as a dealership network, and these guys are routinely expendable.

Pretty soon, Eddie is supplying all the orbital raves which have sprung up like weeds in the deregulated capital-investment zones that rake the late-industrial landscape outside the London ramparts of the M25. He's got bouncers, ex-squaddies and demobbed SAS guys on the payroll wielding shotguns, TAC key codes and CS gas. Things are getting so out of control that the national police net wants to take over his drug ring. The Doctor is running interference for him with wild cover stories about Sirian black ops and psychological warfare test programmes. But no one is buying his nuclear monotheism number and when the cops send out their HOLMES encryption guys he shrugs and fucks off to Glastonbury on the Hypnosis trail.

Meanwhile Eddie is coining it. He's opened an account in a snide name at an EC4 branch of Barings run by an old Oxford chum and finds himself on the receiving end of unlimited borrowing privileges. Time for the Church's brogues. He funds his whole thing out of Queer Street on a mobile phone and routes his profits through a nested hierarchy of shell companies on the forex markets until they pay out from the Transatlantic Corporation registered in a Virgin Islands tax haven. Then it's bags of cash flying back over the Atlantic pond in note form. A quick bung to Customs and the money's in his clip near fresh as the day it was minted.

Neat little scam, eh? Eddie lets it run on automatic pilot and rearranges his shoe closet. But then his bagman throws a wobbly at

Terminal 4 and coughs him up. Suddenly the Inland Revenue sniffer dogs are wanting to go through his pockets and fucking Anubis cuts in to tell him the jig is up. Eddie siphons off his remaining assets into a Swiss holding account – no names, just numbers – and steps back to watch his entire operation go into meltdown.

Que se-fucking-ra. Looks like the scarcity economy has arrived. Eddie pulls in his remaining stash and starts cutting it with amphetamine, synthetic opiates, toilet cleaner, strychnine . . . any fucking shit he can find. So this is the really bad Substance G that produces a void where there should be ecstasy. Eddie don't care. He spears 500 boys in a field in Buckinghamshire. He files his toenails. So what the fuck is happening in Glastonbury anyhow . . . ?

Full Motion Video
The Doctor dropping science with a bunch of nomadic anarcho-occultist sound-system jugglers sporting close crops and black combat gear. He is deep under cover.

DOCTOR: So did I ever tell you kids 'bout the time I worked for government intelligence rat-fucking the Algonquins . . . ?

Narrative voiceover
Eddie pulls on some twelve-hole Docs with rainbow laces and slots in alongside his mentor. The pair receive their marching orders and fall in behind the Dogstar Tribe. These crazy jugglers are wandering the countryside hitting on all the old Afro-Atlantean sites in an effort to rouse the Afro-Celtic gods and challenge the powers of the Old Ukanian Combine. It seems to work. The tribe gets buzzed by Tornado jets as they dance up a storm in Cornwall while reports file in that Osiris is getting moody. The Doctor is in his element working both sides of the track. He boosts his Crown rating by calling in the scores to the HOLMES boys but then gets Eddie to throw the Sirians round the place to keep the Dogstar folks on their toes. It gets so he starts handing out tips on the best domains to hack.

So this is how the Battle of Mudchute came down. The Dogstar Tribe are fronted by this charismatic turntablist called Mark 23. He travels the countryside with a band of merry people, their kids and their dogs. Mark 23 knows how to dig the crates of history as he pumps the wheels of steel. Eddie synchs him into the Raleigh network and pretty soon he's switching the pitch on European techno tracks and animating them with escaped Atlantic drum loops using Caribbean voodoo techniques. The beats are dark and fast.

Osiris is listening. He's trying to get past the lock Eddie has on his box:

Real Audio stream
'Blown minds of screaming-dancing-tattooed-sorted-armed-feathered Dogstar People are only the sparks of a revolutionary implosion and devolutionary planetary regeneration.'

Narrative voiceover
Righty-ho! The Doctor has evolved a strategy of tension and is mouthing off rumours of an insurrection led by Gogmagog. Mark 23 wants the showdown at a stone circle in Wiltshire but the Doctor has other plans. He uses HOLMES to cast an exclusion zone around the meeting place in Wiltshire and sneaks the Dogstar Tribe into Mudchute's green and pleasant land. Mark 23 throws down a mad groove with Eddie slipping him the vinyl. They throw a Stop the City party J21 as the planet turns around the sun. The people are doing a ghost dance and their dogs are going crazy.

The City of London cuts off the green with a secret police roadblock and hits back at the symbolic terror with black helicopters, FM rock and searchlights. The Dogstar folks are pinned down. Eddie has his finger on the page in the Anubis manual that deals with the conjuring of spirits. He gets the nod from the Doctor. It's time to download Osiris. Bingo! All hell breaks loose from Mark 23's decks as Osiris fucks with the infrasound and takes out a building near the Canary Wharf tower.

There's pandaemonium on the Crown's black datanets. The

Dogstar Tribe seize the day. They set their dogs on the coppers and swarm over the roadblocks into the City. Eddie wrestles with his Anubis manual and gets Osiris back in his box. The Doctor hits Mark 23 with a chloroform pad and hauls him off the scene. He might need a hostage. Mudchute empties out.

Next day Mark 23 wanders Threadneedle Street in a daze. He is being led on a rope by this cute little devil dog knows which way is up. The Dogstar Tribe been celebrating with motion tactics in the City. Getting loaded and doing it in the road. Breaking finance-house windows, spilling garbage, setting fire to cars . . .

Full Motion Video
The Doctor and Eddie hooked up on the sacred mound at Parliament Hill engaged in an emergency failsafe procedure. Lots of thunder and lightning.

DOCTOR: This is a recoverable situation.

[Steve Beard]

WALK ON GILDED SPLINTERS
In Memorandum to Memory, 13 April 1969

The mid-1960s poetry extravaganza that posthumously became known as 'Wholly Communion' after the film Peter Whitehead made about it is often viewed as acting as midwife to the emergent hippie culture in London. To some 'Wholly Communion' was the last and greatest hurrah of the London beatnik scene, its fabulous death rattle, while for others it was the birth cry of psychedelia. Regardless of which view you take, for most of the 7,000 punters who trooped into the Albert Hall on 11 June 1965, 'Wholly Communion' was a spectacular success. That said, the individual poetry readings were less inspiring than their ability to attract a huge crowd, since even the appearance of beat stalwart Allen Ginsberg was viewed as disappointing. More spectacularly, the British visionary poet and acidhead Harry Fainlight was singularly unable to complete a recital of his own work. Likewise, depending on which historical commentator is taken at their word, the British beat novelist and ungentlemanly junkie Alex Trocchi either succeeded admirably or failed miserably in his role as MC. Regardless, 'Wholly Communion' is now a mythical event in the annals of the British counter-culture, the first mass gathering of the tribes, and no recent history of London in the swinging sixties appears complete without its reverential invocation.

By way of contrast, the zombification of the British counter-culture at the end of the sixties has for too long remained a taboo subject. Fittingly enough it was the 'Wholly Communion' MC who acted as chief somnambulist at the London Arts Lab slumber party of Sunday 13 April 1969 that exposed the 'Age of Aquarius' as a complete non-starter. This, the apotheosis of post-hippie burn-out, was promoted to an indifferent public as 'Alex Trocchi's State of Revolt'. The evening featured among others Trocchi, William Burroughs, R. D. Laing and Davy Graham. What went down during 'The State of Revolt' wasn't as immediately horrific as the murder of Meredith Hunter at the Rolling Stones' Altamont concert, or as self-consciously staged as the 'Death of Hippie' happening organized by the San Francisco Diggers, or even the Manson murders; and it is precisely this that makes Trocchi's 1969 Covent Garden debacle such an iconic event. 'The State of Revolt' marks the onset of counter-cultural rigor mortis and this living death occurred not with a bang but a smacked-out whimper. It is also a death with implications that we won't fully comprehend until the chatter of neo-critical production about the 1960s ceases to mask the violent silence that lies at the core of that decade, and which will yet prove to be its most enduring legacy.

While smackheads failed to constitute a majority among those present at 'The State of Revolt', both punters and participants shuffled through the Arts Lab looking like reanimated corpses intent on eating living human brains. And I say that knowing my mother, who was present, had been a vegetarian, as well as a junkie, since the mid 1960s. Footage of this Arts Lab death ritual makes up a good portion of the documentary *Cain's Film* (1969) by director Jamie Wadhawan; and my mother, Julia Callan-Thompson, is visible in four separate audience shots. My mother was actually on the hippie trail in India from the beginning of 1968 until the summer of 1969, but she made at least one lightning trip back to Europe during her sojourn to the East. Both she and a number of her boyfriends were heavily involved in Trocchi's drug dealing, and this probably accounts for her presence in the audience at 'The State of Revolt'. Although opium was readily available in India, heroin was harder to come by and so this more powerful sedative was highly prized by those my mother hung out with in Goa, all of whom returned to Europe strung out. They also had an omnivorous appetite for LSD.

I sent a copy of *Cain's Film* to native New Yorker Lynne Tillman because, after arriving in Europe straight from Hunter College, she'd asked Jim Haynes if she could put on a lecture series at the Arts Lab, and he not only agreed but also immediately suggested it should feature Trocchi. Tillman, who went on to become America's greatest living novelist, quickly lost organizational control of the lecture to Trocchi, who was determined to transform it into a junkie jamboree. Being new to London, Tillman knew virtually nothing about Trocchi at the time she first contacted him, and was unaware of his reputation as a dope fiend. On 28 February 2004, Lynne emailed the following observations about the DVD she'd received from me: 'It's the weirdest thing to watch – and sad and I can't find the words – much of it was shot in the basement cinema after I had to move everyone downstairs out of Theatre 1 or 2 by 10 p.m. to let the play go on, whatever it was . . .' *The Tale of Atlantis Rising* was advertised in the underground press as taking place in the theatre spaces, while there was a screening of *The Magnificent Ambersons* in the cinema prior to its being overrun by Trocchi's horde of bloodsucking freaks. Tillman concluded this email by saying: 'I remember many faces . . . if I watched it with Jim H(aynes)., he'd remember more names . . . several of the women are very familiar to me, none was a close friend – seeing Lynn Trocchi and the children was deeply upsetting – and seeing their apt. was so weird and sad and empty – one of the strangest experiences seeing a night and remembering and not . . .'

Jim Haynes, who'd set up and run the Arts Lab, responded to my queries with the following email message sent on 25 April 2004: 'I wish that I could help you, but my mind is a blank . . .' Jim's amnesia is a fitting tribute to the nihilism of those times. 1969 is the year in which many of those involved with the infamous Notting Hill activist group King Mob got seriously into smack. King Mob were best known for the nihilistic political graffiti they sprayed around West London, including the slogan CHRISTIE LIVES on the former home of the notorious sex murderer, and for contributing a float to the 1969 Notting Hill Carnival that featured a junkie beauty queen with a giant syringe protruding from her arm. My mother, of course, was on more than merely nodding terms with several King Mob activists, and the connections were through drugs rather than politics. Trocchi's connection with King Mob had as much to do with politics as smack, since Chris Gray, one of the mainstays of the group, was a former member of the Situationist International, as well as being a drug-scene acquaintance of my mother.

An unidentified underground-press article about 'The State of Revolt' is reproduced within Jim Haynes's copiously illustrated memoirs, *Thanks for Coming!* It didn't take long to discover that the feature entitled 'Alex Trocchi Gives a Party' and bylined to Felix Scorpio had been culled from issue 55 of *IT* (25 April–8 May 1969). Further inquiries revealed that Felix Scorpio was a pen name used by Felix de Mendelsohn. He is described in David Leigh's unreliable authorized Howard Marks biography, *High Time*, as: 'a Jewish Austrian . . . hippie entrepreneur'. De Mendelsohn was editing *IT* at the end of the 1960s with Peter Stansill, and he went on to involve himself with another London underground publication, *Friends*. One of the editors at *Friends* was Charlie Radcliffe, who got to know my mother in the latter part of 1969 when they were both regular visitors to the Notting Hill pad of their fellow dope smuggler Graham Plinston. Radcliffe had previously been a member of the English section of the Situationist International and had fleetingly come into contact with Trocchi as a result of this. De Mendelsohn went on to found the hippie sex paper *Suck* with Jim Haynes. Despite being arrested as a result of a journalistic tour of Belfast with the Republican firebrand and future international dope smuggler Jim McCann, de Mendelsohn had a reputation on the freak scene as a gentle and intellectual dude.

In his *IT* article, de Mendelsohn mentions Ronald Laing (celebrity anti-psychiatrist), William Burroughs (beat novelist and junkie), Ken Kesey (psychedelic novelist and Merry Prankster), Dan Richter (poet and junkie), Feliks Topolski (artist), Davy Graham (guitarist and junkie), Sean Philips (folk guitarist) and a whole camera crew as being present at 'The State of Revolt'. Unfortunately, he's insufficiently hip to name-check my mother as a member of the assembled cognoscenti, quite possibly because her leading role in Ladbroke Grove's weirdest drugs and magic scene (which co-starred Terry Taylor and Detta Whybrow, among others) is the stuff of reforgotten legend . . . In an email of 24 March 2004, Lynne Tillman commented: 'I don't remember Ken Kesey's being there – he was in London at some point . . . if Kesey had been there, I bet he'd have been filmed by Jamie, the cameraman, don't you think?' That said, Lynne did clock Phil Green in Wadhawan's footage, despite his almost criminal omission from the *IT* listing of luminaries. Green is another Trocchi satellite and was also a close friend of my mother.

Rather than setting up a standard lecture with questions afterwards, Trocchi insisted 'The State of Revolt' should be considerably more experimental; de Mendelsohn describes the result as being like a hip version of the then current BBC television talk show *Late Night Line-Up*. In the end what Trocchi did was read a few of his own poems and leave most of the real talking to his friends. The discussion took place mainly upstairs in the theatre space, with Burroughs speaking on the underground media and R. D. Laing banging on about soft drugs. An *IT* feature on squatting also came in for some savage criticism. The event was transformed into a New Orleans-style wake in the downstairs cinema, with wailing folk guitars, deranged dancing and Trocchi's poems. In an email sent on 26 April 2004, Chris Oakley, who was at that time connected to the freak scene and later got involved in anti-psychiatry, recalled: 'I was at that Arts Lab thing, the only time that I ever saw Trocchi in the flesh . . . inevitably the memories are considerably jaded . . . I was far less impressed by the bands than your man from *IT*. Nor was I particularly enamoured by Alex Trocchi that evening as I recall him coming across as unhappy, irritable, as if he didn't really want to be there . . . Burroughs and Laing made far more of a favourable impression.'

Virtually everyone who encountered Trocchi seems to have a horror story to tell about it and the following report emailed to me by Lynne Tillman on 26 August 2003 is a relatively mild example: '. . . as to Trocchi: when I met him . . . he was considered the most evil man in England – people blamed him for bringing heroin in, not Burroughs – one day at his flat, I witnessed a weeping father sitting on his couch, hoping to find his daughter – it was a terrible scene, and one that probably happened often in their big apt on Observatory Gardens – I don't think Alex felt much – and his "fate" was terrible, if you think about how not feeling landed him into having to feel something, when his wife, Lynn, died and their very young and beautiful sons – it was all horrible – I wasn't around him then – as I told you I saw him once later, on the street, and don't remember much – by then he had a bookstore, I think, and was drinking – and fat – his indifference to others, his selfishness, was ugly – how he could've handled all those sad parents coming to their flat looking for their kids, I don't know – but you'd have to have something turned off in you, absolutely – and it was he who got Lynn started on drugs, too, and she couldn't "handle" them as he could – I watched a scene or two between them that was pretty horrific . . .'

Likewise on 21 January 2004, the California-based literary mover and shaker Tosh Berman emailed another relatively mild Trocchi tale: '... my parents knew Alex Trocchi ... I am not sure if they met in LA or San Francisco. But recently we have been going through my father's photographs for an upcoming show – and there are images of Trocchi. At this point I should mention that my father is Wallace Berman, and he was an artist. His creative time-period was mid 1950s to 1976. In 1967 the whole family went to London to see Robert Fraser – who by chance was in prison due to the Rolling Stones bust at the time. But one of the highlights of the trip for me was visiting Alex Trocchi at his flat. What I remember was that there was a small baby and just him. He was shooting up junk – and I was shocked/intrigued at the time. I think I was twelve years old. All my young life I was surrounded by drug addicts of all sorts (strangely enough not my parents – but some of their friends were into it), but this was the first time I actually saw someone shoot up drugs. Again my take on it was typical twelve years old – disgusting and kind of neat to see!'

There are legions of stories doing the rounds about Trocchi nodding out, and during 'The State of Revolt' he was almost doing so in public. He'd come a long way from his native Glasgow. Trocchi relocated to Paris in the early 1950s where he edited the literary review *Merlin* and was involved in the early English-language publication of several influential writers including Samuel Beckett and Jean Genet. Simultaneously, Trocchi assumed membership of the Lettrist International, a group which mixed a revolutionary praxis with excessive drinking and which later transmogrified into the Situationist International. As well as writing high Modernist literature of his own, Trocchi was churning out porn both to make money and as a vehicle for subversion. Trocchi's best dirty book was a faked fifth volume of *My Life and Loves* by the philanderer and literary middleman Frank Harris. To secure publication for his first serious novel, *Young Adam*, Trocchi added some pornographic touches. Trocchi moved to the US in 1956, which is where he became a fully fledged smackhead with all the accompanying lifestyle trappings, including prostituting his American wife, Lynn, to raise money for skag. Trocchi's magnum opus, *Cain's Book*, was published in New York in 1961 and shocked conservative reviewers with its audaciously autobiographical descriptions of the drug underworld. Almost simultaneously, Trocchi was charged by the American authorities with supplying drugs to a minor, and with the aid of various people, including future rock star Leonard Cohen, he fled the US, returning to the UK via Canada. After a brief spell spent in Scotland, Trocchi found himself in London, where he became a fixture of the 1960s counter-culture. As a famous literary drug casualty, one of the many ways in which Trocchi demonstrated his disdain for the bourgeois book trade was by copying out his own novels in longhand and then selling these hoax productions as his 'original' manuscripts. Likewise, Barry Miles in his autobiography, *In the Sixties*, describes Trocchi in a way that creates the impression Alex was a kleptomaniac, illicitly stuffing stock under his shirt more or less whenever he visited a London bookshop.

From the early 1960s onwards Trocchi could no longer be bothered to write novels, although he did do translations and compose some impressive occasional pieces, such as the manifesto *The Invisible Insurrection of a Million Minds*. Instead of writing fiction Trocchi would come up with a synopsis of a planned work, take an advance from a gullible publisher who wanted the completed book, and then move on to his next mark with a new abstract. Less admirably, Trocchi also took great delight in turning people – and particularly beautiful women – on to heroin, and he used drug dealing as a nice little earner. Towards the end of his life Trocchi appears to have been getting about a thousand pounds a day for the drugs he supplied his key dealer, 'Grainger', and there would have been other outlets for his gear. Not a bad turnover for a smack broker in the 1970s or even the early 1980s. Given that Trocchi managed to avoid being busted in London, it is possible he was bunging the notoriously corrupt but nonetheless remarkably well-informed Metropolitan Police drug squad of that era a regular drink. I have no hard evidence to prove this, and the circumstantial case that can be made should not be treated as conclusive. Moving on,

Trocchi greatly exaggerated the size of his habit, telling whopping fibs to doctors in order to score large quantities of drugs on prescription, most of which he would sell on. When Trocchi was hospitalized this caused him some problems since medical staff directly administered him with far greater quantities of skag than he would normally take. Still, Trocchi survived such ill-advised medical assistance and the risk of an overdose no doubt palled in comparison to the possibility that the size of his drug script might be reduced.

Denis Browne emailed me the following observations about the scene around Trocchi on 18 September 2002: 'I knew Alex (AT) from late '78 up to his death in '84. From early '83 I worked with him as a kind of PA – the idea was that I'd help him get it together for a triumphant return to writing. I soon realized that this wasn't going to happen, but at that time I wasn't going to turn down the chance to hang out doing smack with such a cool guy (also helped run his 2nd hand book biz).

'By the time I met him he'd become a rather De Quincey-ish recluse, mainly due to Lynn & Mark's deaths I think. Funnily enough I'd been introduced to Alex by a very straight relative who ran a club where he drank. They'd got talking & she insisted he meet her wannabe writer nephew. I'd been into smack & AT's writing for quite a while, so it seemed a meeting which went beyond coincidence, & still seems strange to this day. I'd been hoping for Alex the mad beat writer, full-on junkie, 60s sigma activist/associate of Michael X, etc., but by then experience had made him a much more withdrawn type (tho not affecting his drug of choice). I'd been hoping for all-nite drug sessions laced with exclusive tales of Burroughs & co., but Alex was more into sitting down with a drink & some Roman history . . . One time he did yield to my pressure & took me to Eric Clapton's country mansion with him. My main memory of the visit is the Great Bluesman grouching out all afternoon over an Airfix kit he was trying to make (Lancaster bomber, I think) . . . Once I slagged off Colin Wilson as a typical hack who'd churn out books by the yard – turned out Alex had known him in the 50s & I was firmly & publicly slapped down – Alex told me that CW had lived on a tin of beans, 2 slices of bread & a can of Heineken a day while writing *The Outsider* as opposed to my half-hearted, excuse-ridden attempts to get my writing together (still true!).

'Feliks Topolski used to have a kind of "open day" at his house every Friday. I always wanted to go, but it was the same old story: – a few drinks at the Catherine Wheel, back to Alex's for a hit en route to Topolski's & that was that. I never knew Lynn – by the time I met Alex he'd got together with Sally Childs (much younger, didn't use at all), who'd been living in as a kind of au pair. She always had a fantasy of straightening Alex out & turning him into a Proper Writer, whatever that is. She & I never got on – she regarded me as a junkie hanger-on . . .'

Browne's portrait of Trocchi matches those of most other commentators who actually knew him. Despite this, Trocchi has recently undergone a kind of posthumous drug rehabilitation. The footage of 'The State of Revolt' in *Cain's Film* shows enough bad craziness to make it glaringly obvious that this is the first and best in an endless series of somnambulistic wakes for full-on long-haired freakdom. A few scraps of the Arts Lab slumber party as shot by Wadhawan were recycled in Tim Niel and Allan Campbell's disappointing 1996 BBC TV documentary about Trocchi entitled *A Life in Pieces*. Here 'The State of Revolt' is made to look like a literary reading rather than the hippie die-in it really was, although Niel and Campbell did have the good taste to leave in one piece of audience footage featuring my mother. The casual viewer is given no indication that what they are actually looking at is the onset of counter-cultural rigor mortis. Leaving aside the brief glimpse it affords of my mother, *A Life in Pieces* is not quite on a par with watching paint dry and considerably less educational. For anyone wanting to take a fresh look at the putrid corpse of the counter-culture, 'The State of Revolt' in its dead-to-the-world anti-glory (the fuller-length Wadhawan version rather than the Niel and Campbell re-edit) is the place to start. What you see is not so much the death of revolt, as death reified into a means of revolt; a Baudrillardian short-cut to postmodernity where Marx's critique of commodity fetishism is simultaneously preserved and reversed. This is the destiny of objects, leading to cultural black holes, antimatter and implosion. It goes without saying that the proto-yuppies who went on to reanimate the corpse of hippie chic in the form of lifestyle consumer items (health foods, kung fu magazines, 'alternative' rock music, etc.) self-consciously embraced rather than combated alienation. Objects are transformed into subjects and vice versa, and it's not done with smoke and mirrors. The inhuman reality of alienated social relations is not so much *Wholly Communion* as incommunicado. Burroughs was wrong about many things but correct to portray heroin as the penultimate commodity.

Asking around about the fate of student director Jamie Wadhawan, I was unable to find anyone who knew what had happened to him. The consensus of opinion was he must have disappeared into Trocchi's somnambulistic black hole. Wadhawan made one further documentary short with Trocchi and no one seems to have heard of him since. My mother followed a similar trajectory, eventually shacking up with Trocchi's key dealer, Grainger, in the late 1970s and soon afterwards being found dead in their shared Notting Hill bedsit. She was thirty-five and the authorities didn't consider it suspicious that she was found naked on her bed with the street door to her basement flat open. Inevitably the man who handled the inquiries was Paul Knapman, who subsequently became the centre of public disquiet about the coroners' system due to his handling of the *Marchioness* disaster. Incidentally, while both my mother and the anonymous go-go dancer featured in Wadhawan's 'State of Revolt' footage are also visible in Peter Whitehead's *Wholly Communion* documentary, they haven't to date featured in any account of the 1960s that I've read. Similarly, memories of Trocchi's Observatory Gardens pad have been exorcized from the Kensington psyche, with the building he lived in being renumbered in an attempt to fox those searching out the melancholy ghosts of his smacked-out bad craziness. About all that now needs to be said is that I remain almost literally Alex Trocchi's illegitimate son; and, since the counter-culture is dead, we are postmodern zombies . . .

[Stewart Home]

MADNESS IN SOMERS TOWN

The toad-faced man in the green coat has just slipped out of sight through the blue door into the estate office in Godwin. Last week, he told me that years ago he'd listened to Zappa's 'Valley Girl' on a ghetto blaster with a Moroccan friend, lying on a sand dune staring at the Saharan stars, smoking kif. Mohammed liked the music so much, he'd had to give him the cassette. Obviously a plant by the Medical Board, they want me to think I'm surrounded by cultural initiates. His coat looked crisp and smart in the sunlight, that kind of nuanced colour which spells this season, ochre green, is it, or a touch of olive? Then, right on cue, keeping the set alive, Uri passes just under my window, with his inevitable blue baseball cap and his mop and the big blue plastic detergent bucket on rollers. Everything is blue round here, just to rub in the implications of 'Crowndale': real estate as monarchy. Ground rent. Silver service reflecting a blue tablecloth. Royal blue rules all of you. Silence glowering over empty courtyards. Sweet meadows aswim with buttercups and daisies surveyed by armoured thugs on carthorses.

A kid exits the blue door, cheerful in the sunshine. He's wearing a brand-new baseball cap, Uri-chic. He grins and waves at Uri, his role model. Except his cap's peak is longer and sharper, a vicious, pecking point, no one can hold back that nestling cockiness. A kidscad buttending a bland old isaac. A middle-aged guy in white overalls walks by slowly, intimating the dignity of labour. Street ballet on the estate precinct, every move scripted by filmic omni-science. The brain spins despite the stunning dose of Largactyl. When will they splash water on my window and pretend it's rain, let me believe the roofman is pissed off and angry? The woman in

409

a cream-coloured robe has pulled down her veil, she's talking to Xena and Uri, shrugging shoulders in the late March sunshine. Buds on the twigs to give me the tip-off it's spring. The scene-setters provide so many clues, I can use the world as my calendar, it's practically medieval. Oh your starry Almanac, put me right back in the torture rack, Jack. 'Can you read the signs?' is all the signs say, finally, that surly emphasis tipping you slowly into mental illness, a sick soundtrack by the Specials. Hello, Jerry Dammers, here come your bullets . . .

Guy with a paunch and a navy-blue fisherman's slop, his belly welded like he's about to give an after-dinner speech, a weapon worthy of Lawrence Upton. In his cups, he worships Odin. There's a white van parked in front of the brick wall of Godwin Court. It shines blandly in the sun, bonnet and door emblazoned with a logo for 'Key Elevators Ltd': the letter 'K' in an octagon. It's a scenery flat, the Medical Board reminding me of the eleventh letter of the alphabet, the primitive counter starting on a new set of fingers, the same anew. Their rationale for this 'cheer up' message is the chronic problem with the lifts, they're always breaking down. One day they'll fix them so you push the top button, and you'll shoot straight into the sky, a jet-pack roaring at your back, azure blue studded with golden Kays, my mother smiling at me through brilliant white clouds flossed by Manzoni.

Now a middle-aged woman with dark hair and a square red shopping bag on wheels: Godwin and Crowndale are busy this morning. Wheels, the great advance on lifting things. Two workmen, young, going to fat, one with Billy Idol hair, bleached yellow, the other flips his cigarette still alight on the steps before they enter: 'I might have to do some work, doesn't mean I have to like it.' Parked cars in front of the white van, shiny like tiny models. The great escape for all of you. Woman in black with a black headscarf, walking by the bottle-bin, black metal wheelie-bin with CAMDEN COUNCIL embossed in gold. After Eight-style to raise the tone of the neighbourhood. Black to tone my mood down, damp the manic volume, alleviate my greedy rise to the champagne skies. Poor Ben's in the big sweet jars: licorice reminders of the big black nothing which waits for me when the manic fizz dies down. OWN ASS ON, EAR ASS ONLY, APE ON: the kids love finding gawky obscenities hidden inside the council's utility lingo. Me too.

Girl passes with grey coat, striped socks, folded arms: 'I'm cold and I don't have to like it.' Blank blue sky behind untidily sketched branches. Red stop light in front of the Working Men's College, green council sign for the estate on the other side of Crowndale Road, temporary yellow sign with an arrow: DIVERTED TRAFFIC. Red/green/yellow prints a hieroglyph inside my eye, green/red, stop/go . . . eco/socialism adding up to yellow action: Go Go Go!! The 46 swings out of Camden Street and the red zone into Crowndale Road with the double yellow lines, the bus's signage an oblong of detail moving just above the wall. Blossom, branches, window frames, bay tree. Camden Onyx dustcart, everything moving according to the street's grid, all those hefty right-angles. What I thought was 'abstract' in the painting of the 1920s was just the actual moving around me, those agglomerations of intent, the real thing beneath the rim of my hot ideological bubble'n'spume. Bubbles break off in the form of postcards made with torn scraps of paper and Pritt Stick, shots of density sped to their targets by post office payments of 28p. £3.36 for a wallet of gold oblongs, reach bar-none in those instant days . . .

Toad-faced man emerges again, walks across the car park with the dignity of an animal observed from a naturalist's bunker. I imagine him catching a fly with a three-foot sticky tongue, decide that's de trop, I'll lose my readers. Three veiled women, all reds and blacks, scarves waving raggedly in the icy wind. A cab zips by, up Crowndale, a bright pink stripe across the wall: the grey drear cracks, lets some dayglo wetness in. The Medical Board prickles my waiting knowledge-buds with sherbet powder, a trail of citric sparks and formal stings. Down here below, the groaning machinery shines nature's lights within its walls, lets go flocks of miners' lamps into the pump room. What a dish to set before a king.

[Ben Watson]

THE GAZETTEER OF
DISAPPEARANCES & DELETIONS

OLD NIGHTCLUBS

St Dunstan's-in-the-East/Idol Lane/Dagon

Three and a half centuries ago, the Charles One reign
came to an end in the Years of Civil Disturbance. It was
then that St Dunstan's-in-the-East was occupied by the
Church of Dagon. St Dunstan's was a wooden building
in the City just north of the wharves at Balin's Gate,
where bright fishing boats loaded with herrings and shell-
fish used to tie up. The Church of Dagon worshipped
the ancient fish-god, whose wooden statue was set up in
the nave. Dagon reared himself up on his tail, his hands
like flippers and the hair on his head shaped in corn-rows.
His priests wore tall mitres painted with fish-eyes and long
green capes. Fishmongers, ironmongers and animal skin-
ners came to the services. They lay in hammocks made of
nets and muttered their prayers as the priests cracked their
bones. The grounds of the church were thick with imported vegetation and the moss on the gravestones was wet.
There was once an alligator kept in the yard, a runaway
from the menagerie at the Tower. Outside the church in
Idol Lane, the streets were crowded with amulet vendors
and incense makers, their rugs spread out on the mud.
The Church of Dagon disappeared when St Dunstan's
was consumed in the Dreaded Fire at the start of the
Charles Two reign. It is said they went into the River.
The Architect Royal, Christoph Wren, built a stone min-
aret on the site to prevent them reappearing. St Dunstan's
today is a Corporation garden with pleasing effects.

St Leonard's/Eastcheap/Moloch

It was in the Years of Civil Disturbance at the end of the Charles One reign that the Reformist Church of Moloch moved into St Leonard's. Now, St Leonard's was a wooden building with a high chimney, on the corner of Eastcheap and New Fish Street in the City. Its Eastcheap front entrance was imposing, with high steps, bolted oak doors and flaming lamps over the porch. People avoided it in this busy area full of bakeries, ale houses and snack bars. There were rumours that the Church practised infant sacrifice, but these were dismissed by the scholars of the time. Its vespers were attended by the shame-faced wives of wine merchants and bankers and single women dressed in veils. They used the back door on New Fish Street. The priests of Moloch wore leather aprons caked with blood. They attended to their congregation with kettles of hot water heated on the stoves raised before their idol. The effigy of Moloch comprised a brass furnace in the shape of a squatting woman with the head of a bull. Her lips were apart to reveal the fiery grate in the hole between her legs. The priests of Moloch eased bloodied offerings from their frightened devotees and placed them tenderly on the flaming lips of their idol. Trumpets were sounded to cover the sounds of the women's cries. The Church of Moloch left the City and went south of the River to the Liberties when St Leonard's was destroyed in the Dreaded Fire at the start of the Charles Two reign. Some say they hid themselves in a basement of St Thomas's Hospital, others that they set up shop outside the Bullring. The corner of Eastcheap and New Fish Street is now occupied by the Syndicate Bank.

St Margaret's/New Fish Street/Chemos

St Margaret's was home to the Temple of Chemos in the Years of Civil Disturbance that followed the Charles One reign. A wooden building just north of the Bridge in the City, St Margaret's stood between New Fish Street and Pudding Lane. Its altar boys had painted faces and sported finger-cymbals and silver toe-rings. They loitered at the wharves and lured merchant seamen back to the Temple with promises of ecstasy. Here, initiates were made drunk with grain alcohol and caressed into signing away their worldly possessions to the Temple. The priests of Chemos kept their sacred papers in a wicker cabinet shaped like a man. This was their idol. They captured the moans of initiates on reed instruments and composed songs of divine love. The initiates were permitted one night of pleasure only. When the altar boys had brought them past the point of orgasm, they were stripped of their clothing and turned out of the building to beg in the streets. St Margaret's was secretly fired by Royal Navy officers at the start of the Charles Two reign. It burned to the ground. This episode is covered over in official histories of the Dreaded Fire that spread through the narrow parts of the City. The Temple of Chemos travelled south of the River to the Liberties, where they re-formed as a transvestite band of players. The Architect Royal, Christoph Wren, drove a stone column into the ground at New Fish Street to banish the memory of the Temple of Chemos. It stands there to this day at a desolate crossroads scoured by the wind.

St Olave's/Tooley Street/Belial

When the reign of Charles One came to an end in the Years of Civil Disturbance, St Olave's was where the Fundamentalist Church of Belial used to worship. St Olave's was a large wooden building south of the River in the Liberties-without-the-City. It stood on Tooley Street opposite a converted stone priory where travellers lodged for the night and backed on to a warren of tenements, wharves and quays. Tooley Street was filled with carts, mounted horses and pedestrians, all moving very rapidly. There were cargoes of leaf tobacco transported from ships in the River, barrels of beer brought in from the Southwark breweries, gangs of sailors with rings in their ears, prostitutes in bright robes, recently arrived Africans, Americans and Indians, all carrying bags over their shoulders. There was tumult. The Church of Belial congregated at night in the sunken crypt of St Olave's. Drums sounded through the cavernous space and bright lights strobed the gloom. There were no priests in this scene. There were only celebrants. They wore black cassocks with cowls and their faces were dusted with white powder. They came together in groups of two or three and invented ceremonies of desire. There were piercings and whippings, beatings and fistings. Belial was incarnated in the throng of knotted bodies. The next day saw celebrants drifting out of St Olave's into the alleys and lanes around Tooley Street. They walked arm in arm and expressed many words of tender love to each other. They kissed in the street. The Church of Belial disappeared from St Olave's at the beginning of the Charles Two reign. The story goes they jumped in the air and took flight for America. St Olave's no longer exists. In its place is an Art Deco office building named St Olaf House, just opposite London Bridge Station.

St Pancras/Soper Lane/Tammuz

During the Years of Civil Disturbance at the end of the Charles One reign, the Cult of Tammuz used to gather at St Pancras. This was a sacred grove in the City just west of the crossroads at the Royal Exchange. It lay next to St Benet Shere Hog and St Scythes in Soper Lane, a narrow stretch of little churches surrounded by tall buildings. The Cult of Tammuz worshipped the nameless Great Swine and made sacrifices to her every spring. Four or five of the most beautiful pre-op transsexuals in the Cult were chosen by the priestesses to become suitors to the Swine. They always screamed for joy and clapped their hands when they were elected. On the Day of Marriage, they were stripped of their garments, plucked to remove all facial and body hair, and led to St Pancras, where the ivy-clad boughs of the myrtle trees entwined to form a shady arbour. Here, they were tied to the trees with leather straps made by the local cordwainers. As the sun rose, the Cult of Tammuz gathered around the myrtle trees at St Pancras, took drugs and danced to the hypnotic drone of the bagpipes. This was primarily a religion of animal-skin workers and there were fellmongers, tanners and curriers among the celebrants. As evening came, the priestesses put on masks made of boarskin and leaped close to the bound men, waving knives made from tusks. They tied a cord round the scrotal sac of each young man to stop the flow of blood to the genitals, dedicated him to Tammuz, god of flowers, and then removed the testicles and penis in one slashing motion. The sudden rush of blood was captured in clay pots. Then the heated end of a myrtle branch was placed into the ragged wound to prevent it closing over. The wailing of the transsexuals lasted through the night as the festivities climaxed with an orgy of mutual masturbation. Some didn't make it through surgery and were claimed directly by the Great Swine. They were buried in the ground beneath the trees, where the genitals of Tammuz were also scattered. The ceremony ended as the sun rose on the first day that was longer than the last night. The surviving post-op transsexuals were cut down and gratefully ensconced in robes trimmed with white fur. They had spent the night with the Great Swine and now possessed the gift of prophecy. They were sought out by the Royal silk merchants, heroin traffickers and pepperers of Bucklebury just round the corner, for news on how their ships fared in Asia. The blood of Tammuz was prized as an aphrodisiac and sold in the grocers and chemists of Eastcheap. In the summer, St Pancras bloomed with a vitality that was obscene. Sweet-smelling gum oozed from the bark of the myrtle trees, which were covered in honeysuckle and wild roses. St Pancras was consumed in the Dreaded Fire at the start of the Charles Two reign, together with St Benet Shere Hog and St Scythes. Exiled from the City, the Cult of Tammuz took ship to America and erected their Maypole at Merry Mount. What remains of St Pancras today are a few trees in a patch of ivy-covered waste ground just up from the Green Man pub. It is backed on to by the Eastcheap grocers Tesco and watched over by a bored security guard.

St Stephen's/Coleman Street/Jehovah

The Moorish Orthodox Tribe of Jehovah camped at St Stephen's during the Years of Civil Disturbance that ended the Charles One reign, three and a half centuries ago. St Stephen's was a tiny wooden chapel at the south-west end of Coleman Street just off from Moorgate, a back door out of the City leading to the marshy fields where people used to walk their dogs and practise their archery. Coleman Street and its surrounds were filled with the halls of various Royal trading companies and craft guilds. St Stephen's was just down from the Wool Exchange on the corner of one of the little alleys that cut through to the City government offices at Guildhall on Basinghall Street. The alley was covered at both ends but open to the skies at its middle and contained an arcade packed with cloth dealers. St Stephen's had wooden shutters outside its front door, with stairs leading up to the place of worship just beneath the roof. The priests of Jehovah covered their heads with brightly beaded kipas and wore scarlet velvet gowns hung with golden chains. They brought the boys of the Tribe of Jehovah to the sacred yurt at the time of their maturity, and circumcised them as the congregation chanted from the script of the Deal prepared for them by their god in ancient times. The foreskins were gathered up, painted with gold leaf and sewn together to make the scrolls on which were tattooed the Notes on the Deal. On the Sabbath Day, the Tribe of Jehovah gathered to debate what shape the Notes should take. At the end of the ceremony, the priests retired to the rooftop to sip coffee and consult their telescopes. When the first five stars were spied in the sky, the Sabbath was over. St Stephen's was destroyed in the Dreaded Fire inaugurating the Charles Two reign. The Tribe of Jehovah saved their yurt from the flames, packed up and moved to America. No distinct trace of St Stephen's remains.

[Steve Beard]

NORTHERN LINES

DEATH OF A CLEANER

I cannot follow them into their world of death,
Or their hunted world of life, though through the house,
Death and the hunted bird sing at every nightfall.

HENRY REED, 'Chrysothemis'

Not everyone has a house cleaner who knew Dylan Thomas and
Francis Bacon, and who was born into an aristocratic family and
went to Wellington College and Cambridge University. I had one,
called Mr Ashburner, and he disappeared from my life as suddenly
as, fifty years before, he had disappeared from the life of his own
family. This is what I know about Mr Ashburner and the strange
period before and after his death, six years ago.

Antony Wentworth Ashburner was born near Lausanne Switzerland in 1921 and fell down the basement steps, outside my house in
Primrose Hill, on a wet and windy April Fool's Wednesday in 1998.
He died on 4 April, in the Royal Free Hospital, Hampstead, never
having regained consciousness. A coroner in the tiny, neo-Gothic
court in Old St Pancras churchyard decided that the fall had been
an accident, leading to severe brain damage, and that internal bleeding was the primary cause of death. There was no sign of a stroke
or heart attack and certainly no suggestion that he was pushed. He
seems to have slipped on a wet step, while wearing rather smooth-
soled shoes.

Mr Ashburner was the son of Harley Wentworth Ashburner, a
retired lieutenant colonel in the British army (born in the 1850s),
and of Beatrice Blanche Adele Julia Emma Doxat de Champvent. She
came from a long line of Swiss aristocrats which can be traced back to
the thirteenth century. The English Ashburners claim that Beatrice's
family were a dark and unstable breed. Both parents were divorcees
when they married, shortly after the First World War. Beatrice Ashburner, a Roman Catholic, was excommunicated after her divorce.

Antony and his sister, Ann, born a year after him, were brought up in the isolated and imposing Doxat family chateau at Champvent, near Yverdon-les-Bains in the Vaud canton. It is a private residence now, but for a while after the last World War it seems to have been open to the public. Brother and sister were brought up by nannies and servants and had little contact with their elderly father – and not much more with his young wife. Letters from Ashburner's mother, written to him just after the Second War, suggest considerable cruelty offered in his direction by his father. The children's summer holidays were spent on the Côte d'Azur and were shared, on occasion, with the offspring of Haile Selassie and a governess.

By the early 1930s the family had moved to Cheltenham. Ann went to Cheltenham Ladies' College, which she hated and was expelled from. Ashburner was sent to Wellington College in Berkshire, an establishment aimed at those intended for the army. In photographs of 'Hardinge Dormitory' in 1936 and 1939, Ashburner looks quite normal and rather more handsome than most of his fellow pupils. In a 1965 letter to the Labour politician Patrick Gordon Walker, following the notorious Smethwick by-election, he recalled that he owed 'a debt of gratitude to [Patrick's brother] Robin Gordon Walker', who was his form master at Wellington and, so he says, the only good influence in his life until he was about twenty years old. Gordon Walker was subsequently to leave the school under something of a cloud. A friend tells me that Ashburner gave him an amusing account of trying to lose his virginity, as a teenager, in a brothel in Tunis.

According to his sister, he went up to Cambridge in 1939 to read law. If he did go to Cambridge it didn't suit him and he transferred to Birmingham, where he probably read English. There is a mysterious and evocative poem by the Birmingham poet Henry Reed, called 'Chrysothemis', which gives an insight into Ashburner's life in the Second City. After his death, I found a galley proof of the poem in his untidy flat at the wrong end of Ladbroke Grove. There was a dedication, handwritten in ink: 'To Antony from Henry,

December 1942'. The poem is darkly Eliotic and casts light on an important, if brief, relationship. It was published in John Lehmann's *New Writing and Daylight* that winter.

In a letter of 1965 – to Dorothy Baker, a BBC Third Programme script-editor – Ashburner recalls this acquaintance during a brief spell when he was living in the basement flat of a house belonging to Professor Sargent Florence, the left-wing economist and sociologist. This was Highgrove, a Birmingham house famous enough to be the subject of a short TV film by David Lodge. Ashburner's flatmate was Dr Bobby Case, a pathologist at St Chad's Hospital. 'I wondered then,' he wrote to Baker, 'and I have sometimes wondered since, how it was that Bobby Case managed to get hold of so much offal for our dinners – in view of wartime shortages . . .'

Highgrove, a large house, now demolished, was the haunt of writers and radicals, such as Auden and Spender, as well as the novelist and Birmingham University lecturer Walter Allen – whose name can be found in Ashburner's surviving address book. Highgrove was a Midlands bohemian hang-out unknown to most metropolitans. Perhaps, like Julian Maclaren-Ross, another acquaintance, Ashburner was one of the misfits and deserters incarcerated in the psychiatric wing of Northfield military hospital in the Birmingham suburbs, one of W. R. Bion's patients (guinea pigs).

What else did he do in the war? Reed went on to work at Bletchley Park. My mother-in-law, who was in the same section, remembers him taking a female colleague out for lunch. Reed's Bletchley Park friend, Michael Ramsbotham, has no recollection whatever of Ashburner. Was he a conscientious objector? In my more fanciful moments I imagine he was a spy, although I'm not sure which side he would have been on. By the end of the war, he was living in Fitzrovia and working at Foyles bookshop. He wasn't keen on Christina Foyle, he told me.

Ann remembers her brother in 1946 at an old haunt of mine, the now celebrated Marquis of Granby pub in Charlotte Street – with its clientele of gangsters, bookies and homosexuals in search of rough trade. She hadn't seen him since the start of the war, until she discovered him drinking in the company of Dylan Thomas and Francis Bacon – like a fugitive character from a novel by Patrick Hamilton. He mentioned to me, while scrubbing my sink, that he had known such people as the 'two Roberts' (the painters Colquhoun and MacBryde) and Tambimuttu, the poet and editor. I hadn't realized how close he had been to them. Walter Allen, who had been in Fitzrovia since the middle of the war, is a likely link to the world he called 'New Grub Street'. Ann says that Dylan Thomas acknowledged her presence by making an outrageous pass.

The last his family heard of Ashburner, until Ann's daughter read the 'Deaths' column in the *Daily Telegraph*, was around 1950, when Ashburner was living in Paris and performing in a British Council theatrical tour. Ann assumed that he had been dead for years and thought it likely he had been a homosexual and thus something of an outcast. I noted with grim humour the name of her house at this time: 'Ashen Faggot'.

In his letter to Dorothy Baker, Ashburner refers to a manic tour of Sheridan's *The School for Scandal*, in which he took part with Barbara Bray (later a commissioning editor for BBC drama). He wonders if it would make a good piece for radio. He tells her that he is about to take a group of American women around the world and hints that the experience might also provide some promising material for comedy: 'Their itinerary alone is a masterpiece of unconscious humour.'

In 1951 Ashburner was reported as a missing person. He had left his flat with no trace. I have found very little evidence of his life between 1951 and 1964. A ration book of 1952–3 gives two addresses: 21 Romilly Street in Soho and 193 Gloucester Place in Marylebone. At some stage in the 1950s he moved west to 14 Cambridge Square in Paddington, to a house which has now been demolished. He talked of an unpleasant landlord.

I have found a rental agreement for a radio from 1953 (the year I was born) and a 1962 court summons for non-payment of five instalments. How he earned a living I can't say. There are a few comedy scripts for radio, some rather good, including one about a ton-up vicar. Henry Reed, as the successful author of the early 'alternative' radio comedy series about the absurd 'twelve-tone composeress' Hilda Tablet, would have been a contact at the BBC. I imagine that Ashburner hung around BBC pubs such as the Stag, just north of Oxford Street. There must have been many part-time jobs. He spoke of a spell as a pressure-cooker salesman, another echo of Maclaren-Ross.

By 1964 Ashburner had moved to 170a Ladbroke Grove, his last address. Suddenly, for a brief period, there is a lot more evidence about his life. At forty-three, he is a prolific letter writer: to newspapers, local council officials and utilities employees. There is a large file of correspondence (1964–5) about the banning of William Burroughs's novel *The Naked Lunch* by the chief librarian of Kensington, Mr S. C. Holliday. Ashburner waged a one-man campaign to have the book restored to the shelves. He wrote to, and received positive replies from, figures such as: Anthony Burgess, Samuel Beckett, Kingsley Amis, Al Alvarez, Kenneth Armitage, Brigid Brophy, Vera Brittain, Cecil Beaton, John Calder and his old friend Walter Allen. He was also in correspondence with the very 1960s-sounding 'Sexual Emancipation Movement'. In February 1965, following coverage in the press – the *Express* referred in a piece about the case to a 'bloke called A. W. Ashburner' – the ban was lifted.

Copious press-cuttings and letters show that Ashburner interested himself in the public reaction to the death of Winston Churchill in 1965. It is not clear why this was so. He seems in general to have been a militant and witty campaigner on behalf of causes ranging from animal welfare to the arms trade. Churchill doesn't fit this profile – maybe the cuttings were research towards a late radio skit? Cheque stubs show regular payments to charities such as Save the Children and Amnesty. Given his likely income in his last years, the sums donated represent considerable generosity. Another significant batch of papers from the early 1960s, found in that dark basement flat, show that Ashburner was cited as a co-respondent in a divorce case. This needs unravelling: was he a legal convenience for a friend or was this a real affair? If so, it leads to his unlikely metamorphosis into a domestic cleaner.

An important facet of his life was his work as an international tour guide. Passport stamps prove that he travelled the world, while employed by a rather dubious-sounding New York company called Gramercy Travel Systems: Honolulu, Tokyo, Manila, Phnom Penh, Bangkok, Colombo, Madras, Calcutta, Agra, Teheran, Beirut, Cairo, Tel Aviv, Athens. The *Hong Kong Star* (22 October 1966) carries the headline WANTED: 16 ESCORTS FOR BACHELOR GIRLS and a photograph of Ashburner surrounded by his earnest and affluent, mainly American, middle-aged charges. He is quoted as remarking: 'The tours are strictly for single people. The only condition is that everyone comes on his or her own . . . We're not a lonely-hearts club, just a company with a gimmick.' He is pictured wearing a shiny mohair suit, looking like a lounge lizard, a professional seducer of naive or willing women.

In a crowded cupboard in Ladbroke Grove – which also contained a leather-bound early edition of *Paradise Lost* – there were many guide books, maps and phrase books from this rather glamorous period of his life. Disturbingly, there were also contact prints showing Chinese soldiers standing over pits full of dead bodies. The photographs must have been taken by Ashburner himself, as they were found among routine shots of tourist sites and lady clients.

At some point in the mid 1960s, just after the documentation dries up, Ashburner became a cleaner, at first working for an agency. I don't know why he did this. Perhaps he felt he'd tried hard enough to be a writer, didn't fancy more travelling, was disappointed in love – or gave up in order to lead a simple, fairly ascetic life. The anguished and moving letters from his mother, after the war, seem to be answers to questions provoked by a nervous breakdown and suggest a seriously disturbed childhood under the shadow of a cruel father. Given the details we have about his life, you don't have to be an over-zealous Freudian to wonder why a man in his forties with so many abilities decides to dedicate the rest of his life to domestic cleaning. He worked for my parents-in-law, Pamela and

Daniel Waley, who found him through a neighbour of theirs in the 1970s – and then he worked for my wife, Cat, and for me from 1980, when we moved to Primrose Hill after our brief exile in South London. There were other clients, though precious few at the time of his death, when he had about £1,500 left in the bank.

Was he a good cleaner? He was very good at floors and all the serious stuff requiring strenuous arm effort and bending down. He was average at dusting and he wouldn't do ironing. He had a marvellous way of asking for new cleaning fluid or Hoover bags, through simple notes left in amusing places which reminded you of your basic duty in a few well-chosen words: 'More Ajax?' He was great fun to be with and became part of our life, spreading his discreet, benign, pragmatic and strangely unworldly charm through the atmosphere of the house. I think he liked the houses he worked in as places of calm and quietness, and one had the feeling that in some odd fashion he had chosen you, rather than the other way round. He was always kind and courteous and would present you with gifts of his homemade jam and marmalade. He was a very serious gourmet and chef. The most impressive part of his dingy flat was the kitchen with its recipe books and huge array of utensils, pots and pans. He was extremely helpful in advice on culinary techniques and on where to buy the best ingredients. He even wrote a charming menu for my parents-in-law's Burmese cat, Pushkin. He had once been a devotee of the cheaper cuts at Harrods and of the Whiteley's Food Hall, as well as a believer in organic meat.

Ashburner was an expert solver of crossword puzzles, like my mother-in-law, Pam. She remembers his first words to her upon entering her flat in 1975: 'Books do furnish a room. The last time I saw Maclaren-Ross was at Maida Vale station.' Although he was friendly and engaging, one never asked him direct personal questions. My mother-in-law can recall only one occasion on which he offered any information about himself – that his father had no brothers. Another time, suffering from an enlarged prostate gland, too ill and depressed to work, he did confide in my father-in-law, who recalls that: 'I talked to him on the phone at some length, trying to reassure him (in particular about the operation involved, which I had undergone myself). I also offered to lend him money if this would enable him to have the operation properly and thus shorten the period of waiting. He politely refused, saying that he had the necessary sum in reserve, if required. Anyway, he had the operation and was soon back at work and in his normal spirits.'

We don't know who his friends, if any, were. He took very carefully planned holidays, alone, for four weeks every summer, usually in a remote part of France, chosen for its cuisine and ornithological interest. He sent amusing postcards. His cleaning seems to have been a way to pay for these summer trips. Spanish was his final linguistic effort, replacing jazz on the Walkman head-phones he wore while scrubbing the floor or bath. He was a good musician, took musicianship classes at the City Lit and had a piano in his flat, on top of which we found sheet music for works by Debussy and Satie, borrowed from Marylebone Public Library. He was fit, if rather overweight, and cycled from Ladbroke Grove to north-west London right up to his death. He always wore cycle clips and a daffodil-coloured cycling cape. He had a knapsack on his back and moved along at a stately pace.

When the portly figure of Mr Ashburner had fallen down the steps that wet Wednesday morning, my wife did not know, as she left the house by our front door to go to work, that he was lying just below her. When she got home at about three o'clock that afternoon she found an ambulance outside the house. Someone had seen him, after six hours, lying unconscious outside the basement front door, his head resting by a large flowerpot, arms outstretched, legs crossed and reaching up the steps. He was taken to hospital and died without regaining consciousness – although a friend and I attempted to get some response by playing Mozart and Sidney Bechet to him. During this time we entered his flat and tried to discover his next of kin. Nothing gave us a clue. When he was pronounced dead on the Saturday, my father-in-law put an announcement in the papers. Ashburner's niece rang from Devon – the last place he had taken a long summer holiday and where he was booked to go again in June – to say that she had been looking for a birth notice and saw his name by chance. She wondered if it was her 'long-lost Uncle Antony'. I met her, and her mother, Ann, with other members of the family, a few days later at the Polish Daquise café in South Kensington, which seemed the right sort of anachronistic setting for such a strange gathering. Slowly, the extraordinary tale unfolded and we were all struck by the astonishing convergence of lives and events we were witnessing. Ann had assumed that her brother was long dead, and was so upset, both by the death and the recollection of his disappearance, that she didn't attend the cremation at Mortlake – where we read some Wordsworth and played pieces by Schubert, Sidney Bechet and bird song. Only five of us were present for the cremation, we found no other friends. In July we went down to Devon to scatter the ashes on a hillside near Colyton. They were picked up by a sudden gust of wind and disappeared into the clear summer sky.

There is a more personal side to this story and one I can't easily describe. Throughout the whole episode of his death I was in a distinctly strange state of mind. I kept reading T. S. Eliot, especially 'The Waste Land', 'Ash Wednesday' and 'Four Quartets', and lines came to me during the period after the accident, each of which appeared to be some morbid sign of a metaphysical drama going on around me in the 'Unreal City'. I was like a frenetic cabbalistic student in my keen attention to patterns of seemingly trivial details and my sense of psychic charge and shape across time and space – although I stopped short of drawing lines over maps to find hidden geometries of fate. Eliot, I later discovered, went to Lausanne to recover from a breakdown, and began to write 'The Waste Land' at the time Ashburner was born there. 'April is the cruellest month,' of course, and man can know only 'a heap of broken images'. There is the figure of the 'drowned Phoenician sailor' shown by Madame Sosostris in her 'wicked deck of cards', and above all the 'Hanged Man' she cannot find – upside down and in exactly the position as Ashburner when he was found. 'Fear death by water' was a line I couldn't keep out of my mind and it still alarms me.

I was also reading Sir Thomas Browne's *Urne Buriall* and *Garden of Cyrus*, and looking closely at Paul Nash's illustrated editions of Browne, as well as his other work of the early 1930s – made when he was living in a mansion flat in St Pancras. Everything had the quality of a sign and I kept seeing, everywhere I walked in London, Browne's famous quincunx – the cross with five points which he believed showed the true Christian-Platonic and geometrical order of creation. When I visited Ashburner's body, draped in gorgeous purple, in a small sepulchral room in the morgue in Old St Pancras churchyard, I noticed the quincuncial security bars on the office windows. When I read an official document, I kept seeing, like William Carlos Williams, the number five. The steps where Ashburner fell had a lattice pattern on them. 'For all things are seen Quincuncially.'

My wife died of a rare sarcoma in January 2001, after a mercifully short illness, and I have always connected that terrible event with Mr Ashburner's fatal accident and the period surrounding it. Such experiences are frightening. At one point, looking desperately for some cause and miracle cure, I was nearly persuaded by a theory linking cancer with natural radiation disturbed by the flow of underground rivers. Cat's consultant looked at me kindly and questioningly when I mentioned it. Cat felt guilty that she had not noticed Ashburner that morning, though she had no reason to blame herself for a death which was certain from the moment of the fall. Maybe she had some other feeling the accident had provoked. There was much in common between them and, for her, he was a very special person. She was shattered by his death in a way I don't think I was. Looking back I can't really say in what way the two deaths were connected, except that in my mind they still are, by a host of words and images and peculiar sensations about fire, the number five, rose gardens, ashes, the years 1596 and 1965, water, exotic birds, the north side of Sidney Sussex College, Cambridge, Wednesday, the letters H. D., and a myriad other things which tantalizingly float around in my psyche and only hint at sense.

[Richard Humphreys]

OLD HAGS

1 Old Mother Red Cap

Maurice Sendak says that the Wild Things in his story were inspired by his aunts and uncles who used to come to tea on Sundays in Brooklyn and loom their whiskery faces close to his and kiss him and sit him on their laps and pet him with their leathery hands; he expresses a kind of Swiftian revulsion at the memory of their huge hairy noses and ears and moles, their bloodshot eyes and rotten teeth. 'I lived in apprehension,' he remembers, 'that, if my mother cooked too slowly and they were getting very hungry, they would lean over, pinch my cheek, and say, "You look so good, we could eat you up." And in fact we had no doubt they would. They ate anything in sight.'[1]

But the Wild Things who roll their terrible eyes and show their terrible claws don't fill Max with disgust, and he glories in his becoming their king. Likewise they inspire anything but revulsion in us, Sendak's devoted readers, child and adult: his clumsy lolloping monsters beckon us to their wild rumpus, just as irresistibly as they call to Max in his wolf suit.

I didn't take any of the Wild Things for females, it must be said, until I read Sendak's memoir, but many much-loved stories are full of old hags: the silhouette of the humpbacked, beak-nosed crone and her wavering wheedling speech bring instant recognition that magical reversals lie ahead. 'Old Mother,' says Cinderella – or Gretchen – or Belle – or the sister who gets to spit diamonds and pearls; the encounter with the hag is always the beginning of something, something that is going to be exciting (even when you know what's coming because this is one of your favourite stories). Of course, the old hag can be a wicked witch, like Baba Yaga or the ancient fairy with the grudge in 'Sleeping Beauty', but as often as not, she's like one of Sendak's Wild Things, and can be tamed.

When I first came to live in North London, there were two pubs called after old hags: Old Mother Red Cap opposite the tube station at Camden Town and Mother Shipton at the corner of Prince of Wales Road and Malden Road.[2] But in the late 1980s, they both changed their names: the old women have disappeared.

Mother Red Cap went back to the seventeenth century: the alehouse appears on old maps, and by the eighteenth century had become a large coaching inn standing on open ground at the three-way junction of carriageways travelling north; in a later engraving, the pub has a large garden to the side. In 1704, a certain Margaret Bartholomew was recorded as the alehouse keeper at Mother Damnable's, and it seems that this legendary figure, aka the 'Witch of Camden Town' or the 'Shrew of Kentish Town', lies behind the pub's name.

Jinney Bingham, she was called, and her mother was a pedlar's daughter in Scotland, who brought her husband, Jacob Bingham, into the family trade when he was serving in the army up there. He was a brickie from Kentish Town, and after they married, they went peddling round the country together. On one of their wanderings, Jinney, aged sixteen, met Gipsy George Coulter, had a baby and went to live with this 'ne'er do well'; but he was done for sheep-stealing, 'from some meadows near Holloway', and hanged at Tyburn.

It is the stuff of ballads; it could be a story by George Borrow or Thomas Hardy or Angela Carter . . . I have it from a local historian, called Harold Adshead, who wrote about Jinney in a small magazine called *Enquiry* in May 1950.

Jinney did become the heroine of a ballad, but not until after Gipsy George swung from the gallows. The hardships of her life gathered: further adventures, further disasters with unsuitable partners followed hard upon one another: first a drunken reprobate called Darby, then another called Pitcher. Between these two men, her parents were accused of bringing about a young girl's death through the black arts. They were both hanged, too.

Then Pitcher died, found burned to a crisp inside their stove.

Jinney's family history did not help: she was charged with his murder. A witness testified – bizarrely – that Pitcher would often take refuge in the oven to escape her tongue-lashings. Somehow, perhaps because this convinced the court, she was acquitted. She became a loner, living in a cottage her father had built on a piece of uncultivated ground near the crossroads at Camden Town. A three-way crossing: *trivia*, which is one of the names of the Goddess of the Underworld, Hecate. The likes of Jinney turn into hell hags; her dangerous reputation grew, and she was shunned.

One night a man on the run took shelter with her, and stayed. He had money, and Jinney began to prosper. But there were reports of fights and words. Then he too was dead. Rumour spread that she had poisoned him, and though no case was brought, her life afterwards became solitary again. Crowd-stirrers and witch-baiters came by to torment 'Mother Damnable'; so did petitioners wanting their fortunes told, their aches and pains mended, their reluctant lovers bewitched. When her nostrums did not do the trick, mobs railed at her, and she 'would lean out of her hatch-door' and let fly a volley of oaths.

Pedlars, gypsies, vagrants, thieves, hanged men; unmarried mothers, unruly women, promiscuous partners, huddling in hovels at crossroads: Jinney's circumstances offer a copybook case for stigmatizing her as a witch. In the early to mid seventeenth century, the fear of witchcraft flared up and flourished at the very apex of society as well as among the poor. King James I was the author of *Daemonologie*, published in Edinburgh in 1597 (and the monarch for whom Shakespeare wrote *Macbeth*), meanwhile, labourers were squeezed by agricultural policies and wars and religious conflicts. The reputation for brawling and cursing and shouting also stuck to many of the women persecuted in the witch craze ('scolds', 'nags', 'shrews'), because, as the historian Christina Larner argued in her book about the cases in Scotland, vulnerable females – especially old women – who fell on hard times for one reason and another did lash out. The tongue has no teeth but a sharper bite, especially if you have no other weapons.[3]

Of course, I accept that Jinney Bingham might well have been a very nasty piece of work, a Bluebeard of the taverns of North London.

This description was published in a pamphlet when she was old: 'She had a red cap, made of a musqueteer's sash; on her head, no hair, neither graceful nor gorgonic appeared; she had a large bottle nose; vast, heavy, black, shaggy eyebrows; her eyes were sunken, and her lank leathern cheeks were deeply furrowed. Her forehead, which was high, was wrinkled; her mouth was wide, and from each corner oozed a white frothy slaver; her look was steadfast and unperturbed; on her shoulders was thrown a dark grey frieze with black patches, which at a distance resembled flying bats.'

There's also a vivid portrait of her from 1676, the year of her death: she's wearing her wrap of shreds and patches, crouching by a stove, with a spilled tankard beside her, broken pots and shattered panes in the mullion window behind her, and on the wall an emblem of rats tied by their tails upside down and grappling. This print bears the legend, 'Mother Damnable the remarkable Shrew of Kentish Town, the person who gave rise to the Sign of Mother Red Cap on the Hampstead Road near London . . .'

In this picture, Jinney Bingham in her rags and tatters looks just like one of the old beggar women in fairy tales who call at the door and ask for food and warmth: when the heroine welcomes her and does her kindness, the old hag turns into the Lilac Fairy or the queenly fairy godmother, and showers her with gifts. This was the image that inspired the pub sign that disappeared in 1985 when the pub changed its name to the World's End. It's a vast barn of a place now, rebuilt on the site in 1820; its interior bizarrely tricked out with olde shoppe fronts, and lots of faux Camden Town heritage tat including a board giving Mother Red Cap's story, and a repro pub sign hanging from an upstairs gallery that makes the old hag look like Lenin.

On the other side of the street there's the Black Cap, a pub famous for its drag nights and carnival mood – one of the early gay and lesbian meeting places (now 'London's Premier Cabaret and Dance Bar'), and already thriving back in the 1980s as part of the scene. I knew someone then who came across it by chance, and I heard 'The Black Cat' instead, which seemed right, witchy and Gothic. But Carol, who became an habitué there, thought it alluded to the black cap a judge donned when he sentenced someone to death.

But this too is a vanishing, because on the old maps the pub was called Mother Black Cap and stood opposite the Mother Red Cap on the site of the present tube station, before moving down the High Street to its present address.

Calling someone Mother didn't necessarily claim her as family: the name was used to address a woman in charge of something, like a tapster or innkeeper, a midwife, a nun. It survived in my childhood in the convent: we called the different ranks and offices of the nuns Mother Superior and Reverend Mother, Mother Bridget, Mother John. This usage has fallen away too in progressive orders. Mother is still sometimes used in collectives, among the sannyasins of gurus. It was a handle, like Dame, and, indeed, in nursery rhymes and ballads, the two are interchangeable: Old Mother Hubbard, Old Dame Trot – the perfect name for an English drag queens' hang-out, according to a long, bawdy, raucous tradition (most recently followed by Sir Ian McKellen completely over the top as Widow Twankey). The appellation and the performance are carnivalesque – they act to turn things topsy-turvy, disgust into attraction, fear into pleasure, a stranger into a friend, hideous old aunts and uncles into stomping delirious cuddly Wild Things. It's an ancient, deep, effective kind of magic – apotropaic, like monsters guarding the threshold. Old Hags are tomb guardians for the mean streets. But they're being put out of sight, because in some commercial quarters, this kind of performative comedy is a survival skill that's too rude, too uncouth, too monstrous.

2 Mother Shipton

When I first came to live in Kentish Town, there was another local pub called after an old hag, the Mother Shipton. She wasn't a local character but a national legend, a famous Yorkshire prophet, who was born Ursula Sontibles (or Sontheil) in Knaresborough in 1488.[4] According to the legend, she was a monstrous Gargantua of an infant, with 'great goggling, sharp and fiery eyes . . . which gave such light that needed not a candle to dress her by'. Her crowing could silence thunder, still a storm . . .

Her mother withdrew to a nunnery when her strange offspring was two; she repented, it was said, of the union with Ursula's father, the devil.

After this unpropitious start in life, the orphaned Ursula flourished: she married Toby Shipton and was happy, though childless, and worked numerous cures and other wonders for her neighbours, prophesying the Fire of London among other things. At that time, even though belief in witchcraft was certainly lively, a wise woman, a cunning woman, an old mother ran much less danger than in later times of religious fervour and terrors, when Old Mother Red Cap lived in Kentish Town.

After her death in 1561, Mother Shipton inspired pamphlets, ballads, chapbooks, engravings; imitators of her riddling sayings and warnings issued almanacs and broadsides filled with apocalyptic doggerel easy to decipher for any time in any place. With a finger raised, a scroll in her other hand, and hairs sprouting from the inevitably large mole on her chin, chapfallen and hook-nosed, Old Mother Shipton is the Nostradamus of the Dales.[5]

The 'Dropping Well' near Knaresborough where she held her surgeries has the power to turn anything to stone. If you hang up your trainers or keys or hat or scarf or football in the mouth of the cave, or put your teddy there among the hundreds of other soft toys that have been left as offerings, you will find them petrified if you come back a few years later, made larger, whiter, smoother, like Niobe turned into a weeping mountain or Lot's wife into a pillar of salt. Mother Shipton has Gorgon powers from beyond the grave, and the limestone rock, steadily dropping its calcifying tears, is still executing her ordinary miracles.

In 1989, the Mother Shipton in Prince of Wales Road was spruced up and renamed the Fiddler's Elbow – another erasure, another witch vamoosed, just like the wicked witch in *The Wizard of Oz*.

Does any of this matter? On the scale of things, with all the other problems near and far, hardly. But there are reasons for minding, apart from the general loss of memories and stories that connect people and places. The new names have so little character compared to the old ones; when the old hags drop from view, so does an idea of human vagaries and fates, of idiosyncratic and oddball people, with strange histories and surprising fortunes – good and bad. Pub names and signs are some of the oldest surviving traces of exchanges and folklore in a particular place. More and more names and phrases in the public arena are tied to adverts and commodities – global creep of meanings for everybody and no one. They've gone because no pub owner wants to admit that there's any link between disreputable winos and what they are selling. Perhaps they've disappeared too because we've become sensitive to the sight of derelicts with their tins of Strongbow and plastic-bagged bottles and don't want to be reminded. Perhaps the old hag is just too rude for the times.

But I think this delicacy reveals a kind of literal-mindedness at work that weakens the spirit of revelry as a form of resistance and an expression of honesty. Old hags are comic, they're burlesque, they're Mister Punch in a dress; perhaps that's indeed not very nice, perhaps it is indelicate and rude and even frightening and ugly. They enshrine terrible attitudes in the past, as Jinney Bingham, 'Mother Damnable', suffered. The new names – the World's End, the Fiddler's Elbow, the Oxford – reveal a turn away from facing this; they're sort of empty, neutral, nicely repressed. That this should have started to happen in the 1980s and continues still in Camden Town – rapidly turning from a backwater into one of the roughest, hardest, nastiest areas of night-time London – shows the depths of deception and double-think that now prevails in our ways of describing and understanding ourselves.

3 Jorene Celeste

A few years ago, I was walking back home past the Catholic church, Our Lady Help of Christians, and found long flower-laden limousines double-parked nose to tail, with the undertakers waiting outside the closed doors while the service proceeded. The pavement was cordoned off, and I couldn't cross to the church side to see what was going on as a row of black-suited men stood in a phalanx on the pavement making sure passers-by passed by. I asked one of them what was going on. He said, 'Never you mind.' Then I realized, this funeral had to be the send-off for the Irish construction boss who had been knifed a few days before in the Vulture's Perch on the Kentish Town Road. He told one of the drinkers in there to show respect for some Nationalist song or some such, and the drinker – so the story goes – was of a different persuasion in the matter of Ireland. He left the pub, went to the nearby steak house, ordered a steak, waited for the steak knife to be laid at his place and then went back to the pub and took on the man who had dissed him.

The pub closed and was bought by Richard Branson. That didn't change its fortunes. Somebody else came along and tried, renaming it the Jorene Celeste. That was a few years ago, and it has muddled

along since, with lots of hanging baskets in Day-Glo colours against walls painted the fiercest hues from the Outdoor Gloss chart. But last month, I noticed it was scaffolded; with a presentiment, I took a photograph of the sign.

With a name that sounds so close to the *Mary Celeste*, that incarnation was perhaps ill-chosen: in 1872, after the ship's name was changed from the *Amazon*, the *Mary Celeste* put to sea with a cargo of tobacco and was later found drifting and empty, the crew and passengers all vanished. I Googled 'Jorene Celeste', and searching didn't turn up any more old hags or crones or witches (or amazons), but it did home in on a Mother – the pub owner's mother, who had been on the stage under that name.

There are other pubs in the chain – one in Islington, one in Dublin – but the Jorene Celeste in my part of London has now been painted upmarket dark grey inside and out, and been renamed the Oxford. The fruit and veg barrows that used to be parked on the pavement outside have been cleared away, and the Bosnian family – aunt, uncle, nephew – who traded there for a decade since they came during the war, have now moved on. I once saw one of our local drunks come by begging; the aunt gave him some fruit, which he took with a flap of his hand, and a cheers.

[Marina Warner]

LONDON FLESH
A Hampstead Legend
by Warwick Colvin

I

Daniel Defoe was the first to write about 'London Flesh', the legendary meat of the hern supposed to 'confer Magical Powers upon those who Partook of it'. Defoe, in fact, invested money in its unsuccessful commercial production. Perhaps that was why he wrote his famous pamphlet which, while pretending scepticism, actually gave the impression that the meat, sold mostly in the form of a paste, had supernatural properties.

De Quincey, Lamb, Dickens and Grossmith all claimed to have sampled London Flesh, usually in pies, sausages or pastes, but only Lamb was convinced that he had briefly become invisible and known the power of flight (over Chelsea Gardens). The Flesh was rumoured, of course, to be human and Dickens raised the name of Sweeney Todd in *Household Words*, but Doctor 'Dog' Donovan of Guy's was convinced that the meat was 'undoubtedly that of the female hern'. That said, the rumour persisted.

The hern was never abundant and the last pair in the London area was seen in Kew in 1950, but legend had it they were raised in captivity in Hackney Marshes up until the Second World War. Patrick Hamilton and Gerald Kersh both claimed to have been taken to a hern farm (Kersh was blindfolded) and seen dozens of the creatures penned in cages hidden behind trees and bushes, where they were offered hern pâté on cream crackers. 'London Flesh,' reports Hamilton, 'as sweet and smooth as your mother's cheeks.'

'There's a book in heaven,' said Coleridge, who was convinced that the Flesh was human, 'in which is recorded the names of all who dishonour the Dead. Graveyard Desecrations and any form of Cannibalism, including the eating of London Flesh.'

London believes it remembers the horrible story of the cannibal tramwaymen of Hampstead Heath and how they devoured on Christmas Day the passengers and crew of the No. 64 tram, which mysteriously returned empty to the Tudor Hamlets terminal. This is the true story of that event.

No complete list of passengers has ever been made but we do know that a party of some dozen revellers left the Red Mill public house on Tufnell Hill and made their way to the tram stop to board the 64. Witnesses saw and heard them, commenting on their cheerful drunkenness and the somewhat lewd behaviour of the young women who, removing hats and veils, bared their entire heads at passers-by. We also know that the vicar of St Alban's, Brookgate, was last seen boarding at the Tessy O'Shea stop, because his brother walked him there. A young mother with three rather boisterous children also boarded, though it was possible they disembarked before the 64 began its crossing of the Heath. The night was foggy. The gas was out across a fairly wide area, due to air in the pipes at Highgate, the GLC said. Indeed the Gas Light and Coke Co. were held partially responsible for police officers not at once investigating after the tram failed to reach Tudor Hamlets. The gas being restored, the tram mysteriously returned to its own terminus. All that was found aboard was a leverman's uniform cap and two ladies' hats, which told their own grim story.

At that time there was no fashion for elaborate headgear or, indeed, the casual doffing of it as there is today. At least two young women had been aboard, yet at first the police tried to treat the case as one of simple abandonment. They thought the overhead power rail had come adrift from its connector and passengers had decided to walk home. But neither the leverman nor the conductor reported for duty. The Home Office decided to investigate the mystery and sent Sir Seaton Begg and his friend Dr 'Taffy' Sinclair relatively late on Boxing Day. Unhappy at being called away from their festivities, the two men came together at Tudor Hamlets, in the office of Mr Thorn, the regional manager of the Universal Transport Company.

Thorn was a red-faced, anxious man whose perspiration made

Best known for its stories of Billy Bunter and the boys of Greyfriars, the *Magnet* ran many 'Tramway' romances during the 1920s. Almost always set in London and its environs, tram tales were enormously popular.

dark stains on his scarlet, gold and white uniform. He was somewhat in awe of Begg and Sinclair, their reputations being familiar to all who followed the news.

'It will be my head on the block, gentlemen,' he reminded them, 'if the UTC determine negligence here. Of course, we are used to tram robbers on the Heath, but in all my years we have known only one killing and that was when a barker went off by accident. It has always been prudent of levermen to obey a command when they receive one, especially since we are insured for material loss but not for the death of our employees. Guild tramwaymen never do more than wound. Those flintlock pistols they affect allow for little else. It is to everyone's advantage that their guild, formed in 1759, laid down strict regulations as to weaponry, masks, mounts, uniforms, and so on. Do you have any suspicions, gentlemen?'

Removing his wide-brimmed slouch hat Sir Seaton Begg brushed at the brim with his sleeve. 'It's rare for a tramwayman to disobey his own strict codes. They would soon lose the goodwill of Londoners and therefore their guarantees of secrecy and shelter. Nor is it like them to abduct women and children. Either this was a gang feigning to be real tramway thieves or we are dealing with rogues who hold their guild honour at nought.'

'It would be yet another sign of the times,' murmured the tall Welshman, the detective's lifelong friend and amanuensis. 'When tramwaymen go against their traditions, then the next thing we'll see will be the looting of graves.'

'Quite so,' said Begg, taking out an enormous briar, filling it with black shag and lighting it from a vesta he struck against the bricks of the terminus. Soon heavy black smoke filled the hall as, puffing contemplatively, he paced back and forth across the stone flags.

'Remarkable,' offered Sinclair, 'that no passengers were reported missing.'

'And only the leverman's wife called in to say he had not come home.' Begg paused frowning. 'The conductor lived alone?'

'A widower,' said Mr Thorn. 'His mother is in Deal with relatives.'

'Young women? A mother with children?' Sir Seaton drew thoughtfully on his briar. 'Could they all have disembarked before the terminus?'

'It's not unheard of, sir.'

'But unlikely, I'm sure you'll agree. I think it's probably time we took a tram back to the Red Mill. Can you spare us a leverman, Mr Thorn?'

'We're still on a skeleton schedule for the holidays, but in these circumstances . . .' Guild rules usually demanded that every tram carry both a driver and a conductor. 'I can't see anyone objecting here if only the leverman takes out the Special. I'll give the appropriate instructions. We should have her connected in fifteen minutes.'

2

Grey clouds regathered over the Heath as the Special began the long climb up Tufnell Hill. The Red Mill's tethered sails strained against air bending foliage across the horizon like mourners in procession.

Snow had melted into the grass and mud puddles reflected the sky. Crows called with mysterious urgency and there was a strong, fecund smell. Dr Sinclair remarked on the unseasonable warmth. Only a few roofs and the steeple of St Valentine's, Hampstead Vale, could be seen below until the Mill was reached. There, they looked on to Tudor Hamlets and the suburbs beyond Highgate, red roofs, green cedars and pines, the bones of elms supporting untidy nests, all gauzed in smoke from the chimneys.

Disembarking, Begg strolled up the path, through the ornamental metal gates and began to ascend worn granite steps to the Red Mill. Sinclair, examining the soft ground, bent to frown over something. 'Hello! That's odd for this time of the year!' He straightened, now giving his attention to something on the other side of the path. 'I wonder why –?'

A bass voice greeted them from the door of the hostelry attached to the Mill. 'I'm sorry, gents, but we're closed until New Year's

Eve.' Sinclair looked up to see the large red-bearded publican standing there.

'Except for guests who ride hunters, it seems.' Dr Sinclair smiled and pointed to the evidence. 'One doesn't have to be a High Mobsman to know that tramway thieves always convene here for the holidays.'

Sir Seaton shared his friend's humour. 'Don't worry, Mr O'Dowd,' he told the publican, 'we're neither peelers nor wildsmen and have no direct business to discuss with your guests. Would I be wrong if I understood Captain Anchovy to be stabling his horse here for the Season?'

A cheerful, handsome face appeared behind O'Dowd's broad shoulder as, with his famous dashing grace, a man in the white wig and elaborate long waistcoat of a guild member stepped forward, lowering and uncocking a huge horse pistol, the traditional tool of his trade.

'Festive greetings to ye, Sir Seaton. I trust you and your companion will take a glass with us?' He smiled as he shook hands with the detectives. Together they entered the heat of a public bar filled with tobeymen of every rank. Any suspicion of the newcomers was swiftly dispelled and within moments the two investigators were imbibing goblets of mulled wine while Captain Anchovy and his men volunteered their aid in solving the mystery. Their own honour, they said, was at stake.

Tom Anchovy in particular was inflamed with disgust. 'My dear Sir Seaton, that 64 was indeed our intended prize as she came up Tufnell Hill. But it was Boxing Day and we had no intention of stealing anything but the hearts of the ladies aboard. All were brought here. Three children were given presents and old men of pleasant humour were presented with a glass of wine. Only a few refused our hospitality – the mother of the children, a good-hearted reverend gentleman whose abstinence we respected, and that sour fellow who had refused to quit the Inn on our arrival and refused to share his vitalls with us. On any other occasion we might have taken him for ransom.'

'And he was –?' Sir Seaton lifted the beaker to his lips.

'Henry Marriage, sir. A humourless walking cadaver if ever I met one. Yet even he was permitted to retain his valuables. I don't mind tellin' ye, Sir Seaton, that had it not been Christmas I would have had his last stitch *and* kept him for ransom!'

'Is that Marriage of Marriage's Opiates by the river?' asked Dr Sinclair, placing his finished beaker on the bar and nodding with approval as O'Dowd refilled it. 'The millionaire who lives in a house on his own wharf?'

'The same, Dr Sinclair. Do ye know him?'

'Only by reputation. A solitary individual, they say. A dabbler in the alchemist's art. He's published an interesting book or two. No charlatan, but no great scientist, either. Many of his findings and experiments have been discredited. He's considered a mere amateur by the medical and scientific guilds.'

'I understand nothing of such things, sir. But I'll swear to this – when that tram left last evening he was safe and sound, as was every living soul aboard. Though he chose to go with them, all but Henry Marriage were as cheerful as when they had embarked. If that 64 was taken, then it would have been on the high stretch of track below the ruined village.'

'Why so?' Begg inquired.

'Because we watched her lights until they were out of sight and young Jaimie Gordon here was on his way to join us, taking the low road up the Vale. He'd have spotted anything untoward.'

Sir Seaton was already slamming down his glass and cramming his hat on to his handsome, aquiline head. 'Then I can guess where the tram was stopped. Come on, Taffy, let's board our Special. I'm much obliged to you, Captain Anchovy.'

'Delighted to have helped, sir.'

After a further quick word with the tramwayman, the two meta-temporal investigators were again on their way.

3

A Blériot 'bat', no doubt taking the day's mail to France, flew high overhead as the 64 rattled to a stop below the ruins of Hampstead Model Village, which lay on the brow of the hill above the tramline whose branches had once serviced the inhabitants of Lady Hecate Brown's failed evangelical dream of a healthy environment where a good Christian life and enlightened working conditions would be the antidote to all the ills of the city. Her failure to supply the model village with familiar recreations, public houses and fried fish shops caused even the most enlightened artisans to view her idealistic community as a kind of prison. The village had flourished as a middle-class enclave until, without servants or city facilities, the bourgeoisie chose the suburbs of Tudor Hamlets and Lyonne's Greene. The tram service had been discontinued, though the tracks were intact, lost beneath the encroaching weeds and brambles.

As Begg and Sinclair disembarked, the sky clouded darker and it began to rain heavily. Peering with difficulty through the ever-thickening mist, Begg quickly saw that his intuition had been right.

Sinclair was the first to observe how the track had been cleared through the swampy ground leading up to the ruins. 'Look, Begg. There's the shine of brass. A tram was diverted at this very spot and went up Ham Hill towards the old village. What do you make of it?'

'The best place to take a tram off the usual routes, Taffy. The emptied vehicle was sent back on its way, perhaps to divert attention from whatever dark deed was done here. Let us pray we are in time to save those poor souls – victims, no doubt, of some rogue band caring nought for the rules and habits of an old guild!'

With difficulty, they followed the line up the muddy terrain, their boots sinking and sliding in ground normally frozen hard.

As the rain let up, Ham Hill's ruins were seen bleak beneath a lowering sky. The air was unseasonably muggy; thunder rolled closer. Melted snow left pools so that the hill might have been the remains of Hereward's Romney fastness. Sinclair suppressed a shiver

447

as a sudden chill crept up his spine. The afternoon's gloom was illuminated by a sudden sheet of lightning throwing the ruins into vivid silhouette.

'Press on, Taffy,' murmured Seaton Begg, clapping his friend on his sturdy shoulder. 'I sense we're not far from solving this mystery!'

'And maybe perishing as a consequence.' The mordant Welshman spoke only half in jest.

Making some remark about the 'dark instincts of the Celtic soul', Begg tramped on until they at last stood on the outskirts of the ruins, looking down at Tufnell Vale whose yellow lights offered distant reassurance.

No such friendly gas burned in the ruins of Hampstead Model Village, yet a few guttering brands lit the remaining glass in the low church chapel, said now to harbour all manner of pagan ritual and devil worship. The nearby Anglican church had been desanctified on orders from Southwark but the ragged walls remained. Close to the church blazed three or four bonfires built from the wood of old pews and other religious furniture.

Begg and Sinclair kept to the cover of fallen walls and shrubbery. Human figures gathered around the fires.

'Vagrants, perhaps?' murmured Sinclair. 'Do such people still exist?'

Signalling his friend to silence, Begg pointed to a collapsing house sheltering the bulky shapes of horses. Rough laughter and uncultured voices told Begg they had found another tramwayman gang. 'Guildless outcasts, Taffy, by the cut of their coats. Rejected by every mobsmen's association from here to York.'

Keeping well down, the detectives crept closer. Unlike Tom Anchovy's men, guildless tram thieves were known for their cruel savagery.

'It's been years since such a gang was seen this close to London,' whispered Sinclair. 'They risk life imprisonment if caught!'

Begg was unsurprised. 'I knew Captain Zodiac was outside Beaconsfield and suspected of several tram robberies in that region. Quickly, Taffy, drop down.' He flung himself behind a broken wall. 'That's the rogue himself!'

A tall, white-haired man in a black greatcoat sauntered towards one of the fires, eyes burning like rubies in the reflected light. A handsome albino with skin the colour of ivory, Zodiac was an old enemy of Begg. The two were said to be cousins who had often crossed swords.

As they watched, Zodiac approached a thin individual, as tall as himself, on the far side of the fire. It was Sinclair's turn to draw in a sharp breath. Henry Marriage, one of the missing passengers, seemed to be on friendly terms with the most notorious tram thief in Europe!

It grew darker and now all the inhabitants of the ruins were mere silhouettes.

'We can't take 'em single-handed,' murmured Begg. 'We'd best return to the depot and telegraph to Scotland Yard.'

Picking their way carefully down the hill, they had scarcely gone twenty yards before dark shadows surrounded them. They heard a horrible, muffled noise.

Moving towards them across the unnaturally damp ground, big pistols threatening, came an unsavoury circle of leering tram robbers.

'Good evening, gentlemen!' The leader doffed his cocked hat in a mocking bow. 'Always pleased to welcome a few more guests to our holiday harum-scarum!' He removed the shutter from his night-lamp, showing the face of their unfortunate tram driver. The leverman's hands were tied before him and a gag had been forced into his mouth. He had been trying to warn his passengers of his own capture!

4

The mobsmen had not reckoned with the two detectives being armed. In a flash Begg and Sinclair produced the latest repeating Webleys! 'Stand, you scum,' levelly declared the investigator. 'You no doubt recognize this revolver which I intend to use to advantage.'

The triumph draining from their decadent features, the mobsmen fell back, knowing full well the power and efficiency of the Webleys over their own antique barkers. Then a voice cut through the misty air. Sharp as a diamond, it bore the tone of a man used to obedience.

'Fire one chamber, Sir Seaton, and count yourself responsible for the death of an innocent woman.'

Turning their heads, the investigators saw Captain Zodiac, a bright lantern in one hand, pressing his barker against the head of a dishevelled coster girl grinning stupidly from under her raised veil, her hat at an unseemly angle.

Sinclair stifled a cry of outrage. 'You fiend!' He did not let his Webley fall, nor did he disengage the safety catch. 'What have you done to that poor young creature?'

'I, sir?' An almost melancholy smile played across the mobsman's pale lips. 'What d'ye think I've done? Murdered her?' The light from the lantern gave his red eyes a savage sparkle.

'Drugged her!' Sinclair muttered in disgust. 'You're cowards as well as kidnappers.'

Captain Zodiac's face clouded for a moment before resuming its habitual mask. 'She's unhurt, sir. But aggressive action on your part might alter her circumstances.'

'No doubt one of the missing passengers, but where are the children?' demanded Sir Seaton.

'Safe and sound with their mother and full of mince pies,' Zodiac assured him.

'Then show them to me.'

'I'd remind you, Sir Seaton, that you are at a disadvantage.'

'And I'd remind you, Captain Zodiac, that I am a servant of the Crown. Harm me or those under my protection and you'll answer to Her Majesty's justice.'

'I have been escaping that justice, sir, for longer than you and I have travelled the moonbeam roads. Put that fancy barker aside and be my welcome guest.' He stepped away from the giggling young woman as Begg and Sinclair reluctantly reholstered their weapons. Then, tucking the woman's somewhat limp arm into his, Captain Zodiac led them back to the central fire, built just outside the ruined chapel where more of his gang and their captives could clearly be seen.

All but the wide-eyed children were in artificially good humour. Another pair of young women wore their hats on the backs of their heads. Sinclair guessed they had been well supplied with alcohol but Begg shook his head, saying softly, 'Not beer or spirits, I think, Taffy, old man. I suspect another hand in this, don't you?'

Sinclair nodded gravely. 'Do we share the suspicion of who it was put Zodiac up to this crime?'

'I think we do, Taffy.'

Then they were standing among the other prisoners. Only the young mother showed signs of concern. Even the reverend gentleman cheerfully led the leverman, the conductor and a youth wearing the cadet uniform of the Farringdon Watch in a rather jolly hymn.

'See how our guests enjoy their Boxing Day?' Captain Zodiac offered Begg and Sinclair a somewhat cynical grin. 'And all with their pocket books in place.'

'Drugged with laudanum.' Sinclair picked up an empty black bottle, sniffing it just as tall lugubrious Henry Marriage stepped into the firelight, extending his hand. Sinclair ignored the gesture, but Begg, ever the diplomat, bowed. 'Good evening, sir. Are these villains holding you to ransom?'

Marriage's hearty manner thinly disguised an evasive expression. 'Not at all, sir.' He stared around him somewhat helplessly.

'Or is Captain Zodiac in your employ?' demanded Sinclair. 'Why do you only bind our driver?'

'He'll be released at once.' Captain Zodiac signed for the leverman to be released. 'He offered my men violence. Whereas these other good fellows accepted our hospitality –'

'And were drugged into doltishness.'

'Please, sir, are you here to help us?' The young mother clutched imploringly at Sir Seaton's sleeve.

With his usual gentle courtesy towards the fair sex, Sir Seaton smiled reassurance. 'I am indeed, madam. What charming children! Is their father here?'

'I am a widow, sir.'

'My dear lady!'

'We have not been mistreated, sir.'

'I should hope you have not!' interjected Henry Marriage. 'I doubt if your children have ever eaten so well!'

'You have been feeding them, Mr Marriage?' Dr Sinclair offered the thin man an intense glare of inquisition.

'I returned from visiting a generous relative who gave me the hamper. It was meant for my family at home.'

'Indeed, sir,' said Sir Seaton. With the toe of his shoe he touched a large, open basket. Stencilled on its side were the words MARRIAGE'S OPIATES, MARRIAGE'S WHARF, LONDON E. 'This is the Christmas Box, eh?'

'The same, sir.'

'You were sharing it on the tram before Captain Zodiac appeared?'

'He was very generous, sir.' The conductor looked up from where he sat beside the fire. 'I know it's against regulations, but the company generally turns a blind eye at Christmas. Of course, we didn't take any alcoholic beverage.'

'Quite so. What did you enjoy from Mr Marriage's hamper?'

'Just a piece of game pie, sir. Some ginger beer. And a couple of sandwiches.'

'Whereupon you reached the old Hampstead Model Village stop, broke down and, at Mr Marriage's suggestion, continued up here, eh, conductor?'

'Such merry yule fires, sir. Who could resist 'em? It was commonly agreed, sir, even by that reverend gent, there could be no happier way of celebrating Boxing Day until rescue came.' A stupid, sentimental grin crossed the conductor's long face.

'Except by you, madam, I take it?' Again Sir Seaton turned to the mother.

'I've been pained by a bit of a dicky tummy since we had the goose at my husband's brother's house. I'd rather hoped the children and me'd be home by now. But it was either come here or stay on the tram.' She was close to tears. Again Begg laid a gentlemanly hand on her arm. 'And Mr Marriage promised you his protection.'

'He did, sir. The tramwaymen have offered us no harm. But they're a bad example, sir, and –'

'Captain Zodiac and his men make no threats. They keep the traditional tramwaymen's Christmas truce.' Marriage was insistent. 'I offered them a handsome fee to act for our safety when the tram broke down. They helped us guide it up the old line to this spot where we could find some sort of shelter.'

'How on earth did the tram find its own way back to the terminal?' Dr Sinclair was clearly not entirely convinced by this story.

'She slipped backwards, sir, once the horses were untethered,' offered the conductor. 'Somehow she must have reconnected to the overhead power line and continued her journey. It has been known, sir, for such things to happen.'

'So I understand.'

'Stranding us here, of course,' explained Henry Marriage. 'Well, it seems you've brought another vehicle to take everyone home and no harm done. We are all grateful to you, Sir Seaton and Doctor Sinclair. I am prepared to stand guarantee for Captain Zodiac. My honour depends upon promising safe conduct to all parties. I shall elect to stay as evidence of good faith and come morning shall board a fresh tram on the regular morning route. This will give Captain Zodiac and his men time to make themselves scarce. A fair bargain, eh, Sir Seaton?'

'Very fair. And very noble of you, Mr Marriage.' Speaking with a certain irony, Sir Seaton was careful not to challenge anything. They were seriously outnumbered and had many innocents to consider. Since Zodiac the Albino was mixed up in this affair Begg was convinced not everything could be above board. He had several reasons to suspect Marriage's tale. Nevertheless, he did not object when the tramwaymen lit the way with their lanterns to lead the happy party back down the hill. At last the passengers were safely aboard and the leverman reinstalled at his controls.

The passengers cheered as the overhead power rail sparked in the darkness. The magnificent Special hummed, lurched and began to move forward. 'A generous soul, that Mr Marriage,' declared the conductor. 'We'd be mighty hungry by now had he not been so free with his hamper.' He reacted with a muttered explanation as Dr Sinclair's eyes stared sternly into his own. 'I speak only the honest truth, sir. I've done nothing against Company tradition.'

'Of course you haven't, conductor,' interrupted Sir Seaton, his hand on his friend's shoulder. 'You must now ensure your charges arrive safely at the terminus.'

'My duty, sir.' The conductor saluted, shaking off his euphoria.

Next, the two detectives returned swiftly to the tram's boarding platform. 'We have to go back, of course,' said Begg.

'Absolutely, old man!'

As soon as the tram took a bend, they dropped quietly from the platform. Ankle-deep in marshy ground, they moved rapidly back to the village.

'You noticed their eyes, I take it, Taffy?'

'Drugged! All but the mother and children. Something in those meat pies, eh?'

'Opium or Indian hemp. That preposterous story of a generous relative!'

'And at least two of the party were not returned to the tram.'

'Two young women? Exactly!'

'No doubt they imbibed more freely from the hamper's contents than any of the others.'

'Hurry, old man! Knowing Marriage's obsessions, you can guess as readily as I what the fiend intends.'

The detectives rapidly regained the camp, creeping carefully up to the ruined chapel where Zodiac's gang continued to make merry. Yet of the leader or Henry Marriage there was no sign.

Drawing his Webley, Begg motioned towards the ruined Anglican church. Sinclair had already noticed lights shining through the broken stained glass. They heard voices, what might have been laughter, a stifled cry and then a piercing scream. Caution abandoned, they rushed the building, kicking open the rotting doors.

'Oh, for the love of God!' Sinclair was almost forced backward by the horrible smell. The scene's bestial reality was unfit to be seen by anyone save the curator of Scotland Yard's Black Museum. Two young women hung in ropes above the remains of the church altar. One was bleeding from deep wounds in her lower extremities. Her blood dripped into two large copper basins placed there for the purpose. She had fainted, but her companion shrieked in terror through her gag. Henry Marriage, long razor in hand, prepared to perform the same operation upon her as the gloating albino placed bowls in readiness.

Marriage seemed completely deranged but Zodiac was fully alert, his face a mask of hatred as he saw Begg and Sinclair. His long white hair hanging loose to his shoulders, he snarled defiantly, lifting a copper bowl to his lips.

Levelling his pistol, Begg snapped off a single shot spinning the bowl from Zodiac's hands. Sinclair darted forward and with an expert uppercut knocked Marriage to the floor. The razor fell with a clatter from the opiate merchant's hands.

Growling like a wild animal, Zodiac produced his own pistol, but Begg's revolver sounded again. Zodiac's weapon went flying. Sinclair jumped up to the altar and, using Marriage's razor, severed the cords, lowering the two young women gently down as he kicked the bowls of blood clear.

Next Begg leaped forward to press the barrel of his Webley against Zodiac's heart. The albino raised his hands, his ruby eyes glaring.

Knowing that the shot would alert Zodiac's men, Sinclair turned to face the door.

Motioning with his revolver Begg forced Zodiac to stand between them and the entrance. Henry Marriage groaned and came to his senses as the first outlaws appeared in the doorway.

'Stand back there!' The metatemporal investigator held his Webley against the albino's head. But Zodiac's gang was already circling the altar.

His lips rimmed with blood, mumbling curses, Marriage climbed to his feet, his eyes staring into space.

'As you guessed, Taffy, he believes he possesses supernatural powers.' Begg motioned with his pistol.

'Let's hope we are not alone, old man. We decidedly need help from those who promised it . . .'

'Without them we're dead men, I agree. Have you any spare ammunition, old man?'

'None.'

Grimly, Begg and Sinclair prepared for the worst. Aware of their dilemma, Zodiac grinned even as Sir Seaton's pistol pressed against his head.

The investigator knew his captive too well to demand he call his men off. Whatever dark evil Zodiac practised, he was no coward and would die before allowing the two detectives to escape.

Ironically, Henry Marriage came to their aid. Drugged eyes rolling in his head, he lifted up his arms and ran for the door. 'I am free!' he cried. 'Free! Invisible, I shall climb like an eagle into the sky.' His long arms flapping at his sides, he stumbled towards the entrance and, before the astonished outlaws, ran wildly into the night. Zodiac laughed grimly. 'He believes the spell has worked. He forgets our ritual was interrupted.'

'Silence, you monster!' Sinclair covered as many outlaws as he could. Savouring anticipated triumph they tightened the circle . . .

From outside came a fusillade of shots and they heard Marriage screaming in frustrated rage. 'No! No! I am invisible. I fly. You cannot –' There descended a sudden silence.

Taking advantage of this unexpected turn Zodiac broke free to join the mass of his own men. Grabbing a pistol from one of them, with his red eyes blazing, he curved his pale lips in a snarling grin. 'You're lost, Begg! Arming the levermen and the vicar won't save you!'

Then a figure appeared in the smashed doorway. A gold-trimmed tricorne on his bewigged head, a black domino hiding his upper face, he had pushed back his huge three-caped coaching coat, two massive barkers in either beringed hand. Captain Tom Anchovy laughed as the guildless tramwaymen fell back in fear. Behind him, in the fancy coats and three-cornered hats of their trade, pressed his men, contemptuous of the outlaws bringing their trade into disrepute.

'Drop your arms, lads, or we'll blow you all to the hell you thoroughly deserve!' rapped Anchovy.

But Captain Zodiac, using the cover of his men, disappeared through the far door.

'After him, quickly!' ordered Tom. Some mobsmen followed the albino into the night.

Realizing how outnumbered they were, the remaining outlaws gave up their pistols with little resistance, leaving Sir Seaton Begg, Dr Sinclair and Tom Anchovy to bind the young women's wounds and get them decently covered.

'Their hats will be waiting for them at the terminus, no doubt,' said Dr Sinclair. 'They owe their lives to that lost headgear.'

'Indeed they do, Taffy. It was our clue that two young women were still held by Marriage and Zodiac. All the others we saw still had their hats, even if worn at a rather unladylike angle!' He warmly shook hands with the tobeyman. 'You turned up in the nick of time, Captain Tom. Thanks for keeping your word to help us. We remain on opposite sides of the law, but I think we share a moral purpose!'

'Probably true, sir.' Captain Anchovy prepared to leave. 'We'll truss those rogues thoroughly. Should we catch Zodiac, he'll also be left for the peelers to pick up. Boxing Day's almost over and we must return to our regular trade if we're to eat. Marriage's hamper out there was sadly empty of all its vitalls.'

'Just as well. You'd best warn your men that those pies and sausages were poisoned with hern meat and opium. They won't die, but they'll be unable to ride for a day or two should they try any.'

'I'll tell 'em at once. Good luck to ye, gentlemen!' The daring tramwayman disappeared into the night.

'That's what I saw at the Red Mill,' said Sinclair. 'The tiny tracks of the crested hern. I've studied the little creatures a fair bit and was surprised to find some still around London. Brought too early out of hibernation by the unseasonal weather and easily caught by Marriage while staying at the Inn. Some opiates, and his food was ready for those unsuspecting passengers.'

'From what I know of his debased brand of alchemy, Taffy, hern meat is only thought efficacious if fed to female virgins first. Partaking of the flesh, or preferably your victim's freshly drawn blood, imparts great supernatural powers, including those of invisibility and flight. Luckily, he proved himself a liar with that tale of his hamper being a relative's gift. It clearly came from his own warehouse.'

The doctor shuddered. 'Thank God we were able to stop him in time.'

The two men strolled from the ruined church to see that Anchovy's men had already bound Zodiac's followers. Anchovy mounted his magnificent black Arab and saluted them as they appeared. 'If I know Zodiac he'll be long gone in the direction of London, to lose himself in the twitterns of Whitechapel. No doubt our paths will cross again! As for Henry Marriage, I could have sworn my men filled him with enough lead to sink the HMS *Victory*, yet he, too, has disappeared. Perhaps his beliefs had substance, eh?' With that the gallant tramwayman doffed his tricorne in a deep bow, then turned for distant Waymering where Begg knew he lived a double life as Septimus Grouse, a Methodist parson.

Though weak from their experience, the two young victims had recovered somewhat by the time another Special arrived towing a hospital car and a prison van full of peelers. Attended by expert doctors, the women were made comfortable in the hospital car while Zodiac's gang were manacled to hard benches, destined for Wormwood Flats.

Thus the tale garbled by the yellow press as 'The Affair of the Hampstead Cannibals' was brought to a successful conclusion and all innocent lives saved. Enjoying their pipes the pair relaxed in the first-class section of the tram's top deck.

'I think I'll be returning to the Red Mill as soon as possible,' murmured Sinclair thoughtfully.

'You're curious to retrace the stages of the case, Taffy?'

'What's more interesting, old man, was finding those London hern tracks when all naturalists are agreed the species became extinct during the latter part of the last century. I'd like to find another specimen.'

'And vivisect it?' inquired Sir Seaton in some disapproval.

'Oh, not at all. I want to see it in the wild for myself and confirm that Henry Marriage, God rest his soul wherever he may be now, did not destroy the entire race. After all, it isn't every day one discovers that the past can yet be recovered, however small that part might be.'

With a sudden rattle the tram began to move forward. Its buzzing electric engine could not quite disguise the sound of Sir Seaton Begg's approving grunt.

Note: Although every effort was made to keep this tale secret, enough of it leaked out to associate a gang of tramwaymen (some say Turpin himself) with stories of cannibalism on Hampstead Heath around the turn of the century.

[Michael Moorcock]

TUFNELL PARK FOOTNOTED

All the things that have disappeared . . . but yet they remain, remain in the past, exist in the past. But what precisely do we mean and understand by saying something exists in the past? Where is my childhood now? Where is the Tufnell Park I knew fifty years ago? Where exactly are they? And can I get a cheap day return there?

First off, Tufnell Park. It hasn't disappeared because it never existed. I don't mean just the park bit, but the whole thing, *Tufnell Park*. Yes, it has an existence now, though it never existed before, and I'm not talking in riddles here.

I'll ask you a question or two. But first, let's all agree that the very centre of Tufnell Park, the epicentre if you like, the cynosure, the *omphalos* even, is the Boston (Arms), the grand Victorian pub surmounted by a cupola that dominates the junction of roads here.

The 'observatory' tower and cupola of the Boston public house rising up in Tufnell Park like a great brick and stone built ship, murmurous of times past and athwart with memories, an unsleeping sentinel . . .

Some may argue that perhaps the Underground station across the way is the centre. It isn't. It doesn't have the commanding presence and exuberant grandeur of the Boston.[1]

Now, having established the centre, start walking south down Fortess Road. Where exactly does Tufnell Park end and Kentish

---

1. Amazingly, unrecognized by Pevsner (and joint editor Bridget Cherry) in *The Buildings of England: London 4: North* (London: Penguin Books, 1998).

Why the *Boston*? Nobody seems to know. A puzzle. Not even Mr Pat Murray, the landlord, knows, though he tells me some hundred or so years ago it was informally known as the 'Cattleman's Hotel' from the herders taking their cattle to the nearby Metropolitan Cattle Market (Caledonian Market). There's a void here. An obvious job for folk etymology.

It first appears in local directories in 1860 and for a brief period was renamed the Boston Hotel.

Town begin? Or try walking northwards up Junction Road. How far does it extend before becoming Upper Holloway, the neighbourhood favoured by Mr Pooter?

Nobody knows the answers to these questions. This is the ontological end of topography.[2]

And the neighbourhood still awaits its chronicler, even of the antiquarian *Tufnell Park in Ye Olden Tyme* style.[3]

Countless memories of childhood, so how about this? It's 1951 and I'm four years old and I'm standing in the tarmacadam playground (long gone) to the fore of a somewhat forbidding block of flats, Faraday House,[4] on York Rise, just a few minutes' walk from the Boston. This is where my grandmother lives, my father's mother.

I'm in my Sunday best and I'm eating a water ice that my mother has just bought for me from Morris's corner café (gone) just across the road. The smell of a hundred Sunday dinners drifts out from the flats and it mingles with the smoke from the steam trains that hurry on by just the other side of the allotments (*they* eventually sprouted a school and a block of flats).

I ask my father whether we can go to the park. He replies that

2. Pevsner/Cherry, as above, claim that it is 'bounded by Camden, Brecknock and Tufnell Park Roads', p. 703, but without explaining their reasoning, which may, perhaps, be based on estate development. However, signing off on this theory would allow Tufnell Park to claim Holloway Prison as its own when we all know it belongs to 'Camden Road' . . . or is it Holloway? Don't be misled by what it calls itself.

3. The style of local history characterized by the late W. G. Hoskins as being the *materials* of history and not history itself.

Of the 21,000 or so items catalogued in a recent London bibliography only one boasts the word 'Tufnell' in its title, a slim volume of family history: Heather Creaton (ed.), *Bibliography of Printed Works on London History to 1939* (London: Library Association, 1994). I haven't been able to trace anything after that cut-off date.

4. One of the five four-storey blocks arranged around courtyards put up by the St Pancras Housing Association and completed in 1938. Prior to that my father and his sister together with their mother lived in Melton Street, hard by Euston Station, but were moved out owing to redevelopment. Their house was in plain sight of the famous Euston Arch or, more correctly, *propylaeum*, which was wantonly demolished in 1962.

we've already been to the park, Parliament Hill Fields. No, I mean I want to go to *the* park, the Tufnell Park. I knew Parliament Hill, but Tufnell Park by now had attained mythical status and held out the promise of somewhere magical with swings and sandpits and boating lakes and streams and rivers and, perhaps, even mountains and wild beasts!

There isn't one, he explains. There isn't a Tufnell *park*.

I couldn't understand this. How could somewhere be called Tufnell[5] Park if there wasn't a park to go to? The world was not what it promised to be . . .

I walked across the playground and saw that a large rectangular manhole cover by the retaining wall had been opened again. I gazed down and saw swiftly running water,[6] sparkling in the sunlight, looking fresh and cold . . .

Stand to the front of the Boston facing away from it and travel back in time, say two hundred or even a thousand years, and what do you see? Fields and open land and trees, but coming up from the direction of distant London and passing to your right and then ascending the heights towards Highgate is a country lane, a lane of great antiquity. It's gone under many names but seems to have settled down as Maiden Lane[7] in the 1700s. The lane began at

5. I always thought it a strange un-English-sounding word, 'Tufnell'. It was the Tufnell family who owned land here from the 1700s onwards. The surname isn't included in three major name dictionaries I checked. The name is frequently seen now on the vans of a parcel-delivery company but spelled with two fs.

As a child I saw many street names here that struck me as strange: Chetwynd, Ingestre, Brecknock (what was a 'brecknock'?), Twisden, Anson, Fortess and Lady Somerset (who she?).

6. Some forty years later I'd be looking at one of the sheets of Edward Stanford's magnificent six-inch-to-the-mile *Library Map of London and Its Suburbs* (1862) and would see that this was the Fleet River.

7. Probably a dignified refashioning of 'midden', meaning a dunghill or manure heap, among other things, and oft applied jocularly to a muddy road.

Maiden Lane's antiquity can be demonstrated by a simple fact: the boundary of the old parish of St Pancras runs up the middle of the road all the way from King's Cross to Highgate. Such boundaries follow existing features. So, as we know, parishes evolved in

Battlebridge (the present-day King's Cross[8]) and ended on Highgate Hill just below the village. It now has a retitled tripartite existence as York Way, Brecknock Road and Dartmouth Park Hill.

Maiden Lane was Tufnell Park's genesis.

In 1813 the Archway Road was excavated and constructed, a sort of Highgate bypass, to avoid the notoriously steep ascent of Highgate Hill. The only approach was up the Holloway Road and it was soon deemed necessary to build another approach for traffic coming from the west. Thus Junction Road was laid out from Kentish Town northwards to the foot of the new road where the Archway Tavern now is.[9]

Junction Road cut across Maiden Lane, so the nascent Tufnell Park now had a crossroads, if nothing else.

In the 1850s, with the unrelenting growth of London, the land hereabouts was being developed and a short road was projected from the west side of the Holloway Road sporting some twenty or so villas for the newly emerging middle class.[10] This road was eventually projected further westwards until it came to a halt at the crossroads of Maiden Lane and Junction Road where, by this time, there was now a Boston Arms (not the present building) and several villas just to the north.

---

the eleventh and twelfth centuries, therefore the lane is at least as old as that. I suspect, however, it may even be pre-Roman in origin.

This, incidentally, puts the Boston and the Underground station in the former parish of Islington.

For a large-scale map showing the St Pancras boundary, see Frederick Sinclair (compiler), *Catalogue of an Exhibition . . . Illustrating St Pancras through the Ages* (London: St Pancras Public Libraries, 1938).

8. The locale has only been known as King's Cross since around the 1830s from a statue of George IV that once stood here. The Great Northern Railway adopted it for the name of their London terminus in 1852 and it was thus perpetuated. The earlier name, Battlebridge, was a corruption of a word meaning 'broad or wide ford' (over the Fleet River). See Gover, Mawer, Stenton, *The Place Names of Middlesex* (Cambridge: CUP-EPNS, 1942), pp. 140–41.

9. The section up to Tufnell Park tube was renamed Fortess Road in 1879, a name taken from a field here. Its etymology is unknown.

10. I base this on Stanford's 1862 map noted above.

Housing now developed at an accelerated rate and to meet up with the growth of population the Boston Arms was pulled down and replaced in 1899 by the magnificent building we now see.

In 1907 the Underground station was to open,[11] but it was opening at a locale that had no name. As was often the case the name would have to come from an adjacent road. The main options were Fortess Road, Junction Road and Brecknock Road. None of them sounded right. Tufnell Park (Road) got it, more euphonious than the others *and* with a promise of a park. Thusly a neighbourhood was conjured out of the ether. But there never was a park.

1951 again and I'm standing outside the Boston with my mother. My father is inside seeing a man about a dog. I have a glass of R. White's lemonade in one hand and a packet of Smith's crisps in the other (I haven't untwisted the little blue salt packet). My mother holds a gin-and-orange and is telling me about a highwayman called Dick Turpin who lived in a cave on Hampstead Heath, or so she was told when a child. I'm wondering whether he still lives there when my attention is attracted to the bells and clacking and the whoosh of the electric motor of a passing trolley bus[12] as it glides down the cobbles of Fortess Road, its pantograph sparking on the overhead power lines.[13]

Can we go on a trolley bus? Yes, we're going to Inverness market in Camden Town . . .

All of my family, on both sides, were from the neighbourhoods here, living in the many streets that sprang up in Queen Victoria's

11. Tim Demuth, *The Spread of London's Underground* (London: Capital Transport, 2003), p. 12. A wonderful book – the development of the Underground-Tube system in a series of schematic maps with copious notes.

12. The last London trolley bus ran in 1962.

13. Yes, there were still cobbles then. Last month, February 2005, I was driving along behind St Pancras Station, where the redevelopment for the Channel train service is taking place, and saw a section of St Pancras Road that had had the tarmac burned and stripped off. There were the cobbles still. They'd never gone away.

Railway Age. They were the working class whose labour made the wealth of the nation. They were hardy, uncomplaining and accepting, and they all spoke in a peculiarly North London accent with broad, flattened vowels that has now disappeared.

Here are some of them:

Auntie Ivy – Wrotham Road; Great Aunt Em – York Rise; Uncle Bill – near the Black Cat, Camden; Eddie Frewin – Melton Street; Alfred Weeks – Royal College Street; Ruby Constance Hodgson – Leighton Road; Cecil Frewin – Little Albany Street; Jessie Pretoria Berry[14] – Faraday House; Auntie Flo – York Rise; Aunt Nell – Churchill Road; Jessie and Jim Bastow – Faraday House; Emma Hatchard – York Way; Aunt Lally – Polygon Buildings; Auntie Dolly – Grafton Road; James and Caroline Frewin – William Mews, Euston Road; George and Ellen Weeks – Werrington Street . . .

. . . all of whom sometimes drank in the Boston and all of whom are now dead with their memories, hopes, fears, ambitions and loves buried with them. But to me their *manes* remain in this part of London.

And, of course, the Boston remains too.

[Anthony Frewin]

CONTINUITY ERROR

Christine rang Maddox on his mobile. A little accident, she said. A bump.

'Was anyone hurt?'

'No, no one was hurt.'

He made his way to the side street in Shepherd's Bush where it

---

14. My maternal grandmother, who was born in 1900 shortly after Lord Roberts's entry into Pretoria during the Boer War, hence her middle name. Her sister, Elizabeth, born two years later, boasted the middle name of Mafeking. We were a patriotic lot.

had happened. A one-way street temporarily blocked off by road-works at the junction with Goldhawk Road. Estate agents on the corner. Christine had reversed away from the roadworks and at five miles an hour hit a silver Toyota coming out of the concealed exit from the sunken car park behind the estate agents.

By the time Maddox arrived, the driver of the silver Toyota was in full magnanimous third-party mode, confident the insurance companies would find in his favour. Maddox hated him on sight. Too reasonable, too forthcoming. Like providing his address and insurance details was some kind of favour.

Maddox's son, Jack, had got out of the car and stood staring at the small pile of shattered glass on the road, seemingly transfixed by it. Christine was visibly upset, despite the unctuous affability of the Toyota driver and Maddox's own efforts to downplay the situation.

'It's only a couple of lights and a new wing. No one was hurt, that's the main thing.'

Two days later, Maddox and Jack were walking past the top of the side street. The roadworks had been removed and a car was exiting into Goldhawk Road without any difficulty.

'Is that where the accident happened, Daddy?' asked the little boy.

'Yes.'

Jack stopped, his big eyes taking in the details. The fresh asphalt by the junction, the concealed exit from the sunken car park behind the estate agents.

'Is it still there?' the little boy asked.

'What? Is what still there?'

'The accident. Is the accident still there?'

Maddox didn't know what to say.

They were getting ready to go out. Christine was ready and Maddox was nearly ready, a too familiar scenario. She waited by the front door, smart, made-up, tall in new boots and long coat, enveloped in a haze of expensive perfume.

'Are you nearly ready, Brian?'

That she added his name to the harmless query was a bad sign. It meant her patience was stretched too thin. But he'd lost his car key. He'd looked everywhere. Twice. And couldn't find it.

'Where did you last have it?' she shouted up the stairs.

The unhelpfulness of the question grated against his nerves.

'I don't know. That's the whole point.'

He started again. Bedroom (bedside drawer, dressing gown). Jacket pockets. Kitchen.

'Have you looked in your box?'

'Yes, I've looked in my box.'

They each had a box, like an in-tray, in the kitchen. Christine never used hers, but always knew where everything was. Maddox used his, but still managed to lose at least one important item every day. Wallet, phone, keys. Chequebook, bank card. Everything always turned up, sooner or later, but in this case, not soon enough.

'I can't find it. I've looked everywhere.'

Heavy sigh.

If the atmosphere hadn't become tense he would jokingly accuse her of having hidden it, of trying to make him think he was losing his mind. But that wouldn't play now. They were beyond that.

'It's probably at the *flat*,' she said, loading the word with her customary judgemental emphasis.

'How could it be at the flat when my car's outside?' he snapped before realizing that *she* must have been joking.

'It's a pity you don't have a spare key,' she said.

'It's a pity your car's in the garage,' he retorted, 'about to be declared uneconomical to repair. Look, Christine, it's very late. I can't find it and I certainly won't find it with you hovering, getting all wound up, so I suggest you get a cab and I'll follow.'

'But what if you don't find it?'

'I'll find it. I'll be there, just a little late, that's all. You go. You'll easily pick up a black cab on the Green. You're only going to Ladbroke Grove.'

Sweating, he listened as the front door was opened and shut –

slammed. Gate clanged. Fading echo of footsteps receding. He felt the tension flow out of him and collapsed on to the nearest chair. He loosened his tie and reached for a glass.

In their bedroom he pressed the power button on his laptop. While waiting, he stared blankly at the framed poster on the wall. A production he'd been in more than twenty years ago. *Colossus*. Clive Barker's play about Goya. He allowed the faces of cast members to run through his mind, particularly those who'd gone on to other things. Lennie James – you saw him on television all the time now. A part in *Cold Feet*. A one-off drama, something he'd written himself. That prison series. *Buried*. Right. Buried in the schedules.

Aslie Pitter, the most naturally talented actor in the cast. He'd done one or two things – a Channel 4 sitcom, guest appearance in *The Bill* – then disappeared. Maddox had last seen him working for a high-street chain. Security, demonstrating product – he couldn't remember which.

Elinore Vickery had turned up in something at the Waterman's. Maddox had liked her, tried to keep in touch, but there was an invisible barrier, as if she'd known him better than he knew himself.

Missing out on a couple of good parts because of his size (five foot five in stocking feet, eight stone dead), Maddox had quit the theatre and concentrated on writing. Barker had helped with one or two contacts and Maddox sold a couple of horror stories. Over the years he'd moved away from fiction into journalism and book-length non-fiction. The current project, *New Maps of Hell*, hadn't found a home. The publishers he'd offered it to hadn't been able to reject it quickly enough. They didn't want it on their desks. It made them uncomfortable. That was fine by Maddox. He'd worry if it didn't. They'd want it on their lists, though, when it was too late. He'd finish it first, then pick one editor and let the others write their letters of resignation.

He read through the afternoon's work, then closed the laptop. He opened his bedside drawer and there was his car key. He looked at it. Had it been there before? Of course it had. How could it not have been? But he'd not seen it, so it might as well not have been. It had effectively disappeared. Hysterical blindness? Negative hallucination?

He pocketed the key and went downstairs. The door closed behind him and the car started first time. He sneaked past White City – the exhibition halls were gone, torn down for a future shopping centre – and slipped on to the Westway. He didn't think of Christine as he approached Ladbroke Grove, but of Christie, John Reginald Halliday. The former relief projectionist at the Electric, who had murdered at least six women, had lived at 10 Rillington Place, later renamed Ruston Close before being demolished to make way for the elevated motorway on which Maddox was now driving. The film, starring Dickie Attenborough as the killer and John Hurt as his poor dupe of an upstairs neighbour, who swung for at least one of Christie's crimes, had been filmed in Rillington Place itself. Maddox understood, from comments posted on ghoulish message boards on the internet, that the interiors had been shot in No. 8 and the exteriors outside No. 10. But when the police, acting on a tip-off from Timothy Evans, yanked open a manhole cover outside No. 10, Attenborough could be seen peering out through the ground-floor window of the end house in the terrace, No. 10, where three of Christie's victims had been walled up in the pantry, his wife, Ethel, being found under the floorboards in the front room. For Maddox it was the key shot in the film, the only clear evidence that they'd gained access to the charnel house itself. The only other explanation being that they'd mocked up the entire street in the studio, which he didn't buy.

The case accounted for five pages in Maddox's book. He concentrated mainly on the interweaving of fact and fiction, the merging of film and reality. Attenborough as Christie. No. 8 standing in for No. 10, if indeed it did. The internet also yielded a piece of Pathé film footage of the demolition of Ruston Close. Two men with pickaxes. A third man speaking to camera. A burning house. Shots of the house at the end of the street with the white (replacement) door. Clearly the same house as that in the film. But there was no sound, the reporter mouthing inaudible commentary. Maddox lured a lip-reader to the flat, a junior editor from one of the publishers that had turned down his book. She reminded him of Linzi with her green eyes and shoulder-length streaked hair. Even in heels she didn't reach Maddox's height, but she had a confident, relaxed smile. She held his gaze when he spoke to her and appeared to be looking into his eyes, but must have been watching his lips, as she relied heavily on lip-reading.

Maddox was careful to make sure she was looking in his direction before speaking to her, probably over-careful. She must have spent a lifetime compensating for situations in which people wouldn't have made such allowances. Working backwards from the first words she managed to lip-read and then having to catch up. So much information assumed rather than known for certain, but Maddox could relate to that. In some areas of life he, too, knew nothing for certain. The deaf woman's name was Karen. He assumed the proposal for his book had been rejected by someone senior who had given Karen the unpleasant job of telling the author, but he didn't know *that* for certain. Possibly she'd read it and rejected it herself and only agreed to provide lip-reading services because she felt bad about it.

When she entered the flat, Maddox felt at ease. In control. He apologized for the loud, bass-heavy music coming from the downstairs flat, but she said she couldn't hear it.

'I thought you might be able to feel it,' he said.

'It's a new building,' she said. 'Concrete floors. Otherwise . . .'

He showed her the footage. She said it wasn't straightforward. The quality was poor and the picture kept pixellating, plus the reporter unhelpfully turned his head to the side on several occasions.

Maddox asked her if she would come back and have another go if he was able to tidy the picture up a bit.

'I don't think I'll be able to get much off it for you,' she said.

'If you wouldn't mind just trying one more time, perhaps when you're less tired,' he said. 'It's very important to me, for my book, you know.'

*

Maddox pulled into one of the reserved spaces outside a block of purpose-built flats in the depressed residential trapezium bordered by Green Lanes and the roads of West Green, Seven Sisters and St Ann's. He listened to the ticking of the cooling engine for a few moments as he watched the darkened windows of the second-floor flat. The top flat.

The street door had been left open by one of his neighbours. He walked up.

Inside the flat, he left the light switched off, poured himself a drink and sat in the single armchair. He pulled out his phone and sent a short text message. Orange street-lighting cast a deathly glow over the cheap bookshelves stacked with pulp novels, true crime, horror anthologies and dystopian science fiction. His phone chimed. He opened it, read the return message and replied to it. When he'd lived here, the room had been dominated by a double bed. Moving into Christine's house had allowed him to turn the tiny flat into the dedicated office he'd always wanted by burning the bed on the waste ground out the back. He'd considered giving it away, since selling it had struck him as tiresome: placing an ad, answering calls, opening the door to strangers. Easier to burn the damn thing and all the memories associated with it. So then he'd moved his desk from the east end of the room, under the Velux window, to the west-facing windows overlooking the street.

Another text arrived. He read it and closed the phone without replying.

As usual, loud music was playing in the downstairs flat.

He drained his glass and let his head fall back against the soft cushion. The Artex ceiling had attracted cobwebs and grime, but he doubted he would ever feel the need to repaint or clean it. Very few people ever came here. Linzi had spent a lot of time in the flat, of course. He laughed bitterly, then chewed his lip and stared at the ceiling, sensitive to the slightest noise in spite of the thump of the bass from the downstairs flat. Christine had hardly stepped over the threshold. She'd been once or twice soon after they'd met, but not since. There was no reason to. It was clear from the odd comment that she resented his keeping the flat, since it was a drain on resources, but as he'd argued, there was no room in the house for all these books and tapes. Not to mention the stuff stored in the loft. He chewed his lip again.

He switched on the stereo and the ordered chaos of Paul Schütze's *New Maps of Hell* clattered into battle with the beat from below. Schütze's 1992 release was the constant soundtrack to any work he did on the book in the flat. (On the rare occasions that he worked on it at the house, he played the follow-up, *New Maps of Hell II: The Rapture of Metals.*) He believed it helped. *It started out as an aid to getting the mindset right,* he sometimes imagined telling Kirsty Wark or Verity Sharp in a television interview, *and soon became a habit, a routine. I simply couldn't work on the book without having the music playing in the background. It was about the creation of a hermetically sealed world. Which, I suppose you have to admit, hell is. Although one that's expanding at an alarming rate, erupting in little pockets. North Kensington, Muswell Hill. London is going to hell, Kirsty.*

He opened a file and did some work, tidied up some troublesome text. He saved it and opened another file, 'Dollis Hill'. Notes, a few stabs at an address, gaps, big gaps. He was going to have to go back.

He replayed the mental rushes. Autumn 1986. A fine day. Gusty, but dry, bright. Walking in an unfamiliar district of London. A long road, tree-lined. High up. View down over the city between detached houses and semis. Victorian, Edwardian.

The entryphone buzzed, bringing him back to the present with a start. He closed the file. He got to his feet, crossed to the hall and picked up the phone.

'The door's open. Come up,' he said, before realizing she couldn't hear him.

He remained standing in the hall, listening to footsteps climbing the interior staircase. When the footsteps stopped outside his door there was a pause before the knock came. He imagined her composing herself, perhaps straightening her clothes, removing a hair from her collar. Or looking at her watch and thinking of bolting. He opened the door as she knocked, which startled her.

'Come in,' he said. 'Thanks for coming.'

All Maddox had done to improve the image on the video was change the size of the Media Player window so that the reporter's mouth, while slightly smaller, was less affected by picture break-up.

While Karen studied the footage, Maddox crossed to the far side of the room. He returned with a glass of red wine, which he placed beside the laptop. Karen raised a hand to decline, but Maddox simply pushed the glass slightly closer to her and left it there. Finally, while she was watching the footage for a third time, her hand reached out, perhaps involuntarily, to pick up the glass. She took a sip, then held the glass aloft while studying the image of the jaunty reporter: Michael Caine glasses, buttoned-up jacket, button-down shirt, hand alighting on hip like a butterfly.

Maddox watched as she replayed the footage again. Each time the reporter started speaking, she moved a little closer to the screen and seemed to angle her head slightly to the left in order to favour her right ear, in which she had a trace of hearing, despite the fact there was no sound at all on the film. Habit, Maddox decided.

Karen leaned back and looked at Maddox before speaking.

'He's saying something like *newspaper reports . . . of the investigation . . . into the discovery of the burned-out bodies of two women . . . Fifteen – or fifty – years ago . . . Something of the century.* I'm sorry, it's really hard.'

Her speech was that of a person who had learned to talk the hard way, without being able to hear the sound of her own voice.

'That's great. That's very helpful, Karen. It would be fifteen, not fifty. I didn't even know for certain that he was talking about Christie's house. *Burned-out*, though, are you sure? That's strange.'

'No, I'm not sure, but that's what it sounds like.'

Karen's choice of expression – *sounds like* – reminded him of a blind man who had asked Maddox for help crossing the road as he was going to *see* the doctor.

Maddox went to fill up her glass, but she placed her hand over it.

'I've got to go,' she said. 'I said I could only stop by for a minute.'

Maddox stood his ground with the wine bottle, then stepped back.

'Another time,' he said.

'Have you got something else you want me to look at?'

'I might have. If it's not too much of an imposition.'

'Just let me know.'

He showed her out, then switched the light off again and watched from the window as she regained the street. She stopped, looked one way, then went the other, as if deciding there and then which way to go. Hardly the action of a woman with an appointment. He watched as she walked south towards St Ann's Road and disappeared around the corner, then he sat down in the armchair and emptied her wine glass. His gaze roved across the bookshelves and climbed the walls before reaching the ceiling. He then sat without moving for half an hour, his eyes not leaving the ceiling, listening to the building's creaks and sighs, the music downstairs having been turned off.

He took a different route back, climbing the Harringay Ladder and going west past the top of Priory Park. He floored the pedal through the Cranley Gardens S-bend and allowed the gradient to slow the car so that he rolled to a stop outside No. 23. There he killed the engine and looked up at the second-floor flat where Dennis Nilsen had lived from October 1981 to February 1983. One of Nilsen's mistakes, which had led to his being caught, was to have left the window in the gable dormer wide open for long periods, attracting the attention of neighbours.

Maddox looked at his watch and started the engine. He got on to the North Circular, coming off at Staples Corner, heading south down Edgware Road and turning right into Dollis Hill Lane. He slowed to a crawl, leaning forward over the wheel, craning his neck at the houses on the south side. He was sure it would be on the south side. He definitely remembered a wide tree-lined avenue with views over central London. Land falling away behind the house. Long walk from the Tube. Which Tube? He didn't know.

He turned right, cruised the next street. He wasn't even sure of the street. Dollis Hill Lane sounded right, but as soon as he'd got the idea of Cricklewood Lane off the internet that had sounded right too.

He'd gone there, to 108/110 Cricklewood Lane, after reading on the net that that was where they'd shot *Hellraiser*. When he got there and found it was a branch of Holmes Place Health Clubs, he worked out it must have been the former location of Cricklewood Production Village, where they'd done the studio work.

Some time in the autumn of 1986, Maddox had come here, to a house in Dollis Hill. A movie was being made. Clive Barker was directing his first film. *Hellraiser*. They were shooting in a rented house and Maddox had been invited to go on the set as an associate of Barker. He was going to do a little interview, place it wherever possible. Could be his big break. It was good of Clive to have agreed to it. Maddox remembered the big white vans in the street outside the house, a surprising number of people hanging around doing nothing, a catering truck, a long table covered with polystyrene cups, a tea urn. He asked for Steve Jones, unit publicist. Jones talked to him about what was going on. They were filming a dinner-party scene with Andrew Robinson and Clare Higgins and two young actors, the boy and the girl, and a bunch of extras. Maddox got to watch from behind the camera, trying to catch Barker's eye as he talked to the actors, telling them what he wanted them to do. Controlling everybody and everything. Maddox envied him, but admired him as well. A make-up girl applied powder to Robinson's forehead. A hairdresser fixed Ashley Laurence's hair. They did the scene and the air was filled with electricity. Everyone behind the camera held their breath, faces still and taut. The tension was palpable. The moment Barker called, 'Cut,' it melted away. Smiles, laughter, everyone suddenly moving around. Maddox noticed the hairdresser, who looked lost for a moment, diminutive and vulnerable, but Steve Jones caught Maddox's arm in a light grip and cornered Barker. The director looked at Maddox and there was a fraction of a second's pause, no more, before he said, 'Brian,' in such a warm, sincere way that Maddox might have thought Clive had been looking forward to seeing him all morning.

They did a short interview over lunch, which they ate on the floor of a room at the back of the house.

'We're surrounded by images which are momentarily potent and carry no resonance whatsoever,' Barker was saying in transatlantic Scouse. 'Advertising, the pop video, a thing which seems to mean an awful lot and is in fact absolutely negligible.'

Maddox noticed the hairdresser carrying a paper plate and a cup. She sat cross-legged on the floor next to another crew member and they talked as they ate.

'What frightens you?' he asked Barker.

'Unlit streets, flying, being stuck on the Tube at rush hour. Places where you have to relinquish control.'

Once they'd finished, Maddox hung around awkwardly, waiting for a chance to talk to the hairdresser. When it came – her companion rising to go – he seized it. She was getting up too and Maddox contrived to step in front of her, blocking her way. He apologized and introduced himself. 'I was just interviewing Clive. We've known each other a couple of years. I was in one of his plays.'

'Linzi,' she said, offering her hand. 'I'm only here for one day. The regular girl called in sick.'

'Then I'm lucky I came today,' he said, smiling shyly.

She was wearing a dark green top of soft cotton that was exactly the same shade as her eyes. Her hair, light brown with natural blonde streaks, was tied back in a knot pierced by a pencil.

'Are you going to stick around?' she asked.

'I've done my interview, but if no one kicks me out . . .'

'It's a pretty relaxed set.'

He did stick around and most of the time he watched Linzi, promising himself he wouldn't leave until he'd got her number. It took him the rest of the afternoon, but he got it. She scribbled it on a blank page in her Filofax, then tore out the page and said, 'Call me.'

The chances of finding the house in darkness were even less than in daylight. He'd been up to Dollis Hill a couple of times in the last few weeks, once in the car and once on foot. Lately, he'd been thinking more about Linzi, and specifically about the early days, before it started to go wrong. He'd spent enough time going over the bad times and wanted to revisit the good. He wanted to see the house again, but couldn't. He needed to locate it for his book. He'd rewatched the film, which contained enough shots of the house's exterior that it should have been easy to locate it, but it didn't seem to matter how many times he trailed these suburban avenues, the house wasn't there. Or if it was, he couldn't see it. He'd begun to think it might have been knocked down, possibly even straight after the shoot. It could have been why the house had been available. In the film there was a No. 55 on the porch, but that would be set dressing, like the renumbering of 25 Powis Square, in *Performance*, as No. 81.

He looked at his watch and calculated that if he was quick he could get to Ladbroke Grove in time for coffee and to drive Christine home, thereby reducing the amount of grief she would give him. Negligibly, he realized, but still.

In the morning, he feigned sleep while she dressed. Her movements were businesslike, crisp. The night before had been a riot, as expected. When he had turned up at the dinner, two and a half hours late, she had contented herself with merely shooting him a look, but as soon as they left she started. And as soon as she started, he switched off.

It didn't let up even when they got home, but he wasn't listening. He marvelled at how closely he was able to mimic the condition with which Karen, his lip-reader, had been born. Thinking of Karen, moreover, relaxed him inside, while Christine kept on, even once they'd got into bed. Elective deafness – it beat hysterical blindness.

When he was sure Christine had left the house – the slammed door, the gate that clanged – he got up and showered. Within half an hour, having spent ten minutes pointing the DVD remote at the television, he was behind the wheel of the car with his son in the back seat. South Tottenham in twenty minutes was a bigger ask by day than by night, but he gave it his best shot. Rush hour was over (Christine, in common with everyone who worked on weekly magazines, finished earlier than she started), but skirting the congestion charge zone was still a challenge.

He parked where he had the night before and turned to see that

Jack was asleep. He left him there, locked the car and walked up. He had decided, while lying in bed with his back to Christine, that it would be worth going up into the loft. Somewhere in the loft was a box containing old diaries, including one for 1986. He had never been a consistent diarist, but some years had seen him make more notes than others. It was worth a rummage among the spiders' webs and desiccated wasps' nests. His size meant he didn't bang his head on the latticework of pine beams.

The loft still smelled faintly of formalin. He suspected it always would until he got rid of the suitcase at the far end. He shone the torch in its direction. Big old-fashioned brown leather case, rescued from a skip and cleaned up. Solid, sturdy, two catches and a strap with a buckle. Could take a fair weight.

He redirected the torch at the line of dusty boxes closer to the trapdoor. The first box contained T-shirts that he never wore any more but couldn't bear to throw away. The second was full of old typescripts stiff with Tipp-Ex. The diaries were in the third box along. He bent down and sorted through: 1974, a shiny black Pocket Diary filled mainly with notes on the history of the Crusades; 1976, the summer of the heatwave, *Angling Times* diary, roach and perch that should have been returned to the water left under stones to die; 1980, the deaths of his three remaining grandparents, three funerals in one year, coffins in the front room, all burials; 1982, his first term at university, meeting Martin, his best friend for a while. Martin was a year older, which had impressed Maddox. The age difference hadn't mattered. Everything was changing. Leaving school, leaving home. Living in halls. Martin was a medical student. They would stay up late drinking coffee and Martin would smoke cigarettes and tell Maddox about medicine, about anatomy and about the bodies he was learning to dissect.

Maddox could listen to Martin for hours. The later they stayed up, the more profound their discussions seemed to become. Maddox watched as Martin dragged on his cigarette and held the smoke in his lungs for an eternity, stretching the moment, before blowing it out in perfect rings. When Martin talked about the bodies in the anatomy lab, Maddox became entranced. He imagined Martin alone in the lab with a dozen flayed corpses. Bending over them, examining them, carefully removing a strip of muscle, severing a tendon. Getting up close to the secrets, the mysteries, of death. Martin said it didn't matter how long he spent washing his hands, they still smelled of formalin. He held them under Maddox's nose, then moved to cup his cheeks in an affectionate, stroking gesture.

'You don't mind, do you?' he said, as his hand landed on Maddox's knee.

'Could you get me in there? Into the lab?' Maddox asked, shaking his head, picturing himself among the bodies, as Martin's hand moved up his thigh.

'No. But I could bring you something out. Something you could keep.'

Martin's hand had reached Maddox's lap and Maddox was mildly surprised to discover that far from objecting, he was aroused. If this was to be the downpayment on whatever Martin might fetch him back from the dissection table, so be it.

'I've got something for you,' Martin said a couple of days later, 'in my room.'

Maddox followed Martin to his room.

'So where is it?' Maddox asked.

'Can't just leave that sort of thing lying about. But what's the rush?'

Martin lay down on the bed and unbuckled his belt.

Maddox hesitated, considered walking out, but he felt certain he'd always regret it if he left empty-handed. Instead, he knelt beside the bed and spat into his palm.

Afterwards, Martin pulled open his desk drawer.

'There you go,' he said.

Maddox withdrew a strong-smelling package. He started to work at the knot in the outermost plastic bag, but it wouldn't come easily. He asked Martin what it contained.

'A piece of subcutaneous fat from the body of a middle-aged man. If anyone ever asks, you didn't get it from me.'

Maddox returned to his own room on the seventh floor, washing his hands on the way. He cut open the bag and unwrapped his spoils. The gobbet of fat, four inches by two, looked like a piece of tripe, white and bloodless, and the stench of formalin made him feel sick and excited at the same time. Maddox was careful not to touch the fat as he wrapped it up again and secured the package with tape. He opened his wardrobe and pulled out the brown suitcase he'd liberated from a skip in Judd Street.

He saw less of Martin after that. At first he contrived subtly to avoid him and then started going out with Valerie, a girl with fat arms and wide hips he picked up in the union bar on cocktails night. He wasn't convinced they were a good match, but the opportunity was convenient, given the Martin situation.

The piece of fat remained wrapped up in its suitcase, which smelled so strongly that Maddox had only to open the case and take a sniff to re-experience how he had felt when Martin had given him the body part. As he lay in bed trying to get to sleep (alone – Valerie didn't last more than a few weeks) he sometimes thought about the man who had knowingly willed his cadaver to science. He wondered what his name might have been and what kind of man he was. What he might have been in life. He would hardly have been able to foresee what would happen to the small part of him that was now nestled inside Maddox's wardrobe.

When Maddox left the hall of residence for a flat in Holloway, the case went with him, still empty but for its human remains. He kept it on top of a cupboard. It stayed there for two years. When he moved into the flat in N15, he put the suitcase in the loft, where it had remained ever since. The piece of fat was no longer in Maddox's possession, but the suitcase was not free of the smell of formalin.

Maddox's 1986 diary was at the bottom of the box. It took only a couple of minutes to find what he was looking for. '*Hellraiser*, 11 a.m.' he'd written in the space reserved for Friday 10 October. A little further down was an address: 187 Dollis Hill Lane.

He drove to Dollis Hill via Cranley Gardens, but on this occasion didn't stop.

'Why didn't I think of checking my old diaries before, eh, Jack?' he said, looking in the rear-view mirror.

His son was silent, staring out of the window.

Turning into Dollis Hill Lane from Edgware Road, he slowed to a crawl, oblivious to the noisy rebuke of the driver immediately behind him, who pulled out and swerved to overtake, engine racing, finger given. Maddox brought the car to a halt on a slight incline outside No. 187. He looked at the house and felt an unsettling combination of familiarity and non-recognition. Attraction and repulsion. He had to stare at the house for two or three minutes before he realized why he had driven past it so many times and failed to recognize it.

Like most things recalled from the past, it was smaller than the version in his memory. But the main difference was the apparent age of the building. He remembered a Victorian villa, possibly Edwardian. The house in front of him was new. The rendering on the front gable end had gone up in the last few years. The wood-framed bay windows on the first floor were of recent construction. The casement window in the top flat, second floor, was obviously new. The mansard roof was a familiar shape, but the clay Rosemarys were all fresh from the tile shop. The materials were new, but the style was not. The basic design was unchanged, from what he could remember of the exterior shots in the film, which he'd looked at again before coming out, but in spite of that the house looked new. As if a skeleton had grown new muscle and flesh.

'Just like Frank,' he said out loud.

'What, Daddy?'

'Just like Frank in the film.'

'What film?'

'They made a film in this house and I came to see them make it. You're too young to see it yet. One day, maybe.'

'What's it about?'

'It's about a man who disappears and then comes back to life with the help of his girlfriend. It happened in that room up there.' He pointed to the top flat. 'Although, the windows are wrong,' he said, trying to remember the second-floor window in the film. 'I need to check it again.'

The only part of the exterior that looked as if they'd taken care to try to match the original was the front door.

As he'd walked from the *Hellraiser* set back to the Tube two decades earlier, he'd read and reread Linzi's number on the torn-out piece of Filofax paper. He called her the next day and they arranged to meet for a drink.

'Why are you so interested in this house, Daddy?' Jack asked from the back seat.

'Because of what happened here. Because of the film. And because I met somebody here. Somebody I knew before I met your mother.'

Linzi lived in East Finchley. They went to see films at the Phoenix or met for drinks in Muswell Hill. Malaysian meals in Crouch End. He showed her the house in Hillfield Avenue where he had visited Clive Barker.

'Peter Straub used to live on the same road, just further up the hill,' he told her.

'Who's Peter Straub?'

'Have you heard of Stephen King?'

'Of course.'

'Straub and King wrote a book together. *The Talisman*. They wrote it here. Or part of it, anyway. King also wrote a story called "Crouch End", which was interesting, not one of his best.'

Maddox and Linzi started meeting during the day at the Wisteria Tea Rooms on Middle Lane and it was there, among the pot plants and mismatched crockery, that Maddox realized with a kind of slow, swooning surprise that he was happy. The realization was so slow because the feeling was so unfamiliar. They took long walks through Highgate Cemetery and across Hampstead Heath.

Weeks became months. The cherry blossom came out in long straight lines down Cecile Park, and fell to the pavements, and came out again. Linzi often stayed at Maddox's flat in South Tottenham, but frowned distastefully at his true-crime books. One morning while she was still asleep, Maddox was dressing, looking for a particular T-shirt. Unable to find it, he climbed up the ladder into the loft. Searching through a box of old clothes, he didn't hear Linzi climbing the ladder or see her head and shoulders suddenly intrude into the loft space.

'What are you doing?' she said.

'Shit.' He jumped, hitting his head. 'Ow. That hurt. Shit. Nothing. Looking for something.'

'What's that smell?'

'Nothing.'

He urged her back down the ladder and made sure the trapdoor was fastened before pulling on the *Eraserhead* T-shirt he'd been looking for.

Whenever he went into the loft from then on, whether Linzi was around or not, he would pull the ladder up after him and close the trapdoor. The loft was private.

When he got back to the flat that evening, he went up into the loft again – duly covering his tracks, although he was alone – and took the small wrapped parcel from the suitcase. The lid fell shut, the old-fashioned clasps sliding home without his needing to fasten them. Quality craftsmanship.

When it was dark, he buried the slice of tissue in the waste ground behind the flats.

As the decade approached its end, the directionless lifestyle that Maddox and Linzi had drifted into seemed to become more expensive. The bills turned red. Maddox started working regular shifts on the subs' desk at the *Independent*. He hated it but it paid well. Linzi applied for a full-time job at a ladies' salon in Finsbury Park. They took a day trip to Brighton. They went to an art show in the Unitarian Church where Maddox bought Linzi a small watercolour and she picked out a booklet of poems by the artist's husband as a return gift. They had lunch in a vegetarian café. Maddox talked about the frustrations of cutting reviews to fit and coming up with snappy headlines, when what he'd rather be doing was writing the copy himself. Linzi had no complaints about the salon. 'Gerry –

he's the boss – he's a really lovely guy,' she said. 'Nicest boss I've ever had.'

They spent the afternoon in the pubs and secondhand bookshops of the North Lanes. Maddox found a Ramsey Campbell anthology, an M. John Harrison collection and *The New Murderers' Who's Who*. On the train waiting to leave Brighton Station to return to London, with the sun throwing long dark shapes across the platforms, Linzi read to Maddox from the pamphlet of verse.

'"This is all I ever wanted/ to meet you in the fast decaying shadows/ on the outskirts of this or any city/ alone and in exile."'

As the train rattled through Sussex, Maddox pored over the photographs in his true-crime book.

'Look,' he said, pointing to a caption: 'Brighton Trunk Crime No. 2: The trunk's contents.'

'Very romantic,' Linzi said as she turned to the window, but Maddox couldn't look away from the crumpled stockings on the legs of the victim, Violette Kay. Her broken neck. The pinched scowl on her decomposed face. To Maddox the picture was as beautiful as it was terrible.

Over the next few days, Maddox read up on the Brighton Trunk Murders of 1934. He discovered that Tony Mancini, who had confessed to putting Violette Kay's body in the trunk but claimed she had died accidentally (only to retract that claim and accept responsibility for her murder more than forty years later), had lodged at 52 Kemp Street. He rooted around for the poetry pamphlet Linzi had bought him. He found it under a pile of magazines. The poet's name was Michael Kemp. He wanted to share his discovery of this coincidence with Linzi when she arrived at his flat with scissors and hairdressing cape.

'Why not save a bit of money?' she said, moving the chair from Maddox's desk into the middle of the room. As she worked on his hair, she talked about Gerry from the salon. 'He's so funny,' she said. 'The customers love him. He certainly keeps me and the other girls entertained.'

'Male hairdressers in women's salons are all puffs, surely?'

Linzi stopped cutting and looked at him.

'So?' she said. 'So what if they are? And anyway, Gerry's not gay. No way.'

'Really? How can you be so sure?'

'A girl knows. OK?'

'Have you fucked him then or what?'

She took a step back. 'What's the matter with you?'

'How else would you know? Gerry seems to be all you can talk about.'

'Fuck you.'

Maddox shot to his feet, tearing off the cape.

'You know what,' he said, seizing the scissors, 'I'll cut my own fucking hair and do a better job of it. At least I won't have to listen to you going on about *Gerry.*'

He started to hack at his own hair, grabbing handfuls and cutting away. Linzi recoiled in horror, unable to look away, as if she were watching a road accident.

'Maybe I should tell you about all the women at the *Independent*?' he suggested. 'Sheila Johnston, Sabine Durrant, Christine Healey . . . I don't know where to start.'

It wasn't until he jabbed the scissors threateningly in her direction that she snatched up her bag and ran out.

The next day he sent flowers. He didn't call, didn't push it. Just flowers and a note: 'Sorry.'

Then he called. Told her he didn't know what had come over him. It wouldn't happen again. He knew he'd be lucky if she forgave him, but he hoped he'd be lucky. He hadn't felt like this about anyone before and he didn't want to lose her. The irony was, he told her, he'd been thinking his flat was getting a bit small and maybe they should look for a place together. He'd understand if she wanted to kick it into touch, but hoped she'd give him another chance.

She said to give her some time.

He shaved his head.

He drove down to Finsbury Park and watched from across the

street as she worked on clients. Bobbing left and right. Holding their hair in her hands. Eye contact in the mirror. Gerry fussing around, sharing a joke, trailing an arm. As she'd implied, though, he was distributing his attentions equally among Linzi and the two other girls.

Mornings and evenings, he kept a watch on her flat in Finchley. She left and returned on her own. He chose a route between his flat and hers that took in Cranley Gardens in Muswell Hill. He parked outside No. 23 and watched the darkened windows of the top flat. He wondered if any of the neighbours had been Nilsen's contemporaries. If this man passing by now with a tartan shopping trolley had ever nodded good morning to the mass murderer. If that woman leaving her house across the street had ever smiled at him. Maddox got out of the car and touched the low wall outside the property with the tips of his fingers.

Linzi agreed to meet up. Maddox suggested the Wisteria Tea Rooms. It was almost like starting over. Cautious steps. Shy smiles. His hair had grown back.

'What got into you?'

'I don't know. I thought we'd agreed to draw a line under it.'

'Yes, you're right.'

At the next table a woman was feeding a baby.

'Do you ever think about having children?' Linzi asked, out of the blue.

'A boy,' Maddox said straight away. 'I'd call him Jack.'

Maddox didn't mention Gerry. He took on extra shifts. Slowly, they built up trust again. One day, driving back to his place after dropping Linzi off at hers, he saw that a board had gone up outside 23 Cranley Gardens. For sale. He rang the agents. Yes, it was the top flat, second floor. It was on at £64,950, but when Maddox dropped by to pick up a copy of the details ('DELIGHTFUL TOP FLOOR ONE BEDROOM CONVERSION FLAT'), they'd reduced it to £59,950. He made an appointment, told Linzi he'd arranged a surprise. Picked her up early, drove to Cranley Gardens. He'd never brought her this way. She didn't know whose flat it had been.

A young lad met them outside. Loosely knotted tie, shiny shoes. Bright, eager.

Linzi turned to Maddox. 'Are you thinking of moving?'

'It's bigger and it's cheap.'

Linzi smiled stiffly. They followed the agent up the stairs. He unlocked the interior door and launched into his routine. Maddox nodded without listening as his eyes greedily took everything in, trying to make sense of the flat, to match what he saw to the published photographs. It didn't fit.

'The bathroom's gone,' he said, interrupting the agent.

'There's a shower room,' the boy said. 'And a washbasin across the hall. An unusual arrangement.'

Nilsen had dissected two bodies in the bathroom.

'This is a lovely room,' the agent said, moving to the front of the flat.

Maddox entered the room at the back and checked the view from the window.

'At least this is unchanged,' he said to Linzi, who had appeared alongside.

'What do you mean?'

He looked at her and realized what he'd said.

'This flat's all different. I've seen pictures of it.'

The story came out later, back at Maddox's place.

'You took me round Dennis Nilsen's flat?'

He turned away.

'You didn't think to mention it first? You thought we might live there together? In the former home of a serial killer? What the fuck is wrong with you?'

'It's cheap,' he said, to the closing door.

He watched from the window as she ran off towards West Green Road. He stayed at the window for a time and then pulled down the ladder and went up into the loft. He pulled up the ladder and closed the trapdoor. He opened the big brown suitcase. It was like getting a fix. He studied the dimensions of the suitcase. It was not much smaller than Tony Mancini's trunk.

*

487

Christine was at work. Maddox read a note she'd left in the kitchen: 'We need milk and bread.'

He went into the living room and took down the *Hellraiser* DVD from the shelf. Sitting in the car with Jack outside the house on Dollis Hill Lane, Maddox had noticed something not quite right about the windows on the second floor. They were new windows and set in two pairs with a gap between them, but that wasn't it. There was something else and he didn't know what. He fast-forwarded to the exterior shot of Julia leaving the house to go to the bar where she picks up the first victim. The second-floor window comprised six lights in a row. For some reason, when rebuilding the house, they'd left out two of the lights and gone with just four, in two pairs. But that wasn't what was bothering him.

He skipped forward. He kept watching.

Frank and Julia in the second-floor room, top of the house. She's just killed the guy from the bar and Frank has drained his body. Julia re-enters the room after cleaning herself up and as she walks towards the window we see it comprises four lights in a row. Four windows. Four windows in a row. Not six. Four.

Maddox wielded the remote.

Looking up at the house as Julia leaves it to go to the bar. Second floor, six windows. Inside the same room on the second floor, looking towards the windows. Four, not six.

So what? The transformation scenes, which take place in that second-floor room at the front of the house, weren't shot on Dollis Hill Lane. Big deal. That kind of stuff would have to be done in the studio. The arrival of the Cenobites, the transformation of Frank, his being torn apart. It wasn't the kind of stuff you could shoot on location. But how could they make such a glaring continuity error as the number of lights in a window? Six from outside, four from within. It couldn't be a mistake. It was supposed to mean something. But what?

'Daddy?'

Maddox jumped.

'What is it, Jack?'

'What are you watching?'

Maddox looked at the screen as he thought about his response.

'This film, the one shot in that house.'

'The house with the windows?'

'Yes.'

'Why is it important?'

'I don't know. No, I do know.' His shoulders slumped. 'I don't know. Maybe it's not.'

He drove to the supermarket. Jack was quiet in the back. They got a trolley. Maddox stopped in front of the newspapers. He looked at the *Independent*. Although he'd first met Christine on the *Independent* arts desk, it wasn't until they bumped into each other some years later, when they were both freelancing on TV listings magazines at IPC, that they started going out. Although they were equals at IPC, Christine had routinely rewritten his headlines at the *Independent* and while he pretended it didn't still rankle, it did. Not the best basis for a relationship, perhaps. Then a permanent position came up on *TV Times*, and they both went for it, but Christine's experience counted. They decided it wouldn't affect things, but agreed that maybe Maddox should free himself of his commitments at IPC. He said he had a book he wanted to write. Together they negotiated an increasingly obstacle-strewn path towards making a life together. If they stopped and thought about it, it didn't seem like a very good idea, but neither of them had a better one.

Maddox looked around to check that Jack was still in tow, then moved on.

He stood silently in cold meats, swaying very gently.

'Gone,' he said quietly. 'All gone. Disappeared.'

'What, Daddy? What's gone?'

'Wait there, Jack. I'll be back. Don't move.'

He walked to the end of the aisle and turned the corner. He walked to the end of the next aisle and then the next, looking at the items on the shelves, familiar brands, labels he'd seen a thousand times. All meaningless. He recognized nothing. What was he looking for? Bread and milk? Where were they? He couldn't remember. He went back to where he'd left the trolley. It was there, but Jack wasn't.

He looked up and down the aisle. The brand names that had meant nothing to him a moment ago now leaped out at him, shouting, screaming for attention. It was as if the two sides of the aisle had suddenly shifted inward. Jack was nowhere to be seen.

'Jack!'

Maddox ran to the end of the aisle and looked both ways. He looked up the next aisle, then up the next and the one after. He kept calling Jack's name. Shoppers stopped and stared, but Maddox moved faster and shouted louder. He looked at the line of tills and wondered if Jack had gone that way. He could already be out of the store, wandering around the car park, about to be run over or abducted. He told himself to calm down, that he would find him, but at the same time another voice suggested that sometimes the worst thing imaginable did happen. It had before, after all. Would this be the next case heard about on the news? A half-page in the paper. London man loses child in supermarket. Brian Maddox, forty-two, took his eyes off his son for one moment and he was gone. But he hadn't taken his eyes off him for just one moment. He'd gone to the next aisle, or the one after. He'd gone away. He could have been gone five minutes. Ten, fifteen.

'Jack!'

'Sir?'

A young lad, a shelf stacker, was standing in front of him. Maddox told him his son had disappeared. The shelf stacker asked for a description. Maddox gave him one and the lad said he would start from the far end of the store and advised Maddox to start from the other. They would meet in the middle and most likely one of them would have found Jack. Maddox did as he was told and neither of them found Jack. Maddox was short of breath, dry in the mouth, his chest rising and falling, unbearable pressure being exerted on his temples. He could no longer call out Jack's name without his voice breaking. More staff were on hand now. They took Maddox's arms and led him to an office where he was sat down and given a drink of water.

'Maybe the boy's with his mother?' someone suggested.

Maddox shook his head.

'Do you have a number for her?'

Maddox produced Christine's number. He was dimly aware of a phone call being made. The office was full of people. Managers, security, cashiers. They swapped remarks, observations. Some expressions hardened. 'What did she say?' a voice asked. 'There is no son,' another one answered. 'No kids at all, apparently.' A security guard replayed videotape on a monitor. Grainy, vivid. Maddox entering the store on his own with a trolley. Standing in front of the newspapers, on his own. Leaving the trolley in cold meats. No unattached children.

They gave Maddox another glass of water while waiting for the police to arrive. The store didn't want to press charges. 'What would be the point?' Maddox was free to go. 'Has this happened before?' Shake of the head. 'If it were to happen again, the store would have to consider taking action . . . Very upsetting for other shoppers . . . You *will* see someone?'

Maddox sat in the car park, behind the wheel of the car. He hadn't got what he'd come for. The milk and the bread. Maybe it didn't matter any more. He sat in the car for a long time and only turned the key in the ignition when he realized the sky over Central London was beginning to get dark.

He didn't go to the house. He didn't imagine Christine would be there, but it was kind of irrelevant either way. Instead, he drove to South Tottenham. He drove through the top of the congestion charge zone. It didn't matter any more. It was rush hour. It took an hour and a half to get to N15. The street door was open. He walked up, entered the flat. Thump-thump-thump from downstairs. He took out his phone and sent a text message, then stood by the window for a while watching the street. He left the phone on the window ledge and pulled down the ladder and climbed into the loft, retrieving the ladder and closing the trapdoor behind him. Stooping, he walked over to the suitcase, which smelled strongly of formalin. He knelt in front of it for several minutes, resting his hands on the lid, then touching the clasps.

He released the clasps and opened the case.

It was empty.

He frowned, then sat and stared at the empty case for some time, listening to the creaks of the beams and the muffled basslines from the downstairs flat. He wondered if Karen would come, how long she might be. He wasn't sure what he would do when she arrived.

Slowly, he rose, then lowered the upper half of his body into the case, folding his legs in afterwards. Inside the case, the smell of formalin was very strong. He stared at the pine beams, the cobwebs, the shadows clinging to the insulating material. He could still faintly hear his neighbour's loud music, which Karen had been unable to hear, and then, rising above it, the clear and unmistakable chime of his phone, down in the flat, announcing the arrival of a text message. He started to uncurl his body and the lid of the case fell forward.

He had twisted his body far enough that the hump of his shoulder caught the closing lid.

He climbed out and lay down next to the suitcase.

A minute later his phone chimed a reminder.

He thought about Linzi. Linzi had been good for him, until things went bad. He wondered where she was. He looked at the empty suitcase again and plucked a long fine strand of fair hair from the lining. He thought about Karen and her need, unacknowledged, to be looked after. He remembered how vulnerable Linzi had seemed when he saw her for the first time.

Karen would be along soon. Probably. She hadn't let him down yet.

He still had options.

[Nicholas Royle]

THE GAZETTEER OF DISAPPEARANCES & DELETIONS

BATTLE BRIDGE

The urban village of Battle Bridge left the London map in 1836 when a monument to George IV was erected at the junction of Euston, Pentonville, Gray's Inn and Pancras roads, and King's Cross was born. As unpopular as the king himself had been, the sixty-feet-high edifice, with the plinth built on to a one-storey building, survived for just nine years. In its short, unloved life it had served as a pub and a police station.

[Sarah Wise]

TOLMERS SQUARE, NWI

Neighbourhood of small, early-Victorian townhouses surrounding church, built on the site of medieval Totten Hall manor, at the north-east junction of Euston and Hampstead roads. Home to around 1,000 people – families, squatters, students, those on low incomes – and subject of bitter, seventeen-year fight against plans to raze and replace with office blocks. Battle won, in the mid 1970s, in landmark victory for better urban planning, but at a price: original square demolished and replaced by banal high-density, low-rise estate.

[Sarah Wise]

THE OLD MILL, TUFNELL HILL, NW5

A popular spot with working-class Londoners from the Edwardian era to the 1920s, especially on weekends and bank holidays. Trams terminated here. The Mill at one stage incorporated extensive dining rooms, a mosaic hall and an hotel. After the tram route was discontinued, the Mill and its outbuildings fell into disrepair – until it was bought by the reclusive Tom 'Tubby' Ollis in 1960 and converted to a recording studio with living accommodation. It has been used by, among others, Bob Dylan, Dave Stewart, Elvis Costello, Martin Stone and Jah Wobble. Ollis gave up touring with the Deep Fix but continued to record for this and other rock bands as a sessions musician. He restored the Mill to full working condition. Passengers on the upper decks of buses can sometimes catch a glimpse of the sails turning, high above the trees (they supply some of the studio's electricity). Public access has been denied for some years.

[Michael Moorcock]

GOING WEST

THE WESTWAY

London is a city that rarely entered the twentieth century, and to find this stretch of motorway little more than a stone's throw from Marble Arch is a poignant reminder of what might have been. Join it by travelling west along the Marylebone Road, not far from 221B Baker Street, Sherlock Holmes's notional address. The Westway is a continuous overpass some three miles in length, running towards White City, home to BBC Television, and then to Shepherd's Bush, where Pissarro's house is still standing.

By international standards the Westway is unremarkable, and affords a view of some of the most dismal housing in London. But that is not its point. Rising above the crowded nineteenth-century squares and grim stucco terraces, this massive concrete motion-sculpture is an heroically isolated fragment of the modern city London might once have become. There are few surveillance cameras and you can make your own arrangements with the speed limits. Corbusier remarked that a city built for speed is a city built for success, but the Westway, like Ankor Wat, is a stone dream that will never awake. As you hurtle along this concrete deck you briefly join the twentieth century and become a citizen of a virtual city-state borne on a rush of radial tyres.

[J. G. Ballard]

THE WESTWAY

[Robinson] took me round the corner to a multi-storey car park. 'Where are we going?' I asked in the lift. We got off at the top floor.

'Fancy a drive?' he asked, throwing me a set of keys. I fumbled and dropped them.

'Is this yours?' I asked, surprised at the shiny black Jaguar. Robinson shrugged nonchalantly. 'Go on. Give it a go. I trust you.'

I unlocked the car and he climbed in the back and stretched out. I was well over the limit and drunk enough not to care.

The car seemed to drive itself, responding to the merest suggestion, whispering forward with us cocooned in leather-bound silence, protected behind the Cinemascope windscreen. We cruised past Warren Street, jumped red lights on the Euston Road and hit eighty on the Westway with Robinson hooting with laughter and shouting 'Faster, faster!' as the speedometer crept towards a hundred. Afterwards I thanked him. I hadn't enjoyed myself so much in a long time.

[Chris Petit]

PLATFORM

In the days when I used to travel the land, I came back late, one bitterly cold night, from Newcastle. Needing to get to Ladbroke Grove, I went underground and stood, shivering, on a seemingly deserted platform. This was before border-control barriers and CCTV that would shame pornographers.

I smelled something appalling and getting worse: a meths-drinker asking for money. When I declined to contribute, he berated me. I was wearing one of my best suits. He tried to push me off the platform. It was like being hit with a wet newspaper, the creature had no strength at all.

I forget what happened next but he fled. When the train came, I was the only person getting on. Secure in my solitary compartment, a thought hit me with more ferocity than the tramp. If I had gone under the train, the police would have come to my flat in Portobello and found all my books on suicide. They would assume that I had done the job myself, made the big jump. The tramp had chosen the only person in London he could kill without consequence. It was the reverse of an Agatha Christie novel. I think this was the single event that put me off collecting books about death. I have never,

even in Calcutta, where water costs more than alcohol, smelled
anybody as bad as that tramp.

[drif field]

MOVING

When I sorted out the objects in our old house, so we could move
out of it, I found that most of what I keep around (chipped
saucepans, out-of-style dresses, bits of handwriting, expired passports) aren't there as things in themselves but as aides-mémoires –
attempts to stop disappearance by a willed remembering. Faced
with a smaller house, and the likelihood of encumbering the future,
I had to ask if this even works. Surely nothing and no one really
disappears?

Rudolf Steiner wrote that in pre-Atlantean times memory was
geographic. People who wanted to remember something had to go
back to the place where it happened. The landscape was punctuated
with little marker sticks to help them locate their memories.

I've been searching for those sticks ever since I left London for
the first time, when I was thirteen. I have disappeared from that
city in the sense that no one sees me now. Every three or four years
I'll manifest for a walk and a meal, always looking for something,
hovering around certain streets, houses, paintings, books. I'm sure
I still live here, appearances to the contrary. And all those bits of
London – the Coal Exchange, certain bus routes, paving stones,
people one has loved or hated – may seem for a while to disappear.
To stay alive, you have to change all the cells in your body every
seven years – and still know who you are.

The life I lived was a moderate, boring one that felt as if it would
continue for ever. The time was the 1950s. The locality what Robert
Louis Stevenson called, in 1878, 'Westbourne Grove' – a meander
through Paddington, Bayswater, Notting Hill, Ladbroke Grove. A
region which was neither 'in town' nor anywhere in particular. We

499

took trips to my father's office (on the top floor of Liberty) or to the City, which was half monument, half ruin.

I remember the transcendent boredom of Sundays. The day went like this. While my mother cooked heavy lunch, my father, my brother Michael and I climbed into the Humber and drove a mile or so to the Kensington Gardens/Hyde Park border. We could have walked but the car was needed to collect my grandmother on the way home, an event which cast a shadow over what went before it. At the park, we usually progressed around the Serpentine (the surfaced Westbourne River), wearing our decorous Sunday clothes. We did math problems and history, sometimes a little philosophy and religion. Why does a dead goldfish float to the surface? If you were transported to the court of Elizabeth I, what would you have to offer from the twentieth century? Social history was provided by people travelling in the opposite direction. A certain Parsi initiated a discussion of sky burial. Mr Claw, a client of my father, whom we met near the statue of Peter Pan, was the prompt for a rudimentary exposure of the inherent nastiness of real-estate deals, and why we were not allowed to play Monopoly at home. I naturally mixed up Claw with Hook – only discovering the error in my spelling when I saw the developer's name attached to the new Turner Wing at Tate Britain. Poor demonized Charles Clore has received a worse press than the pirate.

It was soon time to collect my grandmother from a stucco terrace behind Lancaster Gate. Her sixth-floor flat was reached by wobbly lift. She barely spoke English and sometimes pretended she didn't have a word of this alien language. Michael and I resisted Polish. Good will wasn't evident in my grandmother. She had dignity: firm posture, silver hair in bun, silk paisley shawls over black. Conversation was an outpouring of excited strategy and outraged recrimination – directed at my father, who would kiss her hand on meeting, say 'Dobzhe, dobzhe' at intervals, and that was all.

The house, on our return, was full of roast beef smoke, and my mother, smiling falsely, would be undoing her apron. Over lunch Granny's rage, in deference to my mother, would shift from Polish to German.

The particular degree of boredom had everything to do with matters we never talked about. I didn't know that Granny had used her stratagems, spiky hatefulness and other resources, to pointed effect, in hiding two daughters, two sons-in-law and my two crazy cousins, all of whom emerged more or less alive from the just-passed war – as most Warsaw Jews had not. My guilty father had skipped the whole thing – not by prescience, but because of New Architecture. Walter Gropius, the Bauhaus man he wanted to work for, wasn't popular in the Germany of 1934. He moved to England, just before my father got his degree in Vienna.

After my mother's death, here in America, clearing out the seaside house, I found a forty-year-old paper bag containing my father's ten-year correspondence with the authorities, carbon copies of multiple attempts to renew visas, join the army, coupled with dogged official variations on: 'Go back to Poland.' At the very bottom of the bag was the ironic riposte: an eight-by-ten photograph of my father pointing out labour-saving devices to an ill-looking, but politely interested King George VI. They stood together in the pavilion my father designed for the Festival of Britain. It was called: 'Homes and Gardens'.

While working on that pavilion, my father began our home and garden (employing ideas, materials and friends from the construction of the Ur-British one). I must explain my mother's role. My father supervised every brick and wire, but she had the 'text' or the key. They met on holiday, playing table tennis in a village by an Austrian lake. She was seventeen, he was in his early twenties. Six months later, they met again in a cinema queue in Vienna. I don't know what film. Both were students. They fell in love. After he left for London, she pretended to visit an older sister in Paris, and slipped across the Channel to see him. Evidence for that illicit adventure is found in photos of black barges on the Thames, a group of New Architects eating sandwiches in Green Park, my teenage mother in many hats. The glamour of my future parents seen in profile, a seagull overhead, as they gaze hopefully into the future.

Back in Innsbruck, my mother wrote letters to London and lived

in dread of her parents discovering the stamps in her passport. To her delight, she was ordered back to England – to keep an eye on two younger sisters who had been placed in a boarding school near Slough, where they were suffering from horrible loneliness and English food. Her visa took more than a year to come through. She barely got out in time, surviving a terrifying search at the Italian border. Among the items returned to her, as she got back on the train, was the single book she'd brought, to practise English on the journey: Stevenson's *New Arabian Nights*. Within this volume was the precise address of my future home.

The house my father designed for us was at 32 Chepstow Place. 32 is twice 16. '16 Chepstow Place, Westbourne Grove' was the real address of the depraved Mr Malthus, member of the Suicide Club: in the Stevenson story, with that title, in my mother's book. And 16 Chepstow Place was where I would live much later, in search – like my mother on the train – of independence. But let's start, as we did, with 32.

My first memory is of that house being built: the view from behind my father's trousered leg of white overalled builders, brick dust in the sun. I even know that this is a 'bomb site'. Many years later, when I dared to ask, I was told that the previous house was empty, its owners having gone to Australia.

LCC Rules (with which my left-wing father enthusiastically concurred) ordered a certain number of council houses to be built before the development of private property. Ours was the first private house (more guilt for him) built, after the war, in the then Borough of Kensington. It was as plain and economical as he could make it: no special effects for a pioneer of modern architecture. A major disappointment was the introduction of smokeless fuel; he'd counted on the bricks turning black, but they stayed a raw pink. The house resisted darkness. Hidden from the street, undivided windows ran from the ceiling almost to the floor. You could sit beside the fire and watch frost on the grass or rain on the concrete terrace. Wires hung from white walls for many years. There was hardly any furniture: we waited for my father to design some. A sunny yellow kitchen, with matching canary, opened on to a dining room which opened on to the living room and its wall of windows. In the summer our parents would sit, unEnglishly, under vines on the terrace, sipping their Camparis, watching us play cricket on the mini-lawn. In bed, I would hear their conversation drift through the wisteria. I woke to the sound of steam trains reducing speed for Paddington Station. Pigeons, buses changing gear, church bells: London was entirely safe.

Early photos show two weedy children, in glasses and falling-down socks, squinting into the bleak unfiltered light against a brick wall, beside an empty flower bed. But we lived here long enough to actually eat occasional apples and pears, and every four years or so, some figs. Bee swarms missing from a neighbour's garden chose ours.

Part of the garden's initial rawness and bleak rectangularity was the result of its growing on top of rubble. It was an exemplar of Modern Gardens, designed by an Ideal Home colleague of my father. I didn't know about this until long after we'd left, when my mother mentioned it. 'But what was to design?' Twenty years after that conversation, I talked to this famous landscape architect, just before he died, and wrote an article about the garden for a popular shelter magazine. My brother read it in California and phoned.

'But why did you leave out the river?'

'What river?'

'There was a river under the garden. Or perhaps I dreamed it.'
Inconclusive maps were sent by London psychogeographers. The
No. 30 neighbour, now ninety-two and living in Putney, confirmed.
Oh yes, the river. Terrible nuisance – held up construction about a
year while they put in pilings.

Above that river, Chepstow Place in the 1950s was a no man's land
between several frontiers. The east/west Paddington–Kensington
boundary ran down the middle of the street. The Paddington side
was a row of low houses that backed on to an alley, which came out
next to the Chepstow (the pub opposite us); after which the houses
got taller, grey terraces with no gardens, just areas, porches with
multiple doorbells. The Kensington side had gardens, front and
back. The north/south axis was also divided – with our bomb-site
house at the approximate pivot point of the west side. South from
32, you walked towards Kensington Gardens, past the peeling stucco
of the fat villas of Dawson Place and Pembridge Square. The route
north of our gate led towards Westbourne Grove and the five-

pointed star of Chepstow Corner. As they approached that corner, the houses gradually shrank in size and pretension, dwindling to some desultory businesses: undertaker, laundry, button shop (where the owner had one blue eye and one brown, possibly buttons).

I saw a different place when I travelled alone. For years I blamed myself for seeing weirdly. (I do in fact see weirdly: no depth perception. My optician says this comes from *horror vacui*, an unaccountable fear of space.) Since no one commented on what I saw, I thought it couldn't be there.

My brother and I went to the same, originally arty, kiddy school near Holland Park. A school whose Old Boys included Peter Pan (Peter Llewelyn Davies and his lost-boy brothers). Michael left when he was ten and I went back and forth by myself. There were only 'safe' streets to walk – if I got off at the right bus stop, which I usually did. Gradually, I began to suspect that there might be worse things than being hit by a bus. I don't mean the obvious. When a man in the alley off Ossington Street pointed his surprisingly large and naked penis at me, I wasn't so much bothered as perplexed. Was there something wrong with it? Other things were frightening. When I went with Michael, I let him do the navigating while I dreamed or worried along. No one had caught on, not even me, that I really didn't know where I was going.

Now I know that chill was only the tip of the iceberg. I'd come upon the opposite and necessary complement to my parents' bold venture into the ideal home of all future, no past. According to Barbara Denny's history of *Notting Hill and Holland Park Past*, the Ladbroke Grove Estate – an 1860s development which included the narrow part of Westbourne Grove and Chepstow Place – was described in the *Building News* of 1864 as 'a graveyard of buried hopes'. This was a place of 'crumbling decorations, fractured walls and slimy cement work'. Bad drainage is the least of what you get when you build on and between streams (Coulters Creek, Westbourne River). It takes huge imagination to match above with what lies beneath. When that fails, danger and stagnation follow.

When the safe world disappeared it happened very fast. My parents broke their rule against re-entering their shared past and went to spend a week skiing in the Austrian Alps. Perhaps because they were too high, my father died there. We hung on in Chepstow Place for about eighteen months. Then my mother capitulated, married my stepfather and decamped, with me but not Michael (who didn't want to go), to New York.

Neither of my parents were good at money. My mother once told me that she was over forty before she discovered (I suppose my stepfather broke the news) that not all bank statements are printed in red and black. During her eighteen months of stunned single life, she economized. Then, startling me, she took the life insurance and bought a house with three doorbells, further down Chepstow Place, on the way to Westbourne Grove.

Why did we need two houses? She explained that we wouldn't live there; rent from the flats would help us to pay our way. I felt ashamed, remembering why our father wouldn't let us play Monopoly. But I needn't have worried, my mother never made any money. The rents were council controlled. As a business venture, the operation ran at a loss. But the course of the future had already been set when we, all unknowing, took possession of, or became possessed by, No. 16. The address in a dark fiction by Robert Louis Stevenson.

[Carol Williams]

AT SEAL HOUSE

In 1964 all the nice people were still as poor as they had been in the 1945 of Muriel Spark's 1963 novel, *The Girls of Slender Means*.

My parents had sent their academically inclined only son to a bucolic, defiantly non-academic, muscular Christian bootcamp whose purpose was apparently to make gentlemen of the sons of Somerset farmers and to knock Newbolt into Devon's garagists of tomorrow. There was a better grammar school where we lived, in Salisbury, and for which I had qualified: my 11-plus essay was on

Sir Nigel Gresley. William Golding still taught there, a decade after *Lord of the Flies*; Derek Warner and Gus Barnes were, locally, famously inspirational.

The reason why I went away was never vouchsafed to me. A striving for social cachet may have played some part, though that improbably accords with my parents' habitual mores. And whether social cachet attached to having a son at King's College, Taunton, was, and remains, moot. More likely they didn't want me around (most every school holiday was an 'exchange', often one way, to France). So my mother's wealthy uncle's willingness to stump up the greater part of the fees must have seemed a godsend.

His great-nephew was the son this man coveted and might have sired had he not been a bachelor living with his bulgy-muscled 'chauffeur/valet' Frank in Sandycove – where, at the entrance to the Men's Swimming Association's premises, there is a notice advising that TOGS MUST BE WORN.

He used to watch appreciatively as, prepubescent, I swam in the Nadder in Salisbury, untogged. He was less appreciative when I got self-consciousness and trunks. Thoroughly unappreciative when I walked out of school, though he chided me only gently. Mute Frank scowled. My parents despaired.

The prospect of living with a teenager whose only aptitude, once he had abandoned competitive swimming, was for sullen shirking, was too much to bear. Whose idea was it to send me to a crammer? I forget. But the idea was enticing. And Great-Uncle John was somehow enthused.

I could escape the old, martial, churchy provinces and take myself to London: which had not yet been designated 'swinging' – but that American anointment of course came after the event. There was something going on. Something new, something long-haired and Cuban-heeled. I could grow my hair. I could walk tall in Cuban heels, wear a black PVC mac, dance in clubs, meet fast girls, chain-smoke Kents and Gitanes, take speed – and retake exams.

But where was I to live?

*

At a fancy-dress party in a roadhouse, between Fordingbridge and Ringwood, called the As You Like It, my parents, yet unmarried, had, in the late thirties, met Augustus John. They were introduced by Peter Lucas, a painter who was their contemporary (one of many John acolytes living around that fringe of the New Forest). My father was outdoorsy, an unambitious biscuit company rep, fanatical only about chalkstream fly-fishing. Save for music, he had no interest in art: and that interest probably derived from Schubert having had the predictive good sense to write 'The Trout' for him. Despite this or because of this – surely, because – John took a shine to him and they struck up an improbable casual bibulous friendship, which endured till John died in 1961 and which, inter alia, saw them (with Lucas) getting Salisbury's only drinking club closed down: after-hours beyond after-hours.

(Architectural-historical aside: John's friend, the stylistically various Oliver Hill, had drawn up plans for an extension to this club, the Old Mill, which are shown in Alan Powers's exemplary monograph of that architect. The cause of its not being built is unmentioned; it was almost certainly unknown to Powers – as was the connection which got Hill the commission in the first place.)

April 1964. I am hitching to Bournemouth with Mike B (just expelled from Stowe for masturbating on socks that didn't belong to him). A (white) forty-year-old Evangelical with a beamer and abundant crinkly hair, on leave from his 'mission' in Ghana, picks us up in his open-top Morris Minor.

Despite smoking moodily, Mike and I fail to pull girls in the cafés and the bowling alley where we loiter. We hitch home late in the afternoon. On Holdenhurst Road we are, weirdly, espied by our Ghanaian friend. He's clearly pissed. But not totally badered, not speechschlurred. We climb in nonetheless. At St Leonard's, a decrepit shack colony north of Bournemouth, he insists that we go for a drink in a grim bungalow pub: Mike and I have 'shorts' – the good man is pleased to treat us. Enthusiastically, he gets in another round. We pass the graceful Georgian bridge at Ellingham, the ancient church tower across meadows that are still fulldyke, mad Colonel Crowe's cottage and the now tatty As You Like It. The Evangelist's next stop was a riverside hotel at Fordingbridge. I had sufficient memories of drunken Christian chaplains not to want to hang about with this increasingly chummy sponge whose intentions might prove dishonourable and whose ability to drive would soon be impaired. I nudge Mike.

We walked past dour brick villas and fruit-holdings gone to seed and the thatched restaurant with its own thatched van parked outside on offensively ginger gravel. We had almost reached the bridge over the disused railway at Burgate when Yuri came into my life.

There was a noise behind us, a motor in decline. It passed us, just, then stuttered and stopped, groaning.

Yuri White – big slab head, straight hair, barrel body – turned astride his sick Vespa and bellowed at Mike B: 'Christ, you're that fellow [I shall never get that 'fellow'] that wanked on R's socks.'

Mike B grinned.

We trudged along beside Yuri as he pushed the motor-scooter. Where the rail track and the river run beside ruinous watercress beds, he turned through an aperture in a high hedge. Here was Yew Tree Cottage, cramped and tiny, his parents' weekend house. His grandmother lived near by. He was less than a year older than I was, but his sophistication was obviously immense: bell-bottom jeans and horizontal-striped 'Breton' T-shirt; his self-proclaimed diet was R&B and girls; he lived in London where all the girls were sexually obliging. Unlike the sisters we all knew who lived just across the river. Yuri found some filthy wine. Fastidiously, I took no more than a sip.

A couple of days later Yuri arrived on his mended scooter at my parents' house. My father liked him. His own wretched son was taciturn, offhand, bored, self-conscious, self-preoccupied and a reader. Yuri was exuberant, lusty, outgoing, unreflective.

My father never found in him the neurosis and solemnity which would come to define Yuri for me: but, then, we fashion them as we want them. He found instead an appreciative audience for his fishing lore and the stupendously filthy wine he made from his Seyval vines – an annual five hundred bottles of emetic, fit only for distillation. He found, too, Augustus John's grandson; the elder son – born in Moscow, hence his given name – of the painter's youngest daughter, Vivien, and her husband, the haematologist John White (whom Augustus derided as 'the hospital orderly').

Yuri turned up over and again that spring and summer of 1964. He'd Vespa into Salisbury even when I was away, suffering my last term in Taunton. My mother was a generous, good cook used to catering for people I had picked up. He was a good fit with my parents. Late one afternoon, lying on the scorched lawn beside the river, I looked up from my book to watch Yuri, bottle in hand, and my father, side by side on a bench formed from a broken willow trunk, leaning towards each other in some shared intimacy.

He was not alone in seeking other people's families. Though it is perhaps a trait more developed in only children.

In those days, before a second home was normal, there were provincial people and there were London people. Those who were both were exotics. The sheer worldliness of such siblings as Kate and Carola, Chris and Gay, of Julian . . .

I routinely sought out contemporaries whose family had a London base. And here, reciprocally, in Yuri's, I had found one. I would rent a room from his parents. All the nice people rented.

Vivien White wore a homemade 'geometric' bob. John White wore his very black hair *en brosse*, as much an oddity then in England as now: it lent him the air of a military policeman who had been up to no good in the cellars of Oran.

They lived in Holland Park. A century before this, Holland Park had been one of London's grandest inner suburbs. Twenty years later it would become so again. In 1964 its long desuetude was in its dotage: not that anyone knew. Like most of London's core it had suffered from the bourgeois flight to the outer suburbs through-out the first half of the twentieth century, that hardly chronicled diaspora which abandoned Georgian order and Victorian pomp to the dispossessed, to exploited immigrants, to slum landlords – and to bohemia. There was yet little sign of 'gentrification' and, indeed, that word was uncoined. Holland Park and the adjacent Ladbroke Estate were all crazed paint and encrusted soot. The Hanging Gardens of Northern Kensington (Christopher Gibbs's epithet) were goosegrass and nettles. The Clean Air Acts of a decade before were effective: 1960s smog allowed you to see five yards ahead rather than the three of the 1950s. Smog never swirled the way studio-rendered pea-soupers did. It was still and thick, like stone that one might pass through. There was, however, movement in the air: sooty stucco peelings flew like free-form bats.

Most of Pottery Lane was an anthology of wrecked, burned-out and, at best, semi-ruinous two-storey cottages – a mews hoping for a grand terrace to which it might attach itself. Seal House was, is, at its northern end, and quite different. It adhered to no building line. It gaped down the lane, an imperious punctuation mark built on a different scale, a late-Georgian oddity, flat-fronted, double-fronted, tall, one room deep, exclusively south-lit, occupying a space occasioned by a kink in the lane, with a wedge of garden ahead of it. Vivien and John had bought it in the late 1940s for, presumably, a song: in 1964 friends of theirs bought a house in the neighbouring Portland Road, four storeys and basement, for £2.2. Thousands, that is. The complexion of Britain was different when there was no such thing as 'the house price differential' between, say, undesirable Central London and desirable Salisbury.

This would change that very autumn when Harold Wilson attained power. That most under-appreciated of prime ministers achieved three things. He acted on Walter James's vision of the Open University. He resisted LBJ's increasingly truculent requests for troops rather than for words in support of his no-win war. (A keen former officer in the Fettesian CCF might have died there.) He effected the centralization of Britain. The politicization of newness was on its way.

*

To walk into Seal House was to walk into the chaotic museum of a world new to me, but far from a new world. Metropolitan neophilia was hugely absent. Where were the fresh balms of man-made materials and glossy gadgets? Where were the tokens of the mythic city of the future, the playground of thoughtful hairdressers and getaway people? Elsewhere, evidently.

The newness in Seal House was the newness of the New English Art Club and its contemporaries, the newness of more than half a century before. I had never heard of Matthew Smith before I stepped on the frame of one of his paintings, negligently propped against a flaking wainscot. Nor of Gwen John, who was then largely forgotten, buried beneath the edifice of her brother's still miraculously intact reputation. Although acquainted with Rodin, I had never expected to handle his maquettes. There were sheaves of prints, rolled-up canvases, cairns of precious doodles. The walls were all but invisible behind the works hung on them. Augustus John was everywhere. His omnipotent shade made his having been dead for three years an irrelevance. He oversaw Vivien from the grave. She felt it her inhibiting obligation to second-guess a corpse.

I studied in a desultory way. I strolled four days a week, down streets of multiply occupied former mansions and seedily genteel terraces, to the 'tutorial college', less than half a mile away. I was flattered when, out of the early evening smog, a man's voice asked me from a bench on Holland Park Avenue if I knew a nearby Turkish Bath, sonny: he had obviously taken me for a Londoner. Which didn't happen at the Café des Artistes, where a sullen Mod marked your hand when you entered with ink that showed under ultraviolet light – the idea being that you could come and go. I went. A girl with whom I attempted to talk jokily called me 'Bumpkin'. It still hurt. I had hitherto been unaware of the accent I had acquired in Taunton. I resolved to talk posh.

And to hang out at the London Cavern, Blaise's, the Cromwellian. Oh, the humiliations . . .

My hair wasn't right. My clothes from the Modern Shop, Catherine Street, Salisbury, turned out – despite what Mr Wakeham the fifty-year-old owner had assured me – to be so last year. I had served no apprenticeship in long cool silences and it showed.

My half-provincial, half-metropolitan friends were different when in London – sharper, more assured, familiar with arcane cafés, richer. They knew the form. Their parents' friends designed film sets and owned important bistros. The long nocturnal walks to their flats and to the clubs which daunted me became more attractive than the destinations. Thus they became increasingly circuitous. I didn't want to arrive. Frequently I had no chance of arriving because I was lost in the smog and reliant on the Tube map which I had yet to realize was diagrammatic. It would be years before I read James Thomson's 'The City of Dreadful Night'. Yet here was that very labyrinth where terror lurked in milky pools of light cast through grubby curtains, in alley shadows, in jagged craterous bombsites where flaccid buddleia sprouted, in walls of friable brick and seeping mortar, in the teeming slums of Little Napoli (© Colin MacInnes) where the ten-year-old urchins (© Roger Mayne) were more wised-up than I was: I don't know how I learned that Vince was called Vince. He used to sit up in his hoodless, tyreless pram, eye me and shout: 'Cunt!' Westbourne Avenue was clamorous. The broad avenues of Maida Vale were always deserted. Not everyone had a phone. A couple of times I dropped by a schoolfriend's flat in Observatory Gardens, near the Victorian water tower on Camden Hill. He wasn't there. At a party on 20 November 1964, I learned that he had been killed on the previous Friday, the 13th, when a furniture van was blown over on top of his father's car on the Hog's Back. Patrick was my first friend to die. It was years before I went back to that square of oeil de boeuf windows and heftily French rustication. I guess that superstitious avoidance means that I was marking out my own London, a city of permanent absences and architectonic solaces.

It was a city, too, that was mediated by Seal House. The interior was like an interior by Sickert or Tonks. I know this because I spent hours among the paintings and reproductions. It did not occur to me that the house was oddly anachronistic, that it was unmarked by the fashions of post-war Britain, that the Whites' taste belonged to an era before they were born. Painting was generically francophile, generically post-impressionist, generically splodgy: it was some years before I had the confidence to admit to myself that I prefer the cold northern precision of Fouquet and Schad to enthusiastic impasto.

In the world of Seal House artists were arty, paint-stained, carelessly dressed (in bright colours). Augustus's widow, the sainted Dodo, was still a make-believe gypsy of sixty years before. Her son, Romilly, a priestly man, would sit for hours in quietist contemplation. There was no end to the Johns. Was the thickset man Edwin? There were Johns with Augustus's profile, beanpole Johns, sober Johns. They constituted more than a diffuse family, they made up a tribe with its own lore and traditions. Vivien's elder sister, Poppet, much less cowed by her parents than Vivien, drank and smoked and laughed with appealing abandon.

One day arrived the most beautiful young woman I had ever seen, Poppet's stepdaughter, the starlet Talitha Pol. I gaped, unable to dissemble my amazement. She was, however, entirely atypical of the exotically shabby galère which regularly assembled at the house, then moved down the road to the Prince of Wales. William Morris, founder of the Free University of London (a shed beyond the North Circular, and the first of several dodgily utopian ventures to bear that name), was a grown-up beatnik. He had filthy clothes, a lopsided beard, barley-sugar fingers from cigarettes, a worse scooter than Yuri's and a ginger girlfriend whose myopia forced her to wear glass bricks on her wan face. Morris also had a revolver with which he threatened a friend of mine who wouldn't sleep with him. Happily the great educator passed out and she ran away with a Spanish basketball pro.

The night before I left the crammer (and Seal House), Vivien gave a party for me – and herself – in the pub. It was a generous gesture which cannot have but rankled with John White, a man of fabulous meanness. It was also a curious gesture for even the youngest of the guests was at least twenty years older than I was. But I was now a garrulous expert on Gilman, Ginner, Gore. I could sing for my supper. They had been my age in the war or through the privations of the late 1940s. And it was this world that they carried with them – and whose memory and fascinations they had passed on to me, an intangible keepsake. They sort of made me their contemporary.

Two years later I returned to London, to RADA. I had learned enough, mostly in France, to take part in the rites of the Cult of Youth – regrettably mandatory, and not to be confused with the immemorial rites of youth.

With some cause, Vivien White was more edgily preoccupied than ever and John White more sullen than ever.

Yuri had a daughter. He had also made a shift, from carefree to careless. Talitha Pol, a RADA student seven years before me, was Mrs John Paul Getty.

And they died, within months of each other, from heroin overdoses. Now newness's time had fully arrived, at last.

[Jonathan Meades]

TERRACOTTA POT

I think you should come for a walk in this area, it is strange in ways you would not expect. It is moated on the north by the Cromwell Road/Talgarth Road roundabout – and if you try to cross on a bike it is like going over mini traffic humps. This is caused by permanent waves of poisonous traffic roaring west and east and cutting ruts into the tarmac with the tyres. You can feel the ruts if you walk, but if you cross on a bike they are very distinct. It's like a rehearsal for the Himalayas.

One day I ran into Pete who used to work for Nigel and who went off travelling. He tried to introduce somebody who claimed to know me. He looked just like any fat bloke. The only person he remotely resembled was Jonathan Meades. It turned out to be one of my oldest friends, Charlie Russell. The one who went on the road with us to Scotland and Newcastle and Durham and Stamford. But the great thing about bikes is that they are all-time winners as bore-avoidance devices.

There is a strange sort of communism round here that operates when people throw things out. I was cycling back one night when I saw some beautiful terracotta flowerpots about eighteen inches high. One of them had a handwritten note saying, 'Please Take Away.' I put them on the back of my bike and had to navigate Cromwell Road and the ruts. Halfway over, the pots were about to fall. I dismounted to redo the elastic straps. The traffic lights changed. A policeman got out of a car, stopped the traffic, both ways, and waved me across.

I got the pots home safely but had nowhere in my flat to put them, they were far too large. I decided to return them to the street and went down to where my bike was chained up – to discover that another three pots had now appeared. I decided to put them all on the patio at the rear of my flat.

The following day I was walking to the newsagent and I spotted a large palm in a small plastic pot. It had grown too large and been abandoned. I brought this home and repotted it. I then decided to start hunting for other abandoned plants. Most, I discovered, are nearly dead. I have no idea what they are called, but as long as they are green I bring them in. Only things found for free in the local streets are allowed to go on the patio.

One morning I was getting some earth out of a skip to fill my eight-foot-long wooden window box, using a trowel and a small fork that I had found the previous week, when a lady came out in a dressing gown and asked me what I was doing. I explained that I was collecting earth and that I was only allowed to use things found for free. She looked hard at me and then went back inside.

I made three or four trips to the skip – you wouldn't believe how much earth pot plants take – then I had to go out. That evening, the skip was gone. I was about to cycle off when the lady came out of her house with a bag of compost. According to her, you cannot have potted plants without compost. It counts as cruelty. I do not wish to be accused of abusing plants. But it has created a moral dilemma. It is against my rules to buy anything for the patio – which should also apply to the acceptance of gifts. I am fairly certain that the woman bought the compost, it had a sell-by date. It's a lovely idea that earth should have a sell-by date. I am not even allowed to buy secondhand compost at boot fairs, so now I have to steal earth when I go to the country. I keep looking for bits with earthworms in. I found one worm but he seems to have died of culture shock. I saw some wonderful green wellies at a boot fair, they were only fifty pence for the pair, but it would have broken my rule to buy them. I am not sure how to get around the problem of the compost. I am thinking of writing to *Gardeners' Question Time*. If I can find a stamp for free.

[drif field]

STRANGE MEETING

Seven-thirty in the evening. Duck into West Ken tube to find Charleville Road on map. Not far. We've come on the off chance and aren't even sure he'll be in, but bike chained to railings can only be his, so we know he's there. He doesn't go anywhere without his bike. P rings and cagey voice on intercom says 'Hello?' Cautious 'yes' to follow-up 'drif?' Doesn't sound like him. P introduces himself and voice perks up and now you can tell it is drif. Says come in, but door won't open. P rings again and after some characteristic theatrical moaning drif says he'll come down. Look at each other: unreal. P says it's funny how the people with the books always live on the top floor: bookbuyer's joke. Familiar bulky frame looms towards us through frosted glass and door opens. Drif says 'Come in, come in' and P 'You remember Marco don't you?' Huffed yes. Never got on and I'm only along for the ride. Shake hands on doorstep.

Typical West London bedsit: usual funny smell in hall, usual hall mirror with landlady's tirade stuck to it. P's right: top floor. Drif leads the way, talking. Silence from other flats on way up.

Hair shade greyer but pretty much unchanged: same skinhead haircut and burly figure. (P challenges my recollection: 'I'd describe the hair as a great deal greyer, almost white. I remember salt'n'pepper.') Looks fat but can't be with the cycling he does. Just big: big as a bouncer. Wearing lightblue cotton trousers with rolled-up trouser legs and stained navyblue jumper. Trousers spattered with red paint. No shoes, just thick grey woollen socks. Only real difference is in the way he's talking, loud as ever but sounding punchdrunk now: so blunted I wonder whether he's braindamaged. P's thinking the same thing.

Pile of transparent sheets on table on landing before flat. P asks: 'For wrapping maps?' Yes. We go in. Single-male sweet-sweat smell. Bathroom facing front door across narrow hallway halfblocked by cabinet covered in clutter. Largish front room to left of bathroom. Kitsch pictures and ornaments dotted about. TV blaring out from bedroom at end of hall: stays on all evening. Light off in bedroom: piles of boxes filled with papers in doorway.

Ushered into front room: light and airy, window on to street. Door to kitchen behind bathroom in far right-hand corner. Couple of shelves of books on right, more by window. P looks them over: wholly unremarkable, charity-shop fodder. In middle of room big table with small telescope surrounded by clutter: for stars or people? Gets us to sit at table while sits with back to large computer on long table by window. Shelves with computer parts on wall facing window.

Warming up now and it's clear we're wrong: brain OK. Gummy quality to speech because most of his top front teeth are gone. Also gone that volcanic self-assurance. Old obsessions and hobby-horses remain, but vagueness about him now. Was always the performer, polishing up his act on bookshop tours. Without an audience seems dulled: comedian who's lost his touch. But keen to talk and soon mouth froths at corners like before.

P comes back from bathroom and asks if drif was about to have a bath when we arrived: bath full of water. Says no, was washing something. Just to be contrary?

Gets up to make coffee and profile framed by window. If anything head juts forward at even more implausible angle. P and I look at each other and roll our eyes. Drif returns from kitchen with plate of chocolate digestives and bowl of nuts, then with coffee in glass jug with plunger and two cups, both dirty. P takes cups back into kitchen and cleans them. Having had no lunch I tuck in with gusto and drif says 'Blimey! You're going it a bit. D'you want me to cook something?' I say no and drif says 'I hate to see anyone go hungry.' Offers again and this time I say yes. P goes with drif into kitchen and conversation continues. Sink blocked. P sees drif thrust arm into brown water and clear out plughole with finger: coffee grounds. Drif's huge back reflected through kitchen doorway in mirror in front room. Comes back with bowl of vegetable soup and thick slice of wholemeal bread. Soup spicy and tasty. Heart races. Wonder if he's added something? It's probably the coffee.

Puritan streak still there. P wants a smoke and asks if drif wants him to do it out of window. Drif: 'You can smoke. People can do what they want here. I just don't approve that's all.'

P does most of the talking. Drif wouldn't believe speculation his disappearance has caused: exaggerated surprise. Inquiries from America: quiet amusement. New breed of drif collector: loud guffaws. More laughter at various sightings but silence when I say I saw him a couple of times in Ealing on his bike. As for being seen outside Earl's Court station talking to himself and giving directions to invisible people says that could well have happened.

P reminds him of the time he fell off his bike and acted strange and had brain scans and drif makes out he can't remember. I think he's pretending and so does P. Drif repeats several times he's developed a selective memory: can't remember people and incidents.

Says he didn't disappear just went travelling. So where on earth has he been? India for eighteen months, Calcutta. Hated it: hated the heat, the insects, the way they treat one another. It's all: do this do that. They think all white people are millionaires, not unreasonable considering what money's worth out there. You can live on practically nothing it's so cheap. Only avoided being mobbed by beggars by getting boy to walk in front giving out coins. Can't think of anywhere worse except perhaps Turkey. But the women are gorgeous.

Says it was a real shock coming back. London so expensive now: really changed. People more obsessed with money than ever: even worse than the 1980s. Some of the people in the flats opposite have cabs waiting at six in the morning to take them to the City, and don't get back till late. When do they live?

Finds travelling round London really depressing. Has arguments most days. Man who worked on his bikes taught him the only thing to do if you're riding around and get into bother is apologize. Never mind rights and wrongs just apologize. Public transport just as bad: everyone wound up and aggressive. Lot to do with these automatic ticket barriers they've put up everywhere. Not like before when you could walk out of an unattended station. They're so greedy now. Got into an argument the other week. Wanted him to pay a ten-pound penalty fare. Refused.

Talks about affair with Indian woman. What was her name? Met her on a train. Looking after two boys, relatives of hers. Both awful: one a little gangster and the other just fat. Started when boys came into carriage and asked if he wanted to buy a calculator. A little later conductor came through and announced someone's calculator had gone missing. Had to spend a lot of time trying to entertain the boys and it was tough going. In his experience Indians don't make very good parents, neglect their children.

Odd affair: she'd only meet him on trains. Didn't mind as was doing his guide book at time and it only involved slight detours to Bristol Temple Meads. When they met she was spending eighty pounds a week on fares for her and the boys. Got to know her by explaining how much she'd save by playing the system. In India she'd done an English Literature degree: PhD on Dickens and Film. Came here and was really surprised: hadn't thought white people had to work. Expected everyone to be like a Dickens character, but said drif was only Dickens character she'd come across. Finally decided she wanted to run away and drif took her to this flat in Aberystwyth.

Wasn't impressed when she found out drif bought things second-hand. That goes down badly with Indians: keen on status. It all ended because she was always on the phone. She'd go on for hours and in the end he said she could only make calls in the evening and she didn't like that. One day she was on the phone and there was this thumping on the door and when he opened it the whole of the Aberystwyth constabulary rushed in and pinned him up against the wall. Her relatives in Southall had rung the police, claiming he'd abducted their 'little girl'. Police thought it was a paedophile case, but when they got her passport from the bedroom found she was twenty-two. He'd thought she was eighteen. Once he'd sorted out the fares business it was costing her fifteen quid to travel with the boys, but the family still paid her eighty and she pocketed the difference. And she still expected him to pay for the room in Aberystwyth.

Upset because he can't remember her name. She was really beautiful and it's ridiculous he can't remember. Finally does remember: Rifet. P says that's unusual: were they Muslims? Yes, all her family were Muslims. Just shows: how can anyone call drif racist? He likes Indian women in saris! Has written about why the sari is the world's greatest garment. The one thing you can't get Indian women to do is undress. They just lift up their saris when they do it. They'll do anything you ask but they won't take their clothes off.

Tell drif that Tony Lambrianou [the old Kray footsoldier] died last week. Makes out he doesn't know who he is. After some prompting [about their mutual appearance in a barber shop] he says 'Oh him, he was horrible. I used to say how I wanted to start a club for people who love their mothers. They all turn out to be psychopaths.'

We're flagging but drif still wants to talk. Around nine-thirty and P needs to go – got to get back to Sutton – but drif rattles on: about the London map he's produced and book he's writing. I get drif to autograph two maps and P takes one. As I get up to go notice black button on floor under chair and wonder whether it might have come from my jacket, but drif says it's his: been sorting through a big jar of buttons. Accompanies us into hallway and as we reach flat door says 'Look at this. This is where I'm going to live.' Stuck to back of door is large photo of Charterhouse at Lombardy. Ask if he's been there and says yes. Say I thought he was going back to India and says no this is where he's going. Says he has nothing to do with booksellers now. Has heard the business is pretty well played out. Internet partly to blame. Doesn't read books any more.

Shake hands in doorway and drif walks us down to the street. Stands in socks on pavement next to bike, still talking. Bike of his dreams, a Marin. Long orange canvas holdall strapped to back. Paintwork scraped off frame: says it's because he had two bikes stolen off railings. Woman who lives opposite keeps asking him to fix hers. Swears she breaks it on purpose.

Off to Sudbury tomorrow.

Ask if he'll let me take picture of him in front of bike and says no. Keeping low profile. I remind him how he used to say he was going to commit suicide at a certain time – 9/9/99 – and sold tickets. Says it's no joke: came close.

A woman's hand twitches at net curtain in ground-floor flat behind him. Two girls walk towards us with a pizza, laughing and joking. They pass and drif says 'I don't suppose you know what language they're speaking? I'm keen on finding things like that out at the moment.' I say I think Spanish. Says no in that dismissive way, Eastern European. Then with animated puzzlement 'Why do they all come here? There must be a reason.' I say London's a rich place. Drif: 'That's not it: they all work really hard when they get here. Some of them have two, three jobs. I just don't get it.' As we walk away shouts after us 'Come back if you're in the area.'

[Marc Vaulbert de Chantilly]

MARINE STORES

The decline in civilization began, back in the 1970s, when they took the small mirrors out of red phone boxes. It was not that things were more wonderful then, but it certainly seems to me that they were much, much easier.

In London, a tenner a week would have got you a flat. All you had to do was ring up, go round and view the place, give the landlord the cash. Many of those rooms were out-and-out slums. They had electricity that would have shocked Dr Frankenstein.

Similarly with jobs. They were not great jobs, but they were there. You turned up for the interview, chatted to the foreman and were usually working the following day. I got my first job when I was thirteen. I lied a little and nobody bothered to check up. With my first week's wages I found a room. I was blithely ignorant of almost everything. And yet I managed to survive, not wonderfully, but well enough.

I used to eat out every evening in a grease caff. I had the same meal every day. There are still grease caffs but there are far fewer of them. They used to be everywhere, even in St John's Wood High Street. I wouldn't claim they were all great. I once saw the owner of a grease caff in the Portobello Road filling his face – in a rival establishment, a little further down the road.

What the genuine grease caffs were selling was not so much food as warmth, physical and psychological. There was usually an owner on the premises who knew all his customers and where they came from: Liverpool, Liskeard or lovely Leytonstone. You could spot a truck driver and ask for a lift. The rate of food poisoning was impressive and most of the owners had fags hanging out of their mouths.

There was one place on the corner of Marchmont Street, midway between Euston and King's Cross – an area guide books describe as 'a village' and motorists describe as 'a maze'. The café was run by two elderly pale Italian sisters and their even older brother. There was a brass door handle, a mosaic floor, glass-topped tables with brass corners, and an espresso machine. They also trusted you with the sugar. I think this has to be the definition of a genuine grease caff.

One day a scruffy young man came into the café. Two plainclothes policemen got up from their morning tea and arrested him at the counter. The serving lady wore her hair in a bun. She told the man to drink up his coffee before he left. She refused his offer of payment. There seemed to be some form of permanent warfare going on between the two sisters. They only united forces to rail at their brother. A truce was called when it was necessary to serve customers.

In the Fulham Road, close to Brompton Cemetery, there was one of the few genuine junk shops in London. Its only aspiration was to make a living. It was on a corner. Six mornings a week, at eight o'clock, they used to hang out clothes and distribute junk. In the side window were books with their spines facing the street. The interior was impossible, heaped with clothes that would never be collected. Porn magazines were kept in a cardboard box. I used to examine these intently while listening to the *Jimmy Young Show* – which seemed to be playing morning and afternoon.

There was a sign above the door which said: L. CLARKE MARINE STORES. What a Marine Store was doing in the Fulham Road I never discovered. Further towards South Kensington was a shop that sold speedboats. There must be a lake in Fulham that I have yet to find.

Most afternoons, various council rubbish trucks would pull up in a side street and spectacular amounts of junk would be disgorged. Kensington dustmen would keep back anything, however unlikely, that might have a monetary value. I once bought a genuine silk top hat in its original cardboard box. It had the name of some ancient general on the label.

The pornographic magazines seem to have come from the offices of *Forum*, which were just around the corner. Fresh supplies arrived on Friday mornings. The elderly lady who ran the front of house pulled out a box of Japanese porn mags for me. These were known, to one-handed connoisseurs, as Mange Comics.

'I kept those back for you,' she said.

This shop was a genuine recycling centre. Everybody who went in was known by name or nickname. They called me 'Bookie'. I can't remember the titles of any of the books I found, but I patronized the place on a regular basis; the atmosphere was so wonderful and the supplies of exotic porn were regular as clockwork.

I listen to the radio, even in my sleep. I heard a programme about wildlife in Brompton Cemetery. They were not talking about homosexuals. I decided to visit the place. I went to North End Road and bought myself a large tub of ice cream and some fruit juice. The junk shop, by this period, had closed down. Searching for a single spoon to devour my feast, I tried one of the innumerable charity shops in the area. The lady told me that they did not sell that kind of thing. In the second shop, they had spoons, but only in batches of six. I broached a third establishment. They had a single spoon but it was unpriced. The manageress told me that she would have to check the mark on the back. It must have been my anger that melted the ice cream before I had a chance to eat it.

In many years of visiting charity shops, I do not think that one person has ever learned my real name. There was a place in Brixton that tried to bar me before I stepped inside the door. It was a 'Back to Africa' charity run by an enormous and enormously black lady – who thereafter used to stand on tiptoe to stroke my skinhead cut. She admitted that she had been terrified the first time she saw me, I was the first white person who had come into her shop. She said that I was very brave. In truth, I was oblivious. I never read notices in charity shops. It is a point of principle.

At that time in Soho there were many people who scavenged the vast amount of unwanted office furniture the cleaners left behind them when they finished their shift. I once lived in a room on the south side of Soho, but had to abandon it when the place became too small to hold the stuff I had rescued from the streets.

One of my town planning fantasies is to place a skip at the corner of every street for things people no longer want: old doors, stained mattresses, broken-down radios. Separate skips for genuine junk. Skips for bottles, skips for newspapers. Have you noticed a lack of people sleeping rough who could easily be employed in such schemes? Public toilets should be located in the same zone. With attendants to keep them clean. Then there would be proper phone boxes and other vanished things.

It wasn't just Marine Stores that disappeared. At one time I used to cycle to Edgware, stopping along the way at dozens of junk shops. Numbers declined to the point where I gave up and started to use the Tube. I have always liked trains, even Tube trains.

I once travelled back by train from London to Bristol, late on a Sunday night. I fell asleep and didn't wake until the train arrived in Taunton. Some early-morning rail workers gave me a ride back to Bristol in their van. Nobody accused me of attempting to defraud British Rail. Recently, on London Transport, I asked for a travel pass to a station on the outer edge of the system, Amersham. Two thirds of the way there, three inspectors got on the train and checked my ticket, before announcing that it was not valid. I would have to pay ten pounds or face arrest. They refused to accept as proof of my identity a card which I have used to cross international borders. The general assumption was that I was a criminal for not knowing that Amersham was not included in the travel card zone, despite being on the London Underground Plan.

I hitch-hiked back from Penzance, hoping to reach London, but somehow ended up in Coventry at about three in the morning. I was stopped at a police roadblock. On another occasion, I managed to get myself to Sedbergh in Cumbria on a Sunday afternoon. I decided to see if I could hitch back to London. I had to walk about five miles to the M6. I must have waited at that junction for three hours. I was picked up by the police, to whom I had to give a complete catalogue of all my actions for that day. I also had to explain to a policeman in Sedbergh why it was that I had been deported from the United States of America in the early 1970s. They eventually allowed me to walk to the nearest railway station.

I was on the Northern Line, coming into Central London from Morden, when a faux Teddy boy got on at the Elephant and Castle. I kept looking at him, not because I objected to his dress, but because there was something about his appearance that wasn't right.

He had the swept-back, jet-black, brylcreemed hair in the duck's arse style. Shiny white skin, specially designed to show off the acne. Frilly lilac shirt and bootlace tie. Long, pale, Day-Glo turquoise jacket with contrasting black lapels. Several plasticky rings on his fingers. Drainpipe jeans. Day-Glo socks and brothel-creeper shoes. He had an ornate belt buckle. A handkerchief in his top pocket. He had the bulldog spot on, that swagger, that fake air of revolt Teddy boys always had. But something was definitely wrong.

I am old enough to remember the original Teddy boys, but there never was a Ted who had it all. They either had the swept-back hair, the handful of rings that doubled as knuckle-dusters, the long jacket or the drainpipe jeans. Nobody, outside a magazine, had the lot. Teddy boys were a working-class movement, but no Ted alive was as clean and tidy as the man on the Northern Line.

And this is exactly where those period dramas on TV get it wrong: the crazy idea that everything from a period belongs to that period. I think I wear more colourful clothes now than I did in the 1960s. The 1960s lasted until about 1979. I was at the Rolling Stones free concert in Hyde Park and I do not and did not like rock music. I was at the anti-Vietnam War demonstration in Grosvenor Square but I did not understand the issues. I was invited to Paris during the student riots in 1968, but I did not have the money for the coach trip.

I worked, in the days when I had long hair, for a bookbinder. My supervisor asked how you could tell the difference between boys and girls if everybody wore long hair. I said that one way was to remove all your clothes. At the end of the week, I was asked to leave the firm, because of my dirty mind. This was in London in 1972.

The reason I know the date is because I recently had to apply to the National Insurance Office about a mistake in my number, something had gone wrong with my official records. When I went to the office, the girl showed me my entire history – which does not amount to much. The machine knew more about me than I did. There is something slightly spooky about the accumulation of records by the state. It is now possible for some unknown person in some shadowy organization to look up my records. They will know about my credit rating. They have access to my medical records, my unemployment records. They could easily find out where I live, where I make my money. They would know what my eating habits are. Every day in London the average person is photographed fourteen times. They can tap your telephone calls, download your emails. One in four men in Britain has a criminal record.

The Roman Catholics have abandoned the idea of hell. I am not sure if they have abandoned the Last Judgement, but now we have it here on earth. If I took photographs of my neighbours at a rate of fourteen a day, I would be arrested as a peeping tom.

What, I think, is the crucial difference between life in the 1970s and now is that most people had the optimistic belief that things were bound to get better. This is what has disappeared, leaked away from London. The future is behind us, but we live in hope. What else is there?

[drif field]

MORNING IN ARIZONA

The thing that was wrong with Phoenix, it was in colour. And what colour: out there, coming off the distant hills, the blue-grey of whatever floats behind Lee Marvin's eyes. Metallic brake-fluid

miracled into light. Like a pay-per-view landscape channel. Fastidious pornography arriving without damage to your credit card.
Human sight before curved lenses get old and flawed and scratchy
with text. America the Movie – before the snakes crawled from the
flood to feast on burger-bloated corpses. Before the orange groves
smelled of napalm and gasoline and sweaty bibles.

On the hotel balcony, a privileged platform, I began to appreciate
the fact that I was barely *here*; night arrival, cars and airports, unreal
conversation; some mention of a gun, a wife with a gun. When you
have a commission, to bring back images, words, you start on a
false note. You see people as Xeroxes. This view – concrete irrigation
ditch, empty car park, early cars on the road, palm trees, flag poles
– was quotation, future memory. But it was not Bastrop, Texas.
Where walking, if not forbidden, is a difficulty. Everything you
might need (even if you don't know it) is off-highway; it takes three
days to get to the Mexican breakfasts that make the rest of the
business possible. It takes a week to digest the gin-u-wine chicken-
fried steaks.

My problem is: too many prompts, not enough history. We've
been peddled the dream and have bought it for so long we don't
know how to disengage. I am corrupted to the juice in my bones. I
can only say there was a particular morning, before food had been
taken; a long corridor, a glass elevator. Before we went into the
streets, each of us with our camera, our small technologies. With
Emma Matthews. Who was recording sound and also playing the
part, as a device, of a person in Phoenix: an interesting woman,
walking out of a generic hotel, to record sound, as she searches for
a writer's house.

9 November 1998: I have the date written on a piece of paper.
Not my paper. My papers have gone (back to Texas). My collabor-
ator, Chris Petit, found it in a beach house on the south coast. A
transcript of that morning's conversation. We had come to Phoenix,
Arizona, to film James Sallis. There were two references, in my
memory file, for this town. The first was easy, Hitchcock's *Psycho*,
the opening: opalescent monochrome. You wouldn't believe it in

colour. This black-and-white photography is the colour of newsreels, of posthumous reverie. The film convinces, absolutely, while it stays with the sorrows of lunch-hour hotel rooms, windows, small offices with large men sitting awkwardly on the edges of desks that do not belong to them. Then the faked, backprojected driving: businessmen on the streets in cowboy hats, the pedestrians of drowsy afternoon. The eros of theft, flight. Hot money folded between cool underwear in a case that weighs nothing. The overbright road, the motorcycle cop in helmet and dark glasses. The rain, the motel. My interest, I find, dies with Janet Leigh. The rest of *Psycho* is hokum and perform-ance. And that's why I can't come to terms with this colour: warm, fragrant air, pink blossom, frighteningly clean streets.

The second box was for Sallis: one of the London disappeared, of long ago, an author whose books I always pick up with enthusi-asm, this was his address. (How did he manage it, being here, getting away from Notting Hill and Camden? Leaving short stories for you to come on, unexpectedly, in decent, fading bookshops: used stock. Copies of the *Transatlantic Review*, stuck not stitched, come apart in your hands.)

The book Chris wanted to film was a slender one, a strategic routine Sallis had come up with, of restless movement, frayed nerves, spooks, guns: a mental landscape that defied resolution. Coded fictions on revolving racks in Kansas drugstores. Airport accidents in Chicago. The book's real aim was an absence of borders. You go to an unknown town, pick a name at random and that invented man will come forward to greet you. *Death Will Have Your Eyes*.

We'd heard of Sallis, the dangerous vitality of his younger life, in America and then in London, from Michael Moorcock. His sponsor. We had our own sense, by this time, of what an exile it was to be the kind of writer these men were, active and present, in late America. They were in hiding, long-term sleepers, tolerated by indifference. Sallis, lightly bearded, thin-spectacled, could operate in this place, but he wasn't at home. He took us around in a car with a tinted windshield: the town unfolded into scrupulously managed discriminations; university, coffee house, bookstore – and, back from the road, the palms and expensive glass of high-concept architecture. Spectral elements of the military-industrial state. Corporate sun-deflecting glitter. Money hospitals and reservations you do not penetrate without a laminated badge, a photograph.

The bungalow, spare, functional, could be packed up and reassembled in minutes, so Sallis said. After one phone call. He didn't like phones. He lived in a room with slatted blinds, filtered light. A quiet place in which to work. In the yard, the small patch at the back, was an orange tree.

We recorded our talk. But I was more interested, really, in the fact of our accidental encounter. It wouldn't happen again. It was scarcely happening now. Between writers, a no man's land is established, a landscape of convenience in which neither of them can fix their bearings.

'My favourite part of most stories,' Sallis said, 'is where they describe where the guy lives. I absolutely love to hear what he has on his shelves and what his tea mugs look like. That's the most important thing in the world to me.'

Moorcock, who had his own difficulty about where he now found himself, is the absolute storyteller, a person with an enormous generosity in all his dealings with the past. He will rehearse ancient grievances, with humour, and then forgive: himself as he was then, along with the victim of his telling. The heart is large and the memories, given this opportunity, are immense: hours and hours of words. When I woke in the morning in a strange house, Mike was already waiting, mid-sentence, at the table. He admired Sallis, his perseverance in a collapsing culture, the pains in his life.

He had the American, this young man, arrive in London unprepared, a meteor of complex arrangements and shifting alliances. He handed him an impossible commission: edit *New Worlds*.

'It's always strange to meet people you like,' Sallis told me. 'Ballard and Moorcock were quarrelling. I met Ballard briefly, but we never really had a conversation. I spent a lot of time with Mike. It's really hard to assess what we were doing with *New Worlds* – because, first, we were all pretty good and young. I was a kid. Why

Mike asked me to edit the magazine god only knows – because I didn't know what I was doing. Mike's memory of all this is a little different from mine. That's the fascination of life, isn't it?'

We talked, ourselves ghosts, about the reforgotten, lost reputations. Good writers who, their moment seemingly used up, move into a posthumous twilight of cult reputation, whispers from initiates. They might still be working, perfectly content, but they are no longer, as the world knows it, part of the package. Mike had been stressing how much William Burroughs admired Barrington 'Barry' Bayley (author of *Star Winds* and *Collision Course*). A paperback original. He wanted Bayley in our film. And he was right. But then the film would go on for however many years we had left. We would never come off the road.

'People disappear,' Sallis said. 'That's the way of any artistic or writing career. It really is a throw of the dice. There are a lot of invisible writers.'

He took out his guitar. He sat under the orange tree. We watched, and liked very much, the pattern of shadows the leaves made as they shifted in the faint breeze. Like Moorcock, like all the writers we met in America, Sallis kept a cat. A car, a cat, a gun. The cat was unimpressed.

I found one of Bayley's books and I started at the back. 'In the recessive hypothesis,' Bayley writes, 'space is purely relational; there is no "place" except where a physical body is. When such a body appears to "move" in relation to another, it is the space between them that is modified . . . The same insight is admirably expressed in the zen aphorism: "Nothing moves; where would it go?"'

[I. S.]

RÉCITS

I used to live with a woman who looked like you. She had large breasts that hung down and rolled across the top of her stomach and she always supported them, the weight of them, with the flat of her arms, hugging herself like a toy bear. Her teeth were even, like tiny ceramic tiles, the colour of milky amber. Getting in, out of bed she always kept her legs together.

Afterwards the room seemed so much . . . larger. As I stood looking at the closed door, I was aware for the first time of the space between things.

Her proportions were always astounding; each day, I discovered them as though for the first time. Her buttocks, the short firmness of her legs, the shallow back and small shelf there – these were not the ones expected, my wife's. They startled.

She disliked my smoking in bed. So afterwards, I would sit in the chair across the room by the window, watching her. The electric heater glowed against the wall and sparkled when I lit cigarettes off it. She wore shiny, round-toed shoes, wrinkled on the top, with buckle-straps going across. And tights, always – I never saw her without tights.

At two or three we would reach up in the dark and it was like shutting doors. I would lie watching her dress, then dress myself. Walk four blocks and find a cab. Back to her husband, who wouldn't ask questions. On the street: You don't take care of yourself, you know. On the street: I'm an abstraction, to you, I could be anyone. I am woman. The thing – perhaps even the quality.

When she was gone, the knives would come out of the mirror like sharks.

*

Some of us who come to London never drink coffee again.

We are sitting in a Lyons, having tea in the middle of the morning. Somehow (the way I chew my toast?) the talk has got on to the subject of camels.

'One hump or two?'

*

> You will want to know
> how I am making
> out here in this
> city of penetrating light.

*

533

I should write you letters
explaining that I am in
fact doing well; how pleasant
it is here, how good jobs
are easily come by, how
beautiful the children are.

These letters would make
you smile, know how I miss
you, make you go look
out your window and looking
for men. In your hands,
with all the scribbling
and erasure, my pressured
hand, they would have
the texture of lettuce leaves.

*

When we make love she turns her face to the wall, where blond and grey stripes resemble an abstract cypress forest. She puts a knuckle in her mouth, hears my watch ticking by her ear. The heater glows against the wall. Only in the final moments does she turn her face up and open her eyes, watching me. There is a spring coming up through the sheet. And then she says Hmmmm.

Later, we fold a torn sheet several times and lay it like a bandage, a compress, over the spring.

*

PS. Indubitably.

*

Locust husks! Summers (he thinks it was summers) they'd hang askew all over trees, fences, even the side of the house. Light and fragile as fallen leaves, dead spurs caught in the bark, burst in a split along the back. He collected them; he remembers one summer when a whole wall of his room was covered with them. Lined perfectly, all climbing upward, row by row.

Also: figs, fireflies searching for an honest man, the red veins in shrimp.

*

1. What is the exact nature of their relationship?
   Changeable.

   Is there a word?
   Weighty.

   And is he weary?
   Yes.

   Of?
   Explanations, digressions, rationalizations, endless
   nights of discussion – what should she do?

2. A quality of hers: to live in a maze of
   possibilities.
   A quality of his: to accept as what *can* occur, only
   that which *does* occur.
   The first allows great freedom of movement and
   excludes responsibility; the second, similarly,
   makes guilt impossible. More and more, it is this
   that sustains him.

3. Him, aware of himself – and her, of him moving
   within her.
   He has said in his allusive way that together they
   are long-legged flies. He tries to explain country
   music to her.
   Finally, as so many times before, he falls back to
   Creeley: 'It is only in the relationships men
   manage, that they live at all.'

4. Where does it end?
On the 52 bus, halfway between Notting Hill Gate and
Marble Arch.

Were there prior signals?
Cabs, for them, assumed a large importance. They
began to read the names on bus panels and wonder
about those places, where they might be.

How did it end?
In argument over the respective merits of various
shampoos.

– Across this page of his notebook (as well as many others,
and all the poems) he has scrawled *HA* a number of times,
H rolling lightly like a valley into the *A*'s hill.

*

They trade stories about shells.

She used to find in the Florida ocean, floating branches which,
removed, proved to be covered with clam shells, tiny and white and
perfect as teeth.

He once came across a huge pile of shells on the bank of a bay.
Chalky white and crunching to bits when he walked into them.
Bending to look closer, he discovered that each shell was punched
full of round, button-sized holes; what remained were the narrow
spaces around the holes, looking like a patchwork of nose septums.

*

PS. I love you.
PS. I miss you.
PS. I enjoy mispelling and singing.

*

She swears that roaches live in the Swiss cheese at this delicatessen;
you can see their heads popping out on the hour for a look round.
At night they chew the soft cheese like the wax in your ears. She
points out how very much this cheese resembles sponge – and how

536

roaches, like many deepsea fish, haven't changed in thousands of years. But he doesn't believe her.

*

He was ill. She learned this from friends and came walking down Portobello Road with cheese and apple juice early one morning. That was the first time they tried to end it.

*

> He has said: It's your freedom makes me do this.
> And she: You contain me.

*

He has a knack for aphorism and she, for conjuring disappointment. Often, sitting beside her, he feels he has been in some obscure way defeated. Her preparation of meals for him, or his for her, has somehow come to be like the running-up of flags. Each morning she goes and brings him things: food, cigarettes, soup, soap, shower attachments. You don't take care of yourself, she says.

At night, in the dark room, they open doors to a few more monads; advance to the next chamber of the nautilus. He begins to perceive new relationships everywhere. An evening sky is the colour of kazoos, his brown shoes on the floor are abandoned tanks.

He asks her, What do penises look like? And she answers: mushrooms. One of his favourite foods.

Later she is asleep and he suddenly exclaims, The fish are not afraid!

She starts awake and when he repeats it, this delights her. But he didn't want to repeat it.

*

> – They are in the cab.
>   They are going home.

> – He to his, her to hers.
>   With?

> – Platitudes, gratitudes.
>   But the age demands an image.

537

– True.

Well?

*

Days later: 'The residue of each in all the others.' A warm day, with pigeons in the corners, and rain.

*

PS. I got your letter today and will write again when I can.

*

I shall answer rage with outrage; expect you to collect my words in little wood boxes of parsley or sawdust; require that you follow behind, obligatto? No.

Outside, standing by the cab, I hear his shouts, the clatter of things thrown at the floor. The driver and I talk about last night's rain; how it took him two hours to cross town, generally a fifteen-minute trip; how he got a fare to Brighton, ten quid. You come out the door when streetlights are turning from orange to yellow, you are wearing your cantaloupe-colour coat, the cab's blue light glints in your glasses.

Now, in the cab, you begin to talk.

*

'Selling pieces of my life. Am being, in a sense, auctioned off – but this is of course no truer for me than for others. Just that my bids are recorded.

'Publishers, contracts, agents, a grant here, a fellowship there, royalty statements, letters; half for my wife, son, friends.

'There is 10 per cent left. That, I offer to you.'

*

My speech, too much used: Je me retournerai souvent.

Memory is a hunting horn
It dies along the wind

*

Books, papers and typewriter, flowers in a beer bottle – on his desk.

For him: the texture of the moment, objects in disarray.

For her: a pattern of abstractions.

'I think my period is starting, you may get blood on you.'

'That's fine.'

'I didn't know. Whether it would matter.'

Later, waking in the night, he realizes how participation in the present is always diluted – by memory, by anticipation. He resents this. Against the window and light outside, the flowers are transformed. He is becoming confused. He is terrified of hurting her.

*

Believe, please, that I understand and appreciate your concern but feel it, upon this occasion, somewhat a waste. By actual count there were fifty-seven people directly concerned with my affairs yesterday; and from every indication the number has risen considerably today.

At the top of this page you'll find a small rendering of two cows facing one another across a field of watercress; this is in the nature of a bonus, on your stock in me.

PS. All the flagpoles have bloomed to flowers. The air smells of eggshells and coffee grounds. There are meringue nativity scenes in all the eggshells. I am yours.

*

'The goddamn hot-water heater only heats three cups of water at a time.'

'Yeah.'

*

Things in the world: a series. A drawing.

1. Mozart
2. Watermelon
3. Oil derricks
4. Puce
5. Drambuie

Why, he asks, this urge towards capitalization?

*

She wants to answer but all she can think is *epithesis* – a nonce word. He gives her *micturation* in return and for days, at every opportunity, they are rehearsing one another's words. They often make these trades.

*

Smoking American cigarettes in London. A bit of chauvinism to contrast his adoption of a British accent, British clothes, British mannerisms, always saying 'Sorry.' (When she brings an American penny out of her purse he laughs; dollars, though, he can still accept as authentic, unsuspect.) Five bob a pack: made in Switzerland under American licence. To buy them he puts on his best voice, assumes a business air, gets it over with as quickly as possible. He is embarrassed; she loves it.

*

Conversation becomes for them a kind of verbal semaphore. Sentences need never be finished. A word, a pause – and the other is smiling, responding, thoughtful. Perhaps the sentences *couldn't* be completed; perhaps they were begun – formed – in this certainty of communication. Sometimes she wonders. She considers holding back her response, to see.

*

Toys.

As a child she slept in a bed full of stuffed animals, contorting herself to fit in among them. He once began a poem: We lie down, the menagerie invades our bed.

She doesn't know about gigging frogs, so he tells her. The miniature trident; how he went gigging toads when he was ten, not knowing the difference; how difficult it is to kill a toad (one, he stabbed fifteen times). Then he explains how you can milk a toad using two matchsticks, something his grandmother taught him. She used to find frogs the size of her thumbnail in her back yard in Florida; sometimes they would cover entire limbs. Once, his lawnmower turned up a nest of baby rattlers.

Finally he remembers the plastic cow. It had a balloon udder you could fill and milk. The teats, bucket and tail (which worked the udder) were white. The rest of the cow was brown.

*

More and more, the word *guilt* enters his conversation.

*

Outside, it is getting dark.

Like a marble trapped in a single chute he slides back and forth through the hall between his rooms. Kitchen: milk bottles lined on the floor in one corner, apples and cheese on the table; teapot, strainer, cups and bags, all used, in the sink. Sleeping room: flowers (tulips) in a cup on the desk, returnable bottles stacked like wine bottles (a honeycomb) in the cupboard. Window obscured in a haze of blue lingerie-curtain. On a trunk, two small brass sculptures from a series called *Joy of the Unborn*. They are foetuses entangled in their cords.

As he walks back and forth – pouring beers down the drain, poking at the tea machinery with two fingers – someone traces his steps in the room overhead. Heads and shoulders cant out of windows across the street. Across the street a man stands poking at his belly in the mirror.

Night is falling, filling: he tries various phrases, like strings across his tongue, and abandons them, standing by the window finally, speechless.

The doctor, a woman, Pakistani, arrives and asks what he's on: Meth, pep pills . . . There are several in her list that he's not heard of. Taking his pulse, she pulls his arm down and glances at the inside of his elbow.

*

One morning when it is raining a letter arrives. He wonders, Did he know she would write it, Has he been expecting this letter? Her name is typed in the corner, with a brown ribbon.

By the time he gets it back to his room there are spots all over it from the rain, like an unevenly ripe fruit. He props it against the bottle of flowers while he changes clothes, hanging the damp ones on a chair in front of the electric heater. Then he makes tea and sits on the bed to read the letter.

It is badly typed, on blue paper. There are many *x*-ings out; words break off arbitrarily at the right edge of the page and continue a full inch-and-a-half from the left on the line below. This is the first writing of hers he has seen and he looks over the page with interest, thinking how strangely this refutes her general sense of form and order, how easily the typewriter has confounded her.

Her signature is in pencil at the bottom of the second page – a row of bold printed letters, lightly connected – and he quickly turns to see what remains on the last page. It is half-filled with PSs.

*

    1. The sky is bruised with light.
    2. I have to save us from abstraction.
    3. The knives come out of the mirror like sharks.

*

Can one's obsessive guilt be cancelled by another's innocence?

He thinks so; he tries.

What qualities does she find common in him and her husband?

A certain shyness, which leads him to such ends as falling off chairs to gain attention; a precise inability to mount stairs; in bed, preoccupation with the cleft between her buttocks; a penchant for leaping through the barriers between rooms.

And he, in her and the other?

The sound of their breath in the dark.

How much has he predicted, to himself?

All but the end. That, like regret, would be against his nature.

Lying here now in the dawn, alone, how does he see the city?

As a thing composed of pale, obscene, gone-off neons. Water trucks sailing slowly down the streets. Milk carts gliding and jangling down the streets. And cats. Cats walk along the sidewalk beside them in utter silence.

[James Sallis]

THE GAZETTEER OF DISAPPEARANCES & DELETIONS

URANIA COTTAGE, W12

Charles Dickens and philanthropist millionairess Angela Burdett-Coutts opened this 'Home for Homeless Women' in Lime Grove, Shepherd's Bush, in 1847; it stood one third of the way up the street on the eastern side. An estimated 80,000 women and girls worked as prostitutes in London in the mid-century; 150 of them, to be 'reclaimed', passed through Urania Cottage before its closure in 1862. Dickens chose their dresses himself, and insisted on a policy of 'tempting' the women 'into virtue', as bullying or scaring them would not work. Tempting did not always work either, and many absconded – such as Sessina Bollard, who would 'corrupt a nunnery in a fortnight', according to Dickens, and was last seen flouncing off along Notting Hill Gate one day in November 1849. In later life, Urania Cottage became the Manager's House, when film company Gaumont constructed the Lime Grove Studios alongside it in 1912. In 1949 the BBC bought the Studios, which survived until demolition in 1993 – the rubble being used as foundation material in the widening of the M25.

[Sarah Wise]

THE WHITE CITY, W12

A 140-acre fantasia of pure white constructions, erected in 1908, north of Shepherd's Bush Green, to house the Franco-British Exhibition of that year. Comprised 20 palaces, 120 pavilions, ornamental gardens, lagoons, bridges, tree-lined avenues, the 'Flip-Flap' – a 200-feet-high fairground attraction (6d a ride). Arabian, rococo and Tudor architectural influences evident. Began to disappear in the 1920s; greyhound-racing stadium survived until early 1990s; southern entranceway vanished early 2004.

[Sarah Wise]

CONVENT OF THE POOR CLARES, LADBROKE GROVE, W11

The convent was built during the 1880s, at the time of the Notting Dale development. It was demolished, ninety years later, to make way for blocks of GLC flats. The nuns were moved to Putney. Local legend had it that a tunnel ran from beneath the convent to a mysterious subterranean world known as the 'Middle March'.

[Michael Moorcock]

THE ALHAMBRA, COLVILLE TERRACE, W11

This magnificent public house, with exceptional fabrics in the art nouveau style, was designed by Voysey and built in 1900. For many years it doubled as a theatre, putting on much of the early experimental work of the Notting Hill group of playwrights (Wilson, Locke, Hare, Hopkins, etc.), as well as poetry-and-performance events promoted by Michael Horovitz and Heathcote Williams. Emma Tennant's 'Banana Follies' were a feature of the mid 1970s. It is now a fashionable restaurant.

[Michael Moorcock]

THE HEARST CASTLE, LADBROKE GROVE, W10

Possibly the most grandiose project of property developer Sir Frank Cornelius. He bought William Randolph Hearst's Californian folly and transported it, stone by stone, to London – where he had it reassembled on the site of the Convent of the Poor Clares. For several years the Castle stood empty as Cornelius became embroiled in planning disputes with the Greater London Council – who eventually took over the land for the construction of high-rise flats (designed by Erno Goldfinger).

Hearst Castle was broken up in 2001 and rebuilt at Battle, near Hastings, East Sussex – where Sir Frank now lives in retirement. Castle and grounds are vigorously policed with no public access (despite attempts by the Ramblers Association to establish a right of way across the Deer Park). Sir Frank acquired a great deal of dilapidated property in the Ladbroke Grove area (along with much of James Burton's crumbling marine speculation in St Leonards-on-Sea). He placed fourth in the latest *Sunday Times* Rich List of British-domiciled plutocrats.

[Michael Moorcock]

SPORTING CLUB SQUARE, W6

Escaping the flying bombs which spread so much destruction in the area, this extraordinary project, the brainchild of Sir Oswald Begg, was built, between 1885 and 1895, by Gibbs and Flew. The open square once contained a dozen tennis courts. Each mansion was named for one of Begg's favourite artists – with the exception of Begg Mansions itself, where the architect lived above studios and workshops staffed by a variety of artisans. The mansions were designed in eclectic styles that varied from French Gothic and Arab Baroque to English Art Nouveau. Even the ornamental ironwork of this early gated community was in the complicated 'naturalism' Begg favoured. Completion was delayed, in 1890, when the original builders were declared bankrupt. Begg, through contacts in the City, raised the private finance to see his dream realized. The Square never attracted the respectable 'New Money' for which it had been conceived. It soon became associated with London's bohemian element. The list of music-hall artists, actors, comedians, painters, illustrators, writers, journalists, script-doctors and film persons who lived there, from 1890 to the present day, is astonishing and comprises a secret history of British intellectual life. The Square has been lightly fictionalized in a number of Michael Moorcock's writings: 'The Clapham Antichrist' (*London Bone*, 2001), 'Crimson Eyes' (*Fabulous Harbours*, 1977) and *King of the City* (2000). Moorcock lived there himself until bankrupted by the Inland Revenue. He moved to his uncle's Old Circle Squared ranch in Lost Pines, Texas, and continued to write stories of the real and imaginary inhabitants of his beloved and post-temporal Square.

[Michael Moorcock]

BLACK LETTER SPEAKING

I

I've had men dressed like
gentlemen no doubt they was
respectable when they was sober
bring two or three books
or a nice cigar case
or anything that don't show
in their pockets & say
drunk as blazes give me

what you can for this
I want it sold for
a particular purpose more drink
I should say & I've known
the same men come back
in less than a week
& buy what they'd sold
& be glad if I
had it by me still

2

poor people run to such
as me I've known them
come with such things as
teapots & old hair mattresses
& flock beds & then
I'm sure they're hard up
reduced for a meal I
don't like buying big things
like mattresses though I do
sometimes some are as keen
as Jews at a bargain
others only anxious to
get rid of the things
& have hold of some bit of
money anyhow yes sir I've
known their hands tremble
to receive the money & mostly
the women's they haven't been used to it

3

Last week a man in black
he didn't seem rich
came into my shop
looked at some old books
& said have you any black lead
he didn't speak plain
& I could hardly catch him I said
no sir I don't sell black lead
but you'll get it at No. 27
but he answered not black lead
black letter speaking very pointed
I said no & I haven't a
notion what he meant

[John Seed/Henry Mayhew]

TERMINALS

PROCESS OF TIME

Every time I thought or talked of home, the Atlantic itself opened up within me, between me and anyone I was speaking to who did not know it in such a way that it would not need to be mentioned. I would look at the other person in the conversation, I would feel smiles and expressions chasing themselves across my face, I would feel my eyes liquid and transparent, but inside was an immensity, something that did not measure up, beyond beyond.

It was not worth trying to communicate this. Everyone has memories; and people must not be made to feel distant, especially across a small table in a crowded room.

I thought of the Atlantic as seen from the tilt of the aeroplane, the colour of sharks and dragons and cold and heat and depth and sheer non-human continuity, nothing within the sphere of safety belts and life vests. I thought of the freezing grasp it could fix on your ankle from the depths of a green wave that stretched the width of a bay. It took years for me to feel, not just to know, that Jean Rhys's novel *Wide Sargasso Sea* was partly about having to contain the ocean within one's everyday self. Speaking across it to other people, how not to feel – seem – sad, fey, inconsequential, self-defeated, cynical, *small*? Home is not just up or down a piece of land. It is across water. 'Ring me before you cross water,' the older generation of my Hindu relatives always said. 'Ring me before you go back to London.'

They knew, but could not feel, that 'London' was not 'England'.

London was not the place to which I went back. Visiting London with an Anglo-Italian friend who lived there and knew it well – it was her city – I did not get a feel for it. She took me to the Soane Museum, a house full of curiosities, but I was distracted by the convex mirrors which made all the lookers-on part of what was collected in the room yet more temporary than any of the assembled objects. She took me to the Poetry Café, where people who looked like blokes sat for a long time over the same drinks. In the street was a motorized conference table being taken, or going, to some place where people who worked for money would sit around it. The chairs were attached, and the place mats, and even the potted plants. Not one London head turned as it processed down the middle of the road. Then my London friend took me to a vintage dress shop. Suddenly I was at home.

There were the princess seams to give shape to backs narrow with lack of activity, the bust darts to suggest fullness, the gathers at the shoulders to hide any muscle and softly round off the upper arms. There were the seafood-counter colours, the aching marriage of tangerine and beige with tads and titbits of crimson piping and silver beading. There was the shine of detergent-green satin, like something luminous except that it gave no light. There was midnight-blue velvet with white ostrich feathers, cut long to sweep on the floor, the richness of the pile a texture to pick up every bit of dust. Do not move.

In Trinidad, in what corresponded to upper- or upper-middle-class society, I used to feel that the women who wore such dresses belonged to a different time. In wrathful and deliberately colourless words, Claudette Earle, a journalist in neighbouring Guyana, denounced the press for failing to report on 'the under-privileged in society'. Instead, '[We] see pictures of the country's elite with glasses in hands attending cocktail parties and lavish luncheons and dinners. The regularity with which these pictures are published gives testimony to the fact that the press is pandering to the vocal and visible minority of the society and wilfully ignoring the predicament of the broad masses. And it is against such a backdrop of social contradictions that the responsible media must help women and men in the Caribbean to define and attain a quality of life that is socially, economically and culturally relevant.'[1]

I would have been thirteen in the year she published this, just a few years after I started wearing T-shirts when swimming in the sea because of the verbal assessments and predictions that the older women felt it was time to make about femininity and my 'figure'.

It seemed to me that the women whose ageing bodies were sneaked and tucked into such evening dresses were indeed part of a problem that was relevant to Caribbean society, the problem of ghosts.

Persisting into the Trinidad of the modern world, transforming with its changes but not in accord with them, was a kind of womanhood that belonged to Victorian England not as it had been but as it was in novels and, worse, on the stage. They never left the husbands who locked them up, beat them, gave them syphilis, gambled away the family fortune or spent it on mistresses. They never used certain 'curse words'. They never went to bed without saying their prayers. Most never went to work; if they had a boutique or a beauty salon they ran it from home. Some prided themselves on high-profile jobs but nonetheless were beaten. They liked to open charity bazaars. Then they appeared in evening dress in the papers, and their suffering was no less real for being furtive and poisonous instead of out in the fields, no less real for belonging to a privileged condition to which presumably more realistic characters – the Trinidadian urban poor, if not the peasantry – were encouraged to aspire. When talking over Victorian literature at college, nothing angered me so much as to hear teenagers say that 'nowadays' they could not really 'empathize' with the problems of infidelity, honour and venereal disease. I silently wished on them a fairy-tale childhood in an island paradise. Then they would see. Then they would know. Then the past would speak, making the century-old gestures in the electronically up-to-date, silk-flowered living room.

I brought myself back to the shop in London. I fingered a layer of chiffon. 'It's interesting to see the ideas people had of what would look nice,' I ventured. My friend smiled. 'They still have these ideas.'

The mythical London of the older generation of Trinidadians: how to map that? It was nowhere that I saw.

I had not asked my mother about her past, though she was my main storyteller. I thought of the 1950s and the 1960s as a time when Leila and Deven zigzagged back and forth between England, France and Trinidad; but wasn't that what everybody did then, during the struggle for Independence? I still have to make an effort to remember – to imagine – that many people, especially in England, had families who stayed put in those decades, reassembling a life after the Second World War. Our parents told us unsettling episodes from that time and those places. They never made a whole story of it. Now I too was living in an England, and starting to read more books by West Indians from that time. The men in the books by men felt dislocated and went to whores. Their work of remembering was a way of questioning or forging identity, trying to make sense in a world of bad stations. Such books by women as I had begun to find seemed somehow backward-looking, elegiac or sensual, full of foliage and foods to which I could not relate, though I was interested to learn that these women's ways of living in, or writing about, the place I thought I knew as home also existed. I felt more like the men – trying to make sense – but I never went to whores and these days stations were not so bad.

I had to find a way to stop myself being harsh about this generation of West Indians.

So I asked my mother what it had been like. My father had died some months before. It was hard to get Leila to talk about herself. At first, she didn't, and she left deliberate signs of haste in her long, impersonal reply:

Date: Tuesday, April 27, 2004 21:38:44–0400
Subject: London

In the 1950s there was a need in London for unskilled and semi-skilled workers to do jobs which the English did not wish to do. This was the opportunity for hosts of West Indians to emigrate to Britain, the Mother Country, to look for a better life than they had in the colonies. They came by the boatfuls, arriving at Southampton or Plymouth and taking the boat train to Paddington. They were full of hope for a better future and felt very secure in the fact of their British citizenship.

When the boat train reached to Paddington there was always a crowd of friends and relatives waiting to meet the newly arrived. There would be shouting and loud greetings, people hugging each other and loud inquiries being made about various members of families or friends back home.

They arrived in their best tropical finery in a blaze of colour. I am sure Paddington Station had never seen anything like it before.

The W. Indians arrived before the influx of Pakis and other Asians including the East Africans who came after being expelled by Idi Amin and others like him.

These came mainly in the 1960s when the West Indians had already established themselves to a great extent especially in jobs in London Transport.

Accommodation was a real problem as a great many of the cheaper flats and bedsitters available came with a sign 'NO COLOUREDS'.

Some said 'No Coloureds, No Dogs, No Children'.

However, there were some landlords who saw this as an opportunity. They could let their premises without any trouble, no need to redecorate or to make sure everything was in working order. They let out their houses as flats and bedsitters. For example, in Ladbroke Grove the houses consisted of a basement and three storeys. The basement flat had the use of the small bit of land/garden at the back. The three storeys were let to single people or families. Each floor had two rooms. In one house, for example, the ground floor was let out to a family of four. Up the stairs on the first landing was the bathroom which served the entire house. Then up to the next landing and the two rooms were let separately as were the rooms on the third floor. The landlord had only to get several gas and electricity meters installed and the tenants would put in their shillings or their pennies to get their gas for cooking or electricity for their lights and radio, etc. The gas man and the electricity man came to look after the meters and all the landlord had to do was to collect his rent every week. Tenancies were usually weekly. The tenants often sublet their kitchen or took in paying guests so that the house could be rather crowded.

How could I possibly use this as a reality check? It fit so many stereotypes not allowed into good 'postcolonial' books.

My mother must have sat down, determined to be helpful to her daughter, her amber eyes reminiscent, her back stiff with pained nerves and desiccated discs. Typing as one unaccustomed to keyboards and who wrote as second nature a perfect italic hand, she had tried to be fair and give a representative account, one that did not say 'I'. 'I' had no place in the formal language she had learned. 'I' did not belong in narrative prose. 'I' was a way of putting yourself forward, as a person with words to say and as a woman; and putting yourself forward was – wrong. (Trinidadian woman's joke to put down another woman: 'She is an I specialist, or what?')[2] Writing in her mind from a time in Trinidad when a person of mixed race would answer cheerfully to the nickname 'Reds', not caring this was a short form of 'red nigger', she used unmentionable words like 'Paki' because she wanted to use the word an English person might have used for people like her – us, them – and 'coolie' was taboo, too Trinidadian and never jocular to the coolies themselves. A word like 'finery', an understatement like 'rather crowded': in what 'postcolonial' novel would such word choice not sound mock-English and sarcastic, a condemnation of the character who could speak so? But her generation had the need to be dry, the need to be careful. The world was so absurd. It was never just 'Idi Amin'. To her generation's mind, it always would be Tyrant X *and others like him*. The best you could do was make a few statements that you were sure you could stand behind if you woke up in a court of law.

Wait. Another message had flown in straightaway. This was unusual. My mother's training normally prevented her from volunteering more information until there had been a reply. Turn-taking, that was the decent thing to do. I still had little idea what she might have to say, but it seemed there would be something.

Date: Tuesday, April 27, 2004 22:04:34–0400
Subject: Paddington Bear

Michael Bond's first Paddington book came out in 1957.

It was she who had given us the Paddington books to read when we were children! Why was she telling me this now? Did I need to have second thoughts about Paddington Bear? I had loved the story of how he arrived at the London station that gave him his name: place, plus animal generic. I loved how his suitcase was tied up with string and how he kept marmalade sandwiches for emergencies under his hat. Best of all was Paddington Bear's insistence (how sweet! as if it mattered any longer or ever had meant much!) that he was from *Darkest* Peru. Then an English family adopted him, and he did many things wrong, but by chance and because of how easy it was to fool English people who were richer than his adoptive family and went to the ballet, Paddington came out looking like a hero. In my first year at university, when I was introduced to people my age who seemed pompous (perhaps they were anxious?), sometimes I made a joke and said that *I* was from Darkest Peru. Wasn't Paddington Bear one of their stories – wasn't I handing them something that we held in common? Laughter was on my face and quotation marks in my voice, but often as not the pomposity on the visage opposite would cross into a lost look and no response was made. Soon I stopped this joke.

Date: Saturday, May 1, 2004 21:05:31–0400
Subject: London

When I arrived at Paddington Station in the wee hours of the morning in Sept. 1957 I felt totally dazed. There were people meeting friends and relatives but I had not arranged for anyone to meet me. Since I was on scholarship I thought that I would be looked after. A person, I have no recollection of whether it was a man or a woman, eventually turned up and said that those of us who had no arrangements would be taken by bus to Hans Crescent (a hostel for men) but that we would have to make arrangements to leave after 3 days. This was the max. amount of time that they would keep us there. I felt very alone but I did not panic. Suddenly I saw my brother-in-law's brother. He knew that I would be coming so he turned up at Paddington to see how I was making out.

He then saw me to the bus. He did not offer any other help but his presence there was enough to make me feel a lot more confident.

The following day the few of us who were on scholarship were taken to the Colonial Office to arrange for our tuition and maintenance money to be paid. Of course I had no clue but I went along and since nobody seemed put out I must have done and said what was expected. The problem was that I had not thought about where I would stay for the two weeks or so until the beginning of term in Exeter.

As I was going down some stairs, still not knowing exactly what I was doing, I saw Deven who had found out where I was likely to be and had come to meet me. It seemed very strange as I had not seen him for a year. At home I had always seen him in shirtsleeves, but here he was, wearing a suit, looking, as I thought, very handsome. He said that he shared a flat in Ladbroke Grove with Miss — and that she was willing for me to stay with her until I left for Exeter. It seemed a godsend. D. accompanied me to the various places that I had to go to and then took me to Miss —'s by tube. We got off at Ladbroke Grove station and then there was a short walk to Cambridge Gardens. The whole neighbourhood had an atmosphere of neglect. The air seemed heavy and everything seemed to have a light coating of soot. I did not judge anything. After all, this was LONDON and this must be all right. I had heard that students had meagre living conditions so I was not put off. However, when we got to #— and he opened the front door a smell of curry hung thickly inside. Apparently the Singalese woman who lived on the ground floor was cooking her dinner. The curry was recognizable as curry but totally different in pungency to what we in T&T knew as curry. We went up the stairs past the landing with the communal bathroom and then to Miss —'s first-floor flat. This was comprised of two rooms both with doors opening on to the landing. There was no internal communication between the rooms. I then learned that I was to share the large double room which she used and that Deven's room was a kitchen with a single bed in one corner, a gas stove and a sink in two opposite corners and the door was at the other corner of the room. There was a small table with four chairs, a sort of wooden cupboard and a big radio which belonged to Deven on a chest of drawers.

I put my two suitcases on the floor and had to keep all my stuff in them as there was no place for anything but Miss —'s clothes, books, odds and ends and a paraffin heater about two feet high which she kept between her legs while she sat on a chair to read.

She was quite welcoming but this was a financial arrangement. I paid her for the time I would spend there. She had one double bed which I had to share. She looked dirty and I would know later that she was dirty. Every Saturday she peeled all the layers of flannel vests and jumpers that she wore for the week, washed them, had a bath and was fully clothed again for another week. She resented doing any cleaning or chores. The carpet looked dark grey. When she went to the library I went out and bought a brush and dustpan, went down on my hands and knees (there was no vacuum or broom) and swept all the layers of dust out. Not only was the carpet much lighter in colour but there was a geometric pattern all over it! Deven's room, the kitchen, had no carpet, only linoleum which he kept clean with a mop. I soon realized that she was taking advantage of Deven since he was expected to pay half the rent, to do the shopping, to make her breakfast and a sandwich to take with her and to meet her at the Ladbroke Grove station with an umbrella on rainy nights or just to walk her home if it was very foggy. She was only about 36 years old, a fat, short, Presbyterian spinster. She seemed ancient to our 19-year-old eyes and the fact that she was already a barrister with an LL.B. and that Deven's parents had arranged for him to stay with her gave her power over him psychologically.

I am aware that this should be about London but this was my introduction to London. We saw few and met no English people.

I shall try next time to tell you about our second stay in London when we at last really got around and got to know and like the city.
Love L.

Date: Thursday, May 13, 2004 21:53:21–0400
Subject: London cont'd

London for me in 1957 was a physical reality, but mentally it meant mainly putting up with Miss — and the hold she seemed to have over

D. It was as if he was afraid to leave the set-up arranged by his parents as he thought that they would disapprove. They thought that since she was a barrister and in her mid thirties she would be a suitable person to look after his welfare and to guide him in his legal studies. In fact the only thing she ever wanted to discuss with him was the crime of rape. One had to prove that the alleged rapist had 'capacity' and she kept asking him over and over if he knew what 'cipacity' was, as she pronounced it.

I found that there were reasonably priced students' rooms and I encouraged D. to move out of the flat. He kept saying that he would but never did. That Xmas, my first in England, I spent with them in Cambridge G'dns. I was annoyed because D. made sure to announce that he got gifts of the same value for Miss — and me. We all three went on Xmas eve to Trafalgar Square. It was bitterly cold but the atmosphere was wonderful. The people gathered there were singing carols and the lights were beautiful. The tree in Trafalgar Square was huge.

Date: Thursday, May 13, 2004 22:09:16–0400
Subject: London cont'd

Every year the people of Norway send an enormous Christmas tree to Britain. This tree is put up in Trafalgar Square. It is a present to thank the British for their part in liberating Norway during the second world war. Looking back now I realize that the war had ended only just over a decade before.

I loved the cold weather. It made me feel alert and alive. I loved the cold wind on my face which made my skin tingle. I made sure to keep warm by wearing a woollen vest and I spent a fair amount of money on boots which, lined with lambskin, kept my feet warm as well.

◀ ▶ 1 Copy 1 Delete 1 Reply 1 Forward **Message: 8 out of 71** Show Hdrs

[Vahni Capildeo]

ERNEST SO FAR

On the war memorial at King's Cross Station in London nearly
1,000 names are listed. The citation on the memorial reads:

1914–19
TO THE IMMORTAL MEMORY OF THE MEN OF THE GREAT
NORTHERN RAILWAY WHO GAVE THEIR LIVES
IN THE GREAT WAR

1935–45
TO THE IMMORTAL MEMORY OF THE MEN OF THE NORTH
EASTERN RAILWAY WHO GAVE THEIR LIVES
IN THE SECOND WORLD WAR

ORIGINAL MEMORIAL ERECTED BY THE GREAT NORTHERN
RAILWAY IN 1920.
NEW MEMORIAL INCORPORATING THE ORIGINAL NAME PANELS
ERECTED BY THE BRITISH RAILWAYS BOARD IN 1973.

Nothing else; no clue as to rank or regiment. It is not even clear
from the citation whether the names include men from both wars.

This is the account of an attempt to find out the history of one
of those men, a man who might, or might not, be a relative of mine;
a search to add substance to one name, among so many lost.

We begin, one February morning, Iain and I, by looking for the
memorial. After a few wrong turns, we find it. A wall of marble. A
stark list of names, grey with neglect. The plaque forms one wall of
a wide corridor, a sort of side exit leading out of the station towards
the Great Northern Hotel. The area is dimly lit. There is nothing
else here. And no one, except for two women, sitting on unlikely
chairs, tucked in a corner under the first list of names. They look

at us curiously as we scan the memorial. It is clear that they had not noticed the memorial and that they are uncomfortable with our intrusion. We feel awkward. They have stopped speaking, and our conversation is the only sound in this cavernous place. We have to ignore the fact that every scrap of our discussion, criticisms and wonderings, must be attended to by these strangers.

We scan the lists and find the name we want about halfway down the fifth column: HADMAN E. Hadman is my family name, but we do not know this soldier; he has not been found in our recent researches into my ancestry. Hadman, however, is an unusual surname and the GNR runs right through Peterborough, the area of the country from which my father's family emerged. We feel this lost railwayman is within our reach. There are other surnames on the memorial which are familiar from our investigations in the villages around Peterborough: Bullimore, Hill, Titman, Twelvetrees. But there is nothing else to be discovered from this dank wall of names.

Iain is convinced that, on the station, there will be archives relating to the memorial, or, at least, someone who knows something about it. We set off for 'Information'. A fat man in a tight suit perches on a stool in a sort of open-sided booth. He is continually swooped at by rushing passengers, with dark flapping coats and briefcases. He sweats and blusters. We wait for a quiet moment in which to put our query. The man is programmed to respond only to swoopers, we go in sharpish and grab our turn. He cannot help and is not friendly, but he directs us to the Customer Service Office. This is better. This is the public face of the Great North Eastern Railway. A carpeted office next to the luxurious First Class lounge. Two smiling facilitators. Our question is taken up by the man of the team, who confesses that he has never before been asked about the war memorial. He is completely at a loss, while recognizing that this is something he should know about.

Then he has an idea. On the station is an employee who has worked for the railway for nearly fifty years and who will certainly possess the required folk memory: steam-trains, porters, vanished architecture. Nationalization, privatization, broken promises. Disasters and cover-ups. He has survived them all. At first, I think this man must be retired and we have just been lucky to catch him on a day when he is visiting the station. But no, he is still working, and, yes, he is clamped to his walkie-talkie. We set out to locate him. Our guide strides, professionally, along the platform. He is very tall and walks extremely quickly. I have almost to run to keep up. The veteran is discovered on the main concourse.

He started work here when he was fourteen. Stocky, weather-beaten, in neat uniform with overcoat, hat and several metal badges and insignia, he is obviously proud of his record and pleased to be sought out for his mythical knowledge. He tells us that the main line north was first operated by the Great Northern Railway, and was later amalgamated with many smaller companies into the London and North Eastern Railway. The men on the memorial could have worked for either company in either war. The records are all kept at the headquarters in York or at the National Railway Museum. It is good to talk to him, and the man from Customer Services feels he has done his stuff.

On the way out I remember another, more recent, event that surely must be commemorated: the King's Cross fire of 1987. We approach the man in the booth again. 'Oh, yes,' he says, 'it's somewhere around, either at the top or the bottom of the stairs.'

We look. We search for some time. The walls are covered in grey plasterboard as part of the refurbishment and rebuilding of King's Cross as the Channel Tunnel Terminal. There is no sign of any plaque to the memory of those who died in the fire.

Where now; as the station does not keep any records? The National Railway Museum in York? I have a new toy, a brand-new Apple iBook with internet access. Perhaps this is the moment to join the net surfers, to fly into that magical information mist.

Five o'clock; dusk. Iain is out, trusting to the last of the light, as he runs round the park. The house is quiet and I bring up the Research and Archives section of the National Railway Museum website.

I tap into Railway Staff Records. The first paragraph reads:

The National Railway Museum frequently receives inquiries from the descendants of former railway staff who wish to obtain details of their relatives' careers. The National Railway Museum does not hold the railway company staff records so is unable to give detailed information. In fact, where such records survive, they are held by the <u>Public Record Office</u> for England and Wales and by the <u>Scottish Record Office</u> for Scotland.

Not very encouraging. 'Don't trouble us with your relatives,' it seems to say. 'Go and bother the Public Record Office in Kew, but don't expect too much.'

I think of another approach. I log on to the website of the War Graves Commission and I type in 'E. Hadman'. Immediately the name comes up: twice. There are *two* E. Hadmans commemorated here. Both named Ernest. One died in 1917, aged twenty, and the other in 1944, aged twenty-four. One in each war. I am astonished. Here is:

Ernest Hadman. Trooper. Royal Armoured Corps. 1st Lothians and Border Horse. Age: 24. Date of Death: 21/11/1944. Son of Elijah and Ethel May Hadman, of Balby, Doncaster, Yorkshire. Mook War Cemetery.

He was killed in fighting around Limburg.

And then:

Ernest Hadman. Private. Northamptonshire Regiment. 6th Battalion. Age: 20. Date of Death: 17/02/1917. Son of John Hadman, of Denton Lodge, Stilton, Peterborough. Cemetery: Thiepval Memorial.

There is no known grave. This Ernest was one of the thousands of deaths on the Somme. As he is the son of a John Hadman of Stilton, I believe that he is a member of my family.

Both such young men. Remembered with honour. I am in tears when Iain comes in. Now I have two E. Hadmans, and I cannot be sure which of them is commemorated at King's Cross. I need to identify the railwayman.

*

I think again about the National Archives at Kew and the next day I visit their website. In the Research Guide I find a list of available railway records. I ring them and order up the Staff Records for the Great Northern Railway (1848–1943), and for London and North Eastern Railway (1897–1943), available to view on 8 March. The journey on the North London line from Dalston Kingsland to Kew Gardens is an easy and familiar experience. It used to be one of our favourite outings when we had young children. The sweep around the northern arc of London, looking in on all the back gardens, and over the rooftops of Camden and Islington, past the Heath, into the wastes of Willesden Junction, and the final triumph of the wide river crossing, is as enjoyable as ever. This morning, however, I must resist the temptation to cross through the underpass and walk down the tree-lined street, through the Victoria Gate, and into paradise. Instead, I stand on the pavement, searching for the brown heritage signposts to the National Archives. The route involves a quiet suburban street of prosperous terraced houses, with wide bay windows and interesting front gardens.

As I amble along, I hear rapid footsteps behind me and am overtaken by a thin elderly gent, in pressed beige, with too-short trousers flapping over brown socks and highly polished shoes. He carries a see-through plastic bag, filled with different-coloured files. I do not hear the next walker. She dashes past, a bulging black rucksack bouncing on substantial shoulders. My slow pace is holding up the flow of researchers to the Public Record Office. It is nearly eleven o'clock. The office opens at ten. It takes a while to travel to this corner of London. If you want to avoid rush hour and use your freedom pass, this is the earliest you can make it. I am in Kew's own ancestor-hunting rush hour.

The National Archives are housed in a building that is surrounded by a paved landscape of architectural flower beds, lakes and rills; it looks like an enormous pagoda, a civic temple. A path leads acolytes past catalogue plants – yucca, cordyline – and expansive water features to a wide concourse and up to the great glass doors of the entrance. We hurry forward, revolved into a light-filled atrium. I am so dazed that I float right past the security desk and have to be called back with a loud shout of: 'Check your bag, madam?'

I line up for my reader's card. This little piece of wizardry is your pass to the whole electronic life of the Public Record Office. It is the key to your personal identity, your access to the past. In possessing it you become one of the privileged.

You have to leave your bags and your coat in the locker room and put what you need in a transparent plastic carrier bag. Pencils only. I approach the security barrier at the bottom of the stairs. My carrier is minutely examined and I am turned away. A rubber and a pencil sharpener. I have to go all the way back to the locker room to store these forbidden items.

I approach the unsmiling security person again and this time I am allowed in. Up the stairs to the research room. It is warm, spacious, well lit, beautifully furnished with round tables/desks in expensive light wood. It is very quiet. The floor is softly carpeted. Initiates are sitting at the tables with large record books. There is a breathable air of concentration, of people who know what they are doing. I am at a loss. I approach an information desk and whisper that I think, *possibly*, that I might have ordered some documents and where might I find them?

The reader's card does the trick.

'Yes, Mrs Sinclair, you should find your documents in D4, and that is your seat number for the day.'

D4 is a numbered cubbyhole in a whole bank of numbered cubbyholes, where documents that have been ordered are put for collection. There are wooden squares, with Perspex doors that give access to your books. The backs open on to another room where you can see the workers going about with heavily laden trolleys. The nearest thing to this set-up that I have experienced is the arrangement that you sometimes find in cafeterias where plated meals are put in little cubbyholes from which you help yourself. Empty slots are immediately replenished by robotic kitchen staff.

D4 has three tatty leather-bound folios in it: my railway staff records. D4 is also my reserved place in the research room. A seat at one of the round tables where personal space is protected by radial wooden ledges. You perch within a piece of the pie.

I cannot concentrate. I need to relax, to take in my surroundings, to realize where I am – and to accept that, by the mere fact of occupying my seat, I am now subsumed into the system. I have become part of this living electronic cobweb of the past.

So begins the first of many hours that I shall spend at the Public Record Office as I search through lists of names for any mention of E. Hadman. I trail the service records of clerks, of engineers, of loco drivers, of signalmen. I discover where the indexes for the records are kept. I order up fresh documents; some so huge and decrepit that they are sent to the Map and Large Document Room, which is brisk with professional academic researchers working with digital cameras and laptops.

I examine Office Staff Registers. I have great hopes of Rail 745 (1886–1920), the Register of Clerks' Commencing Dates (which includes Army Reserve List). I go through Goods, Parcels, Passengers and Telegraph. There are entries for Peterborough, Stamford, St James Deeping, Peakirk. Most of the registers are handwritten and falling apart. There seems no reason why some should have survived and others not. I get the feeling that they have been randomly hauled off a rubbish tip at the last minute; which they probably were, given the amount of reorganization and amalgamation of railway companies that went on between 1923 and 1948.

The registers contain little personal information. There are some references to the terms for remuneration of signalmen whose cottages and gardens form part of their wages. There is a curious entry for W. Rowe, who was a railwayman from 5.5.1913 to 15.9.1917 and who 'wishes to be known as W. Wright, his proper name'.

I spent two days at Kew, and in all those hours, and through all those lists, from 1914 to 1944, I found no trace of E. Hadman.

Ernest is still lost.

Dispirited, I investigate the National Railway Museum website, thinking that some more information on the war memorial itself would be helpful, and must be available. I discover a box in which you can type a question for the researchers. I put in 'King's Cross War Memorial/E. Hadman' and send it off.

The next day there are two emails from Martin Bashforth, Access Content Developer, National Railway Museum. The first is quite long and has interesting information about the Memorial.

> The original war memorial was officially unveiled on 10 June 1920 by Field Marshal Earl Haigh and commemorated the fallen of the Great Northern Railway during the Great War. It had marble panels with a granite and lead surround. A further set of names was added commemorating LNER staff who died during WW2. The memorial as a whole was repositioned in 1973 and the original surround was removed.

He goes on:

> Regarding E. Hadman, you do not specify on which of the two war memorials the name appears, so I am not sure if you are seeking information relating to the first or second war.

No, Mr Bashforth, neither am I. Where is 'the further set of names . . . commemorating LNER staff who died during WW2'? Could they have been destroyed, along with the original granite and lead surround, when the memorial was repositioned in 1973?

He cannot find my Ernests. He has looked them up on the Commonwealth War Graves Commission website, as I did, but cannot link them to the railway. Trooper Hadman does not appear on the York LNER Memorial to those who died in the Second World War. Private Hadman's name is not listed in the booklet published by the Great Northern Railway Company to mark the Railway Memorial Service held at St Paul's in May 1919.

Martin Bashforth's second email is timed eight minutes after the first:

Dear Mrs Sinclair,

Having realized that the list for St Paul's is not in alphabetical order, I can now confirm that your man is on the list as a member of staff of the GNR. The only additional information is that he was employed by the GNR as a porter. There is no information as to where he worked, but given the address from the website, I would guess it was most likely at Peterborough. Yours sincerely, Martin Bashforth

Ernest found!

The excellent Mr Bashforth sends me a copy of the photograph of Earl Haigh at the unveiling of the original memorial and a photocopy of the GNR booklet for the memorial service. There he is: E. Hadman. Acting Porter.

Found as a railwayman; but is he a member of my Hadman family? With his father's address in Stilton it seems highly likely. I abandon Kew in favour of the Family Record Office in Clerkenwell, a short bus ride away.

There is a much more informal atmosphere here. Customers bustle in and out. There is no entry procedure. The huge ledgers of

Births, Marriages and Deaths are heaved on and off the shelves, passed from hand to hand. People chat and help each other. I find the record of Ernest's birth – and then, after a long search through the Marriage Ledgers, the date of his parents' marriage: John and Caroline, in 1885, eleven years before Ernest was born.

The information in the ledgers is minimal: the date, names of the principal parties, and a reference number. How can I see the original certificates? I inquire at the desk. I can order copies which will cost £7 each and will be sent out to me in five working days. The original records are kept in Southport.

To hold a copy of Ernest's birth certificate in my hand, would that make me feel as if I had really found him? I order copies of his birth certificate, and of his parents' marriage certificate.

I find a quiet corner and unroll the tatty bundle of names, dates, lines, crossings-out and pastings-over (residue of a previous project) that connects me to my great-great-great-grandfather, Richard Hadman, born in 1768. Can I fit Ernest in? Can I find his place? I search for likely candidates. I trace out indirect routes, looking at uncles and cousins.

If I had the date when Ernest's father, John, was born, I could make some progress. But I won't be able to establish this until I see his marriage certificate, some time next week – unless I find the family on the 1901 census (available online, upstairs, from this building).

The room with the computers is no place for amateurs. But I am determined. I ask and re-ask. I stand in line to purchase a voucher that will let me view the page. I ask again how to use it. Then I have it.

In 1901, in Washingley, Huntingdon, there are recorded: John Hadman, 42, and his wife Caroline, 40, and their three children, Nelly, 14, Elijah, 9, and Ernest, 5.

With this information I can place John Hadman's birth in 1859. On my family tree I have another John Hadman, born in 1826 and married to Susanna. Is he a candidate for John's father and Ernest's grandfather?

My records show that John had only daughters: Mary, Sarah, Eliza, Elizabeth and Alice. But there is a significant gap between

Eliza, born in 1854, and Elizabeth, born in 1865. Have I missed a son? The daughters were found in the original Bishop's Transcripts in Northamptonshire Records Office. I could easily have missed him. I need a birth certificate for Ernest's father, John. Is he a son of John and Susanna? I go downstairs and order it.

By the next week I have completely forgotten about the Ernests and the family. I am busy living among the living. So when the post comes on Tuesday and Iain calls that I have three large envelopes, all the same, I am momentarily dumbfounded. Then I remember. Will this be the morning when I find him?

The certificates are a delight. True copies of the original documents. Only the robustness of the paper betrays them as replicas. Ernest Hadman's birth certificate shows that he was born on 1 March 1896, to John and Caroline Hadman, in Washingley, sub-district of Stilton in the County of Huntingdon. And John Hadman's birth certificate does give *him* as the son of John and Susanna Hadman of Washingley.

E. Hadman is no longer merely a name on a bleak memorial, he is placed firmly in the web of his family: his grandfather, John; his father and mother, John and Caroline; his elder sister, Nelly; and his brother, Elijah.

And his connection to me? He is my cousin. My great-great-grandfather, Robert, and Ernest's great-grandfather, William, were brothers. The names of *my* two brothers? William and Robert.

But all this can still only be 'Ernest So Far'. I now feel a responsibility. I shall have to go back to Kew and search out his war records. And why is he not on the war memorial in the chancel of Stilton church? If we look in Lutton, in Denton, in Glatton, shall we find him?

And what of the second Ernest? Trooper Hadman, killed in 1944 in Holland, son of Elijah and Ethel May. Is this the same Elijah, Ernest's elder brother, who, possibly, named his son in memory of his brother, only to see him also killed? I don't know. Perhaps I shall find out. It is all part of the same story.

[Anna Sinclair]

FALLUJAH LONDON

Research into the background of my wife's family, the Hadmans, brought me up against an obscure wall on King's Cross Station. Anna's father reckoned that the Hadmans were related to the local poet John Clare of Helpston. Our investigation drew many previously unknown Hadmans from ground where they had lain, undisturbed, for hundreds of years. They were known to each other, some of them, but unknown to us: lives summarized by uncertain dates and incompetent transcriptions of that surname. Church records had been chewed by rats, inscriptions on gravestones erased by wind from the Fens. Most of the Hadmans never made it beyond a day's walk from their starting point, the now disappeared settlement of Washingley (on the ridge above Stilton). Two Hadmans, we discovered, did venture further afield. One, Oscar, booked passage for America. He registered his destination as 414 West First Street, Sioux Falls, South Dakota. Unfortunately, his third-class ticket was on the *Titanic*. The other, Hadman E., was recorded among the columns of the dead on the King's Cross War Memorial. Heroic efforts by Anna, trips to Kew, Clerkenwell, days trawling the internet, established a connection. Hadman E. was Ernest. From Stilton, Huntingdonshire. A railwayman in Peterborough, an 'Acting Porter', Ernest died on the Somme in 1917. He is listed on the Thiepval Memorial. There was indeed a remote kinship with Anna. Her great-great-grandfather and Ernest's great-grandfather were brothers. Enough to leave her in tears and to send her on an expedition to the station memorial that I had already visited and photographed. But I needed to come to terms with this episode in my own fashion: by walking a circuit of all the London mainline stations, checking on the visibility and continuing presence of the war dead. How does a preoccupied city remember them, the missing faces of a lost generation? How long do those memories survive the fret of contemporary life?

Stations and war: brass bands, flags, bunting, fumbled embraces. Refugee children with little boxes on strings around their necks. Smoke, steam. Whistles. Troop transports. Pinched faces seen through the slats of cattle trucks. The physical layout of city stations, part civic boast, part open-doored barn, creates a microclimate of suspended anxiety: the urge to fall asleep on an uncomfortable bench, to eat food you don't need, to purchase goods as a token sacrifice against the hazards of travel. Leaving an older self behind, rooted, watching as you walk away, involves an element of risk. Stations are non-denominational places of worship, staffed by pre-occupied disbelievers. The laws of time and space are different here. The narrator of H. G. Wells's *The War of the Worlds* (1898) strolls down to Woking Station to check the latest bulletins on the Martian invasion, news from elsewhere: the London evening papers, gossip with porters, rumours peddled by station casuals. Railway lines, out of the grander urban cathedrals – Victoria, Waterloo – seem to connect, directly, with apocalyptic killing fields. They trench through heavy clay to emerge in the shock of battle. The city shudders from the silent pounding of stone ordnance, the mute thunder of that life-size howitzer by Charles Sergeant Jagger on the Royal Artillery Memorial at Hyde Park Corner. Arranged on obelisks are squadrons of engineless planes that will never achieve flight. Granite battleships hide in alcoves. Ghost armies perch on temporary plinths in a psychosexual romance of heavy cloaks, gas masks, boots and belts. I think of Walter Owen's strange First War fantasy, *The Cross of Carl* (1931), in which Underground trains shunt still conscious corpses from the trenches to industrial units, death camps of the future, where they will be rendered into meat. Silver rails, out of the capital, double as telegraph wires. The hum of manipulated intelligence, into the provinces, country towns, brings noisy echoes of present conflicts. In a mood of communal hallucination, pals from choir or band or football club, labouring brothers, are induced to volunteer. They lay down the plough, the blacksmith's hammer, the slaughterman's knife. Intoxicated with blood-and-flag rhetoric, tales of atrocities committed by a bestial enemy, they willingly march off to alien killing fields. Dreams of posthumous glory. A memorial in the village church.

The First War inflicted still unappeased psychic damage on twentieth-century England: the shockwaves of Modernism, the fracturing of imperial pretension. News was unreadable. You could no longer trust official sources, far better to construct your own narrative from randomly chopped headlines varnished into Cubist paintings. T. S. Eliot's *Waste Land* zombies, flowing over London Bridge, eyes down, have very recently emerged from a railway station. The dead are scattered, unburied, unclaimed in France and Belgium. War memorials are not in place, not yet, to remind Eliot's city workers of what they have lost: fathers, brothers, sons. Memorials came into existence only because there were no bodies, railwaymen could never be returned to their stations. Publishing the pain, cataloguing the names (without vulgar forensic detail), was a necessary ritual of convalescence. Even memorials that now strike us as baroque, hysterical, were criticized, at their unveiling, for unnecessary realism. Death as death: so morbid.

So many.

So many railway workers; faces gone, heat lost. Surnames that are no longer heard: Asplen, Ellege, Ellener, Ellum, Elvidge, Fairminer, Gilderdale, Gladders, Hawnt, Kedges, Markillie, Povah, Rasberry, Shawsmith, Shimelda, Shroff, Smotheringale, Snoxell, Spendiff, Waldie, Waterworth, Wellawise. On the King's Cross panels, they are present, all of them, alongside Anna's distant cousin, Hadman E. The names are here because the dead men, who exchanged one uniform for another, are not. Individual bodies could not be reassembled, bones picked from the mud. 'The government of the time,' Peter Ashley wrote in his English Heritage booklet, *Lest We Forget* (2004), 'refused to acknowledge the concept of the repatriation of the dead, so these monuments became the focal points for grief.' The fallen of King's Cross are uniformly capitalized: a plain design, black on grey: like stone wallpaper for a morbidly themed restaurant. Memorials are small incidents of civic amnesia, a way of letting go. Publish a thing on a high wall and nobody sees it. I'd worked, at night, shifting sacks of Christmas mail, at Liverpool Street, King's Cross and St Pancras, but I had no focused picture of the war memorials, if there were any. A single day, 29 April 2004, would stitch the London termini together into a circuit of remembrance. Anna decided that she'd like to come with me, some of the way, until her interest or her energy flagged.

As I crunched my muesli, I watched a drama being enacted just outside the window; a magpie was driving its beak into the belly of a mouse, which was alive but helpless, turned on its back, legs pedalling. Anna was delighted: one less rodent to poison. Before I could call her to actually witness this savagery, the bird flew up to the shed roof, the better to enjoy its morsel. A passing squirrel startled it. The dying or dead mouse fell from its grip and rolled down the mildewed slope.

London anticipates disaster. And, in that fearful anticipation, incubates it. Visible tanks patrol the perimeter fence, signalling the boundaries of risk: Heathrow, Bluewater Shopping Centre. American service personnel, based in Suffolk, it is announced, will not be allowed to step inside the M25 orbital motorway. By asserting that future horrors are inevitable, politicians invite us to make an accommodation with present blight. Timid pressure groups call for more CCTV cameras: the better to witness the dreadful thing, after it has happened. By seven-thirty, on this April morning, cruise cars are loud on the streets, performing the fake alertness of the pre-election limbo, shaking down recidivists, invading crack dens that relocate before the snatch squad have the sacrificial dealer banged up, sniffling in the cells. A major disappearance is the railway bridge that once carried, along with promos for George Davis and Reggie Kray, passengers from Dalston Junction to Broad Street: a lovely aerial view of industry, canal, domestic and commercial property, Shoreditch to City. You saw, precisely, where you were. For a token fee (often no fee), you became a privileged spectator. Now grander plans are afoot and we have the block developments, the dust and noise and cancelled rights of way, to prove it. All that is left, raw stumps heritaging the memory of the bridge, is a set of pink, circular pillars, topped by flat pedestals on which nothing stands. The pillars have been customized by inelegant spray-can signatures, the aerosol equivalent of the dog's upraised leg.

From the canal – the deleted Gainsborough Film Studios (revamped with waterfall steps and angular apartments), faded trade signs on brick (designed to be read from passing barges or trains) – we emerge on the heights of Islington: that famous view down towards the crazy, bat-chewed spires of St Pancras. An example of architecture intended to be fabulous, but unworkable. Grey spikes on red brick. A thousand Gothic revival windows with a yellow hard-hat in every one of them. As far as this stylistic Babel, bedlam of novelty, is concerned, memory is firmly on the agenda: the destruction of it. There is a residual nostalgia for grunge, smack, crack, skunk, discarded rubbers, black-glassed massage parlours, Mao cartoon on high, begging bowls, flea-bitten dogs, muggers, shunters, fast-food banditry, snoop cameras optimizing car-fine revenue in the name of that corrupt god, ecology. The area stinks: of hair in hot fat, man-sweat, spastic movement. Of non-specific fear leaking out of surveillance monitors. The urban condition: suspension of reality. A thick Harry Potter filter between consumer and world. A multitude of travellers avoid touch and collision. They apologize. Or argue the toss with uniformed invaders of privacy. The whole mess is underwritten, yet again, by a notional futurology. The Radiant City that is still to come, Brussels-connected, Euro-buttered. And somewhere, behind all this, Antony Gormley has a factory-ashram dedicated to processing naked Gormley off-cuts. Which are required everywhere to validate oil-rich Cities of Culture: deserts, airports, highways, retail parks, museums and malls. Gormley is not a sculptor of consoling monuments, a grief technician healing trauma. He is a hands-on mystic, a philosopher of otherwise unconsidered spaces: roadside mounds, riverbank platforms. He works ahead of the next development. Challenged about the obsessive reproduction of his own body shell, he replies: 'I want to confront existence.'

*

We can't, for the moment, get at the memorial wall; a stacked trolley has been parked in front of it, brightly coloured bundles of today's giveaway publication. FREE LAUNCH ISSUE! A TV guide that morning commuters are unwilling to accept. Tourists, staggering under John Bunyan packs, are reluctant to add to their burdens, but they suspect that it might be compulsory. They take the magazine, sniff it, then bin it as soon as their benefactor has moved on. Rucksacks are SAS-issue, Bergens last seen on Falklands War footage: travel is a military operation, an endurance test. Most of tonight's television schedules, it appears, will be given over to the Hitler franchise. He may have lost the war, but he's walking away with the ratings. Two and a half hours of *Hitler in Colour*, followed by *Uncle Adolf* (a 'fact-based' drama focusing on the Führer's clammy relationship with his niece Geli Raubal). BBC2 is offering *The Nazis: A Warning from History*. Otherwise, it's all snooker. And repeats of *Dad's Army*.

The panels advertising the war dead are invisible to through-shuffling station users, clients of apathy. The false ceiling doesn't help. Nor the perch of CCTV cameras keeping eternal vigil on the queue for the hole-in-the-wall cash machine. Search the list for a lost relative and you are bang in the middle of the surveillance frame. Cameras are spiked like hedgehogs. Anybody withdrawing money, buying a railway ticket, is guilty. You are in the station's memory loop, on tape: part of the involuntary cinema of metropolitan life. This occulted corner is designed to be restless, to keep you moving. It bristles with the 'Security Awareness' notices that signify a contrary condition: the impossibility of free transit. Exhausted travellers spurn the memorial plaque: eleven columns with around eighty-six names in each.

The point of the conveniently located 'Information' kiosk is to soothe panic by establishing a small island of calm in an ocean of chaos. There are no porters. High boards, with mythical destinations, click and spin like fruit-machines. The nature of the information that the laminated informers are allowed to give out is a secret: they can't tell you what they don't know. And they don't know what they do tell you. They are conduits; relaying, to correctly delivered personal applications (in English), smooth and unflustered evasions. They offer therapy, analgesic reassurance, not hard facts.

'Fire?' said the man, affronted. 'What fire?' The woman, younger, knew something about it. 'Ask Wally,' she suggested. But we'd done that, sought out the station's longest-serving uniform, in our earlier quest for the placement of Hadman E. Don't trouble Wally again. His local knowledge is a badge of honour. The infamous Underground fire, from 1987, shames the place; bad times best forgotten. We slither down the ramp towards a labyrinth of subterranean corridors. 'There *was* a fire,' the woman shouts after us. 'The station burned to the ground.'

We find no trace of this still potent fable. Plasterboard panels disguise earlier walls. There is no obvious plaque, no memorial to that loss of life. But, as we emerge into daylight, into Euston Road, I spot a mature functionary, younger than Wally, a man standing very still. A rare official who knows exactly where he is, who he is, and what he should be doing: impersonating officialdom, lending a general air of authority to a nervous stairwell. The man explains: the memorial to the King's Cross disaster has been removed, put into store. Refurbishment. If we search hard enough we'll find an information poster: a memorial to the memorial. The fire, beneath the Piccadilly Line, on 18 November 1987, killed thirty-one people. The plaque has been taken to Acton, the London Transport Museum's Depot, where it can be viewed, by arrangement, on 'open weekends'. The fire memorial, we are promised, will be returned. 'It will be reinstated on completion of Project in a public area of the station.' And there is one thing more: 'We will employ experts to reinstate the name of Mr Alexander Fallon on the Plaque, previously identified as unnamed victim.'

Fires, rail crashes, bombs and blitzes: the mainline stations, unconsciously, have become our museums of melancholy. With the passage of time, monuments lose their original function, giving place to the honoured dead; they become street furniture, obstacles, curiosities. Decommissioned memorials are offered for sale, to private collectors, on the internet. Or they are removed to the National Memorial Arboretum in Staffordshire, a theme park of redundant symbols: lions, bears, eagles. There is even a ghostly white, blind-folded man that Peter Ashley thinks might be a late tribute to soldiers executed for walking away from the battle.

The next station, on our walk to the west, leaves us frustrated. The marzipan-and-betel-juice grandeur of St Pancras is impenetrable, ring-fenced, security guarded. You can visit the old station on Saturdays and Sundays at 11 a.m. and 1.30 p.m.: as a tourist. And of course I do. In recent times, the vast corridors, decaying public rooms and dramatic staircase have been a favoured set for fashion shoots and music promos. The Spice Girls were launched here and a dank basement was converted into an opium den for Johnny Depp in the film version of Alan Moore's *From Hell*. The war memorial remains off-limits while the conversion takes place that will magic the former servants' quarters into luxury apartments for the Manhattan Loft Corporation and the rest into a flagship Marriott Hotel. St Pancras is not about going anywhere, not now, it's about architecture; once admired, later despised, now restored. It's about the Channel Tunnel Rail Link: yet another grand project. 'The largest transport hub in Europe,' so the brochures tell us. The station was bombed in 1917, but the trains kept running. Our mistake, it is evident, is in living in the crease between the antiquated fog of a city that blundered along (privileges for the privileged) and a city that is promised, but which never quite arrives (leaves on the line).

If the old St Pancras is a stranded reef, the virtual, computer-generated bit is a rehearsal for what is coming when the monstrous makeover is completed, when the twin stations, eco-park, repos-itioned gas holder, hotels, canalside flats, make this 'one of Europe's most accessible locations'. Accessible to hype, fast money, Olympic dreams and every cell and splinter group of international terrorism. Because now the terrorists, like other businessmen and corporate foot-soldiers, bond at whitewater rafting sessions in North Wales, in convenient body-building gyms. For the moment, in this lethargy of future boasts and current frustrations, we join a straggle of flustered passengers carrying bags down a ditch between building sites. Red-and-white plastic barriers are like conceptual artworks moonlighting as blast-deflecting shields. Hurt buildings have been bandaged for elective cosmetic surgery. Wind puffs gauze like the last breath of a dying man, puffs red dust around our feet. There are no memorials on the temporary station. Present wars are unmentioned and old wars forgotten. A 'Security Policy Statement' promises full CCTV coverage of public areas and the 'physical security' of all plant and equipment.

Negotiating passage to Euston, the last of the Euston Road triad, a Sickert among stations, we inspect the steroidal and broken-backed Blakean geometer by Eduardo Paolozzi, on his plinth in front of the British Library, in the pertinent shadow of the Novotel. Naked Newton (sponsored by Vernons football pools) is the true architect of this warped vision. Here indeed is a proper symbol for the corporate city, Blake's Jerusalem reimagined by a committee determined to cover every cultural shift and marker. The giant's compasses make their terrible calculations in the dirt of building works. In his prophetic poem *Europe*, Blake writes that it is the 'mighty Spirit . . . from the land of Albion, nam'd Newton' who alone has the power to sound 'the Trump of the last doom'.

The courtyard of the British Library is like a grazing ground for muggers: dozens of harmless and woolly academics, waiting to be let in, clutch very obvious laptops, software in soft bags. They have adapted to the concept of the forum, the civic space dressed with its sculptural prompts. They sit where they can, on low walls, on the curved stone benches of a bijou amphitheatre dressed by eight Gormley rocks: *The Planets*. The Gormley zone validates the development, a cultural imprimatur: serenity, medieval cosmology making its treaty with contemporary physics. Planets as humours, as our guides and mentors. Human dust led to acknowledge its own mortality, the infinite spaces within the smallest cells of our bodies.

Body parts are pressed into Gormley's cannon balls, his rocks on plinths; arms, legs, hands. The eight stones are like calcified lumps recovered from the ashes of Pompeii or Herculaneum. Living traces printed into basalt.

Beside the amphitheatre is a box hedge, in which is contained a gold-red tree, a Japanese Acer; a tree of sharp-edged coins. You can't approach the tree through the maze of the tightly clipped hedge; it is closed off, solitary. This tree has its plaque, it is a living memorial, planted on 12 June 1998: 'To commemorate Anne Frank and all the children killed in wars and conflicts this century.' The plaque quotes from Frank's diary, the entry for 15 July 1944. 'I see the world being slowly transformed into a wilderness, I hear the approaching thunder that, one day, will destroy me too.'

At which point, going back over the account of the war memorial walk, what was found at Euston, Marylebone, Paddington, Victoria, Charing Cross, Waterloo, London Bridge, Liverpool Street, my pedestrian anecdotes became suddenly redundant, overtaken by the events of 7 July, the four London bombs. With four more to follow, exactly two weeks later. Explosions seemingly orchestrated by Newton's compasses: north, south, east, west. The numerology, contemplated in this setting, alongside Gormley's *Planets*, was disturbing. The original expedition, recording the names of dead railwaymen, the erasures, was an hallucination, a sleepwalker's fugue in the lull before the attacks on London that would use King's Cross as the trigger for a malignant chain reaction.

By 14 July, transport was moving, the No. 30 bus trundled up the hill from King's Cross as I walked down, once again, to the station. There were more pedestrians, certainly, more rucksacks, but bus passengers were as stoic, preoccupied, chemically adapted as ever. They waited impatiently for the new Harry Potter to blot out the view from the window, a comforting lump in the hand, a weapon. Potter makes use of Platform 9¾ at King's Cross. Trainee magicians have to learn how to pass through the solid barriers between platforms 9 and 10. They are capable, I suppose, of circumventing surveillance systems. The invisibles of the city do not appear on CCTV until they are dead, until it is all over and a suitable fiction of the past is being edited by politicians and judiciary.

The normal queue of transients, many being ostentatiously frisked by dozens of yellow-jacket police, by station security in gooseberry-custard tabards, was infinitely extended by mourners. They waited patiently, with plastic water and floral tributes, for their turn in the small, spontaneous garden of remembrance which had established itself around a tree, in a fenced-off corner of the station frontage, between Euston Road and York Way. This multi-faith shrine, despite the sombre aspect of the witnesses, felt Mexican; a mass of conflicting colours, adapted football shirts, written-over flags, pink bears, white dogs. Sunlight dazzled on cellophane. The trunk of the sturdy whitebeam disappeared into a mound of banked flowers. A woman in a Red Cross uniform stood beside the tree with a Kleenex box held discreetly behind her back. At the point of entry, further boxes of Twin Ply tissues were stacked, ready to cope with an outpouring of confused emotion. An unnoticed accident of railway architecture, a suitable nowhere, was the sanctioned memory site, a cloister of mummified flowers. The death of Princess Diana was the template for public grief in the city. A fence, protecting a royal palace, buried in carnations, lilies, roses, professionally pack-aged, or lavender bunches picked from private gardens. Now this generally off-limits walkway was the focus for ranks of cameras, which were forbidden access, held back; interviewers interviewing each other, talking to the police, yawning and waiting. The faces of the missing, some serially reproduced, fly-pitched plasterboard, the glass partitions of bus stops. In phone boxes, portraits of the van-ished competed with cards for prostitutes. Some were slick laptop productions, others as crude as punk-era fanzines. 'Can You Help?' One sad triptych of video-grab memories, highlights in a lost life, displaced the tattered flyer for the now forgotten tsunami disaster.

Shortly before midday, I return to the plaza of the British Library. A gang of men, shirtless, loudly tattooed, uttering very audible obscenities, are playing pitch-and-toss in the Gormley amphitheatre. It lends itself very well to this activity. Nervous tourists steer around the sunken pit and make for the open-air café. But then, quite unexpectedly, as the two-minute silence is announced, the gamesters freeze and draw themselves up as if on parade. The tourists, bemused, are caught mid-stride, in groups, couples, moving across the courtyard. They are Lowry figures, black against the dominant red brick, the chequerboard squares. London is unused to such silence, no squad-car sirens, ambulances, drills; the Euston Road in gridlock stasis without the undertow of frustration and peevishness, phone-babble, honking. The stillness of something sucked from the atmosphere, a breath taken and held. Two minutes, then, is a long, necessary time: in which to experience Gormley's projection of the emptiness of our bodies, the difficult mechanism of standing firm on a piece of moving ground.

This seemed, before I made my way to the canal and home to Hackney, a day to circumnavigate the Channel Tunnel Rail Link building site, the flattened and protected acres around the stations. Familiar loops at the back of King's Cross and St Pancras have been off-limits for years, only glimpses from the elevated North London Line give a sense of the progress of this immense work of civil engineering. Rookeries such as Somers Town have long ago vanished. The dust heaps are an urban memory invoked by fresh piles of rubble, giant cranes. Marooned and disregarded, at the secret centre of all this activity, stands St Pancras Old Church, on its mound above the now submerged and piped Fleet River. The developers and consortiums and quangos associated with the grand scheme held many private and semi-public meetings, discussions, presentations. They were careful not to appear as earth-rippers, mindless exploiters of the fabric of the city. Every new block had its eco-park shadow, every piracy an artist in residence. The poet most deeply implicated in the visionary geography of King's Cross was Aidan Dun. His long-meditated cycle, *Vale Royal*, was published in a handsome, limited edition in 1995. Dun was invited, and indeed paid, to address the developers. 'King's Cross,' he pronounced, 'has exerted a magnetic attraction down the centuries. The artists, the poets have made this forgotten place royal with their presence.'

Given Dun's poetic manifesto, based on a reading of Blake, an interpretation of the pattern of hills and rivers, the events of 7 July can be seen as the inevitable consequence of our refusal to remember, our communal amnesia. Blake's city of gold, its pillars aligned with the specifics of London topography, has been wilfully ignored or set aside. The legends of Chatterton and Rimbaud, of Shelley, their association with old St Pancras, are forgotten. Dun recognizes that pastoral invocations of Fleet River, swimmers, cattle, fishermen, are no more than nostalgic engravings hung on the locked church in the teeth of the coming storm. 'The bitter-sweet stench of the combustion of child-flesh/ floats through London streets.' He sees a repeated pattern of sacrifice deriving from our refusal to recognize the originating myths of this spurned site. 'The poisoned flower of a military necropolis,/ with perfumes of sulphur.'

The church on its mound now appears as a slightly embarrassed pensioner, hovering at the outer limits of the development zone. A protective wall of green has been erected by the Channel Tunnel Rail Link operatives, who also provide a '24-hour helpline', along with a skirting of that ubiquitous red-and-white plastic: more blast-deflecting shields. A protected but half-hidden enclave, shady and attractive to picnicking urban transients. I'm drawn in – as I was, frequently, in the days when I worked as a railway postman. I gained access to the church interior for the first time on 16 May 1973. I made a note of the fact, my viewing of St Augustine's sixth-century stone under the altar cloth, the pattern of plain crosses. 'The church,' I wrote, 'is part of that northern rail. It drinks from ancient Christian sources.' A week after the first bombs, I have come back, by chance, at the one hour when the doors are again open. Incense, taped chanting, dim light: a young woman kneeling, absolutely still, beside the rack of burning candles. She is Czech and leaves, as I notice in the visitors' book, a message about how she finds consolation here. Private rituals are enacted with none of the drama of the King's Cross shrine: the flowers, shirt-offerings, colours. The church is stone and sand, everything bleached and smoky. Two men march in together. One, smart in a striped shirt, buys his candle, drops to his knees, makes his gestures, leaves. The other, filthy, tattered, angry, borrows the price of his candle, slumps, drops his head, staying in place for a few moments before reeling out. In the Parish Room, he kicks against the door of the toilet. The walls of the church are dressed with engravings, watercolours: Old St Pancras as it never was. The most unexpected icon is a photograph of the Beatles, posed in the frame of the west door; Ringo, George and Paul lounging against the toothed Norman arch, while John lurches at the camera, his raised fist a blur. It's my belief that this shot, a frozen frame, derives from a session with the war photographer Don McCullin on 28 July 1968. It is referred to in the reference books as the 'Mad Day'. The posthumous troop moved on a strange, random trawl across London, a version of the dictated geography of Aidan Dun or William Blake. St Pancras Old Church to Old Street Roundabout to Farringdon Road to Wapping Old Stairs: where Lennon lay on the ground and played dead.

St Pancras was a child martyr who gave his name to numerous churches, a hospital, a railway station. He is pictured on a wall-hanging in the Sacrament House of the Old Church (from which the Tabernacle was stolen in 1985). In his left hand he holds a Byzantine cross, an extension of the tau cross. It is hard not to recall the theory, suggested by various commentators, that the 7 July bombings (and indeed the second wave of 21 July) were intended to mark out a specific pattern on the skin of London. An Islamist website exulted in this symbol of the 'burning cross' – with King's Cross railway station as the pivot, the gathering point from which the bombers would embark on their deadly missions. A failure on the Northern Line Underground service spoiled the conceit.

A green-shirted, ponytailed gardener, spotting me looking at the faded gravestone tribute to 'one of the few Persons who came out of the Black Hole at Calcutta', gives me the full tour: John Soane, William Godwin and Mary Wollstonecraft, the Hardy tree. Building work now, as at the time of the laying out of the railway, is causing havoc at the burial ground. Tombs are splitting, monuments tilting drunkenly, holes appearing in the earth. You could, stepping carelessly, tumble into a vault. The fabric of the city cannot be shaken, bored into, trenched, day after day, without cost. It is not always as banal as a Tesco Superstore collapsing into a cut-and-cover railway tunnel. London, in its totality, is deafened, red-eyed, traumatized. Making the best of it. We are telling our stories to the camera as to a sanctioned confessor. Victims replay horrifying incidents as a form of video exorcism. Accused men are watched and recorded by instruments designed to make no moral judgement. The city is paralysed while contrary fictions struggle for credibility.

Back on the canal, returning home, there are more walkers than ever, more bicycles. Nothing disturbs London's sense of the absurd: an entirely naked black man exercises on a bench, stretching, bending, grunting, as he looks across the water at the unresolved development zone, the eco garden and the cranes. Beside him, a middle-aged woman sits eating her sandwiches, ignoring the sweating man, folding down the corners of her penultimate Harry Potter into neat, finger-licked triangles. As I approach Hackney, I record a black newly stencilled slogan: FALLUJAH LONDON. BOMBS = BOMBS.

It wasn't easy, but I persisted, I had to see the King's Cross fire memorial in the London Transport Museum's Depot at Acton. The functionaries at this hangar were pleasant, helpful but somehow damaged: like combatants removed from the front line. 'My back,' said the milky-eyed man who led us to the aisle where the two memorial tablets were stored. The depot is an Ikea warehouse of transport memorabilia, docketed, wrapped and hidden away. The storeman fetched a stool so that I could photograph the slate panels with their thirty-one deaths. Andy Burdett, BA (Hons), Jane A. Fairey, BA (Hons): academic distinctions added to the scroll of capitalized names and initials. Mohammed Shoiab Khan, Rai Singh, Ivan Tarassenko. The lettering is plain; the memorial, funded by the King's Cross Disaster Fund, is protected under layers of plastic sheeting. The slabs will stay in this quiet place, this store, until present developments at the station are complete.

The depot is uncanny. We are free to wander, free to examine whatever takes our fancy among the shrouded and unwitnessed exhibits, the preserved fragments of an earlier London. There are bucolic, Metroland lithographs by Lawrence Bradshaw and John Mansbridge. A black-and-white photograph of passengers on the upper deck of a bus: all white, women with tightly permed hair, men with white shirts and ties, no luggage, no burdens. Another era, so remote and self-contained: an interlude between wars. Then there is an extraordinary device like an up-ended torpedo with a door in its side. This grey metallic husk is a bomb-shelter for one or two persons, members of staff only. The shelters were kept at 'vulnerable sites', so that railwaymen could enjoy the experience of being buried alive: a double coffin with a flap that should open from the inside.

Deep-red buses gleam, their windows shine. Immaculate antiques like the 236 to Leyton High Road, by way of Highbury Barn, Queensbridge Road, Hackney Wick. London Transport is perfected at last: it doesn't go anywhere. The horrors of a collapsing system, the nightmare journey to reach here from Dalston-Kingsland, is refuted by this citadel of wonders. We stroll down empty Underground platforms, a cinema of exemplary objects and no script. J. G. Ballard, in an essay on the director Michael Powell, suggested that drama in the 'serious' novel of the future would 'migrate from the characters' heads to the world around them'. No interior monologues, no social satire: meaningless and cruel happenings reported without emotion. He seems to predict the steady stare of the full-face snapshots on the 'Missing' posters, the soft-focused video-pulls of suspects, running, stumbling, ducking: in movement. Footage stitched together from mobile-phone improvisations. Home movies of hostage executions downloaded from the internet. First you notice the camera on the rooftop and then the bomb goes off. The new fiction of the city is edited from unauthored fragments, while the self-serving fantasies of politicians are left to decay in obscure sheds and sponsored warehouses. Down these virtual platforms, we stroll past the Crossrail prototype, past clean, cool trains that will never leave their moorings. And then Anna, who dislikes Underground travel, notices that the sliding doors to one of the compartments are open. She hesitates, steps inside. She's not alone. Others have preceded her. Dummies. The dead-in-life. Figures used to test bomb blasts: they are dressed, posed, cryogenically frozen. Among all of these stalled trains, in the silence of the vast hangar with its rounded roof, these are the only passengers, waiting patiently for doors that will never close. Summer dresses, accurate in every fold and pleat, in colour and flowered-texture, are made from plaster. Hair is too luxuriant. The vamp at the door, standing, even when there are plenty of free seats, is scarlet-mouthed. Eyes like a cat. A soldier sits, trying to make sense of a map of the Underground system. A woman, grinning hideously, points at the floor. Another autistic smiler, open-necked shirt, grey suit, reads a Festival of Britain brochure. A real Londoner, on the razzle, splash of American tie, combs dead hair. They are, in the low light, more than realistic, but there has been a miscalculation with their feet: they don't reach the ground. And here they remain, before the show begins or after it is finished, the ultimate audience. The ones who sit and smile, without memory, or time, or words. The ones who have no obligation to make sense of the city that contains them.

[I. S.]

LAST TRAIN

See them coming out of Soho, Old Compton Street, Covent Garden: accountants, copy-editors, junior executives, waitresses, heads of development. See them helping their wounded, arms around shoulders, laughing lurching singing. China Town, Five Corners, St Martin's Lane. Glassy-eyed, burbling. From pubs and wine bars, unimaginable dives: systems analysts, programmers, designers, nurses, manicurists, dental assistants, floor managers. From cinemas theatres street corners. Leicester Square, Trafalgar Square, the Strand.

To Charing Cross.

See them converging on automatic turnstiles held open, piling into waiting carriages, finding and losing each other, calling out to friends, spilling coffee from plastic cups, staring blearily at their mobile phones. Ecstasy cocaine cannabis nicotine alcohol anti-depressants magic mushrooms uppers downers Red Bull. A couple draped, intertwined: exchanging spit. Ketamine horse tranquillizer kicking in. Wedged eyelids.

THE TRAIN TO HASTINGS IS CALLING AT WATERLOO EAST LONDON BRIDGE ORPINGTON SEVENOAKS HILDENBOROUGH PLEASE STAND CLEAR OF THE DOORS

Slam slam slam slam. Slam slam. Slam. 'I like the Eye.' 'You fucking don't.' 'I fucking do.' 'Fuck the Eye.'

THIS IS TONBRIDGE THE NEXT STATION IS HIGH BROOMS PLEASE STAND CLEAR OF THE DOORS

'See what she done?!' 'Serves you fucking right mate!' 'Mind the fucking ketchup.' Slam slam. Slam.

THIS IS TUNBRIDGE WELLS THE NEXT STATION IS FRANT PLEASE STAND CLEAR OF THE DOORS

They've gone, the live ones. The young bucks have rolled off, away. Still looking about, sniffing the night.

See them staring blankly, straight-backed sentinels, the left behind. The middle-aged on limited incomes who haven't been to clubs, not tonight, not ever. Retired airline pilots. School teachers. Doctors dentists solicitors. Theatregoers still flinching from the bright lights. An old man stretches, snores: necklace of pearly snot decorating the table.

THIS IS WADHURST THE NEXT STATION IS STONEGATE PLEASE STAND CLEAR OF THE DOORS

Slam. Slam. Slam. Faster greyer: emptier. *Downward to darkness on extended wings.* The journey gets older, poorer. 'Tickets please!' 'What have you done with your life, sir?' 'Fuck you!'

They avoid each other, the downwardly mobile. Last one off the train's the biggest failure. It's you or him, that Old Tosser sleeping stiffly in the corner. A ringer for Dublin's Judge Kelly – with his baggy pants and bloodshot eyes, loitering around the toilets between Players Theatre and the Main Gate. His bladder range was limited. Rumoured to have been a High Court judge until one day he sentenced a student to death for riding a bicycle without lights.

THIS IS ETCHINGHAM THE NEXT STATION IS ROBERTSBRIDGE PLEASE STAND CLEAR OF THE DOORS

See the Old Tosser rouse himself, totter on to the empty platform. Papers. Bags. Stink of pee. Scruffy shoes. Nobody left in the world. Russian roulette of the ghost train.

THIS IS BATTLE THE NEXT STATION IS CROWHURST PLEASE STAND CLEAR OF THE DOORS

Silence. Nobody to get off. Nobody left to bear witness. To see the face reflected in the night window; hollow, hooded eyes. Through whose shadowed half-head escarpments of unseen forest go sliding by. Beyond whose blind sockets spark distant stars and galaxies. *Mother, do the train thing please. First, up the hill. I wish I could I wish I could I wish I could I wish I could.*

Ecstasy cocaine cannabis alcohol heroin. I wish. Imagine. The big one. Ketamine.

Now nearly at the top, slower. I think I can I think I can I think I can I think I can.

It happens when it happens. Does it really matter where? Isn't here as good a place as any?

Down again. Really fast! I knew I could I knew I cou –

THIS STATION IS ST LEONARDS WARRIOR SQUARE THE NEXT STATION IS HASTINGS PLEASE STAND CLEAR OF THE DOORS

Slam.

[Ranald Graham]

EDGE-LANDS

RACIST SPARROWS

Wednesday, 23 March 2005

It's the middle of Holy Week. Three days ago Jesus rode into Jerusalem on his donkey. The day after tomorrow they will be nailing him to his cross. Today the table is being booked for the Last Supper, and I'm standing in a field pulling up a broad bean plant, putting it into a plastic bag and putting the bag into my jacket pocket.

The remit for this piece was vague but simple: did I want to write about things in London disappearing?

'How many words?'

'However many you want.'

'OK. When do you need it for?'

I can't remember the answer to that but today I'm attempting to fulfil my side of the deal.

The trouble is, I don't really give a shit about London. Never lived there. Wouldn't mind if the whole lot disappeared in front of my eyes and we were left with a huge wild forest at the heart of south-east England with red squirrels leaping from tree to tree, clean-running chalk streams, wild deer roaming the glades – all that sort of stuff. And I certainly wouldn't mind if it was this that I would be strolling through for the next couple of days, after I get myself out of this bean field, instead of trudging over very ungolden pavements for the next however many hours it's going to take me.

For that's what I'm going to be doing. All my life it has been 'if in doubt, go for a walk'. The bigger the doubt, the bigger the walk. At some point I started to try to justify these walks, aggrandize them, anoint them with meaning, when in fact they are just me getting out of the house away from any number of responsibilities, to give myself time to mull things over. Then there is my fixation with maps. It was when I was a teenager that I started to draw lines across them and follow the lines on foot. Sometimes the line went around in a circle, sometimes they squiggled and sometimes they were just regular straight ones. I have written about this bent at length elsewhere. The line that I am going to be following for the next couple of days is a straight one, across London from north to south, passing through Charing Cross Station at the Queen Eleanor Cross.

At school we were taught something about Queen Eleanor's crosses. She was the wife of one of England's medieval kings and when she died, somewhere up-country, she was taken to London to be buried. After she was buried the king commissioned these elaborate monuments to be sculpted and positioned at the various points along the route where her body had lain for the night. One of these places was called Brigstock in Northamptonshire. This village was only a few miles from Corby, where I spent my secondary school years. I used to pass this Queen Eleanor Cross when I took the bus to Kettering. It held a romantic place in my imagination.

The teacher also told us that the last Queen Eleanor's Cross is outside Charing Cross Station and that this point is considered to be the centre of London, rather than Buckingham Palace or Westminster or Piccadilly Circus or any of the other more famous landmarks. It was one of those useless facts that has stayed with me down through the decades when all the ones that would have come in handy have departed my memory.

Yesterday I tried to buy the two Land Ranger Ordnance Survey maps that cover London. The shop I was in had only one of them, Sheet 177, which covers East London. Luckily for me, Charing Cross Station just made it on to the page, about a quarter of an inch from the left-hand edge. I got my rule out and drew a line which followed the longitude that would cut through Charing Cross.

I'm standing on that line in this bean field, right now. It's the line that I'm going to follow on my feet for the next couple of days. What I imagine I will be doing with this walk across London is slicing the capital in two. Symbolically speaking, anyway. Like slicing an apple or an onion in two so you can see the inside. That way I can have a better look at it. See what's rotting, see how far the worm has got, count its rings and thoroughly mix my fruit and vegetable metaphors before I reach the end of this paragraph.

The idea was that I would start my walk in the first bit of proper open country at the top of London. And when I say open country I don't mean parkland or golf courses and definitely not paddocks used by riding stables. Proper open country that farmers use to make a living growing crops or with sheep or cows in. Proper farmers who hate people from towns 'cause they don't understand their ways. Farmers who support the Countryside Alliance and all that sort of stuff.

As for the disappearing London bit, I didn't have a clue. So I asked friend, colleague and film-maker Gimpo to come along with me with his camera. Among other things Gimpo is a good walking companion and we both need to get in shape for our forthcoming walk across Iceland.

I had this half-baked idea that on our walk south across London Gimpo would film cars, buses, taxis, lorries, motorbikes, rickshaws and any other form of transport driving around corners. Then we would have a short film of vehicles disappearing from view, one after the other from the top of London to the bottom. I can't say that the idea for this film fills me with any sort of great creative enthusiasm. It's not something that is going to set a new benchmark in the art-film genre, let alone change the face of art history, but it's what we are going to do.

Gimpo gets out his camera and takes a 180-degree shot of the rural landscape to the north of where we are standing. Then we head for the barbed-wire fence and hedge we clambered over earlier.

Ten minutes later we are well into our stride down the pre-war suburban streets of an area of London my map reliably informs me is called Oakwood. It's Janet and John country. I could get cynical about these streets and all they represent: a white, safe, backward-looking England. But I won't because there are golden daffodils everywhere trumpeting the coming of spring, cherry blossom is already out, the streets are empty of people and moving vehicles. Gimpo and I stride on down the middle of this, following my detailed and meticulously planned route down the hill and up into Southgate. All virgin territory as far as I'm concerned. Down the hill towards Broomfield Park, up Powys Lane and Brownlow Road to Bounds Green tube station, then on to Bounds Green Road.

That's where I'm standing now, staring at the pavement. It's not flagstones but tarmacadam. I'm staring at all the ring-pulls from cans of drink which have become embedded into it. Dozens of them. I take a few more paces. No, it's hundreds of them. I've always enjoyed the patina of spat-out chewing gum that decorates our pavements, but this is the first time I've seen a similar pattern created by ring-pulls. Then it hits me. Not only do I not give a fuck about disappearing London, I'm interested only in what I haven't seen before, the new things, what's going to happen next, what's appearing now. And what's appearing now is ring-pulls embedded in the pavement. I look up. Above is a horse chestnut, its large sticky buds are within a week of bursting. Within a few weeks their candles will all be out on display. I don't give a shit about the past, not now spring is here anyway. All that seeking out the traces of what's gone before. Give me the new, the this year, the way it's gonna be. I was going to say the new order but that smacks of Germany in the late 1930s and that's the past.

I don't let on to Gimpo how I'm feeling. He's diligently filming every car that is disappearing around a corner as we tack our way south across the map.

We keep going. Alexandra Palace looms then disappears, then Wood Green where Turnaround Books who distribute a good chunk of the underground and suspect books in the country is based. We pass a school where Gimpo reckons his girlfriend teaches. It might pep this text up if I could be documenting some banter between the two of us. Stuff that might make you smirk, even disgust you. But no, Gimpo and I trudge on mainly in silence. This is partly because Gimpo is still in recovery from his annual 25-hour

M25 spin and all the attendant intake of stimulants which goes with this pilgrimage of his to nowhere.

More and more celandines and dandelions. They are now beaming their golden smiles at me from the most trashed and unkempt gardens. That's what I like about spring, however much we trash things, you just can't stop it. Mind you, there are not that many birds about. I'm sure you've heard on the radio or read in your newspapers about the dwindling sparrow population. In the couple of hours that have passed from standing in that bean field to lurching down Middle Lane into Crouch End, I've not heard the friendly chirrup of a single sparrow.

We are getting into familiar territory. I know these streets well. Crouch End looks very desirable to the upwardly mobile arty type who wants to hold on to something of their supposed bohemian roots. We nearly moved here ourselves a few years back but the house sale fell through.

Gimpo and I stop off at a café to rest our legs and quench our thirsts. It's all laptops and shaved heads. This may not be the quintessential suburbia of Oakwood where we started but it's suburbia still, with affectations of hipness.

I want to carry out a survey of the other clients of this café. I want to ask them what they think is disappearing from London right now, what is disappearing this very moment as we sip our espressos and freshly squeezed orange juices. Not what has disappeared since their childhood. That would be too easy, all that eel pie shop sense of community stuff. Is there a sparrow out there in a Crouch End garden thinking 'Fuck it! I've had enough with all the wogs and Pakis. I'm moving to Milton Keynes.' Are sparrows racist? Am I allowed to use words like 'wogs' or 'Pakis' in a book like this?

The trouble is I've not got the front to carry out my survey and I'm more concerned with a blister coming up on the heel of my right foot. Gimpo sups the dregs of his coffee granules, I drain my freshly squeezed orange juice and we head back out. To carry on with our mission to slice London in two.

Up and over Crouch Hill we get our first panoramic view of London. The day is a good one for walking, dry with a light breeze. But there is a hint of mist in the air which stops the panoramic view from delivering all that it could do on a clear day. The only major landmark that we can make out is the Gherkin. I don't know what I feel about this building. Theoretically I should love it. It's new, it's of a design I've never seen before. But something stops me wanting to embrace it in the way I've instinctively embraced all Modernist architecture since I first saw a documentary on TV in the mid 1960s about Brasilia. I suppose some building or other must have been made to disappear to make way for the Gherkin. I have always had an urge to flatten whatever house I have been living in and build a Modernist eyesore in its place, the more glass the better. I can't believe I have ended up living in a timber-framed house that was built in the 1500s.

Just noticed that while we are surveying the city spread out before us we are standing on a railway bridge. I love to look over railway bridges at the lines below. We all do, don't we? Even if we don't want to lob bricks over the side into the windshields of oncoming trains. I look over. No oncoming train, no glistening lines, no rail lines whatsoever. It's all overgrown, brambles, feral sycamores and a path where once the glistening track was. They must have disappeared when Beeching did his thing. I check the map: this is the Parkland Walk. I wonder if there are any racist sparrows down there planning to move to Milton Keynes. In the mid 1980s I briefly worked with a rock band who came from the far east end, the bit that's over the border in Essex. They and their families felt the need to keep moving further and further out of London to stay clear of the onward march of those who are not us. I never had what it took to confront their blatant racism. Mind you, it is always so much easier to be aware of racism in others than what you have got knocking around in your own head. Is racism hardwired? A survival instinct or just a learned thing? Do Darwin or his finches know the answer to these questions? They were a great band. They never made it.

We move on down into Upper Holloway, edge around Tufnell Park, into Holloway proper and past the prison down into Kentish Town. This is all proper urban multicultural stuff, proper London. Graffiti, bendy buses, marauding gangs of school kids, Asian-owned mini-markets with a few hundredweight of fresh fruit and vegetables all polished and stacked up in boxes outside the shop front, bill-boards for mobile-phone network providers, discarded B&H cartons and empty Sunny Delight bottles roaming free. This is the way inner cities should be. Sod what they were like when you were a kid, this is the way they are today. And I like it. But that's easy for me to say, I've never lived the inner-city multicultural thing. I've only lived in (almost) all-white communities. Even in Liverpool it was all white, unreconstructed working class as far as the eye could see. It's easy for me to be a left-leaning liberal when I've never had to watch where I live completely and utterly change culturally within my own lifetime. To feel everything I hold true slip away for ever. Easy for me to say 'Well, we live in a country that grew rich out of going wherever the fuck we wanted in the world not giving a toss for the native cultures as long as they learned English, read the Bible and bought our stuff.' We were the biggest drug dealers in the world, literally peddling opium to the masses in China and we freak out about so-called Yardie gangs, with their drive-by shootings, their attitude and their drum-and-bass music, coming over from Jamaica selling crack cocaine on our streets to our kids. It's all easy for me to say when I am now living in a leafy suburb of Norwich. Norwich? You don't get more fucking radical than Norwich.

Have you noticed that since I have been tramping along the inner-city streets my language is getting more out of control?

Down York Way, but it's blocked off for major roadworks. Gimpo knows a detour. A desolate 1970s estate, then over a foot-bridge over the main lines into St Pancras. We are now on the edge of Agar Grove Estate, which is primarily made up of three tower blocks. Gimpo used to live in one of them, and it's where his daughter and ex-partner still live, but they are away so we don't get the lift and knock on their door for a cup of tea.

Down Camley Street. Under another rail bridge. Hundreds of thousands have been spent doing up this bridge, not strengthening it, or widening it, or anything practical like that but just tarting up all the Victorian brickwork. All part of the millions that are being pumped into the King's Cross area. Past the locked gates of an inner-city wildlife sanctuary. My mind is going, I'm beginning to lose it. I keep forgetting where I am and where I'm going and what I'm doing. Is this what begins to happen as you get older? We have been pounding the pavements non-stop now for three and a half hours. That is apart from the ten minutes in the café in Crouch End.

Gimpo is trying to engage me in conversation about how the King's Cross gas works have been lovingly dismantled and neatly stacked up, every Victorian nut and bolt of them ready to be reconstructed.

Then he goes on about all the rebuilding of St Pancras for the EuroStar. I try to take in what he is saying. I look up and nod. This is how my mum must feel. She had a stroke about four years ago and when you talk to her you see her struggling to make sense of what you are saying. Is the pavement pounding knocking out thousands of brain cells with each step? Maybe that is what is disappearing in London – my sanity.

We are now squeezed in between the two mighty stations of King's Cross and St Pancras and we are being met by a flood of commuters. All of them dressed in black suits, black jackets, black dresses, black skirts, black shoes, black socks. Black, black, black. Except their faces; most of them are white. We are swimming against the tide of them and their blackness.

'Where are they going, Gimpo?'

'Home, Bill.'

'But why this way?'

He explains something about the entrance to St Pancras being changed because of all the building work.

We somehow cross Euston Road. I remember to look the right way and not get run over. Down Judd Street and into Bloomsbury. My sanity is returning with the calm that Bloomsbury always seems

to exude with its Georgian squares and University of London buildings. Past the front of the British Museum where there used to be
a magic shop that I loved going into as a kid on the occasional
family visit to London. That's long disappeared. Maybe that's it.
The magic of London has disappeared.

Gimpo has been diligently filming every car, cab, bus and bike
which has been disappearing around corners. The problem for him
is that with every one of these disappearances at least two other
vehicles come into frame when what we had been hoping for was a
nice empty frame.

Maybe I should read something into this, something about what
appears is always more . . . No, fuck it! I won't try to read anything
into anything. I will just keep walking.

Out of the peace and quiet of Bloomsbury, across New Oxford
Street, a few yards down Shaftesbury Avenue and into Monmouth
Street and St Martin's Lane. The lights are on, bars are full, res-
taurants filling up, theatres open for business. All around us are
people with lives and friends and things to do and talk about. Shiny
faces laughing and smiling, getting rounds in, having a laugh, having
a life. I can feel the madness creep up on me again. Where's Gimpo?
I'm lost, I'm sinking. My feet keep going. Keep striding. Keep
wading through the people. St Martin-in-the-Fields. Horatio
Nelson. Where the fuck is that Queen Eleanor's Cross? Have I
made the whole thing up? Turn into the Strand. Cross the road
to Charing Cross Station. That must be it, standing behind the
wrought-iron fencing. Between the two gates, where the taxis go in
and the taxis go out. The top half is covered in netting to stop the
pigeons shitting all over it. It is all grimy and sooty. I walk around
it. There is no notice or placard or anything telling us what it is or
why it is here. Nothing to say that I am now standing at the very
epicentre of this city, once the greatest city in all the world. All
around me hundreds, thousands, millions of people getting on with
. . . no, positively rushing through their lives, and I'm just standing
right here in the centre of it all.

Where's Gimpo? There he is. He is trying to film taxis as they disappear out of the gate at the other side of the cross. I sit down on the ground, my back against the cross, and stare up into the sky. Still no sparrows.

The plan had been for us to bring sleeping bags and sleep down under the arches by Embankment tube station, where all the homeless used to sleep. Then we would carry on with the second half of this London Slicing In Two walk in the morning, but family commitments mean I have to get the train back to Norwich tonight and we will finish the walk the day after tomorrow. That's Good Friday. I wonder if Judas has done his deal yet.

Gimpo and I disappear down into the tube station.

Thursday, 24 March 2005

Can hardly climb out of bed. Legs stiffer than ever in lifetime. Signs of ageing multiply by the day. Put 'Queen Eleanor's Cross' and 'Charing Cross' into Google and get '1–10 of possible 20'. I click on the second one, www.rodcorp.typepad.com, and up comes the information.

At the exact centre of London on the site now occupied by the statue of King Charles was erected the original Queen Eleanor's Cross, a replica of which now stands in front of Charing Cross Station. Mileages from London are measured from the site of the original cross.

When Queen Eleanor of Castile died in 1290, Edward I commissioned 12 crosses, each sited at one of the stopping places her burial procession passed from Lincoln to Westminster. The original cross was replaced, then demolished (the stone was reused to make paving along Whitehall) and in 1863 a rather ornate version was put up in front of Charing Cross Station, a couple of hundred yards away.

You fuckin' arsehole, Drummond. Why the fuck didn't you check Google the day before yesterday? I spent all of yesterday walking down a longitude 'a couple of hundred yards' from the one I should have been following. All that William Blake visionary madness and me giving it 'at the very epicentre of blah blah blah' is just bollocks now. It might be only 200 yards to you but to me it has made all those pavements pounded and words written on the hoof pointless.

Best not to tell Gimpo.

Friday, 25 March 2005

'Morning.'

'Morning.'

'Fancy breakfast before we start?'

'Yeah.'

We enter an empty Garfunkels around the corner on Northumberland Avenue. I have never been in a Garfunkels before. Hate the idea of them. Strictly for foreign tourists. The full English is surprisingly good.

Plates cleaned, we get to work. Striding down Whitehall, through the swarms of foreign tourists. Past the crap and embarrassing statues of irrelevant generals outside the Ministry of Defence. I mean, obviously they weren't irrelevant in their day, whenever that day was, but they are to me today and, I guess, to all the tourists. The one of Monty looks good, with his hands behind his back in some non-heroic pose. At least his soldiers loved and respected him. At any rate my dad did when he was out in the desert in 1944.

Anyway, enough of the past. On to Parliament Square. Can't believe that bloke protesting against the war in Iraq is still there with his ever-growing wall of placards and banners of all shapes and sizes. What he is doing is brilliant. Pisses all over my pack of pointless Silent Protest cards and more importantly pisses over most art being produced in the here and now. Visually, it is stunning. It has an audience of hundreds and thousands. It is seen daily by the people who run our country and all those foreign tourists who don't. But best of all he doesn't get moved on. He doesn't shut up shop. He doesn't disappear. He just keeps appearing, more and more of him. Or at least more and more of his placards and banners.

Gimpo tells me that he doesn't make them all himself. Other people make them and bring them down to add to his collection. Why doesn't someone come along and burn the lot? Why don't the police do something about it? It's a national embarrassment, that's why it's brilliant.

Fuck the badly done replica Queen Eleanor's Cross that's not even in the right place. As far as I'm concerned, this man – whatever his name is – is the centre of London. He is the point that all this madness that is London revolves around. Right now, on this Good Friday morning as they are driving the nails through Jesus's flesh, it's him, the bloke on Parliament Square, who is my modern Blake and he is building our New Jerusalem with dog-eared placards and tatty banners.

We move on down Millbank, the Thames on our left sparkling in the sunlight. Gimpo films the Tate boat. The one with the Damien Hirst spots on it. The one that takes art lovers from Tate Britain to Tate Modern and back again. Gimpo is filming it disappearing around Millennium Pier.

We cross Vauxhall Bridge, down South Lambeth Road, past all the Portuguese shops. Past Stockwell tube station, which I used to come out of nearly every weekday morning in the late 1980s on my way to Jimmy's house for us to be getting on with our Justified Ancients of Mu Mu things.

'There used to be a baker's in the parade of shops in the next block. I would go there every morning on my way to Jimmy's for a bag of doughnuts.'

It's still there. It hasn't disappeared. I go in. They've got a deal going. Four doughnuts for £1. I get four. Gimpo doesn't want one. Gimpo's on some sort of no-wheat diet, says wheat saps your strength. I eat two doughnuts, one after the other. Save the other two for later. Feel like Homer Simpson.

Gimpo is wearing his new hearing aid. He started to go deaf after being a gunner in the Falklands war. It's a pink flesh-coloured one. He wants to get one of the dark brown ones that are made for black people. We pass the National Centre for Deafness on Clapham

Road. Turn on to Bedford Road at Clapham North tube station. The legs are feeling good. We should have attempted to do the whole lot in one day. That was my original idea. Walk across London in a day. Green fields to green fields between dawn and dusk. It was Gimpo who thought we couldn't do it.

'You know, Gimpo, we should have done this in a day.'

'Fuck off!'

'What d'ya mean?'

'I'd 'ave ended up carrying you.'

'Fuck off!'

King's Avenue. Cherry blossom, daffodils, as well as the cheeky dandelions and saintly celandines I was going on about before. We take a turning on the left, Thornbury Road. And there it is, the back wall of Brixton prison. Gimpo's home for a few months at the back end of 2002, where he spent Christmas banged up for crimes against himself.

'They used to throw tennis balls over the wall from here.'

'What for?'

'With drugs inside.'

'What, the prisoners?'

'No. Friends or family would throw them from the outside, from here in the street. And them on the inside would have volunteered for sweeping up the perimeter yard, between the wall and the block. It was mainly to sweep up all the crap and bog paper we would throw out of our cell windows. But you would phone your friends or family to let them know when you would be doing the sweeping up so they could throw the tennis ball at the right time.'

'Makes sense.'

We keep walking. Past one of the prison wardens that Gimpo remembers, he's obviously on his way to work.

'He was a cunt. Always got the other officers to do the dirty work, sent them in to sort things out when it all started going off.'

We keep walking. No sparrows. Where the fuck have they all gone? And why?

*

Cross the South Circular into Tierney Road and on to Streatham Hill. The A23. The road south to Brighton. Past the Megabowl. Lots of people out and about on this Good Friday morning. Not that many people look too bothered that Jesus is now hanging on his cross, a gash on his side, some blokes throwing dice for his clobber while he is dying for our sins. Yours, mine and all these people looking fine and dandy on this lovely spring day.

I could never work out what it meant that Jesus died for our sins. Did it mean that I could do whatever I wanted and when I got caught I could say 'It's OK, you don't have to punish me 'cause Jesus has already died for my sins.' It didn't seem to work out that way. My sins didn't disappear. I still got a clip round the ear.

We move on. Streatham Ice Skating Rink, home of the Streatham Raiders Ice Hockey Team. I used to love going to ice rinks. Not for the skating, not even for checking out the girls, but for listening to the over-cranked pop music reverberating around the hall. Hearing Telstar by the Tornados in Ayr Ice Skating Rink is one of my all-time pop moments, up there with doing stage security for the Damned at Eric's Club, Liverpool, in 1977.

Don't get me started on pop moments or I'll be here all day. We've got to keep going.

I like Streatham. This is going to sound patronizing and maybe even racist. When I am in Brixton, I think it must be shit to be black. When I am in Streatham, I always think it must be great to be black. And don't ask me why, that would take longer than categorizing the pop moments thing.

Still no fucking sparrows. I wonder whether Jesus was able to watch any sparrows while he was up on the cross. When he said that thing about not worrying 'cause God that feeds the little birds in the fields will surely look after you, I always imagined it to be sparrows. Sparrows always look so happy as they squabble about in gangs, chirruping away. It always makes me feel good when I see them getting on with life, whatever their surroundings. So where the fuck are they? What do they know that we don't and does Jesus know this and should he be told before he dies later this afternoon?

We move on past Streatham Common where a poster is advertising Kite Day 21 April. Gimpo has taken to filming low-flying passenger jets that are flying above us as they make their descent into Heathrow. He is filming them in a patch of blue sky as they disappear behind a cloud.

Pounding down a long straight section of the A23, cars ploughing by, heading for the coast. We take a detour from the A23 but we are still keeping close to our chosen longitude, the one that your man on Parliament Square is on. Down a couple of lower-middle-class suburban streets, Leander Road, Silverleigh Road. Families out in the sunshine. I'm feeling chipper.

Back on the A23, skirt around Broad Green. Somewhere down here is the Mechanical Copyright Protection Society (MCPS) or the Performing Rights Society (PRS) or one of those other official music industry things that used to make my life difficult but now endeavour to make it pleasant. Not that pleasant, but a few bob in the post before Christmas because a song you had a hand in writing has been getting a few radio plays in South America helps pay for the turkey.

On to Purley Way. Croydon rises in the east. I've never been to Croydon. Driven past it loads of times, but never got out and had a look around. I like the idea of Croydon.

Gimpo points out a couple of towering chimneystacks to our south-west.

'There's an Ikea there.'

Gimpo and I have, over the past few months, been building up a mental map of the country based on where Ikeas are located. No other information is on this map other than Ikeas and their proximity to major centres of population. I think the theory is that you can measure your distance from the heart of modern civilization by timing how long it takes you to drive to the nearest Ikea. I'm not claiming this as an original theory, it sounds more like one a journalist would come up with. I wonder how long it will take before the concept of Ikea will disappear as a conversational topic within certain classes in London?

Gimpo was right, there is an Ikea.

'I'm fuckin' starvin'. We must be more than halfway. Do you reckon there's any cafés down this stretch?'

'Just around this bend, Bill, there's one, but you won't want to go there.'

'Why?'

'You wait.'

And before we round the bend I can see the golden arches peeking over the fence. I start singing 'McDonald's, McDonald's, Kentucky Fried Chicken and a Pizza Hut'. I love singing that song. It has got to be both the most inane song and the one that captures a strand of our culture more precisely than any other in this decade. Was it the Cheeky Girls that sang it? I wonder what happened to them.

I am now resigned to walking into a McDonald's for my lunch. The place is chocker: kids, dads, young couples, lonely lost souls, gangs of gum-chewing teenage girls and me and Gimpo. I'm fooled into ordering something from their new healthy range. Some sort of chicken wrap thing with chilli sauce and side salad. It's shite. At least the chips are OK. I really resent the fact that I like McDonald's chips. I wonder if people will get nostalgic about McDonald's when they disappear, like my parents' generation get nostalgic for Lyons Corner Houses? Will the thought of a McDonald's Happy Meal conjure up warm feelings inside the children of today in fifty years' time?

We leave McDonald's and most of my chicken wrap. The two doughnuts are still in my jacket pocket. I eat them. That makes me feel better.

We take another detour off the A23, through an area called South Beddington according to the map. This is all new landscape for me. We are going up Mollison Drive when I hear something familiar. Something it seems I haven't heard for some time. It's sparrows chirruping, just three or four of them in a garden shrub squabbling away like sparrows do.

'Where have you been? Why didn't you tell me you were going? What's going on? Is Jesus dead yet?'

Of course, it must have just gone three o'clock and the temple curtain has been rent asunder.

'Don't be fuckin' daft, Bill,' says one of the sparrows. 'Palestine is at least four hours ahead of us. Jesus died ages ago. They've already got him in the tomb at the garden of Gethsemane.'

'Shit, you're right. I hadn't thought of that. But look, while I'm doing my Doctor Dolittle bit and you are going along with it, can you tell me why you have all been buggering off?'

'No, Bill, we can't. We are sworn to secrecy. And no, it's got nothing to do with the rumour about the giant sparrow hawk in the sky about to swoop down and kill us all. Or the racist crap that we understand that you have been going on about. Any other questions?'

Talking to birds is a bit of a habit of mine while out walking by myself. Obviously I wouldn't want to be seen doing something as alarmingly stupid as talking to birds in front of a companion. So today I've restrained my chatting to the sparrows to the confines of my notebook. What is liberating about this is that in the confines of the notebook the sparrows can chat back. Down on to Foxley Lane and up into Woodcote Lane. Everything is looking decidedly stockbroker beltish. I hate using tired old clichés like stockbroker belt, but you know what I mean, leafy and wealthy.

There is nobody about, the streets are empty, the gardens are empty, the houses look like they are empty.

'You can tell only whites live here, none of the others have got this far yet. Maybe in ten or fifteen years' time.'

'What do you mean, Bill?'

'Well, you know, as ethnic minorities climb the social ladder they move further out of any metropolitan centre and deeper into the suburbs. It will be some time before they reach here and even longer before they reach the supposed traditional English village. Ethnics hate the countryside. They're frightened of it.'

'You're talking shit, Bill. What do you know?'

'When was the last time you saw a black man in the countryside?'

Gimpo doesn't answer. I notice that the daffodils in the gardens we are walking by are already past their best. I hate the visible signs of the passage of spring. Without trying to be profound, decay follows the promise of spring all too soon. It's all so fleeting. One moment you see your first snowdrop of the year, the next thing you know the swifts are packing up and heading south again.

We pass through some gates at the top end of Woodcote Lane. A village green opens up in front of us. The green is surrounded by wealthy and wooded gardens. At one corner is an old village shop with a red pillar-box outside. Picture postcard stuff. A war memorial with a long list of the glorious dead from the parish.

'Looks like you were wrong, Bill.'

'What do you mean?'

'The lads playing football.'

I look over. About a dozen lads are kicking a ball about, every one of whose grandparents came from some other part of the globe. I find this somewhat inspiring, that nowhere is safe in this backward-looking country from the multicultural ethnic thing. Wonder what the lads on the war memorial would have thought if they could see this. Embrace change or you're fucked, that's what I say. Trouble is, I can say it but I can't always do it. All that embracing gets harder as you get older.

On to Woodcote Grove Road. Lurching down into a place called Coulsdon. We catch glimpses of open country ahead of us. That's London almost sliced in two. According to the map there is an overground station here. Gimpo gets out his mobile and phones rail inquiries. Seems the trains run at 49 minutes past the hour. It's 12 minutes past four. That gives us just 37 minutes to get out into the country and back down the hill to the station.

We cross the A23, take a short cut across some major road works, on to the B276. It's not that I expect you to be thinking, 'Oh yes, the B276, I know it well, often take that route myself when walking across London.' I'm only writing it down 'cause that's what it says on the map. It's all uphill now. We turn off on to a lane that according to the map will take us on to Farthing Downs. We cross a cattle grid. Rough grass, cowpats on the ground. Does this count as open country or is this just parkland? A fresh cowpat smells good. We walk on up the hill. We reach the top. Rural Surrey stretches out before us. A black man strolls past with a pair of walking boots on, clutching an Ordnance Survey map.

'Look, Gimpo, up there. Are those cows or horses? If they are only horses, it doesn't count. But if they are cows, then this, in my book, is open country.'

Even with my specs on my eyesight is pretty fucked. Gimpo only needs his specs for reading.

'I'm not telling you. And anyway if they are cows, you've got to touch one of them for it to count.'

Whatever these beasts are they are about 400 yards away and we've got only about 29 minutes before the train comes. I pull the bag containing the broad bean plant from my jacket pocket. Scoop a small hole in the ground and plant the beans, in the hope . . . well, in the hope of something. Get back up and start lumbering towards the beasts. They are cows, big brown ones. When I'm about 20 yards away I stop then start to sidle up to one and place the palm of my hand on her surprisingly warm flank. She turns her large head around and looks me straight in the eye, as if to say 'So what does that prove?'

Just then I notice a small flock of sparrows heading south. And I say 'Hang on a minute lads, I've got something I need to ask you.'

But if they heard me, they don't want to stop and find out what it is. The cow moves off and I'm left standing, wondering what the fuck that was all about.

[Bill Drummond]

BEDFONT COURT ESTATE

All through the summer, drawn by the raw, unswerving energy of the jets, I returned obsessively to Heathrow Airport and environs. I was fascinated by the squat utility buildings of the 1940s and 1950s, but it was the unmapped zone, out beyond the airport's Western Perimeter Road, that attracted me most.

I would edge up from Feltham Station, through the old railway yards and along the River Crane, towards the sound of the planes. At Hatton Cross I would skirt the southern edge of the airport, aiming for the River Colne. Martin S. Biggs, writing in 1934, in his book *Middlesex Old and New*, described this area as a 'veritable Middlesex Mesopotamia'. As a dweller on the Northern Heights, I found that this alluvial plain, with its ditches and hatches, had the feel of another country.

I would take my camera and my plant recognition manuals and set out with an eye open for roadside skips and empty houses. I have spent years building up an archive of material – old photos, documents, household objects – recording traces of lives lived in the old county of Middlesex. Retrieving discarded letters, diaries and borough guides from these unofficial time capsules was one of the pleasures of my walks.

It was while exploring the land around Spout Lane North that I discovered Bedfont Court Estate, a colony of derelict smallholdings set up by the Middlesex County Council in the 1930s. For years this little enclave of farmhouses remained hidden beneath the Heathrow flight paths. Later the M4 wormed out from London, while the M25 slashed around to the west, closing in on the farms and concrete tracks.

The estate pre-dated the airport. At the time of its construction there was nothing more than a small aerodrome belonging to the Fairey Aircraft Company. Since the Second World War, Heathrow and its attendant facilities have spread outwards in successive waves.

Airport perimeter roads have been laid down – one of them cutting through the edge of the estate as recently as 1947.

I first stumbled across the Bedfont Court Estate during an attempt to visit Perry Oaks, a sludge-disposal works set up by the County Council in the 1930s as part of the West Middlesex Main Drainage Scheme. Liquidized sewage was pumped down the Bath Road from Mogden, near Isleworth, and dried out at Perry Oak – for use on the rich farmlands of the region. During the 1980s concerns about heavy-metal contamination by industry put paid to the recycling of waste and, ultimately, to Perry Oaks.

The sewage works featured in that record of urban wildlife Richard Mabey's *The Unofficial Countryside* (1973). Though he doesn't name the site (in keeping with his precursor Richard Jefferies's policy of being unspecific about the locale of his subjects), it is clearly Perry Oaks he is discussing. Mabey drew attention to the rare waders using the works as a halt on their migratory flights. Being interested in birds (and sewage farms) I decided to check the place out. I was shocked to find that where Perry Oaks should have been, according to my OS map, there was now a massive building project.

Instead of austere 1930s blockhouses and sediment lagoons, I saw what looked like an aluminium frame for a vast greenhouse. Cranes sliced through the stark horizontal of the airport. Eerie half-glass half-tent structures shimmered across the landscape. Gigantic ramparts curved out of the construction site. Gravel mounds towered over the trees. Checking my map, I found that this area of tracks and buildings was described as the Bedfont Court Estate.

I hadn't realized that work on BAA's new flagship fifth passenger terminal was so advanced, or that Perry Oaks had been earmarked as its location. A glance at the security fence around the main site confirmed that access was impossible. Crossing the Western Perimeter Road, I turned up Spout Lane North, where kennels have been established to board pets while their owners are out of the country.

Spout Lane is obviously old. Ditches run down one side. Tall oaks wrapped in ivy, and dense patches of bramble interspersed with wild rose, line the lane. You could be entering a traditional farming community circa 1914. I found out later that the Spout in question was an ancient fish pond formed by the confluence of several streams and field ditches. In its place is a reservoir holding the drainage from the airport runways.

To the right a little track ran towards some scattered pines. The baying of dogs from the boarding kennels could be heard through dense hedges. On the left I saw the first of the smallholdings: small white houses, their roofs steeply pitched. Desolate scraps of land broken by ramshackle sheds and greenhouses. Signs warned of trespass and surveillance.

Behind the houses, across land dense with thistles and docks, a flimsy wire fence marked the lower slopes of the gravel mounds. It was hard to shake off the feeling that something disastrous had happened here. It was as if a major contamination of the site had occurred, an unreported Chernobyl emptying the area of its inhabitants. Folk memories had been replaced by the blur seen in a moment's glance from cars speeding through to the new terminal.

Yet the particular resonance didn't arise from relics left behind by previous users: the broken fences lost in weeds, a burned-out caravan parked in a yard, the dying damson bushes. There was a knotty multifariousness, a strata of cultural associations, evident in the broader brushstrokes of the place. The farmhouses, for instance, seemed to come straight out of the Ukraine in the middle of the last century. There was something of the kolkhoz, of enforced participation, about these buildings, all identical, each plopped firmly within its allotted area of land. The concrete track with telegraph poles had the makeshift feel of militant, revolutionary policy farming: 'we must feed the cities'. The dumpy little tractors standing by disintegrating shacks might have been loaned out by the authorities for communal use (an impression I later found was correct).

And the piles of gravel: these instantly shifted me to an Industrial North of the mind. I found out, while subsequently researching the site, that the mounds had been heaped up to provide material for the construction of T5. Some of the gravel had been dredged from the River Colne. The mounds also included the crushed remains of Perry Oaks. Under EU legislation, smashed concrete has to be recycled as aggregate.

I climbed over the fence of house No. 6 and wandered around its garden. I opened the door of a small storage shed and looked inside. A battered upright piano, keys like uneven teeth, topped with three old canary cages. A wire basket with flower bulbs, their meristems visible in the dim light. A yellowed newspaper discussing Peter Shilton's rejection from the England football team.

The weight of years was concentrated in this hidden patch of west Middlesex. Lives, brushed aside by vast economic forces, had formed a residue here. Decades of family activity were implicit in that piano, the memorials to dead pets. Outside once more, I looked in through a window at the front of the house. A little bed was neatly made up in a well-swept room. The smoothed lines of the pink counterpane contrasted with the untidiness of the external landscape. A small extension to the rear contained armchairs, a

padded footrest, plastic flowers on a folding table. By the inner door a pair of green wellington boots stood side by side.

I climbed one of the mounds and gazed across at the North Downs and the Guildford Gap far to the south. The Harrow petit massif looked tiny, off to the north-east. I could see the glowering dome of Beacon Hill, over near Tring in the Chilterns. Best of all, the half-built T5 stood little more than a third of a mile away, partly screened by some trees. I had accidentally stumbled upon an historic moment: the construction of T5, its spur road displacing the estate at my feet. I tried to take a photograph or two but found that I had run out of film.

Two weeks later I took my friend Mark to the estate. Mark is the kind of topographic commando who has no fear of climbing over obstacles to gain a more intimate view of his surroundings. I have seen him balance precariously above the Thames on a ladder, while boarding a derelict boat. I have swung around just in time to see him disappear through corrugated iron or through a smashed window into some dangerous structure.

Our visit started badly: we were accosted by a vanload of police while walking the concrete track that slices through the estate, providing its main thoroughfare.

A sharp-eyed officer leaned his head out of the van: what were we doing, in what he described as 'a sensitive area'? I had done enough background research to be aware of the local population of tree sparrows and pipistrelle bats. I said that an interest in bird life had brought us to this backwater. The police drove away, shocked but satisfied. We climbed the mound and Mark took some shots of T5 and the bespoiled zone.

Minutes later we were climbing through a window into No. 8. Any hopes I'd had of finding documents for my Middlesex archive vanished with the sight of the bare rooms, the dusty echoing staircase. The house had been meticulously stripped of its fittings. The plinth for a vintage sewing machine and a stainless-steel spoon with an ornate handle were all that we found. Mark reckoned he could smell asbestos. I sensed troubled, uncomfortable lives, wheezing years spent wrestling a livelihood from the surrounding acres. We hung around a minute or two listening to the scraping of birds' claws on the roof, then we got out.

There was a barn and a breeze-block fallowing sty attached to one of the houses. Rusting clamps were fixed to steel worktables. A hepatic bodkin or two lay in the dust. I picked up some photographs of old folk playing with dogs and a stained copy of Summerhay's *Encyclopaedia for Horsemen* (newly revised 1975). Mark did me a favour, wrenching a cast-iron wheel from a cement-topped gatepost that guarded a moulded resin fish pool and a grove of planted cypresses.

Ghosts flitted about as the sun set and tree sparrows settled down for the night. The houses were sad in the evening light, their chimneys pointing accusingly at the passing jets. I gazed at my retrieved photos and wondered at the years spent beneath flight paths, the stoicism it required to endure in that economic and social gap between coarse-faced smallholders with decrepit tractors and the international pilots and svelte hostesses in fuel-devouring machines overhead.

A bat flew up and down the tree line seeking out moths. Mark – ever the product of his rural Irish upbringing – snapped some pears from a tree at the garden's edge. It was the best pear I'd ever eaten. We watched the yellow trucks and bulldozers, still trundling across the Bailey bridge, heading for T5. It was a small triumph that these fruit trees had managed to keep a grip on their rightful inheritance in the face of this rampant onslaught.

T5's brief includes the eventual 'rehabilitation' of the site. Presumably this will involve utilizing the type of applied ecology that makes BA's landscaping of their HQ at Prospect Park in Harmondsworth such a joke. Groves of 'traditional' trees, sculpted tumuli and enforced hedgerow biodiversity (in accordance with Hooper's dictum that you can tell the age of a hedge from the number of tree and shrub species per 30 metres, averaged across the length of the hedge) seem an insufficient salve for the greed being enacted here.

I returned a few weeks later with Michael Collins, a photographer who specializes in highly detailed studies. In one of his prints, of a railway yard in Purfleet, a specimen of charlock is clearly visible from a hundred yards off.

I ran into Michael at the London Metropolitan Archive while researching the Bedfont Court Estate. He mentioned the difficulty he was having accessing T5 for one of his shots. By introducing him to the gravel mound, I could provide him with an unsurpassed shot and, hopefully, gain a high-quality print or two for my Middlesex Archive.

The following Saturday Michael picked me up in his van and we sped down to Heathrow. We carried out a quick reconnaissance while waiting for the weather to shift. A nod from Michael and we were hauling his heavy plate camera and tripod up the side of the mound. There was a heart-stopping pause while the camera was set up, then Michael applied the mysteries of his craft. We were perched above T5 and one of the airport runways, in clear view of traffic rolling along the Perimeter Road below.

Michael took twenty minutes over a couple of shots. Far below, a white police van drove southwards along the Perimeter Road. As we were packing up I saw the vehicle edge in along the track running off Spout Lane. We tumbled down the slope, rehearsing our explanations.

The police were waiting for us. They were armed. I didn't help by asking one of the officers if he would hold our box of film while I struggled over the fence. He refused. Slinging their submachine-guns across their chests they separated us. Michael got the nice cop while I was left with an embittered cynic, intent on aggravating the already tense situation.

While my documents were being scrutinized and the radio crackled back info on my (impressive) criminal record, a jeep pulled up. A burly guy from T5 told us that he was going to photograph us. If we had any objections, it was pointed out that they had the power to detain us, intimately search our persons and confiscate the expensive photographic equipment. Satisfied that we weren't armed with hand-held Blowpipe surface-to-air missiles, Michael's police-man relaxed and discussed the finer points of photography. My man was determined to extract a shame-filled apology. 'Are you aware of the current international situation, sir?'

The man from T5 Security took our portraits with a digital camera. I was advised to stay out of the area – irritating, given my devotion to old Middlesex. Though I made brave and resistant noises on the journey back to London, I never returned. Those submachine-guns had taken the pleasure out of the project.

For all I know the estate has since gone the way of Perry Oaks. Soon BAA will begin the push for Runway Three and the villages of Harmondsworth, Sipson, Longford and Harlington will also disappear, swept aside by the urge to find depth and richness else-where in this world. Always elsewhere.

[Nick Papadimitriou]

STALKING THE TIGER

22 June 1906

. . . a female patient, Catherine Muller, admitted on the 14th Novem-
ber, 1904, and who, therefore, has been in the Asylum about one year
and seven months, is found to be pregnant. On the 17th December last,
as reported to the Committee, she escaped from the Asylum, from which
she was absent rather less than an hour and a half. The condition of
the pregnancy and the medical record points exactly to this time as the
date of conception. She will give no reason, either to her husband or
myself, as to the cause of her condition.

. . . The patient being of German nationality and unable to speak
English, arrangements had been made at Dr Bryan's request for Mrs
Freedman, Interpreting Attendant, from Colney Hatch Asylum, to
attend with a view to obtaining particulars from the patient.

According to the neuroscientists, when we see a tiger's tail,
stretched out, gold and white and muscular from behind a rock,
our brain at once jigsaws in the invisible body-parts, so that we
think *Ah yes, a tiger*, and take to our heels or reach for the camcorder.
We have an inbuilt jigsaw-fetishist, that can't let a length of fur on
the ground be a length of fur, but searches its memory for the
missing pieces, and makes up a whole it thinks it can relate to.

You start with lined pages of fuzzy type, bound into a great
decaying ledger, red-brown leather-dust on your clothes and hands,
and something inside you tries to fill in the tiger.

Matron entertained a visitor last night. Except for ten in the extreme
cold weather, no chicks above one day old have been lost; this is
attributed to the use of Chikko dry chick food for all under one month.
1,800 cauliflower plants have been transferred to the colony at three
shillings per thousand. The habitual frequenting of public houses by
female staff should be strongly discouraged.

Reading the minutes is a thinned-down version of living as a
patient in the asylum. There's too much going on, the asylum farm,

the production of calico drawers in the needle room; the activities that are held to be therapeutic but end up simply sustaining the institution. Two thousand patients and as many staff. How do you get these people to take notice?

George Grundy escaped from a walking party at about noon on 3rd August. This is probably the case which has given rise to reports in the local paper that a patient was at large in a nude state. Several parties were sent out to search but were unsuccessful.

Or perhaps it's like being on the Sub-Committee. Mr Chairman, I have a few questions for the Medical Superintendent. When Catherine was brought back after her escape, did she seem particularly distressed? What support is she having through her pregnancy?

28 September

The Medical Superintendent reported that patient Catherine Muller was safely confined of a female child on the 13th instant and that she now gave the information that the sexual congress took place in the Horton Lane on the night of her escape.

Questions for the Medical Superintendent (soon to be fired), the Poor Law Guardians of St Giles Parish: their concept of care and treatment, their neutron-bomb failure of imagination, vaporizing humans, leaving the walls intact. Questions, more to the point, for Catherine. How have you been coping? What do you want to happen?

26 September

READ letter from London County Asylum, Horton, intimating that Catherine Muller gave birth to a female child on the 13th instant.

RESOLVED that in acknowledging the letter they be informed that the Guardians take it that the London County Council will make provision for the maintenance of the child, as in their opinion the trouble has been brought about owing to the neglect of duty of the Officers of the Asylum in allowing the patient to escape.

24 October

READ letter from the Asylums Committee, London County Council, intimating that they have no legal power to pay for the maintenance of the child of Catherine Muller, born in Horton Asylum.

Questions for her daughter, whisked off to the workhouse.

Sometimes you catch a tiger by the tail and all your brain offers you is a few stripes, the musculature of a thigh, a plushy paw. It's not clear if your fingers can't let go, or if your arm is caught in not-yet-visible jaws.

Subsequently, the patient, who was in bed, was seen by members of the Sub-Committee. The patient was afterwards dressed and taken to the grounds with a view to ascertaining which road she took when she escaped. No reliable information could however be elicited from the patient and finally she stated that she was not going to have a baby.

You understand that questions are not the answer.

*

And why this particular tiger, anyway? Why not naked George Grundy in the streets of Epsom? Or Minnie Crawford, whose unnamed husband is addicted to morphine, and threatens to poison her and kill himself if the doctors put Minnie 'under restraint'? The asylum minutes are full of terrible stories, in direct language, among the farm yields and insubordinate nurses: and more stories there, and still less information.

Catherine Müller (just once she is given the courtesy of an umlaut) is German and speaks no English; though she 'appears to understand what is said to her'. (The reverse does not seem to be expected.) From December 1904 till April 1905 her husband didn't come to visit her; now again, she has had no male visitors for a year. For a year and seven months, nobody in the asylum has felt it necessary to communicate with her at anything beyond the most basic level. She is pregnant for six months before anyone notices; and when they do, all their communication, through the hastily summoned interpreter from Colney, is designed to prove they are not responsible.

Catherine, come away from the dark wards.

Come out of the laundry, the desolate bleached aprons,
gasp of the steam pushed out of seamed sheets

and trapped behind windows. Look,
out here in the rosebeds the crinkled frost has fallen

and covers hope like an overall. Catherine,
Katharina, slip through the gates to your own language.
Here in the lane the beech-trees know everything:

how you must lift
up through your body again, how you will find
in the frost on the bright beech-leaves your own voice calling.

Just so far imagination can take you. Is it her own voice Catherine meets in the lane, the long-missed surrender to another body, penetration as the essence of being known; or some chancer who comes upon a bewildered young woman, and finds it no effort at all to grab and rape her?

The London Metropolitan Archives and the Family Records Centre are two minutes' walk apart, behind Exmouth Market. The same people busy themselves in both buildings: neatly dressed white people of a certain age, single men, couples, siblings, mothers and daughters, with notebooks and the requisite soft pencils. These are the resurrectionists, digging for grandparents and great-grandparents in parish records and marriage registers. The shop at the Family Records Centre sells family-tree posters, ready for completion. To be in either place, rifling through the tomes, without a provable DNA connection feels reprehensible; illegitimate.

The Parish of St Giles Camberwell has left two bluntly titled *Registers of Lunatics Chargeable*, from 1890 to 1906 and 1906 to 1912. In the first of the huge landscape ledgers, four inches thick, with the front cover missing, the pages loose and grubby, is *Muller, Catherine, aged 23, married, Church of England, housewife, of 68 Landcroft Road. Husband's name: John Muller.* The printed columns of the register speak to the Poor Law authorities' expectations: *Age on first attack: 21. Where previously treated: Horton. Duration of existing attack: 3 weeks. Supposed cause: unknown. Epileptic: no.*

Suicidal: no. Danger to others: no. Admitted: 14.11.04. In the second volume the details are the same; but John has moved house, from Camberwell to Ebury Street, Pimlico. There is no date of discharge.

The asylum admissions registers, with patients' personal details, are closed till 2017 and 2021. (Poor Law records don't seem to have the same restrictions.) The agendas and resolutions of the Sub-Committee are marked in the index *unfit for consultation*. The Board of Guardians has a little more to offer.

1 August 1906

We saw Catherine Muller, and looked carefully into the facts of her disease, and inspected the record books. The fact of the escape was reported to the Lunacy Commissioners on December 18th, that is within two clear days. Mrs Muller looked ill and anaemic.

What did the Committee do with that information? Did anyone in the asylum act on it?

6 December 1907

We have this day visited the Horton Asylum and seen the 72 inmates chargeable to the Parish, and are sorry to say very few show any sign of ever being discharged.

They all appear to be well cared for.

*

A German woman with an anglicized name, not speaking English, still in the asylum in 1912 and perhaps later, during the First World War.

If not the person, perhaps at least the context.

At the time Catherine was admitted to the asylum, German people made up the second-largest immigrant community, after Russian Jews: around 56,000. Most were economic migrants, from the impoverished regions of Germany. Many worked in East London in sugar refining, hard, unhealthy work; or as waiters, clerks, bakers. The German Hospital in Hackney (now the Metropolitan Workshops) had 120 beds, nearly always full, and saw 20,000 to 30,000 outpatients a year.

Already in the years before the war, when Catherine was living in Landcroft Road and later in Horton, there was growing hostility towards German people. The usual cries: they were paupers; they worked for low wages. Prejudice as ever was licensed by politics, the diplomatic tensions between the countries. The paranoia could have been from Horton: all these bakers and tailors were working for the Kaiser, preparing for the German invasion of Britain. By September 1914, with the war just started, the Met had received 8,000 to 9,000 reports accusing Germans in London of espionage. A lurid spy literature appeared and flourished. The same mad speeches in the same locations: Joseph Chamberlain, Limehouse, a hundred years ago:

And behind those people who have already reached these shores, remember there are millions of the same kind who . . . might follow in their track, and might invade this country in a way and to an extent of which few people have at present any conception.

Petty racism doesn't reach the chronicles. Still we have seen this twitching tail before: graffiti, insults shouted down the street, children beaten up on the way to school. You could hardly live in East Dulwich and not know it.

With the war, prejudice gained full expression, in Parliament as much as on the streets. Day two produced the Aliens Restriction Act, enabling a series of regulations to control where Germans could live and travel, who they could meet. John Muller perhaps in one of the long queues at police stations for compulsory registration. The *Daily Mail*, already xenophobic, complained that some Germans were changing their names – perhaps to avoid being taken for spies – and in October 1914 this too was outlawed. Internment of men of military age began; over 13,000 by 23 September, at which point there was no more accommodation.

Anti-German riots began to flare, the most sustained racist disorder ever in Britain. Someone threw a brick at a shop in Deptford High Street, and the building was torched; two other shops were attacked, the contents destroyed. In the usual logic of blame-the-victim, the response was to start internment all over again, though some were released later for lack of space. Women, children and men over military age were deported.[1]

There is no indication of the nature of Catherine's illness, nor what the asylum considered to be its cause. For all the women committed for enjoying sex, or having illegitimate children, for all the lack of cure and the brutal treatment, some at least of the 100,000 asylum patients in 1900 must have been suffering from what we too would describe as mental illness; or, if we mistrust our own time's diagnoses, from distress that they couldn't find relief for. Whatever the label the asylum gave Catherine, however we might describe her state of mind, we know being hated is bad for the mental health. Day-to-day racism can get under the skin, erode the self-confidence, make it harder to maintain the sense that one is active, contributing to the well-being of the planet. The riots, ten years after she was committed, were within a few miles of Catherine's home: Deptford, the Old Kent Road, Brixton, Lee Green, Catford.

Or perhaps the neighbours were specially kind to her.

Which would be better: four more years in Horton, till the end of the war, or to be deported? Would anyone bother to deport a woman who had already spent ten years in an asylum? If she's going back, she will need to recover at least by the time she's fifty. Among the Jews and Roma and homosexuals, the first victims in the camps of the Holocaust were the psychiatric patients.

*

She sits still.

The rocking-chair tilts her gently back, then forward. She sets her feet firmly on the pink-and-blue rug. The chair stops, in mid movement: just there.

Now the only movement is her lungs, steadying; the blood flowing past the pulse-points in her wrists.

She sits still in her rocking-chair, in her rented rooms: in her land-lady's house, in what is now her street. Although she was brought here, not knowing where it was, it seems that now she has chosen all this: the bright sunlight slanting down from the dormer window, the two attic rooms with their sloping ceilings, the smell from downstairs where her landlady is cooking, the front garden, the suburb. She sits like a stone dropped in a pond, and feels the concentric circles spread around her.

I hope I will not fall to the bottom.

Outside on the street some children are playing a game. She can hear their heavy jumps, between ragged pauses, their voices calling out words she doesn't understand. A bicycle judders over the cobbles. A woman calls to someone. A dog squeals.

Nobody here will ask her to do anything, except pay five shillings to Mrs Pilgrim the landlady on Fridays. At first Mrs Pilgrim seemed to hope she would talk; but she shakes her head. Later she will start to put English words to things. Thank you, she says when the tray is brought to her door.

If she goes out of the house she will start to say Good morning. So far she does not want to leave the house.

So far I do not have the strength to leave it.

I can choose not to do what I say I have no strength for.

The rocking-chair is made of dark varnished wood, and upholstered in worn brocade. The smooth wood cools the spread palms of her hands. The rug at her feet is faded pinks and blues, knitted from soft rags. In the bedroom there is a patchwork counterpane.

She thinks: no one else has just this bedspread, made by a woman, Mrs Pilgrim perhaps, from old summer dresses. It will not return from the wash and be allocated to another patient.

I am not a patient.

The light pours in with a torrent of bright dust. The room smells of dust and lavender-bags. When she has eaten, the smell of boiled potatoes and casseroled meat will fade from the air slowly.

She sits here waiting to find who she has become. Though she thinks to find out she will have to get to her feet, tilt the rocking-chair forwards; go out of the door and down the two flights of stairs. When the front door latches behind her, she will be a person, in a street with children and dogs and bicycles, a city where there are men apart from doctors. There she will be one particular person, in the way that the pieces of dress have become a quilt.

While I sit here I do not need to be anyone.[2]

*

Upstairs at the Family Records Centre are the census findings. The 1901 census survives in gunmetal drawers full of microfiches.

Landcroft Road is on RG13/501, folio 134, page 138; or RG13/501, folio 169, page 173; or possibly RG13/502, folio 17, page 25.

Dark replicated pages lurch across the screen. Either the census-takers recorded answers just as they walked, along one side of a road, down a turning and another turning, then back on the opposite side to the main road; or the pages have been copied in nil order. There are bits of Landcroft Road scattered here and there. You come close to 68 and turn the fiche on to the following page, but that proves to be blank, or you're somewhere else completely. You can't tell if you're skipping pages. You can't remember which fiche you've seen already. Then abruptly you see it, 68 Landcroft Road, and whoever is living there it's not the Müllers.

There are other places to look for a tuft of fur. Marriage certificates list husband's occupation, and even occasionally wife's. You have to scour.

Downstairs is filled with the percussion of metal shelves struck by heavy ledgers being removed, replaced. You heft down the register on to the tilted desk, turn the thick pages, run a finger down to the surname; then close the volume again, back on to the shelf and find the next, K–S or S–Z, quarter by quarter, year by year. In 1904 Catherine was twenty-three; she could have been married from 1897 on.

No	When Married	Name and Surname	Age	Condition	Rank or Profession	Residence at the time of Marriage	Father's Name and Surname	Rank or Profession of Father
194	Twenty fourth April 1901	John Müller	21 years	Bachelor	Baker Journeyman	27 St James Road Bermondsey	William Müller (deceased)	General dealer
		Catherine Nockel	20 years	Spinster		27 St James Road Bermondsey	John Henry Nockel	Brush Manufacturer

A baker; one of the main occupations open to Germans. Is a journeyman one who's done his apprenticeship, and works in someone else's bakery, one of those shops to be torched thirteen years later? And then they are living at the same address, before the marriage; living together; or recent immigrants, perhaps, both in lodgings in the same house; or Catherine as the lodger of Mrs Müller, senior, now a widow, or . . .

If Catherine in her twenties speaks little English, the chances are that she came to the country as an adult, or at least a teenager. The shelves of red birth registers stretch back to the far reaches of the room: 1960, 1940, 1920, 1900. Catherine was born in 1881. The records start, mercifully, in 1880. The heft of ledgers, the finger down the page, the slot into place again. There are no Nockels; or rather there is the occasional Nockels, plural, but no baby Nockel, Katharina or Catherine.

Names	When born	Condition	Calling	Religious creed	Address of friends	Date of admission	discharge
							infirmary
37 *Müller*	*13.9.06*	*illgt child of Catherine*		*CE*	*Child brought from Horton Asylum*	*21.11.06*	*11.3.07*

The Creed Register lists admissions to the workhouse, those who have come to the end of their own resources and find themselves submitting to this shame, to be unable to fend for themselves, their families. Domestic servants, bricklayers, housewives, retired factory workers; and this child. Everyone else, however destitute, has a given name. In two months surely her mother named her? Even the child of a rape, once she was born; even the child resented for bringing even more punishment upon her mother.

The red ledgers again.

Muller, Katherina .... **Epsom 2a 24**

Katherina: of course she was Katherina, her mother's real name, her given name, before she or her father or husband or some official at the port of entry decided she had to be English. In German it's Katharina, with an a. Like the umlaut on Müller, the subtleties, the distinctions by which you know yourself as a person with a past, a culture separate from this one, are ignored.

Assuming Catherine was literate, and cared. Assuming she didn't choose the variant, and spell it out herself.

When and where born	Name, if any	Sex	Name and surname of father	Name, surname and maiden surname of mother	Occupation of father	Signature, description and residence of informant	When registered	Signature of registrar
Thirteenth September 1906 Horton Asylum Epsom	Katherina	Girl		Catherine Muller formerly Nockel of no occupation of 68 Landcraft Road East Dulwich		David Ogilvy Acting Medical Superintendent Horton Asylum Epsom	Twenty third October 1906	James Andrews Registrar

Katherina, two months old, in late autumn, leaving Horton, the indoor world of the ward and the day room; abruptly weaned from her mother's milk and her mother's consoling or reluctant arms; carried on a cart or bus or train to Gordon Road, Peckham, and the grim workhouse. It had to be grim: the Poor Law principle of less eligibility required conditions to be worse than any its inmates would otherwise live in. Is there a baby ward, a row of cots, a wet-nurse brought in? Then four months later, another move, to the infirmary, wherever that is: out of the workhouse care.

Nothing in the Horton list of baptisms. Nothing more in the workhouse register. There were children's homes, run by the Board of Guardians. Workhouse children lived in the homes till they were seven or eight, then were boarded out. Workhouse children stood out awkwardly in school, in ill-fitting clothes, not knowing how to play. After boarding out the boys were sent to work on the land, or to training ships. At fourteen the girls came back again to work unpaid in the homes, on the slim pretext that this would prepare them for domestic service. This could have been Katherina's childhood: children's home, private household, children's home.

The Poor Law girls were incapable of doing the ordinary work of a house, such as lighting a fire or laying a cloth. They had little knowledge of ordinary household equipment . . . They had no idea of the value of money or shopping.

A Poor Law girl would scrub a floor well enough if told, 'Begin here, and go up to there.' This she would do more patiently and ploddingly than the local girl, but as soon as she was told, 'Make the kitchen look nice and bright,' she had not the least idea how to set about it.

The results of such a childhood were traits which made it difficult for the girls to get on with other people.[3]

Without parents to stick up for them, or a mother's advice on dealing with harassment, young women leaving the children's homes were vulnerable to seduction or rape by the master of the house where they worked, or his sons. Many went into part-time prostitution:

They were usually small and looked younger than their age. Moreover, they were broken to direction, had little knowledge of the world and were hungry for affection . . . If they disappeared, there was no one to make a fuss.[4]

Broken to direction. Was that what happened?

The register of children maintained at the workhouse care. The register of children boarded out. The register of children adopted or emigrated (a transitive verb).

Clara and Jane Dark, aged seven and ten, admitted to the workhouse children's home on 6 January 1906, when their parents enter Gordon Road Workhouse. Discharged 13 January. Back the next day till the 25th; Clara discharged and readmitted the same day. They both stay till 1 February: this time their father in the infirmary, the mother at home. Back again the same day, this time till 10 March. In July the two sisters are 'adopted', which seems to be something less than permanent.

Other children are in and out the whole time. Four-year-old Albert Miller is there on every page, from October onwards. Rosina, Alfred, Ernest and Beatrice Davis, aged between nine and four, have an alternative surname, Churchill, and a 'reported' father, Alfred Churchill, carpenter, in Gordon Road with all the other parents, except their mother, Rose, address unknown. Alice, Frances and Lily Marshall, aged eleven, six and three, father dead, mother in Bexley Asylum, boarded out and then adopted. Henry Mason, aged eleven, foundling, emigrated to Orleans, Ontario. Rose Clarke, aged sixteen, adopted by Reverent Perdue in Ontario from the Waifs and Strays Home, Whitehaven.

No Katherina.

Then there is only one way left to try to trace her. The death rate of illegitimate Poor Law children was twice as bad as for the legitimate. Back across Exmouth Market, behind the bank become a pizzeria, to the black ledgers. If Katherina isn't recorded among the living, perhaps you can find her among the dead.

1907. 1908. 1909; April, June, September, December of each year. Every year that her name isn't there with the other Mullers, three or four in each volume, you have kept her alive. The clack of ledgers returned to the metal shelves, the aftershave and perfume of other searchers, the weight of the tome as you lift it from the shelf and turn with it in your arms to the reading desk. 1910. 1911. At 1914 you are competing with a man in a tweed jacket and sunken unsmiling cheeks, who grabs each volume as if you might scarper with it. You're tired; perhaps you'll give up for today. You leapfrog to 1919, on the other side of the shelving unit, and begin working backwards.

*

It isn't Katherina that you find.

Muller, Catherine 37 .... Epsom 2a 40

Catherine dead; presumably still in Horton; perhaps in the great influenza epidemic. No lodging with Mrs Pilgrim, no rocking-chair; no afterlife of trying to find her daughter, and not finding her and living anyway, rediscovering music and food and sex and friendship. No learning to live without the institution, no flashbacks to the terrible treatment there, no difficulty with other people or herself to be ascribed to Horton, thirty years later. It's the day before the Bank Holiday weekend; urgent to get hold of the death certificate, whatever paltry facts are there to console you. You pay twenty-three pounds for an express search, and wait and wait even so, the three-day weekend, the Tuesday when it is printed, the two days that first-class post takes to reach Tottenham.

| 344 | Twenty fourth September 1918 Banstead Mental Hospital Banstead | Catherine Muller | Female | 37 years | of 68 Landcroft Road East Dulwich Wife of - Muller Name unknown | Tuberculosis of Lung no P-M Certified by (Illeigible) | JE Viney Resident Medical Officer Banstead Mental Hospital Banstead | Twenty seventh September 1918 | (Illegible) Deputy Registrar |

Not influenza, which at least was shared with some equity across swathes of the world and all kinds of people, not least Dr Lord, Medical Superintendent of Horton, though he survived and worked long after the war. TB, the disease of the poor and overcrowded.

And Banstead. Horton, to the satisfaction of Dr Lord, was a military hospital for most of the war, the patients – the ordinary, mad patients – dispersed to other asylums around London. In spring 1915, 2,143 people were evacuated, each with a medical report and a case paper (but not the detail of Catherine's husband's name), 'a full personal kit and as far as possible a change of clothing'.

GPs refused to certify patients to the remaining asylums, because the conditions were known to be so bad.

More Sub-Committee minutes, for Banstead this time. No mention of the transfer of Horton patients; but in November 1917, the year before Catherine died, a special report from the Medical Superintendent.

ACCOMMODATION

As the Sub-Committee are aware, it was at the end of last year that our death rate began to rise to alarming proportions . . .

In 1916–17, the death rate among male patients is 21 per cent, and 12.5 per cent among women. This is before the flu epidemic has started. As a man you have a one in five chance of dying, as a woman one in eight. He goes on to chart the principal causes of death:

	Male		Female	
Pneumonia	82	35.8%	65	34%
Phthisis	47	20.5%	52	27%
Dysentery	16	7%	6	3%

. . . It is not for a moment suggested that overcrowding was the sole cause of the increased death rate and as I have previously reported a number of factors have had their share. The reduction in the amount and the unsuitability of food, the lowering of the standard of cleanliness by the stoppage of all decorating work, the reduction in number and in experience of the Nursing staff are all probably causes which have had the effect of lowering the vitality of the inmates.

I am not opposing the re-admission of patients, but I would ask the Sub-Committee to realize that as long as these various factors remain combined, our death rate will, in all probability, continue to rise.

Catherine.

Nothing more about deaths in 1918. Dying doesn't get your name into the minutes any more. There's a volume of burial records, but too late.

*

And what is left in your hands after all this? A few hairs, a footprint, the rank carnivorous odour on the air. A woman who may have spent fourteen years of her life in the asylum, and died there because the care of the mentally distressed was least of all priorities during the war. Whether it continued to be terrible, whether she made friends and learned some English, if her husband visited again or was interned, cannot now be resolved in the factual world, only in the pages of fiction, where assertions are true because the writer makes them and the reader colludes. A daughter vanished from the bureaucracies of London, who may have died in the infirmary and the death not been registered; or lived on, beyond the age of twenty, as far as I have searched in the registers. If you have read this, you may know more of her mother than she did.

Think: perhaps you had a grandmother called Katherina or Kitty or Kay or Katie, whose maiden name was Müller, or even Miller.

Perhaps she was your old aunt's next-door neighbour, a shop assistant in the local baker's, your mother's best friend from the Poor Law children's home. If so, please tell me.

She'd be ninety-eight. Perhaps she's still living.

Perhaps nobody now alive has heard of her.

[Ruth Valentine]

DEREK RAYMOND CONSIDERS HIS NOVEL *I WAS DORA SUAREZ* AND TALKS OF DEATH
Silvertown, 1992

The dead, their faces remain in my mind much longer than the faces of living people. That's because, by definition, a dead face never changes. You see it for the last time and the last time never leaves you. *Never leaves you.* They say the dead don't come back. Sometimes I'm glad when they do and sometimes I wish they didn't. But they come back anyway. It's not like in real time, going down to the pub where you might get on well with a geezer or you might get on badly – the dead come back either loving you or hating you. It's a terrible thing when they hate you. You can't keep the dead out. You can't keep them out of a room, never mind out of your head. They come anyway. They rest on your shoulder, whatever you're doing, they weigh *nothing*. Not a feather of weight. But they have no new word to say. It's always the same thing: 'Join us. The river is open. All you have to do is cross it, be with us, you never were with them.' Death lasts much longer than life. Life really is an illusion. I don't cry for the dead, I speak to them and they speak to me. And that's the end of it. Amen. Mark that with a cross.

They're cardboard, two-dimensional. They're flat. If you knew them, living, you would realize how quickly solid people can become nothing. And yet be as solid as they ever were, as solid as the future is black – for all of us. Or they might turn and say to you, living or dead, 'We are all part of the General Contract, join us. *Join us.* Nothing can touch you any more. Not a bullet, not a fist, not a prayer. We don't need their prayers, we're here now.'

And I say to them, 'Is it true you can pass through walls?'

And they say, 'Of course – if we need to. Like angels or villains, really, we can go anywhere. We can go all over town for a mate.'

People say to me, 'Why do you spend so much time alone?' And I say, 'Well, I'm never alone, I keep my own company.' I'm a close man, but I'm open to a dark that most living people are far too busy to see. You have to find it to know it. But to know it you have to want to find it. Or, if not, they'll come to you because they want to find you. The living say, 'It's bad news to be wanted by the dead.' But I don't think so. No, I don't think so at all.

NOTES

THE GAZETTEER OF DISAPPEARANCES & DELETIONS

The Regent Street Colonnade, SW1 [Sarah Wise]
1. Retrieved from the *Builder* magazine and the *Daily News*, November 1848.

AVRAM NACHUM STENCL [Rachel Lichtenstein]

1. 'Stencl's Berlin Period' by Heather Valencia, *The Menele Review: Yiddish Literature & Language*, Vol. 07.004 (Sequential No. 130), 6 April 2003. Translated from *Loshn un Lebn*.
2. Taken from interview with Stencl in the film *Lively Arts: Whitechapel*, made for the BBC in July 1979 by Bristol Arts Unit. Director: Dennis Marks.
3. 'Stencl of Whitechapel' by David Katz, *The Menele Review: Yiddish Literature & Language*, Vol. 07.003, 30 March 2003.
4. *Lively Arts: Whitechapel*, BBC. British Arts Unit, 1979.

Bibliography

Kathi Diamant, *Kafka's Last Love: The Mystery of Dora Diamant* (London: Secker & Warburg, 2003)
Bill Fishman, 'Stencl', *Elam*, 1965
Leonard Prager, 'A. N. Stencl – Poet of Whitechapel'. The first Stencl lecture, given at the Oxford Centre of Postgraduate Studies, 4 August 1983
S. S. Prawer, 'A. N. Stencl – Poet of Whitechapel', *TLS*, 3 May 1985
Maurice Rosenbaum, 'Poet of His People', *Guardian*, 10 July 1964
'Avrom Nokem Stencl'. Obituary, *Jewish Chronicle*, 28 January 1983
Heather Valencia, 'Czeladz, Berlin & Whitechapel: The World of Avrom Nokem Stencl', *Edinburgh Star*, Vol. 5, May 1993

THE QUAYSIDES OF BRICK LANE: WALKING WITH EMANUEL LITVINOFF [Patrick Wright]

1. Emanuel Litvinoff, 'A Jew in England', ed. J. Sonntag. 'More Jewish – or less?', First Anglo-Israeli Dialogue, Special Issue, *Jewish Quarterly*, Spring 1967, p. 8. The present text incorporates material from my earlier article about Litvinoff. See 'Ghetto Blaster', *Guardian Weekend*, 27 March 1993, pp. 16–23. It draws on interviews with Emanuel Litvinoff, held in November 1992 and February 2002. It also includes quotations from unpublished manuscripts borrowed from Emanuel Litvinoff in 1992, including *Travels in a Mind Machine*, an autobiographical sequel to *Journey through a Small Planet*.

2. Litvinoff, *Journey through a Small Planet* (London: Michael Joseph, 1972; repr. Robindark, 1993).

3. Litvinoff, 'A Jew in England', p. 8.

4. Ibid., p. 9.

5. Ibid., p. 9.

6. Litvinoff, *The Lost Europeans* (London: Heinemann, 1960), pp. 92–3.

7. Louis Golding, *To the Quayside* (London: Hutchinson, 1954), p. 222.

8. Golding, *The Bare Knuckle Breed* (London: Hutchinson, 1952), p. 13.

9. Litvinoff, *Journey through a Small Planet*, p. 30.

10. Litvinoff, *The Lost Europeans*, p. 171.

11. Quoted from Raymond Gardner, 'Behind the Covers of History', *Guardian*, 21 May 1973.

12. 'To T. S. Eliot' is collected in Emanuel Litvinoff, *Notes for a Survivor* (Northern House, 1973).

13. Dannie Abse, *A Poet in the Family* (London: Hutchinson, 1974), p. 203.

14. Litvinoff, 'A Jew in England', p. 10.

COAL HOPPER, NINE ELMS LANE, 1979 [Patrick Keiller]

1. Sir Ove Arup (1895–1988), founder of Ove Arup and Partners, one of the largest and most widely respected consulting engineering practices in the world.

2. When coal gas was phased out during the 1970s most of the structures

associated with its production became redundant apart from gasometers, many of which survive as storage for natural gas, which is largely methane.

3. Wolfgang Schivelbusch writes: 'The speed with which the gas industry took hold varied with the speed of industrialization in the different European countries. England was the first to come under its thrall, and the industry developed most quickly there; the Continent lagged behind. Within a few years, London became the first metropolis to be largely supplied with gas. In 1814 there was one company, founded by [Frederic] Winsor, which possessed a single gasometer with a capacity of 14,000 cubic feet. Eight years later, in 1822, there were already four companies and forty-seven gasometers with a total volume of almost one million cubic feet.' *Disenchanted Night: The Industrialization of Light in the Nineteenth Century* (Oxford, New York, Hamburg: Berg, 1988), pp. 30–31.

4. 'Coal gas is produced by the destructive distillation of coal, with a composition by volume of (average) 50% hydrogen, 30% methane, 8% carbon monoxide, 4% other hydrocarbons and 8% nitrogen, carbon dioxide and oxygen. The by-products of the process include coke, coal-tar, ammonia, sulphuric acid and pitch. Carbon monoxide is very poisonous, combining with haemoglobin in the blood to produce bright red carboxyhaemoglobin, so that the haemoglobin is no longer available to carry oxygen.' *A Dictionary of Science* (London: Penguin, 1964).

OLD HAGS [Marina Warner]

1. Maurice Sendak, 'An Informal Talk' (1987), in *Caldecott & Co.: Notes on Books and Pictures* (New York: Farrar Straus & Giroux, 1988), p. 214.

2. John Richardson, *Camden Town and Primrose Hill Past* (London: Historical Publications, 1991), pp. 9, 21, 90–91; Gillian Tindall, *The Fields Beneath* (London: M. T. Smith, 1977), pp. 84–5.

3. Christina Larner, *Enemies of God: The Witch-Hunt in Scotland* (London: Chatto & Windus, 1981).

4. Anon., *The Life and Prophecies of Ursula Sontheil, better known as*

Mother Shipton, ed. Dropping Well Estate, Knaresborough, Yorkshire, n.d. From the Local History Library, Camden Town.

5. John Ashton, *Chap-Books of the Eighteenth Century* (London: Chatto & Windus, 1882), pp. 88–91.

PROCESS OF TIME [Vahni Capildeo]

1. Claudette Earle, 'Media Concepts for Human Development in the Caribbean with Special Reference to Women', in *Women of the Caribbean*, ed. Pat Ellis (London and New Jersey: Zed Books, 1988), p. 116.
2. Leila emailed me this after reading how I took her words: 'Also, the reason I don't use the "I" is because in French a common saying was "Le moi est haïssable" [the use of the first person is odious]. That is why we say "on dit" [one says] rather than "je dis" [I say], or "on est toujours heureux quand on est . . .", etc. [one is always happy when one is . . .]. I guess that that is different now . . . forty years on!'

STALKING THE TIGER [Ruth Valentine]

1. Panikos Panayi, *The Enemy in Our Midst: Germans in Britain during the First World War* (New York and Oxford: Berg, 1991).
2. Ruth Valentine, *The Jeweller's Skin*, unpublished.
3. Nigel Middleton, *When the Family Failed* (London: Gollancz, 1971), p. 121.
4. Ibid., p. 125.

ACKNOWLEDGEMENTS

My thanks to Anna Sinclair for submerging herself in the complicated fret of this project: format conversions, disintegrating or fast-breeding emails, wearisome scanning sessions, self-cannibalizing disks. The whole landfill of unanchored words. To say nothing of the eccentricities of the local postal service (sacks in the canal, packages stacked on doorsteps, thwarted deliveries that were never recaptured). If a potential contribution to our *City of Disappearances* failed to reach me, its fate should be seen as a very proper response to the enterprise.

I'm grateful to all those who responded to my impossible demand: *demonstrate disappearance*. And I'm especially grateful to Michael Moorcock and Sarah Wise, who understood – better than I did – just what was required: entries for an ever-expanding encyclopaedia of loss.

The support and enthusiasm of my editors at Hamish Hamilton – Simon Prosser, Juliette Mitchell, Francesca Main, Sarah Coward – is much appreciated. Discussions with my agent, John Richard Parker, helped me to shape the way the book evolved.

[I. S.]

'Battle of Mudchute' by Steve Beard is extracted from his novel *Meat Puppet Cabaret*, published by Raw Dog Screaming Press in 2006.

'Dora's Story: Lost and Found' by Kathi Diamant is extracted, with the author's permission, from *Kafka's Last Love: The Mystery of Dora Diamant* (London: Secker & Warburg, 2003).

Extracts from *Place* are published by permission of Allen Fisher. *Place* was reissued in a handsome new edition by Reality Street (Hastings, 2005). Our thanks to the editor, Ken Edwards.

'The GLC Abolished' by Bill Griffiths was first published in the collection *Future Exiles: 3 London Poets* (London: Paladin, 1992).

'The Cellar in Gray's Inn Road, WC1' is extracted from *The Old House (A Generation of Lawyers)* by Malcolm Letts (London: Frederick Muller, 1942). With thanks to Amanda Sebestyen for bringing this to my attention.

Rachel Lichtenstein gives thanks to Miriam Becker, Avram Stencl's great-niece, for permission to publish the poem 'Where "Whitechapel" Stood' (translated by Elinor Robinson from the sequence 'Whitechapel' in *Yoyrl Almanakh* (1956); a special celebratory edition of *Loshn un Lebn*, with a cycle of forty-one poems about Whitechapel, to mark 300 years of continuous Jewish life in England); and to Susannah Rayner, Head Archivist at SOAS, for permission to look at the Stencl archives. To Majer Bogdanski, Derek Reed, Bill Fishman and Tony Laurence for interviews conducted with Rachel Lichtenstein. Special thanks to Bill Fishman for his support and advice.

Alexis Lykiard's 'Vanishing Hero, Vanished Place', written for May Day 2004, was originally published in a longer version in the periodical *Tears in the Fence* (Autumn 2004). Our thanks to the editor, David Caddy, for permission to reprint.

Jeff Nuttall's 'The Singing Ted' was originally published, in a fuller version, in *Poetry Information*, 9/10 (Spring 1974). Thanks to the editor, Peter Hodgkiss, to Nuttall's estate and to Jill Ritchie.

Extracts from *Robinson* (London: Jonathan Cape, 1993) are published by permission of the author, Chris Petit.

Tom Raworth's *A Serial Biography* was originally published by Fulcrum Press (1969). The extracts used here are by permission of the author.

The interviews with Derek Raymond are taken from *The Cardinal and the Corpse*, a documentary made by Chris Petit and Iain Sinclair for

Illuminations Films. With thanks to Martin Stone for permission to revive his Silvertown elegy from that production. (And to Madeleine Sinclair for elegant and accurate transcripts.)

'Récits' by James Sallis was first published in the *Transatlantic Review* (1970).

John Seed's poems are extracted from *Pictures from Mayhew (London 1850)*, published by Shearsman Books (Exeter, 2005). Our thanks to author and publisher.

'Fallujah London' by Iain Sinclair was originally published in the *London Review of Books* as 'Museums of Melancholy'.

'Grub Street' by Alan Wall is indebted to *Grub Street: Studies in a Subculture* by Pat Rogers (London: Methuen, 1972).

Marina Warner gives many thanks to Tom Fisher for making inquiries in local pubs on her behalf for 'Old Hags'.

'The Life of It' by John Welch first appeared in *PN Review*.

'Nova Scotia Gardens' is extracted from *The Italian Boy* by Sarah Wise, published in 2004 by Jonathan Cape and in 2005 as a Pimlico paperback. Thanks to Will Sulkin (publisher), Sarah Wise and Jonathan Cape for permission to reprint.

With thanks for the photographs and illustrations to: Paul Buck (*Hairdressers' Journal*, photo: Michael Barnett, 1965), N. Diamond, Nick Frewin, Patrick Keiller, Andrew Kötting, Rachel Lichtenstein, Claire McNamee, Michael Moorcock, Jill Richards, Marina Warner, Carol Williams and the National Railway Museum (BTC Clapham 911/54). (Other photographs were taken by Iain Sinclair.)

NOTES ON CONTRIBUTORS

ANN BAER writes: 'I am the daughter of Frank Sidgwick (the publisher of Sidgwick & Jackson). I had an art student training in London in the 1930s. After the war I worked for Turnstile Press and then, from 1949 to 1980 (when it closed), for Ganymed Press, in which I became a director. I am the author of *Medieval Woman* (London: Michael O'Mara, 1996).

'I am very grateful to you for having stimulated in my memory events from so long ago. It has made me realize how enduring one's self-consciousness is. I know I am still the same person amused at being haunted in the London art galleries, and the same person freezing and puzzling about Ossian in a Golders Green attic – and yet so many decades of difference have flowed over me since.'

J. G. BALLARD's novel *Millennium People* (London: Flamingo, 2003) is a story of bomb outrages among the disappearing middle classes of a Chelsea gated community. His latest book, *Kingdom Come*, published in September 2006, compares motorway culture with the rise of consumer fascism.

One of the pleasures for Ballard enthusiasts lies in finding authorial offcuts in unexpected places: art catalogues, colour supplements, brochures, underground magazines. Writing of the artist and film-maker Tacita Dean, Ballard notices how 'the spectator's imagination flows into these cryptic and eventless spaces, trying to decode and make sense of them'.

STEVE BEARD used to write for the style mags. Then he wrote the cyberpunk science-fiction novel *Digital Leatherette* (Hove: Codex, 1999). His extreme fantasy novel *Meat Puppet Cabaret* is published by Raw Dog Screaming Press in 2006.

KIKI BENZON is a Canadian-born freelance writer and footwear advocate living in London. A doctoral candidate in English Literature, Benzon has published essays on works by Paul Auster, Alejo Carpenter, Mark Z.

Danielewski, Don DeLillo, Manuel Puig and David Foster Wallace. She has contributed articles to periodicals such as *The Times Literary Supplement* and *Books in Canada*. She is currently editing a book on the fiction of Curtis White for the Dalkey Archive Press.

PAUL BUCK is a writer, translator and editor. His most recent book is *Spread Wide* (Paris: Dis Voir, 2005), a textual enjoyment generated from his correspondence with Kathy Acker. He is currently committing highway robbery, in the company of Rebecca Stephens and other associates, using the exploits of Dick Turpin as an excuse. He anticipates the pillory, if not the gallows.

VAHNI CAPILDEO came to England from Trinidad in 1991. Her book-length sequence, *No Traveller Returns* (Cambridge: Salt, 2003), explores place and voice. In December she completed *Say If You Have Some Place in Mind* (non-fiction). Her work appeared most recently in the *Oxford Magazine*, in *Poetry Salzburg Review* and *Tears in the Fence*. She took a doctorate in Old Norse at Oxford and held a Research Fellowship at Cambridge.

KEGGIE CAREW is an artist. She hopes to publish her first novel in the near future.

PETER CARPENTER is co-director of Worple Press and co-author of the original guide to our replikit football kultur, *At the End of the Day*; on his own he has produced four books of poetry, the latest, *Striking Distance*, published by Shoestring. He reviews and writes essays for many journals, learned and otherwise, including *London Magazine* and *Metre*; he is currently writing a novel with the working title of *The Hornby Set*.

BRIAN CATLING is a sculptor, poet and performance artist, who has made installations and video works for many countries, including: Spain, Norway, Germany, Iceland, Japan, France and Switzerland. In 2005 Catling had his fourth solo show, 'Antix', with Matt's Gallery in East London, and premiered *The Cutting*, a narrative video-film made with Tony

Grisoni. He has been commissioned by Historic Royal Palaces to make a monument for 'The Site of Execution' at the Tower of London. He is Professor of Fine Art at the Ruskin School of Drawing, University of Oxford, and a Fellow of Linacre College.

MARC VAULBERT de CHANTILLY is not English, but he is a Londoner. The London that he knew has disappeared. The London that he knows will reappear.

KATHI DIAMANT is the author of *Kafka's Last Love: The Mystery of Dora Diamant* (London: Secker & Warburg, 2003), a biography that took two years to research, in England, Germany, the Czech Republic, Russia, Poland, Switzerland, France and Israel. Kathi is also the founder and director of the Kafka Project (www.kafkaproject.com) at San Diego.

DRIFFIELD wishes to be known as 'drif field' (lower case). He says: 'Write what you please about me, as long as it is not the truth.' Over a number of years, and numerous revisions, he has wrestled with a magnum opus, the documentary-confessional-novel-polemic ATAMARA (upper case).

BILL DRUMMOND was born in 1953 and grew up in Galloway and Corby. Now an independent writer/walker/anti-artist, he rose to prominence in the late 1970s when he formed the Merseyside trio Big in Japan. He later managed Echo and the Bunnymen and Teardrop Explodes. In 1987 he formed the KLF with Jimmy Cauty. By 1993 it had become the K Foundation.

GARETH EVANS is a writer and film programmer. He edits the moving-image journal *Vertigo*. He conceived and curated the season 'Here Is Where We Meet', a London-based exploration, in all media, of the work of John Berger.

TIBOR FISCHER, a self-confessed Booker judge, says that he 'is looking forward to disappearing from London'.

ALLEN FISHER started writing poetry at the City Lead Works in 1962 and teaching Art and Art History in 1983. He is now Professor of Poetry and Art at Manchester Metropolitan University. He was part of the British Fluxus in the early 1970s, which led to the work currently owned by the Tate. He started painting in 1978. His work is owned by museums and private collectors in Iceland, Britain and America. His last three substantial books were *Gravity* (Cambridge: Salt, 2004), *Entanglement* (Ontario: The Gig, 2004) and the collected books of *Place* (Hastings: Reality Street, 2005). He is currently working on *Assemblage & Empathy*, a book-length study of composition in post-war American art and literature.

ANTONY FREWIN was born in London in 1947. His family are all from Kentish Town and Camden Town ('When you couldn't give the neighbourhood away!'). He was an assistant to the film director Stanley Kubrick for over thirty years and is the author of several novels and screenplays. He recently wrote the original screenplay for the John Malkovich film *Colour Me Kubrick*.

RANALD GRAHAM spent his childhood years as a Japanese prisoner of war in Borneo. The atom bombs on Hiroshima and Nagasaki saved his life. Otherwise: a nomadic professional writer in Edinburgh, Los Angeles, New York, Europe, Australia. He wrote cult-director William Castle's final film, *Shanks* (which starred Marcel Marceau). Having taken the last train to the coast, Graham has developed a profound antipathy to seagulls.

BILL GRIFFITHS was born in Middlesex in 1948 and continued to live there until the 1970s, when he started to move around (East London, Paderborn, Little Clacton, Morden, Uxbridge . . .), finally settling in Seaham, Co. Durham, in 1990. His poetry was first published in *Poetry Review* under the editorship of Eric Mottram and he subsequently produced many booklets through Bob Cobbing's Writers' Forum. More recent work has included a series of short stories, some studies of Old English, and books on local history and dialect in the North-East as a member of the Centre for Northern Studies, Northumbria University. Latest poetry publications: *Durham & Other Sequences* (Sheffield: West House, 2002) and – with Tom Pickard – *Tyne Texts* (Seaham: Amra, 2004) and *Mud Fort* (Cambridge: Salt, 2004).

LEE HARWOOD lived in Stepney from 1958 to 1968, before moving to Brighton ('London by the Sea'). He has published several volumes of poetry – the latest being his *Collected Poems* (Exeter: Shearsman Books, 2004) – as well as translations of the Dada poet Tristan Tzara.

STEWART HOME is the author of twenty-one books of fiction and cultural commentary, including *69 Things to Do with a Dead Princess* (Edinburgh: Canongate, 2003) and *Down and Out in Shoreditch & Hoxton* (London: The Do-Not Press, 2004). According to the London *Evening Standard* he may also have penned the best-selling 'autobiographical' account of his alleged 'day job' as the female prostitute Belle de Jour.

RICHARD HUMPHREYS is a curator at Tate Britain. He has written books on Ezra Pound and Art, Wyndham Lewis, Kurt Schwitters, Futurism and British landscape painting.

PATRICK KEILLER's films include *London* (1994) and *Robinson in Space* (1997), the latter extended as a book in 1999. His most recent project is *The City of the Future*, an exploration of urban and other landscapes in early (1895–c.1905) film.

MARIUS KOCIEJOWSKI is a poet, essayist and travel writer. His three collections of poetry are: *Coast* (Warwick: Greville Press, 1991), *Doctor Honoris Causa* (London: Anvil Press, 1993) and *Music's Bride* (London: Anvil Press, 1999). Most recently, he published *The Street Philosopher and the Holy Fool: A Syrian Journey* (Stroud, Glos.: Sutton Publishing, 2004). He is currently working on another book about Syria, *The Pigeon Wars of Damascus*.

ANDREW KÖTTING was a lumberjack and market trader and is now an artist and film-maker. His two feature films, *Gallivant* and *Filthy Earth*, have won prizes and international critical acclaim. He has published books, pamphlets and music CDs. He is currently in receipt of an AHRB Research Fellowship (through the Kent Institute of Art and Design, where he is a Senior Lecturer in Time Based Media).

RACHEL LICHTENSTEIN is an artist and writer, recently appointed the British Library's first Creative Research Fellow. Her publications include *Rodinsky's Room*, co-written with Iain Sinclair (London: Granta, 2000), *Rodinsky's Whitechapel* (commissioned by Artangel, 1999), *Keeping Place* (from a show on 'Older Women of the East End' curated at the Women's Library) and *Add. 17469 (A Little Dust Whispered)*. Rachel is currently working on a series of three topographically based London books for Hamish Hamilton.

ALEXIS LYKIARD, between the 1950s and 1970s, lived mainly in London. His novels include *The Summer Ghosts* (London: Blond, 1964), *Zones* (London: Blond, 1966), *The Drive North* (London: Allison & Busby, 1977). In 2000 he published the memoir *Jean Rhys Revisited* (Devon: Stride Publications). His main poetry books are *Selected Poems 1965–96*, *Skeleton Keys* (Bradford: Redbeck Press, 2003), *Judging by Disappearances* (2006). He is also a prolific translator of poetry and prose by poets.

JONATHAN MEADES was conceived in Seathwaite, in what was then Lancashire. He was born in Salisbury. His last books were *The Fowler Family Business* (London: Fourth Estate, 2002) and *An Encyclopaedia of Myself* (London: HarperCollins, 2003). His most recent TV film, *Joebuilding*, is about Stalin's architecture.

MICHAEL MOORCOCK was born in London at the beginning of the Second World War. He enjoyed a good Blitz, endured the 1950s and made the most of the 1960s and 1970s, especially the sex, drugs and rock and roll. He edited *New Worlds*, fronted Hawkwind, won some prizes for his fiction, including *Gloriana* (London: Allison & Busby, 1978), *Mother*

London (London: Secker & Warburg, 1988) and his Pyat quartet. His most recent London fiction has been *King of the City* (New York: Scribner, 2000), a semi-autobiography, and *London Bone* (short stories) (New York: Scribner, 2002). He lives between Austin, Texas, and Paris, France, and is working on a new sequence of novels called *Pete's Rules*.

ALAN MOORE, after working mostly in the comic-book medium for the past twenty-five years, is currently getting down to some serious writing with a second novel, entitled *Jerusalem*. He lives in Northampton with his fiancée, Melinda Gebbie, and his hairstyle.

JEFF NUTTALL died on the first Sunday of 2004 – as Michael Horovitz wrote – 'suddenly and peacefully with a glass of wine in his hand on leaving his weekly jazz gig at the Hen and Chicks pub in Abergavenny'. Poet, painter, teacher, musician, actor, performer, Nuttall lived through a cultural trajectory that was remarkable for its diversity. *Bomb Culture* (London: MacGibbon & Kee, 1968) remains a valuable source book on the period, mixing confessional anecdotes with quirky synopses of counter-cultural manifestations.

The man who invented, published, composed his own newspaper (in order to give William Burroughs space in which to operate) also played Friar Tuck in John Irvin's 1991 film, *Robin Hood*. The 'People Show' performer from the basement of Better Books, the apocalyptic poet, will be most familiar to contemporary audiences as a wheezy judge, a bent brief (parts that Ken Campbell didn't get): or as sidekick to Lenny Henry in a television series about a celebrity chef.

NICK PAPADIMITRIOU was born in Finchley (Middlesex) in 1958. Sentenced to Borstal training in 1976, he went on to serve his sentence in Feltham. After completing a degree in Philosophy at Middlesex Polytechnic in the late 1980s, he spent several years in Gdansk, north Poland, studying the fortifications and narrow-gauge railways of the region. He is obsessed with the topography of his county of birth and with drawing out its easily overlooked inner poetry.

CHRIS PETIT is a film-maker and writer. His films include *Radio On*, *Chinese Boxes* and – with Iain Sinclair – *London Orbital*, *Asylum* and *The Falconer*. Subjects otherwise covered include: air stewardesses, bank managers, money-laundering, Soho, Kilburn and, in his latest book, air disaster and the career of James Jesus Angleton.

TOM RAWORTH grew up in South London, leaving school at sixteen 'out of boredom' and gravitating towards jazz clubs where, briefly, he played the piano. In 1965 he founded Goliard Press with Barry Hall. When he is not travelling in Europe or America, he lives in Cambridge with his wife Val. Among his books are *The Big Green Day* (London: Trigram, 1968), *Lion Lion* (London: Trigram, 1970), *Writing* (Berkeley: The Figures, 1982), *Tottering State* (Berkeley: The Figures, 1984; rev. edn Paladin, 1988).

DEREK RAYMOND was born in London (as Robin Cook: the name under which he originally published). He lived abroad for many years in Morocco, Spain, Italy, Turkey and the US. During an eighteen-year spell in France he reinvented himself as Derek Raymond, a writer of *noir* London thrillers. He died in July 1994.

NICHOLAS ROYLE was born in Manchester in 1963. He is the author of five novels: *Counterparts* (Barrington, 1993), *Saxophone Dreams* (London: Penguin, 1996), *The Matter of the Heart* (London: Abacus, 1997), *The Director's Cut* (London: Abacus, 2001) and *Antwerp* (London: Serpent's Tail, 2005). He is also a prolific short-story writer and editor. He writes about books, film, art and music for a wide range of publications. He has won the British Fantasy Award three times and the Bad Sex Prize once. He lives in Manchester with his wife and two children. More at: www.nicholasroyle.com.

ANTHONY RUDOLF, born in Hackney in 1942, now lives in Wood-side Park, N12 – via sojourns in NW11, NW3 and N19. His books include autobiography, poetry, poetry translation and literary criticism. He recently completed a volume of short stories. He is an occasional broadcaster and founder of Menard Press. He has appeared as Mr Rochester on postage stamps issued to commemorate the 150th anniversary of Charlotte Brontë's death.

JAMES SALLIS writes: 'London was the other city where I came into my own; the first was New Orleans. Living off Portobello Road at the rag-end of the 1960s, in self-exile from the US and helping to edit *New Worlds*, I recognized that I was to be a kind of interloper in whatever society I lived in, and began writing my first good poems and stories.'

Sallis has recently published *A City Equal to My Desire* (poems) (Point Blank, 2000). *Cripple Creek* (a novel) will be published by No Exit Press in 2006. *A James Sallis Reader* (a selection of work, fiction and poetry) was published by Point Blank in 2005; *Drive* (a novel) was published by Poisoned Pen Press in 2005.

SUKHDEV SANDHU is the author of *London Calling: How Black and Asian Writers Imagined a City* (London: HarperCollins, 2003) and chief film critic for the *Daily Telegraph*. He also writes for *Vertigo*, *Modern Painters* and the *London Review of Books*.

JOHN SEED teaches History at Roehampton University in London. *Pictures from Mayhew* and *New and Collected Poems* were both published by Shearsman Books in 2005.

WILL SELF is the author of four novels, four collections of short stories and four novellas. He is a regular contributor to numerous newspapers and magazines, and has published three collections of non-fiction writing. He lives in South London with his wife and four children.

ANNA SINCLAIR is a qualified minibus driver and the author of *How to Succeed in an Inner City Classroom* (based on thirty years' experience of Hackney primary schools). She is presently completing *How Not To Cook*.

WILLIAM SINCLAIR's short film *The Last Days of Dobson* opened the 2004 Portobello Film Festival. A dystopian fantasy, *The Pantheon Project*, was acquired for distribution by Universal/Hypnotic. His most recent films are *Automaton* (featuring Brian Catling) and *Tell It to the Fishes* (featuring Dylan Moran).

STEPHEN SMITH is a correspondent for BBC's *Newsnight*. He is the author of *Underground London: Travels Beneath the City Streets* (London: Abacus, 2005).

MARTIN STONE, a celebrated musician and book-dealer, stays on the move: France, England, America.

RUTH VALENTINE has published four collections of poetry, two books on social welfare for schools, and a history of Horton Asylum: *Asylum, Hospital, Haven* (London: Riverside Mental Health Trust, 1996). She grew up in Bognor Regis, but came to London at the earliest opportunity. She lives in Tottenham.

ALAN WALL is a novelist, poet, short-story writer and essayist. His books of fiction include *Bless the Thief, The Lightning Cage, Richard Dadd in Bedlam, The School of Night* and *China*. His book of poetry *Jacob* was shortlisted for the Hawthornden Prize. *Bless the Thief* was translated into nine languages. His latest book is *Writing Fiction* (London: Collins, 2007). He is Professor of Writing and Literature at the University of Chester.

CLAIRE WALSH is an editor, researcher and lifelong Londoner.

MARINA WARNER's most recent book is *Phantasmagoria* (Oxford: OUP, 2006). 'I have been writing it for a decade,' she says. 'It's the one about psychic photography and ectoplasm as well as the hypnotism of telly phantoms.' She is a Professor of Literature, Film and Theatre Studies at the University of Essex.

BEN WATSON was born in Kingston in 1956 and now lives in Somers Town, where he runs the website www.militantesthetix.co.uk with Esther

Leslie. The couple have recently produced *Shadowtime*, Brian Ferney-hough's dismal opera about Walter Benjamin, and issued *Academy Zappa: Proceedings of the First International Conference of Esemplastic Zappology* (SAF), an attempt to use the pleasure principle to electro-convulse celebrity morbidity.

JOHN WELCH was born in 1942. He lives in London. In 1975 he founded The Many Press with the intention of publishing new poetry. His own poems have appeared in four main collections, the most recent being *The Eastern Boroughs* (Exeter: Shearsman Books, 2004).

CAROL WILLIAMS was born in London. She has lived in Sag Harbor, New York, for thirty-one years. She devoted much time to researching (and writing about) the life and work of the painter N. H. Stubbing. She is the author of *Bringing a Garden to Life* (New York: Bantam, 1998).

SARAH WISE grew up in West London and now lives in the West End. *The Italian Boy* (London: Jonathan Cape, 2004) won the Crime Writers' Association Golden Dagger for Non-Fiction and was shortlisted for the 2005 Samuel Johnson Prize.

PATRICK WRIGHT's books include *On Living in an Old Country* (London: Verso, 1985 & 1991), *A Journey through Ruins* (London: Radius, 1991; rev. edn Flamingo, 1993) and *The Village that Died for England* (London: Jonathan Cape, 1995; rev. edn Faber & Faber, 2002). He lived in East London from 1980 to 1992.

LIST OF CONTRIBUTIONS

LIST OF CONTRIBUTIONS